Industry Comes of Age

Business, Labor, and Public Policy

1860 - 1897

The Economic History of the United States

I. Colonial Period to 1775
II. 1775–1815
III. The Farmer's Age: Agriculture, 1815–1860
IV. The Transportation Revolution: Industry, 1815–1860
V. The Farmer's Last Frontier: Agriculture, 1860–1897
VI. Industry Comes of Age: Business, Labor, and Public Policy, 1860–1897
VII. The Decline of Laissez Faire, 1897–1917
VIII. Prosperity Decade: From War to Depression, 1917–1929
IX. Depression Decade: From New Era through New Deal, 1929–1941

INDUSTRY COMES OF AGE

Business, Labor, and Public Policy

1860 - 1897

By EDWARD C. KIRKLAND

VOLUME VI
The Economic History of
the United States

HOLT, RINEHART AND WINSTON
New York

PUBLISHED SIMULTANEOUSLY IN CANADA BY
HOLT, RINEHART AND WINSTON OF CANADA, LIMITED

LIBRARY OF CONGRESS CATALOG CARD NUMBER: 61-9816
24961-0111
PRINTED IN THE UNITED STATES OF AMERICA

To

Arthur H. Cole

COUNSELOR, CRITIC, COMFORTER

Foreword

WHEN this series of nine volumes on the economic history of the United States was first conceived, the nation's economy had reached a critical stage in its development. Although the shock of the depression of 1929 had been partially absorbed, the sense of bewilderment which it produced had not yet vanished, and the suffering and the bitterness of its first years were being transformed into less substantial, though still anguished, memories. Reform measures, either in operation or proposed, were being actively debated, but with less sense of urgency than earlier.

To the Editors of this series a fresh consideration of America's economic history was justified by more than the experiences of the recent past or the obscurity of the future. Rich contributions to the literature of American history had been made through cooperative series dealing with the political, social, and cultural aspects of American life. Numerous single-volume surveys of the country's economic development have been written. But, as late as the end of the fourth decade of the twentieth century, the world's foremost economic power had not yet produced an integrated, full-length, and authoritative treatment of its own economic history.

Scholarly concern with American economic history has been constantly growing during the past half century, and chairs of economic history have been established in leading universities. A more profound understanding of the role of economic forces in the nation's history has not only been developed by historians and economists, but has also won some measure of popular acceptance. The earlier thin trickle of monographs has broadened in recent years into a flood of publications. At present, such specialized studies, the many collections of documentary materials, and the mountains of government reports on different facets of American economic life, are staggering in their richness and scope.

This series has been planned to utilize these available sources in the preparation of a full-scale, balanced, cooperative, and readable survey of the growth of American economy and of its transformation from one of primitive character to world pre-eminence in industry, trade, and finance. Clearly, in nine volumes all aspects of the nation's economic life cannot be treated fully. But such a series can point the way to new fields of study and treat authoritatively, if not definitely, the main lines of economic development. Further, the series is intended to fill a present need of those professionally concerned with American economic history, to supplement the economic materials now available in general school and college histories of the United States, and finally to provide the lay reader with the fruits of American scholarship. If these objectives are attained, then the efforts which have gone into the creation of this economic history of the United States will have been amply repaid.

Contributors to the series have been chosen who have already established their competence in the particular periods they are to survey here; and they are, of course, solely responsible for the points of view or points of departure they employ. It is not intended that the series represent a school of thought or any one philosophical or theoretical position.

Industry Comes of Age is the arresting and appropriate title for Volume VI of the series, devoted to "Business, Labor, and Public Policy" from 1860 to 1897. In this work Professor Kirkland advances the thesis that the "Age of the Robber Barons" was one of the great and fruitful periods of American history. He does so, however, not by *a priori* reasoning but rather by seeking to find how the period looked to those who took part in its events. Every reader knows that the United States moved somehow from *The Farmer's Age* and *The Transportation Revolution,* so vividly described in the volumes by Professors Gates and Taylor, respectively, into the present era of industrial marvels. One might infer from this fact that there was a causal connection between economic policy, public and private, and economic performance. It would be hard to escape the further inference that the transition period must have enjoyed a considerable degree of economic cooperation, which in turn must have been based on a considerable measure of social consensus. The special merit of Professor Kirkland's volume lies in his *demonstration* of such harmony among business, labor, and government—both in thought and in action.

The conditions for economic progress existed between our Civil and Spanish Wars, to be sure, but we would be selling our forbears short—on the evidence of the present volume—to assume inevitability in the result. "Industry came of age" under the parental guidance of men with ideas as well as energy. Frictions and setbacks developed, but the general thrust was forward. Critics and reformers played their role in exposing injustice and inefficiency, sometimes real and sometimes imagined, but the general mood was bullish. Any reader of this book who has felt the lure of economic determinism will be more resistant hereafter. And every student of economic growth must reckon with Professor Kirkland's striking findings about a colorful era.

The Editors

Preface

A preface is an opportunity to be personal. I do not claim that the method I have used in this volume is the only, or even the most valuable, one for treating the controversial period it covers. For instance, the period might be treated statistically or in terms of the currently popular theory of economic growth. As for the former approach, there is no need of dispute about methodology; the statistical data simply do not exist. While some series have been thrust back into the later decades of the nineteenth century and there is a promising current effort to enlarge their number, an excursion through the period as a whole is, as one statistican has wittily put it, one "through the badlands of statistics." My preference for some approach other than a theory of economic growth is based upon the conviction that most interpretations of the period have already suffered enough from the retrospective application to the data of hypotheses, presuppositions, patterns, and stereotypes.

On the contrary, my desire has been to find out how the period actually looked to contemporaries who participated in its activities: politicians and businessmen and labor leaders. Two previous short works of mine sketched some of the preliminary results of this quest. This large and final volume is a history of economic policy, public and private, and its relationship with economic performance. I hope it will loosen up the economic determinism so frequently and so exclusively applied to the events and appearances of these years. The scriptural observation "As a man thinketh in his heart, so is he" seems to promise that the approach to economic development through the avenue of thought may be fruitful.

I am deeply grateful for assistance. The John S. Guggenheim Foundation helped me inaugurate these studies with a fellowship. Of all the libraries in which I worked, the Dartmouth College Library had to bear the heaviest burden in providing facilities and services; its officers and rank and file alike showed hospitality and resourcefulness. Professor George Rogers Taylor, who read the entire manuscript, brought his fine sense of perspective to its many problems. My wife, Ruth Babson Kirkland, gave indispensable aid in the preparation of the manuscript and in seeing it through publication.

April, 1961 Edward C. Kirkland

Contents

Illustrations

BETWEEN PAGES 144 AND 145

Between Pages 336 and 337

Industry Comes of Age

Business, Labor, and Public Policy

1860 - 1897

CHAPTER I

Business Vicissitudes

GENERAL FEATURES OF THE ECONOMY IN 1860

IN a nation with such immense resources of undeveloped land as the United States had at its founding, agricultural operations were the natural basis of its economy; from the Revolution to the Civil War the United States had a largely agricultural civilization. As the decades passed, however, changes began to cause disintegration of the agrarian way of life. One change was the beginning of industrialization. To be sure, machine production had fallen far short of touching all fields of manufacture. But a cotton textile industry, which began to be transformed as early as the last decade of the eighteenth century, had matured enough both to supply the domestic market and to ship some of its products to foreign markets, where they successfully competed with goods turned out by industrially more advanced nations. In the fifties, stirrings in the iron industry seemed to hold out the promise of extensive progress in the metallurgical industries. More important, the United States had secured a modern transportation system. After a period of experimentation with canals, the country had directed its enthusiasms, energies, and means to the locomotive. This concentration met with such success that by the sixties the United States had a longer railroad mileage than any other nation in the world. It was nearly three times that of Great Britain, the "inventor of the railroad." Of course American distances and wide-open spaces had compelled construction on this scale.[1] In spite of these considerable modifications in its agricultural civilization, the value of farm lands, livestock, farm machinery, and tools in 1860 was still roughly seven times the capital in manufacturing.[2]

At the outbreak of the Civil War, the United States was in truth an

[1] George R. Taylor, *The Transportation Revolution, 1815–1860* (New York: Holt, Rinehart and Winston, Inc., 1951), pp. 102–103, 143–149; M. G. Mulhall, *The Dictionary of Statistics* (London: George Routledge and Sons, 1899), p. 495.

[2] Bureau of the Census, *Historical Statistics of the United States, 1789–1945*, p. 2.

"undeveloped" country. It still relied, for instance, upon imports of manufactured articles and, for its own growth, still brought in investments, immigrant workers, and ideas from overseas. In the Atlantic community the United States was peripheral in terms of wealth and population. The center of that community was still in the more advanced countries of western Europe and Great Britain. Though the position of the United States was on the fringe, it did not thereby escape the marked alternations of prosperity and depression which had come to mark the economies of western capitalist nations. These cycles did not necessarily take place everywhere at precisely the same time, nor were their features and courses necessarily everywhere identical; nonetheless it seems possible, at least with the tools of later analysis, to distinguish periods of good and bad times and to describe in a general way their history. Many of the disputes characteristic of erudition on this subject, for instance the timing of "turning points," are best left to technicians.

THE PROSPERITY OF THE CIVIL WAR AND AFTER

Be that as it may, by the time of the Civil War the country's economy was shaking off the aftereffects of the panic of 1857. Although cycle theorists often prefer to exclude war from their patterns as an "exogenous event" or "random perturbation,"[3] the Civil War had repercussions upon the prospects and activities of business enterprise. Under inflationary pressures and an imbalance between supplies and demands, prices rose. Though some industries such as cotton textiles, which was deprived of its raw material, were for a time prostrated, others thrived. Between 1861 and 1865, the annual tonnage of coal mined rose from approximately 15,500,000 tons to 22,792,000; between 1861 and 1864 that of pig iron from 731,344, to 1,135,996. The multiplication by nearly six times of bank clearings in New York City testified to the quickening and expansion of production and trade.[4]

Within a few years after the war, one contemporary was recalling how the national government became the great consumer of agricultural and industrial goods, and how, though manpower was diverted to conflict, machinery and the more efficient employment of the remaining labor sprang to satisfy the national needs.[5] In the Treasury, David A.

[3] Joseph A. Schumpeter, *Business Cycles, A Theoretical, Historical, and Statistical Analysis of the Capitalist Process* (2 vols.: New York: McGraw-Hill Company, 1939), I, 314–315; Wesley C. Mitchell, "Business Cycles," *Encyclopedia of the Social Sciences,* III, 93.

[4] Bureau of the Census, *op. cit.,* pp. 142, 149, 270; Willard L. Thorp, *Business Annals* (New York: National Bureau of Economic Research, 1926), pp. 128–129.

[5] J. B. Hodgskin, "Financial Condition of the United States," *North American Review,* CVIII (April, 1869), 526–527.

Wells, the best informed among government officials on business conditions, cited a textile company in New England to show how in wartime property or claims to property rose rapidly in value: if at the beginning of the war the company had burnt its mills, lost its insurance, and relied instead upon the funds already invested in purchases of raw cotton which would be sold later at higher prices, "the result would have afforded the stockholders a permanent annuity of at least twelve per cent on their original investment." [6] A young correspondent of Charles F. Adams, Jr., chronicling the wartime speculative fever in Boston, cited the fabulous profits of stockholders in New England mills and the quick gains to be made in urban real estate speculation, where desirable plots of land were sold again and again in a day. He added, "Wealth stalks openly, but mostly it rides." [7] All this, of course, did not prove that the prosperity of the era was prosperity in depth nor conceal from the discerning that war destroyed rather than created real values.[8]

Those temperamentally suspicious of prosperity as "unsound" were suspicious of the economic activity of the Civil War and anticipated its collapse with the return of peace. Yet in 1867 Wells was asserting there was "great activity—industrial or speculative—in nearly every section of the country." There was at work "a spirit of enterprise which seems to redouble its energy with every additional burden placed upon it." [9] Though later analysts have isolated two occasions in the postwar era when the forward progress stumbled,[10] contemporaries usually were more impressed by the wonderful persistence of prosperity. The civilian economy with its pent-up needs hurried to satisfy them. Railroad and housing construction were cases in point.[11] Established industries, like cotton textiles, added annually an unprecedented amount of plant; new industries, such as petroleum and steel, burst into flower. The stream of immigrants, thinned during the war, quickened to a confident flood. The revival of the cotton trade brought some prosperity to the prostrate South. Government disbursements for arrears in soldiers' pay, for bounties and pensions, and for the settlement of contracts totaled $700,000,000

[6] "Report of the Special Commissioner of the Revenue," *Senate Executive Document* No. 2 (s.n. 1276), 39th Cong., 2d Sess., p. 21.

[7] Edward C. Kirkland, "Boston during the Civil War," *Proceedings of the Massachusetts Historical Society*, LXXI (1953–1957), 200–202.

[8] "Report of the Special Commissioner of the Revenue," *House Executive Document* No. 27 (s.n. 1416), 41st Cong., 2d Sess., p. xlv.

[9] "Report of the Special Commissioner of the Revenue," *Senate Executive Document* No. 2 (s.n. 1276), 39th Cong., 2d Sess., p. 10.

[10] Rendig Fels, *American Business Cycles, 1865–1897* (Chapel Hill: University of North Carolina Press, 1959), p. 84.

[11] [Poor's] *Manual of the Railroads of the United States for 1875–76* (New York: H. V. and H. W. Poor, 1875), p. xxvii.

in a little less than four years and "were immediately invested in the purchase of food, clothing, shelter, implements, transportation and business." [12]

THE "NEW ERA" OF DEPRESSION

As usually happens in human affairs, something went wrong. Though in 1872 and early 1873 the exceptionally foresighted or the easily frightened had premonitions of business disaster, the collapse held off until September 18, 1873. On that day the public learned that the firms of Jay Cooke, the most noted financier of the American Civil War, could not meet their bills: Cooke's little empire of brokers' offices and banks in New York, Philadelphia, and Washington closed its doors. Excitement shook the stock exchange, railroad and industrial concerns, and the money market. So great and rapid was the collapse of security values that the Governing Committee of the New York Stock Exchange closed their institution two days after Cooke's downfall. When the Exchange reopened ten days later, the severest spasm of the crisis had passed.[13]

After a considerable interval of prostration and recovery, the distressing phenomena of panic recurred in the mid-eighties. To be sure, the descent into the maelstrom was gradual. In the second half of 1883 business took a downturn; continued financial uneasiness characterized the months that followed; and finally in early May, 1884, a panic brought down in ruins a welter of banks and brokers. Among the brokerage houses was that of Grant and Ward, distinguished by the presence of a former President of the United States among its partners and by liabilities in excess of $17,000,000. A contemporary declared that the blackness of this moment was "even more unexpected to the country than that of September 1873." [14]

In 1890 the spectacular collapse in Great Britain of the Barings, an imperial firm of international bankers long associated with the United States and its economic development, was a storm signal; though American financial institutions and money markets felt the shock, a bumper

[12] D. A. Wells, "The Meaning of Revenue Reform," *North American Review*, CXIII (July, 1871), 112–113; "Report of the Special Commissioner of the Revenue," *Senate Executive Document* No. 2 (s.n. 1276) 39th Cong., 2d Sess., pp. 9–10; "Report of the Special Commissioner of the Revenue," *House Executive Document* No. 81 (s.n. 1332), 40th Cong., 2d Sess., pp. 18–19; "Report of the Secretary of the Treasury on . . . the Finances . . . 1871," *House Executive Document* No. 2 (s.n. 1507), 42d Cong., 2d Sess., p. viii.

[13] *Commercial and Financial Chronicle*, CVII (September 6, 1873), 301; (September 13, 1873), 33; (September 20, 1873), 275–276, 383; (October 4, 1873), 448.

[14] "Report of the Comptroller . . . 1884," *House Executive Document* No. 2 (s.n. 2291), 48th Cong., 2d Sess., pp. 148–150.

crop of American wheat and its export at high prices to European consumers short of grain warded off in 1891 and 1892 the full force of the blow. The next year this brief interval of immunity ended. In February, the failure of the first of a string of important railroads marked the onset of panic; in May, one of the most conspicuous of the new industrial trusts, National Cordage, "collapsed like a bursted meteor," and by the end of the next month the traditional week of black disaster strained and tortured the nation's financial and business structure. A few months of financial tension and successive cyclones on the stock market ensued.[15]

Since the most dramatic and frightening aspect of business vacillations was the banking "panic" or "money crisis," contemporaries were apt to see here a cause for business misfortunes. American business, they discovered with some degree of astonishment, increasingly relied, as did business in other advanced countries, upon borrowed capital. Once, so it was said, those who owned capital had managed capital; the post-Civil War structure of bankers, brokers, and other middlemen of money and credit was something new and dangerous. If these lenders on a large scale once suspected the inability of debtors to meet their obligations, whether interest on railroad bonds, farm mortgages, or bank loans, the panic began. The first wave of terror crashed upon the exchanges and the banks. In the stock market, values of securities sank. From the banks depositors hastened to withdraw their funds. The banks called in their loans and hesitated to extend old ones or make new; and when the banks' resources, including their reserves, were exhausted, they stopped shoving money over their counters and swung their doors shut.[16] Hard-pressed debtors tried to borrow anew and to turn their property into liquid funds for discharging existing obligations at the very moment it was difficult to do so. Interest rates, particularly on call loans, fluctuated widely—during the brief crisis of 1890 the figure reached 186 per cent a year.[17]

The first rescue measures were naturally those taken to stay the panic. In the chief cities of the United States the clearing-houses, those new associations of banks, resorted to concerted action to save themselves. In New York the clearinghouse banks in 1873 pooled their specie reserves and issued to distressed members, on acceptable collateral, clearinghouse certificates by which they were able to discharge their obligations to each other without the transfer of cash. Thus the banks

[15] *Commercial and Financial Chronicle,* LVI (February 25, 1893), 311–312, 322; (May 6, 1893), 728; LVII (July 1, 1893), 2–4; (July 29, 1893), 162; (August 19, 1893), 272; (August 26, 1893), 321–322.

[16] *Commercial and Financial Chronicle,* XX (January 23, 1875), 72; (March 20, 1875), 276–277.

[17] *Commercial and Financial Chronicle,* LI (November 22, 1890), 692–693.

freed money to quiet the public pressure. In 1884, 1890, and 1893, the banks again resorted to this device for settling their inter-bank balances. Such emergencies were of short duration. Somewhat less than five months after the first certificate issue in 1893, the New York Clearing House was holding a jubilee meeting to celebrate the cancellation of the last of the loan certificates issued that year.[18]

Much less easy to account for was the long period of "languor," "lassitude," "stagnation," or "depression" which followed a panic. For one thing, being less intense and headlong than a crisis, the depression required a different standard of measurement. Since fantastic rates on call loans and the frightening decline of reserves were no longer characteristic, some observers chose to measure the long aftermath of depression in terms of imports and exports, including shipments of gold, and asserted that an increase in exports and a favorable balance of trade was the signature of American prosperity. Others resorted to that great human referendum on American conditions, the number of immigrants. With peculiar appropriateness, for instance, arrivals reached their high tide of the nineteenth century in 1882, a peak of temporary prosperity.[19] Though some contemporaries resorted to another social test, the extent of unemployment, national figures on this matter were unfortunately untrustworthy.

One of the more precise mathematical tests for measuring the ebb and flow of the economy was change in the totals of bank clearings. Thus New York's totals fell from $35,461 millions in 1873 to $21,597 millions in 1876; and in the nation as a whole from $61,054 in 1882 to $37,770 in 1885 and from $60,884 in 1892 to a low point of $45,028 in 1894. As a measure of the volume of business, these astronomical figures were somewhat tainted in the eyes of the purists by the inclusion of speculative transactions on the stock exchange.[20] Perhaps the statistics of the transportation interests of the country, "the cut water to commercial prosperity," were more revealing. New railroad construction, which in the early seventies once attained 7,379 miles in a single year, fell in the middle of the decade to a low of 1,711; in 1882, new mileage was 11,569; in 1885 only 2,982; in 1895 only 1,519.[21]

[18] Fritz Redlich, *The Molding of American Banking. Men and Ideas* (New York: Hafner Publishing Company, 1951), Vol. II, Part II, pp. 165–167; *Commercial and Financial Chronicle,* LVII (November 4, 1893), 740, 749.

[19] *Commercial and Financial Chronicle,* LVI (January 28, 1893), 145–147; *First Annual Report of the* [U. S.] *Commissioner of Labor, March, 1886,* pp. 245–247.

[20] Bureau of the Census, *Historical Statistics of the United States, 1789–1945,* p. 270; *Commercial and Financial Chronicle,* LVIII (January 5, 1894), 5.

[21] C. S. Smith and F. B. Thurber, "What Will Bring Prosperity?" *North American Review,* CLXIV (April, 1897), 428; *Poor's Manual of the Railroads of the United States . . . 1897* (New York: H. V. and H. W. Poor, 1898), p. vi; Charles Hoffman,

The performance of individual industries varied in significance. In the seventies the cotton industry furnished the favorite figures for those who wished to read the present and forecast the future. By the nineties the annual tonnages of pig-iron were more esteemed as a "barometer of our industries." Production declined by very nearly 800,000 tons between 1873 and 1876; by 649,000 tons between 1882 and 1885; and by almost 2,800,000 tons between 1892 and 1894.[22] Since business downswings were also periods of liquidations, observers brooded over the figures of business failures, obligingly provided by a firm in which, no matter how titled, the name of Dun always appeared. Though its quarterly and annual compilations did not include railroad or bank failures, Dun's reports were a significant measure of the mortality among American commercial and industrial enterprises.

In a rough way all these evidences pointed to the conclusion that periods of business prostration lasted four or five years: 1873–1878, 1882–1885, 1893–1897.

Contemporary commentators went through a corresponding cycle of emotions. At first they were sure that the differences from previous depressions meant the current one would not be so bad; later, as hopes were deferred and patience strained, each depression became the most severe in American or all history. Thus Andrew Carnegie currently observed of 1893, "It is doubtful if a more disastrous cyclone ever blasted a country to such an extent in so short a time."[23] From the detached vantage point of later scholarship, it was possible to discern that among the depressions in the late nineteenth century the one of the seventies was the most severe.[24]

Though short periods of revival and prosperity in 1878–1882, and less certainly in 1886–1892, separated the major depressions from one another, the predominance of years of business stagnation increasingly impressed beholders. Consequently, whereas the unthinking continued to look upon prosperity as the norm, the more perceptive frequently concluded that a "new epoch" confronted Americans. In the eighties, Carroll D. Wright, first United States Commissioner of Labor, asserted with appropriately hopeful reservations that the fifty years of building

---

"The Depression of the Nineties," *Journal of Economic History*, XVI (June, 1956), 141–142.

[22] *Commercial and Financial Chronicle*, LVII (November 11, 1893), 785; Bureau of the Census, *Historical Statistics of the United States, 1789–1945*, p. 149.

[23] Andrew Carnegie, "The Silver Problem: A Word to Wage Earners," *North American Review*, CLVII (September, 1893), 355; *Commercial and Financial Chronicle*, LVI (February 25, 1893), 322.

[24] A. R. Eckler, "A Measure of the Severity of Depressions, 1873–1932," *Review of Economic Statistics*, XV (May 15, 1933), 77, 81; Charles Hoffman, "The Depression of the Nineties," *loc. cit.*, pp. 137–138.

up the economy of western industrial nations was at an end: "The day of large profits is probably past. . . . The market price of products will continue low." A decade later David A. Wells, who whether in public or private life liked to play Cassandra, collected in his *Recent Economic Changes* a series of articles emphasizing, among other themes, the continued dominance of depression phenomena.[25] At the same time, as the additional returns from the mid-nineties came in, J. W. Jenks, a professor at Cornell, described what had happened in terms of "great waves covering a score or more of years and bearing the panic fluctuations on their surface like mere ripples." [26]

The course of prices reflected these long downward swings in the economy. Later rather than contemporary analysis has furnished the most widely accepted index of price performance. According to it, the "general price index" stood at 100 in 1873 and declined to 77 in the depression which followed; the downturn in the mid-eighties carried the figure from 87 to 76; that of the early nineties from 78 in 1890 to 71 in both 1894 and 1896. At the last two dates, for the first time since Appomattox, the general price level fell to the position it had occupied when Abraham Lincoln was first elected President of the United States.[27]

THE CAUSES OF DEPRESSION

Since the long deflation deeply disturbed relationships between creditors and debtors, employers and employees, buyers and sellers, contemporary thought worked hard to fit the perilous years into some generalized pattern of cause and effect; for, though it was quite willing to christen the debacle of 1873 the "Jay Cooke panic," it was reluctant to explain the lean years that followed in terms of the misdeeds or mistakes of a single tycoon, no matter how formidable. Depression theory on the popular and business level—no attempt is made here to soar to the scholarly level—even before the Civil War had compiled a considerable body of data and explanation; after the experience of the late nineteenth century, the record of opinion was longer and more varied.[28] In general

[25] *First Annual Report of the* [U. S.] *Commissioner of Labor, March, 1888*, pp. 254–258; David A. Wells, *Recent Economic Changes* (New York: D. Appleton and Company, 1899), pp. 1, 6.

[26] J. W. Jenks, "Causes of the Fall of Prices since 1872," *Journal of Social Science*, No. XXXV (1897), 34 ff.

[27] Bureau of the Census, *Historical Statistics of the United States, 1789–1945*, pp. 231–232.

[28] Harry E. Miller, *Banking Theories in the United States before 1860* (Cambridge: Harvard University Press, 1927), pp. 187–207; Paul Barnett, *Business-Cycle Theory in the United States, 1860–1900* (Chicago: University of Chicago Press, 1947), *passim.*

this body of doctrine leaned more heavily on analogy than analysis. Thus the oscillations of good and bad times were compared to the swing of the pendulum or were said to be subject to the "wave-law" which "appears to play a part in human activities as important as the place assigned to it in the physical sciences." [29] Meteorology furnished metaphors; economic affairs built up to the tension of the tropical atmosphere preceding a storm, and once the blow was over, fair weather returned.[30] From horticulture came the idea of "a sequence of causes as the seed follows from the bud, the flower, and the fruit." [31] From physiology, anatomy, and medicine came the comparison of disease and health, and sometimes more detailed specifications. "Like some forms of organic life, our economic system, when weak members are lopped off, quickly puts forth newer and stronger members to take their place"—this of the process of liquidation.[32]

Though such verbalisms were frequent, they were far from constituting the whole body of contemporary thought on the causes of prolonged depressions. When Carroll D. Wright and his agents in the Bureau of Labor tallied in the eighties the "alleged causes" of depression, they arranged their findings under seventy-one headings. Nonetheless Wright concluded that the great cause of the "industrial disease" was underconsumption. Meager returns on crops, lower wages, the decline in railroad building, and the consequent unemployment, all impaired the community's capacity for making purchases. "Any disturbance in the monetary affairs of our country by which the purchasing power of money is decreased cripples the consuming power of the people, and when the people, through apprehension or through real results, feel that their consuming power is crippled in ever so slight a degree, individual retrenchment begins and corresponding stagnation follows." [33]

Others viewed much the same facts under a different aspect: overproduction. Americans found it hard to accept this possibility. As was natural in a new country with huge undeveloped resources and vistas of gain before every eye, Americans had feared scarcity and had made a god of production. One of the most American of economic thinkers in this era, Henry George, the author of *Progress and Poverty* and crusader

[29] Henry Clews, "The Late Financial Crisis," *North American Review,* CLII (January, 1890), 105; *Commercial and Financial Chronicle,* XVIII (May 23, 1874), 515.

[30] *Commercial and Financial Chronicle,* XVII (October 11, 1873), 479.

[31] Gamaliel Bradford, "Lombard and Wall Street," *North American Review,* CXIX (October, 1874), 350.

[32] *Commercial and Financial Chronicle,* XVII (November 29, 1873), 710; XIX (September 29, 1874), 305; (October 4, 1874), 410.

[33] *First Annual Report of the* [U. S.] *Commissioner of Labor, March, 1886,* pp. 76–79, 243–246, 291–292.

for the single tax, announced: "I do not think there can be any such thing as an over production until everybody has more than enough." [34] Still the upshot of Wells' argument in *Recent Economic Changes* was that "the use of the word 'over-production,' stripped of its looseness of expression . . . is not inappropriate in discussing the economic phenomena under consideration." Wells was cautious in defining overproduction and the methods which brought it about.[35]

Diverging at many points from these analyses was the conclusion that panics and depressions emerged from the course of investment. As capital and savings were sunk in economic enterprises, optimism and speculation led to mistakes in the calculations as to which were likely to be profitable; and, once suspicions were aroused, it was discovered that the business community had put too large a share of its resources into fixed, long-time commitments; there were not enough liquid funds to carry on current business. This explained the financial stringency that was the herald of depression. While waiting for "latent" capital to earn a return, the community lived frugally, saved, and recreated a new fund for loaning and investment. As bankers, brokers, and capitalists once again enjoyed more funds than they knew what to do with, interest rates declined and enterprising men with an eye open for new opportunities borrowed them. In so far as lenders were surfeited with money and interest rates fell, the facts were indubitable. But the process of borrowing and investment did not necessarily follow.[36] For that, confidence was a needful prelude. People must believe that money would make more money. With typical metaphor, the *Commercial and Financial Chronicle* declared: "If the monetary circulation is compared to the circulation of the blood, the movements of economic confidence resemble those of the nerves. . . . Depression and weakness cannot give place to buoyancy and vigor until the deep-seated trouble in the nervous centers has been relieved." [37]

SOLUTIONS

In the diversity and tentativeness of these diagnoses there was a handicap to remedial action. Horace White observed in 1887, from the

[34] Testimony of Henry George, *Report of the Committee* [on Education and Labor] *of the Senate . . . 1885,* I, 471.

[35] Wells, *Recent Economic Changes,* pp. 70–113, 291.

[36] *Commercial and Financial Chronicle,* XIX (December 12, 1874), 585; XX (January 2, 1875), 1–2; Bonamy Price, "The Stagnation of Trade and Its Cause," *North American Review,* CXXVII (June, 1879), 587–601; *Nation,* LXII (January 30, 1896), 93; T. C. Cochran, *Railroad Leaders, 1845–1890: The Business Mind in Action* (Cambridge: Harvard University Press, 1953), p. 103.

[37] *Commercial and Financial Chronicle,* XXIV (January 20, 1877), 50.

vantage point of journalism and business, that "at present it must be admitted that economists themselves are not sufficiently agreed upon the fundamental principles of commercial crises to command strict attention from the unprofessional classes." [38] And the habit of discussing depressions—even if it were rhetorical—in terms of mechanics, meteorology, and health implied that depressions were subject to natural law and about all that could be done was to wait, be patient, and perchance recover.[39] There were occasional signs of a breach in this policy of resignation and endurance. Ideological consistency alone helped incline the advocates of a protective tariff to accept a resort to government action. At any rate the statement of Justin Morrill, Republican Senator from Vermont, was conceivably of wider application than to the many protective tariff bills bearing his name. He dissented from "the idea . . . that nothing should be done by any people through legislation to change or to elevate and increase their industrial power." [40] Others felt that, at the very least, general policy or specific legislation could remove obstructions to business expansion and even directly stimulate, revive, and enlarge it.[41]

Pummeled by direful experience, members of the business community seemingly moved toward the idea that government policy could relieve, if not solve, the depressed state of affairs. The greenback program, as the next chapter notes, enlisted support among capitalists. At the tail end of the depression of the seventies, the orthodox *Commercial and Financial Chronicle* bemoaned "the bad habit induced by our war finance" which had led businessmen to look "to Congress and to its daily debates for assistance in the work of forecasting the future of business and of the money market." A generation later, in 1893, the same journal seemed to take it as axiomatic that the economic welfare of the nation depended upon what was done or undone at Washington and that businessmen, together and singly, were to be commended for their efforts in securing the repeal of harmful legislation.[42] Since the focus in the last

[38] Horace White, "Commercial Crises," J. J. Lalor, ed., *Cyclopedia of Political Science, Political Economy, and Political History* (New York: Charles E. Merrill and Company, 1885), I, 530; Wells, *Recent Economic Changes*, p. 81n.

[39] A. T. Hadley, *Railroad Transportation: Its History and Its Laws* (New York: G. P. Putnam's Sons, 1885), p. 49; *Commercial and Financial Chronicle*, XVIII (March 28, 1874), 307.

[40] J. S. Morrill, "Free Trade or Protection," *North American Review*, CL (March, 1890), 283.

[41] David A. Wells, "How Shall the Nation Regain Prosperity?" *North American Review*, CXXXV (September, 1877), 284; William S. Russell, "Political Causes of the Business Depression," *North American Review*, CLVII (December, 1893), 641–642.

[42] *Commercial and Financial Chronicle*, XXII (February 12, 1876), 145; LVII (September 2, 1893), 356–360.

instance was upon a specific measure, the Sherman Silver Purchase Act, the shift in business attitude must not be overemphasized. The thick-and-thin advocates of government intervention to meet the depression were other groups: farmers,[43] laborers to some extent, and reformers.

[43] F. A. Shannon, *The Farmer's Last Frontier* (New York: Holt, Rinehart, and Winston, Inc., 1945), pp. 185–188, 314–326.

CHAPTER II

Government Finance, Banking, and Currency

PONDERING one of the unexpected business downturns in the post-Civil War era, David A. Wells commented, "It is not easy . . . to see in what manner the shrinkage of values . . . could have been averted by any present legislation of Congress . . ."[1] The statement might be taken to express either perplexity over effective policy or an uncertainty about Congressional power to act in such matters. While doubts over Congressional authority to regulate or direct the economy were legitimate in the sixties, there was one field, government finance, in which the founding fathers had delegated to the central government an ample area for action. Congress had the right to levy certain taxes and incur debts, to "coin money," and "to regulate the value thereof." These and other relevant constitutional clauses the Supreme Court had interpreted as far back as 1819 broadly enough to permit the national government to charter a National Bank.[2]

Although it is a mistake to believe that the Civil War initiated every change in the economy of the United States, there is no doubt that the financial needs of that conflict compelled the North to innovate on a wide scale. In matters of currency and banking it took several new departures. Some of the resulting institutions lasted into the twentieth century; the debate over their performance, and their relationship or usefulness to a period of baffling business fluctuations, was continuous throughout the decades between the Civil War and the turn of the century. Not until the late nineties was the nation monetarily put upon

[1] "Report of the Special Commissioner of the Revenue, 1868," *House Executive Document* No. 81 (s.n. 1332), 40th Cong., 2d Sess., p. 28.

[2] H. S. Commager, editor, *Documents of American History* (New York: F. S. Crofts & Co., 1940), pp. 141, 213–220.

a relatively stable course. In summary, the financial exigencies of the Civil War put everything in flux. Old landmarks and old courses were submerged by the tide of change. As early as 1868 Wells was lamenting, "It is now nearly seven years since gold and silver disappeared from circulation among us. During this time a large proportion of young men and women of the country have come upon the stage of active life. They have grown up without any practical knowledge of the values of a metallic currency. Their ideas and habits have been formed in the most vicious school of economy; and it is exceedingly desirable that specie should reappear among us before the harmful education shall have ripened into its natural fruit of universal extravagance and insolvency."[3] It is time now to turn to the measures, circumstances, and policies that induced this despair.

HANDICAPS AND INSUFFICIENCIES

The Mexican War, the most recent conflict in men's minds when the Civil War began, had been relatively easy to finance. The Treasury had met its costs from duties on imports, customarily the chief source of government revenue, and from the sale of less than $100,000,000 in government securities, a large portion of it to European investors.[4] The prospect facing the Treasury in 1861 was less hopeful. For one thing, government finances were showing deleterious deficits, an aftermath of the panic of 1857.[5] For another thing, few were in a position to forecast the length and intensity of the Civil War. Consequently on July 4, 1861, when Salmon P. Chase, Secretary of the Treasury in the Lincoln cabinet, presented his matured financial program for dealing during the next twelvemonth with the "flagrant violence" of a "vast conspiracy," he had to hope the sheer wickedness of the rebellion would soon bring the Confederacy down in ruins. For the rest he approached his problems rather gingerly and conventionally. Chase felt loans must pay for the war. Taxes were to meet only the ordinary expenses of government, the interest on the debt, and payments toward the gradual extinction of the principal.[6] He justified this preference, at least in retrospect, on the ground that it was unwise to increase the tax burdens of the people

[3] "Report of the Special Commissioner of the Revenue, 1868," *House Executive Document* No. 16 (s.n. 1372), 40th Cong., 3d Sess., pp. 63, 65.

[4] Fritz Redlich, *The Molding of American Banking. Men and Ideas,* Vol. II, Part II (New York: Hafner Publishing Company, 1951), 347–351.

[5] "Report of the Secretary of the Treasury . . . July 4, 1861," *Senate Executive Document* No. 2 (s.n. 1112), 37th Cong., 1st Sess., pp. 11–12.

[6] *Ibid.*, p. 6; "Report of the Secretary of the Treasury on . . . the Finances . . . 1861," *Senate Executive Document* No. 2 (s.n. 1121), 37th Cong., 2d Sess., pp. 20–21.

when a "flagitious rebellion had deranged their business, and temporarily deranged their incomes." [7]

If loans were to be the chief method, the nearness or remoteness of their due date, the rate of interest, the method of sale, the "money" for which indebtedness was to be sold, all involved cognate and complicated decisions. The Treasury dreamed of selling short-term securities directly to the people—this was loyal and democratic—through government agencies at a rate of interest, 7.3 per cent, by which the lender could easily calculate his return, a cent a day on fifty dollars. When these visions did not materialize, the government and certain banks in New York, Philadelphia, and Boston made an arrangement by which the banks were to take government securities through a loan of $150,000,000 in three installments.[8] The bankers expected that they would enter this sum on their books as a credit to the government; that the Treasury would draw on it for expenditures; that these expenditures, flowing back into the banks, would form the basis for further credits. In the end "the people . . . loaned their capital to the government by giving credit to the bank promises, while the banks held the security in government bonds." To this inflationary process there was some check, in that the banks planned to tap the capital of private investors by selling them the government securities.[9] On this last count, the banks were not particularly successful.

Either because Chase did not understand this arrangement, or could not execute it in the face of his scruples about statutory restrictions, or because a dismaying military and diplomatic situation led individuals by the end of 1861 to withdraw gold for hoarding or for export, the specie reserve of the banks fell so low that they could not meet the demands made upon them by their depositors. They suspended specie payments on December 20, 1861. In this setting it was quite impossible for the government to continue to pay out coin for its expenditures or for the redemption of its notes. With promptitude it likewise announced its own inevitable departure from a specie basis.[10] Chase's policy of paying for the war through loans came to a standstill. This was not all. The government had no money and the banks had no "legal money" to constitute the reserves many state laws required them to carry wherewith to redeem their notes.

[7] "Report of the Secretary of the Treasury on . . . the Finances . . . 1863," *House Executive Document* No. 3 (s.n. 1186), 38th Cong., 1st Sess., p. 10.

[8] Redlich, *op. cit.*, Vol. II, Part II, 86–92.

[9] [Hunt's] *Merchants' Magazine and Commercial Review*, LI (July, 1864), 31–32.

[10] *Ibid.*, XLVI (January, 1862), 101–102; LI (July, 1864), 32; Paul Studenski and H. E. Krooss, *Financial History of the United States* (New York: McGraw-Hill Company, 1952), p. 143.

SOFT MONEY

In these desperate circumstances, Congress took over. E. G. Spaulding, a member of the Ways and Means Committee in the House and formerly Treasurer of the State of New York, made the original suggestions which, in February, 1862, bore fruit in a bill authorizing the national government to issue $150,000,000 in Treasury notes.[11] These notes, soon christened greenbacks because of the ink they were printed with, were not convertible into gold or silver—though they were redeemable in government bonds bearing interest in gold—for the government had suspended specie payments. It was the understanding, however, that their inconvertibility was temporary; that after the war these United States notes would be canceled or redeemed in one fashion or another.[12] To give the notes a current acceptability, the act made them legal tender in the payment of all private and public debts, except duties on imports and interest on the public debt: for these purposes coin was still required. In answer to those doubtful about the constitutionality of this legislation, or disturbed by the previous experience of the country under an inflated paper currency, the cry of necessity rang through the House and Senate.[13]

The legal tenders or greenbacks became such a heated issue in American politics and economics that their opponents drenched the origin of the greenbacks in obloquy. According to the argument, the legal tender act was the result of financial ignorance or of loose Western radicalism, the two explanations overlapped each other. Henry Brooks Adams, the young Easterner returning from Europe in 1866 in search of an education and job, wielded with the help of economist F. A. Walker, the most merciless pen of those who felt the greenbacks wrong or unnecessary.[14] Adams censured Spaulding because he came from upstate New York and was a "country banker," thus having "the advantage or disadvantage of a certain sort of financial experience." Thaddeus Stevens of Pennsylvania, chairman of the influential House Committee on Ways and Means, "was as little suited to direct the economic policy

[11] 12 *United States Statutes,* 345; E. G. Spaulding, *History of the Legal Tender Paper Money* (Buffalo: Express Printing Company, 1869), pp. 5–14.

[12] Max L. Shipley, "The Background and Legal Aspects of the Pendleton Plan," *Mississippi Valley Historical Review,* XXIV (1937–1938), 334–339.

[13] W. C. Mitchell, *A History of the Greenbacks* (Chicago: University of Chicago Press, 1903), pp. 91–98, 117–118; "Report of the Secretary of the Treasury on . . . the Finances . . . 1862," *Senate Executive Document* No. 1 (s.n. 1149), 37th Cong., 3d Sess., pp. 8–9.

[14] Henry B. Adams, *The Education of Henry Adams* (Boston: Houghton Mifflin Company, 1918), pp. 234, 247–250, 277–278.

of the country at a critical moment, as a naked Indian from the plains to plan the architecture of St. Peters or to direct the construction of the Capital. . . ." [15] Unremarked in this tirade was the fact that among the most influential advocates in the House was Samuel Hooper, one of the wealthiest men in Massachusetts, and that some of the direst prophecies of the doom inherent in paper money came from spokesmen of the West.[16] On the other hand, Chase, who was a hard-money man, paradoxically pronounced the measure an administrative must.[17]

In 1862 supporters of the legal tenders promised restraint in further issues. These commitments were soon broken. Within a year two additional issues were authorized. Pessimists felt justified. "To grant any earthly power the legal right, under any circumstances, to issue notes which it is not obliged to pay in coin, and to expect this right not to be abused, is like putting an open cask of wine before a thirsty laborer, with the expectation he will confine himself to a single glass." [18] By June, 1865, there were $462,687,966 in greenbacks outstanding.[19] Meanwhile, because of the suspicion of greenbacks and the continued need for gold —for export, customs duties, and for the settlement of previous gold contracts—gold had risen to a premium. Trading in this commodity had resulted on July 11, 1844 in a price of $100 in greenbacks for $35.09 in gold. This was depreciation's highest point.[20] Prices for goods in terms of paper currency had also mounted. In 1860 the general price index stood at 71; in 1864 at 129.[21] For a time the proponents of the greenbacks denied there was an increase in prices; later—blaming the gold premium on speculators, Southern sympathizers, and rebel agents—they sought to prohibit trading in gold and ascribed the inflation to economic maladjustments of war and to the expansion of credit by the banks.[22] As in all wars, the cause for a price rise could not be singular. Wartime shortages in raw materials—for example, cotton—and in finished goods and more extravagant wants joined an expanded currency to boost prices.

[15] Henry B. Adams, "The Legal-Tender Act," *North American Review*, CX (April, 1870), 302–304.

[16] "Samuel Hooper," *Dictionary of American Biography*, IX, 203–204; Spaulding, *op. cit.*, pp. 73–74, 78, 89–90.

[17] "Report of the Secretary of the Treasury on . . . the Finances . . . 1862," *Senate Executive Document* No. 1 (s.n. 1149), 37th Cong., 2d Sess., pp. 6–9.

[18] "Our Financial Future," *North American Review*, CII (January, 1866), 106.

[19] "Report of the Secretary of the Treasury on . . . the Finances . . . 1865," *House Executive Document* No. 3 (s.n. 1254), 39th Cong., 1st Sess., pp. 52–53.

[20] Mitchell, *op. cit.*, p. 427.

[21] Bureau of the Census, *Historical Statistics of the United States, 1789–1945*, p. 232.

[22] "Report of the Secretary of the Treasury on . . . the Finances . . . 1862," *Senate Executive Document* No. 1 (s.n. 1149), 37th Cong., 3d Sess., pp. 12–15; Mitchell, *op. cit.*, pp. 183–189, 209–210.

The issue of the greenbacks interlocked with the loan policy of the government. The legal tender statutes also authorized the Treasury to sell batches of securities in large amounts. The greenbacks provided the currency which, being legal tender, could be used again and again in the course of circulation to purchase the loans. As the greenbacks depreciated, the interest rate on government bonds was actually much higher than stated. When a gold dollar bought two greenback dollars and the latter were in turn invested in government securities, the stated interest rate of 6 per cent payable in gold was really twelve. Spaulding and Chase were in agreement that to float the government loans, the government must first make sure that enough greenbacks were in circulation.[23]

THE NATIONAL BANKS

Civil War finance bestowed upon the United States the greenbacks. It also gave the nation its national bank system. In one sense the two devices were complementary: in another, alternatives. Perhaps the latter aspect was uppermost in Chase's plans. As a hard-money man, he had an instinctive alarm at the prospect of government paper money. As early as his report of July, 1861, he wrote that an irredeemable paper currency was a certain and "fatal expedient for impoverishing the masses and discrediting the government."[24] He much preferred bank notes issued by private corporations: these notes, as in the case of banks in New York State and elsewhere, were to be based upon government bonds and a specie reserve. Unhappily, existing notes, issued by banks chartered in the states and regulated by a variety of state statutes, were neither uniform in value nor necessarily safe. What was needed, Chase thought, was a banking system which was national in scope and at the same time not a monopoly of one central bank. Under ideal arrangements the national government could exercise, through a number of national banks, its undoubted authority "to control the credit circulation which enters so largely into the transactions of commerce and affects in so many ways the value of coin."[25] Though clearly Chase had in mind advantages which would operate for a period longer than the war emergency, his proposed arrangements would also serve the Treasury in

[23] Spaulding, *op. cit.*, pp. 190–197; "Report of the Secretary of the Treasury on . . . the Finances . . . 1862," *Senate Executive Document* No. 7 (s.n. 1149), 37th Cong., 3d Sess., p. 14.

[24] "Report of the Secretary of the Treasury on . . . the Finances . . . July 4, 1861," *Senate Executive Document* No. 2 (s.n. 1112), 37th Cong., 1st Sess., p. 14.

[25] "Report of the Secretary of the Treasury on . . . the Finances . . . 1861," *Senate Executive Document* No. 2 (s.n. 1121), 37th Cong., 2d Sess., p. 17.

its current operations. Government securities would be sold to the banking corporations, and the resulting bank notes, as legal tender for bond purchases and for all taxes except customs, would be acceptable to the Treasury, as the supplanted state bank notes were not.[26] With help and advice from government servants, from Congressmen, and from some bankers, Chase's plan for a national banking system was enacted early in 1863 in a bill fittingly enough characterized as the "National Currency Bill." The next year another statute, making national incorporation more attractive to bankers, really got the system under way.[27]

The aim of these enactments was to transform existing banks into or to found new ones under national rather than state charters. The institutions were to issue bank notes, secured from a Comptroller of the Currency, by depositing with him a somewhat larger value of government bonds. Each bank was to keep on hand a redemption fund of lawful money—greenbacks qualified—equal to 25 per cent of its circulation and deposits. As a crude stab at relating government control of credit to the needs of the country, a provision apportioned the bank note issue among the states and territories in proportion to their population, resources, and business needs.[28] The total of these proposals aroused opposition. Banks under state charters saw little gain in transforming their institutions into national ones with fewer privileges; dreaded a host of small-scale competitors, since the capital requirements for national banks were not high; and saw fewer possibilities of profit under the new system than under the old. Furthermore, regions and communities with an ingrained localism dreaded a national system with fewer safeguards than in some of the older sections and with an indifference to local needs which the existing banks, no matter how poorly run, had understood and tried to serve.[29] Was this the time to innovate? Francis Bowen, a Harvard professor, thought not. "A great war is the very time for making trial of newly invented cannon and iron-clad ships; but it is no more a proper reason for experimenting with a new banking system than with a new religion." [30]

As an aid to financing the war, the national banking system arrived on the scene late. Toward the end of 1863 there were only 138 banks

[26] *Ibid.*, pp. 18–20; "Report of the Secretary of the Treasury on . . . the Finances . . . 1862," *Senate Executive Document* No. 1 (s.n. 1149), 37th Cong., 3d Sess., pp. 14–15, 19–20.

[27] A. M. Davis, *The Origin of the National Banking System*, pp. 36–101; Redlich, *op. cit.*, Vol. II, Part II, 100–105.

[28] Davis, *op. cit.*, pp. 155–196.

[29] Redlich, *op. cit.*, Vol. II, Part II, 105–108; Francis Bowen, *American Political Economy Including Strictures on the Management of the Currency and Finances since 1861* (New York: C. Scribner & Company, 1870), pp. 369–371, 381.

[30] Bowen, *op. cit.*, p. 368.

under national charter. Ohio had more than Pennsylvania, and Indiana than New York. In truth, the West with its inadequate banking welcomed the new dispensation; private bankers, hitherto without charters, also took the leadership in incorporation. Revisions of the act, strenuous preachment of patriotic duty, and leadership by government officials or bankers associated with government financial operations then made breaches in the inflexible East.[31] Finally an Act of 1865 taxing state bank notes 10 per cent on the amount every time any bank paid them out spurred the changeover.[32] In mid-1865 there were 1,294 national banks: their resources included $393,988,000 in government securities.[33]

JAY COOKE AND LOAN POLICY

As the general situation and existing institutions grew better adapted to a successful loan policy, the government also resorted to more effective ways for disposing of loans. Sale through the banks and through government offices "to the people" had failed in 1861, and in 1862 the Treasury saw fit to sell through an agent. After all, in other areas of government procurement the agency system was at work; perhaps it would function in the field of finance. Furthermore, as it turned out, the new departure offered a blend of methods—sale through a banking house and its allies, but to the people. This method was conceived by Jay Cooke of Jay Cooke and Company of Philadelphia. Cooke was somewhat an outsider in the banking world. He was enterprising, pious, patriotic, and well supplied with able relatives and associates: he also had access to the Treasury. On one occasion his father wrote of another son, Henry, "I took up my pen principally to say, that H. D.'s plan in getting Chase into the Cabinet & Sherman into the Senate is accomplished, and that now is the time for making money, by honest contracts out of the govt." [34] In 1862, when Chase was casting about for a way to sell $500,000,000 of the government's 6 per cent five-twenties—bonds callable in five years and maturing in twenty—Jay Cooke got the contract. He was to receive on the bulk of the sales a commission of three-eighths of one per cent and pay all expenses.[35]

With characteristic optimism, he flung himself into a bond crusade. He recruited a small army of 2,500 subagents among bankers, insurance

[31] Redlich, *op. cit.*, Vol. II, Part II, 109–112; "Report of the Secretary of the Treasury on . . . the Finances . . . 1863, Comptroller of the Currency," *House Executive Document* No. 3 (s.n. 1186), 38th Cong., 1st Sess., p. 49.

[32] 13 *United States Statutes*, 484.

[33] *Annual Report of the Comptroller of the Currency, December 7, 1931*, p. 1021.

[34] Henrietta Larson, *Jay Cooke* (Cambridge: Harvard University Press, 1936), p. 103.

[35] *Ibid.*, pp. 116–120.

men, and community leaders and kept them inspired and informed by mail and telegraph. He taught the American people to buy bonds, using lavish advertising in newspapers, broadsides, and posters. God, destiny, duty, courage, patriotism—all summoned "Farmers, Mechanics, and Capitalists" to invest in loans which supplied "the ready, *present* and *required* means to strike the death blow at rebellion, and the foul disturbers of the Nation's peace." [36] As the campaign gained momentum, the apparatus frequently disposed of over a million dollars a day. Early in 1864, after fifteen months of effort, the loan was oversubscribed. For his part Cooke gained a net commission of one-sixteenth of one per cent on his sales, some incidental return from his speculations in government securities, and an undying prestige as the financial titan of the North.[37] He had also stimulated the enmity of rival bankers and the popular suspicion of having made too much money. These handicaps operated to exclude him for about a year from major government financing. Finally in 1865 the need for money led the Treasury to appoint him once again agent for the sale of three-year notes bearing 7.3 per cent interest. When the campaign, which surpassed the previous one for efficiency and emotionalism, closed six months later, the total sale of "seven-thirties" was $830,000,000.[38]

By June, 1865, the national debt incurred during the war amounted to $2,616,446,199. The largest single item, constituting a third of the total, was the seven-thirty Treasury notes, running for three years. The five-twenty bonds were roughly a quarter of the nation's indebtedness, and the greenbacks, if looked at as a loan without interest, almost a sixth.[39] As to who held the greenbacks, only partisans were sure enough to hazard a surmise and a slogan. Knowledge about the ownership of other notes and bonds was only a little less imprecise. Government officials had chosen not to sell such issues abroad, largely because informed advice had pointed out that the terms would be onerous. Nonetheless, toward the end of the war, national securities began to move across the Atlantic and by 1866 estimates placed the amount held abroad at $350,000,000. Criticism found this outcome distasteful. It reflected upon American "self-reliance," placed bonds in the hands of foreign speculators interested primarily in a profit, and by transferring interest payments overseas diminished the money available for the payment of taxes to meet the debt. It was better to owe the debt to ourselves.[40] As for

[36] *Ibid.*, pp. 129–130.

[37] *Ibid.*, pp. 120–151, *passim.*

[38] *Ibid.*, pp. 160–174.

[39] "Report of the Secretary of the Treasury on . . . the Finances . . . 1865," *House Executive Document* No. 3 (s.n. 1254), 39th Cong., 1st Sess., pp. 50–53.

[40] Larson, *op. cit.*, p. 117; "Report of the Secretary of the Treasury on . . . the Finances . . . 1866," *House Executive Document* No. 4 (s.n. 1287), 39th Cong., 2d

American purchasers, Jay Cooke and the Secretary of the Treasury were obviously bound to picture them not as large capitalists but as patriotic, hard-working people of moderate means.[41] Direct evidence is not available to contradict the assertion. But national banks, as has been seen, in 1865 owned very close to one-eighth of the national securities; the heaviest sales had been in the financial and industrial cities of the Northeast; and thither the bulk of the indebtedness soon gravitated.[42]

TAXES

Throughout the Civil War a continuous din from officials and bond salesmen affirmed that loans, bearing interest or not, were based upon the faith and credit of the United States. Specifications of what the phrase meant relied upon the wealth of the United States. A commonly repeated measurement was the value of property within the nation, appraised for taxation purposes, and the annual product flowing from capital and industry: since statistics are lifeless things, the symbols of the national resources were our rich fields, generous crops, miles of railroads, and humming spindles.[43] The usefulness of these resources, as far as the government was concerned, depended upon the taxes the owners of wealth and the recipients of income could and would pay. At first the formulators of policy were slow to tax the nation's abundance. On certain items, public policy had actually discarded sources of revenue. In 1862, for instance, Congress passed a homestead act which theoretically arranged to give away rather than sell the public domain. This lavishness Secretary Chase and others lamented as they gradually realized that increased taxation was essential to the preservation of the nation's credit. Bankers also insisted upon this point.[44] Naturally resort was made to increased customs duties, for the machinery to collect them was in existence and the country was used to this form of taxation. Every

---

Sess., p. 12; "Report of the Secretary of the Treasury on . . . the Finances . . . 1868," *House Executive Document* No. 2 (s.n. 1370), 40th Cong., 3d Sess., pp. ix–x.

[41] Larson, *op. cit.*, p. 174; "Report of the Secretary of the Treasury on . . . the Finances . . . 1867," *House Executive Document* No. 2 (s.n. 1328), 40th Cong., 2d Sess., pp. xxvii–xxviii.

[42] "Report of the Secretary of the Treasury on . . . the Finances . . . 1864," *House Executive Document* No. 3 (s.n. 1222), 38th Cong., 2d Sess., p. 52; Larson, *op. cit.*, p. 144.

[43] "Report of the Secretary of the Treasury on . . . the Finances . . . 1865," *House Executive Document* No. 3 (s.n. 1254), 39th Cong., 1st Sess., pp. 24–25.

[44] "Report of the Secretary of the Treasury on . . . the Finances . . . 1863," *House Executive Document* No. 3 (s.n. 1186), 38th Cong., 1st Sess., pp. 9–13: "Report of the Secretary of the Treasury on . . . the Finances . . . 1864," *House Executive Document* No. 3 (s.n. 1222), 38th Cong., 2d Sess., pp. 15–16; Redlich, *op. cit.*, Vol. II, Part II, 94.

year saw a new tariff act; some saw more than one. Duties were levied upon articles such as tea and coffee, hitherto on the free list; and tariff rates were raised on imports of foreign manufacture, largely to compensate for the increased taxation that an internal revenue system placed upon American producers.[45]

For the novelty of the Civil War was the resort by the national government to direct domestic taxes. The principle was a simple one: "Wherever you find an article, a product, a trade, a profession, or a source of income, tax it." [46] There was an excise tax on manufacturing, and since often every stage in the making of a product was taxed, the government sometimes collected 20 per cent of the sale price of a finished industrial product. In addition to the excise on manufacturing, which was the largest single source of internal revenue, the government taxed insurance, communication, transportation, banking, and advertising businesses and required from an impressive number of sources, including teachers, brokers, banks, and owners of stallions and jacks, the annual payment of a license fee.[47] To these taxes on business and occupation, Congress added one on incomes. For a time toward the close of the war, the statutory exemption was $600, the sum required to provide a family "with the bare necessities of life," and the rate reached 10 per cent upon incomes between $600 and $5,000, 12.5 per cent on the excess above $5,000, and 15 per cent on the excess above $10,000. In 1865 the income tax furnished 23.4 per cent of the internal revenue.[48] By this time domestic taxation had far outpaced the returns from customs, and total taxes, which in 1861–1862 bore a ratio to government expenditures of about 1 to 9, were in 1864–1865 about 1 to 4.[49] For the whole war government tax receipts met 21 per cent of expenditures, excluding the redemption of the public debt.[50] These figures of course did not reveal the real burden and glory of the nation. Those desiring to celebrate its achievement properly pointed out that in 1865–1866 direct and indirect taxation amounted to $11.46 in gold per capita, a larger sum than in

[45] "Report of the Special Commissioner of the Revenue, 1867," *Senate Executive Document* No. 2 (s.n. 1276), 38th Cong., 2d Sess., p. 9; F. W. Taussig, *Tariff History of the United States* (New York: G. P. Putnam's Sons, 1888), pp. 162–169.

[46] David A. Wells, quoted in D. R. Dewey, *Financial History of the United States* (New York: Longmans, Green & Co., 1903), p. 301.

[47] "Report of the United States Revenue Commission, 1866," *House Executive Document* No. 34 (s.n. 1255), 39th Cong., 1st Sess., pp. 20–23.

[48] *Ibid.*, pp. 22–23, 27; 13 *United States Statutes,* 281, 417.

[49] "Report of the Secretary of the Treasury on . . . the Finances . . . 1862," *Senate Executive Document* No. 1 (s.n. 1149), 37th Cong., 1st Sess., pp. 31–32; "Report of the Secretary of the Treasury on . . . the Finances . . . 1865," *House Executive Document* No. 3 (s.n. 1254), 39th Cong., 1st Sess., pp. 17–18.

[50] Dewey, *op. cit.*, p. 330.

any country in the world, and the national debt of $74.28 per capita was exceeded only in Great Britain and Holland.[51]

The demonstrated capacity to pay for an increasing part of the war carried confidence to every part of the financial system. Banks, greenbacks, the gold premium—all in their way reflected this accomplishment. But the emotions of warfare are not mathematical. Less measurable but weighty influences were at work to induce investors to subscribe to war loans and the gold dealers and the public to place a differing value upon the greenback. These influences were political and military. "A Union victory on a battle-field or at the polls depresses the price of gold; a Rebel victory in the South or at a northern election sends it up. Jefferson Davis, the Southern Armies, Generals Longstreet and Lee, and the Northern Democrats are the bulls of the gold market; Lincoln, Chase, Grant, Meade, our brave troops, and the loyal and patriotic men of the North, are the bears."[52]

SHOULD THE INNOVATION BE TEMPORARY OR PERMANENT?

At the end of the war, Hugh McCulloch, by then Secretary of the Treasury, professed to believe that it had been fought without an increase in the centralizing tendencies or change in the powers of government.[53] In the realm of finance nothing could be further from actuality. The government had departed from principles of finance as old as Thomas Jefferson, Albert Gallatin, and Andrew Jackson, principles sturdily held and rigorously applied.[54] Now it had so far departed from a standard of gold and silver in its own operations as to suspend specie payments and issue paper money. So far were government financial operations mingled with the banking system—once deemed an abhorrent alliance—that the Treasury used the bankers to sell its obligations and placed its funds in private banks as depositories. Congress also established a national banking system, bestowing upon banks the precious privilege of issuing notes based upon government bonds. The establishment of an extensive system of internal taxation completed the circle of innovation.

To the question after the war whether this new system was to be liquidated and the country return to normalcy, or whether parts of what

[51] "Report of the Special Commissioner of the Revenue, 1867," *Senate Executive Document* No. 2 (s.n. 1276), 39th Cong., 2d Sess., p. 27.

[52] "A National Currency," *North American Review*, XCIX (July, 1864), 228.

[53] "Report of the Secretary of the Treasury on . . . the Finances . . . 1865," *House Executive Document* No. 3 (s.n. 1254), 39th Cong., 1st Sess., p. 5.

[54] George R. Taylor, *The Transportation Revolution, 1815–1860* (New York: Holt, Rinehart and Winston, Inc., 1951), pp. 359–360.

had been done should be repealed and parts retained, the response of those in charge of formulating policy in the Treasury and elsewhere was likely to be conservative. Chase's traditional beliefs were continued by those who succeeded him in the immediate postwar era. McCulloch asserted that the Almighty had ordained the precious metals "as the only true measure of value"; and though he accepted banks, he occasionally doubted if he were to start things all over again whether he would include banks.[55] Sherman, in the Treasury during the late seventies, gave sound money men moments of alarm, but as an Ohio politician and the master of the possible, he usually ended as the foe of financial heresies.[56] As late as the nineties, John G. Carlisle, Secretary of the Treasury under a Democratic President, was writing with a grey goose quill and following policies of financial orthodoxy. The chief subordinates in the Treasury were the Comptrollers of the Currency. When John Jay Knox, who held this position under Sherman, and James H. Eckels, who held it under Carlisle, resigned, both became bank presidents.[57]

While contemporaries of this persuasion marveled at the stamina and loyalty of a nation which had been able to finance a four-year Civil War, they were often disturbed not so much by the economic consequences of what the nation had done as by its moral disadvantages. In their verbalisms, "evil" and "wickedness" were frequently employed. In every sector of the economy and in every class in the community, these critics detected an infection. Employers were sure their employees did not work as hard as before the war. Businessmen were less interested in production than in speculation. The way to fortune was through the exchanges and commercial dealings. Instead of prudence, there was ostentation and extravagance.[58] "Gold which had disappeared from circulation, reappeared in harness and livery. . . . Four-in-hands came into use, and costly club-houses grew up like mushrooms; and . . . America became the great buyer of all high-priced articles the world over, drained all Christendom of its diamonds, drank more Champagne than ever grew on French soil, and ran its importation bills from three hundred up

[55] Hugh McCulloch, *Men and Measures of Half a Century* (New York: C. Scribner's Sons, 1888), p. 201; "Report of the Secretary of the Treasury on . . . the Finances . . . 1866," *House Executive Document* No. 4 (s.n. 1287), 39th Cong., 2d Sess., p. 15.

[56] A. D. Noyes, *Thirty Years of American Finance* (New York: G. P. Putnam's Sons, 1900), pp. 27–29.

[57] "James Herron Eckels," *Dictionary of American Biography,* VI, 3; "John J. Knox," *ibid.*, X, 477–478.

[58] "Report of the Secretary of the Treasury on . . . the Finances . . . 1865," *House Executive Document* No. 3 (s.n. 1254), 39th Cong., 1st Sess., p. 9; "Report of the Special Commissioner of the Revenue, 1867," *Senate Executive Document* No. 2 (s.n. 1276), 39th Cong., 2d Sess., pp. 22–25; *ibid.*, 1869, *House Executive Document* No. 27 (s.n. 1416), 41st Cong., 2d Sess., pp. xxxi–xxxiii, xlv–xlvi.

to four hundred and fifty millions per annum."[59] The resulting persistent surplus of imports over exports, the payment for the former by the transfer overseas of American securities, the decline of the American merchant marine—all these reflected in the eyes of contemporary criticism a departure from a sturdy national self-reliance and an inability to supply overseas markets in the face of international competition. In turn these defects in productive apparatus and national spirit meant the failure of America to fulfill its mission of being a great manufacturing nation able to compete in the international arena.[60] In short, the nation must get back to the hardpan of work, frugality, stability, and order.

Not everyone agreed with this melancholy diagnosis or with the prescription. For one thing, certain interests and groups found they had benefited from the ephemeral financial arrangements made during the war and saw little reason now to undo them. For another thing, the hardships of panic and depression compelled a reappraisal of policies taken or proposed. There was a powerful strand of opinion which believed that a shortage of money explained all. In hard times banks obviously lacked money to pay their depositors; the failures of businesses to pay their debts and of landowners to meet their mortgages reflected a lack of money on their part. Since prices were the value of commodities or services expressed in terms of money, the decline in prices, according to the quantity theory of money, represented a shrinkage in the volume of money and a rise in prices represented an increase in its amount. "The true and only cause of the stagnation in industry and commerce now every where felt is the fact every where existing of falling prices, caused by a shrinkage in the volume of money." At least this was the dogma announced by a United States Monetary Commission in 1876.[61]

DEBT AND TAXES

The tax structure was the first part of the war's heritage to be dismantled. The hasty improvisations of the war years had admittedly erected a taxation system which did not accord with "financial science" or the "laws of political economy." Consequently Congress soon repealed the domestic taxes on production and business enterprise. The income tax, assertedly a tax upon thrift and energy as well as upon accumulation

[59] J. B. Hodgskin, "Financial Condition of the United States," *North American Review*, CVIII (April, 1869), 526–527.

[60] "Report of the Special Commissioner of the Revenue, 1868," *House Executive Document* No. 16 (s.n. 1372), 40th Cong., 3d Sess., pp. 10–11; "Report of the Special Commissioner of the Revenue, 1869," *House Executive Document* No. 27 (s.n. 1416), 41st Cong., 2d Sess., pp. xxvi–xxxi, xxxvi–xxxviii.

[61] "Report of the United States Monetary Commission . . . 1876," *Senate Report* No. 703, Vol. I (s.n. 1738), 44th Cong., 2d Sess., pp. 119–121.

and abundance,[62] was first modified and then in 1870 extended only through that year and the following one. Of the internal revenue system, taxes on liquor and tobacco remained; majority opinion esteemed these products luxuries, if not downright immoral, and thought practitioners of "indulgence" might well help the Treasury erase its deficit.[63] The external tariff system remained largely unaltered, until in 1872 a tariff act reduced most duties by 10 per cent. In the depression years which soon followed, Congress erased this reduction. In the remaining decades of the century continued agitation sought tariff reduction, but whether under Democratic or Republican administrations it met with negligible success.

The outcome, as a whole, was not surprising. The internal revenue system was new; customs duties were historic. The collection of sums through domestic taxation involved immense difficulties for the bureaucracy. Evasion, fraud, and corruption were so rampant that one expert in a position to know, David A. Wells, concluded: "Not over fifty per cent, of the amount of the assessed, internal revenue taxes is received in the national treasury." [64] On the other hand, though customs houses had their scandals, the collection of duties was generally easy, efficient, and equable. Finally, since the stimulation of production was one object of tax reform, it seemed more plausible to collect revenue from imports of foreign merchandise than from excises on domestic. Such abatements from the protective duties as were made—for instance on salt, coal, hides, and pig iron—McCulloch and others argued aided American production by giving it cheaper raw materials.[65] That the advocates of protection applied an adroit strategy to legislation also helped in preserving the tariff.

[62] "Report of the Commission of the Revenue System, 1866," *House Executive Document* No. 34 (s.n. 1255), 39th Cong., 1st Sess., pp. 16–17, 27–28; "Report of the Secretary of the Treasury on . . . the Finances . . . 1865," *House Executive Document* No. 3 (s.n. 1254), 39th Cong., 1st Sess., pp. 22–25, 27–28; "Review Article," *North American Review,* CV (October, 1867), 674–676.

[63] "Report of the Secretary of the Treasury on . . . the Finances . . . 1867," *House Executive Document* No. 2 (s.n. 1328), 40th Cong., 2d Sess., p. xxxv; David A. Wells, "Reform in Federal Taxation," *North American Review,* CXXXIII (December, 1881), 621–622; 16 *United States Statutes,* 256.

[64] "Report of the Special Commissioner of the Revenue, 1868," *House Executive Document* No. 81 (s.n. 1332), 40th Cong., 2d Sess., pp. 11–15.

[65] "Report of the Secretary of the Treasury on . . . the Finances . . . 1865," *House Executive Document* No. 3 (s.n. 1254), 39th Cong., 1st Sess., pp. 27–29; Report of the Secretary of the Treasury . . . on the Finances . . . 1866, *House Executive Document* No. 4 (s.n. 1287), 39th Cong., 2d Sess., pp. 18–22; "Report of the Special Commissioner of the Revenue, 1866," *Senate Executive Document* No. 2 (s.n. 1276), 39th Cong., 2d Sess., pp. 34–68; *Commercial and Financial Chronicle,* XVII (August 23, 1873), 239–240.

Since the enactment of even the earliest of these measures took some time, revenue continued to pour into the Treasury; even when changes were made, the decline in receipts was not as marked as had been anticipated.[66] Receipts were unhesitatingly applied to reducing the national debt. It was uniquely American to do so. Since the days of Jefferson and Gallatin, policy had turned away from the theory that a public debt was a public blessing. After the Civil War this attitude was given new specifications. The debt was a danger to republican institutions. A bureaucracy to collect taxes enhanced the power of presidential patronage and filled the country with snoopers and informers; the presence of the debt unhinged the will to conduct public business economically, concealed the hardships of current expenditures by postponing their payment, weakened the attachment of taxpayers to the government, and stimulated the formation of popular parties bent upon the spoliation of bondholders.

Furthermore it was important to preserve the ability of the national government to go into debt, for future generations would have their own wars to finance. Finally the debt was a burden on industry. Directly it created a class of bondholders who lived on interest payments and did no useful work; indirectly through taxes it increased costs of production and decreased consumption. Also, it discouraged European migrants who fled hither to escape the crushing burden of taxes in their home countries.[67] Since "old debts are hard debts to pay," the sooner the reduction of the debt began the better.[68] Consequently the managers of debt policy looked askance at the comfortable advice that, since the nation was increasing in wealth, it would in time "grow up" to the debt and bear its burdens more easily.[69]

By its lights, the Treasury was extraordinarily successful. It first employed its surplus to pay off its short-time Civil War loans. Concurrently it was refunding old securities with new ones which bore a lower rate of interest. It thus reduced annual interest charges. Eventually

[66] "Report of the Secretary of the Treasury on . . . the Finances . . . 1866," *House Executive Document* No. 4 (s.n. 1287), 39th Cong., 2d Sess., pp. 1–8.

[67] "Report of the Secretary of the Treasury on . . . the Finances . . . 1865," *House Executive Document* No. 3 (s.n. 1254), 39th Cong., 1st Sess., pp. 15–16; "Annual Report of the Treasury on . . . the Finances . . . 1870, *House Executive Document* No. 2 (s.n. 1451), 41st Cong., 3d Sess., p. xvi; "Our Financial Future," *North American Review,* CII (January, 1866), 101; Simon Newcomb, *A Critical Examination of Our Financial Policy during the Southern Rebellion* (New York: D. Appleton and Company, 1865), pp. 64–65; Henry C. Adams, *Public Debts, An Essay in the Science of Finance* (New York: D. Appleton and Company, n.d.), pp. 240–241.

[68] "Report of the Secretary of the Treasury on . . . the Finances . . . 1867," *House Executive Document* No. 2 (s.n. 1328), 40th Cong., 1st Sess., pp. xxxv–xxxvi.

[69] "Report of the Commission of the Revenue System, 1866," *House Executive Document* No. 34 (s.n. 1255), 39th Cong., 1st Sess., pp. 41–42.

the Treasury was buying back government securities before they came due, sometimes at a premium. In August, 1865, the debt stood at a peak of $2,845,907,626; by July 1st, 1891, it had sunk to a low of $1,560,772,784.61; annual interest charges, once $150,997,698.87 were $23,378,116.23 in 1892.[70] This achievement officialdom believed to be "an example" of righteousness to debt-ridden nations throughout the world.[71]

Its continuance stopped in the mid-nineties. Then the depression bit so deeply into government receipts that annual surpluses became deficits.[72] For another thing, prudence in government expenditures, along with abundant revenues, had explained the Treasury's success. Government expenditures were esteemed "unproductive," a genuine fixation of the era. At the end of the eighties the Harrison administration had abandoned this carefulness for political reasons. Pensions were the chief item in its enlarged expenditures. When the old Americanism, stirring restlessly at such extravagance, indicted the Republican Congress of 1889–1890 as the "billion dollar Congress," Czar Reed, Speaker of the House, airily dismissed the charge by quoting "the complete reply, the best in kind ever evoked, was that this is a Billion-Dollar Country." [73] This may have been cleverness; it was hardly the expression of a sober, socially-orientated program to lift depression by fiscal policy. That purpose, if such existed, was to be found in the controversy surrounding other aspects of the government's post-Civil War financial program.

BANKING

Paradoxically, controversy surrounded the one feature of Civil War finance intended to be permanent, the national banks. In addition to the disquiet attending their conception, experience during hard times convinced critics that banks and those who operated them were responsible for the financial stringencies of panics, for the contraction of the currency and the fall of prices, and for either causing depression or delaying recovery from it. It was true that defects in the system and

[70] "Annual Report of the Secretary of the Treasury on . . . the Finances . . . 1884," *House Executive Document* No. 2 (s.n. 2291), 48th Cong., 2d Sess., p. xxvii; "Annual Report of the Secretary of the Treasury on . . . the Finances . . . 1897," *House Document* No. 8 (s.n. 3654), 55th Cong., 2d Sess., pp. xciv–xcvi.

[71] "Annual Report of the Secretary of the Treasury on . . . the Finances . . . 1884," *House Executive Document* No. 2 (s.n. 2291), 48th Cong., 2d Sess., pp. xxvii–xxix.

[72] Bureau of the Census, *op. cit.*, p. 296.

[73] T. B. Reed, "Spending the Public Money," *North American Review,* CXLIV (January, 1887), 80–82; W. M. Grosvenor, "What Shall be Done with the Surplus?" *North American Review,* CXLIV (January, 1887), 80–82.

the pursuits of unfortunate policies aggravated the distress of hard times. But attacks went far beyond sober analysis. They charged that bankers lived a voluptuous existence indifferent to the public interest, that the national banking system was a "monopoly" (dread echo of Jacksonian days) and that it made extravagant profits, in part because it received a double interest on its notes through interest on the government bonds which were their basis and interest on the loan of the notes themselves. Indeed it was sometimes charged that the banks brought on panics for sinister purposes. Demagogues voiced such sentiments; so did the wise and the good. A contributor to the *American Journal of Politics* soberly declared that the bankers conspired to precipitate the panic of 1893 in order to compel the repeal of the Sherman Silver Purchase Act.[74] Many of such charges were baseless. Bankers do not deliberately shatter the prosperity which yields them profits; the average dividends on bank stock declined from 10.5 per cent immediately after the Civil War to a low in 1897 of 6.7 per cent; the returns on capital and surplus together ran nearly 2 per cent less. The banks were no monopoly, unless it be meant that charters were open only to those who had money to invest. On the contrary there was some democratization of investment in the banks; between 1876 and 1897 the number of shareholders increased from 208,486 to 281,225.[75] The defenders of the banks, of course, resorted to their own symbolism: the system had been the savior of the nation during the perils of the Civil War.[76]

But the process of damnation and sanctification could not obscure the fact that national banks actually failed during hard times. In 1873–1878 the number was 43; in 1883–1886, 22; and in 1893–1897, 186.[77] In the last period one of the failures was of a national bank with a branch on the grounds of the Columbian Exposition in Chicago; the managers of the Fair decided they did "not desire an exhibition of a failed bank among the interesting collection on the Midway Pleasaunce."[78] More seriously, during the nineties the Comptroller of the Currency made a reputation as an executor of closed banks.

[74] William Knapp, "An Artificial Panic in Retrospect," *American Journal of Politics,* IV (June, 1894), 656–666; F. J. Scott, "Our National Banking System," *North American Review,* CXLI (September, 1885), 197–201.

[75] *Annual Report of the Comptroller of the Currency . . . 1912,* p. 278; "Report of the Comptroller of the Currency, 1897," *House Document* No. 8 (s.n. 3654), 55th Cong., 2d Sess., pp. 351–352.

[76] "Annual Report of the Secretary of the Treasury on . . . the Finances . . . 1884," *House Executive Document* No. 2 (s.n. 2291), 48th Cong., 2d Sess., p. xliii; H. W. Boutwell, "Our National Banking System," *North American Review,* CXLI (September, 1885), 202.

[77] Bureau of the Census, *op. cit.,* p. 273.

[78] F. C. James, *The Growth of Chicago Banks* (New York: Harper & Brothers, 1938), I, 582.

Sometimes the reasons for failure were the malfeasances or mistakes of bank officials which bank examiners did not detect in time or could not correct. Grim vignettes of bad banking and bad bankers [79] filled a portion of the Comptroller's annual reports. But there were defects more fundamental than human weakness. The national system was merely an aggregation of individual banks. The number, which had reached a figure of 1,968 in 1873, mounted to a peak of 3,807 twenty years later.[80] Although legislation gave them common characteristics and centralized supervision, it did not give them centralized control—except indirectly and incidentally.

Country banks had to keep a 15 per cent reserve in lawful money against deposits; three-fifths of this reserve could be kept by banks in a large number of reserve cities or in central reserve cities; banks in reserve cities had to keep a reserve of 25 per cent, half of which could be kept in banks in central reserve cities. New York was the only one of the latter until 1887, when Chicago and St. Louis were added. Banks in central reserve cities had to keep a reserve of 15 per cent against all deposits. Banks relished these arrangements, for they received interest on their deposited reserves; if the reserves had been in their own vaults, they would not have done so. As arrangements worked out, a few great New York banks centralized the system. The reserves deposited with them they loaned on call. Nominally the latter were highly liquid, since the customary security for call loans was a transaction on the stock exchange. Inasmuch as the latter provided a continuously functioning market, call loans could be liquidated instantly.[81] In times of crisis, however, pressures that could not be met converged upon the New York banks. After their reserves were drawn down, they had no means of meeting the demands of their local and out-of-town depositors without calling loans at the precise moment when the stock exchange itself was whirling downward. Such arrangements hardly placed a rock of Gibralter under the banking system.

Unhappily the national banks were in general unable to minister to the regions and economic interests which felt that hard times were due to a lack of money—the agricultural areas of the South and West. Legislation forbad national banks to loan on real estate. Furthermore, for short-time loans these regions preferred bank notes; national banks everywhere increasingly found such issues unprofitable. Be it recalled

[79] "Report of the Comptroller of the Currency, 1884," *House Executive Document* No. 2 (s.n. 2291), 48th Cong., 2d Sess., pp. 156–160; "Report of the Comptroller of the Currency, 1887," *House Executive Document* No. 2 (s.n. 2548), 50th Cong., 1st Sess., pp. 442–445.

[80] Bureau of the Census, *op. cit.*, p. 264.

[81] O. M. W. Sprague, *History of Crises under the National Banking System*, pp. 10–24.

that the security behind them was government bonds. As the Treasury bought up government bonds with its surpluses, the base for bank notes contracted. Lower interest on government bonds and taxation on circulation further diminished the gains from issuing notes.[82] Comptrollers of the Currency in the eighties were calculating that the banks were making a profit of one-half on 1 per cent on note circulation or that note issue was an actual loss to the banks.[83] In the circumstances the total of national bank notes declined. The amount, reaching about $340,000,000 in 1874 and 1875, held at over $300,000,000 for about a decade and then fell sharply to a low point of $162,221,000 in 1891.[84] Here indeed was ammunition for those troubled by the scarcity of money. From all the proposed legislation, Congress between 1870 and 1882 elected only to pass provisions giving a greater share of the note issue to the banks in the South and West; to raise and then repeal all limitations upon the national maximum of bank notes; to reduce the currency reserve held in the Treasury for bank notes, already amply enough protected by government bonds; and to discourage the banks in the curtailment of note circulation.[85]

Among the proposals failing to win Congressional approval was the repeal of the punitive tax of 10 per cent on the notes of state banks. Much to the surprise of some observers, the number of banks under state charter and other banking institutions outside the national banking system multiplied so rapidly in the later part of the century that by 1897 the state banks and private banks, resting "on the common law right and privilege of banking," numbered 5,847 and their combined deposits were 19 per cent greater than in the national banks.[86] The first two categories of banks generally operated under lighter restrictions than national banks and performed some functions the latter did not.

Whether totals of bank notes were declining or the reverse was relatively a matter of indifference to the business community, for it had developed instrumentalities more sophisticated than precious metals or bank notes. After the Civil War contemporaries were continually ob-

[82] "Report of the Comptroller of the Currency, 1884," *House Executive Document* No. 2 (s.n. 2291), 48th Cong., 2d Sess., pp. 127–135.

[83] *Ibid.*, p. 134n; "Report of the Comptroller of the Currency, 1889," *House Executive Document* No. 2 (s.n. 2734), 51st Cong., 1st Sess., p. 396.

[84] Bureau of the Census, *op. cit.*, p. 275.

[85] 16 *United States Statutes*, 250–251; 18 *ibid.*, Pt. 3, 123, 196; 22 *ibid.*, 164–165.

[86] "Report of the Comptroller of the Currency, 1875," *House Executive Document* No. 2 (s.n. 1683), 44th Cong., 1st Sess., pp. 246–248; "Report of the Comptroller of the Currency, 1884," *House Executive Document* No. 2 (s.n. 2291), 48th Cong., 2d Sess., p. 166; "Report of the Comptroller of the Currency, 1897," *House Document* No. 8 (s.n. 3654), 55th Cong., 2d Sess., pp. 353–356; Redlich, *op. cit.*, Vol. II, Part II, 177–180.

serving that the trend in advanced countries was toward an economy "in the use of money." The same amount performed more exchanges. As early as 1867 the Secretary of the Treasury stated there was less need for currency in view of the growing reliance upon other credit arrangements. "In all the cities and towns throughout the country, checks upon credits in banks, and bills of exchange, have largely taken the place of bank notes. Not a fiftieth part of the business of large cities is transacted by the actual use of money. . . ." [87] This trend so broadened and extended that by 1890 bank money—drafts, checks, bills of exchange—practically monopolized wholesale trade and large payments. It constituted two-thirds of the payments in retail trade and about the same figure for wages and salaries. That such instruments played a smaller role in the South and West did not mean that those regions relied upon money. Mining regions depended on store orders, agricultural regions on store orders and book accounts which exchanged the commodities of the purchaser for those of the store.[88] As for money itself, there had been a slight shrinkage in the supply after Appomattox; it did not continue long. In the seventies the trend took an upward turn and, in spite of tiny fluctuations, the supply reached a sum in 1897 just over twice what it had been in 1873.[89] Even gold contributed to this outcome, for in the nineties the development of new gold mines in South Africa and the application of the more efficient cyanide process of extraction greatly enlarged the production of that metal [90] whose "tyranny" the advocates of inflation deplored.

THE GREENBACKS

While the attempt to force the national banking system into a policy of inflating or deflating its circulation resulted in little more than legislative nibbling, the apostles of thoroughgoing measures proposed to set

[87] "Report of the Secretary of the Treasury on . . . the Finances . . . 1867," *House Executive Document* No. 2 (s.n. 1328), 40th Cong., 2d Sess., p. xii.

[88] "Report of the Comptroller of the Currency, 1881," *House Executive Document* No. 2 (s.n. 2022), 47th Cong., 1st Sess., pp. 195–201; "Report of the Comptroller of the Currency, 1890," *House Executive Document* No. 2 (s.n. 2849), 51st Cong., 2d Sess., pp. 386–392; "Report of the Comptroller of the Currency, 1896," *House Document* No. 8 (s.n. 3498), 54th Cong., 2d Sess., pp. 490–495; *Commercial and Financial Chronicle,* XVIII (June 27, 1874), 641; XXI (September 11, 1875), 241; "Minority Report from House Committee on Coinage, Weights, and Measures," *House Report* No. 3967, Pt. 2 (s.n. 2889), 51st Cong., 2d Sess., p. 12; A. T. Hadley, "Commercial Crises," *Johnson's Universal Cyclopedia* (New York: D. Appleton and Company, A. J. Johnson Company, 1893–1897), p. 425.

[89] Bureau of the Census, *op. cit.,* pp. 274–275.

[90] Robert E. Preston, "The Future of Gold," *North American Review,* CLX (January, 1895), 39–43.

the amount of money without the agency of private corporations. One group of such believers turned to the greenbacks. The ambiguous position of these legal tenders certainly raised questions of policy and legality. Actually they were serving as a portion of the nation's currency. According to orthodox finance they were also a part of the national debt, "a promise to pay when the promissor was able." McCulloch and Wells consequently felt the redemption of the greenbacks was the only honorable and honest course.[91] In 1866, with Congressional authorization, they began to contract the amount of greenbacks in circulation. Regretting this step, Congress for several years put the brakes on contraction or dallied with the idea of expanding the amount in circulation. Finally in 1875 it passed an act promising to redeem the greenbacks in specie on January 1, 1879. Astute management on the part of John Sherman, Secretary of the Treasury, and a great influx of gold from Europe to pay for purchases of American grain made necessary by disastrous harvests, insured the success of this policy. With the resumption of specie payments, the gold premium disappeared and the nation and the banks returned to a specie basis.[92]

The halts and reversals of policy along the road to resumption arose from depression and a resulting clash between debtors and creditors. Contraction and resumption, real or proposed, was deflationary. Such an outcome benefited creditors, for the dollars they were receiving would buy more products; it injured debtors, who to pay their debts had to work harder or longer to produce more at the lower prices. Creditors were unpopular, as money-lenders usually are; they did not seem to work; they constituted a minority in the community.[93] But they had a classic defense. Henry Adams stated it explicitly and patronizingly: "It is less injurious to national wealth when the creditors are benefitted at the expense of the debtor . . . because, as a general rule the creditor class are disposed to save their money, and the debtor class to spend it; and when the debtor pays more than he justly owes, he is compelled to be more frugal, while the creditor receives a greater reward for his frugality and is therefore encouraged to be more frugal. Frugality being the foundation of all national wealth and strength, the habits which conduce to wealth and strength are encouraged by an appreciation of

[91] Newcomb, *op. cit.*, pp. 90–107.

[92] 14 *United States Statutes*, 31; 15 *United States Statutes*, 34; 16 *United States Statutes*, 1; 18 *United States Statutes*, 296; W. C. Mitchell, *Gold, Prices, and Wages under the Greenback Standard* (Berkeley: University Press, 1908), p. 4; Noyes, *op. cit.*, pp. 22–23, 43–58.

[93] Henry C. Carey, "The Public Debt, Local and National: How to Provide for Its Discharge While Lessening the Burthen of Taxation." *Miscellaneous Works* (Philadelphia: H. C. Baird, 1872?), p. 10.

the currency. . . . Eras of depreciating paper money have always been those of luxury, extravagance, and waste of wealth." [94]

Ordinarily the debtor class was thought of as consisting of the underprivileged, farmers and laborers. But businessmen, even corporations, were debtors. Every bond was a debt. A substantial contraction of the currency would also lower the value of previous investments in inventories, mills, or railroads, and, by possibly increasing interest rates, retard the activity of business. Businessmen who supported the greenbacks have customarily been identified with the ironmasters, who persuaded themselves that prices stated in paper currency gave them an extra protection against dreaded imports from abroad. Ironmasters from Peter Cooper of New York, who ran for the presidency on a greenback ticket in 1876, to those in Wisconsin seemed to affirm the coupling of "Protection and the Greenback," the slogan of Henry C. Carey of Pennsylvania, the protectionist spokesman for the iron industry.[95] Actually the businessmen for greenbacks were not confined to the iron industry. The *Nation* observed that the debtor class lived "in large mansions, in Beacon Street, Fifth Avenue, and Chestnut Street, with huge safes stuffed full of stocks and bonds, but especially stocks." [96] Historically speaking, no horny-handed son of toil, no "plow holder," had formulated the doctrinal statement for the greenbackers. Its author was Edward Kellogg, an eastern merchant punished by the panic of 1837. In a volume entitled *Labor and Other Capital. The Rights of Each Secured and the Wrongs of Both Eradicated,* published in 1849, he elaborated the theory that money secured its value not from the scarcity of the materials from which it was made, but from the law which gave it a legal tender. To implement his theories of justice, he proposed that the government issue fiat currency to individuals through a central office with branches; real estate would be the security for these loans. Government policy would also set the interest rate.[97]

That these opinions were later viable the 1878 platform of the National Party, commonly called Greenback, demonstrated. That document

[94] Henry B. Adams, "Our Financial Future," *North American Review,* CII (January, 1866), 110–111; Newcomb, *op. cit.,* pp. 124–130.

[95] H. C. Carey, "The Currency Question," *Letters to the Hon. Schuyler Colfax* (Philadelphia: Collins, 1865), pp. 5–6, 24–33; Allan Nevins, *Abram S. Hewitt with Some Account of Peter Cooper* (New York: Harper & Brothers, 1935), pp. 288–290.

[96] *Nation,* XIX (December 17, 1874), 394–395; XIX (December 24, 1874), 414–415.

[97] C. M. Destler, "The Influence of Edward Kellogg," *American Radicalism, 1865–1901, Essays and Documents* (New London: Connecticut College, 1946), pp. 51–55.

announced as a general principle: "It is the exclusive function of the General Government to coin and create money and regulate its value. All bank issues designed to circulate as money should be suppressed. The circulatory medium, whether of metal or paper, shall be issued by the government and made a full legal tender for all debts, duties, and taxes in the United States at its stamped value. . . . Congress shall provide said money adequate to the full employment of labor, the equitable distribution of its products, and the requirements of business, fixing a minimum *per capita* of the population as near as may be, and otherwise regulating its value by wise and equitable provisions of law, so that the rate of interest will secure to labor its just reward." The party polled just over a million votes in 1878.[98]

Proposals to put the government into banking were more likely in the last resort to tighten than to divide the ranks of businessmen. Such proposals meant a multiplication of bureaucrats, an intrusion of partisan motives into commercial affairs, ignorance, confusion, inefficiency, and waste. The pulling and hauling over the number of greenbacks and over resumption were more than peripheral skirmishes between creditors and debtors; they were assaults against the inner fortress of the business structure.

WHO'S FOR SILVER?

The definitive triumph of resumption in 1878 and the reappearance of prosperity—no causal connection between them is implied—took the starch out of the greenback movement, but "the free and unlimited coinage" of silver at once offered a way to apply a similar philosophy and seek much the same objectives. Alone among financial issues silver was not a heritage of the Civil War; a quirk of discovery and technology thrust it to the fore. In the seventies the great silver mines of Nevada, the bonanza mines, began pouring out immense quantities of metal. Between 1870 and 1873 American production more than doubled; between 1873 and 1890 it doubled again. World production also increased.[99] As the flood of silver mounted, European nations demonetized it. In 1893 India followed suit. The next year the average price of silver on the

[98] *Appleton's Annual Cyclopedia and Register of Important Events of the Year 1878,* New Series, III, 806–808.

[99] Bureau of the Census, *op. cit.,* pp. 151–152; Oscar Lewis, *Silver Kings* (New York: Alfred A. Knopf, 1947), pp. 3–45; A. B. Parsons, ed., *Seventy-five Years of Progress in the Mineral Industry, 1871–1946* (New York: The American Institute of Mining and Metallurgical Engineers, 1947), pp. 42, 45, 55–56; "Report of the Director of the Mint," *House Document* No. 8 (s.n. 3634), 55th Cong., 2d Sess., pp. 312–313.

London market fell for the first time below 30d an ounce.[100] As it happened, the United States had in 1873 also dropped silver coinage except for subsidiary coins, because no silver was being presented at the mint. Its owners preferred to sell it in the more profitable public market. In the changed circumstances after 1873 the silver miners and their inflationist allies began once again to hanker for the Treasury market, for the "free and unlimited coinage of silver" at some ratio to gold, for example 16 to 1, that is, the comparative weight of metal in the coins. The Act of 1873 became the "Crime of 1873."

Though many greenbackers hesitated to embrace "the barbarism of specie," from the agitational point of view silver had many superiorities over paper. No matter how rapidly silver production increased, there was an eventual natural limit to it: to wit, the deposits in the earth and the costs of extraction. Since printing presses made paper money, the trivial costs of production placed no limits on greenbacks. Silver currency was in accord with natural law; indeed it was divinely appointed.[101] Ideologically also, all the light of sacred shibboleth could gather about the silver story. It had served as currency during the nation's youth from Alexander Hamilton to Andrew Jackson. In the late nineteenth century, Europe by electing gold had enhanced the Americanism of silver. Finally silver production was production; as an industry like others it could call on government for protection and aid. The silver lobby, so often execrated, included the railroads, which served the silver states from Montana to Colorado, and the coal mine owners and merchants who supplied fuel and provisions to the silver miners.[102]

Though the greenbackers had enlisted in their crusade the white-haired philanthropist and ironmaster Peter Cooper, it is doubtful if his respectability and influence equaled that of Francis Amasa Walker, the first president of the American Economic Association and president of Massachusetts Institute of Technology. As Walker diagnosed the situation, "Purposed inflation, by act of government, having for its object the raising of prices and the scaling-down of debts, is subject to the gravest impeachment on grounds . . . of social justice. . . . It carries with it the sting of fraud. . . . An inflation of the money-supply due to the discovery of new mines and fields . . . whatever hardship it may bring

[100] "Report of the Director of the Mint," *House Document* No. 8 (s.n. 3634), 55th Cong., 2d Sess., pp. 286–303.

[101] W. M. Stewart, "Contraction and the Remedy," *North American Review*, CXVI (March, 1888), 827–833; "Report of the Secretary of the Treasury on . . . the Finances . . . 1877," *House Executive Document* No. 2 (s.n. 1883), 45th Cong., 2d Sess., pp. xvi–xxv; *Commercial and Financial Chronicle*, XXIII (December 30, 1876), 632–634; United States Monetary Commission, *op. cit.*, pp. 6–14.

[102] *Commercial and Financial Chronicle*, LVII (July 15, 1892), 105.

on certain persons or classes of persons, carries no sting of injustice."[103] With well-established claims to "conservatism and Common sense," bimetallism won support from journalists, presidents and professors in academe, businessmen, and Secretaries of the Treasury in or out of office.[104] By the nineties, of course, the geographical centers of its political strength were the silver states and the newer agricultural ones.

The more cautious of the silverites came to the conclusion that international action on behalf of silver was essential. Bimetallism in one country was impossible. The silver in the world would gravitate thither for coinage; the price would continue to fall; the silver coin, unless its weight and coinage ratio were continually changed, would become less valuable than gold and the latter would leave the country through foreign trade. A silver currency and that alone would result. To escape from this dilemma, American officials took the lead in calling a series of international monetary conferences, those at Paris in 1878 and 1881, and at Brussels in 1892–1893. Agreement upon opening the mints of the world to the unlimited coinage of silver at a common ratio to gold proved quite impossible of attainment. While Europeans were willing to let America have her prejudices, they were unwilling to surrender theirs.[105] All this policy of "Stop, wait, negotiate"[106] filled the more fervid of American silverites with impatience. Internationalism was identical with inaction. As "Silver Dick" Bland, Congressman from Missouri, put it, "Standing among the nations of the World as a giant among pygmies, why should we ask the aid or advice of baby England, baby Germany, or lilliputian France, in establishing for ourselves a bimetallic system?"[107]

They hadn't waited. But they had to compromise. In 1878 the Bland-Allison Act compelled the Secretary of the Treasury to purchase between two and four million dollars worth of silver a month and coin it into dollars of 412½ grains. Holders of these dollars could exchange them

[103] F. A. Walker, "The Relation of Changes in the Volume of Currency to Property," American Economic Association, *Economic Studies,* I (1896), 32–33.

[104] Hugh McCulloch, "Our Future Fiscal Policy," *North American Review,* CXXXII (June, 1881), 528–529; F. A. Walker, "Shall Silver Be Demonetized?" *ibid.,* CXL (June, 1885), 490; S. D. Horton, "A Chapter of Monetary Policy," *ibid.,* CXLI (November, 1885), 555–563; "Annual Report of the Secretary of the Treasury on . . . the Finances . . . 1886," *House Executive Document* No. 2, Pt. 2 (s.n. 2472), pp. xix–xxii; *Commerical and Financial Chronicle,* XII (April 29, 1876), 410–411, 527.

[105] R. P. Bland, "In the Interests of Shylock," *North American Review,* CLVI (February, 1893), 172–173; Charles Foster, "The Brussels Conference Reviewed," *ibid.,* CLVI (April, 1893), 493–500.

[106] "Annual Report of the Secretary of the Treasury on . . . the Finances . . . 1885," *House Executive Document* No. 2 (s.n. 2384), 49th Cong., 2d Sess., p. xvii.

[107] R. P. Bland, "What Shall the Ratio Be?" *North American Review,* CLV (July, 1892), 12.

for certificates of deposit, silver certificates. The lonely eminence of gold as the only legal tender for the payment of customs duties and of interest on the public debt disappeared; the silver dollars were legal tender in the payment of all debts and dues, public and private, if there were no contract to the contrary.[108] Since silver fell in price during the twelve years of the act's operation, the Treasury, though it purchased the minimum prescribed value, actually bought more silver to make more and more dollars. The total amount thus added to the currency was $378,166,793.[109]

In 1890 the Sherman Silver Purchase Act placed purchasing on a quantity basis. Every month the Secretary of the Treasury was to buy 4,500,000 ounces of silver bullion with Treasury notes which, as a part of the money supply, were known as Treasury notes of 1890. These notes were legal tender in payment of all debts public and private and could form a part of bank reserves. At his discretion, the Secretary of the Treasury could redeem these notes on request from the holder, in gold or silver, "it being the established policy of the United States to maintain the two metals on a parity . . . upon the present legal ratio."[110] The number of ounces designated in the act equaled the amount of domestic silver production at the moment.[111] The *Banker's Magazine* thought the act "a good thing for the silver block and a good thing for business generally."[112] By June 30, 1894, there were outstanding $152,584,417 in Treasury notes of 1890.[113] The act had been repealed toward the close of 1893.

Whatever the words of the statutes, quite often ambiguous, or the assertions of advocates and enemies, what did the silver purchase policy mean in practice? Did it mean through the promised redemption of everything, including silver, in gold, gold monometallism? Did it mean, through the impossibility of redeeming everything in gold, silver monometallism? Consistently since the passage of the Bland-Allison Act and the resumption of specie payments, Secretaries of the Treasury had warned that the government had been able successfully to promise redemption in gold only thanks to the special circumstances of a favorable balance of international trade and investment, which was bringing gold into the country or keeping it there, and thanks to the existence of a government surplus, in part composed of payments to the government

[108] 20 *United States Statutes*, 25–26.

[109] "Report of the Director of the Mint," *House Executive Document* No. 2 (s.n. 3219), 53d Cong., 2d Sess., p. 314n.

[110] 26 *United States Statutes*, 289–290.

[111] Bureau of the Census, *op. cit.*, p. 151.

[112] *Banker's Magazine and Statistical Register*, XLV (August 18, 1890), 96.

[113] "Annual Report of the Secretary of the Treasury on . . . the Finances . . . 1897," *House Document* No. 8 (s.n. 3654), 55th Cong., 2d Sess., p. 99.

in gold.[114] The business crisis of the early nineties shattered these foundations. Tax policy and the decline in imports cut down government revenues, now payable in silver or its representation; government expenditures continued pretty much at their old level; and the Treasury to meet its bills had to pay out greenbacks and even the gold reserve kept to redeem them. Gold began leaving the country—for several reasons. The central banks of European countries when the depression hit in 1890 in order to protect themselves raised interest rates and drew gold whence they could find it. England, the center of world finance, was highly vulnerable because of the Baring collapse and the accompanying disasters to investments in the Argentine and Australia. American export trade—particularly in agricultural commodities—shrank in quantity and value, and the inflow of gold to pay for them, so vital to the achievements of 1879, ceased.[115]

As always in times of panic, gold began leaving the banks for hoarding by individuals and corporations. In addition to the run upon the banks, another and more prolonged one upon the Treasury exchanged greenbacks and Treasury notes for gold. Naturally the intensity of this run increased with the fear lest the government go onto silver, intrinsically less valuable than gold. To meet this crisis of fact and of opinion, President Cleveland and his Secretary of the Treasury Carlisle forced in 1893 a repeal of the Sherman Silver Purchase Act and in 1894–1896 sold almost $300,000,000 worth of government bonds for gold. Bankers and investors, here and abroad, furnished the gold; some of it they drew from the Treasury by presenting greenbacks and Treasury notes for redemption.[116] Harrowing and humiliating as this test of government solvency was, it demonstrated that the policy of gold redemption was gold monometallism and that of bimetallism was silver monometallism. Platform planks for a double standard, as in Bryan's campaign of 1896, however sincerely believed, were impossible to carry out. Out of the mouth of petulance or excitement sometimes comes candor: "They can't

[114] "Annual Report of the Secretary of the Treasury on . . . the Finances . . . 1878," *House Executive Document* No. 2 (s.n. 1853), 45th Cong., 3d Sess., pp. viii–xvii; "Annual Report of the Secretary of the Treasury on . . . the Finances . . . 1881," *House Executive Document* No. 2 (s.n. 2022), 47th Cong., 1st Sess., pp. xiv–xv; "Annual Report of the Secretary of the Treasury on . . . the Finances . . . 1889," *House Executive Document* No. 2 (s.n. 2734), 51st Cong., 1st Sess., pp. lx–lxi; "Annual Report of the Secretary of the Treasury on . . . the Finances . . . 1896," *House Document* No. 8 (s.n. 3498), 54th Cong., 2d Sess., pp. lxxv–lxxvi.

[115] "Report of the Comptroller of the Currency, 1891," *House Executive Document* No. 2 (s.n. 2943), 52d Cong., 1st Sess., pp. 234–237; "Annual Report of the Secretary of the Treasury on . . . the Finances . . . 1893," *House Executive Document* No. 2 (s.n. 3219), 53d Cong., 2d Sess., pp. lxix–lxxiv.

[116] James A. Barnes, *John G. Carlisle, Financial Statesman* (New York: Dodd, Mead & Company, 1931), pp. 150–424.

exhaust the gold reserve too quickly to suit me," said Cockerell of Missouri. "We can go to a silver basis without as much as a ripple in our financial system." [117]

Whether he or the gold men who differed with him were right can only be surmise. In any case the discontent engendered by hard times, rising in the nineties to a climax in the campaign of 1896 when Bryan carried the banner of silver against gold, stiffened attitudes and alignments and convinced conservatives, whether Republicans or Democrats, that the national government should curtail its concern with banking and currency policy. On the first count, the national banks should through their own safety funds and reserves guarantee the safety of their notes; legal requirements for reserves for deposits should be left to the judgment of the bankers; and the Treasury should have less to do with the banks than formerly.[118] As for currency, men of conservative temper were just as aware as greenbackers and silverites of the need for elasticity. Currency should expand and contract with the legitimate business needs of the country. For instance, the moving of the crops in autumn or the time of spring trade required increased currency for the increased transactions. Government currency was at fault precisely because it lacked elasticity. Since the notes of national banks depended on government bonds, and since the amount of greenback and of silver currency was set by political considerations, government currency was forced into the channels of commerce rather than responding to its needs. The banks should issue an asset currency based, for instance, on discounted short-term paper, "good business notes." To govern the currency in terms of the needs of private enterprise through the banks was sounder than to use government power.[119]

In the light of the level the economy had reached, the crusades over the greenback policy and silver coinage had a certain anachronistic air; the controversies would have been more appropriate to the days of

[117] *Ibid.*, p. 367.

[118] "Annual Report of the Secretary of the Treasury on . . . the Finances . . . 1890," *House Executive Document* No. 2 (s.n. 2849), 51st Cong., 2d Sess., pp. xli–xliv; "Annual Report of the Secretary of the Treasury on . . . the Finances . . . 1894," *House Executive Document* No. 2 (s.n. 3312), 53d Cong., 3d Sess., pp. lxviii–lxxxii.

[119] W. M. Springer, "The Financial Muddle," *North American Review*, CLX (February, 1895), 147–148; J. H. Eckels, "The Duty of the Republican Administration," *ibid.*, CLXIII (December, 1896), 698; "Report of the Comptroller of the Currency, 1894," *House Executive Document* No. 2 (s.n. 3312) 53d Cong., 3d Sess., pp. 394–395; "Annual Report of the Secretary of the Treasury on . . . the Finances . . . 1896," *House Document* No. 8 (s.n. 3498), 54th Cong., 2d Sess., pp. lxii–lxxiv; "Report of the Comptroller of the Currency, 1897," *House Document* No. 8 (s.n. 3654), 55th Cong., 2d Sess., pp. 337–339; Clews, "The Late Financial Crisis," *loc. cit.*, pp. 110–113.

Jackson and perhaps even to colonial times, when land banks had been an issue. Evidence already cited seems to demonstrate that linking hard times with the money question was shadow-boxing, and some but not all present-day analysts of cycle theory have come to a similar conclusion. While monetary factors aggravated situations, for example the silver debacle in the nineties, they were generally secondary or contributory.[120] Instead theorists lean, albeit with more subtlety, to the hypothesis held by contemporaries that what was fundamental in generating good or bad times was the rate and extent of investment—particularly in railroads.[121] But railroads were, of course, important for broader reasons.

[120] Rendig Fels, *American Business Cycles, 1865–1897* (Chapel Hill: University of North Carolina Press, 1959), pp. 212, 218, 224–225; Charles Hoffmann, "The Depression of the Nineties," *Journal of Economic History,* XVI (June, 1956), 164.

[121] Fels, *op. cit.,* pp. 213–222, 223; Hoffmann, "The Depression of the Nineties," *loc. cit.,* pp. 139–142; Joseph A. Schumpeter, *Business Cycles. A Theoretical, Historical, and Statistical Analysis of the Capitalist Process,* 2 vols. (New York: McGraw-Hill Company, 1939), pp. 325–341.

CHAPTER III

Railroads: Building and Finance

AMERICAN railroads, whose triumphs before 1860 had been impressive, played a critical role in the Civil War. From the early days of 1861, when maintenance of rail communication between the northern states and the Capital was essential for the movement of troops for its protection, until the end, which was hastened by the transport of a Federal army of 30,000 men from central Tennessee to the North Carolina coast in three weeks time, the iron rail and the iron horse were fundamental to tactics and strategy.[1] Railroads, even in states untouched by military operations, found their business quickened and enhanced by the transport of men and materiel.[2] Though all this was normal enough, the war years generally slowed further construction. In 1861 and 1865 the railroad mileage of the country stood respectively at 31,286 and 35,085.[3]

Except in the areas immediately affected by military operations, the Federal government remained aloof from railroad construction or control. Its railroad war policy relied upon the activity and loyalty of private railroad corporations and the ability of their officials.[4] This governmental railroad policy of the war years in general mirrored prevalent peacetime,

[1] G. E. Taylor, *Victory Rode the Rails. The Strategic Place of the Railroads in the Civil War* (Indianapolis: Bobbs-Merrill Company, 1953), pp. 47–60; Edward Channing, *A History of the United States* (New York: Macmillan Company, 1925), VI, 409.

[2] *Twenty-first Annual Report of the Directors of the Concord Railroad Corporation . . . 1862* (Concord, N. H.: McFarland & Jenks, 1862), p. 9; *Twenty-fourth Annual Report of the Directors of the Concord Railroad Corporation . . . 1865* (Concord, N. H.: McFarland & Jenks, 1865), p. 12; *Twenty-fifth Annual Report of the Directors of the Concord Railroad Corporation . . . 1866* (Concord, N. H.: McFarland & Jenks, 1866), p. 7.

[3] Bureau of the Census, *Historical Statistics of the United States, 1789–1945*, p. 220.

[4] Taylor, *op. cit.*, pp. 246–247.

civilian preferences. Whereas early in the nineteenth century, when the railroad system was getting under way, individual states had established Boards of Improvement to plan a transportation system and had financed and operated "public works," usually canals, this policy had generally petered out or been repudiated by 1860. Though afterwards state and municipal governments, in exceptional circumstances, owned railroads, and states sometimes continued to operate canals as an heritage from an earlier day, public opinion and its official reflection in legislative and executive action favored the construction of the nation's railroad system through the agency of corporations.[5] This decisive preference was of immense importance, for the great transportation achievement of the United States following the Civil War was the construction and improvement of a national railroad network. Quite largely this achievement was the work of private corporations.

CHARTERS AS RAILROAD PLANNING

Railroad corporations, of course, required charters. Therefore it was theoretically possible for the governments which granted them to select the railroads to be chartered and to pay heed in their choice to considerations of public welfare or public exigency, as it was usually called. In the earlier railroad era an occasional attempt had been made to do so. But the process ran into all sorts of difficulties. Since a charter authorizing the incorporators to exercise the right of eminent domain to secure a right of way without necessarily paying the owner's price was a valuable privilege, railroads vied with one another for charters for particular routes. Cities and towns, merchants, shippers and farmers demanded charters for enterprises which would serve their individual interests and promote community welfare. The result was a legislative free-for-all. All sorts of pressures, often quite demoralizing, were brought to bear upon governors, railroad committees, and legislators; favoritism and log-rolling obscured the sweet concept of the general will. Furthermore, if promoters and investors were willing to risk their money in an enterprise which promised to bring so much good to the community, why should the state hamper them?

At first each charter was an act of special legislation. While the assignment of a unique route and the grant of special privileges seemed to dictate this individualistic arrangement, the prelude of demonstrating

[5] Edward C. Kirkland, *Men, Cities, and Transportation: A Study in New England History*, 2 vols. (Cambridge: Harvard University Press, 1948) I, 97n; Carter Goodrich, "The Revulsion against Internal Improvement," *Journal of Economic History*, X (November, 1950), 145–169.

a public exigency had degenerated into a mere routine. Newspapers along the proposed line editorialized upon the necessity and blessings of the road; petitioners on paper or petitioners in person supplicated the railroad committee for a charter, and persuasive railroad counsel with maps and pamphlets demonstrated how advantageously the project would rearrange traffic for the benefit of all concerned.[6] "Free trade" in railroad charters in fact existed long before most states enacted general incorporation laws by which a specified number of incorporators could automatically secure a charter by conforming to certain preliminary conditions in reference to surveys, capitalization, and subscriptions.

In the East, New York led the procession in 1850 with a significant act for general incorporation; in the West, Illinois had already taken a similar step in 1849. In behalf of a practice which became the common one after the Civil War, it was argued that removal of temptations to special legislation would preserve the purity of republican institutions and establish democracy in the distribution of charters. The connection of such legislation with the preference for competitive railroading will be mentioned later.[7] Though in some jurisdictions an effort was made to wed general incorporation with the determination of public exigency, the latter objective administratively amounted to little more than a suspicion of unsound, small-scale enterprises.[8]

Though state jurisdictions might thus dissociate themselves from railroad planning or dilute their responsibility, the different circumstances of the Federal government compelled a different policy. In 1860 the nation still possessed an immense area in the Great Plains, in the Rockies, and in the extreme Pacific Northwest, organized in territories or organized not at all. In the fifties in order to connect the more settled East with California and to populate and develop the intervening areas, the national government through its military engineers discovered four feasible routes for a transcontinental railroad.[9] In 1862 Congress chartered the

[6] C. F. Adams, Jr., and Henry Adams, *Chapters of Erie and Other Essays* (New York: Henry Holt and Company, 1886), pp. 363, 422–424; Kirkland, *op. cit.*, I, 267–270.

[7] B. H. Meyer, *Railway Legislation in the United States* (New York: Macmillan Company, 1903), pp. 91–92, 99–100, 108–126; Kirkland, *op. cit.*, II, 257.

[8] Massachusetts *Eleventh Annual Report of the Board of Railroad Commissioners. January, 1880,* pp. 41–48; Massachusetts *Twelfth Annual Report of the Board of Railroad Commissioners. January, 1881,* pp. 46–59; Massachusetts *Twenty-second Annual Report of the Board of Railroad Commissioners. January, 1891,* pp. 207–214; 160 *New York,* 202; 227 *New York,* 248.

[9] G. L. Albright, *Official Explorations for Pacific Railroads. 1853–1855* (Berkeley: University of California Press, 1901), pp. 10–28, 157–158; R. R. Russel, *Improvement of Communication with the Pacific Coast as an Issue in American Politics, 1783–1864* (Cedar Rapids, Iowa: The Torch Press, 1948), pp. 323–325.

Union Pacific Railroad to run from the Missouri River to California along what was generally called the central route. The western connection of the Union was the Central Pacific, a corporation chartered in California. Between 1864 and 1871 Congress incorporated three other transcontinentals to proceed by varied northern and southern routes across the Great Plains. Of them the Northern Pacific was the only one to reach the coast under its incorporated name.[10]

Aside from such special instances and modifiying circumstances, visionaries, promoters, boosters, merchants, manufacturers, and capitalists in their private capacities largely planned the railroad network of the United States and planned it piecemeal. It was just as well. Except in special circumstances the Federal government did not possess power to act. The separate states, while their transportation and commercial antagonisms had softened since the fifties, were primarily provincial in outlook and the differences in policy between many jurisdictions would have produced delay and confusion in the matter of overall planning.[11] Meanwhile the achievement of corporations under free trade in railroads was breathtaking in terms of geographical extent and rapidity of construction. Between 1865 and 1897, corporations increased the mileage of track in operation within the United States from 35,083 to 242,013.[12]

THE NATIONALIZATION OF THE RAILROAD NETWORK

More specifically the railroad frontier, a line connecting the railheads of completed construction, had pressed just before the Civil War across the Mississippi and into the first tier of states beyond. Missouri and Iowa constituted the main salient of advance. Thirty-seven years later the rail network had reached the Pacific coast and had provided California at least with an extensive state system. The threads of five transcontinentals connected the Pacific mileage with the eastern railroads, which like the advance of population, had thinned out along a wavering line between the 98th and 100th meridians of longitude.[13]

Spectacular as it was, the advance of the railroad frontier, taken alone, concealed the real accomplishment of corporate activity. While the transcontinentals were breaking through to the Pacific's shore, the rails

[10] 12 *United States Statutes,* 489–498; 13 *ibid.,* 365–372; 14 *ibid.,* 292–299; 16 *ibid.,* 574–579.

[11] Frederick Merk, "Eastern Antecedents of the Grangers," *Agricultural History,* XXIII (January, 1949), 2–6.

[12] Bureau of the Census, *op. cit.,* pp. 200, 202.

[13] Eliot Jones, *Principles of Railway Transportation* (New York: Macmillan Company, 1925), maps opposite pp. 54, 58, 64; George R. Taylor and Irene D. Neu, *The American Railroad Network, 1861–1890* (Cambridge: Harvard University Press, 1956), maps at end of volume.

consolidated their conquest of the two tiers of states west of the Mississippi. In this area between 1870 and 1880 mileage more than doubled, and in the next decade more than doubled again. In 1890 Iowa, Texas, and Kansas each had a mileage roughly a quarter greater than all the New England states. The old Northwest, which in 1860 had the largest regional mileage in the nation, increased its figure in 1870–1880 by 70 per cent. In the next decade the states of the Confederacy east of the Mississippi, at last shaking off the long fatigue of war and reconstruction, roughly doubled their railroad network. Perhaps with sounder analysis the railroad's achievement should be stated in terms of density rather than frontiers. If the test were sheer mileage, Illinois in 1897 was the rail state of the nation; if it were mileage in relation to acreage, New Jersey, Massachusetts, and Pennsylvania held priority in that order.[14] In short the years of prosperity and depression after 1865 not only extended but filled in the railroad network.

The mere extension of mileage, however, could not complete the nationalization of the railroad network nor alone account for the distinguishing achievements of American railroads. Certain European countries, for instance, might equal or surpass America's facility in the mass transport of passengers; none carried bulky freights for low costs and for continental distances. To do this American railroad corporations had to connect their systems physically, adopt certain uniform conditions of practice and operation, and to mute in some measure the antagonisms inherent in corporate aggrandizement and competition. That a regiment of corporations, numbering in 1897 some 1,158 operating railroads, came to any solution of the technical and operational innovations involved was a tribute to the advantages of agreement and an indication of the pressures making for it.[15]

In the technical realm, the railroads proceeded first of all to achieve a large measure of physical connection with one another, often to the intense distaste of local opinion dreading to lose the designation or advantage of being "the end of the line." [16] In some instances this meant the laying of rails along some city street. In other instances it involved bridging the great watercourses which interrupted the land. In 1860, for instance, the through rail route along the Atlantic coastline was broken at the Thames in Connecticut, not bridged until 1889; at the Connecticut River, not bridged until 1870; at New York where tunneling and bridging postponed a connection until the twentieth century; at the Susquehanna, bridged in 1866; and at Washington where steamboat and stage con-

[14] Interstate Commerce Commission, *Eleventh Annual Report on the Statistics of Railways . . . 1898*, pp. 12–13.

[15] Bureau of the Census, *op. cit.*, p. 202.

[16] A. F. Harlow, *The Road of the Century. The Story of the New York Central* (New York: Creative Age Press, 1947), pp. 267–274.

nected with a rail line from Richmond until after the Civil War.[17] Though before 1860 railroad bridges had crossed both the Ohio and the Mississippi, the great period of building came later. When the Eads bridge across the Mississippi at St. Louis was opened with a civic celebration on July 4, 1874, the event concluded a decade in which ten railroad bridges crossed the Mississippi, either for the first time or in sturdier rebuilding.[18]

More important was the standardization of gauge. Though during the seventies the Canadian roads, and trunk lines such as the Erie with a broad gauge of six feet, had shifted to the standard 4′8½″, the Federal census of 1880 found 22.3 per cent of the mileage still outside the standard width. In 1886 the great holdout, the old South east of the Mississippi, shifted in twelve dramatic hours one rail inward to a gauge of 4′9″.[19] In such changes the larger share of expense was incurred in altering the rolling stock. The standardization of cars and their appurtenances was a larger problem than the obtaining of a standard gauge. In the case of the coupler, for instance, a multitude of variants, many very rudimentary, endangered railroad workers, slowed the coupling and uncoupling of cars, and hampered the interchange of equipment between roads. In the eighties, spurred by a safety movement and the desire for efficiency, the Master Car Builders' Association endorsed an improved automatic coupler, standardized its links, and recommended with some success that their members and principals install the device.[20]

A national railroad system also required business innovations facilitating joint and through operations. Passengers must make connections with tolerable certainty and ease; the freight cars of a corporation must not come to a stop at some corporate terminus where an agency would have to unpack their cargo and transfer it to the cars of another carrier, like as not just across the street. Almost unchronicled and undated, the railroads introduced through bills of lading, and though shippers still carped at their limitations, these bills became the accepted method of freighting in the seventies; on them a local trader at Cedar Rapids, Iowa,

[17] Kirkland, *op. cit.*, II, 83, 92; H. D. Dozier, *The History of the Atlantic Coast Line Railroad* (Boston: Houghton Mifflin Company, 1920), p. 91; G. H. Burgess and M. C. Kennedy, *Centennial History of the Pennsylvania Railroad Company, 1846–1946* (Philadelphia: Pennsylvania Railroad Company, 1949), p. 393; Taylor and Neu, *op. cit.*, map I.

[18] W. F. Switzler, "Report on the Internal Commerce of the United States . . . 1888," *House Executive Document* No. 6, Pt. 2 (s.n. 2552), 50th Cong., 1st Sess., pp. 19–26, 41–46.

[19] *Tenth Census of the United States, 1880,* IV, 294; *Commercial and Financial Chronicle,* XLII (May 29, 1886), 649–651; W. F. Switzler, "Report on the Internal Commerce of the United States . . . 1886," *House Executive Document* No. 7, Pt. 2 (s.n. 2476), 49th Cong., 2d Sess., p. lxxxiv.

[20] Kirkland, *op. cit.*, II, 372–374.

for example, could ship to Liverpool, London and Europe.[21] At the same time fast freight lines were undertaking to run cars over the lines of several companies. In one variety of these organizations a transportation company, apart from the railroad, provided the cars, collected the freight money, and paid the roads a percentage of the freight money or a fixed sum per mile. In part because such companies were open to abuse by insiders, they were giving way by the mid-seventies to the cooperative fast-freight companies. The railroads involved contributed their proportion of cars to the line, usually designated by some color—the Green Line promoted by the Louisville and Nashville was a famous one. On its part the fast freight line solicited cargo and, after deducting the modest administrative expenses, adjusted mileage balances between roads on the basis of a fixed charge per car per mile.[22] If the total mileage run by a line's car exceeded that proportioned to the individual road's mileage in the line, that road was credited; if the opposite, debited. The next step as the period ended was to agree upon car interchanges and rentals on a per diem basis.[23]

There were other steps toward uniformity. Though bulky products usually bore the lower rates, each road classified its freight so as to enlarge its own returns or develop its own particular territory. Throughout the decades after the Civil War the railroad associations in the chief traffic regions worked for the establishment within their jurisdictions of a uniform freight classification. Six thousand items were involved: the peculiar circumstances of local rates and inter-state regulation were baffling. Nonetheless by 1890 three major classification systems emerged: official classification in territory north of the Ohio and Potomac and east of a line drawn north and south through Lake Michigan and extended south from Chicago to St. Louis; the Southern Railway and Steam-ship Association classification in the South, east of the Mississippi; and Western classification in an area radiating west from Chicago. But

[21] Joseph Nimmo, Jr., "Report on the Internal Commerce of the United States . . . 1879," *House Executive Document* No. 32, Pt. 3 (s.n. 1857), 45th Cong., 3rd Sess., pp. 148–149; Joseph Nimmo, Jr., "Report on the Internal Commerce of the United States . . . 1881," *House Executive Document* No. 7, Pt. 2 (s.n. 1966), 46th Cong., 3rd Sess., pp. 44–45; Testimony of Albert Fink, *Report of Committee* [on Education and Labor] *of the Senate . . . 1885,* II, 477–478.

[22] J. L. Ringwalt, *Development of Transportation Systems in the United States* (Philadelphia: J. L. Ringwalt, 1888), pp. 192–193; Joseph Nimmo, Jr., "First Annual Report on the Internal Commerce of the United States . . . 1876," *House Executive Document* No. 46, Pt. 2 (s.n. 1761) 44th Cong., 2d Sess., appendix pp. 49–51; New York Legislative Assembly, *Proceedings of Special Committee on Railroads* [Hepburn Committee] . . . *1879,* III, 2960–2970.

[23] W. F. Switzler, "Report on the Internal Commerce of the United States . . . 1886," *House Executive Document* No. 7, Pt. 2 (s.n. 2476), 49th Cong., 2d Sess., appendix p. 681.

there were many exceptions—some on paper and some in the minds of managers and agents.[24] More tangible was the orderly formulation of passenger schedules through consultation between the roads. In 1883 following a decade of time table conventions, the railroads agreed to substitute for the fifty-four different times with which they were working four time zones across the country with uniform time in each. In 1891 these conventions graduated into the American Railway Association, which was to become in its own right a great unifying influence.[25]

Applause saluted these advances—applause and preachments. According to a government report, the railroads established the facilities for through business "voluntarily," following "the leadings of the natural evolution of the railroad system, with no other guide than the promptings of self-interest, and the suggestions of the constantly-extending commerce of a country of vast extent, and almost illimitable resources."[26] From the financial fortress of metropolitan New York, an editorial writer inferred from the attainment of standard time and standard gauge that "the laws of trade and the instinct of self preservation effect reforms and improvements that all the legislative bodies combined could not accomplish." Furthermore the railroad accomplished these innovations without delay, frustrations or complaint.[27]

As a matter of fact, railroad legislation from the beginning had sought, albeit awkwardly, to promote through traffic. In the states, charters and general legislation permitted roads to enter upon and use the tracks of one another and frequently enforced arrangements for a joint traffic with forceful particularity, while Congress, in 1866, authorized interstate roads to form continuous lines.[28] The Interstate Commerce Act of 1887, echoing historic experience, enjoined the railroads to provide facilities for the interchange of traffic without charging discriminatory rates.[29] State administrative bodies and legislatures over the opposition of many corporations compelled uniformity of freight classifications, the Interstate Commerce Commission early assuming the seemingly hopeless

[24] *Second Annual Report of the Interstate Commerce Commission . . . 1888*, pp. 34–41, 176–184; *Fourth Annual Report of the Interstate Commerce Commission . . . 1890*, pp. 197–210; *Commercial and Financial Chronicle*, XLVII (November 10, 1888), 545.

[25] Robert E. Riegel, "Standard Time in the United States," *American Historical Review*, XXXIII (October, 1927), 84–89; *Commercial and Financial Chronicle*, XXXVII (November 17, 1883), 523–525.

[26] Joseph Nimmo, Jr., "Report on the Internal Commerce of the United States . . . 1879," *House Executive Document* No. 32, Pt. 2 (s.n. 1857), 45th Cong., 3rd Sess., p. 143.

[27] *Commercial and Financial Chronicle*, XLII (May 29, 1886), 651.

[28] 14 *United States Statutes*, 66.

[29] 24 *United States Statutes*, 380.

task.[30] As for standardization of equipment, when the Interstate Commerce Act was finally passed, the state railroad commissioners, with an almost audible gratitude for promised relief from the frustration they had experienced on this count, passed the burden to the Interstate Commerce Commission. In the nineties a series of Congressional enactments at last compelled the holdout railroad corporations to install such beneficent devices as the air brake, the improved coupler, and uniform handholds on freight cars.[31] In short, the railroads, for all their success, neither could nor would have achieved the complete uniformity they needed without legislative prodding.

The national railroad system undoubtedly brought immense benefits to the economy. If a new traffic—grain in the states west of Chicago, lumber in Wisconsin, petroleum and its derivatives in western Pennsylvania, soft coal in Virginia, West Virginia, Tennessee and Kentucky—promised returns, the railroads, if they were at all strategically located, rushed to participate in it. At the same time they reached restlessly toward the great markets and shipping points. Much to the pain of merchants in New York, Philadelphia, and Baltimore, railroads once projected and built to enlarge the wealth of a single favored metropolis, the New York Central, the Erie, the Pennsylvania, and the Baltimore and Ohio, now sought to carry goods wherever their shippers wanted them sent, particularly if it were a long carriage. New York and Chicago drew all railroads to them. In short, the roads were shedding their local chrysalis.[32] But this did not mean that any shipper anywhere could send his goods by the road of his own choosing to any market. There was a limit, a variable one, to the distance commodities could feasibly travel. But these limits and restrictions, far from being fixed solely by the "natural law" commentators so often celebrated, were set by the rate structures adopted by the railroads in their competitive struggles or their efforts to abate them. Invisible barriers and embargoes of this sort fractured the national railroad system, regardless of how "connected" it appeared on maps.[33]

[30] *Seventh Annual Report of the Interstate Commerce Commission . . . 1893,* pp. 50–56.

[31] *Fifth Annual Report of the Interstate Commerce Commission . . . 1891,* pp. 337–340; *Seventh Annual Report of the Interstate Commerce Commission . . . 1893,* pp. 261–264; Henry C. Lodge, "A Perilous Business and the Remedy," *North American Review,* CLIV (February, 1892), 189–195; H. S. Haines, "Railway Safety Appliances," *ibid.,* CLV (July, 1892), 121–124.

[32] Joseph Nimmo, Jr., "First Annual Report on the Internal Commerce of the United States . . . 1876," *House Executive Document* No. 46, Pt. 2 (s.n. 1761), 44th Cong., 2d Sess., pp. 74–78.

[33] *Seventh Annual Report of the Interstate Commerce Commission . . . 1893,* pp. 44–45; *Eighth Annual Report of the Interstate Commerce Commission . . . 1894,*

THE SCOPE OF RAILROAD FINANCE

The American railroads led lives of noisy desperation. For one thing their demands for capital were urgent and insatiable. In 1860 the combined total of their stocks and bonds was $1,849,481,000; in 1897 it was $10,635,000,000. It should be recalled that at the former date the national debt was only $64,844,000 and at the latter, $1,226,794,000.[34] In short, the conditions under which the first two sums were incurred and the manner in which they were handled would be bound, even if no other considerations than numerical totals were involved, to have a greater effect upon the economy than the management of the national finances.

In the nature of the case the cost of constructing an American railway was highly uncertain. Though engineering and construction experience had brought greater precision in estimates than was true in earlier eras of promotion and building, when costs usually exceeded original calculations, grave uncertainties remained. It took time to build these huge enterprises; seven years intervened between the chartering and the completion of the Union Pacific, nineteen between similar landmarks in the history of the Northern Pacific. In such intervals the costs of rails, equipment, and labor vacillated unpredictably. Furthermore a good share of the roads built in this era were pushed through unsettled territory or territory in the course of rapid development. There was no knowing what the traffic would be or what unforeseen changes would compel a new scale of construction even as construction was going on. These were old American dilemmas. Coupled with the customary dearth of capital for investment, they dictated a type of construction and method of finance well described by one of the capitalists on the Northern Pacific: "We must get a cheap line and a safe road, but at the outset we must in grades and curves try to save—and trust to the future for the higher finish." [35] Without too much exaggeration it may be said that American railroad builders as soon as they got a road done threw it away and built another.[36] In addition, competitive circumstances compelled all but a few fortunately situated railroads, whose directors were secure in a favored location, continually to finance extensions and branches either at first hand or through purchase. This was expensive business.

---

pp. 54–60; *Tenth Annual Report of the Interstate Commerce Commission . . . 1896*, pp. 33–37.

[34] Bureau of the Census, *Historical Statistics of the United States 1789–1945*, pp. 203, 204, 305, 306.

[35] T. C. Cochran, *Railroad Leaders, 1845–1890* (Cambridge: Harvard University Press, 1953), p. 132.

[36] Testimony of T. F. Woodlock, *Report of the Industrial Commission . . . 1901*, IX, 459.

By the 1850's a pattern of railroad financing had emerged which some of its expositors regarded as a great departure from the conventional method of selling common stock to raise building funds. After the Civil War, the new method with considerable variations became the accepted one. Once the road had drawn the first breath of corporate life through a token subscription to the capital stock, it proceeded to issue bonds to raise the funds to build the road. There were all varieties of bonds. To give the investor reassurance, these bonds were usually made a mortgage upon the road and its property. Often railroads resorted to successive mortgages with some form of priority or they placed their property in categories and issued bonds based upon land grants or upon equipment or they issued "income bonds" with a lien upon income. To expect a railroad man to regard the last as having any legal rights would have been extraordinarily naive.

The character of the common stock was in the circumstances quite unpredictable. A preliminary even if nominal subscription was of course necessary to get the road under way. In order to induce possible bond purchases, conservative opinion thought it desirable to show a considerable further stock subscription, if possible along the line, as an evidence that promoters had faith in the project and that those whom the route would serve believed in its usefulness and profit. Those who did things more directly or impetuously issued the stock and sometimes income bonds to purchasers as a bonus for their subscription to other bonds. Both stocks and bonds were sold at a discount or for what they would bring. Sometimes while the constructors and financiers were waiting to make a sale, a process acutely difficult when money was tight or the economy was heading toward one of its financial crises, they deposited securities with banks as collateral for loans. Thus bank credit, which the cautious felt should be restricted to short-time commercial transactions, went actually into permanent investments.[37]

These expedients for raising money became systematized after the Civil War through the construction company. In spite of its name, this organization was less concerned with moving dirt than with moving securities. Primarily it was a fiscal agency, its origins diverse. Often in their financial needs railroads in course of construction had paid the contractors in part with the securities of the road and the latter had used them as a basis for credit or had sold them. At other times hard pressed railroads, in order to give their securities tone or to sell them at all or

[37] James P. Kirkwood, "Railroad Enterprises and their Detractors," *Hunt's Merchants' Magazine*, XXXII (April, 1855), 404–410; Interstate Commerce Commission, *First Annual Report of the Statistics of Railways in the United States . . . 1888*, pp. 12–16; *Commercial and Financial Chronicle*, XXXV (November 4, 1882), 506; XXXVII, 293; Cochran, *op. cit.*, p. 100.

to borrow money, had relied upon the superior credit of individual directors or had enlisted some "money doctor" or "financial wizard" in order to utilize his.[38] Now the construction company, with a charter and stock of its own, institutionalized these devices.

At the very outset of the postwar period the details of such arrangements were revealed to the public gaze through the publicity unloosed by the participation of the Crédit Mobilier in politics. The organization in question was the construction company of the Union Pacific. The chief stockholders and officials of the railroad company generally occupied the same role in the Crédit Mobilier. According to the terms of the contract the latter took the various bonds of the former (with the exception of the government subsidy bonds, of which more later) at progressive discounts and received the stock for nothing. It used these securities as collateral for loans or for sale. In the end the Crédit Mobilier successfully completed a road through unknown territory, occupied largely by hostile Indians, during an era of high prices at a profit which the construction company asserted was only twenty-five per cent greater than the cost of construction.[39] Other computations, proceeding on the assumption contrary to fact that the securities should be figured at par, calculated profits of between 80 and 100 per cent, the last figure being not infrequent for construction companies.[40] The variation in such estimates of profits after construction reveals how imprecise must have been the calculation of gains in advance. Here as elsewhere profits were not foreordained. The financiers took awesome risks,[41] which were lessened by a construction company, limiting the liability of stockholders for debts. No wonder the device built all the transcontinentals. Railroad officials of high reputation used it to provide their main lines with branches. Even in the East, where risks were more calculable, the construction company held sway.[42]

[38] Cochran, *op. cit.*, p. 63; Kirkland, *op. cit.*, I, 332–333; II, 449.

[39] Crédit Mobilier Investigation, Poland Committee, Testimony of Horace F. Clark, *House Report* No. 77 (s.n. 1577), pp. 430–436; Nelson Trottman, *History of the Union Pacific, A Financial and Economic Survey* (New York: Ronald Press Company, 1923), pp. 30–43, 52.

[40] Trottman, *op. cit.*, pp. 44–46; Crédit Mobilier Investigation, Poland Committee, *op. cit.*, p. 433.

[41] H. V. Poor, "The Pacific Railroad," *North American Review*, CXXVIII (June, 1879), 677–678; R. C. Overton, *Gulf to Rockies. The Heritage of the Fort Worth and Denver-Colorado and Southern Railways, 1861–1898* (Austin: University of Texas Press, 1953), pp. 89–106.

[42] Cochran, *op. cit.*, pp. 99–100, 111–112; E. P. Oberholtzer, *Jay Cooke, Financier of the Civil War* 2 vols. (Philadelphia: George W. Jacobs & Co., 1907), II, 158–165, 244; *Commercial and Financial Chronicle*, XIX (July 11, 1874), 29; XX (February 20, 1875), 184–185; XXXV (Investor's Supplement, October 28, 1882), i–iii; *Bradstreet's* XI (April 25, 1885), 274–277.

In spite of its necessity, it had, however, grave disadvantages. Men operating in one capacity gave themselves contracts in another; eventually the risks were so infinitesimal that high profits were certain. On the one hand, speculation and manipulation under this device stimulated the building of roads and the weakened enterprises were left for others to operate. On the other, the chief subscribers to the construction company built with other people's money, bonds for instance, and then by the retention of the stock divorced investment from management, with the possibility of further managerial irresponsibility. In one contract company job, as criticism mounted, defenders were driven to the assertion: "We . . . do not claim to be immaculate, beyond expediency [but] are content with right intentions and good results obtained on the whole. . . ." [43] By the late eighties a less speculative approach to railroad financing, a comparative elimination of risk-taking, and the ability to estimate costs more accurately contributed to the diminishing use of the device or to abating its worst features.[44]

"WATER, WATER EVERYWHERE. . . ."

To determine whether the incorporators of the Crédit Mobilier received a greater reward than merited involved resort to moral abstractions. There was no doubt, however, that the face value of stocks and bonds issued to the Union Pacific was roughly twice the amount of money put into its construction. Nor was this situation unique. Everywhere commentators recognized that in the case of stocks there was a wide divergence between the stated par value and the amount of money originally paid for them. This difference was stock inflation or stock watering, the result of the sale of stock at a discount or of giving it away or of the declaration of a stock or scrip dividend. Strictly speaking the latter process, if it reflected earnings stockholders had previously foregone and ploughed back into the enterprise, was not water. Such reinvestment of earnings, at a time of rapid technological change, was common.

Nonetheless, in the absence of restraint, stock issues might well represent nothing at all.[45] Officials occasionally issued stock simply to escape from a jam into which mismanagement or dishonesty had forced them. Sometimes, as on the Erie Railroad under the speculative sovereignty of Daniel Drew, Jay Gould, and Jim Fisk from 1864 to 1872,

[43] Cochran, *op. cit.*, pp. 113–114.

[44] *Ibid.*, p. 115.

[45] C. F. Adams, Jr., and Henry Adams, *op. cit.*, pp. 398–399, 405–406; C. F. Adams, Jr., "Railroad Inflation," *North American Review*, CVIII (January, 1869), 130–136, 139–144.

members issued stock to further their market speculations and win their Wall Street engagements against competitors or rival speculators. In these eight years the common stock of the Erie, without comparable investment in money, increased from $24,228,800 to $78,000,000.[46] The great opponent of the "Erie gang" was Cornelius Vanderbilt, who by the sixties had turned definitely from water to land transportation. In 1868 he secured control of the New York Central between Albany and Buffalo (itself a consolidation of the fifties) with watered stock; he immediately increased its stocks and indebtedness of $40,000,000 by a stock dividend of $23,000,000. In the next year he consolidated the Central with the Hudson River, increasing the stock of the former by 27 per cent and of the latter by 85.[47] In one of their revels, Wall Street brokers unveiled a statue of Vanderbilt equipped with a watering pot, and a spokesman of the fraternity declared, "It is the use of water, not as a beverage but as an element of public wealth, which has been the distinguishing characteristic of the achievements of Commodore Vanderbilt's later years." [48]

Risibilities aside, the complex fashions in which stockwatering took place made it impossible to determine with any precision what portion of the nominal value of American railroad securities represented actual investment and what did not. While all figures were guesses, there was general agreement. Writing in 1869, Charles F. Adams estimated that for a selected sample of roads over the previous four years, half the increase in their stock "may be set down as pure, unadulterated 'water.'" [49] In the early eighties Henry V. Poor, certainly the outstanding railroad expert of the country not in the pay of the railroads, ascribed the panic and depression of that period to the cumulative effect of waterings and concluded that of the increase in railroad capital and indebtedness from 1880 to 1882 only 52 per cent represented actual cash expenditure.[50] This outcome seemed highly regrettable to those who felt that railroad earnings and the rates, which presumably supplied them, should be based upon actual investment.

At the other extreme were those who felt that the latter figure was an irrelevance. Instead of capitalization fixing earning power, earning power should fix capitalization. Vanderbilt's waterings represented what

[46] Stuart Daggett, *Railroad Reorganization* (Cambridge: Harvard University Press, 1908), p. 36.

[47] C. F. Adams, Jr., and Henry Adams, *op. cit.*, pp. 401–404.

[48] New York *Tribune*, Nov. 10, 1869, quoted in Lewis Corey, *The House of Morgan* (New York: G. H. Watt, 1930), p. 103.

[49] C. F. Adams, Jr., and Henry Adams, *op. cit.*, p. 409.

[50] Poor's *Manual of the Railroads of the United States for 1883* (New York: H. V. and H. W. Poor, 1883), p. iii; *ibid. . . . 1885* (New York: H. V. and H. W. Poor, 1885), pp. iv–v.

his road could earn. The dividend on the stocks in the New York Central and Hudson River Railroad remained at 8 per cent or better through the depression seventies. Admittedly it was earned.[51] Earnings depended upon investors' foresight and managerial skill and the expansion of the economy brought about in part through construction of railroads. If actual capitalization fell short of capitalized earnings, prudently calculated over the years, management or promoters would find ways to increase the stock; if capitalization exceeded capitalized earnings, bankruptcy and reorganization would restore the proper proportion.[52]

GOVERNMENT AID

In the absence of abundant capital resources, communities and individuals, hungry for transportation and alert to its effect on production and commerce, had long aided canals or railroads as best they could. Some gave a right of way; others contributed labor and material; and, since land was an abundant resource, state legislatures and Congress gave acres away. At their disposal some states had an acreage from the national domain, transferred by Congress for "internal improvements"; others, such as Maine and Texas, possessed public domains of their own. In 1867 the governor of Maine asked, "Why should private individuals be called upon to make a useless sacrifice of their means, when railroads can be constructed by the unity of public with private interests, and made profitable to all?" The next year the legislature granted somewhat over 700,000 acres to a road going through the state's eastern wilderness.[53] From the fifties on, Texas followed the general policy of granting sections of land for each mile of railroad constructed; in 1882, when it was discovered that these donations exceeded by 8,000,000 acres the land left in the public domain, the policy came to an end.[54] Later calculations have placed the total of all state grants at 48,883,372 acres.[55]

The big giver, however, was the Federal government. The policy,

[51] *Commercial and Financial Chronicle,* XXV (August 11, 1877), 126–127; (August 18, 1877), 149.

[52] Testimony of T. F. Woodlock, *Report of the Industrial Commission . . . 1901,* IX, 456–459; Sidney Dillon, "The West and the Railroads," *North American Review,* CLII (April, 1891), 446.

[53] Kirkland, *op. cit.,* I, 466, 472–475.

[54] Aldon S. Lang, "Financial History of the Public Lands in Texas," *The Baylor Bulletin,* XXXV (July, 1932), 101–107.

[55] "Public Aids to Domestic Transportation," *House Document* No. 159 (s.n. 10963), 79th Cong., 1st Sess., p. 110; Thomas LeDuc, "State Administration of the Land Grant to Kansas for Internal Improvements," *Kansas Historical Quarterly,* XX (November, 1953), 545–552; Bureau of Corporations, *The Lumber Industry,* Pts. II and III, 222–236.

initiated by the historic land grant to the Illinois Central in 1850, had for all practical purposes ceased to operate seven years later,[56] but the construction of transcontinentals gave the program new incarnation. Since these roads were built through territories, Congress granted the land directly to the corporations rather than to states for transfer; and since the risks of these untried projects were so great and the value of the land, at least in the semi-arid and arid regions, so uncertain, Congress considerably increased the area of these donations. The original Union Pacific Act of 1862 gave the corporation, in addition to its right of way, five odd-numbered sections on each side for each mile of track. Because of the rectangular system of survey for the government domain and the method of numbering sections, the railroads actually ran across a checkerboard twenty miles wide in which the government retained the even numbered sections. To secure its grant and other assistance, the road had to be completed within twelve years.[57] By the time of the Northern Pacific grant in 1864 the beneficiary was entitled to twenty odd-numbered sections a mile on each side of the track in the territories and ten in the states; in case any of these designated sections of the "base" land had been otherwise disposed of, the railroad could indemnify itself with sections from a zone ten miles wider. These were known as "lieu" lands. The checkerboard could be 100 miles wide. Again the road had to be built within twelve years.[58]

Since these and other grants were embodied in special acts, it is impossible to describe with complete accuracy details of a generalized land grant policy. In instances the indemnity areas were wider than those for the Northern Pacific; quite frequently the time limit was ten rather than twelve years. Sometimes the government sold its reserved sections for $2.50 an acre, twice the minimum elsewhere in the public domain (if the land were sold rather than homesteaded).[59] During the Civil War the statutes on this matter of grants quite naturally emphasized military necessity and the usefulness of projected roads. Though neither the Union nor the Northern Pacific Acts placed explicit military obligations upon the corporations, other enactments frequently required the aided roads to carry troops and government property "free from toll or other charge." [60] The ambiguity and cunning with which statutes were

[56] Thomas Donaldson, *The Public Domain. Its History with Statistics,* pp. 269–270; George R. Taylor, *The Transportation Revolution, 1815–1860* (New York: Holt, Rinehart and Winston, Inc., 1951), pp. 95–96.

[57] 12 *United States Statutes,* 492.

[58] 13 *United States Statutes,* 367–370.

[59] William L. Greever, "A Comparison of Railroad Land-Grant Policies," *Agricultural History,* XXV (April, 1951), 83–84.

[60] David M. Ellis, "Railroad Land Grant Rates, 1850–1945," *Journal of Land & Public Utility Economics,* XXI (August, 1945), 211–213.

phrased and the bewildering variety of special provisions placed upon the agencies which administered them, notably the General Land Office in the Department of the Interior, a heavy and thorny burden. Those prone to view outcomes in terms of railroad lobbying and pressures were likely to interpret the resulting decisions in terms of an ingrained pro-railroad bias if not dishonesty.[61] Actually Congressional neglect and executive inertia and incompetence better accounted for the administrative failures of the subsidy policy.[62]

In 1871 Congress gave its last donation, though a year earlier the House had enthusiastically declared against the principle of this policy.[63] Throughout the eighties, legislation secured the forfeiture of specific grants which the railroads had not earned, and in 1890 a general but mild act systematized the process of repossession by the national government.[64] Decades later a governmental agency calculated the railroads had by 1940 secured from the Federal government title to 130,401,606 net acres of the national domain. The gross totals, since the railroads had lost some acreage through forfeiture or surrender, had been somewhat larger.[65]

The Federal land-grant policy had collided with events and ideals which were bound to undo it. On the first count, the long depression of 1873–1877 was critical. By postponing construction it prevented many railroads from earning their grants within the statutory time limits and compelled them to seek an extension of their privileges.[66] On the second count, the land grant policy contradicted the surface philosophy of the Homestead Act of 1862, by which lands were practically given away in holdings of 160 acres to actual settlers. The public lands belonged to the people.[67] Yet Congress was bestowing "fabulous" donations, usually compared in extent to some state or European country, upon corporations. Since the lands were frequently unsurveyed, the General Land Office customarily withdrew from settlement all the land in the base and lieu zones. In some instances the government held its own land out

[61] George W. Julian, "Railway Influence in the Land Office," *North American Review*, CXXXVI (March, 1883), 237–256.

[62] J. B. Rae, "Commissioner Sparks and the Railroad Land Grants," *Mississippi Valley Historical Review*, XXV (September, 1938), 211–230.

[63] *The Congressional Globe*, 41st Cong., 2d Sess., 1869–1870, Pt. 3, p. 2095; John B. Sanborn, *Congressional Grants of Land in Aid of Railways* (Madison: Wisconsin University Press, 1899), pp. 68–70.

[64] David M. Ellis, "The Forfeiture of Railroad Land Grants, 1867–1894," *Mississippi Valley Historical Review*, XXIII (June, 1946), 36–56.

[65] "Public Aids to Domestic Transportation," *op. cit.*, p. 110.

[66] *Commercial and Financial Chronicle*, XXX (April 24, 1880, Investor's Supplement), 3.

[67] F. A. Shannon, *The Farmer's Last Frontier* (New York: Holt, Rinehart and Winston, Inc., 1945), pp. 52–58.

of the reach of its own citizens for as long as thirty years. The case against land grants was able to summon powerful arguments: it was a fight for the individual against the corporation, for the ordinary settler against the construction company which used the land grant as a guarantee of land grant bonds and made off with "enormous" profits; the purity of republican institutions was endangered by the luxury and corruption of subsidy and favoritism.[68]

Such arguments were too simple and generally speaking too extravagant. The railroads with the largest land grants established land companies or departments and promoted settlement. Settlement meant traffic for the road. "No settlers, no trains," one western railroad executive put it. The railroads charged moderate prices, granted long credits, and, though some large land holdings emerged, usually sought to hold off the speculator and the monopolist.[69] Though the land programs of government and of railroads both developed shortcomings, apparently the policy of the latter was at least as successful as the former in attaining desirable social objectives, the rapid peopling of territory and a democratic dispersal of ownership. From the narrow business point of view, the railroads according to informed but probably overestimated guess, had by the end of 1941 a net gain from the disposal of land grants from state and nation of $434,806,671 and still retained land valued at $60,684,032.[70] Four present-day systems, the Northern Pacific, the Santa Fe, the Southern Pacific, and the Union Pacific accounted for 73 per cent of the land granted to railroads.[71] Perhaps these and other railroads would not have been built at the time they were without land grants, a policy that also speeded the development of the West.

But land is not money. Returns from the former depended upon skill in its sale and the growth of the country. Consequently, to enable the first transcontinental to start at once upon its untried way, Congress decided to make it a loan of government bonds. These securities bearing 6 per cent interest and maturing in thirty years were to vary in amount with the ruggedness of the terrain: sixteen thousand dollars a mile over

[68] "The Truth about Land Grants," *Nation,* XI (December 22, 1870), 417–418; *The Congressional Globe,* 41st Cong., 3d Sess., 1870–1871, Pt. 2, pp. 1471–1473.

[69] R. C. Overton, *Burlington West: A Colonization History of the Burlington Railroad* (Cambridge: Harvard University Press, 1941), pp. 98–121, 158–163, 186–217, 237–271, 290–390, 412–479; Cochran, *op. cit.,* pp. 151–152; P. W. Gates, *The Illinois Central Railroad and Its Colonization Work* (Cambridge: Harvard University Press, 1934), pp. 149–352; P. W. Gates, *Fifty Million Acres: Conflicts over Kansas Land Policy, 1854–1890* (Ithaca: Cornell University Press, 1954), pp. 249–294; J. B. Hedges, "The Colonization Work of the Northern Pacific Railroad," *Mississippi Valley Historical Review,* XIII (December, 1926), 311–342; Shannon, *op. cit.,* pp. 66–71.

[70] "Public Aids to Transportation," *op. cit.,* p. 119.

[71] Ellis, *op. cit., Mississippi Valley Historical Review,* XXXIII (June, 1946), 29n.

the Great Plains and in the farthest West, forty-eight thousand a mile for the penetration of the mountain ranges, and thirty-two thousand a mile in the great interior basin between the Rockies and the Sierra Nevadas. To secure these loans Congress declared them a second mortgage upon the property of the beneficiaries. To assure their payment, principal and interest, the government was to retain half the money paid the roads for the transport of mail, troops, and government material and the roads were "to apply" "annually" 5 per cent of their net earnings to paying this indebtedness.[72] Under the provisions of these and other acts the United States advanced $64,623,512 to western railroads; much the largest proportion was for the main line of the Union-Central Pacific and the remainder largely for its branches.[73]

Thirty years of litigation and court decisions, of legislative quarreling and new statutes, ensued. When the Union Pacific won the right to postpone payment of principal and interest until the loans fell due between 1895 and 1899, those in control of the road improvidently declared large dividends and made no provision for anticipating the government loan. When Congress compelled the Union Pacific to make payments to a sinking fund and competition thrust down rates, the road had to pass its dividend and the stock became the plaything of speculators.[74] To find out what was going on, Congress supplemented the Pacific Railway Committees in House and Senate and the five government directors on the Union's board with an Auditor of Railroad Accounts, later Commissioner of Railroads, who could prescribe the form of report from railroads aided by bonds or land grants and under a roving commission determine whether the companies were keeping their books correctly and obeying the law.[75] All the while the interest on the loan, in the usual inexorable fashion, mounted, until its sum, $114,137,761, was considerably greater than the principal.[76]

Pay day came in the late nineties. For one reason or another the sinking fund proved to be inadequate to meet the government's bill and the depression of 1893 forced the Union Pacific into a receivership. Curiously this misfortune proved to be an advantage. The puissant financiers engaged in the road's reorganization were eager to eliminate the interference of the government and their successively higher offers finally resulted in the complete repayment of principal and interest on

[72] 12 *United States Statutes*, 492–493, 495; 13 *ibid.*, 359, 360.

[73] Office of Federal Coördinator of Transportation, Section of Research, *Public Aids to Transportation*, v. II, Pt. 1, p. 59.

[74] "Reports . . . of the United States Pacific Railway Commission," *Senate Executive Document* No. 51 (s.n. 2505), 50th Cong., 1st Sess., pp. 52–68, 86–96; Trottman, *op. cit.*, pp. 123–146, 206–211, 221–229, 238.

[75] 20 *United States Statutes*, 169–170; 21 *ibid.*, 409.

[76] Office of Federal Coördinator of Transportation, *op. cit.*, v. II, Pt. 1, p. 138.

government loans for its main line. A settlement with the Central Pacific followed easily. Although some of the smaller items remained undischarged, the government regained all but 6 per cent of its principal and accumulated interest.[77] A contemporary hailed the result as "financially not less than brilliant." [78] Actually the better word was "lucky," though government officials certainly negotiated with shrewdness. Thus ended an experiment which enabled the first transcontinental in the days of its construction to borrow more cheaply for its construction than if it had had to resort to the investment market; in the uncertainties of the sixties reliance upon private capital without the confidence engendered by the government's advances would in all likelihood have been fruitless. From those who felt the government should keep out of railroading, severing the tie between the Pacific railroads and national politics brought a sigh of relief.[79] To find an event of comparable significance in government railroad financing we must go back to 1857, when Pennsylvania sold to the Pennsylvania Railroad the "main line" of its public works.

Even as the former divorcement was consummated, the *American Railroad Journal* was chronicling with approval the continuance of states aiding railroad construction through their superior credit. At least ten states were following this policy [80] in many forms. The state might give an outright donation of cash or state securities; through guarantees or endorsements of railroad bonds it might engage to meet the principal and interest in case the railroad defaulted; it might by an exchange of its own securities or through funds raised by the sale of its own bonds subscribe to the securities of the railroad; or it might loan railroad corporations its securities. These devices might come to the aid of particular enterprises or take the form of a general policy of assisting all roads in proportion to their mileage. The last procedure has in the long history of state assistance been the most popular.[81] An outright donation, of course, usually involved no continuing connection between railroad and state and all the other methods, at least in the minds of their more optimistic advocates, carried little risk for the state since the railroads obligated themselves to meet interest payments on the former's advances and to repay the principal eventually, and gave the state some form of lien upon their property.

[77] Office of Federal Coördinator of Transportation, *op. cit.*, v. II, Pt. 1, p. 138; Trottman, *op. cit.*, pp. 261–272; H. R. Meyer, "The Settlements with the Pacific Railways," *Quarterly Journal of Economics*, XIII (July, 1899), 442–443.

[78] H. R. Meyer, *op. cit.*, pp. 443–444.

[79] *Ibid.*, 444; "Reports . . . of the United States Pacific Railway Commission," *op. cit.*, p. 19.

[80] Goodrich, "The Revulsion against Internal Improvements," *loc. cit.*, pp. 148–149.

[81] Office of Federal Coördinator of Transportation, *op. cit.*, v. II, Pt. 1, pp. 57, 60, 61, 65, 139–159.

In the period after 1860 the Southern states as a group were the outstanding practitioners of state aid. The dispersed and agricultural nature of Southern civilization had led even before the Civil War to an exceptional reliance upon state credit; some states, Virginia, for example, had developed a widely embracing and highly successful system.[82] After 1865 compelling directives to the same end were at work. The Civil War had devastated two-thirds of the railroad network of the South; even so crucial a line as the Central of Georgia did not run a through train for over a year after Appomattox. Since in the circumstances Southerners had little capital for investment, railroad conventions summoned Northern capitalists to the harvest, and the proffer of state assistance was a supplementary and more tangible inducement. Nor was the South immune from the railroad boom of other sections.[83] On the surface the Southern constitutions, reformed in the early years of reconstruction, seemed likely to hamper or perhaps kill through prudential clauses a widespread application of state aid. But where the prohibitions were the most stringent, as in Mississippi, legislatures discovered they did not prevent outright gifts; elsewhere assistance was possible if special taxes were levied to meet the state's obligations or if the grants were ratified by two-thirds of the legislature or by a popular referendum which, as in Arkansas, with a convenient absence of detailed information asked the electorate simply to vote "For Railroads" or "Against Railroads." [84]

So far it has proved to be impossible to measure with any precision the resulting extravaganza of railroad aid. Debts for all purposes of the Southern states mounted from $111,413,000 in 1865 to $247,578,000 toward the end of Reconstruction in 1872–1874.[85] Though clearly the largest share went to railroad enterprises, other expenditures are included in this figure. It has been equally difficult to apportion responsibility for the increase. Years before President Hayes in 1877 withdrew troops from the last portions of the occupied South and before Southern whites "redeemed" their governments from Negro and carpetbag domination, states here and there began an examination of their debts and the high taxes involved in paying the interest thereon. They came gen-

[82] Carter Goodrich, "The Virginia System of Mixed Enterprise," *Political Science Quarterly*, LXIV (September, 1949), 355–387; E. M. Coulter, *The South during Reconstruction, 1865–1877* (Baton Rouge: Louisiana State University Press, 1947), p. 150; Goodrich, "The Revulsion against Internal Improvements," *loc. cit.*, p. 168.

[83] Robert C. Black, II, *The Railroads of the Confederacy* (Chapel Hill: University of North Carolina Press, 1952), pp. 289–292; Coulter, *op. cit.*, p. 3.

[84] B. U. Ratchford, *American State Debts* (Durham: Duke University Press, 1941), pp. 167–168; R. C. McGrane, *Foreign Bondholders and American State Debts* (New York: Macmillan Company, 1935), p. 294; J. W. Garner, *Reconstruction in Mississippi* (New York: Macmillan Company, 1901), pp. 288–289.

[85] Ratchford, *op. cit.*, pp. 172, 183.

erally to the conclusion that neither their resources, wealth nor strength could bear the burden. In the vernacular of the time they decided to "repudiate" some of their obligations and "readjust" the remainder through "scaling" or some other device. In other words investors would not get their money. An outcome so contrary to "state honor" and "public faith" required justification, and the history of an era, in which one Southern governor had declared that "corruption is the fashion," was able to provide a mountainous assortment of bribes, carelessness, and misappropriation of funds to exculpate reversing the policy of state aid.

For a long time it was customary to blame Northern bankers and promoters and ignorant blacks and rascally carpetbaggers for the noisome aspects of reconstruction railroad policy. Such explantion hardly accorded with the several instances when both political parties supported state aid, and Southern bankers and businessmen lobbied in its behalf and popular referenda gave it thundering majorities.[86] Nor was the charge of unusual wastefulness compatible with the recorded reconstruction of the Southern roads and the extension of their mileage from 9,182 in 1860 to 13,872 in 1877.[87] But when the tide turned toward repudiation in the seventies, only Texas and Mississippi in the old Confederacy remained untainted. Many states enacted constitutional amendments forever preventing the levying of taxes to pay interest and dividends on their discarded debts.[88] Elsewhere the battle was prolonged. Virginia, whose debt was the largest and state credit men strong, did not settle the issue until 1892 when the debt was scaled down to 35 per cent.[89] Repudiation wrung from injured or unsympathetic Northerners the cry of "naked rascality."[90] Conservative financial opinion, however, appreciated the plight of the South and begged for compromise on both sides. It was agreed, nevertheless, that the South should pay something to "exhibit the genuine grit characteristic of Americans."[91]

Experience with state aid in the North hardly predisposed the

[86] *Ibid.*, pp. 168–183, 193–196; W. E. DuBois, *Black Reconstruction* (New York: Harcourt, Brace, 1935), pp. 407–408, 475–477, 493–494, 531–532; Coulter, *op. cit.*, pp. 152–153; C. Vann Woodward, *Origins of the New South, 1877–1913* (Baton Rouge: Louisiana State University Press, 1951), pp. 89–92; Carter Goodrich, "Public Aid to Railroads in the Reconstruction South," *Political Science Quarterly*, LXXI (September, 1956), 407–442.

[87] H. V. Poor, *Manual of the Railroads of the United States for 1868–69* (New York: H. V. and H. W. Poor, 1868), p. 21; H. V. Poor, *Manual of the Railroads of the United States for 1880* (New York: H. V. and H. W. Poor, 1880), p. v.

[88] Ratchford, *op. cit.*, pp. 183–193.

[89] *Ibid.*, pp. 197–218; Woodward, *op. cit.*, pp. 92–98.

[90] New York *Times*, quoted in Woodward, *op. cit.*, p. 88.

[91] *Commercial and Financial Chronicle*, XXV (August 25, 1877), 174; XXVIII (April 26, 1879), 412–413.

region to sympathize with the South. The old Northwest had abandoned it and along the Atlantic seaboard Massachusetts, whose investments at one time or another in the Hoosac Tunnel Route and more feeble enterprises had amounted to nearly $18,000,000 and had made her the most conspicuous state investor in the North, enjoyed an impeccable credit rating in comparison with the Southern states, some of whose bonds were going for two cents on the dollar.[92] Even in the trans-Mississippi West where frontier conditions had perpetuated state assistance, Kansas, Nebraska, and Missouri were retreating from the policy by means of constitutional provisions.[93] Only in Minnesota, where in 1858 the government projected a loan of $5,000,000 to four railroads and two years later forbad by constitutional amendment the payment of principal and interest on this debt without popular ratification, was there any repetition of Southern experience, including the electorate's call for formal and complete repudiation. A maneuver by state officers outwitted the popular will and finally scaled the debt to 50 per cent.[94]

LOCAL AID

Meanwhile counties, cities and towns were beseeching state legislatures for permission to adopt their own policy of financial assistance to railroads. Though there were some who believed that these localities as the primordial unit of government had the inherent right to make such decisions anyway, a different conception prevailed.[95] In the end the result resembled in some respects state policy. Through special or general legislation—the latter method being more convenient became common—legislatures allowed local governments to extend their credit to railroad corporations. Through donations, loans, guarantees, or subscription to railroad securities—the last the most usual form—the local governments proceeded to act. Legislatures customarily hedged their permission with prudential clauses requiring the assent of local voters and sometimes of property owners to railroad grants and limited the

[92] Goodrich, "Revulsion against Internal Improvements," *loc. cit.*, pp. 147–148; *Commercial and Financial Chronicle,* XXIV (June 2, 1877), 504; Kirkland, *op. cit.*, I, 431, II, 43, 310.

[93] Goodrich, "Revulsion against Internal Improvements," *loc. cit.*, pp. 156–159.

[94] G. W. Green, "Repudiation," J. J. Lalor, ed., *Cyclopedia of Political Science, Political Economy, and of the Political History of the United States,* III, 608; McGrane, *op. cit.*, pp. 322–334; *Commercial and Financial Chronicle,* XXIV (July 16, 1877), 552–553.

[95] Louis Hartz, *Economic Policy and Democratic Thought: Pennsylvania, 1776–1860* (Cambridge: Harvard University Press, 1948), pp. 103–122; *Commercial and Financial Chronicle,* XIX (July 18, 1874), 51–52.

debt incurred for railroads to a percentage of the assessed valuation of the community's property. In view of the jurisdictions involved there was a wide variety of provisions.[96] In any case, they were not necessarily binding, for local governments eager to have railroads sometimes made grants in advance of permissive legislation, or after it had been withdrawn, or when it had never been given at all.[97]

On the whole the policy of local aid exhibited more contrasts to than identities with state aid. Sometimes it preceded state assistance; sometimes it was contemporary with it—Massachusetts, for example—and sometimes it was an alternative, as in the old Northwest, for a state policy abandoned or forbidden. No state in the Union entirely escaped the practice of local aid. In terms of time, the passage of statutes permitting local aid was concentrated in the years of the great railroad mania, 1865 to 1873. By 1890 fifteen states still retained their general laws, and even later local aid often helped build or extend a railroad.[98] One explanation for the persistence of this device lay in the more sharply felt needs of local communities. A state could be reasonably sure of having some railroads. But it was fatal for a small community to be left aside by a projected railroad or to have no branch to a main line, and for a metropolis to fall short of the stature of railroad center or to be at the mercy of one railroad was to invite discrimination and economic stagnation. As a Cincinnati newspaper put it, when the city was considering building the Cincinnati Southern Railroad, "When it comes to a matter of life and death, where our future prosperity or decay is in such scales, then extreme cases need extreme remedies."[99]

The urgent note of "life and death" was sounded by all parties interested in local aid: railroad promoters, often seeking quick profits from dubious enterprises, repeated it and so did communities yearning for railroad connections. What did it matter if they lost money upon their direct investments? They had indirect benefits. Obviously the technique of winning local aid differed from that of winning assistance from the legislature. In the latter case suppliants had to resort to lobbying; in the former, to convert the electorate. The necessary prelude to local aid was consequently a revivalistic campaign with damnation or salvation present on the platform. The local press, the best citizens, and assorted spell-

[96] Carter Goodrich, "Local Government Planning of Internal Improvements," *Political Science Quarterly*, LXVI (September, 1951), 418–423.

[97] 94 *United States*, 256; *Commercial and Financial Chronicle*, XXV (August 11, 1877), 138.

[98] Goodrich, "Local Government Planning of Internal Improvements," *loc. cit.*, pp. 412–413.

[99] J. H. Hollander, "The Cincinnati Southern Railway: A Study in Municipal Activity," *Johns Hopkins University Studies in Historical and Political Science* (Baltimore: Johns Hopkins Press, 1894), 12th Series, Pts. 1–2, p. 22n.

binders united to mesmerize the electorate.[100] But those sufficiently jaundiced about public moods or outside the area of excitement were sure that good sense was likely to be the victim. It outraged the law of supply and demand and the principles of the Republic to substitute "the voice of the majority for the hard, calculating instinct of the moneyed man." [101] Be that as it may, local governments through loans, endorsements and subscriptions, according to an estimate which is clearly too low, aided railroads to the tune of $86,816,209.[102] The number of small communities which bonded themselves for this purpose is legion. Of the great cities, some, such as New York, Chicago, and Boston, refrained from assistance; others, such as Milwaukee, Philadelphia, and Baltimore, forked up.[103] Over a period of nearly sixty years Baltimore, for instance, authorized $20,767,500 for railroads, including the Baltimore and Ohio.[104]

As in the case of state aid, disillusionment generally set in after the collapse of 1873. In some cases the aided "railroads" had not materialized at all. More usually they had cost more than had been estimated; often they failed to earn enough to pay the interest on the securities which local governments had endorsed or to which they had subscribed. Towns and cities were confronted with the grim specter of increased taxation or diminished appropriations for other purposes, from schools to sewers, or with finding some way to avoid meeting their obligations.[105]

Luckily for would-be defaulters, the impetuousness of town proceedings and the well-known inability of elected officials to act strictly in accordance with the minutiae of enabling legislation offered an occasion for asserting that grants did not accord with the law and hence were hardly a legal responsibility of the communities.[106] The states had been able to bring off a similar evasion largely because the eleventh amendment of the Federal Constitution in effect barred creditors from bringing direct action against the delinquent states.[107] No such shelter protected counties, municipalities and towns. Though local judges and

[100] Harry H. Pierce, *Railroads of New York: A Study of Government Aid, 1826–1875* (Cambridge: Harvard University Press, 1953), pp. 41–58; Kirkland, *op. cit.*, I, 481.

[101] *Nation*, X (February 17, 1870), 101; *Commercial and Financial Chronicle*, XX (April 10, 1875), 345–346.

[102] Office of Federal Coördinator of Transportation, *op. cit.*, v. II, Pt. 1, pp. 60, 61, 65.

[103] *Ibid.*, v. II, Pt. 1, pp. 139–145; Hartz, *op. cit.*, p. 106; A. M. Hillhouse, *Municipal Bonds; A Century of Experience* (New York: Prentice-Hall, 1936), p. 153.

[104] Carter Goodrich and Harvey H. Segal, "Baltimore's Aid to Railroads: A Study in Municipal Planning of Internal Improvements," *Journal of Economic History*, XIII (Winter, 1953), 1, 8.

[105] Kirkland, *op. cit.*, I, 476–478, 484–486; II, 313; Pierce, *op. cit.*, pp. 58–59.

[106] Pierce, *op. cit.*, pp. 82–104.

[107] Ratchford, *op. cit.*, pp. 232–241.

lower state courts, sensitive to the moans of citizens who had elected them, sometimes came to the rescue of communities which had plunged injudiciously, the Federal courts took the matter out of their hands.[108] In plowing through a stupendous docket of municipal bond cases, the justices of the Supreme Court declared a few municipal issues clearly invalid; in the main they held such debt must be paid.[109] The difficulties in forcing payment at the local level under law or judicial decision were another matter.[110]

An estimate of aid from state and local governments in terms of measurable financial contributions on the one hand and repudiation, scaling and repayments on the other is beyond formulation. In any case it could shed little light on the purpose or accomplishments of policy. State and local communities aided railroads because of their quickening effect upon production, land values, and commerce. Of course it might have been sounder to have waited for direct investment by private citizens, but such restraint would have meant some roads would not have been built at all, or not as soon as they were. For governmental units furnished the risk capital; their contributions paved the way for private investment and gave the latter confidence and assurance. Beyond this the policy did not go. Majority opinion in the era insisted that the railroads, whatever their public obligations, be predominantly financed and controlled by private capital. Nearly everywhere governments feared participation in railroad management; when their representation on railroad directorates did not actually terminate with the construction of the road it became innocuous and ineffectual; and communities sold their stock to private investors or distributed it to their citizens.[111] According to the canon, once the pioneering stage was over, public participation should cease.[112]

TRENDS AMONG PRIVATE INVESTORS

Private investment came in part from abroad, indirectly through the purchase of government issues in behalf of railroads, directly through the purchase of railroad securities themselves. For the former category there is no overall approximate guess of the sums involved; for the latter, estimates of variable authenticity are available. In 1853 foreigners owned

[108] *Nation,* XXVIII (January 2, 1879), 5; *Commercial and Financial Chronicle,* XXV (August 25, 1877), 187.

[109] Hillhouse, *op. cit.,* pp. 159–165.

[110] *Commercial and Financial Chronicle,* XIX (July 18, 1874), 51–52; Pierce, *op. cit.,* pp. 88–90; Hillhouse, *op. cit.,* pp. 169–176.

[111] Kirkland, *op. cit.,* I, 364–366, 377–379, 415–419; Pierce, *op. cit.,* pp. 105–129; Goodrich, "Local Planning of Internal Improvements," *loc. cit.,* pp. 428–429.

[112] Goodrich, "The Revulsion against Internal Improvements," *loc. cit.,* p. 168.

$51,914,742 in railway securities; in 1869 the sum was $243,000,000.[113] Unluckily the most authoritative analysis at the end of the century did not always break down its totals into categories. There seems little reason to doubt the conclusion, however, that of the $3,145,000,000 foreigners had invested in this country "the vast mass . . . could only be in railroad securities." [114] The British were the largest investors. At the earlier date foreigners preferred bonds to stocks; by the eighties huge blocks of railroad stocks were crossing the Atlantic and becoming a favorite object of international speculation. In addition to their long-standing investments in roads such as the Illinois Central and the Erie, foreign investors owned more than half the shares in the Central Pacific, Louisville and Nashville, Norfolk and Western, two-fifths of those in the Pennsylvania, and one-third of those in the Union Pacific.[115]

The course of foreign investments did not always run smooth. When depression tore away the façade from American enterprises and revealed mismanagement and miscalculation, owners of pounds sterling kept them at home and called back some they had already sent overseas. At such times, also, foreign investors uttered loud cries of censure and woe and, largely ignoring the responsibility of their countrymen who had sold them their American securities, sought to prescribe remedies for ailing American railroad management. Proposals for transferring to London the business of the corporation, including corporate records, a portion of the directors, and the disbursements of dividends, and for holding annual meetings there were not adopted.[116] Instead the English or other investors despatched investigators and occasionally appointed representative directors, helped turn out undesirable managements, and brought about receiverships and foreclosures.[117] Aliens could resort to the American courts for redress, and could utilize responsible American banking firms to represent them. When counsel rang the changes on the evils of foreign influence, the *Commercial and Financial Chronicle* characterized this appeal as a "perfect abomination." [118] Those committed to the development of the American economy saw in the vast reserves of investment funds overseas an essential element in their success.

[113] "Report of the Secretary of the Treasury . . . on American Securities held in Europe . . . 1853," *Senate Executive Document* No. 42 (s.n. 698), 33rd Cong., 1st Sess., pp. 36–50; "Report of the Special Commissioner of the Revenue, 1869," *House Executive Document* No. 27 (s.n. 1416), 41st Cong., 2d Sess., p. xxviii.

[114] N. T. Bacon, "American International Indebtedness," *Yale Review*, IX (November, 1900), 266, 269, 270, 276.

[115] Leland H. Jenks, "Britain and American Railway Development," *Journal of Economic History*, XI (Fall, 1951), 376–377.

[116] *Commercial and Financial Chronicle*, XXI (August 7, 1875), 137; XXIV (March 24, 1877), 260–261.

[117] Jenks, "Britain and American Railway Development," *loc. cit.*, pp. 379–381.

[118] *Commercial and Financial Chronicle*, XXIV (March 31, 1877), 297.

The great majority of American railroad securities were, however, American owned. In 1853, for instance, foreigners owned about 11 per cent of the outstanding securities of American railroads; it probably was as high as 25 per cent by 1899.[119] Little is known about the number of American investors. In 1893 the editor of an important railroad journal asserted the total number was about 1,250,000, in the light of later enumeration an overestimate.[120] Nor is it crystal clear that the number of investors was increasing and that, consequently, stock ownership was gaining a broader base. At the outset of its corporate life a railroad might start with a widespread subscription, particularly if it were a local road and enlisted small investors along the line. On the other hand, if it were taken in hand by a tight group of driving capitalists the stock-ownership, as on the Central Pacific, might be highly concentrated. When a road of the former type proved profitable or strategic, larger investors might buy up its securities; for a road of the latter type, stock-ownership for any one of a number of reasons might become more dispersed. Early in the eighties, for instance, a banking syndicate began selling widely a portion of W. H. Vanderbilt's 87 per cent holding in the New York Central; on the Boston and Albany the number of stockholders grew from 4,880 to 8,531 between 1872 and 1890.[121] As far as available figures show, there would seem to have been a general trend away from the railroad "king," "magnate," or "monopolist" and toward ownership by "hundreds of thousands of plain people," but the case is by no means proven.[122] Also, the figures ignore holdings by banks, insurance companies, and other railroads.

As the railroads moved into the West and South, a corps of capitalists from the Northeast planned their extension, undertook their construction, provided the funds, and, on completion, ran them. The symbol of this process was location of the main office of such enterprises in Boston, New York, or Philadelphia. Representative of this type of entrepreneur were John Murray Forbes of Boston, who with a fortune gained in the foreign trade and the aid of a powerful group of relatives and business peers moved westward over the Michigan Central to the roads making up the Chicago, Burlington and Quincy; Jay Gould of

[119] "Report of the Secretary of the Treasury . . . on American Securities," *loc. cit.*, p. 50; *Poor's Manual of the Railroads of the United States, 1900* (New York: H. V. and H. W. Poor, 1900), p. ii.

[120] H. S. Robinson, "A Railway Party in Politics," *North American Review*, XLVI (May, 1893), 553; Lewes H. Kimmel, *Share Ownership in the United States* (Washington: Brookings Institution, 1952), pp. 111–112.

[121] Pierce, *op. cit.*, pp. 8–10; Kirkland, *op. cit.*, II, 340–341; "Report of the Pacific Railway Commission," *Senate Document* No. 51 (s.n. 2505), 50th Cong., 1st Sess., p. ii.

[122] *Nation*, XXXVIII (January 31, 1884), 91.

New York City, who after a start during the Civil War on some tiny railroads upstate, became an overlord of the Erie—until the English investors ousted him—and then the "directing mind," variously titled, of the Union Pacific and a whole system of roads in the Southwest; Jay Cooke, the titan banker from Philadelphia, who made of the Northern Pacific his pride; and Tom Scott of the Pennsylvania Railroad, whose restless energy found outlet in the Union Pacific and Texas and Pacific. Even railroad kings less absentee than these, the Californians C. P. Huntington and Leland Stanford of the Central and Southern Pacific, for example, were born in the East, had eastern interests, eastern offices, and even eastern railroads.[123]

The way to fortune from railroading might run through promotion, construction, the changing value of the property or returns on the investment. On the last count, certainly, the averages were a mean far from golden. In 1869 the yield on railroad bonds ranged from a low of 5.8 to a high of 6.4 per cent; in 1897 from 3.2 to 3.4 per cent. While this continuous descent took place, the index of dividends on railroad common stocks fell irregularly from a high of 6.98 per cent in 1873 to a low of 3.47 per cent in 1897.[124] Nor was this erosion the only evidence of the fate befalling one of the most highly respected of investments. At no time in the decade 1888–1897 did the portion of railroad stock paying dividends exceed 40.36 per cent; once it fell as low as 29.83 per cent.[125] The proportion of the funded debt which paid no interest varied, so far as figures are available, from 9.90 per cent in 1891 to 18.19 per cent in 1889.[126] "It is as frivolous to cite a fortune made in the manipulation of stocks as an evidence of the profitableness of the operation of railways as it would be to advance a fortune made in the wheat ring as a proof that farming pays," commented an observer.[127]

Clearly loss as well as gain attended the overproduction of American railroads. The periods of depression, failure, and reorganization raised questions of what caused the failure, who should pay for it, and how the corporation could return to a profitable and fruitful life. To the first query there was at least one convincing answer. Within the framework

[123] "Jay Cooke," *Dictionary of American Biography,* IV, 383–384; "John Murray Forbes," *ibid.,* VI, 507–508; "Jay Gould," *ibid.,* VII, 454–455; "Collis Peter Huntington," *ibid.,* IX, 408–412; "Thomas Alexander Scott," *ibid.,* XVI, 500–501; "Leland Stanford," *ibid.,* XVII, 501–505; Cochran, *op. cit.,* pp. 266–267, 325, 364.

[124] Bureau of the Census, *op. cit.,* p. 280.

[125] Interstate Commerce Commission, *Eleventh Annual Report on the Statistics of Railways . . . 1898,* p. 60.

[126] Interstate Commerce Commission, *Second Annual Report on the Statistics of Railways . . . 1889,* p. 29; Interstate Commerce Commission, *Fourth Annual Report on the Statistics of Railways . . . 1891,* p. 65.

[127] Robinson, "A Railway Party in Politics," *loc. cit.,* p. 558.

of alternating good and bad times, construction by bonds and floating debt imposed inflexibility and pressing expense upon railroads and the interest on such borrowings had to be met. On the second point matters were somewhat less clear. According to the pattern of mercantile enterprise, an unsatisfied creditor could foreclose the debtor's business, sell the property, and recompense himself for his advances. On the railroads a first mortgage bondholder, or his official representative, the trustee of the bonds, was unable to proceed so directly. The community demanded that a railroad be kept in operation. To do so it was often necessary to recognize as a prior lien to the first-mortgage bonds, rentals on leases of branch roads, interest on equipment bonds—for without rolling stock the roads could not run—and also payments for current expenses. Nor was it foreordained that bondholders could avoid losses by installing a more efficient administration, for failure might well be due to unavoidable circumstance.

What was needed was a receivership to improve the property, reconcile the various interests, and perhaps checkmate the immediate emergency. But receiverships of this sort were also devices by which an unscrupulous management could avoid paying debts it did not wish to meet, break contracts it did not wish to honor, feather its own nest by loans to the corporation at high rates of interest, and keep itself in power. Thus many interests, righteous or unrighteous, rushed into receiverships and circuit judges of the United States courts were pried out of bed at midnight to grant them. Sometimes these receiverships, instead of passing through a quick foreclosure of the property and the reorganization of the concern with a debt structure better adapted to its capacities, took years, and the resulting "endless and titanic litigation" might lead to a new company with heavier burdens than the original debtor. The final outcome for the bondholders, who once fancied they had security, was a postponement of interest payments and the payment of current expenses to maintain their rights.[128] The *Commercial and Financial Chronicle* derided the eight pages of printed foolscap of one such reorganization as quite unsuited for the "consideration of widows and orphans and other small holders"—a plain summary of it, if forthcoming, would have been "easily comprehensible to the average understanding." [129]

In truth the release of an injured corporation from the bondage of bankruptcy was a task for the expert. From the unprecedented wreckage

[128] Simon Sterne, "Railway Reorganization," *Forum,* X (September, 1890), 37–53; *Commercial and Financial Chronicle,* XVIII (January 24, 1874), 76–77; (February 7, 1874), 131–132; (February 21, 1874), 181–182; XIX (October 3, 1874), 339–340; (October 17, 1874), 387–388; (October 24, 1874), 411–412; XXXIX (August 30, 1884, Investors' Supplement), 1–3; Kirkland, *op. cit.,* II, 48–49, 56–64.

[129] *Commercial and Financial Chronicle,* XXV (November 10, 1877), 456.

of the depression nineties, the investment banking house of J. P. Morgan emerged as the most skilfull and systematic resuscitator. Its formula was to consolidate bond issues at lower interest rates and thus reduce fixed charges upon the enterprise, exact from existing stockholders heavy assessments to discharge the floating debt and provide funds for improvement, and replace existing junior liens with an enlarged issue of new stock, common and preferred, entitled to make money only in contingencies.[130] In this fashion, it was hoped, a new financial structure would correct the misjudgments and misdeeds of the past. Such readjustments certainly entailed less hypocrisy and proportionately no more litigation and loss than had attended the repudiation of their railroad bonds by the southern states and by the municipalities of the North. Be that as it may, the reorganizations of the nineties gave a new status to bankers in railroad management, further concentrated in the Northeast the control of the railroad network, and through the imperial handling of leases, branches, and connections hastened the trend toward large-scale railroading and consolidation.[131]

When they reflected upon their stupendous accomplishments in the decades after the Civil War, those who had constructed the railroads and invested in them were understandably stirred to pride and to an estimate of themselves as benefactors of the community and of the nation.[132] Though only one railroad titan, J. J. Hill of the Great Northern, gained the sobriquet of "The Empire Builder," most railroad men would have echoed the words of Sidney Dillon, contractor, promoter, investor: "The world should therefore thank the railway for the opportunity to buy wheat; but none the less should the West thank the railway for the opportunity to sell wheat." [133]

But American democracy was unlikely to accept railroads as a matter of grace. Nor did shippers and travelers refrain from criticizing railroad performance in general and in particular. For the influence of the railroads penetrated every cranny of the economy and touched every man's interest. Furthermore democratic governments had aided the railroads in wholesale fashion. Though the dream of a transcontinental as a "Peoples Railroad to the Pacific Ocean," built by the investments of

[130] *Commercial and Financial Chronicle,* LVI (May 27, 1893), 858–860; (June 3, 1893), 905–907; E. G. Campbell, *The Reorganization of the American Railroad System, 1893–1900* (New York: Columbia University Press, 1938), pp. 145–189; Daggett, *op. cit.,* pp. 334–386.

[131] Campbell, *op. cit.,* pp. 326–334; W. F. Switzler, "Report on the Internal Commerce of the United States . . . 1886," *House Executive Document* No. 7, Pt. 2 (s.n. 2476), 49th Cong., 2d Sess., appendix, pp. 28–29.

[132] Cochran, *op. cit.,* pp. 203–205, 250.

[133] Sidney Dillon, "The West and the Railroads," *North American Review,* CLII (April, 1891), 444.

thousands of everyday Americans was wholly unrealizable, the concept of the railroads as peoples' roads in a somewhat different and wider sense persisted. These antithetic conceptions of insiders and outsiders were bound to lead to conflict and changing policy.[134]

[134] E. V. Smalley, *History of the Northern Pacific Railroad* (New York: G. P. Putnam's Sons, 1885), pp. 102–103; Testimony of Joseph Medill, *Report of the Committee* [on Education and Labor] *of the Senate . . . 1885,* II, 968–969.

CHAPTER IV

Railroad Pricing Policy

A MULTIPLICITY OF RATES

IN contrast to a tendency, general during the era, toward a fixed price for an article or service, railroads followed a policy of many prices. While this was true of passenger fares, it was more marked in the case of freight charges. Unlike passengers, who load and unload themselves, freight has to be handled and stored at both ends of the journey. Since these terminal charges were the same whether the commodity traveled ten or a hundred miles, freight rates for most hauls at once departed from a strict mileage or pro-rata basis. On through traffic, railroads discovered, as had the canals before them, that if they were to move heavy commodities selling at a low cost they had to grant low rates. The rates for coal, wheat, livestock, and metals were, therefore, lower than those for groceries or suits of clothes. These distinctions accounted, as we have seen, for the classification system. On through traffic over long hauls it was especially desirable to carry full cargoes both ways, since it cost something to haul back empty cars. Railroads also had a fixed investment in roadway, terminals, and rolling stock; these costs went on, business or no business. Thus for several reasons, railroads resorted to a pricing system contemporaries christened as "charging all the traffic will bear." Albert Fink, a railroad expert, thought a fairer description of railroad practice would be that the roads did not "charge more than the article will bear." [1]

Nor could the strategist of railroad pricing merely consider short-time gains or losses. Railroads in the United States were built in advance of traffic and, if they were to make money from traffic not yet in existence or communities not yet populated, they had to establish developmental rates. In the seventies Charles Francis Adams, Jr., Railroad Commissioner of Massachusetts, was lecturing the railroads of the Commonwealth on the wisdom of low coal rates: "a cheap and reliable source of power

[1] Testimony of Albert Fink, *Report of the Committee* [on Education and Labor] *of the Senate . . . 1885,* II, 519–527.

[for industrial growth] is the prime essential. It is, in fact, to the manufacturer all that manure is to the agriculturist, and it has seemed to the Commissioners, and during the last year they have repeatedly urged it on railroad officials, that it was as bad economy for them to insist upon receiving large profits from the carriage of coal along the lines of their roads, as it would be for a farmer to insist upon being handsomely paid for the carriage of every load of manure which he spread upon his fields. In the one case, as in the other, the carrier should look for his reward in the increased production of his territory,—it is the crop he seeks for and not his pay as a carter." [2]

COMPETITION

Railroad managers, however, were not able to work out a rate by slide rule in an ivory tower. They were running their roads in competition with each other and the setting of rates was dictated by the necessity of getting their share of the business. Once, in a few places, a railroad charter had granted monopoly of a route. This generally unpopular privilege the states had by the post-Civil War period generally succeeded in voiding. Thus in the early seventies the carriage of passengers and freight across New Jersey between New York and Philadelphia was no longer the monopoly of the Camden and Amboy.[3] Inferred, rather than granted monopolies disappeared. The immense cost of its construction and the degree of government sponsorship had convinced many investors in the Union Pacific that it was to have a monopoly of transcontinental traffic, but the chartering and completion of the Northern Pacific in 1883 disillusioned them. By this time the Southern Pacific and the Atchison, Topeka and Santa Fe had traversed the supposedly reserved area, and in 1893 the Great Northern joined the parade west.

Nor was the appearance of major competitive lines confined to the wild, undeveloped country of the Far West. The railroads fanning westward from Chicago had once been content to reach ports on the Mississippi; now they sought to push across the river to meet at the Missouri River gateways the eastern railheads of the first transcontinental and to traverse states, such as Nebraska, whose fertility wrung from Charles E. Perkins, president of the Burlington, the report: "I never saw such a land for farming in my life." [4] The whole topography of these

[2] Massachusetts *Third Annual Report of the Board of Railroad Commissioners. January, 1872*, pp. clvii–clix.

[3] John W. Cadman, Jr., *The Corporation in New Jersey. Business and Politics, 1791–1875* (Cambridge: Harvard University Press, 1949), pp. 58–59.

[4] R. C. Overton, *Burlington West* (Cambridge: Harvard University Press, 1941), p. 230.

regions was so favorable to building that road branches and extensions spread out like quicksilver. Lacing and interlacing each other, the so-called Granger roads—the Chicago and Northwestern, the Chicago, Rock Island and Pacific, the Chicago and Alton, the Chicago, Milwaukee and St. Paul, and the Chicago, Burlington and Quincy—competed in the carriage of livestock and cereals.

The grand theatre of competition was, however, in trunk-line territory. Here five immense corporations—the Grand Trunk, the New York Central, the Pennsylvania, the Erie, the Baltimore and Ohio—all with western allies and connections, stretched from Chicago, Cincinnati, and St. Louis to the Atlantic ports or bent every effort to do so. Here was the heaviest concentrated traffic in the country. Within or along the boundaries of this area were specialized types of competition. One was the enclave of the anthracite coal carriers. Though once canals, rivers, and coastal waters had been thought the only feasible means for carrying this bulky commodity profitably, by 1860 the anthracite roads had demonstrated their ability to do so. They went on to engross the traffic. The Philadelphia and Reading, the Lehigh Valley, the Delaware and Hudson, the Delaware, Lackawanna and Western, the Central of New Jersey, as well as the Erie and the Pennsylvania carried anthracite from the mining area of northeastern Pennsylvania to New York, Philadelphia and Baltimore; from sprawling, grimy tidewater installations, sailing vessels distributed the coal to the New England and other markets. The "coalers," embedded in trunk-line territory, were not as long as the soft coal roads, the Chesapeake and Ohio and the Norfolk and Western, which after the Civil War penetrated eastward from Norfolk and Newport News to the deposits of Virgina and West Virginia and became partial rivals of the trunk lines as they pushed westward to the Ohio and the Great Lakes.

The competitive traffic patterns of the Old South were unusual. In 1888 the Interstate Commerce Commission commented upon the fact that the territory "is substantially surrounded by the ocean and the mighty rivers which bound it on the North and West, while it is penetrated to a considerable extent by other navigable streams . . . in addition to these elements of diversity it is characteristic of this section that many lines exist over which traffic to or from distant markets may be taken in either direction with equal facility." [5] Railroads from the interior, as far west as the Mississippi and as far north as the Ohio, came down to the Atlantic at Charleston and Savannah and regular steamship lines connected these ports with New York, Philadelphia, Baltimore and Boston. In addition, north and south, "Palm to Pine" lines, such as the Illinois Central and the Louisville and Nashville, traversing the interior river

[5] 3 *Interstate Commerce Commission,* 24.

basins connected the Northwest with Gulf ports or carried goods, including coal and great shipments of overland cotton, northward to the Ohio River gateways or other points of traffic interchange with the trunk lines.

Calling the roll of sectional competitors by emphasizing major roads is to understate the ubiquity of competition. By the mid-eighties it could be said that "hardly a town or city of any magnitude in the United States, which has not two or more tributary railroads, which, with their connections, constitute direct or indirect routes to almost every other trade center in the United States. Through such facilities for transportation each commercial town and city has become directly and forcefully the competitor of very many other towns and cities, near and far." [6] Nor was competition largely between obvious rivals and parallel routes. Long detours and indirect transportation was possible once goods were placed on the cars. As the Industrial Commission commented in 1902, "Twenty-five years ago there were 20 competitive routes between St. Louis and Atlanta, varying in length from 526 to 1,855 miles respectively. . . . Freight transported from New York to Denver may be carried more than 3,100 miles via New Orleans, as against 1,940 miles direct, one route being 62 per cent longer than the other." [7]

While it might be possible to describe for almost any area the effect of competition in determining rates, the experience in trunk-line territory was most significant because of the intrinsic importance of the area and the resulting publicity of what was done in it. Since the Baltimore and Ohio and the Pennsylvania had shorter routes to the West than had the Erie, New York Central, or Grand Trunk, the first two argued that the shortest line should set the rates, between the interior and the seaboard and should enjoy a differential over their northern rivals. The Central, disdaining an argument which if allowed would have permitted its southern competitors to engross the trade, asserted that costs of operation should determine the proper charge. Though the Central's route was longer, its absence of grades and the greater density of its traffic gave it lower costs. When the Pennsylvania and the Baltimore and Ohio deigned to acknowledge this reasoning, they asserted their own costs were lower because of cheaper coal.

The argument then wandered far afield. For instance, the arguments presented by the Grand Trunk for lowering and cutting rates

[6] Joseph Nimmo, Jr., "Report on the Internal Commerce of the United States . . . 1884," *House Executive Document* No. 7, Pt. 2 (s.n. 2295), 48th Cong., 2d Sess., p. 8; Joseph Nimmo, Jr., "Report on the Internal Commerce of the United States . . . 1879," *House Executive Document* No. 32, Pt. 3 (s.n. 1857), 45th Cong., 3rd Sess., p. 4.

[7] Industrial Commission, *Final Report,* XIX, 356.

exhibited an interesting peculiarity of railroad operation. It was the longest of the competing roads. One justification for low rates, the presence of water competition along its line, the New York Central could as reasonably invoke. But the Grand Trunk was a weak road, continually trembling on the verge of insolvency and often going over: "It is well known that a road in bankruptcy is just so much stronger [for competition] than one that is not . . . because it is relieved from the obligation, for the time being, of paying interest upon its bonds and dividends upon its stock." [8] "Railroads, unfortunately, seem to reverse the rule of the 'survival of the fittest' to the 'survival of the unfittest' . . . when they go into the hands of receivers, they are to be run so long as operating expenses can be paid." [9]

Before all these routes had been either opened or extended to Chicago, wars of rates had broken out. The first at the end of the fifties was a mere preliminary bout, for it was confined to westbound high-class freight. After the Civil War such engagements recurred with the certainty of "small pox or the change of seasons." [10] They reached a climax in the rate war of 1876–1877, "the fiercest, the most determined, and perhaps the most wasteful contest ever known in the history of railroad management . . . between the trunk lines connecting the West with the seaboard." [11] The reasons for the original outbreak and its recurrence were various. The president of the Baltimore and Ohio, opening a connection to Chicago in 1874, had pictured its arrival as a savior to an agricultural region oppressed by extortionate freight charges and had announced that "with the completion of his lines, like another Samson, he could pull down the temple of rates around the heads of these other trunk lines." [12] The merchants of New York were pressing for rate reductions, and Vanderbilt, president of the New York Central, declared his unalterable opposition to any differentials in favor of New York City's rivals. The Grand Trunk was also encroaching upon the Boston traffic of the New York Central. The long depression of the seventies made roads desperate for traffic. During these railroad fights, rates sank abysmally. In 1876–1877, first-class freights from the East to Chicago

[8] Testimony of Edwin D. Worcester, N. Y. Legislative Assembly, *Proceedings of Special Committee on Railroads* [Hepburn Committee], . . . 1879, I, 1074; Speech of Simon Sterne, *ibid.*, IV, 3895–3898.

[9] *Manual of the Railroads of the United States for 1885* (New York: H. V. and H. W. Poor, 1885), p. v.

[10] *Commercial and Financial Chronicle,* XXIV (April 7, 1877), 308.

[11] Joseph Nimmo, Jr., "First Annual Report on the Internal Commerce of the United States . . . 1876," *House Executive Document* No. 46, Pt. 2 (s.n. 1761), 44th Cong., 2d Sess., p. 62.

[12] Testimony of George R. Blanchard, *Proceedings of Special Committee on Railroads* [Hepburn Committee], III, 3171–3172.

and other Western cities, which had once been 75 cents sank to 25 cents; on fourth and fifth class to sixteen; on eastbound goods, once $1.00 a hundred, the rate "went down to seventy-five, it went down to fifty; it went down to twenty-five; it went down to thirteen, it went down to ten." Fifteen was a more accurate minimum. Passenger fares between Boston and Chicago very nearly halved.[13]

Such struggles of titans were not to the taste of investors. Though the contestants were loath to admit they lacked "staying power," the war of rates in 1877 compelled both the Baltimore and Ohio and the Pennsylvania to pass dividends. Angry observers chided railroad managers for being so oblivious to the interests of stockholders and raised the question how money from Americans and from abroad was to be tempted into enterprises harassed by such intemperate competition.[14] Nor were shippers satisfied when rates sank to levels undreamed of by the wildest visionaries of cheap transportation. The truth was that the vacillation and uncertainty of rates challenged that quest for certainty and calculability which was so dominant a note in the economy of the period.

In the mid-eighties Joseph Medill, proprietor and editor of the Chicago *Tribune,* gave a realistic picture of the disadvantages of railroad fights. "We will say that the cost of conveying wheat or corn or any agricultural product from Chicago to this city [New York] is 25 cents per hundred pounds, to-day. On the strength of that rate our merchants proceed to buy wheat, corn, or oats all over the West . . . and farmers make their bargains based on this cost of transportation from Chicago to tide-water. Suddenly, or with brief notice, the charge goes up to 30 cents. Every merchant who holds that grain, and it may amount altogether to tens of millions of bushels, has instantly lost 5 cents on each hundred pounds. That 5 cents is wiped out as completely as if it had been burned, or sunk without insurance. Then, if there is a fall suddenly of 5 cents a hundred pounds, that affects not only the grain that was bought by the merchants, but the entire stock of produce remaining in the hands of farmers. At once, of course, there is a natural dissatisfaction throughout the whole farming community at this artificial fall. . . . The first thing you know they are carrying grain to New York from Chicago for 20 cents per hundred pounds instead of 30 or 35 cents. All at once there is a tremendous 'boom' in the market. Every man's grain rapidly advances. Then the farmers are all angry because they sold

[13] *Commercial and Financial Chronicle,* XXII (June 17, 1876), 582; *Proceedings of Special Committee on Railroads,* [Hepburn Committee] IV, 3769; Massachusetts *Eighth Annual Report of the Board of Railroad Commissioners. January, 1877,* p. 52; Interstate Commerce Commission, *Railways in the United States in 1902,* Pt. II, p. 44.

[14] Lewis Corey, *The House of Morgan* (New York: G. Howard Watt, 1930), pp. 145–146, 150.

out before the cut in transportation. . . . There is no steadiness, no system, no fixedness for anything, and the whole country is kept in a tremor of expectancy as to whether prices are going up or going down from this unregulated cause." [15]

RAILROAD COOPERATION

Least of all were such vacillations or uncertainties to the taste of most railroad managers, and throughout these decades they experimented with various devices to bring them to an end. Cooperation in one form or another was the answer. The resort to these devices, the withdrawal from competition, raised for railroad businessmen a real dilemma. In the individualistic tradition of American life they had been the celebrants of competition. In 1891 Sidney Dillon, president of the Union Pacific, informed his readers that "prices [rates] will always be taken care of by the great law of competition, which obtains wherever any human service is to be performed for a pecuniary consideration. . . . Calculations based upon the law of competition have this advantage: that the foundations on which they rest are immutable, and not only so in their own right, but they cannot be changed by any process whatever . . . no power can prevent one man or set of men from offering to perform a lawful service at lower rates than another." [16] Affirmations of this sort were not merely a handy stick to beat the dog of governmental rate regulation; private communications between railroad men expressed the same dogma. Charles E. Perkins wrote to a Chicago merchant, "There is no other business so sensitive to the natural laws of competition as the business of transportation by rail." [17]

If competition were ordained by natural law, little could seemingly be done to avoid it. One avenue for escaping this painful dilemma was to draw distinctions between "legitimate" or "healthy" competition, both advantageous and unavoidable, and cut-throat competition, "the result of mismanagement." [18] Or perhaps there was a law other than competition. In short, the true gospel had been enunciated long ago by George Stephenson, the "sagacious father of locomotion by steam," when he said, "where combination was possible, competition was impossible." Railroads were a natural monopoly; the law of gravitation and central-

[15] Testimony of Joseph Medill, *Report of the Committee* [on Education and Labor] *of the Senate . . . 1885*, II, 965–966.

[16] Sidney Dillon, "The West and the Railroads," *North American Review*, CLIII (April, 1891), 447–448.

[17] Cochran, *op. cit.*, p. 448.

[18] *Ibid.*, p. 161; Joseph Nimmo, Jr., "First Annual Report on the Internal Commerce of the United States . . . 1876," *loc. cit.*, appendix, p. 12; Robert Garrett, "The Railway Problem," *North American Review*, CXXXIX (October, 1879), 370.

ization was upon them.[19] "There may be, and probably is, some subtle law of evolution governing the whole. Why do railroads consolidate? . . . Plants grow because a law of their nature prompts; may it not be also true that capital joins capital in tacit obedience to a law which has made such union the condition of success? If so, nobody is responsible, for nobody is at liberty to disobey. Could Mr. Vanderbilt or Mr. Scott or any other of the managers avoid consolidating and hindered operations if he would? Could any critic avoid it, in their place? If not, then they too are obeying a subtle law which is above them."[20]

In the world of here and now, destiny had to be implemented. It occurred to some railroads they could avoid the war of rates by controlling the shippers. One means, of course, was to own the latter. The chief practitioners of this art were the anthracite railroads. They were following an old tradition, for the first miners of coal in northeastern Pennsylvania had been compelled to incorporate and to invest in canals in order to get their product to market. As railroads superseded canals, they became the heirs of this inter-relationship. Railroads without coal lands began their acquisition. Of this policy, Franklin B. Gowen, president of the Philadelphia and Reading, originally a railroad without coal lands, was the most conspicuous exponent. By devious maneuvers he obtained from the Philadelphia legislature in 1871 the incorporation of a concern which became the Philadelphia and Reading Coal and Iron Company. Within a short time it owned 100,000 acres of coal lands. Tempted into the iron industry, Gowen provided money to build iron furnaces along the railroad's route. A local wit even suggested that the Reading proposed "buying and running all the pea-nut stalls on the line of their road." The railroad furnished all the money for these acquisitions and expansions by issuing huge amounts of its own bonds. Gowen hoped to secure a return by renting his resources to operators as well as by eliminating rival carriers.[21]

This whole program ran into difficulties. One was ideological; a strain of public opinion in Pennsylvania had long feared corporate

[19] C. F. Adams, Jr., "Railroad Inflation," *North American Review,* CVIII (January, 1869), 150–152; C. F. Adams, Jr., "Railroad Problems in 1869," *North American Review,* CX (January, 1870), 133–134.

[20] *Commercial and Financial Chronicle,* XXX (March 13, 1880, Investors' Supplement), p. 2.

[21] M. W. Schlegel, *Ruler of the Reading: The Life of Franklin P. Gowen, 1836–1889* (Harrisburg, Pa.: Archives Publishing Company of Pennsylvania, 1947), pp. 14, 32, 35–36, 52–54; Eliot Jones, *The Anthracite Coal Combination in the United States* (Cambridge: Harvard University Press, 1954), pp. 4–22; Julius I. Bogen, *The Anthracite Railroads* (New York: Ronald Press Company, 1927), pp. 94–95, 119–121, 161–164, 187–189; *Report of the Industrial Commission on Transportation,* IX, xxv–xxvi.

power.[22] The Philadelphia and Reading Coal and Iron Company, a corporation embracing several enterprises, was peculiarly frightening. A new constitution in 1872–1873 included a ban on mining and manufacturing by the state's railroads.[23] Nor were the financial results commensurable with the expenditures. In five years Gowen multiplied the bonded indebtedness of the Philadelphia and Reading twelve times; after borrowing money to pay interest not earned and manipulating statements through deceiving entries, the road passed into receivership in 1880. Though its policy had assured it a regular source of traffic, a decline in coal prices and the consequent decline in rates for carriage, usually a percentage of the selling prices, did not assure that this traffic would be profitable. Though less spectacularly, a similar policy by the Central Railroad of New Jersey and by the Delaware and Hudson led also to financial difficulties.[24] The boom and bust cycle of the seventies was hardly a favorable time for these experiments.

In bituminous coal, the pattern of control was different. Instead of the railroad owning coal mines, coal companies, established by officers, investors, and promoters of the railroad or their associates, purchased large holdings of coal-bearing lands and then entered into agreements with the railroad to send all their coal over it. At least such were the arrangements on the Chesapeake and Ohio and the Norfolk and Western as these roads penetrated into the magnificent, undeveloped coal fields of Virginia and West Virginia.[25]

These arrangements of the "coalers," anthracite and bituminous, for meeting competition were of limited or local application. Far more widely used were the special rates, "special contracts," by which railroads sought to secure a shipper's traffic by granting him a rebate or drawback from the usual or published price of carriage. Though such rebates might take many subtle forms, underbilling, underclassification, the performance of services such as cartage of goods or their storage in cars, the customary form was pecuniary. From trunk-line territory, where the New York Central alone furnished six thousand cases of special contracts, to California, where rebating was standard operating procedure, such "methods of meeting the market" might result in reductions from published rates as high as 50 per cent.[26] In the passenger field, the equivalent to the

[22] Louis Hartz, *Economic Policy and Democratic Thought: Pennsylvania, 1776–1860* (Cambridge: Harvard University Press, 1948), pp. 67–79.

[23] Schlegel, *op. cit.,* p. 60.

[24] Bogen, *op. cit.,* pp. 164–167, 195–197.

[25] Joseph T. Lambie, *From Mine to Market: The History of Coal Transportation on the Norfolk and Western Railway* (New York: New York University Press, 1954), pp. 37–41.

[26] Testimony of C. F. Adams, Jr., "Report of the Senate Select [Cullom] Committee on Interstate Commerce," *Senate Report* No. 46, Pt. 2 (s.n. 2356), 49th

rebate was the free pass. The railroads did not always initiate these favors; they were demanded by travelers and shippers and the railroads complied for fear of losing their "share of the business" and because rebates promised that certainty and calculability which business wished to introduce into its operations. "A man may say, 'I can give you so much business.' If you can depend on that you may make definite arrangements accordingly." [27]

Sometimes railroads took a further step and organized their rebate receivers into groups to apportion shipments among railroad competitors. Apparently impressed by the example of the anthracite roads but unable to resort to a like device, the railroads which were desperately competing for the new traffic in petroleum, the first deposits of which were worked in western Pennsylvania, relied in 1871–1872 upon a corporation, the South Improvement Company, to regularize the shipments of this product. Officials in the Pennsylvania Railroad were the first promoters of this scheme; a group of refiners, including the Rockefeller interests, later joined the enterprise, and it was thought all refiners and oil producers would eventually become members. The railroads apportioned the freight, 45 per cent to the Pennsylvania, 27.5 per cent each to the Erie and the Central; the refiners were to act as "eveners" by making shipments in accordance with these percentages. In return for performing these functions they were to get rate concessions that might run as high as 50 per cent; the eveners also received drawbacks on all shipments made by those outside the agreement, and since they evened shipments they received waybills of all shipments whether made by themselves or their competitors.[28] Although this particular application of the evener-rebate device aroused so much hostility that railroads and oil refiners jettisoned it, the railroads proceeded in 1875 to give to three eveners the division of the traffic in livestock from Buffalo and all points west. In return they gave the eveners a rebate of $15 a car, an arrangement which lasted four or five years.[29]

Cong., 1st Sess., p. 1210; James F. Hudson, *The Railways and the Republic* (New York: Harper and Brothers, 1886), pp. 56–59.

[27] Testimony of E. D. Worcester, "Report of the Select Committee on Transportation-Routes to the Seaboard . . . 1874," *Senate Report* No. 307, Pt. 2 (s.n. 1589), 43rd Cong., 1st Sess., p. 136.

[28] Allan Nevins, *Study in Power. John D. Rockefeller, Industrialist and Philanthropist* (New York: Charles Scribner's Sons, 1953), I, 95–131; C. M. Destler, "The Standard Oil, Child of the Erie Ring, 1868–1872," *Mississippi Valley Historical Review,* XXXIII (June, 1946), 89–114.

[29] Testimony of R. C. Vilas, *Proceedings of the Special Committee on Railroads* [Hepburn Committee], I, 396–404; Testimony of J. B. Dutcher, II, 1742–1748; Testimony of G. R. Blanchard, III, 3328; "Report of the Select Committee on the Transportation and Sale of Meat Products," *Senate Report* No. 829 (s.n. 2705), 51st Cong., 1st Sess., pp. 2–4.

But this comparatively inexpensive substitute for owning the shipper's business was not the most common way in which railroads sought to prevent competition. No matter how widespread rebating was, it aroused for quite obvious reasons popular hostility and among railroad managers considerable distaste. "It is not," wrote Albert Fink, "the province of railroad companies to make themselves partners in private enterprise. Even if they had the legal right, it is questionable whether it would be good policy to do so." [30] Rebates lowered gross earnings. Fink and others were apostles of a program by which the railroads themselves in competitive matters would exercise "self-control"; for warfare they would substitute "cooperation" by voluntary agreements among themselves. Though these pooling agreements included mechanisms for fixing rates, their chief innovation was a means to enforce these rates. Some pools apportioned the territory between railroads. In the early eighties Gould and Huntington divided Texas between them, the system of the former taking the northern part of the state; and in 1893 the Boston and Maine and the New Haven divided New England, with the route of the Boston and Albany serving as a sort of northern Mason and Dixon line.[31]

Since historical accidents of railroad construction and development somewhat limited the useful area for territorial divisions, pools more generally sought their ends by a division of the traffic and assignment to each road of the share it should carry. Essential to the pool's inception and later administration was the collection of statistics and other data. Even when the returns were all in, the members of the pool had to have some device for making traffic flow in accord with agreed percentages. They could divert traffic or manipulate *"the rates from time to time, so as to insure the desired result."* [32] Sometimes it seemed easier to fix rates and let traffic flow as it would and then adjust the returns in accordance with the agreed upon percentages. In other words the roads pooled the earnings derived from the business in question; to roads which carried more than the allowance, the pool paid a sum merely covering the costs of carriage; to roads which did less than their allowed share was transferred a sum to make good the deficiency. In all cases the railroads, rather than shippers, were the eveners.

The proponents of pools tried to give them every possible consecration. One was tradition. American pools in their organization imitated the national government or the railroad clearing-house which had worked

[30] Joseph Nimmo, Jr., "First Annual Report on the Internal Commerce of the United States . . . 1876," *loc. cit.*, appendix, p. 9.

[31] W. Z. Ripley, *Railroads, Finance and Organization* (New York: Longmans, Green, and Co., 1915), p. 584; Kirkland, *op. cit.*, II, 31.

[32] Joseph Nimmo, Jr., "First Annual Report on the Internal Commerce of the United States . . . 1876," *loc. cit.*, appendix, p. 21.

so well and justly in England. The theme of order and calculability did wonderful service in behalf of the pools. As Fink expressed it, the unfettered competitive system of fixing rates was unbecoming an intelligent people in a civilized age. "Rates of transportation should be reasonable: they should be uniform and permanent. . . . Intelligent cooperation between all the transportation lines which can influence the tariff [rates] . . . becomes absolutely necessary. . . . The principles of competition would still remain in force, but this competition would be regulated intelligently, and in accordance with natural laws." [33]

The first example of a great pool was that established in 1870 by three roads competing for the traffic between Chicago and the western gateways along the Missouri River and for the traffic in between. The Chicago, Burlington and Quincy, the Northwestern, and the Rock Island by an unwritten understanding arranged for the division of earnings from the Chicago–Council Bluffs traffic. Each road retained 45 per cent of its passenger and 50 per cent of its freight receipts and the remainder was divided equally among the members. Most observers did not expect this "Great Pool" to last, but it did, with modifications, until 1885.[34]

Meanwhile other traffic areas had applied the pool in more detailed and embracing fashion. In 1875 twenty-two railroads of the South and a smaller number of associated or allied coastal steamers running to Baltimore, Philadelphia, New York and Boston established the Southern Railway and Steamship Association. They selected as their executive head or commissioner Albert Fink. Fink, born in Germany and educated as an engineer there, had come to this country in 1849 and obtained administrative experience on the Baltimore and Ohio and the Louisville and Nashville. Of speculative mind, he had turned with statistical precision to the formulation of an economic science of railroading and had become the persuasive advocate of railroad pooling. His immense erudition, capacity for labor, and strength of personality, as well as the need of the railroads for some solution of their competitive difficulties, explained the success of the agreements he was associated with. Over the years of its operation the Southern Railroad and Steamship Company attempted a herculean task: setting through rates via steamship and connecting railroad from northern Atlantic ports to an array of southern basing points, evening the pooled earnings between routes "over" and "under," and trying to allot between centers in the Northeast and Midwest the business of supplying the Southeast. The Northeast was to supply the manufactured products required by the South, and the West was to supply the western produce, for example hay, grain, flour, liquor, and

[33] *Ibid.*, appendix, pp. 12–16.

[34] Julius Grodinsky, *The Iowa Pool. A Study in Railroad Competition, 1870–1894* (Chicago: University of Chicago Press, 1950), pp. 17, 110, 160–162.

livestock. On the whole the pool worked well until the Interstate Commerce Act of 1887 forbad railroad pooling.[35]

After a year's experience Albert Fink went north to attempt to lower the competitive fever of titan trunk lines with the same medicine, a pooling agreement. In 1877 after the fiercest of their spasms, the New York Central, Baltimore and Ohio, Pennsylvania, and Erie formed the Eastern Trunk Line Executive Committee; a little later the western connections established the Western Executive Committee. Fink was chairman of the Joint Executive Committee uniting the two. Representatives of the roads voted on policy and practice; if they were not unanimous Fink decided the issue and his decision was final. Though roads could appeal to disinterested arbitrators, Fink deserved the sobriquet "Napoleon" or "Caesar" contemporaries applied to him. Before his advent the trunk lines had adopted a systematic rate structure in which the Chicago–New York rate was basic and rates between other termini varied proportionately. Probably the most controversial feature of this arrangement was a lower rate or differential permitted on eastbound shipments to Baltimore and Philadelphia vis-à-vis New York and Boston which enjoyed New York rates. Fink's great contribution was the means of enforcing agreed upon rates; the division of traffic, the pooling of receipts, and the evening of payments by the pool authority. Though there were long periods of unprecedented rate stability, Fink and the Joint Executive Committee were unable entirely to scotch rate wars in trunk-line territory.[36]

For this pool, like others, possessed certain defects. The more unscrupulous of railway managers were always ready to cut corners and wiggle through loopholes. More honest pool participants could wearily resign themselves to these hazards—for a time. John Murray Forbes once wrote, "We can stand a great deal of cheating better than competition." [37] But the complexity of regulations to forestall sharp practices burdened pools with bureaucratic difficulties and heated managerial impatience. During one tangle in the Iowa Pool, an exasperated participant wrote, "Can't we get that celebrated 'Philadelphia Lawyer' to figure out this pool and its complications?" [38] One of the most important innovations in Fink organizations was the chairmanship with its power of interpretation and final decision. Still defects remained. Pooling agreements were unenforceable at law and the participants could not call upon

[35] Kirkland, *op. cit.* II, 179–182; Joseph Nimmo, Jr., *loc. cit.*, appendix, pp. 16–24; Testimony of T. M. B. Talcott, *Report of the Industrial Commission,* IX, 626–627.

[36] W. Z. Ripley, *Railroads: Rates and Regulation* (New York: Longmans, Green, and Co., 1912), pp. 355–363, 374–375; Kirkland, *op. cit.*, I, 510–515, 520–521.

[37] Cochran, *op. cit.*, pp. 162–163, 166.

[38] Grodinsky, *op. cit.*, p. 26.

the authority and machinery of the state to secure their observance or punish non-compliance. Fink and others labored to reverse this situation, but in vain.

Another defect was that most pools were for limited periods, and at stated times there was a new division of traffic among their signers. In such negotiations the much vaunted test of justice was a "fair share of the traffic" according to a "natural division." In practice the "natural division" was that in existence. Accordingly, in the intervals between adjudications each road labored by fair or foul means to increase its business in order that the new agreement would recognize the new achievement by accepting a new *status quo.* Since these expansive and upsetting tendencies were at work among the pool members, it is not surprising that railroads outside the pool should strive desperately to acquire a high share of the business in order to be taken into the pool on their own favorable terms. In trunk-line territory, for instance, the Grand Trunk continually played the blackmailing marauder. Indeed the favorable rate levels which the pools brought into existence or stabilized might tempt the speculative to construct new roads either to compete their way into the pool or to sell out to some member. Thus during the "paralleling mania" of the early eighties, a group of promoters through consolidation and new construction extended the New York, West Shore and Buffalo up the west bank of the Hudson and then across New York as a competitor to the New York Central and Hudson River Railroad; the same role farther west the Seney syndicate, named after a speculative New York banker, undertook with the New York, Chicago and St. Louis Railroad, alias the Nickel Plate, which paralleled the Lake Shore and Michigan Southern, Vanderbilt's western arm, from Buffalo to Chicago.[39] W. H. Vanderbilt, who regarded with public nonchalance this latter threat, first gave it as his opinion that the Nickel Plate "will be taken into what is commonly called the pool" and somewhat later bought the road.[40] He determined to fight the other "raider road," the West Shore. Finally in 1885 J. P. Morgan induced him to purchase it as part of a general settlement of the competitive situation in trunk-line territory. Incidental to this agreement the Pennsylvania Railroad bought the South Pennsylvania which Vanderbilt and allied capitalists were promoting as a parallel to it.[41]

[39] H. V. Poor, *Manual of the Railroads of the United States for 1883* (New York: H. V. and H. W. Poor, 1883), pp. 181–182; H. V. Poor, *Manual of the Railroads of the United States for 1882* (New York: H. V. and H. W. Poor, 1882), p. 559.

[40] Taylor Hampton, *The Nickel Plate Road: The History of a Great Railroad* (Cleveland: World Publishing Company, 1947), pp. 171–189.

[41] Corey, *op. cit.,* pp. 147–152.

RAILROAD CONSOLIDATION

Though by 1887 railroads throughout the nation had pooled nearly all classes of traffic for which they competed,[42] pools had shown they were not an impregnable way of attaining that harmony among competitors which evangelists such as Fink had assumed. Their grave defects were the unavailability of the law to prevent their violation and the popular hostility they excited, for as Fink confessed, "the Government or the people . . . fear that such association will lead to abandonment of competition, and to extortionate rates. The catchword 'combination' will be used against them." [43] Indeed in trunk-line territory some of the wars of rates in the era of the pool reached a severity reminiscent of that in the days of "illegitimate" competition. Innovators were, therefore, applying other methods. One customary device was the lease either of branches or competitors. The exact moment when to lease was a question. Perhaps it was more sagacious to bide one's time patiently and strike with Napoleonic suddenness after traffic deficiencies or a Wall Street raid had demonstrated the weakness of the lessor's property; more often the lessor forced the lessee to an agreement by the pressure of some competitive situation or the need for acquiring a link in some scheme of expansion. Such emergencies could be expensive. Charles Mellen, president of the New Haven once wrote of his road's past: "The New Haven has always been prone to underestimate the value of a competitor, and as a result of delay, in very many instances, has paid a tremendous price, when, with very little effort, the competition could have been stopped in its inception and with very little expenditure. The road has been extremely fortunate, in being so rich it could afford to pay the prices it has for its acquisitions, but is there not a limit beyond which even a property like the New Haven can go?" [44]

The payments under the lease, of course, varied with the document. The lessee might merely guarantee to pay the lessor the earnings minus the costs of operation. This was consolidation on the cheap. More customarily the lessee had to guarantee to pay the interest on the leased road's bonds and under less happy circumstances dividends on its stock. If earnings were not enough to meet these charges, the lessee had to meet them from its own returns. This might well be ruinous. Sometimes a rail-

[42] Cochran, *op. cit.*, p. 170; Charles S. Langstroth and Wilson Stilz, "Railroad Cooperation," *Publications of the University of Pennsylvania. Series in Political Economy and Public Law No. 15* (Philadelphia, 1899), p. 53.

[43] Joseph Nimmo, Jr., "First Annual Report on the Internal Commerce of the United States . . . 1876," *loc. cit.*, appendix, p. 45.

[44] Quoted in Kirkland, *op. cit.*, II, 108–109.

road chartered an affiliate to hold and operate the leased roads. In 1870 the Pennsylvania Railroad the year after leasing its western extension chartered the Pennsylvania Company to operate leased properties. The architect of these acquisitions was Thomas A. Scott, coadjutor and later successor to J. Edgar Thomson, president of the Pennsylvania Railroad Company. Such high earnings were guaranteed to leased roads that in 1875 and 1876 the Pennsylvania had to reduce its own dividend from 10 to 8 per cent. The *Commercial and Financial Chronicle,* conceding that Scott like Gowen was a person of "extremely sangine temperament," announced: "We have, however, no admiration for that dead conservatism which spends itself in croaking over the Scotts and Gowens of the world: like the hermit crab it would rather live in another's cast off shell than build for itself. And yet, while enterprise is essential and an air of rashness inseparable from it, sooner or later accounts must be balanced, and the balance sheet is the inevitable test. . . . Policy [should be] aggressive, of course, but not reckless." [45]

As less threatening to corporate credit, the same editorial expressed a preference for consolidation and cooperation through stockownership by individuals in several railroads and the resulting interlocking of directorates and unity of management. The great practitioner of this method was Commodore Vanderbilt. In the base of his railroad pyramid, the New York Central and Hudson River Railroad, he owned 84 per cent of the stock. His first foray outside this charmed circle was disastrous. In 1868 he tried to purchase a controlling interest in the Erie Railroad. To assure that the procedure have some finite limit, he first obtained a court injunction prohibiting the overlords of Erie, Daniel Drew, Jim Fisk, and Jay Gould, from increasing its outstanding stock. Then he entered Wall Street. After making immense purchases, he found he had underestimated the ingenuity and recklessness of his opponents. They issued to themselves $10,000,000 worth of convertible bonds, converted them into stock, and dumped them upon the market. All in all, Vanderbilt purchased 100,000 shares of Erie stock and still lacked control. After a series of forays in courts and legislatures, the extravagance of which bordered on the comic, Gould induced the New York legislature to pass a bill forbidding the consolidation of the Erie and Central, and the contestants came to an agreement which relieved Vanderbilt of some of his losses.[46]

But one failure did not discourage the Commodore. Indeed the loss of the Erie compelled him and his advisors to seek closer ties with western roads to serve as connections with either the Erie or Central. In 1869

[45] *Commercial and Financial Chronicle,* XXXII (May 28, 1881), 563–564.

[46] C. F. Adams, Jr., "A Chapter of Erie," *North American Review,* CIX (July, 1869), 35–75.

the Vanderbilt interests bought stock in these extensions and in the next year Vanderbilt's lieutenants became officials in the new consolidation, the Lake Shore and Michigan Southern. Before his death in 1877 the Commodore built up an outright stock control of the Michigan Central, and his son a year or so later was a large stockholder in the Chicago and Northwestern.[47]

Everywhere that Vanderbilt went Gould was sure to go. The latter was another examplar of the practice of railroad hegemony through large personal holdings, complaining on one occasion under the prodding of examination, "I am in so many things." [48] Almost against his will, according to his story, Gould began a career on western railroads by purchasing about 370,000 shares of stock in the Union Pacific; then to "protect" the Union Pacific he purchased 40,000 shares in a parallel, the Kansas Pacific, and to "protect" the Kansas Pacific acquired over $20,000,000 of stock in another parallel, the Missouri Pacific.[49] The last became the nucleus of a great southwestern system. At the same time he acquired lines east of the Mississippi, and by means of the Wabash Railroad extended his empire to the Great Lakes and trunk-line connections.[50]

At the turn of the century contemporary opinion was greatly impressed "by the tendency recently manifested toward the establishment of great consolidated railway systems and toward community of interest between railroads hitherto competing." [51] As usual the "primary motive in forming these combinations has been to prevent excessive competition"; the method, a "community of interest," was regarded as a novelty. Broadly construed, a "railroad king's" controlling ownership of stocks in several roads might be regarded as affecting a "community of interest"; more narrowly considered, the latter phrase meant at this time the ownership by one railroad corporation of the securities of another. Such a wedding of interest early legislation had generally forbidden. Railroads, particularly competing ones, were not to own stocks in each other. But as usual there were statutes permitting a railroad to subscribe to the

[47] Wheaton J. Lane, *Commodore Vanderbilt. An Epic of the Steam Age* (New York: Alfred A. Knopf, 1942), pp. 264–274, 300; Grodinsky, *op. cit.*, p. 124.

[48] Testimony of Jay Gould, "Report of the Commission and of the Minority Commissioner of the United States Pacific Railway Commission . . . 1887," *Senate Executive Document* No. 51 (s.n. 2505), 50th Cong., 1st Sess., p. 459.

[49] *Ibid.*, pp. 451, 463, 509; Testimony of Jay Gould, *Report of the Committee* [on Education and Labor] *of the Senate . . . 1885*, I, 1066–1068.

[50] Grodinsky, *op. cit.*, pp. 114–115; S. F. Van Oss, *American Railroads as Investments* (New York: G. P. Putnam's Sons, 1893), pp. 503–505, 590–593; Interstate Commerce Commission, "Intercorporate Relationships of Railways in the United States as of June 30, 1906," *Special Report* No. 1, pp. 20–44; *Commercial and Financial Chronicle*, XXXI (September 4, 1880), 240.

[51] *Report of the Industrial Commission*, IX, v.

stock of a branch or extension in order to assure their construction.[52] At the very moment the prohibition of pooling by the Interstate Commerce Commission Act and decisions of the Supreme Court sent railroad managers searching for other means of cooperation, states began softening prohibitions against interlocking stockownership.[53]

Who "the inventor or the crystallizer of the community-of-ownership principle" was is a matter of dispute. One author ascribes the trend to J. P. Morgan, who decided in the mid-eighties to preach and enforce "harmony among the trunk lines"; [54] another witness asserts that C. P. Huntington was "generally understood" [55] to be the discoverer and prophet of the new dispensation; a third possibility is Alexander J. Cassatt, who became president of the Pennsylvania in 1899. Distressed by the demoralization of rates on bituminous coal, Cassatt prevailed upon the New York Central to join in the purchase of 40 per cent of the stock in the Chesapeake and Ohio Railroad. Each of the purchasers forthwith had four directors on the board of the latter railroad. The Pennsylvania went on to purchase large holdings in the Norfolk and Western and in the Baltimore and Ohio and through the latter secured 1,100,000 shares of Reading stock.[56] Sometimes this interlocking of ownership and direction was accomplished by means of a separate company—after 1896 the Reading Company was an example—a holding company which issued securities for the purchase of securities in the controlled concerns.[57] Although community of interest or community of ownership did not reach its peak until the twentieth century, it had gone so far by 1897 that nearly one-fifth of the total railroad stocks and one-tenth of the total of railroad bonds were owned by railroad corporations. While the railways' habit of carrying their surplus funds in such securities and the desire to control the administration of dependent lines partly explain this accomplishment,[58] the figures also represent the trend toward a community of interest among competitors. This process of consolidation fulfilled the expectations of prophets such as Perkins, who had written in 1879, "I have long been of the opinion that sooner or later the railroads of the country would group themselves into systems and that each

[52] Interstate Commerce Commission, *Railways in the United States in 1902,* Part IV, pp. 171–179.

[53] *Infra,* pp. 204–205.

[54] Corey, *op. cit.,* pp. 150–153.

[55] Testimony of T. F. Woodlock, *Report of the Industrial Commission,* IX, 462.

[56] George H. Burgess and Miles C. Kennedy, *Centennial History of the Pennsylvania Railroad Company* (Philadelphia: The Pennsylvania Railroad, 1949), pp. 458–461; Jones, *op. cit.,* pp. 59–73.

[57] Interstate Commerce Commission, "Intercorporate Relationships of Railways in the United States . . . 1908," *loc. cit.,* pp. 22–26.

[58] Interstate Commerce Commission, *Tenth Annual Report on the Statistics of Railways in the United States for . . . 1897,* pp. 50–51.

system would be self-sustaining. . . . This law, like other natural laws, may work slowly, but it is the law nevertheless." [59]

To explain the resort to lease and interlocking stockownerships solely in terms of prim managerial decisions to avoid competition and introduce rate stability would be an oversimplification. Other motives were at work, motives which involved ways of making money for those who could bring off a successful maneuver. Railroad managers bought up shoddy enterprises and then made them worth something by leasing them to sounder corporations in which the managers were also interested—a process appropriately known as "saddling." Jay Gould amassed holdings in the West and put separate roads together into systems in the hope that he would make himself such a nuisance or danger that he could sell out his securities at an advanced figure to some other person or to other concerns in which he was also interested.[60]

A REDUCTION IN RAILROAD CHARGES

Amid all the buffetings of competition and attempts to flee from it, amid railroad stategy of acquisition and integration, rates went down. This was the primary fact through all the period. Freight rates are, of course, more fundamental to the welfare of the economy than passenger fares and for that reason have perhaps elicited more attention. The outright markdown of nominal rates, it must be cautioned, was not the only method of rate reductions. Another was the constant shifting of commodities from classifications with high rates into classifications with lower ones; another, the growing proportion of commodities traveling under the lower rates for carload lots rather than the higher ones for less-than-carload shipments. Certainly the most significant area in which to note these trends is the trunk-line area.

In 1887, following the Interstate Commerce Act, the freight agents of the trunk lines introduced a new official classification. Of the total number of items in the old westbound classification, 66.78 per cent had been in a class higher than fourth; after 1887, 53.21 per cent was higher than fourth class. Before 1887, 14.11 per cent of the items westbound were entitled to quantity rates when shipped by car loads; in the revision of 1887, 55.1 per cent had the same privilege.[61]

[59] Cochran, *op. cit.*, p. 138; H. T. Newcomb, "The Present Railway Situation," *North American Review*, CLXV (November, 1897), 599.

[60] Kirkland, *op. cit.*, II, 13–15, 29–31; Adams, "A Chapter of Erie," *loc. cit.*, pp. 19–20; Van Oss, *op. cit.*, pp. 503–506, 591, 594.

[61] "Wholesale Prices, Wages and Transportation. Report of Mr. Aldrich from the Committee on Finance . . . 1893," *Senate Report* No. 1394, Pt. 1 (s.n. 3074), 52d Cong., 2d Sess., p. 419.

These changes reflected a real reduction in rates. Actual figures of the stated rates reinforced the trend. Consider the westbound rate between New York and Chicago, the rate to which all other rates in that direction were adjusted. At the end of the Civil War in 1865 the rates in cents per hundred pounds for this distance on the four highest classifications were:

	1	2	3	*4*
May, 1865	215	180	106	96

These figures reflected the paper money inflation; they were not in terms of gold. In 1888 rates lasting into the twentieth century came into operation; they were, in cents per hundred pounds:

	1	2	3	*4*
December 17, 1888	75	65	50	35

Even allowing for the resumption of specie payments, this was a notable reduction.[62]

Goods westbound were high class goods. For the raw materials of the interior whose carriage by the railroads was the real triumph of this era, the railroads made "commodity rates" lower than the "class rates." Between July, 1866, and the same month thirty-one years later, the Chicago to New York rate per 100 pounds of wheat fell from 65 cents to 20 cents. In the dressed beef trade, which was created during this period the rates fell per 100 pounds from 90 cents in May, 1872, to 40 in February, 1899. Rates on anthracite and bituminous, not trunk-line business, fell approximately 40 per cent from the mid-seventies to the mid-nineties.[63]

One explanation of these declines in rates was, of course, the general deflationary character of the decades. Prices were coming down, once the post-war years of good times were over, and railroad prices were no exception. The adjustment of railroad rates to the new levels of panic and depression was neither immediate nor complete, but chronological rate charts show a notable decline in the late seventies, another less marked in the mid-eighties, and a resumption of the decline in the nineties. It is impossible to disentangle the effects of depression from the cognate ones of competition, for, as the *Commercial and Financial Chronicle* pointed out, rate wars came in poor times, "the roads being indifferent about maintaining rates, each expecting in fact, to increase its proportion of business by carrying on lower terms. When, however, the times are good and the roads have pretty near all they can do, there

[62] Interstate Commerce Commission, *Railways in the United States in 1902*, Pt. 11, p. 44.

[63] *Ibid.*, pp. 79, 86, 88–89.

is no such inducement to carry at lower rates. . . . The managers are shrewd business men and they are not disposed to let slip an opportunity to make money for themselves and their stockholders." [64] Be that as it may, depressions usually inaugurated an enduring lower level of rates. After the business hurricane passed railroads did not entirely rebuild their former rate structure.[65]

Railroads were able to stand the reduced rates because of reduction in costs of operation, which might be secured by reducing wages, work forces, and profits; but there were limitations to such methods. In depression years, of course, the prices of materials purchased and used by the railroads declined: the average price of steel rails per ton at the mill, for instance, declined 50 per cent between 1873 and 1876, broke below $50 a ton for the first time in 1877, below $40 in 1883, below $30 two years later and in 1897 below $20.[66] The reduction in the price of fuel was equally helpful. Furthermore technical and operational innovations reduced the costs of carriage. "Necessity has been teaching [railroad] managers, just as it has the farmers and manufacturers, how to find ways of getting more out of materials in hand. In the struggle for existence, they have had to do this, and they have done it. This is one of the ways in which trouble works out good results for offset. . . ." [67]

The mounting efficiency of these years was based upon better utilization of existing techniques and upon adoption of new and better ones. "Steel rails . . . form the very 'cornerstone' of the great improvements which have taken place in railroad efficiency." [68] Larger locomotives, longer trains, cars of greater capacity with a more favorable ratio between cargo space and dead weight, higher speeds, all followed. When railroad managers and investors sought to embody such accomplishments in more precise measurements, they relied, in spite of its deficiencies, upon the "operating ratio," the proportion operating expenses formed of operating income. For the period, the nineties, for which figures are available, the average operating ratio for all American railroads varied from a low, termed a desirable ratio, of 65.34 per cent in 1888 to 68.14 in 1894.[69]

[64] *Commercial and Financial Chronicle,* XXXI (September 18, 1880), 292; *supra,* notes 62, 63.

[65] Massachusetts *Twenty-sixth Annual Report of the Board of Railroad Commissioners. January, 1895,* pp. 9–13.

[66] Kirkland, *op. cit.,* II, 383.

[67] *Commercial and Financial Chronicle,* XXVIII (May 17, 1879), 490.

[68] Joseph Nimmo, Jr., *Report on the Internal Commerce of the United States for . . . 1881–'82,* appendix, pp. 297–320.

[69] Interstate Commerce Commission, *Second Annual Report on the Statistics of Railways in the United States . . . 1889,* p. 35; Interstate Commerce Commission, *Tenth Annual Report on the Statistics of Railways in the United States . . . 1897,* p. 82; D. P. Locklin, *Economics of Transportation* (Chicago: Business Publications, Inc., 1938), pp. 581–582; Van Oss, *op. cit.,* pp. 118–119.

In short, in the midst of a critical decade of hell and high water, a commentator observed "The Americans are admitted to have no equals in the art of moving freights cheaply." [70]

Through the thickets of explanation for these lower rates stalked impalpable figures of competition and combination. No doubt it could be demonstrated that competition lowered rates. The continuing contrast, on a per mile basis, between local, non-competitive rates and through or competitive rates is one indication. The sudden descents of rates during railroad wars is another. But it should be noted that during these decades local rates as well as through ones came down—the former from 10 to 50 per cent.[71] When a railroad war ended, though rates were raised, they were not set back to the old level but to "a figure considered by the railroads as the normal rate . . . the maximum rates which could then be obtained." [72] Though combinations were often bewailed by critics as likely to lead to the imposition of "extortionate" and "monopoly" rates,[73] the large corporations were precisely those which were the most enterprising in the adoption of cost-saving devices. They exemplified, it has been said, "a universal law that by doing business on a vast scale it became practicable to effect the economies in purchases and operating expenses and it is these conditions which make low rates possible." [74]

Finally this reduction of rates was "voluntary," in the sense that legislation did not bring it about. With few exceptions, railroad management set rate policy. Nonetheless it would seem that business depression and outbursts of competition spurred managers to rate reductions which they themselves in moments of unharassed calculation would have thought both unfeasible and undesirable. In this they were acknowledging an "obedience to the 'higher laws' of competition and business, which statutes can never repeal or materially alter, and which, therefore, legislation should learn not to meddle with at all." [75] At least, so it was written.

[70] Van Oss, *op. cit.*, p. 120.

[71] "Wholesale Prices, Wages, and Transportation. Report of Mr. Aldrich for the Committee on Finance . . . 1893," *loc. cit.*, p. 629; Interstate Commerce Commission, *Railways in the United States in 1902*, Part II, pp. 150–191.

[72] "Wholesale Prices, Wages, and Transportation. Report by Mr. Aldrich for the Committee on Finance . . . 1893," *loc. cit.*, p. 527.

[73] Langstroth and Stilz, *op. cit.*, pp. 52–53.

[74] *Commercial and Financial Chronicle*, XXX (March 13, 1880), Investors' Supplement, 2; XXXI (August 28, 1880), Investors' Supplement, i–ii; Lane, *op. cit.*, p. 299.

[75] *Commercial and Financial Chronicle*, XXVIII (May 17, 1879), 490.

CHAPTER V

Railroad Reform

THE EVILS OF DISCRIMINATION

IN view of the reduction in railroad rates, the frequent charge in anti-railroad agitation that rates were "too high" is a curiosity. Such a conception implies, of course, a comparison with a "just" or "proper" rate. As it turned out a convenient test was at hand in the years following the Civil War. A rise in taxes and in the price of materials had forced the railroads in war time to raise their tariffs. In the post war years the national taxes had evaporated and prices the railroads paid had come down. To call for a general revision downward of railroad rates seemed logical. On the local scene critics made this point firmly.[1] On the national scene the Windom report on "Transportation-Routes to the Seaboard" developed in 1874 the same case. This document, christened after a conservative senator from Minnesota and often cited as one of the classic landmarks in the drive for national regulation, was in its indictment of extortionate rates far from impressive. The evidence was based either upon dubious premises or the constructive manipulation of statistics which in themselves demonstrated that nominal railroad rates on grain to the seaboard had actually declined between 1868 and 1872. A rather fumbling comparison of this decline with that in the price of wheat and corn suggests that the yardstick for measuring the justice of rates was that they had not declined proportionately with the decline in the prices of agricultural commodities.[2]

The Windom report also accused the railroads of "unfair discrimina-

[1] Massachusetts *Third Annual Report of the Board of Railroad Commissioners . . . 1872,* pp. xxiii–xxxiv, ccxix–ccxx; "Summing up by Simon Sterne," N. Y. Legislative Assembly, *Proceedings of Special Committee on Railroads . . . 1879* [Hepburn Committee] IV, 3923–3924.

[2] "Report of the Select Committee on Transportation-Routes to the Seaboard," *Senate Report* No. 307, Pt. 1 (s.n. 1588), 43d Cong., 1st Sess., pp. 14–23, 71–78.

tions."[3] One phase of this discrimination was that between places. As has been seen, the pricing policy of the railroads had resulted in local rates distinctly higher than through rates in proportion to the distance. This arrangement perplexed and endangered the small towns and villages without competing railroads. Even cities as large and important as Pittsburgh, served only by the Pennsylvania Railroad, paid 25 cents on grain from Chicago, while New York, farther from the center of production, paid 15 cents.[4] In Massachusetts, buyers of grain at Worcester paid for their freight as if the shipments passed through the city on through rates from the West to Boston and then returned from the latter to Worcester at local rates.[5]

Not only did these arrangements seem an inexplicable departure from a common-sense way of doing business—"each reduction in the distance for which the freight is hauled brings with it a more than proportionate increase of charges"[6]—they were disastrous for enterprises in unfavored localities. The low through rates on flour from the West to New York City built up the Minneapolis millers at the expense of millers in Rochester, for "the [former] had his cereals produced at his door and had the flour carried to New York at twenty cents a hundred, when they [the latter] were compelled to pay more than that for the mere carriage of the wheat to their mills, and a higher absolute rate for the carriage of the product of their mills to the seaboard."[7] Again, prior to the invasion of the trans-Mississippi West by railroads from Chicago, the river towns of Iowa along the Mississippi were markets for grain and livestock; afterwards, Dubuque, Davenport, and Burlington were mere stations on lines which carried agricultural products on through bills of lading from the interior of Iowa to Chicago. The rate structure thus had the power to determine whether the Chicago market would submerge those at Iowa river towns. Sometimes the rate from the interior towns to the river was apparently greater than between the former and Chicago.[8] In Massachusetts the railroad commissioners forecast with alarm the possible extinction of decentralized manufacturing. To survive, fac-

[3] *Ibid.*, p. 71.

[4] S. F. Van Oss, *American Railroads as Investments* (New York: G. P. Putnam's Sons, 1893), p. 25.

[5] E. C. Kirkland, *Men, Cities, and Transportation: A Study in New England History, 1820–1900* (Cambridge: Harvard University Press, 1948), II, 283.

[6] James F. Hudson, *The Railways and the Republic* (New York: Harper & Brothers, 1886), p. 52.

[7] Simon Sterne, *Railways in the United States* (New York: G. P. Putnam's Sons, 1912), p. 118.

[8] George H. Miller, "Origins of the Iowa Granger Law," *Mississippi Valley Historical Review*, XL (March, 1954), 661–662.

tories would have to move to the Massachusetts ports enjoying low through rates.[9]

Nor were termini of through routes without grievances. In New York City merchants and shippers and other businessmen were enraged when railroads such as the Central and the Erie, supposedly run exclusively for New York interests, permitted a differential in rates with the West to the roads serving Philadelphia and Baltimore. Such a differential enlarged the foreign commerce of these rival Atlantic ports and contributed to their greater prosperity.

Onerous as these discriminations between places were, they seemed easier to explain than the discriminations granted certain shippers through drawbacks, special contracts, and rebates. The Hepburn investigation in New York in 1879 "discovered that a single flour-mill at Niagara, during the extraordinary contest for freight between the railway companies—which pulled down the freight rate on flour from Minneapolis to New York to ten cents a hundred—had continued to work, and ship its flour to New York from Niagara when every other mill within the limits of the State of New York had been compelled, under the pressure of this competition, to close its doors. . . . [The mill] had a private contract which gave to the proprietors . . . a pro-rate of the Minneapolis rate, whatever it might be, and therefore enabled it to live, whilst every competitor . . . was compelled to close."[10] Also, rebating arrangements with eveners among packers and oil refiners helped to build up the favored and the strong, the leviathans of industry.

Though farmers everywhere might criticize railroad practices, railroad discrimination bore upon their interests in a fashion varying with the region where they lived. For farmers in the West, low through rates were essential if they were to send their agricultural commodities to the markets of the East and of Europe. By the eighties at least the farmers of the interior, if the Secretary of the National Farmers' Alliance was an authoritative spokesman, felt "through rates are reasonable enough."[11] For their part, Western farmers protested the high local rates and also the discrimination in favor of large shippers which gave advantages to speculators shipping many cars of grain and thus increased "a surplus of middle-men at the expense of the producer and consumer."[12] On the other hand, many farmers in the East, without the advantages of the

[9] Kirkland, *op. cit.*, II, 283.

[10] Sterne, *op. cit.*, p. 190.

[11] Testimony of Milton George, "Report of the Senate Select [Cullom] Committee on Interstate Commerce . . . 1886," *Senate Report* No. 46, Pt. 1 (s.n. 2356), 49th Cong., 1st Sess., p. 117.

[12] *Ibid.*, p. 120.

lower production costs of the West, saw floods of cheaply carried commodities undercutting them in their "natural" markets near at hand. Not only did Eastern farmers shipping to these centers at comparatively high local rates suffer a loss of markets, they experienced as well a depreciation of land values. "This phenomenon is explained when we find the railways charging sixty-five or seventy-five cents on a tub of butter to New York from a point one hundred and sixty-five miles away, while the rate from Elgin, Illinois, one thousand miles away, was thirty cents." [13]

In a few instances railroads and farmers had worked out devices easing the way for the latter to buy railroad securities and all over the country, as we have seen, governmental units had invested in railroad enterprises. This experience had not been a happy one, for the railroads frequently failed to provide public and private investors the returns which promoters, boomers, and organizers had promised. Sometimes the investor had made a simple misjudgment; sometimes he was the victim of jobbery and deals by the officials of the corporation in which he had invested. Consequently, along with the small producers, merchants, shippers, and farmers interested in railroad rate reform, the investor, for a quite different reason, became a railroad reformer. These groups constituted an impressive and national phalanx. Their influence upon railroad policy was greatly enhanced by the fact that in this period the small town and city exerted a disproportionate political influence and leadership.

Though high rates were at times to the forefront of anti-railroad agitation, the primary continuing objective was discrimination.[14] Though rates were constantly lowered, they remained discriminatory. Also, the charge of discrimination was early assimilated to the charge of exorbitant rates. A comparative yardstick for a fair and just rate was always available in the low rates favored places and shippers received. This gave tactical strength to the agitation against discrimination. Complainants on this score could also summon to their aid deep seated American attitudes: rebate systems deprived American would-be producers of that "real industrial equality" which was their birthright. Discriminations between individuals were "corrupt and criminal." [15] Though a similar moral condemnation was more difficult to apply to discriminations between places, the Master of the Michigan State Grange could "hardly

[13] Hudson, *op. cit.*, p. 42; Lee Benson, *Merchants, Farmers, and Railroads: Railroad Regulation and New York Politics, 1850–1887* (Cambridge: Harvard University Press, 1955), pp. 80–93.

[14] Jonathan Periam, *The Groundswell: A History of the Aims, and Progress of the Farmer's Movement* (Chicago and Cincinnati: F. Hannaford & Company, 1874), pp. 453–454.

[15] Hudson, *op. cit.*, p. 55; John M. Bonham, *Railway Secrecy and Trusts* (New York: G. P. Putnam's Sons, 1890), pp. 10–11.

imagine a case where it would be right or proper for a railroad to charge more for a shorter than for a longer distance for freight like in kind and quantity and over the same road or roads."[16] All in all, "common justice, sound policy—every sense of duty, the whole spirit and letter of the law require an equality of right . . . sacred and fundamental."[17]

The censure of discriminatory practices on democratic grounds had another version. Favors of this sort were not necessarily inherent in the railroad business; they were often due to "the arbitrary will" of officers or even worse "were granted as the caprice, the whim, or the interest of the railway freight agent dictated." There was a wholesome dread of being at the mercy of such unrestrained power.[18] Be it remembered railroads were the first large corporate enterprises to appear in this period. As a foreign observer said in the nineties: "The American people, although on the whole, I think, by no means unreasonable, are opposed to large corporations. . . . Hence the people are 'hard on railways.' "[19]

"PHYSICIAN, HEAL THYSELF."

Since the railways were corporations, perhaps the path of railroad reform was that of corporate reform. In essence this meant wresting the governance of the corporation from an inner ring of directors and officials and placing it in the hands of the stockholders. Any such program required reversal of historical process. The growth in the size of railroad organization and the warlike character of competition had necessitated a centralization of management; only in this fashion could the corporation take expert, prompt, secret, and firm decisions. The duties of a railroad president, it was said, "require more than ordinary business capacities; they demand extraordinary talent and even this must fail if it is not backed by arbitrary power. As a rule this is given, and in America we usually find that blind support of the management without which the latter would lack strength."[20] The able railroad leader was a "railroad king." The return to corporate democracy, it was anticipated, would put an end to the speculations, deals, and frauds so frequently engineered by the insiders to the disadvantage of the owners of the property and, since democracy was equated with honesty or represented a wider sampling of the community, might abate some of the grievances visited

[16] Testimony of C. G. Luce, "Report of the Senate Select [Cullom] Committee on Interstate Commerce . . . 1886," *loc. cit.*, Pt. I, p. 110.

[17] Chauncey F. Black, *Essays and Speeches of Jeremiah S. Black* (New York: D. Appleton and Company, 1883), pp. 178–179.

[18] Hudson, *op. cit.*, pp. 28–29; "Summing up by Simon Sterne," *loc. cit.*, IV, 3971.

[19] Van Oss, *op. cit.*, pp. 130–131.

[20] *Ibid.*, pp. 13–14; Kirkland, *op. cit.*, II, 438–439, 444.

upon the public by compelling management "to follow the old-fashioned ways of procedure which have been so often proven to come out best at the end." [21] Besides, proposals enabling the owners of a property to manage it better and in their own interests avoided many of the ideological difficulties involved in state intervention in business affairs.

The battle to restore corporate government to the majority of the stockholders had begun before the Civil War. Afterwards further legislation continued the effort and added refinements. Acts placed limitations upon the solicitation or voting of proxies by management or sought to assure for stockholders outside the managerial circles the same facility in assembling proxies. There were proposals for proportional representation in voting for directors; and critical corporate decisions, such as making of leases and issue of securities, had to have assent of stockholders as well as directors.[22]

"PITILESS PUBLICITY"

Clearly if stockholders were to participate intelligently in election of directors and other decisions at annual or special meetings, they would have to be informed of the condition and doings of their corporation, for railroad statements covered a multitude of sins. The desire of investors for guidance and of the state for an informed basis of regulation were other factors in the demand for accurate information.[23] Before the Civil War, general statutes or individual charters had done something in many jurisdictions to compel annual railroad reports to some state officer; and private agencies, notably the *American Railroad Journal* under the editorship of Henry V. Poor, collected information and published it. After the Civil War, Poor began the annual publication of his *Manual of the Railroads of the United States,*[24] and business periodicals such as the weekly *Commercial and Financial Chronicle* made available more current happenings. Editors of such publications had a vested interest in railroad publicity, and chastised, directly or by innuendo, railroad officials who held back information. Commodore Vanderbilt and his

[21] *Commercial and Financial Chronicle,* XXIII (September 23, 1876), 292; T. C. Cochran, *Railroad Leaders, 1845–1890: The Business Mind in Action* (Cambridge: Harvard University Press, 1953), p. 109.

[22] Kirkland, *op. cit.,* II, 428–432; *Commercial and Financial Chronicle,* XXIV (June 23, 1877), 577–578.

[23] Henry Clews, "Legislative Injustice to Railways," *North American Review,* CXLVIII (March, 1889), 323–324; *Commercial and Financial Chronicle,* XXIV (May 12, 1877), 431.

[24] A. D. Chandler, Jr., *Henry Varnum Poor, Business Editor, Analyst, and Reformer* (Cambridge: Harvard University Press, 1956), pp. 247–278.

"inflexible purpose to give to the public no more information than was required by law"[25] was a favorite target.

The post-Civil War regulatory movement in the several states also improved annual reports. In Massachusetts, for instance, the Railroad Commission, with the aid of a committee of railroad accountants, specified and defined the items of a model report and, under legislative authority, prescribed it for the railroads; the Commission also took the leadership of a movement for uniform reports on the Massachusetts pattern throughout the New England states.[26] After 1887 provisions of the Interstate Commerce Act compelled the railroads of the nation to file reports in accordance with the standards set by the Commission's statistician. The first appointee was Henry C. Adams, the first recipient of a Ph.D. from Johns Hopkins University and a onetime teacher of economics at Cornell and Michigan.[27]

In this complicated business of reducing reports to order and meaning, trained public accountants had an essential role. The concept of an audit by impartial and expert outsiders came to this country from England in connection with the purchase and combination of breweries by English investors and brewers. Also, English investors, bewildered by the intricacies of American railroad finance and stunned by unexpected failures and reverses, sent over accounting missionaries and prevailed upon railroads to use their services.[28] Advocates of railroad reform saw that "a new profession of railway accountants, wholly independent, officially, of any railway system, must be developed before entire frankness and absolute truthfulness can be secured as between the owners, the public, and the administrators."[29]

So much was achieved that by the century's end the reports of American railroads "might serve as an example for those issued by English railways."[30] As a means of general betterment, however, the concept of self-reform had great limitations. It was based upon the incorrect premise that there was a genuine gap between the interests of managers and stockholders. Actually the vicious financing of railroads was due to "the greed for dividends on the part of stockholders of railways and the consciousness of directors that their places are largely

[25] *Commercial and Financial Chronicle,* XXIII (September 23, 1876), 291–292; XXIV (May 12, 1877), 434.

[26] Kirkland, *op. cit.,* II, 328–339; *Commercial and Financial Chronicle,* XXIII (September 23, 1876), 291–292.

[27] "Henry Carter Adams," *Dictionary of American Biography,* I, 67–68.

[28] *Commercial and Financial Chronicle,* XXV (December 15, 1877), 580.

[29] Simon Sterne, "Recent Railroad Failures and their Lessons," *Forum,* XVII (March, 1894), 31.

[30] Van Oss, *op. cit.,* pp. 169–170.

dependent upon satisfying this greed." [31] Though transportation to annual meetings was free, stockholders traveled the distance not to be present and vote but to have a good time shopping or seeking entertainment.[32] "Investors in railways nowadays no longer desire to be participants in the enterprise, as though they were partners, dependent upon its success for their profits, and losing their money in the event of failure." They preferred to hold bonds, to be "investing creditors" rather than entrepreneurs.[33] Nor was corporate reform, however beneficial to investors, likely to remedy matters of discrimination and of other railroad practices about which there was so much complaint.

Actually during this period, opinion and policy placed more reliance for railroad reform upon "one of the best laws known to economics and most beneficial to the public . . . the law of competition." [34] Reform would simply unfetter the natural forces of competition; besides, the alternatives to competition as regulator were frighteningly formidable. "The attempt to regulate the business of transportation by general congressional enactments establishing rates and fares on 1,300 railways, aggregating nearly one-half the railway mileage of the world, and embracing an almost infinite variety of circumstances and conditions, requires more definite and detailed information than is now in the possession of Congress. . . ." [35] So concluded the Windom Committee in 1874.

The whole of this report as well as its specific recommendations reveal a more powerful reason for reliance upon competition. For the report is not so much a reforming as a promotional document. It sounds the note of a community not so much desirous of regulating a matured transportation system as one eager to secure in one way or another the construction of additional transportation facilities. Its spirit is more akin to land grant and local aid policies than to the Interstate Commerce Act. In sum, the policy of competition meant that transport facilities should become "ample," as the Windom report demanded, among other things.

WATERWAYS AS COMPETITIVE SALVATION

Among possible competitors, a considerable fraction of American opinion preferred waterways. The nominal rates were often lower than by rail, and even so puissant a paladin of railroading as Albert Fink stated more than once that the water route of the Lakes, the Erie Canal,

[31] Sterne, "Recent Railroad Failures," *loc. cit.*, pp. 28–29.
[32] Kirkland, *op. cit.*, II, 433–434.
[33] Sterne, "Recent Railroad Failures," *loc. cit.*, p. 36.
[34] *Report of the Industrial Commission*, IX, 777.
[35] "Report of the Select Committee on Transportation-Routes to the Seaboard," *loc. cit.*, Pt. I, p. 240.

and Hudson determined the rates the railroads charged for the Chicago–New York haul.[36] Furthermore, during the historic period when canals and rivers provided the chief pathways for American commerce, the system was primarily government-owned.[37] Waterways did not enter into combinations, pools, and conspiracies to manipulate rates. It was easy for groups which believed that agriculture was a superior way of production because it worked with nature to embrace the cognate illusion that "water routes are nature's thoroughfares" and the "natural channels which seem to be so plainly indicated by the hand of the Great Architect of the continent."[38] The fact that nearly everywhere except along the coast or on the Great Lakes, railroads were proving their superiority by taking traffic away from waterways would seem to put considerable strain upon this line of thinking; but this difficulty was countered by asserting the railroads triumphed because of their "malign influence" and conspiratorial methods of competition.[39]

The Windom report envisaged the construction or improvement of four great waterways from the interior to the coast—the Great Lakes and the Erie and Canadian canals, the James River and Kanawha Canal, the Atlantic and Great Western Canal between the Tennessee River and Savannah, and finally the Mississippi River. In the period here under discussion only the first and the last enlisted any real governmental or popular support. As the New York Central and Erie Railroads improved their services and lowered rates in the fifties, the decline of the traffic on the Erie Canal disturbed New York officials, for the state, which had to pay interest on its debt for the canals, saw the revenue from tolls fall off. Perhaps the best thing to do was to reimpose upon the tonnage of the offending railroads the canal tolls which they had once had to pay if they carried freight. This obscurantism reached its acme in a delineation by the state engineer in 1856 of the "appropriate

[36] Testimony of Albert Fink, "Report of the Senate Select [Cullom] Committee on Interstate Commerce," *loc. cit.*, Pt. II, p. 100; "Report of the Select Committee on Transportation-Routes to the Seaboard," *loc. cit.*, Pt. I, pp. 51–70; Albert Fink, "Report upon the Adjustment of Railroad Transportation Rates to the Seaboard Cities," in J. B. Daish, Editor, *The Atlantic Port Differentials* (Washington: W. H. Lowdermilk & Co., 1918), pp. 31, 32, 37, 38.

[37] Carter Goodrich, "National Planning of Internal Improvements," *Political Science Quarterly*, LXIII (March, 1948), 16–28; Carter Goodrich, "Public Spirit and American Improvements," *Proceedings of the American Philosophical Society*, XCII (1941), 305–309.

[38] "Report of the Senate Select [Cullom] Committee on Interstate Commerce," *loc. cit.*, Pt. 1, appendix, p. 109; "Report of the Select Committee on Transportation-Routes to the Seaboard," *loc. cit.*, Pt. I, p. 188.

[39] *Manual of the Railroads of the United States for 1881* (New York: H. V. and H. W. Poor, 1881), pp. xxvi, xxxi–xxxiv; L. C. Hunter, *Steamboats on the Western Rivers* (Cambridge: Harvard University Press, 1949), pp. 603–605.

functions" of each method of transport: "The passenger traffic belongs exclusively to the railroads, *while the transport of cheap and heavy articles of freight belongs to the canal.*" [40]

After the Civil War it was discovered that the Erie was losing out because it was technically backward. The canal should be enlarged and perhaps steam applied to its navigation. The merchants of New York also saw in the canal the one means which kept them on a par or ahead of their competitors in Philadelphia or Baltimore. "Wipe out the canal from the map of New York, and if the railways persist in continuing the discrimination of from two to six cents a hundred, that would wipe out the commerce of New York as effectually as though a bed of rock were by one of nature's convulsions to block up our channels to the sea." [41] This prophecy of doom came at the end of a decade during which state officials wrestled with the difficulties of preventing frauds and collusion in the work of improving and maintaining the canal and commercial interests secured exemption from tolls on the commodities in which they were interested. Finally in 1882 a constitutional amendment, vigorously supported by merchants angry at railroad differentials against New York City, abolished canal tolls entirely and placed the support of the waterway on revenues from taxation.

When this "liberal, catholic spirit" which "had abolished tolls entirely and had thrown open the canal to the commerce of the world" proved unable to match the "infernal activity" of competing railroads, a favorable legislative enactment cleared the way in 1895 for a popular ratification of a program increasing the state's aid by $9,000,000 in order to deepen the Erie's channel to nine feet and to double the length of short locks.[42] Logically enough, this departure in policy occurred during a period of depression, when spokesmen from the Middle West were agitating for a ship canal between the Lakes and the Atlantic in order that American farmers might match "the agricultural competition we have been compelled to meet from India" and from "the entrance into the world's market of the rising States of the South of our continent." The United States was required to examine "the manner we can lighten the burdens of our agriculture and keep pace with the world's progress by facilitating and cheapening our internal transportation. The limit of reduction in railroad freight seems to have been reached." [43] During these years of clamor and change, the tonnage on the Erie Canal de-

[40] *Manual of the Railroads . . . 1881,* p. xxvii.

[41] "Summing up by Simon Sterne," *loc. cit.*, IV, 3934.

[42] Noble E. Whitford, *History of the Canal System of the State of New York,* I, 316–357; *Manual of the Railroads . . . 1881,* pp. xxiv–xxxviii.

[43] "Report of the United States Deep Waterways Commission," *House Document* No. 192 (s.n. 3527), 54th Cong., 2d Sess., p. 9; *Manual of the Railroads . . . for 1881,* p. xxxiii.

clined only from 2,523,490 in 1865 to 2,356,084 in 1895. It had touched a high point of 4,608,651 in 1880.[44]

On the great Mississippi River system of internal navigation the decline, noted in the fifties, continued after the Civil War. The steamboat business shrank to short journeys in smaller vessels, and although acres of rafts and barges laced together with a single towboat enabled the river to carry coal and lumber considerable distances, the deliberate attempt after 1880 to ship grain for export south from St. Louis to New Orleans under these new economies failed to provide more than enough grain for southern consumption. As railroads parallelled the rivers or lanced the traffic higher and higher upstream, on the Missouri for example, partisans of these western waters were reduced to celebrating the regulatory character of their rates.[45] There was no doubt railroad rates responded to conditions of navigation. Railroads put up the rates during the long periods of chronic drouth and water shortage and in the winter. "One reason they give for it is that it costs more to move freight in winter by rail than it does in summer; but the principal reason is that there is no water competition, no lake, no canal to interfere with them, and of course there is more business for the road. It is one of these things which is peculiar to human nature to get all you can."[46] All the while the movement to improve the western rivers at federal expense by providing a minimum depth of navigation ran into controversies between engineers over methods and into conflicting self-interests. By the late nineties the national government had completed the improvement of the Ohio between Marietta and Pittsburgh and of the upper Mississippi to St. Paul; it had even earlier made New Orleans a deep water port by building the Eads jetties to scour out a passage below the city; elsewhere on the lower Mississippi, improvements remained inadequate.[47]

Government expenditures on rivers and harbors increased steadily after the Civil War. In 1867 they had been $1,217,000; their peak in the years before 1897 was $19,944,000 in 1895.[48] Relative to what the railroads were spending this sum was trivial. The latter in 1895 devoted $143,976,344 to maintenance of way and structures and increased the total cost of roadway and equipment, representing a more permanent form of investment, by $174,961,586.[49] Though the government undoubt-

[44] Bureau of the Census, *Handbook of Historical Statistics 1789–1945,* p. 219.

[45] Hunter, *op. cit.,* pp. 561–591, 600–603.

[46] Testimony of Richard Smith, "Report of the Select Committee on Transportation-Routes to the Seaboard," *loc. cit.,* Pt. II, p. 510.

[47] Hunter, *op. cit.,* pp. 207–215.

[48] Bureau of the Census, *Historical Statistics,* p. 169.

[49] Interstate Commerce Commission, *Eighth Annual Report on the Statistics of Railways . . . 1895,* p. 65; *Poor's Manual of the Railroads . . . 1898* (New York: H. V. and H. W. Poor, 1898), p. ii.

edly spent its funds with more system than the critics of pork-barrel legislation would admit and shipping men regarded puttering with breakwaters, channels, and harbors in a more charitable fashion than did land-tied critics, expenditures were frequently for unimportant and wasteful and piecemeal projects. For example, the Chief of Army Engineers, to whose Corps these tasks were assigned, reported in 1897, "The river and harbor act of June 3, 1896, ordered an examination made of the Bartrand River, South Carolina. Diligent search and inquiry has failed to show where such river is located, and it has been impracticable to make the examination." [50]

WAYS TO COMPEL COMPETITION

Since on the whole the railroad as transportation agency was clearly in the ascendant, it seemed more sensible to rely upon competition between railroads than from waterways. "Our people are not reduced to absolute slavery. There never was a time," wrote Poor in 1881, "in which they were so completely masters. If they do not like a railroad they will not patronize it, or will build another. . . . The whole question of the power of railroads to oppress was settled when their construction was thrown open to all. *One* road might oppress; twenty, competing for the same business, cannot. *One* capitalist might oppress; twenty, competing in the same line, cannot." [51] Such reassuring generalizations required implementation in policy. Consequently state after state substituted for the practice of chartering by special act that of chartering under general law. In so doing the legislature usually acted on an imperative contained in the constitution. On this score New York was "the great examplar State." The convention "that formed the constitution of 1846 became . . . intent on removing from corporate agency its monopoly character. . . . It retained corporate agency as an allowable and valuable facility of social progress, but removed its monopoly feature, by permitting, under general laws, every person to obtain a corporate organization who desired the facility. . . . And thus was consummated the greatest triumph that our American experiment of equal rights has ever achieved in practical results." [52] Four years later the New York legislature passed a general incorporation law for railroads. The "wise policy" of this statute enabled "25 or more persons . . . without any application to the Legislature, [to]

[50] "Annual Reports of the War Department . . . 1897, Report of the Chief of Engineers," Part 1, *House Document* No. 2 (s.n. 3631), 55th Cong., 2d Sess., p. 24.

[51] *Manual of the Railroads . . . 1881,* pp. lxii–lxiii.

[52] A. B. Johnson, "The Legislative History of Corporations in the State of New York," *Hunt's Merchants' Magazine,* XXIII (December, 1850), 613; Charles A. Lincoln, *The Constitutional History of New York* (Rochester; Lawyers Cooperative Publishing Company, 1906), II, 184–195.

associate themselves and, by so doing, become a body corporate, authorized to do any act necessary to the construction, operation, or the maintenance of a railroad. . . . Railroads could be built anywhere and everywhere—a dozen parallel lines running side by side if parties could be found silly enough to construct them." [53] This reliance upon "free trade" in railroads spread from state to state until by 1902 railroads could be incorporated only under general law in forty-one states.[54]

The regime of competition between railroads, thus seemingly assured, convinced Poor "that the people of the United States had at last, in the construction and management of such works reached the very acme of social, economical and practical wisdom." [55] Be that as it may, since competitors and parallels still continued to combine, enactments or constitutions in half of the states forbad the combination of competing lines and in a third prohibited pooling. In themselves consolidations were "evils of such magnitude as to demand prompt and vigorous measures for their prevention." [56] As for pooling, so inherently hostile was popular opinion to this device that the Interstate Commerce Act of 1887 continued the tradition of state legislation when in Section 5 it declared, "it shall be unlawful for any common carrier subject to the provision of this Act to enter into any contract, agreement, or combination with any other common carrier or carriers for the pooling of freights of different and competing railroads, or to divide between them the aggregate or net proceeds of the earnings of such railroads, or any portion thereof. . . ." [57]

Perhaps a sounder method of assuring railroad competition was to permit the government to own and operate key roads set in the larger network of private ownership and operation. Since the government would not combine or pool, it would act independently and fairly in setting rates; it might through its efficiencies serve as a yardstick for rates in private enterprise. Usually a mere coincidence of circumstances rather than overarching hypothesis unloosed such proposals. Thus in Massachusetts, when the legislature was forcing the consolidation of the Boston and Worcester and the Western into a through route across the state, Josiah Quincy, a railroad reformer, proposed the state buy the roads under the charter provisions permitting such acquisition and run them under a special corporation.[58] A few years later in 1873, when the

[53] *Manual of the Railroads . . . 1881,* p. xlviii.

[54] Interstate Commerce Commission, *Railways in the United States in 1902,* Pt. IV, pp. 23–24, 118–128.

[55] *Manual of the Railroads . . . 1881,* p. 1.

[56] "Report of the Select Committee on Transportation-Routes to the Seaboard," *loc. cit.,* Pt. I, p. 241; Interstate Commerce Commission, *Railways in the United States in 1902,* IV, pp. 29, 298–304; *Report of the Industrial Commission,* IX, 928–929; Van Oss, *op. cit.,* pp. 35–37.

[57] 24 *United States Statutes,* 380; Van Oss, *op. cit.,* pp. 35–37.

[58] Kirkland, *op. cit.,* I, 365–366.

Commonwealth was debating the disposition of the Hoosac Tunnel, which its finances had largely constructed, young Charles Francis Adams, Jr. of the Railroad Commission and one of the great dogmatists in behalf of private ownership lent piquancy to the proceedings by advocating state operation. "We rely on competition to preserve us from red tape on one side and corruption on the other, and so we do not want to destroy competition by State ownership, but we want to get back to it through mixed ownership. When we stand upon competition, we feel the solid ground under our feet."[59] The state rejected this proposal.

Yet in 1874 the Windom Committee, when it could get its eyes away from waterways, recommended that the national government build or control double-tracked freight railroads from the interior, perhaps Council Bluffs, to the seaboard, perhaps New York. "One or more railroads, economically constructed, and operated, or controlled by the Government in the interest of the public, would regulate all the others on fair business principles, remedy the abuses that now exist, check combinations, and thereby reduce the cost of transportation to reasonable rates. . . . The only means of obtaining efficient and permanent competition, is through Government ownership or control, of certain lines, with which combination will be impossible."[60] Later in the eighties and nineties when the question of what the Federal government should do with its claims to the Union and Central Pacific vexed Congressmen and others, a considerable body of opinion, particularly in California, advocated that the government foreclose the two properties, combine them, and then operate the road to break the railroad monopoly of the Southern Pacific.[61]

By the nineties proposals such as these were more properly a part of a movement for government ownership of public utilities, including railroads, than for the creation of some competitive government elements spotted about in an essentially private enterprise system. Reformers had inspired and organized the new trend. Frank Parsons, trained as engineer and lawyer, professor at Boston University and "deeply interested in general social philosophy, ethics, and sociology," was the moving spirit in the National League for Promoting the Public Ownership of Monopolies. The League recruited members from the clergy, colleges, settlement houses, labor unions, and reform movements in general and asserted

[59] *Ibid.*, I, 416–417.

[60] "Report of the Select Committee on Transportation-Routes to the Seaboard," *loc. cit.*, Pt. I, pp. 140–141, 156–161.

[61] H. R. Meyer, "The Settlements with the Pacific Railway," *Quarterly Journal of Economics,* XIII (July, 1899), 437; "Report of the Commission and of the Minority Commissioner of the United States Pacific Railway Commission . . . 1887," *Senate Executive Document* No. 51 (s.n. 2505), 50th Cong., 1st Sess., pp. v, 125–126, 152–153.

private railways had a "wrong aim, private profit in place of the public good," whereas public railways had as their "true aim . . . service and public interest first" and would lower rates, abolish discrimination and watered stock and obey the law.[62] The Populists in their national platform in 1892 called for government ownership of railways.[63]

Advocates of such measures cited foreign experience. For the competitive yardstick of government ownership, Belgium for a time provided the chief illustration.[64] For government ownership, Prussia was the pattern. Indeed, B. H. Meyer, a professor at the University of Wisconsin who became in 1911 a member of the Interstate Commerce Commission, announced in 1900 that the Prussian system of railways had earlier exhibited the same tendencies as railways elsewhere, but the state legislation leading toward government ownership "affords instructive lessons to those countries in which legislative bodies pursued a different course."[65] Opponents, though willing to examine foreign experience, rejected it. Charles Francis Adams, Jr., elaborated a theory that to the primal and ubiquitous railroad competition nations reacted in accordance with the "differing economical, social, and political habits and modes of thought of the people." The outcome in Prussia was natural, for "the inclination of the German mind, especially the North German mind, is bureaucratic." Their governmental system was executive and administrative, not parliamentary and legislative.[66]

Although the movement for government ownership of some or all railroads came to a dead end, the debate had put a finger upon sound objections to the program. They were partly political. Even those sensitive to railroad abuses recognized that the current system of government patronage would reduce the efficiency and integrity of government owned roads and that the dispersion of functions among judicial, legislative and executive branches would prevent the centralization of decision necessary for a well-run enterprise.[67] Severer critics asserted government ownership

[62] Testimony of Frank Parsons, *Report of the Industrial Commission*, IX, 123, 168–171; "Frank Parsons," *Dictionary of American Biography*, XIV, 266.

[63] H. S. Commager, *Documents of American History* 2 vols. (New York: Appleton-Century-Crofts, 1949), II, 144.

[64] C. F. Adams, Jr., *Railroads: Their Origin and Problems* (New York: G. P. Putnam's Sons, 1876), pp. 94–100; Arthur T. Hadley, *Railroad Transportation: Its History and Laws* (New York: G. P. Putnam's Sons, 1883), pp. 257–258.

[65] *Report of the Industrial Commission*, IX, 962.

[66] Adams, *op. cit.*, pp. 109, 115, 205–206; Hadley, *op. cit.*, pp. 187–189, 236–239.

[67] "Report of the Select Committee on Transportation-Routes to the Seaboard," *loc. cit.*, Pt. I, pp. 157–158; Testimony of P. J. McGuire, *Report of the Committee* [on Education and Labor] *of the Senate . . . 1885*, I, 345–346; *Commercial and Financial Chronicle*, XXIX (September 27, 1879), 314; E. R. A. Seligman, "Railway Tariffs and the Interstate Commerce Law," *Political Science Quarterly*, II (June, 1887), 235.

was inherently incompatible with an expanding economy. "All men in office belong to the past. Their ideals are easy berths, good pay, and long terms of place, secured by political cajolery. . . . In the matter of rates, government is . . . incapable. When it establishes them it must go upon the evidence of the past. It has no instinct for the future. It has no right to attempt to forecast. It must proceed upon evidence." [68]

In the United States the idea of free trade in railroads, of competition as natural regulation of their practices, collided with somewhat paradoxical objections. On the one hand, it was clear that competition was the chief cause of grievances, for example, discrimination and undependability in rates against which so many Americans were protesting. On the other hand, competition was diminishing and a dreaded and inevitable combination was increasing. From this dilemma the escape was government control or regulation.[69]

OBSTACLES TO REGULATION

However plausible on the surface, this program in turn was confronted by obstacles inherent in American politics. Was regulation legal or constitutional? On this point judicial decisions before the Civil War had given decisive answers. Most jurisdictions had concluded that railroad corporations, though privately owned, were public service corporations and as such subject to state regulation. The state bestowed the right of public domain upon such corporations only with the understanding that the acquired property would be used for a public purpose.[70] On the other hand the decision in the Dartmouth College case in 1819 seemed to imply that the charter of a railroad corporation was a contract between the corporation and the state which the latter under the contract clause of the Federal constitution could not alter. Later Supreme Court decisions had ruled, however, that courts should construe such charters narrowly, and state constitutions or legislation, general and specific, had made the granting of charters conditional upon the state retaining the right to amend, alter, or repeal them. The courts had upheld this reservation.[71] Whether the fourteenth amendment in its first section, "no State shall deprive any person of life, liberty, or property without due process of law, nor deny to any person . . . the equal protection

[68] *Manual of the Railroads . . . 1881*, pp. xxxvi, lxi.

[69] "Report of the Senate Select [Cullom] Committee on Interstate Commerce," *loc. cit.*, Pt. I, pp. 52–63.

[70] Edwin Dodd, *American Business Corporations until 1860, with Special Reference to Massachusetts* (Cambridge: Harvard University Press, 1954), pp. 44, 158–160; Leonard W. Levy, "Chief Justice Shaw and the Formative Period of Railway Law," *Columbia Law Review*, LI (March, 1951), 328–330.

[71] Dodd, *op. cit.*, pp. 16–31, 124–129.

of the law" threw a new guarantee around railroad rights was, of course, left to the decades here under scrutiny to judge.

Be that as it may, some felt "a higher law" than state or constitution forbad railroad regulation. Of these higher laws, upon whose formulation the generation focussed so much energy and thought, one was the natural law of private property: railroads "belong to those who built them . . . property in railroads is as sacred as in farms; . . . government has no more right to impair their value than it has a right to impair the value of the farm of any citizen"; and others were "the law of supply and demand,—a more potent law than that of legislatures," and the law of competition. "So should government forbid railroads charging more than one-half cent per ton per mile, they would do no business unless it could be done at a profit. They would not do business at a loss, no matter who commanded. It is impossible in the long run, that rates should be excessive." [72]

Even when these "verities" were shunted aside by counter argument, practical difficulties remained. Legislatures or Congress seemed deaf to demands for reform. Since the reformers were convinced of the persuasive righteousness of their own case, this indifference to or rejection of salvation was explicable only in terms of railroad control of the government. Not the strength of the railroad's case but their influence —champagne and cigars were the favorite symbols—accounted for the *vis inertiae* of those who should have been servants of the people rather than of the corporations.[73]

Unquestionably, railroads concerned themselves with the creation of a favorable opinion among those of influence. They lavishly issued the free pass to journalists, judges, governors, and legislators. As a realistic president of the Boston and Maine put it, "Men are a good deal like hogs; they don't like to be driven, but you throw them down a little corn, and you can call them most anywhere. That is all there is to it." [74] Railroads retained the ablest lawyers in most jurisdictions—ostensibly to handle damage suits and the like—and the most able lawyers later gravitated to legislative chambers or to the bench.[75] Railroads made contributions to political parties—sometimes for a *quid pro quo* and sometimes on general principles. Jay Gould of the Erie informed an investigating committee of the New York legislature: "We had to look after four states, New York, New Jersey, Pennsylvania, Ohio and have helped men in all of them; it was the custom when men received nomi-

[72] *Manual of the Railroads . . . 1881,* pp. lxii, lxxiv.

[73] Sterne, *Railways in the United States,* pp. 163, 165, 166–167, 169; *Commercial and Financial Chronicle,* XVIII (February 28, 1874), 204.

[74] Quoted in Kirkland, *op. cit.,* II, 21.

[75] *Ibid.,* I, 442.

nations to come to me for contributions and I made them and considered them good paying investments for the company; in a Republican district I was a strong Republican, in a Democratic district, I was Democratic, and in doubtful districts I was doubtful; in politics I was an Erie Railroad man every time. . . ."[76] From the charges of opponents and from *lapsis linguae* of "railroad kings," one could collect a sizable anthology of similar utterances.[77]

Proved instances of corruption by railroads were frequent enough.[78] But boastfulness by railroad leaders about their influence and the public naïveté concerning the new phenomenon of lobbying probably account for the belief that the railroads stalled the regulatory movement by graft. In any case, the frequently empty victories and outright failures of the railroad reform movement led Americans to import from England and paraphrase in many forms the observation that the railroads would manage the state if the state did not manage the railroads.[79] In view of these obstacles to reform there was great jubilation whenever the proponents of regulation scored a point. When the Supreme Court of Wisconsin validated, on July 4, 1876, the key enactment of the regulatory movement in that state, the Potter Law of 1875, the governor ordered a salute of one hundred guns.[80] The people had triumphed over their enemies. Penetrating observers were convinced that "the direction must be toward governmental control, but this imposes upon the people of the United States the duty of making the governmental machinery fit to exercise such control."[81]

STATE REGULATION

Although state regulation came in time to deal with a wide spectrum of ills arising from the community's experience with the railroad, at the heart of railroad regulation was rates. Even before individual railroads came into existence, legislators were foresighted enough to realize the crucial importance of the prices railroads charged. Some of the early charters

[76] Quoted in Benson, *op. cit.*, p. 62.

[77] *Twenty-third Annual Report of the Corporation of the Chamber of Commerce of the State of New-York, for the Year 1880–'81* (New York: Press of the Chamber of Commerce, 1881), Part I, pp. 115–166.

[78] Testimony of C. P. Huntington, "Report of the Pacific Railway Commission," *loc. cit.*, I, 38–39; C. F. Adams, Jr. and Henry Adams, *Chapters of Erie and Other Essays* (New York: Henry Holt and Company, 1886), pp. 42–57; L. H. Haney, *A Congressional History of Railways in the United States* (Madison, Wisc.: Democrat Printing Company, 1910), II, 256–257.

[79] C. F. Adams, Jr., *Railways: Their Origin and Problems,* p. 86.

[80] *Commercial and Financial Chronicle,* XIX (July 11, 1874), 27.

[81] Sterne, *op. cit.*, p. 142.

of railroads in Massachusetts had, for instance, specified maximum rates per mile for freight and passengers; later the Commonwealth fell into the habit of regulating rates through railroad earnings: if over a period of years "net income exceeded 10 per cent upon the cost of the road, the legislature could reduce the rate of tolls and other profits in such a manner as to take off the overplus. . . ."[82] In New York, an example often cited in this connection, the directors could set the passenger rates within maxima ranging from the 3 to 6 cents per mile stated in the charters.[83] In the Middle Western states carefully drawn charters contained maxima for both freight and passengers.[84] In the end, regulation of rates by this method worked out badly. Where rates were limited by returns, the prosperous corporations did not distribute their earnings but built up surpluses and occasionally transferred them to the stockholders in stock dividends or other forms of security inflation, or the roads were allowed to stagnate, since aggressive business policy would yield profits "painfully large."[85] Stated maximum rates per mile were usually so generous as to be no restriction at all. Later various state jurisdictions embodied rate regulations in general laws governing railroad matters.[86]

[82] Kirkland, *op. cit.*, I, 118.

[83] F. W. Stevens, *The Beginnings of the New York Central Railroad: A History* (New York: G. P. Putnam's Sons, 1926), pp. 266–293.

[84] B. H. Meyer *Railway Regulation in the United States* (New York: Macmillan Company, 1903), pp. 56–62.

[85] C. F. Adams, Jr., "Railroad Legislation," *American Law Review* (October, 1867), II, 30–32.

[86] B. H. Meyer, *op. cit.*, pp. 92–96, 152–158.

CHAPTER VI

Railroad Commissions: Breakthrough or Stalemate?

FORCE OR PERSUASION

B. H. MEYER was writing in 1903 that "the general statement . . . holds true that the regulative features of railway legislation of the different states of the Union are embodied in our commission laws in all states in which commissions exist."[1] This sentence chronicled a revolution, not in the concepts of the powers the state possessed over railroads or ought to exercise, but in the means by which the state administered its policy. Hitherto the chief agencies of the state in dealing with railroads had been the legislatures, operating usually through their railroad committees, and the courts, to which those who were injured under the common law or the statutes repaired for redress.

Neither had been particularly effective. Cases in court entailed formality, expense, and delay. Still some judges became experts in railroad affairs. Similar competence was rare in legislatures, for members served short terms and were frequently retired by elections,[2] thus leaving little chance to acquire the experience and expertness that regulation of the complicated railroad business required. The good intentions and democratic purposes of legislatures could not compensate for the deficiencies of the legislative process. In that process the key was the railroad committee, and Charles F. Adams, Jr. was observing truly in 1868 that legislative committees "are eternally fluctuating, are not peculiarly well-informed, judiciously selected, or free from bias. As a

[1] B. H. Meyer, *Railway Legislation in the United States* (New York: Macmillan, 1903), p. 164.

[2] James W. Hurst, *The Growth of American Law. The Law Makers* (Boston: Little, Brown, 1950), pp. 51–68 makes the same analysis for a later period.

consequence, the lobby becomes more and more powerful; greater opportunities are afforded for corruption, and legislation becomes yearly less systematic and founded less on principle." In general the legislators possessed few qualifications for their tasks. In this country "every man can legislate, even if he can do nothing else. . . ." [3] To many contemporaries, therefore, a reform and regeneration of political administration had to precede railroad reform.[4]

The solution was a board or a commission, "a new phase of representative government. Work hitherto badly done, spasmodically done, superficially done, ignorantly done, and too often corruptly done by temporary and irresponsible legislative committees, is in future, to be reduced to order and science by the labors of permanent bureaus and placed by them before legislatures for intelligent action." [5] Actually there were several sources for the commission technique. Adams asserted that "the legislative committee is the embryotic American bureau." [6] Legislatures and courts had likewise appointed temporary commissions to handle specific railroad tangles; many American states on the eve of transportation improvements in the nineteenth century had started out with boards of internal improvements; county commissioners had aided in the taking of lands for railroads; and the states had already resolved difficulties, ranging from those involved in harbors to schools, through bureaus and boards.[7] Nor were European patterns, particularly English ones, without influence. In 1873 Parliament after forty years of investigation and legislation established in the Regulation of Railways Act a commission of three men to deal with grievances and to compel obedience to previous regulatory legislation.[8]

Because the railroad system came earliest to maturity there, the first commissions in the United States were in New England. New Hampshire, the first state to have a commission, established one in 1844. By 1897 the number of state commissions, which had been four in 1860,

[3] C. F. Adams, Jr., "Boston," *North American Review,* CVI (January, 1868), 15–19.

[4] Simon Sterne, "Legislation concerning and Management of Railways in the United States," John J. Lalor, editor, *Cyclopedia of Political Science* (New York: Charles E. Merrill & Company, 1888), II, 524, 530–531; *Nation,* XIX (June 4, 1874), 356.

[5] Adams, "Boston," *loc. cit.,* pp. 15–19.

[6] C. F. Adams, Jr., *Railroads: Their Origin and Problems* (New York: G. P. Putnam's Sons, 1878), p. 110.

[7] E. C. Kirkland, *Men, Cities and Transportation: A Study in New England History, 1820–1900* (Cambridge: Harvard University Press, 1948), II, 231–232; Adams, "Boston," *loc. cit.,* pp. 17–19.

[8] Adams, *Railroads: Their Origin and Problems,* pp. 81–94; A. T. Hadley, *Railroad Transportation: Its History and Its Laws* (New York: G. P. Putnam's Sons, 1885), pp. 163–186.

had increased to twenty-eight.[9] After their sporadic establishment before the Civil War, they came in spurts. In the late sixties and seventies the demands of the Grangers, "when nothing short of . . . sturdy, forceful methods . . . could have allayed the gathering storms of public indignation [with] the then existing methods of management," carried the commission to the Midwest and the South.[10] Though the Illinois statute was the preeminent exemplar in the Granger states, the movement for regulation through this device was neither wholly Granger nor Western, as the creation of the significant Massachusetts Commission in 1869 and the New York Commission in 1882 demonstrated. In the mid-nineties, an observer was bemoaning that in the Southwest "roads are in that state which Northwestern lines were in some 20 or 30 years ago, . . . and it seems even that the hostile, injurious, and injudicious legislation which has caused so much difficulty in Iowa, Wisconsin, etc., will be repeated throughout the Southwest." [11]

Whatever merits underlay the reasons for their establishment, the effectiveness of regulation depended upon the commission personnel and work conditions. Commissioners usually held office for stated, overlapping terms, received salaries comparable to those in other state positions, and had their impartiality partially guaranteed by the proviso they should not be "interested in any railroad." Whether they were unbiased in other directions was another and perhaps inconsequential question. Some commissions were so set up as to include representatives of the agitational groups which had brought them into being. New York went about as far in this direction as possible. Its act of 1882 required the Governor to appoint a person jointly representing the Chamber of Commerce of the State of New York, the New York Board of Trade and Transportation, and the National Anti-Monopoly League. In a few instances the people elected the commissioners.[12] However motley these statutory requirements, the success or failure of a commission usually depended upon the ability and force of a single railroad commissioner, often the chairman. Rather than legal provisions, it is the man that "is the power that lies behind the throne which vitalizes the machine," observed B. H. Meyer.[13]

[9] Interstate Commerce Commission, *Railways in the United States in 1902,* Pt. IV, pp. 54–60.

[10] "Report of the Senate Select [Cullom] Committee on Interstate Commerce," *Senate Report* No. 46, Pt. 1 (s.n. 2356), 49th Cong., 1st Sess., p. 64.

[11] S. F. Van Oss, *American Railroads as Investments* (New York: G. P. Putnam's Sons, 1893), pp. 556–557.

[12] Interstate Commerce Commission, *Railways in the United States in 1902,* Pt. IV, pp. 54–61; "Report of the Senate Select [Cullom] Committee on Interstate Commerce," *loc. cit.,* Pt. I, p. 75.

[13] Meyer, *op. cit.,* p. 167.

In Massachusetts, for instance, C. F. Adams, Jr., made the commission what it became. There were other illustrations.[14]

Contemporaries of the Commission movement made a frequent distinction between commissions which were "advisory" and those that were "regulative," or in words of even less precision, "weak" and "strong." [15] The Massachusetts Commission was the archetype of the first category. Upon its own initiative or upon petition from outsiders it was to investigate the operation of the railroad system or specific grievances; it could then suggest to the railroads a course of action and report its findings. In an oft-quoted sentence, Adams declared, "The law could not have been improved. Had it not been a flagrant legislative guess, it would have been an inspiration. The only appeal provided was to publicity. The board of commissioners was set up as a sort of lens by means of which the otherwise scattered rays of public opinion could be concentrated to a focus and brought to bear upon a given point. The commissioners had to listen, and they might investigate and report; they could do little more." [16] Most of the New England states and New York copied the pattern of Massachusetts.[17]

Arrangements in Illinois exemplified the other pole of regulation. Here the first step was a constitutional provision asserting the paramount rights of the state over railroads and the former's obligation to act on the premises. Thus section 2 of the Illinois constitution in 1870 declared: "Railways . . . are hereby declared public highways. . . . And the General Assembly shall, from time to time, pass laws establishing reasonable maximum rates of charges for the transportation of passengers and freight on the different railroads in this state." Section 5 added, "The General Assembly shall pass laws to correct abuses and to prevent unjust discrimination and extortion in the rates of freight and passenger tariffs on the different railroads in this state. . . ." [18] The next step was the passage of a regulatory act fixing fares and prohibiting certain discriminations, and the capstone was the establishment of a board of railroad commissioners to enforce the legislative directions and to penalize infractions. A few years later Georgia imitated Illinois and most Southern states imitated Georgia.[19] This type of regulation led Adams to assert

[14] Kirkland, *op. cit.*, II, 245–247.

[15] E. R. A. Seligman, "Railway Tariffs and the Interstate Commerce Law," *Political Science Quarterly*, II (September, 1887), 410.

[16] Adams, *Railroads: Their Origin and Problems*, pp. 138–139.

[17] Meyer, *op. cit.*, p. 167; Kirkland, *op. cit.*, II, 249–256.

[18] S. J. Buck, *The Granger Movement . . . 1870–1890* (Cambridge: Harvard University Press, 1913), pp. 129–130.

[19] "Report of the Senate Select [Cullom] Committee on Interstate Commerce," *loc. cit.*, Pt. I, p. 78.

that "in the West the fundamental idea behind every railroad act was force; the commission represented the constable." [20]

In Adams' judgment, such regulation was in contrast to Massachusetts', but it is doubtful that the Massachusetts Commission even in conception was as advisory as he and other contemporaries asserted. The Cullom Committee of 1887 pointed out that the Massachusetts Commission had made decisions as to rates and discriminations and that these decisions the railroad managers of Massachusetts had observed "simply because self-interest admonishes them of the supreme folly of encouraging or engaging in a losing contest with the forces of public opinion as concentrated and made effective through the commission. It is not because the managers, directors, or stockholders personally shrink from public criticism, but because back of the commission stands the legislature and back of the legislature stand the people, and they realize that they themselves will inevitably be the sufferers when they invoke or provoke a contest with those forces." [21] Another competent contemporary was observing that "so far as a formal statutory enumeration of specified powers goes," there was a distinction between the advisory and regulative commissions, but that in actuality the first might accomplish as much as the latter.[22] The Massachusetts type, however, was less likely to antagonize the railroads; the commission gave them a hearing and might persuade them it was acting as arbitrator between them and complainants. It also proceeded to regulatory measures with less impetuousness and with more emphasis on cooperation.[23] The so-called Granger legislation inaugurated "a contest between the people and the railroads." [24] Since capitalists, strangely enough, are very sensitive to rhetoric they preferred commissions which gave them a hearing rather than punished them with words.

RATE POLICIES OF REFORM

Although the state railway commissions dealt with service, station toilets, safety devices, and a host of other matters, the nub of their duty was rates. Like the railroad managers they had to have a pricing policy. In view of popular discontent this policy, not surprisingly, was somewhat different. If provisions of charter and statute on this count were proper precedent, the thing to do was to prescribe maximum rates per mile. These, of course, could be set so high as to be meaningless. If com-

[20] Adams, *Railroads: Their Origin and Problems,* p. 138.

[21] "Report of the Senate Select [Cullom] Committee on Interstate Commerce," *loc. cit.,* Pt. I, p. 69.

[22] Meyer, *op. cit.,* pp. 167–168.

[23] Adams, *Railroads: Their Origin and Problems,* p. 140.

[24] Buck, *op. cit.,* p. 128.

missions employed greater precision, a host of complications ensued. It was impossible to set fares justly without ascertaining what proportion passenger and freight or local and through traffic furnished to costs and revenues and what the actualities and potentialities of a road's region were. Maximum rates, for instance, which would make one road prosperous would bankrupt another.[25] Therefore genuinely subtle and just railroad regulation put railroads in classes and assigned to each group rates graded to its circumstances. The Illinois commissioners in 1873 divided the state's railroads into five categories according to the degree of their business opulence or lack of it and set varied maximum fares for each category. By 1881 when the more prosperous roads had absorbed the poorer ones, the commissioners simplified the schedule to two classes. Such distinctions took the place of a cast-iron tariff formulated largely on surmise.[26]

Perhaps it was simpler to establish and enforce a pro-rata charge in which the mileage covered was the chief determining factor. A per-mile rate would demolish the irritating differences between local and through charges and, if enforceable, do away with discriminations between places and persons. Such a program accorded superficially with the proper way of doing business—the longer journey should cost more—and it also harmonized with American notions of what was right and proper. "The limitation of the charges to rates, perfectly and uniformly proportioned to weight and distance, must be apparent to anyone who will consider the nature of the contract [between the state and the railroad]. . . . Whenever, in those acts of incorporation, any mention is made of rates, taxes, or tolls, they are spoken of as proportioned to the use made of the road by him who pays them—so much per ton per mile, whether the miles be many or few, up grade or down, without regard to the number of tons carried at one time, or at different times, for the same shipper." [27] Between 1858–1861, pro-rata laws of this general type had been introduced into the legislatures of the Middle Atlantic states, and had been defeated. They clearly ignored the economics of rail transportation.[28] With more subtlety those who later

[25] C. F. Adams, Jr., "Railroad Legislation," *American Law Review*, II (October, 1867), 42–45; Massachusetts *Fourth Annual Report of the Board of Railroad Commissioners. January, 1873*, pp. 55–64.

[26] Testimony of J. S. Schultz, "Report of the Senate Select [Cullom] Committee on Interstate Commerce," *loc. cit.*, Pt. II, p. 264; Testimony of G. M. Bogue, *ibid.*, Pt. II, p. 734; Massachusetts *Fifth Annual Report of the Board of Railroad Commissioners. January, 1875*, pp. 50–57.

[27] Chauncey F. Black, editor, *Essays and Speeches of Jeremiah S. Black* (New York: D. Appleton and Company, 1885), pp. 184–185.

[28] Frederick Merk, "Eastern Antecedents of the Grangers," *Agricultural History*, XXIII (January, 1949), 7–8.

regulated the railroads sought to reconcile by a tapered rate schedule the distance principle with the fact of fixed overhead costs at terminals and elsewhere. Thus the Illinois commissioners in 1881 substituted for a one-mile base rate for a distance "up to 150 miles a 5-mile unit. After we passed 150 miles we made a 10-mile unit, and then, when we get up to over 200 miles, we adopted a 20-mile unit." [29] The upshot of these tapered mileage systems was that total rates for long hauls were greater than for short but the per mile rate was lower.

More popular than these refinements were legislative and commission decisions to regulate local and through rates by prohibiting a greater charge for the short than for the long haul. Ostensibly a simple device—in "principal" [sic] "just and right"—the Cullom Committee of 1886 declared no question had given them "more perplexity than that relating to [its] utility and expediency." [30] In many states short-haul legislation was loosely and extravagantly drawn. The Illinois law of 1871, for instance, provided that a railroad company should not charge the same or larger rate for the transportation of freight over a longer distance than it was charging at the same time for freight of the same class over a lesser distance anywhere on the road.[31] An Illinois Court reminded the railroads and their regulators that the common law of carriers forbad carriers to make unreasonable and excessive charges and obligated them to render "service to all without injustice" and that discrimination between places was as bad as discrimination between persons and was indeed very much the same thing. Only a "peculiar state of affairs, among which the presence of competition is not one, can justify discrimination. It was never intended or expected that these corporations should use their power to benefit particular individuals or build up particular localities by arbitrary discriminations in their favor that must cause injury to other persons or places engaged in rival pursuits or occupying rival positions." Since the law in question forbad all discriminations, not merely unjust ones, and did not permit the railroads to advance evidence to justify theirs, it violated the state constitution of Illinois.[32] Forthwith, the Illinois legislature defined unjust discrimination as a difference in rates between places if the freights were going in the same direction and permitted the railroad to produce evidence in behalf of the justness of its discrimination.

Adams had pointed out that one reason for the ruggedness of West-

[29] "Report of the Senate Select [Cullom] Committee on Interstate Commerce," *loc. cit.*, Pt. II, pp. 735–736; 45 *Interstate Commerce*, 257, 258.

[30] "Report of the Senate Select [Cullom] Committee on Interstate Commerce," *loc. cit.*, Pt. I, p. 195.

[31] Buck, *op. cit.*, p. 133.

[32] Chicago and Alton Railroad Company *v.* People *ex rel.* Koerner, 16 *American Reports*, 607, 608.

ern legislation had been that it was directed against enterprises owned by Eastern rather than local investors. These absentees were pictured as "robber barons," "bloated bondholders," "money sharks." [33] Not unnaturally the reaction in the East to this Western legislation was severe. One line of attack was its inexpediency. The "ruinous" regulation of rates prevented railroad securities from earning money and discouraged Easterners and foreigners from further investments in the improvement and extension of the roads.[34] The stocks of the Granger roads in Wisconsin responded sensitively to the changes of railroad legislation in that state,[35] and when the legislature repealed the Potter Law, the annual report of the Chicago, Milwaukee and St. Paul congratulated the legislature on restoring the road's "credit in the markets of the world." [36]

But the attack upon these Western laws generated real fire when it ascended to the realm of righteousness. The *Nation* announced that Wisconsin's prescription of reasonable rates was "spoliation as flagrant as any ever proposed by Karl Marx or Ben Butler." [37] One trouble was, of course, that state regulation violated the fundamental tenets of self-help: "agriculture at the West has been overdone and farmers are now asking industrious people in the East to help them out—they want the railroads by carrying at low or no rates to protect [them] against the consequences of their own mistakes." [38] Be that as it may, businessmen and their counsel determined to test the laws in the courts; in the meantime they assumed a lordly attitude, deliberating as to whether they should obey the laws. In some instances they graciously informed a state governor that they would do so "under protest" or "experimentally." [39] Even in the passive East, a railroad president chided the advisory commission of Massachusetts when it pressed for lower rates: "I have supposed that your honorable Commission was created to, in some measure, stand between the railroad corporations and their patrons . . . I have not supposed . . . that the Commission intends . . . to seriously attempt advising the trained and experienced managers of roads in this Commonwealth upon the details of their duty." [40] The more arrogant of such statements certainly furnished ammunition for

[33] Adams, *Railroads: Their Origin and Problems,* p. 145.

[34] *Commercial and Financial Chronicle,* XIX (July 11, 1874), 33; (July 25, 1874), 83; Buck, *op. cit.*, p. 154; Mildred Throne, "The Repeal of the Iowa Granger Law," *Iowa Journal of History,* LI (April, 1953), 122–124.

[35] *Commercial and Financial Chronicle,* XXII (January 15, 1876), 57.

[36] *Commercial and Financial Chronicle,* XXII (April 29, 1876), 421.

[37] *Nation,* XVII (July 17, 1873), 36–37.

[38] *Nation,* XVII (July 31, 1873), 68.

[39] Buck, *op. cit.*, pp. 137, 144, 149, 154–155; Throne, "The Repeal of the Iowa Granger Law," *loc. cit.*, p. 103.

[40] Massachusetts *Third Annual Report of the Board of Railroad Commissioners. January, 1872,* pp. xxxii–xxxv.

those who charged the railroads regarded themselves as an *imperium in imperio*, equal if not superior to the state.

THE JUDGES TAKE A HAND

A series of decisions in state or lower Federal courts on Illinois, Wisconsin, and Iowa laws [41] would have warned railroad interests of impending peril, if they had not been so convinced of their righteousness and so accustomed to find protection in the greater intelligence and conservatism of judges and their comparative remoteness from popular agitation.[42] If a judge in Wisconsin went astray and declared the Potter Law constitutional it was because "he was living in the midst of this fever district, and it is far from impossible that the miasma has secreted itself in his blood without his knowing it." [43] The decision validating this law "fell like a bombshell on the railroad men of Chicago. They were in a perfect state of demoralization." [44]

Seven years later, in March, 1877, the justices of the Supreme Court of the United States, with two dissenting, summed up in Munn vs. Illinois, a case involving the regulation of warehouse charges by Illinois, and in a review on appeal of certain railroad cases, the correct legal and constitutional principles. "Railroad companies are carriers for hire. They are incorporated as such, and given extraordinary powers, in order that they may better serve the public in that capacity. They are, therefore, engaged in a public employment affecting the public interest." To be sure, a railroad charter is within the meaning of the Federal constitution and the state cannot abrogate that contract. But the railroad accepted its charter subject to the limitations and reservations in the charter and in the laws and constitutions that govern it. Common carriers "can charge only a reasonable sum." Until legislatures act, the courts must decide what is reasonable. But when the legislature acts, its decision on reasonable rates is overriding. Even if the legislature has not used this power for years, it makes no difference. "A good government never puts forth its extraordinary powers, except under circumstances which require it. That government is the best which, while performing all its duties, interferes the least with the lawful pursuits of its people." It is no plea that the regulation of railroads by state law is prohibited by the clause

[41] Chicago and Alton Railroad Company *v.* People *ex rel.* Koerner, 16 *American Reports,* 599; Peik *v.* Chicago and North-Western Railway Company, 94 *United States,* 164; Chicago, Burlington and Quincy Railroad Company *v.* Iowa, 94 *United States,* 155.

[42] Hurst, *op. cit.,* pp. 122–124; *Commercial and Financial Chronicle,* LVIII (February 3, 1894), 214.

[43] *Commercial and Financial Chronicle,* XIX (July 25, 1874), 129.

[44] Throne, "The Repeal of the Iowa Granger Law," *loc. cit.,* p. 104.

of the constitution conferring the regulation of interstate commerce upon Congress: "Until Congress acts, the State must be permitted to adopt such rules and regulations as may be necessary for the protection of the general welfare of the people within its own jurisdiction, even though in so doing those without may be indirectly affected." On the wisdom of such legislation, courts must not pass: "our province is only to determine whether it could be done at all, and under any circumstances." [45] In view of this wholesale validation of the state regulatory movement, perhaps the railroad men, like the proprietors of the grain elevators in Illinois, not surprisingly considered themselves, according to the Chicago *Tribune*, "thoroughly reconstructed." [46] Charters, contracts, fourteenth amendment, did not avail against the public nature of the railroad calling as stated in the common law of carriers. Actually in view of the common law and of earlier decisions in many jurisdictions, the findings of the Supreme Court in the Granger cases lacked novelty.

Although the Supreme Court now gave benediction to the state regulatory movement, the decision came at a time when there was considerable dissatisfaction in general with state action. For one thing the commission method of regulation was falling into disrepute. The popular aversion to governmental expense and to bureaucratic aloofness aroused suspicion of commissions. Since they were also deemed too friendly to the railroads, the old cry of corruption was raised. Finally, reformers noted that in Wisconsin, Iowa, and Minnesota the opponents of railroad regulation threw an advisory commission of the Massachusetts type across the path of thorough state control and substituted the former for more stringent measures.[47] Some leaders of the Grange were informing the Cullom Committee in the mid-eighties that "positive law is best to suppress palpable wrong." "The people want no board of railroad commissioners. They want just and wholesome laws, with well-defined provisions for enforcing them. . . . The people prefer to trust the courts rather than a commission." [48] State regulation proved, furthermore, wasteful and inefficient. It failed to touch rates of railroads passing through many jurisdictions. Though rate regulation by western states, for instance, successfully governed local rates and fares, the vital through rates were unaffected. Indeed the railroad sometimes raised them as

[45] Chicago, Burlington and Quincy Railroad Company *v.* Iowa, 94 *United States,* 161, 163, 164; Munn *v.* Illinois, 94 *United States,* 126, 130.

[46] Bessie L. Pierce, *A History of Chicago* (New York: Alfred A. Knopf, 1957), III, 76.

[47] Throne, "The Repeal of the Iowa Granger Law," *loc. cit.,* p. 121; Buck, *op. cit.,* pp. 164, 194–195.

[48] Statements of J. S. Woodman and P. P. Bois "Report of the Senate Select [Cullom] Committee on Interstate Commerce," *loc. cit.,* Pt. I, appendix, pp. 109, 116.

compensation for lowering the former.[49] The multiplicity and contradiction of state legislation naturally also antagonized railroad managers.

One solution might be national regulation, and the Supreme Court in 1886 made the desirable necessary. In Wabash, St. Louis and Pacific Railway *v.* Illinois, the learned justices, throwing overboard part of the Granger case baggage, declared that the application of an Illinois short-haul statute to consignments from Illinois points to New York City violated the clause of the Federal constitution conferring upon Congress the right to regulate commerce among the states. The last sentence of the decision was almost a directive: "A regulation of commerce . . . must be of that national character, and the regulation can only appropriately exist by general rules and principles, which demand that it should be done by the Congress of the United States under the commerce clause of the Constitution." [50]

INTERSTATE COMMERCE ACT: BACKGROUND AND PRINCIPLES

The national note was, of course, characteristic of the period. In the seventies, the Windom Committee had resorted to the commerce clause of the Constitution as justification for national regulation, and in the eighties the Cullom Committee was to do likewise.[51] However cogently such assertions justified a grant of power to the national government, local suspicions and rivalries persisted. Many states were as particularistic as the most rugged of businessmen; they had peculiar interests or circumstances which only state policy could wisely handle.[52] If these and other obstacles were to be overcome, politically powerful economic interests had to support national regulation. On this count by the eighties the Granger movement was relatively insignificant.[53] By then American producers, shippers and merchants, many of them in the East, had assumed the chief burden of agitation and lobbying. Memorials, petitions, and representations from Chambers of Commerce or Boards of Trade were manifestations of this interest. Prominent in the movement were F. B. Thurber, a member of a wholesale grocers firm in New York, and Simon Sterne, representing the Board of Trade and Transportation

[49] Buck, *op. cit.*, pp. 163–164, 175; "Report of the Senate Select [Cullom] Committee on Interstate Commerce," *loc. cit.*, Pt. I, pp. 43–45.

[50] Wabash, St. Louis and Pacific Railway Company *v.* Illinois, 118 *United States*, 560, 577.

[51] "Report of the Select Committee on Transportation-Routes to the Seaboard," *loc. cit.*, I, 79–99; "Report of the Senate Select [Cullom] Committee on Interstate Commerce," *loc. cit.*, Pt. I, pp. 28–39.

[52] Massachusetts *Thirteenth Annual Report of the Board of Railroad Commissioners. January, 1882*, pp. 35–43.

[53] Buck, *op. cit.*, p. 230.

of New York, both of whom had played a major role in initiating and conducting the Hepburn Investigation of 1879 in New York, the prelude to enactment of a commission law in that state.[54]

Nor was the railroad interest a unit in opposition. Railroad managers saw in national regulation a substitute for the anarchy of control by multiple state jurisdictions and a means of countering the irresponsibility of rate-cutters, railroad speculators, and financial freebooters, whose irresponsible activities and large fortunes were "leading to what is called communism in this country." [55] It was a former vice-president of the Erie Railroad who informed the *Commercial and Financial Chronicle* by letter: "It has always been the fashion in this country to argue that the less government we have the better, and that this constitutes the main advantage of this country over Europe. But there are some things that the Government must do if society is to hold together." In the case of railroads the do-nothing policy was a "despairing conclusion." [56] In short the apostles of order among railroad managers called upon the national government for assistance. Their program involved the governmental authorization of pooling and the governmental enforcement of rates agreed upon by the railroads.[57] Competing railroads also saw gains in government regulation if they could, under the guise of general principles, call in the government as an ally against their competitors. Thus the short-haul legislation held the seed of pro-rata rates. The shortest line between points could use this law to secure advantages over rivals with longer routes.[58] All in all, "let-alone" purists were aghast at the unanimity with which various business interests were all crying "for the same soothing syrup—legislative enactment." [59]

For years most attempts did not get far in Congress. In the late

[54] Lee Benson, *Merchants, Farmers & Railroads. Railroad Regulation and New York Politics, 1850–1887* (Cambridge: Harvard University Press, 1955), pp. 60–75, 115–121; Gerald D. Nash, "Origins of the Interstate Commerce Act," *Quarterly Journal of the Pennsylvania Historical Association,* XXIV (July, 1957), 4–8.

[55] Statement of Albert Fink, "Report of the Senate Select [Cullom] Committee on Interstate Commerce," *loc. cit.,* Pt. II, p. 126; Statement of George R. Blanchard, *ibid.,* Pt. II, pp. 161–162; Statement of F. B. Thurber, *ibid.,* Pt. II, p. 292; Statement of Charles F. Adams, Jr., *ibid.,* Pt. II, p. 1202.

[56] *Commercial and Financial Chronicle,* XLI (July 4, 1885), 7.

[57] Statement of Albert Fink, "Report of the Senate Select [Cullom] Committee on Interstate Commerce," *loc. cit.,* Pt. II, pp. 91–92, 107–112, 114; Statement of George R. Blanchard, *ibid.,* Pt. II, pp. 163, 170, 172.

[58] L. H. Haney, *A Congressional History of Railways in the United States* (Madison, Wis.: Democrat Printing Company, 1910), II, 307; In the Matter of the Export Trade of Boston, 1 *Interstate Commerce,* 24; Boston and Albany Railroad *v.* The Boston and Lowell Railroad Company *et al.,* 1 *Interstate Commerce,* 158.

[59] *Commercial and Financial Chronicle,* XL (June 6, 1885), 666–668.

seventies and early eighties the Reagan bill, named for John H. Reagan, ex-confederate cabinet official and now representative from Texas, gained considerable support and passed the House.[60] With ample definitions of the specified offenses, it forbad rebating, the pooling of freights or proceeds from carrying them, and included a crudely drawn short-haul clause. The courts were to enforce the act in response to private suits and complaints by those who felt they were injured by the railroads.

Finally in 1887 Congress passed the Interstate Commerce Act. There had been a thorough preliminary investigation of the railroad situation by a Senate committee, the chairman of which, S. C. Cullom, had participated in Illinois politics during the Granger era and had enforced the regulatory act of 1873. While the Reagan bill had stressed chiefly the matter of discriminations, then the dominant concern of railroad reformers, the Interstate Commerce Act covered other matters as well and provided a new means of enforcing and administering the policy. As for discrimination, the bill prohibited rebates and contained a carefully worded section which read "that it shall be unlawful for any common carrier . . . to charge or receive any greater compensation . . . for the transportation . . . of passengers or of like kind of property, under substantially similar circumstances and conditions, for a shorter than a longer distance over the same line in the same direction, the shorter being included within the longer distance." Another clause enacted the common law injunction that "all charges" "shall be reasonable and just." The act established an Interstate Commerce Commission of five members who could investigate either on complaint or their own initiative, bring their findings to the attention of the railroad, and if the latter remained obdurate, resort to the Federal courts to compel obedience. So far the act had largely proceeded on the assumption that it was the duty of the government to remedy specific abuses.

There was another aspect to the Interstate Commerce Act, for it continued to rely upon competition for the protection of public and private welfare. Section 5 prohibited the pooling of freights and earnings. Not the Cullom Committee, but the efforts of Congressman Reagan and popular clamor inserted this clause in the bill of 1887.[61] Among the witnesses before the committee, C. F. Adams, Jr. powerfully stressed the impossibility of securing competition and the unhappy consequences of an enforced competitive regime. "Everlasting warfare among railroads would be provided for by statute." Bankruptcy and combinations would

[60] Haney, *op. cit.*, II, 281–290; "John Henniger Reagan," *Dictionary of American Biography*, XV, 432–433; Nash, *loc. cit.*, pp. 9–11.

[61] 24 *United States Statutes*, 379–387; "John H. Reagan," *loc. cit.*, XV, 432–433; Haney, *op. cit.*, II, 298–309; E. R. A. Seligman, "Railway Tariffs and the Interstate Commerce Law," *Political Science Quarterly*, II (September, 1887), 393.

follow. The railroad company evolving from this process would represent "the natural survivorship of the fittest." [62] This bogeyman did not frighten everyone. Thurber, the representative of the New York merchants, exhorted the committee to "hold fast to the sheet anchor of competition. I believe that is the only salvation for the people of this country." [63] The resulting clash of concepts was to be expected in an act which stirred together the heterogeneous ingredients of American state legislation and foreign precedents, particularly English ones. For the Interstate Commerce Act was the American manifestation of a shift in railroad policy in the Western World. Hitherto the aim had been promotion; now it was restraint.[64]

For the next ten years railroad legislation proceeded on two levels. Neither the Supreme Court decisions nor the Interstate Commerce Act did away with state regulation. For one thing, national action did not embrace all matters of concern to railroad reformers, matters for instance as important as capitalization and watered stock. Since states had given the charters and passed the subsequent legislation they might continue to regulate their own corporations in certain matters.[65] Consequently, state legislatures frequently fixed the amount of stock and bonds and their relative proportion and prescribed the fashion in which they could be marketed and the purposes for which the funds were used. The agencies of the states continued to busy themselves with matters of safety and convenience and with intra-state rates. In this process the differences between regulatory and advisory state commissions, never very great, diminished. When the Massachusetts commission in the nineties criticized freight rates as too high, the *Commercial and Financial Chronicle* lamented that the most "enlighted" commission "in the country" had begun to sound "Western." [66] Perhaps one explanation was contagion by association, for the railroad commissioners held annual conventions to deal with their common problems.

Nonetheless decisions of Federal courts considerably diminished the effectiveness of state regulation, not on the grounds stated in Wabash, St. Louis and Pacific Railway Company *v.* Illinois, but by reversing the ample justification for governmental interference as stated in Munn *v.* Illinois. When the Railroad and Warehouse Commission of Minnesota,

[62] Statement of C. F. Adams, Jr., "Report of the Senate Select [Cullom] Committee on Interstate Commerce," *loc. cit.*, Pt. II, p. 1204.

[63] Statement of F. B. Thurber, "Report of the Senate Select [Cullom] Committee on Interstate Commerce," *loc. cit.*, Pt. II, p. 293.

[64] Benson, *op. cit.*, pp. 204–207; Hadley, *op. cit.*, pp. 22–23; Seligman, *loc. cit.*, II, 392.

[65] Testimony of Simon Sterne, "Report of the Senate Select [Cullom] Committee on Interstate Commerce," *loc. cit.*, Pt. II, pp. 56–57.

[66] *Commercial and Financial Chronicle,* LVIII (February 10, 1894), 243–246.

established in 1887 within a month of the Interstate Commerce Commission, set just and reasonable rates for the carriage of milk from Minnesota points to St. Paul and Minneapolis, the Supreme Court of the United States in 1890 declared the commission's act violated the fourteenth amendment of the Federal constitution. It deprived "the company of its right to a judicial investigation, by due process of law, under the forms and with the machinery provided by the wisdom of successive ages for the investigation judicially of the truth of a matter in controversy, and substitutes therefor, as an absolute finality, the action of a railroad commission which, in view of the powers conceded to it by the state courts, cannot be regarded as clothed with judicial functions or possessing the machinery of a court of justice." [67] Clearly this opinion substituted judicial infallibility for the legislative prerogatives vouchsafed in the earlier Granger decisions. Seven years later in a cluster of cases arising from a Nebraska statute, the Supreme Court affirmed in the strongest possible manner the public nature of the railroad business and a government's right to regulate its charges, but asserted a judicial right to pass upon the reasonableness of rates and laid down various criteria to be employed in such a test.[68] The Nebraska Act of 1893 authorizing legislative rather than commission action, was declared invalid because among other things the prescribed rates compelled the railroads to do business at a loss; this was not just compensation to the property owners; the fourteenth amendment prohibited such arbitrariness. However comforting on the right of regulation the statements in this case were, they introduced complications in the administration of the process.

THE COMMISSION AND THE COURTS

Meanwhile at the national level the Interstate Commerce Commission had been organized under T. M. Cooley as chairman. Cooley had been a professor of constitutional law in the Law Department of the University of Michigan, a writer on constitutional questions, and at the time of his appointment to the Commission was a receiver for a portion of the Wabash Railroad.[69] He was no ranting revolutionary. The railroad movement in his eyes was likely to fall short of wisdom because of "the want of popular information" on railroads and the changing character of railroad science. Moreover the reform drive represented "hostility to

[67] Chicago, Milwaukee and St. Paul Railway Company *v.* Minnesota, 134 *United States,* 457.

[68] Smyth *v.* Ames, Smyth *v.* Smith, Smyth *v.* Higginson, 169 *United States,* 466.

[69] Lewis G. Vander Velde, "Thomas McIntire Cooley," *Michigan and the Cleveland Era,* E. O. Babst and L. G. Vander Velde, eds. (Ann Arbor: University of Michigan Press, 1948), pp. 79–99.

railroad management [which] tends also, in some degree, to strengthen a troublesome, if not dangerous, feeling of antagonism to acquired wealth." [70] Whatever the ideology of its chairman, the commission faced a mountain of business.

As was to be expected, "the regulation of railroad rates . . . constituted from the outset the Commission's central task and most prolific activity." [71] On this score one problem was the general level of rates so often characterized by railroad opponents as "extortionate." The common law phrase in the Interstate Commerce Act, "all charges shall be reasonable and just," was "no self-executing formula." In search of greater precision the Commission in its first annual report came quickly to the conclusion that the proper test was the "relative value of the service," which bit of semantics was quite indistinguishable from the railroad's "charging what the traffic will bear." Such a system "would be best for the country because it would enlarge commerce and extend communication; it would be best for the railroads, because it would build up a large business." [72] In a later report the Commission inveighed against unreasonably low rates—"so unthinkingly prized by public sentiment"—as unfair to investors and likely to lead to impairment of service.[73] The Commission proceeded to apply its criteria to specific cases, and, if the rates were judged unjust and unreasonable, to prescribe ones meeting the standard of the Act.

After some preliminary rumblings, the Federal Supreme Court turned its attention to this performance in Interstate Commerce Commission *v.* Cincinnati, New Orleans and Texas Pacific Railway Company. In this so-called Maximum Freight Rates case, decided in 1897, justices said there were three agencies which might set railroad rates—the company, Congress, or some subordinate agency. Congress did not exercise this right nor did it assign in "unmistakable terms," as in many state laws, this legislative function to the Interstate Commerce Commission: other sections of the Interstate Commerce Act showed that Congress intended that the managers of the roads should prescribe rates. The Commission "has no power to prescribe the tariff of rates which shall control in the future." [74]

[70] Statement of T. M. Cooley, "Report of the Senate Select [Cullom] Committee on Interstate Commerce," *loc. cit.*, Pt. I, appendix, pp. 8–9.

[71] I. L. Sharfman, *The Interstate Commerce Commission: A Study in Administrative Law and Procedure* (New York: The Commonwealth Fund, 1936), III B, 3.

[72] *First Annual Report of the Interstate Commerce Commission. December 1, 1887*, pp. 30–32.

[73] *Second Annual Report of the Interstate Commerce Commission. December 1, 1888*, pp. 26–33.

[74] Interstate Commerce Commission *v.* Cincinnati, New Orleans and Texas Pacific Railway Company, 167 *United States*, 493, 505–506.

The other phase of rate regulation was relative rates or discriminations. Since on this point the provisions of the Interstate Commerce Act had given precise definitions, it would seem to have been easier for the Commission to fashion criteria for action. But vague wording, for instance "under substantially similar conditions and circumstances" in the short-haul clause, caused difficulties, and the railroads were authorized to ask the Commission to make exceptions to Section 4. Most railroads, except the transcontinentals or those in the Southeast where water competition had operated extensively, revised their rate structure to conform to the long-and-short haul prohibition.[75] As it applied this section to particular cases, the Commission permitted lower rates for long hauls in instances where water competition had compelled their necessity; it refused to admit that the presence of competition from other railroads was justification for exception. To do so would be to permit the discriminations, which had caused the enactment of the section, to serve as an excuse from its operation.

In 1897 the Supreme Court reviewed Section 4 in Interstate Commerce Commission *v.* Alabama Midland Railway Company. This case was brought before the Commission by the Board of Trade of Troy, Alabama, because, among other things, goods from Baltimore, New York, and other eastern sources paid more freight to Troy than to Montgomery, the latter being fifty-two miles farther on; and cotton from Montgomery passing east through Troy to the Atlantic shipping ports in the South paid 40 cents a hundred pounds, while from Troy the rate was 47 cents a hundred pounds. All this the Supreme Court, overruling the Commission, permitted on the ground that "competition between rival routes is one of the matters which may lawfully be considered in making rates, and that substantial dissimilarity of circumstances and conditions may justify common carriers in charging greater compensation for the transportation of like kinds of property for a shorter than for a longer distance over the same line." [76]

During the early nineties the Supreme Court was passing not only upon state regulatory measures and the Interstate Commerce Act, but also upon "An act to protect trade and commerce against unlawful restraints and monopolies" passed July 20, 1890. The important case applying this Sherman Anti-Trust Act to the railroad network was United States *v.* Trans-Missouri Freight Association, decided in March, 1897. The Association in question was one of the groupings formed after the prohibition of pooling in the Interstate Commerce Act. These regional

[75] *First Annual Report of the Interstate Commerce Commission. December 1, 1887*, pp. 20–21.

[76] Interstate Commerce Commission *v.* Alabama Midland Railway Company, 168 *United States*, 146, 147, 170.

"associations," professing a desire to further the equal, just and reasonable rates of the Interstate Commerce Act, arranged for common action in setting rates and for departing from them, and for penalties for violating their rulings: they scrupulously refrained from pooling freights or the returns therefrom.[77] Agreements of this sort or ones more elaborate increasingly won authoritative support. Railroad men were loud in their statements that the prohibition of pooling was the single greatest mistake or weakness of the Interstate Commerce Act; a considerable body of opinion among state railroad commissioners and shippers favored pooling under supervision of the Interstate Commerce Commission.[78] Such a policy would do away with the "destructive competition" of rate wars and unjust discriminations. By 1897 a majority of the Commission was favorable to the experiment of permissive pooling under "suitable safeguards." [79]

While such distinctions might appeal to the four judicial dissenters in the Trans-Missouri Freight Association case who asserted the Sherman Act did not forbid "reasonable restraints of trade," they had little influence upon the majority, who stated with considerable vigor that the Sherman Anti-Trust Act applied to transportation as well as other forms of business enterprise, that its first section forbidding "every contract" in restraint of trade and commerce meant quite literally what it said, and observed that "the public" and "those who assume to defend its interests both in and out of Congress" believed that "competition is a necessity for the purpose of securing in the end just and proper rates." [80]

In the Alabama Midland Case, Mr. Justice Harlan issued a single pungent paragraph of dissent. Its general tenor was that the Court had improperly interpreted the Congressional intent of the Interstate Commerce Act and had defeated "many of the important objects designed to be accomplished by the various enactments of Congress relating to interstate commerce." [81] Taking cue from this or from other analyses, later commentators, including not surprisingly the Interstate Commerce Commissioners, have frequently written of the "emasculation" of the act

[77] United States *v.* Trans-Missouri Freight Association, 166 *United States,* 292; United States *v.* Joint Traffic Association, 171 *United States,* 506, 507; *Tenth Annual Report of the Interstate Commerce Commission. December 1, 1896,* pp. 86–88.

[78] *Sixth Annual Report of the Interstate Commerce Commission. December 1, 1892,* pp. 47–55, 219–265; *Commercial and Financial Chronicle,* LVIII (February 3, 1894), 206; (May 26, 1894), 885–887.

[79] *Eleventh Annual Report of the Interstate Commerce Commission. December 6, 1897,* pp. 48–51.

[80] United States *v.* Trans-Missouri Freight Association, 166 *United States,* 311, 333.

[81] Interstate Commerce Commission *v.* Alabama Midland Railway Company, 168 *United States,* 176, 177.

and implied that the Court threw itself as an obstacle across the path willed by Congress and the public.[82] This is far from certain. The Interstate Commerce Act naturally lacked the fire of a crusading document; to secure the Congressional majority it did, it had to contain many compromises of phraseology and contradictions in concept.

When the cluster of Supreme Court decisions from Smyth *v.* Ames to Trans-Missouri Freight Association are taken as a whole, it is clear that the judges preferred a reliance upon natural forces to those of administrative regulation. "Competition, free and unrestrained," they said, "is the general rule which governs all the ordinary business pursuits and transactions of life. Evils, as well as benefits, result therefrom. . . . That free and unrestricted competition in the matter of railroad charges may be productive of evils does not militate against the fact that such is the law now governing the subject. No law can be enacted nor system be devised for the control of human affairs that in its enforcement does not produce some evil results, no matter how beneficial its general purpose may be." [83] When it came to abating these evils, the Court professed to believe that judges, not commissions, should apply the common law of carriers or individual statutes. That the Court's attitude hampered the swift effectiveness of railroad regulation is indubitable.[84] That it was a defiance of popular will is another question. If the spokesman for the Grange, who had opposed a commission on the ground "the people" did not want it and preferred regulation under the laws by the courts "which are within convenient reach of the people, and with whose methods of procedure they are familiar" was representative, a considerable number of people, even among reformers, were as eager to secure justice from the railroad through the courts as judges were eager to oblige.[85]

THE RESULTS OF REGULATION

The Commission had the misfortune to begin work on the eve of a difficult era. Soon the depression of the mid-nineties would do more to rearrange the structure of railroad organization and practices than the orders and findings of commissions, but meanwhile harassed railroad

[82] W. Z. Ripley, *Railroads: Rates and Regulation* (New York: Longmans, Green and Co., 1913), pp. 456–486; *Sixth Annual Report of the Interstate Commerce Commission. December 1, 1892*, pp. 5–7.

[83] United States *v.* Trans-Missouri Freight Association, 166 *United States*, 337.

[84] *Fourth Annual Report of the Interstate Commerce Commission. December 1, 1890*, pp. 9–21; *Fifth Annual Report of the Interstate Commerce Commission. December 1, 1891*, pp. 14–23.

[85] Note 48 *supra.;* Haney, *op. cit.*, II, 307–308; United States *v.* Trans-Missouri Freight Association, 166 *United States*, 319, 320.

presidents complained that the decisions of the Commission invaded their managerial functions and substituted for expertness and training control by "inexperienced theorists," and business-minded journalists were certain that the diminution in the number of dividend-paying roads and the decline of dividends was due in part to "meddlesome action" of public authorities in scaling down rates.[86] All this the Commission was quick to deny. In its second report, the Commission asserted that rather than being "harmful," the administration of the Act was "beneficial" to the carriers, and five years later with statistical particularity demonstrated the Commission was not responsible for current railroad receiverships and that low dividends were due to stockwaterings rather than Commission decrees. In any case, the Commission found arguments of this sort a distasteful irrelevance. Railroads had been guilty of "practices which operated to the public detriment," whose "prohibition was demanded on grounds of common justice and public morality . . . even though the profit from such practices were unquestionable." [87]

On the larger question of the results of the railroad reform drive, the movement over the period as a whole had achievements of the first order which were necessary preliminary to the more trumpeted ones of a later era. In the realm of theory, the courts had placed beyond assail the right of the government to regulate the railroads as public enterprises. On this point, Smyth *v.* Ames in 1898 was just as firm as Chicago, Burlington and Quincy Railroad Company *v.* Iowa in 1877. Even conservative public opinion which thought the Granger laws misguided and mischievous felt the Granger movement was justified because it impressed upon the railroad leaders their obligation to serve the public.[88] Furthermore in the realm of practice the railroad reformers had introduced, extended and refined as an instrumentality of regulation the railroad commission. Throughout the whole period, the concurrent civil service reform movement in state and in nation made strides toward the goal of competence in government officials and elimination of partisanship and favoritism.

The railroad reform movement failed, however, to solve the dilemma as to whether competition or railroad cooperation under governmental control was the better way to end the abuses against which it protested. This was understandable. "Rome was not built in a day. . . .

[86] C. F. Adams, Jr., *Railroads: Their Origin and Problems,* pp. 136–137; Seligman, "Railway Tariffs and the Interstate Commerce Law," *loc. cit.,* II, 409; *Commercial and Financial Chronicle,* LVIII (February 3, 1894), 206–207; *ibid.,* LVII (November 25, 1893), Investors' Supplement, pp. 1–2.

[87] *Second Annual Report of the Interstate Commerce Commission. December 1, 1888,* p. 17; *Seventh Annual Report of the Interstate Commerce Commission. December 1, 1893,* pp. 36–38.

[88] Adams, *Railroads: Their Origin and Problems,* pp. 136–137; Seligman, "Railway Tariffs and the Interstate Commerce Law," *loc. cit.,* II, 409.

A system of laws under which the people of the United States and their railroad system are to grow and prosper together, the rights, duties, and obligations of each being defined and regulated, I do not . . . believe that this system of laws will result from the labors of any one Congress or indeed of ten Congresses. A body of legislation of any permanent value has got to grow up slowly. The railroad system of to-day is the growth of fifty years."[89] As it turned out, a change in the circumstances shaping policy led to a growing decisiveness of legislation. Some Congressmen in 1886 were foresighted enough to realize that the prohibition of pooling in the Interstate Commerce Act would spur the move toward railroad consolidation.[90] That movement, the Interstate Commerce Commission noted, was taking place both before and after the passage of the Interstate Commerce Act.[91] In due time salvation by inter-railroad competition would come to seem an anchronism.

[89] Statement of Charles F. Adams, Jr., "Report of the Senate Select [Cullom] Committee on Interstate Commerce," *loc. cit.*, Pt. II, p. 1217.

[90] Haney, *op. cit.*, II, 302.

[91] *Third Annual Report of the Interstate Commerce Commission. December 1, 1889*, pp. 76–80.

CHAPTER VII

Natural Resources: Finding and Development

THE NATION'S ENDOWMENT

IN the struggle for railroad reform, commentators often referred to railroad rates as a tax upon production. Such a statement usually implied the superiority of production to transportation and is thus but another indication of American emphasis on productivity, so ubiquitous in this period. The farmer's calling, of course, was the supreme embodiment of this virtue, for the cultivator mingled his labor with the earth, he worked with nature's potential bounty. The same superiority, with distressing modifications to be noticed later, inhered in the discovery and development of America's natural resources. These were part of the nation's endowment; to search them out and to put them to use was to fulfill intentions almost divine. It was no accident that William Jennings Bryan, playing upon so many symbols in his famous cross of gold speech in 1896, should, immediately after celebrating the farmer, pay tribute to "the miners who go down a thousand feet into the earth, or climb two thousand feet upon the cliffs and bring forth from their hiding places the precious metals to be poured into the channels of trade."

Since the "peerless leader" was avowedly discussing finance, his exclusive gaze on the precious metals was perhaps excusable. Actually the economy of the nation was based upon other resources: timber, coal, iron, the minor metals, and petroleum. These, along with agricultural products, were the foundations of American industry. The extraction or procurement of these resources not only gave employment directly to labor and capital. The materials they furnished brought into being further production by saw mill, iron and steel works, and refinery. Thus judged by the value of their products, the most important manufactures in 1860 were flour and cotton goods. Then came lumber. Luckily the value of pig-iron, in fifteenth place, exceeded that of malt, though not of spirituous liquors. These last two branches of manufactures, in varied degrees "pernicious in their effects," were somewhat redeemed—with the exception of New England rum, dependent upon imported molasses—by utilizing "materials of domestic production." [1] The same generalization fortunately applied to most supplies of raw material.

DISPERSAL AND MOBILITY IN RESOURCE PRODUCTION

In the sixties usable natural resources were with few exceptions concentrated in the eastern half of the country. Though the hardwoods everywhere furnished fuel for heating and simple industrial operations, the commercial lumber industry was a soft-woods one, based largely upon white pine. Throughout the first half of the nineteenth century, Pennsylvania had usually led the nation in the production of board feet and in the number of saw mills. New York, in spite of the fact that Maine boasted the title of Pine Tree State, was generally the runner up. By 1860 the "inexhaustible" resources from the pineries of the states bordering the Great Lakes had dented the statistical columns of production.[2] At least ten or fifteen years earlier the more foresighted or "Napoleonic" among the lumbermen of the East had set their course toward these Western resources.[3]

Over the American resources of metals and coal, Abram S. Hewitt, a noted iron master, grew lyrical in 1867. "The position of the Coal-Measures of the United States suggests the idea of a gigantic bowl filled with treasure, the outer rim of which skirts along the Atlantic to the Gulf of Mexico, and thence, returning by the plains which lie at the eastern base of the Rocky Mountains, passes by the great lakes to the place of beginning on the borders of Pennsylvania and New York. The rim of the basin is filled with exhaustless stores of iron ore of every variety, and of the best quality. . . ." Scattered here and there within the "bowl" were coal-seams, equally inexhaustible, "for all the coal of the rest of the world might be deposited within this iron rim, and its square miles would not occupy one-quarter of the coal area of the United States." [4]

[1] "Preliminary Report on the Eighth Census, 1860," *House Executive Document* No. 116, 37th Cong., 2d Sess., pp. 65, 191.

[2] R. G. Wood, "A History of Lumbering in Maine, 1820–1861," *University of Maine Studies.* Second Series. No. 33 (Orono: University Press, 1935), p. 30.

[3] Isaac Stephenson, *Recollections of a Long Life, 1829–1915* (Chicago: Privately Printed, 1915), pp. 56–57; A. M. Larson, *History of the White Pine Industry in Minnesota* (Minneapolis: University of Minnesota Press, 1949), pp. 17–28.

[4] R. W. Raymond, "The Geographical Distribution of Mining Districts in the United States," *Transactions of the American Institute of Mining Engineers,* I (May, 1871), 38–39.

When this lofty generalization descended to mundane geological precision, the great iron districts were still those which in 1860 made Pennsylvania, as it had been for years, the great ore producing state of the nation. In the forties on the iron rim of the treasure bowl, the first of the Lake Superior iron ranges, the Marquette, Gogebic, and Menominee, came into production in the upper peninsula of Michigan, and in 1860 that state was the fourth in production. Neither the remarkable ore deposits in northern Alabama, "over which a horseman may ride for more than one hundred miles," nor Iron Mountain and Pilot Knob in Missouri had placed either state among the first five producers.[5] In coal production, too, Pennsylvania was preeminent, mining in 1860 over three-quarters of the whole value of all coal in the nation.[6] In her northeast coal regions—the Wyoming, Lehigh and Schuylkill—the state possessed a virtual monopoly of the nation's anthracite deposits.[7] At the other end of the state the bituminous fields in Allegheny, Westmoreland, Clearfield, and Fayette counties, formed the northeastern tip of the great Appalachian deposits, which farther south in Virginia had stimulated as early as 1790 the "first systematic coal mining operations in this country." [8] In 1860 Virginia followed Pennsylvania, Ohio, Illinois, and Maryland as a producer. Alabama, with its thick seams of coking coal was far in the rear.[9] All of these states, with the exception of Illinois, were in the Appalachian field. Though the mines in Illinois, Indiana, and western Kentucky, taken together, constituted a separate central district, geologically its coals resembled those of the Appalachians.[10]

In 1860 a mineral newcomer, petroleum, appeared for the second time in the statistical columns of American production. The total output was 500,000 barrels. The previous year when the first oil well was drilled at Titusville on Oil Creek in northwestern Pennsylvania, the total had been 2,000 barrels.[11] For some years thereafter the production of petroleum was confined to this Pennsylvania region and an adjacent area in New York.

By the end of the nineties the industries of the United States rested on a much wider geographical base of natural resources. Until 1890 white pine dominated the lumber markets of the nation: nonetheless,

[5] R. S. Tarr, *Economic Geology of the United States* (New York: Macmillan, 1894), pp. 144–145.

[6] "Preliminary Report on the Eighth Census. 1860," *loc. cit.*, p. 173.

[7] H. M. Chance, "Report on the Mining Methods and Appliances Used in the Anthracite Coal Fields," *Second Geological Survey of Pennsylvania, 1883*, AC, 4–5; D. T. Day, *United States Geological Survey, Mineral Resources of the United States . . . 1891*, pp. 305–306.

[8] Chance, *op. cit.*, p. 4.

[9] "Preliminary Report on the Eighth Census. 1860," *loc. cit.*, p. 173.

[10] Tarr, *op. cit.*, p. 318.

[11] *Mineral Resources of the United States . . . 1891*, p. 408.

cheap transportation by the sailing vessels in the Atlantic coasting trade and by the interior railroads enabled the rival yellow pine of the South to encroach upon markets from eastern seaports to the prairies. At the same time the Northern Pacific, and a few years later the Great Northern, brought east at low rates the fir and pine of the great Pacific forests.[12] By the century's end, however, Wisconsin, Michigan, and Minnesota, in that order, still led the nation in the value of lumber production. Washington, the first Far Western state to place, was fifth below Pennsylvania.[13]

Meanwhile the mining of ore had moved westward along Abram Hewitt's "iron rim." In the later seventies, exploiters dug into the Vermilion iron range north of Duluth; toward the end of the next decade the development of the Mesabi deposits, somewhat nearer Lake Superior and destined to become the greatest producers in the United States and in the world, began. By the close of the century when the "production of iron ore" in the United States was "in excess of the amount previously reported in any year for this or any other country," Minnesota had almost overtaken Michigan as a producer, and Alabama far exceeded Pennsylvania, where totals sometimes receded to those of 1850.[14] The Mesabi range, the youngest, easily led the list of producers.

In the minor metals production certainly moved about. In 1861 the copper region in the upper peninsula of Michigan after only two decades of development was providing 89.5 per cent of American production, a percentage which it occasionally surpassed after the war.[15] "Lake copper," however, soon found rivals farther west. In the late seventies capital, largely from the East, began to open and develop the magnificent deposits in southern and eastern Arizona, and the expansion transformed tatterdemalion mining camps such as Berber and Morenci into somewhat more settled copper producing centers.[16] Far away in Montana, foresighted pioneers such as George Hearst, Marcus Daly, and W. A. Clark were shifting a silver mining industry to copper, and by the early eighties Butte was on its way to metallurgical eminence.[17] By 1900

[12] E. C. Kirkland, *Men, Cities and Transportation: A Study in New England History, 1820–1900* (Cambridge: Harvard University Press, 1948), II, 151; Larson, *op. cit.*, pp. 397–399.

[13] *Twelfth Census of the United States . . . 1900. Manufactures.* Part II, pp. 835, 874.

[14] Tarr, *op. cit.*, pp. 144–145; Day, *Mineral Resources of the United States . . . 1900*, pp. 39, 43.

[15] William B. Gates, Jr., *Michigan Copper and Boston Dollars. An Economic History of the Michigan Copper Mining Industry* (Cambridge: Harvard University Press, 1951), pp. 195, 197–198.

[16] Robert G. Cleland, *A History of Phelps Dodge, 1834–1950* (New York: Alfred A. Knopf, 1952), pp. 80–90.

[17] T. A. Rickard, *A History of American Mining* (New York: McGraw-Hill Company, 1932), pp. 350–352.

Montana was providing nearly twice as much copper as Lake Superior and Arizona was in third place, not far behind.[18]

In the realm of fuels, Pennsylvania retained to an extraordinary degree its primacy in coal. She maintained her classic superiority in anthracite and in bituminous as late as 1900 easily led the Union.[19] The Appalachian coal region, of which the state was a part, constituted the greatest storehouse of high-rank coal in the United States, if not in the world.[20] Nevertheless there had been within this region a production movement toward the southwest. Before the Civil War western Maryland had joined Pennsylvania as producer; by the nineties, while the former's tonnage totals showed little change, the figures for West Virginia expanded dramatically.[21] Its mountains held some of the finest bituminous in the country; Pocahontas coal, for instance, had a high rating in terms of British thermal units and a great virtuosity, for it coked well, yielded on distillation a large volume of gas, and was admirably suited to raise steam in transportation and industrial plants.[22] In spite of the advantages of West Virginia's resources, however, Illinois, in second place, surpassed her as producer in 1900. By that date the various fields beyond the Mississippi contributed approximately 16 per cent of the national production, a figure a little less than that of the late eighties.[23]

For a time it seemed likely that Pennsylvania's control of petroleum might rival hers in coal. For the Titusville well was in northwestern Pennsylvania and the first oil region developed thereabouts. At one time, it was alleged, John D. Archbold, one of the most important of the Standard's directorate, had offered to drink all the oil ever found outside of the state of Pennsylvania.[24] Luckily he was not called upon to execute this careless commitment. On the Pacific coast there was some dispute as to when the region of southern California really entered production. Indeed for some years after the Civil War, the state imported kerosene from the East by way of Cape Horn. By 1875, however, the California petroleum industry began to develop.[25] Contemporaneously

[18] Day, *Mineral Resources of the United States . . . 1900,* p. 144.

[19] *Ibid.,* pp. 278–279.

[20] J. T. Lambie, *From Mine to Market. The History of Coal Transportation on the Norfolk and Western Railway* (New York: New York University Press, 1954), p. 43.

[21] Day, *Mineral Resources of the United States . . . 1900,* pp. 276–279, 285–287.

[22] Lambie, *op. cit.,* pp. 41–46.

[23] Day, *Mineral Resources of the United States . . . 1900,* pp. 281, 300.

[24] P. H. Giddens, *The Birth of the Oil Industry* (New York: Macmillan, 1938), pp. 46–87.

[25] R. W. and M. E. Hidy, *History of Standard Oil Company (New Jersey). Pioneering in Big Business, 1882–1911* (New York: Harper & Brothers, 1955), p. 758, n. 2.

the Appalachian area was spreading into western New York, southeastern Ohio, and West Virginia, and in the mid-eighties eastern production took a long stride into the midlands, when the difficulties of using the oil in the Lima-Indiana field were solved.[26] Wildcatters in the nineties were meanwhile probing the areas of eastern Texas; one of the most persistent of them struck oil in 1901 at Spindletop. Until it was capped the well flowed continuously in a column of petroleum six inches in diameter to an average height of 160 feet. This strike amazed American producers, as gushers of such strength and munificence had rarely been seen outside the famous Russian fields.[27] In 1900, however, the Appalachian field still produced 57 per cent of the petroleum of the country, while the percentages for the Lima-Indiana, Southern California, and Texas fields were respectively 34, 6, and 1.[28]

In the case of natural resources, production as a whole throughout the United States greatly increased in this period. An index of physical production in mining, based upon ten metals, coal, and petroleum, for the years since 1879 showed production multiplied very close to five times between 1879 and 1900.[29] In the longer period between 1860 and 1897 coal production multiplied approximately fourteen times and pig iron eleven times. Between 1869 and 1899 lumber production in board feet multiplied nearly three times; and between 1876 and 1896 barrels of petroleum nearly seven.[30] By the test of international rather than domestic standards, the United States over the decades was the largest producer of petroleum, until at the end of the century Russia surpassed her for a few years. In coal and pig iron, the United States in the nineties passed Great Britain, the traditional leader in industrialization and purveying of coal. After 1883 the United States was the leading producer of copper in the world.[31] Better processing or refining of raw materials, as we shall see, explained in part these increases. But the first step was, in every instance, an improvement in the methods of locating raw materials. The geographical expansion, hitherto described, would seem to demonstrate the United States had met this challenge successfully.

[26] *Ibid.*, pp. 155 ff.

[27] Day, *Mineral Resources of the United States . . . 1900,* pp. 579–580.

[28] *Ibid.*, pp. 540–545.

[29] Edmund E. Day, "An Index of the Physical Volume of Production," *The Review of Economic Statistics,* II (October 25, 1920), 294.

[30] Bureau of the Census, *Historical Statistics of the United States, 1789–1945,* pp. 125, 142, 146, 149.

[31] E. W. Pehrson, "Seventy-five Years of Progress in Mineral Production. The Statistical Record," A. B. Parsons, ed., *Seventy-five Years of Progress in the Mineral Industry, 1871–1946* (New York: American Institute of Mining and Metallurgical Engineers, 1947), pp. 361, 365; Day, *Mineral Resources of the United States . . . 1900,* p. 316.

PRACTICE AND SCIENCE IN MINING OPERATIONS

In a sense this was unexpected, for exploration and exploitation were far from systematic or scientific. To a surprising degree the first hints as to the location of natural resources can be traced back to the American Indians or to literary sources such as the *Jesuit Relations*.[32] At a later period individual prospectors traversed a promising terrain looking, in the case of minerals, for outcrops bared by erosion or metallic stains and coloration. Even more accidentally, observant soldiers fighting Indians in the Southwest located some of the most important copper fields in that region.[33] Acquiring some scientific repute from an analogy with the compass needle, which behaved erratically in the presence of iron ore, water wizards pretended to locate petroleum through the use of forked sticks, and spiritualists had informative seizures as they passed over promising territory.[34] The government survey of the public domain in the West would have offered an opportunity for a more systematic approach to the problem of finding, but these surveyors were primarily interested in running the boundaries of lands to be disposed of to agricultural settlers. Occasionally they might note on their maps, relying upon their observation or upon local statements, the presence of forests or other natural resources, but theirs was not a geologic survey.[35] Actually the agents in the land offices, through their sources of information or personal examination, could build up a more complete picture of possibilities.[36]

Aside from occasional reports of exploration financed by the national government, the first systematic appraisals of natural resources were undertaken by the states. Massachusetts was the pioneer. In 1830 the General Court, in response to the request of the Governor for a policy which would discover "the presence of valuable ores, with the localities and extent of quarries, and of coal and lime formations, objects of inquiry so essential to internal improvements, and the advancement of domestic prosperity," made an appropriation for a state geological sur-

[32] F. P. Wirth, *The Discovery and Exploitation of the Minnesota Iron Lands* (Cedar Rapids, Iowa: Torch Press, 1937), p. 7; Gates, *op. cit.*, pp. 1–2; Giddens, *op. cit.*, pp. 1–3.

[33] Cleland, *op. cit.*, pp. 80, 84–87.

[34] Wirth, *op. cit.*, pp. 25–26; S. W. Tait, Jr., *The Wildcatters. An Informal History of Oil-Hunting in America* (Princeton: Princeton University Press, 1946), pp. 70–74.

[35] "Testimony before the Joint Commission to Consider the Present Organizations of the Signal Service, Geological Survey, Coast and Geodetic Survey," *Senate Misc. Doc.* No. 82 (s.n. 2345), 49th Cong., 1st Sess., pp. 10–12, 35, 45.

[36] P. W. Gates, *The Wisconsin Pine Lands of Cornell University: A Study in Land Policy and Absentee Ownership* (Ithaca: Cornell University Press, 1943), pp. 91–93.

vey.[37] Before the end of the decade most states in the eastern portion of the country and some midwestern ones had followed suit.[38] Some of these enterprises, as in Massachusetts, worked over territory originally not richly endowed; others, as in the Pennsylvania anthracite and oil regions, perpetrated so many errors as to limit their usefulness; [39] still others, such as that of Dr. Douglas Houghton, publicized accurate and conservative knowledge of the copper deposits in the Upper Peninsula of Michigan, but not of its iron resources.[40] With the Civil War the administrative problem shifted, for the extensive Far Western regions had territorial and not state governments. After a series of regional surveys, Congress in 1879 appropriated money for a Geological Survey to examine and classify the public lands, their "geological structure, mineral resources, and products." [41] About a decade later all restrictions confining the survey to the national domain were removed.[42]

This governmental activity, state or national, faced the conventional difficulties: limited and sporadic appropriations and a clash between theoretical and practical objectives. If the Geological Survey were attacked, it advanced not only the usual and persuasive defence that its work was essential for the development of the country, but also the doctrine that only governmental funds were adequate to the immensity of the task and only governmental activity on the premises was democratic, for the maps, reports, and findings were available to everybody at only moderate expense.[43] This last observation was true also at the state level. When the Pennsylvania state survey was re-created in the seventies, no charge was to be made to any citizen of the state for any information the survey could communicate, nor was verbal information withheld until publication. The acceptance of fees from capitalists or companies for taking up one line of survey in preference to another or out of its proper order was forbidden.[44] In short, there was here an area of conflict between public or equalitarian and private or individual priorities and preferences.

Those who were going to risk their money in unknown enterprises

[37] George P. Merrill, "Contributions to a History of American State Geological and Natural History Surveys," Smithsonian Institution, United States National Museum, *Bulletin* No. 109, pp. 149–152.

[38] *Ibid.*, pp. 537–538.

[39] *Ibid.*, p. 432; Tait, *op. cit.*, p. 81.

[40] E. K. Rintala, *Douglas Houghton, Michigan's Pioneer Geologist* (Detroit: Wayne University Press, 1954), p. 110.

[41] "Testimony before the Joint Commission to Consider the Present Organizations," *loc. cit.*, pp. 16–17; 20 *United States Statutes*, 394–395.

[42] 25 *United States Statutes*, 526.

[43] "Testimony before the Joint Commission to Consider the Present Organizations," *loc. cit.*, pp. 1071–1075, 1078–1080, 1082–1084.

[44] Merrill, *op. cit.*, p. 443.

W. H. Vanderbilt. (Collection of Mrs. Byron Dexter) ➤

▲
Cornelius (Commodore) Vanderbilt (seated) at Saratoga, 1866. (Collection of Mrs. Byron Dexter)

Jay Cooke. (Collection of Mrs. Byron Dexter) ➤

John D. Rockefeller in 1888.

Andrew Carnegie. (Carnegie Endowment for International Peace)

A. L. Holley. (American Society of Mechanical Engineers *Memorial of A. L. Holley*, Frontispiece)

F. W. Taylor. (F. B. Copley, *Frederick W. Taylor,* 1923, I, Frontispiece)

George Westinghouse. (Westinghouse Electric Corporation)

Edison and His Principal Assistants at Menlo Park, 1878. (F. L. Dyer and T. C. Martin, *Edison: His Life and Inventions*, 1910, I, p. 275)

Edwin L. Drake. (Museum, Drake Well Park, Titusville, Pennsylvania)

Company Housing: Block of Overseers' Houses at Nashua, N. H. (Collection of Mrs. Byron Dexter)

Better Class of Company Housing in the Anthracite Region. (John Mitchell, *Organized Labor,* p. 216)

Worst Class of Company Housing in the Anthracite Region. (John Mitchell, *Organized Labor,* p. 185)

Cable Cars and Elevated Trains in the Nineties, Herald Square, New York City. (Waldemar Kaempffert, *Popular History of American Invention,* 1924, Vol. I, p. 115)

Harper's Iron-Front Office Building, New York City. (Collection of Mrs. Byron Dexter)

Typical Old-Law Tenement Houses of the Better Class, Chrystie and Delancey Streets, New York City; probably erected in the 1890's. (James Ford, *Slums and Housing*, 1936, I, p. 192)

Brownstone Fronts, 38th Street East from 5th Avenue, in the Sixties, New York City. (Collection of Mrs. Byron Dexter)

Building the Eads Bridge at St. Louis. (Collection of Mrs. Byron Dexter)

Railroad Bridge on the Portland and Ogdensburg—1870's. (Edward C. Kirkland)

A Trestle on the Union Pacific. (Collection of Mrs. Byron Dexter)

naturally sought to find out all they could about the resources, their location, richness, and extent if for no other reason than to protect themselves from fraudulent proposals and from designing promoters. In the case of lumber, it was feasible for purchasers to take to the woods themselves and find out. Often they did.[45] Even here, however, most preferred to rely upon the acquired skill of timber viewers and land-lookers who, it was said, could tell with precision how many board feet there were in a clump of white pines.[46] In the case of earth materials, private enterprises sent out exploring parties including geologists; their achievements were considerable. In the debate over reviving the Pennsylvania survey, new industries such as petroleum were in favor of the proposal; established industries such as anthracite, bituminous, and iron-mining, which had their own geological advisers, had made their own surveys, and understandably preferred to keep the information to themselves, were hostile.[47]

Alexander Agassiz, one of the great scientists and scientific promoters of the country and a man whose knowledge and management had lifted a prostrate copper industry of Michigan to the bonanza level,[48] assailed the United States Geological Survey as "wasteful and extravagant" and as an agency from some of whose work "private individuals have learned nothing."[49] For his part, the head of the Survey implied that Agassiz hoped to substitute for public enterprise in this area private activity by collecting from "gigantic business enterprises a great fund" to be used for scientific research and publication.[50]

Nor was this quarrel the only handicap upon public enterprise in this area. As had been true in the states, appropriations were frequently irregular and inadequate; there was a disturbing difference of opinion as to whether surveys should enlarge the knowledge of natural history or seek immediately utilitarian objectives. And public as well as private exploration faced a shortage of trained men. Both relied at first upon "chemists" and "geologists" from academic circles or upon individuals who had been self-trained in practice or in theoretical science.[51] Since European mining had a longer history than American, it was not sur-

[45] Stephenson, *op. cit.*, pp. 77–78; R. N. Current, *Pine Logs and Politics: A Life of Philetus Sawyer, 1816–1900* (Madison: State Historical Society, 1950), pp. 22–23.

[46] P. W. Gates, *op. cit.*, p. 92.

[47] Merrill, *op. cit.*, p. 436.

[48] W. B. Gates, Jr., *op. cit.*, p. 41.

[49] "Testimony before the Joint Commission to Consider the Present Organizations," *loc. cit.*, pp. 1014–1016.

[50] *Ibid.*, p. 1078.

[51] Giddens, *op. cit.*, pp. 31–36; Hal Bridges, *Iron Millionaire. Life of Charlemagne Tower* (Philadelphia: University of Pennsylvania Press, 1952), pp. 141–154.

prising that schools of mining engineering had appeared there. The most famous of these, the Bergakadamie at Freiberg, had begun instruction in 1702,[52] and American mining enterprises often relied upon its graduates. One of them saved silver mining in the Comstock by his innovations.[53] The foreign accent, the close clipped hair and the glasses of the Prussian engineer soon became a feature of American mining areas. Even American experts could be exotic. John Hays Hammond, who combined Yale and Freiberg, once arrived on location "with the highest and shiniest boots . . . ever seen in the gold camps." To part one's hair in the middle was also to invite the suspicion of those who graduated from the academy of pick and shovel.[54] A concatenation of circumstances incredible except to an academician, enabled Columbia University to establish in 1864 a School of Mines,[55] which by 1890 had probably awarded more than half of the total number of mineral industry degrees in the United States.[56] In spite of on-the-spot suspicion of the "theorist," scientific education made impressive headway. James Douglas, trained in minerology, chemistry, and geology at Laval University, developed the immense copper interests of Phelps Dodge in Arizona;[57] and William A. Clark, merchant and capitalist, took the precaution of attending the Columbia School of Mines for a year before he began the large undertakings in Montana which earned him the sobriquet of the "Copper King." One of his competitors, F. A. Heinze, was a graduate of the same school.[58]

As early as 1871 the considerable number of mining engineers with a developed sense of professional status and of distinctive competence, had organized the American Institute of Mining Engineers. The immediate impulse to this action came from the coal regions. One objective of the Institute was "the more economical production of the useful

[52] T. T. Read, "Seventy-five Years of Progress in Mineral Industry Education," Parsons, ed., *loc. cit.*, p. 376n.

[53] Oscar Lewis, *Silver Kings. The Lives and Times of Mackay, Fair, Flood, and O'Brien, Lords of the Nevada Comstock Lode* (New York: Alfred A. Knopf, 1947), pp. 14–15.

[54] Quoted in C. C. Spence, *British Investments and the American Mining Frontier, 1860–1901* (Ithaca: Cornell University Press, 1958), pp. 103, 107; Rowland T. Berthoff, *British Immigrants in Industrial America, 1790–1950* (Cambridge: Harvard University Press, 1953), p. 60.

[55] Allan Nevins and M. H. Thomas, editors, *The Diary of George Templeton Strong* (New York: Macmillan, 1952), III, 403–404, 429–430, 528–529, IV, 91, 185; T. T. Read, *The Development of Mineral Industry Education in the United States* (New York: American Institute of Mining and Metallurgical Engineers, 1941), pp. 43–50.

[56] Read, "Seventy-five Years of Progress in Mineral Industry Education," Parsons, ed., *loc. cit.*, pp. 388–389.

[57] Cleland, *op. cit.*, pp. 93–94.

[58] Rickard, *op. cit.*, pp. 356–357, 360.

minerals and metals." One of the founding fathers also emphasized the wisdom of going beyond the "merely practical man" to the creation of a science of mining through research and the delivery and discussion of papers. Like all fledglings this society depended upon a man to keep it alive and direct its growth. Whatever his official position, Rossiter W. Raymond fulfilled this function for decades. In 1871 he was U. S. Commissioner of Mining Statistics.[59]

The judgment of how far science had really gone by the end of this period in the field of prospecting is difficult. When even trained lumber viewers had repeatedly underestimated the board feet on some of the Wisconsin pine-lands entered by Cornell University,[60] it was not surprising that knowledge of material resources underground was highly speculative. In this area probably the greatest advances during the period were made in the location of petroleum deposits. For both "rock-hounds" and wildcatters were busy trying to correlate the presence of supplies with structural geology or geophysical location. The theory of "creekology" that petroleum lay in the valleys was superseded by the realization that underground sandstone reservoirs were porous enough to hold oil and that drilling should be along anticlines or undulations in the rock formation.[61] Spindletop was epochal, for it was the first giant well brought in by an engineer.[62] In spite of accumulated knowledge, dry wells were commonplace. Even in a field as well understood as the Appalachian, between 1877 and 1900 about one in six wells failed to strike oil in paying quantities.[63]

All in all, finding depended upon a growing body of accurate knowledge about earth structure and the means by which ores were deposited and upon the employment of new techniques of exploration—for example, the diamond drill imported from France and applied in the lead regions of Missouri in 1869.[64] Though the total of such contributions might enable the prospector and miner to map underground ore bodies and to run shafts and drifts other than by the hit-or-miss methods of going down and branching out, much was still conditional even at the end of the century. As an eminent geologist confessed, prospecting depended upon

[59] A. B. Parsons, "History of the Institute," Parsons, ed., *loc. cit.*, pp. 403–413.

[60] P. W. Gates, *op. cit.*, pp. 236–237.

[61] Read, "Seventy-five Years of Progress in Mineral Industry Education," Parsons, ed., *loc. cit.*, pp. 398–399; J. V. Howell, "Historical Development of the Structural Theory of Accumulation of Oil and Gas," W. E. Wrather and F. H. Lahee, editors, *Problems of Petroleum Geology* (Tulsa, Oklahoma: American Association of Petroleum Geologists, 1934), pp. 1–20.

[62] Tait, *op. cit.*, pp. 116–123.

[63] Day, *Mineral Resources of the United States . . . 1900,* p. 539.

[64] Rickard, *op. cit.*, pp. 173–174, 300; L. C. Groton, "Seventy-five Years of Progress in Mining Geology," Parsons, ed., *loc. cit.*, pp. 28–29.

"lines of probability." "Every rule has exceptions, and this is especially true of rules for prospecting. Much must always be left to the experience and judgment of the men in immediate charge." [65] In short, theory was not enough: general experience, local knowledge, and luck had to supplement it.[66]

OWNERSHIP AND DEVELOPMENT POLICY

Although natural resources were associated with land, those who worked to develop them did not necessarily wish to own the earth. They were after the resources. Conversely owners, though they usually had an exaggerated idea of the value of their possessions, often had neither the interest nor the ability nor the means to capitalize upon their ownership. In an expanding country like the United States, where there were many demands and opportunities for capital investments, it was difficult to raise the large funds required for ownership. Consequently, it seemed simpler all around to enter into some sort of arrangement by which the process of development itself financed the transfer of the resources to the developers. Perhaps the earliest of these arrangements were the ones by which an operator purchased stumpage rights to fell trees. Contracts or "permits" specified the limits of the tract to be lumbered and the price to be paid the owner for each thousand feet of board measure. Provisions, sometimes explicit but sometimes indirect, made sure that the lumbering would take place within a certain time and that the operator would get out, if growth permitted, a certain amount of product.[67] Such transactions might run to big figures. The last big sale of stumpage rights in 1887 from the Cornell white pine-lands in Wisconsin brought in $746,561 on 35,809 acres.[68]

On mineral lands the cognate arrangement was the lease. These appeared early in the oil industry. The lessee usually agreed to drill a hole of a certain diameter and depth on the leased property; the land-owner-lessor received a royalty varying conceivably from one-tenth to one-half of the value of the oil, and perhaps an immediate cash bonus.[69] Speculation in leases was an organized feature of the oil regions. The lease appeared also in the iron regions of the Great Lakes. Such leases

[65] H. F. Bain, "Preliminary Report on the Lead and Zinc Deposits of the Ozark Region," *Twenty-second Annual Report of the United States Geological Survey . . . 1901*, Pt. II, p. 216.

[66] Rickard, *op. cit.*, p. 378.

[67] J. S. Springer, *Forest Life and Forest Trees* (New York: Harper and Brothers, 1856), p. 54; Wood, "A History of Lumbering in Maine, 1820–1861," *loc. cit.*, pp. 59–65; P. W. Gates, *op. cit.*, pp. 212–213.

[68] P. W. Gates, *op. cit.*, pp. 236–238.

[69] Giddens, *op. cit.*, pp. 30–31, 63–64, 132.

specified a royalty, perhaps 25 cents a ton on ore, guaranteed a minimum production a year, and agreed to mine out all the property within a certain period. Leases on petroleum and iron lands might run for a specified period, say twenty years, or into infinity.[70]

In disposing of its great timber resources in the upper Middle West, Cornell University sold stumpage on some 190,000 acres, and sold land, including the timber, to the amount of 512,428 acres.[71] In short, those who developed the natural resources of the country were not always content to purchase the resources alone but wanted the land on which they were found as well. Complete ownership gave complete control and stability.

Since in this period a good share of the resources was west of the Mississippi on the public domain, the government land policy was of primary importance. At the time of the Civil War that policy was ill-adapted to an orderly or intelligent disposal of landed property. As it had been for decades, one objective of that policy was the transfer of the national domain to private ownership; another was to manage this disposal in a fashion to encourage settlement and ownership in farms of 160 acres, deemed a proper family-sized farm. The general Preemption Act of 1841 and the Homestead Act of 1862 had permitted specified classes of individuals to secure 160 acres of public land, in the first Act on the payment of the minimum price, $1.25 an acre, in the second on the payment of a fee of ten dollars. In both Acts such an entry had to be lived upon and improved by the applicant; in the case of the Homestead Act this period was for five years previous to the final patent. The ideological tilt of these enactments was revealed in the provisions that the applicant could exercise his right to preempt 160 acres only once, that a homestead grant was for "settlement and cultivation" and not for speculation, that it was patented by the applicant for his own use and not "directly or indirectly" for anyone else.[72]

Among the lands to which the Preemption Act was not to apply were those on which were "known salines or mines." In accordance with the practice of sovereigns over the ages, the national government had early reserved for itself a portion of the metals and minerals found on the public domain; in terms of administration, this meant the national government reserved mineral lands and leased them to developers at a rent or royalty. At least this was the procedure in the most extensive application of the leasing policy, that to lead mines in the upper Middle

[70] H. R. Mussey, "Combination in the Mining Industry. A Study of Concentration in Lake Superior Iron Ore Production," *Columbia University Studies in History, Economics and Public Law* (New York: Columbia University Press, 1905), XXIII, pp. 84–85, 87, 113.

[71] P. W. Gates, *op. cit.*, p. 242.

[72] 5 *United States Statutes*, 455–456; 12 *United States Statutes*, 392–393.

West. According to a President of the United States, this system cost the national government more to administer than it took in and caused a great deal of discontent and friction in the mining regions. Accordingly in the late forties Congress began authorizing the public sale of mineral lands at certain minimum prices higher than those for agricultural lands.[73]

Whatever the motives leading to this departure in policy, they were reenforced after the Civil War by the massive size of the government debt and the dream of debt administrators and planners that they could meet their difficulties by turning the natural resource lands of the West into a source of government revenue.[74] Within a little over a decade Congress passed a series of enactments for dealing in a specialized fashion with the variety of government land. In 1866 and 1872, codifying and formalizing local customs that had grown up in the previous mining regions of the Far West, enactments arranged for the sale of mineral lands at minimum prices between $2.50 and $5.00 an acre. The universal preference for actual developers was revealed in provisions of the statutes favoring patents for those who had expended certain sums in labor and improvements and permitting those who had discovered a lode or vein not only the right to enter the surface tract but also "to follow such vein to any depth with all its dips, variations, angles." [75] This so-called "apex rule" protected the discoverer even if his discovery extended under the surface ownership of another person. It was a fruitful source of litigation.[76] A somewhat similar provision underlay the law governing petroleum deposits. The surface owner who got his well driven first was entitled to drain the pool, not only under his own land but also under that of adjoining owners. As one California operator expressed it, "We all try to get the oil out of each other's land." The first step was to drill wells along the boundary edge of one's holding.[77]

In 1873 Congress set for coal lands minimum prices ranging from $10 to $20 an acre.[78] In 1878, by the Timber and Stone Act, Congress partially filled a vacuum of legislation by providing a minimum price

[73] B. H. Hibbard, *A History of the Public Land Policies* (New York: Macmillan, 1924), pp. 512–515.

[74] "Report of the Secretary of the Treasury on . . . the Finances . . . 1862," *Senate Document* No. 1 (s.n. 1149), 37th Cong., 3rd Sess., p. 22; "Report of the Secretary of the Treasury on . . . the Finances . . . 1864," *House Document* No. 3 (s.n. 1222), 38th Cong., 2d Sess., pp. 15–16.

[75] 14 *United States Statutes,* 251–252; 17 *United States Statutes,* 91–96; R. W. Paul, *California Gold: The Beginning of Mining in the Far West* (Cambridge: Harvard University Press, 1947), p. 230.

[76] Paul, *op. cit.,* pp. 234–238; Rickard, *op. cit.,* pp. 360, 362–364; Cleland, *op. cit.,* pp. 101, 113n., 122–123.

[77] John Ise, *The United States Oil Policy* (New Haven: Yale University Press, 1926), pp. 215–217; Hidy and Hidy, *op. cit.,* p. 8.

[78] 17 *United States Statutes,* 607–608.

of $2.50 an acre for land chiefly valuable for timber and stone. The agricultural orientation of this enactment was revealed in the limitation of sale to areas of 160 acres and in the provision that the purchaser must certify his purchase was for his own use. It was an attempt to recreate "the wood-lot" in the West.[79]

These enactments were of far from universal application. Often the original statute applied only to certain states and territories. Often special bills—that of 1873 adjourned the Mineral Land Acts in Michigan, Wisconsin and Minnesota—exempted whole regions from general legislation.[80] Around many such instances there was an implication of corruption or at best special interest legislation. Such deviations, however, paled in comparison with the many cases of outright fraud and illegality. Lumbermen, as they had since colonial days, trespassed upon government property, cut down trees, and carried away logs—all without payment.[81] If a recourse to legality seemed desirable or prudent in case of timber or even ore on government property, the favored path toward possession was by way of the agricultural land acts. Purchasers could still acquire land for cash at government auction sale or they could recruit small armies of individuals, brief them on procedures, and put them on the march through the local land offices as preemptors and homesteaders. These new landowners later transferred their claims to their employers.[82]

While those who initiated such perversions must bear opprobrium, it was not theirs alone. The legislators of this land policy had in the original enactments the naive notion that a legal conformity with prerequisites could be assured through affidavits,[83] as if lawbreakers of any variety could establish their innocence by taking an oath they had not committed a crime. At last in the eighties Congress and the General Land Office made more nearly adequate efforts to enforce legislation through a larger bureaucracy of investigators and special agents.[84] Then a new difficulty arose. Communities did not want the strict enforcement of the law lest it slow their development. There was real difficulty in getting jury verdicts to convict spoliators of the government domain.[85] As one government servant reported from the Vermilion

[79] 20 *United States Statutes,* 89–91.

[80] 17 *United States Statutes,* 465.

[81] Wood, "A History of Lumbering in Maine, 1820–1861," *loc. cit.,* pp. 65–75; P. W. Gates, *op. cit.,* pp. 70–73, 211–212.

[82] Wirth, *op. cit.,* pp. 136–152, 155, 159; John Ise, *The United States Forest Policy* (New Haven: Yale University Press, 1920), pp. 74–75, 77, 79.

[83] 5 *United States Statutes,* 456–457; 12 *United States Statutes,* 392–393.

[84] J. B. Rae, "Commissioner Sparks and the Railroad Land Grants," *Mississippi Valley Historical Review,* XXX (September, 1938), 211–213, 230; P. W. Gates, "The Homestead Law in an Incongrous Land System," *loc. cit.,* p. 680.

[85] Ise, *The United States Forest Policy,* p. 83.

Iron Range in Minnesota, where Charlemagne Tower and his associates used entrymen on a large scale: "When brought to the point they [most people in the region] will admit that none make the improvements contemplated by the law—but they seem to argue that custom has made a higher law, and that they have a right to the land, if they don't get it some one else will." [86]

Meanwhile, as the decades passed, some voices doubted the wisdom of a policy focussing so exclusively upon the rapid exploitation of natural resources. The early agitators on this score came from an elite of scientists, educators and government servants. A more diffused influence came from those who "loved nature"—artists, savants and educators.[87] As customary, the reform group was riven by schisms. Their first objective was the forests, perhaps because their disappearance was most evident. Furthermore, in the eastern states which had been lumbered over and in the prairie states which, lacking timber, had tried to encourage its growth—Arbor Day was first celebrated in 1872 in Nebraska [88] —there was a willingness to try a different policy or at least an indifference to the continuation of the old.

The movement, which eventually gained the name of conservation,[89] has always had cosmic and ecstatic overtones. As early as 1873, F. B. Hough, a New York doctor-scientist who had been impressed by the danger of forest depletion through his work with the Federal census,[90] formulated the arguments for a new forest policy in a paper before the American Association for the Advancement of Science. The speaker emphasized that the preservation of forests was essential to prevent flood and drouth, for canal navigation and water power, and for the reservoirs which all American cities required for adequate and wholesome water supplies. Forests modified the climate; their presence prevented the return of the desert. Adequately preserved and protected forest lands had recreational possibilities, and, finally, wood as fuel and construction material was of immense economic importance to the nation.[91] On the whole the last motive did not receive emphatic notice in Hough's paper.

[86] Wirth, *op. cit.*, pp. 121–122.

[87] Hans Huth, *Nature and the Americans. Three Centuries of Changing Attitudes* (Berkeley: University of California Press, 1957), pp. 30–53; David Lowenthal, *George Perkins Marsh, Versatile Vermonter* (New York: Columbia University Press, 1958), pp. 246–276.

[88] Ise, *The United States Forest Policy*, pp. 29–30.

[89] Gifford Pinchot, *Breaking New Ground* (New York: Harcourt, Brace and Company, 1947), pp. 319–326.

[90] A. D. Rodgers, III, *Bernhard Eduard Fernow, A Story of North American Forestry* (Princeton: Princeton University Press, 1951), p. 37.

[91] F. B. Hough, "On the Duty of Governments in the Preservation of Forests," *Proceedings of the American Association for the Advancement of Science. Twenty-second Meeting, Held at Portland, Maine, August 1873*, XXII, Pt. 2, pp. 1–10.

Some years later Gifford Pinchot, the young Yale zealot who had been trained in forestry abroad, came to believe that one of the greatest lessons he had learned from his European mentors was that trees were a crop and that you must manage a forest and make it pay.[92]

The title of Hough's paper pointed to one way to change: "On the Duty of Governments in the Preservation of Forests." But the analysis was stronger on the duty than on the means to it. Private land tenure in America daunted innovators. Hough, for instance, pointed out that the absence of large entailed estates descending from father to son, meant that one generation was not spurred to plant and protect for the next.[93] B. E. Fernow, another professional prophet of conservation, opposed government control over private timberland owners as "not only unsatisfactory and distasteful, but as it means reduction of private gain, unjust." [94] Such generalizations circumstance contradicted or modified. In the nineties, George W. Vanderbilt, a grandson of the Commodore, built himself a great chateau, Biltmore, in North Carolina, which he surrounded with an estate and a forest, to the over 100,000 acres of which he attempted to apply forestry practices. Biltmore was to become an educational center to which American lumbermen would send their sons for practical forestry training.[95] Apart from this spectacular example, American owners of large lumber tracts occasionally employed foresters to examine or manage their tracts. Rather than businessmen in general it was the "lumbermen on the job" who doubted the wisdom of new methods.[96]

Meanwhile government enterprise had stepped into the same area. As usual, individual states, notably New York, took the lead in establishing public forests.[97] The years of agitation and education in the eighties also influenced some leaders in the national government. In 1891, taking advantage of a codification of the national land laws, Congressional maneuvering slipped into the act, while it was in committee, a provision permitting the President to withdraw from entry forested areas on the public land. This authorization appealed greatly to the Presidents of the nineties. Harrison immediately created forest reserves, and Cleveland did so even more generously.[98]

Since the Forest Reserve Act of 1891 represented the tactical success of "doing good by stealth" rather than the convictions of a majority,

[92] Pinchot, *op. cit.*, p. 11.

[93] Hough, *op. cit.*, p. 4.

[94] Quoted in Pinchot, *op. cit.*, p. 34.

[95] C. A. Schenck, *The Biltmore Story. Recollections of the Beginning of Forestry in the United States* (St. Paul: American Forest History Foundation, 1955), p. v.

[96] Pinchot, *op. cit.*, p. 36; Rodgers, *op. cit.*, pp. 23–24, 28.

[97] Hough, *op. cit.*, pp. 8–9; Rodgers, *op. cit.*, pp. 253–258.

[98] Ise, *The United States Forest Policy,* pp. 31–33, 45, 110–122.

it is not surprising that it aroused intense hostility. Those lumbermen who interpreted "forestry as an interference with their constitutional liberties" [99] were obvious opponents; dealers in lumber and railroads which carried it joined the phalanx; miners who could not cut freely for fuel and mine timbering, stockmen who could not graze their cattle where they willed, agricultural settlers seeking lumber for houses through trespass were other opponents. A sectional cleavage between the Far West, where the reservations were, and the East appeared. The legislature of Wyoming prayed for the abolition of a reserve within its boundaries "lest it seriously cripple and retard the state's development." [100]

Such clamor was surprising in view of how little government policy had accomplished. While by 1897 reservations of timber land totaled 39,103,030 acres,[101] the policy of reservation had not yet been extended to coal, petroleum or minerals.[102] Even within the specific area of forestry there were in 1897 less than ten professional foresters in the country and no real understanding of forestry except among a few pioneers who were usually either foreigners come to this country or Americans trained abroad. By 1900 both Cornell and Yale had established Schools of Forestry which were to help in remedying this deficiency in training, and Gifford Pinchot had made his way to the headship of the Bureau of Forestry in the Department of Agriculture.[103]

MINING TECHNOLOGY

The larger national reliance upon natural resources required not only innovations in finding but improvements in extracting and in processing. Thus new industries such as petroleum came into being as the result of absolutely new methods of mining. The lessee who held the first oil lease at Titusville had proceeded by archaic methods; he dug lakes and trenches in the locality of the oil springs and used a pump to skim the oil from the oil-and-water collected in a central basin. Improvement upon this method came about almost by chance. Since one of the incorporators of a concern created to exploit the oil deposits around Titusville, George H. Bissell, a kind of jack-of-all professions and a lawyer, was impressed by the fact that oil was an unsought by-product of the salt wells which were drilled or bored around Pittsburgh and in West Virginia, the group despatched E. L. Drake, ex-farmer and railroad

[99] Schenck, *op. cit.*, p. 75.

[100] Ise, *The United States Forest Policy*, pp. 38–43.

[101] C. R. Van Hise, *The Conservation of Natural Resources in the United States* (New York: Macmillan, 1913), p. 215.

[102] Hibbard, *op. cit.*, pp. 520–528.

[103] Ise, *The United States Forest Policy*, p. 143; Schenck, *op. cit.*, pp. iv–v.

conductor, to Titusville to drill for oil. In 1859 Drake, after examining the methods in the salt regions and collecting equipment and an operator, finally punched a hole through the subsurface rock and found oil at 69 feet. He had attached an iron bit to a cable, working down from a "derrick"; steam power churned the bit in the earth; he had lined the well with iron pipe or casing to keep out earth and water.[104] The Drake well became the pattern for the essential devices in petroleum extraction.

Instead of using the methods of percussion and puncture, some innovators had experimented with apparatus for boring through the earth with a cutting bit rotated by a constantly lengthening stem. Water was forced down the resulting hole to carry the bit cuttings and earth to the surface. Drillers at first sought to line such holes with casing, but this complicated matters. Finally a mud solution was used to wall the hole. Rotary drilling, which oil men seemed to have derived from water well drillers, was especially useful in soft rocks, and the development of the Gulf Coast and Texas fields depended upon its use. In the twentieth century it finally invaded the Appalachian area, the stronghold of cable tools.[105]

For centuries the holes from which coal had been dug had been known as pits and those who worked them were pitmen. In this country the open quarrying of stone continued this tradition. Superficially this method should have been the easiest and cheapest for the extraction of coal and ores. But though pits appeared in the anthracite regions and in the Gogebic iron district, the method was expensive, for workers had to shovel and cart away in wheelbarrows or dump carts the unwanted overburden of earth and stone or drag it aside with horse-drawn scrapers. Gradually, as the depth of the overburden increased and water filled the pits, it seemed cheaper to follow the outcrop down or in with a shaft to which a series of horizontal drifts and slopes were subsidiary. Workers with pick or drill prepared the deposit for an explosive, and, when it had shaken down the material, shoveled the debris into the carts or cars, horse or mule drawn, of a subterranean transportation system. Elevators or skips in the shafts raised these containers to the surface. A supply of needed trained workers was at hand in the immigrants from the British and Welsh collieries and from the Cornish mines, who rose to positions of responsibility in the iron and copper regions of the United States. When the Nobel firm solved the problem of using nitroglycerin

[104] "Letter from the Secretary of the Treasury on Petroleum as a Source of Natural Wealth," *House Executive Document* No. 51 (s.n. 1256), 39th Cong., 1st Sess., pp. 4–5.

[105] E. L. De Galyer, "Seventy-five Years of Progress in Petroleum," Parsons, ed., *loc. cit.*, pp. 288–291; Tait, *op. cit.*, pp. 43–44.

without the customary hazards of premature explosion, dynamite took the place of black powder in bituminous coal mining. Spear-like picks, usually driven by compressed air, undercut the coal seam, which was then brought down by an explosive; later power-driven chains, armed with bits and traveling at high speeds, did the work.[106]

In mining as a whole the advance of technology was uneven. Every mine presented its own problems. In the Mesabi region, since the deposits of ore were shallow and near the surface, it was possible for extraction to regress to open pit or strip mining. The steam shovel did the work. Into these vast devastated areas the cars which carried away the product could be shunted as on a railroad.[107] In mining for anthracite, copper, or the precious metals, where deposits had to be followed down into the ground, as in the Comstock or at Butte, in a portion of the Pennsylvania anthracite region, and in the upper Michigan peninsula, engineering apparatus to remove the water, ventilate the shafts, and transport workers and material vertically had to be installed.[108] The unevenness of technical advance was demonstrated in a single industry, coal, in which anthracite was mined in 1900 much as it had been at the end of the Civil War; meanwhile in the five years from 1891 to 1896 the percentage of bituminous mined by machines increased from 5.3 to 12 per cent.[109]

Except in exceptional cases such as some copper deposits in Michigan, minerals were so mixed with deleterious substances that they had to be processed before they were available for use. Luckily the iron ores of the Lake Superior region were so low in phosphorous and sulphur that they could be made into steel by the Bessemer acid-process, the one usually employed in this country. The introduction of the basic process toward the end of the seventies made usable ores with a higher phosphorous content and indeed turned the phosphorous into a valuable by-product.[110] The Bessemer process also stimulated the use of coke in smelting iron, for coking partially removed the handicap of sulphur present in uncoked coal. The availability of coking coal in Alabama, in the Pocohontas field, in the Connellsville area of Pennsylvania thus

[106] Edward W. Parker, "Coal-Cutting Machinery," *Transactions of the American Institute of Mining Engineers,* XXIX (1899), 411–449.

[107] Mussey, "Combination in the Mining Industry," *loc. cit.,* pp. 104–108.

[108] Chance, "Report on the Mining Methods and Appliances used in the Anthracite Coal Fields," *loc. cit.,* AC, 60–337; W. B. Gates, Jr., *op. cit.,* pp. 4–5, 24–25, 30–31, 89; Mussey, "Combination in the Mining Industry," *loc. cit.,* pp. 100–102.

[109] Cadwallader Evans, Jr., "Seventy-five Years of Progress in the Anthracite Industry," Parsons, ed., *loc. cit.,* pp. 250–255; Parker, "Coal-Cutting Machinery," *loc. cit.,* XXIX, 406–407.

[110] V. S. Clark, *History of Manufactures in the United States* (New York: McGraw-Hill Company, 1929), II, 243, 267–268.

became an important factor in the localization of the iron and steel industry.[111]

One of the most spectacular dramas in the conquest over refractory materials occured in the Lima-Indiana oil field. Its petroleum, in comparison with that from Pennsylvania, contained on the average .65 per cent of sulphur. This sulphur imparted so vile an odor to the crude that the latter earned the sobriquet of "skunk oil," and kerosene distilled from it by conventional methods burned rapidly, crusted lamp wicks, and smoked chimneys. The Standard Oil capitalists who became interested in the new field employed Herman Frasch, a German-born chemist-inventor, to devise a workable method of refining this oil. It seems to have taken him somewhat over two years to find a solution,[112] a triumph which cost the Standard Oil group about $200,000.

TRANSPORTATION OF RAW MATERIALS

In considering the utilization of natural resources, one might well recall the dictum of one of Biltmore's first foresters: "Forestry, like any other business, is essentially a problem of transportation." [113] The fact that most of the areas of untapped natural resources after the Civil War were in wilderness or desert presented an acute challenge. It was met in part by a regression to or perpetuation of earlier solutions—waterways. The development of the anthracite regions in Pennsylvania had for instance depended upon the canalization of rivers and the construction of artificial waterways, and the lumber industry of Maine had relied upon the rivers to hurry the logs down from the interior to the mills near the sea-coast harbors; in New York, Albany had become a great lumber market because the Erie and Champlain canals brought the material thither and the vessels of the Hudson carried it away.[114]

After the Civil War, the pineries of the Midwest developed because a whole series of rivers—the Cass and Flint in Michigan, the Wisconsin, Fox and Chippewa in Wisconsin, the Red River of the North, the St. Louis and St. Croix in Minnesota—constituted supply routes for sawmills. Along with stands of timber, possession of sites for storage booms and for improvements of navigation became strategic points in the lumber

[111] *Ibid.*, II, 251.

[112] Hidy and Hidy, *op. cit.*, pp. 157, 160–161, 163–165.

[113] Schenck, *op. cit.*, p. 76.

[114] Wood, "A History of Lumbering in Maine, 1820–1861," *loc. cit.*, pp. 10–17; Chester L. Jones, *Economic History of the Anthracite-Tidewater Canals* (Philadelphia: Published for the University, 1908), *passim;* James E. Defebaugh, *History of the Lumber Industry of America* (Chicago: The American Lumberman, 1907), II, 315–321, 325–326, 346–349, 408–418.

business.[115] Down the lower reaches of these rivers and along the upper Mississippi, logs or lumber were rafted to further destinations. These sprawling rafts, at first dependent solely upon the downstream current, were by the time of the Civil War pushed ahead by steam towboats.[116] When the lumber industry leapt to the West coast, it depended upon rivers, such as the Columbia, and on Puget Sound. The lumber centers were often at places christened with the prefix "Port." On the Pacific as well as the Atlantic the coastal trade marketed the product.[117]

Not the least of the advantages of the mineral district in upper Michigan, Wisconsin and Minnesota was its nearness to the Great Lakes. Though the exploitation of some of these deposits was not hampered by the absence of improved navigation around the falls or rapids at Sault Ste. Marie between Lake Superior and Lake Huron, this barrier certainly interdicted expansion in the Lake Superior area. The need as well as the remedy was so plain that promoters in the forties fashioned plans for a canal around this obstruction. In 1850 Congress gave Michigan 750,000 acres of public land to defray the cost of construction; the state accepted the grant and transferred it to a private corporation, the Saint Mary's Falls Ship Canal Company, to finance and construct the waterway. When this work was completed in 1855, the company had spent $1,000,000 and built a magnificent pioneer ship canal.[118] In spite of its dimensions, peculiarly impressive in view of the ditches serving contemporaneously as canals in the United States, it had to be enlarged. Possession was transferred to the Federal government, and on two occasions, 1881 and 1896, enlarged locks, built by Congressional appropriations, were opened. By 1900 the cargo in many ore vessels was averaging 8,000 tons as contrasted with 1,100 in the largest vessel of the early seventies.[119] The parade of carriers at the Sault was one of the moving pictorial dramas of the nation.

For fuels, water transportation had always had a critical importance. The anthracite miners had to demonstrate this product could be burned

[115] Larson, *op. cit.*, pp. 9–10; P. W. Gates, *op. cit.*, pp. 121–136; Frederick Merk, *Economic History of Wisconsin During the Civil War Decade* (Madison: State Historical Society of Wisconsin, 1916), pp. 59 ff.

[116] L. C. Hunter, *Steamboats on the Western Rivers: An Economic and Technological History* (Cambridge: Harvard University Press, 1949), pp. 574–578, 581–582.

[117] U. S. Commissioner of Corporations, *Report on Transportation by Water in the United States* (1909), II, 19, 35–38, 332–336.

[118] "Annual Report of the Corps of Engineers" in the "Annual Report of the Secretary of War," *House Executive Document* No. 1, Pt. 2 (s.n. 1796), 45th Cong., 1st Sess., pp. 922–923; Harlan Hatcher, *The Great Lakes* (New York: Oxford University Press, 1944), pp. 301–304; U. S. Commissioner of Corporations, *op. cit.*, II, 152–161.

[119] Mussey, *op. cit.*, pp. 82–83, 95–96; Harlan Hatcher, *Lake Erie* (New York: Bobbs-Merrill Company, 1945), p. 327.

in a grate and, equally important, promote and finance canals to carry their coal to market.[120] For the carriage of bituminous coal three great water-borne traffics developed in the post-Civil War era. One was the Atlantic coastal trade which brought grimy cargoes by sail or steam collier from the Delaware and Chesapeake Bay northward to New York and New England.[121] The back cargoes of coal on the Great Lakes formed a second.[122] The third was a downstream traffic on the western waters, to which the coal mines of the western Appalachians were adjacent. Wooden coal boats from the Monongahela and upper Ohio floated down with the current, and Pittsburgh on the eve of the Civil War had a flourishing coal trade with cities on the Ohio and Mississippi. Just before the Civil War towboats were used in this regularized traffic. Like the lumber tows on these western thoroughfares, coal tows were so large that the coal trade furnished the chief opponents to proposed improvements of navigation. To pass through the locks tows would have to be broken up. As it turned out, ingenious mechanical arrangements or experience abated this inconvenience. A private company first improved navigation on the Monongahela, and between 1879 and 1896 the national government completed a slackwater system of navigation between Pittsburgh and Marietta on the Ohio.[123]

At first the carriage of Pennsylvania petroleum bade fair to recapitulate the history of anthracite and lumber. The oil from the wells was usually placed in barrels, which in turn were stowed away on barges along Oil Creek; a sequential opening of the dams on the upper reaches of the creek provided a "pond freshet" which carried these boats into the Allegheny, down which they either floated or were towed to Pittsburgh.[124] Such arrangements lasted only a brief period, for the railroads were at the borders of the oil regions and soon local capital began constructing subsidiaries and feeders. By 1866 the railroads were substituting for the barrel a tank car, a flat car with two vertical wooden tanks; five years later the horizontal iron-boiler type of car was in use.[125]

Since oil could flow, it seemed natural even in the sixties to run it through pipes to water or railroad shipping centers. By 1865 Samuel Van Syckel had financed and operated a pipe line through whose five-mile

[120] Jones, *op. cit., passim.*

[121] Kirkland, *op. cit.*, II, 157–162; U. S. Commissioner of Corporations, *op. cit.*, II, 31–35.

[122] Hatcher, *Great Lakes*, p. 336; U. S. Commissioner of Corporations, *op. cit.*, II, 187–189.

[123] Hunter, *op. cit.*, pp. 206, 210–213, 570–572.

[124] Giddens, *op. cit.*, pp. 101–111.

[125] *Ibid.*, pp. 111–113, 151–152; S. F. Peckam, "Report on the Production, Technology, and Uses of Petroleum and Its Products," *Tenth Census of the United States, 1880,* X, 92.

length pumps forced the crude oil.[126] By 1874 a pipe line from the Pennsylvania oil region to Pittsburgh was in operation, and four years later the Tidewater Pipe Company succeeded in dispelling the doubts that pumps could push petroleum over the Alleghenies. The oil moved about as fast as a man could walk. The new method of transportation proved so flexible and so suitable that by 1900 there were 18,000 miles of pipe line in operation.[127]

While railroads might be eager to build connections into the oil regions, the construction of logging railroads involved a different judgment of risks and investment. The lumber companies built them. Also the developers of the copper and iron deposits around Lake Erie frequently had to provide their own railroads. Before Charlemagne Tower could get iron ore out of his holdings on the Vermilion Range he had to construct a sixty-nine mile railroad inland through the forest from a harbor on Lake Superior. The road cost him just under $2,000,000.[128] Contrarily the Merritt clan, "finders" of the Mesabi deposits, lost their holdings to Rockefeller in part because they could not successfully finance a railroad to them.[129]

In the carriage of petroleum, since the railroads either would not or could not provide tank cars, the oil companies did so.[130] Furthermore the first pipe lines were built and operated by buyers of crude oil—Van Syckel was the prototype. Somewhat later the railroads, worried lest pipe lines deprive them of the carriage of oil, entered the business. The Pennsylvania Railroad, for instance, in 1865 organized the Empire Transportation Company to acquire and manage pipe lines. Somewhat more belatedly the Standard Oil group and the New York Central met this challenge by creating the United Pipe Lines.[131] As time went on the railroad dropped out of this business and in operational ownership the pipe lines became adjunct to oil refineries. They were a step in

[126] Giddens, *op. cit.*, pp. 141–147.

[127] G. S. Wolbert, Jr., *American Pipe Lines. Their Industrial Structure, Economic Status, and Legal Implications* (Norman: University of Oklahoma Press, 1951), pp. 7–8.

[128] Bridges, *op. cit.*, pp. 172–194, 213–239; W. B. Gates, Jr., *op. cit.*, pp. 60–63, 73; W. G. Rector, *Log Transportation in the Lake States Lumber Industry, 1840–1918* (Glendale, California: Arthur H. Clark Company, 1953), pp. 193, 203, 215–223.

[129] Allan Nevins, *Study in Power. John D. Rockefeller, Industrialist and Philanthropist* (New York: Charles Scribner's Sons, 1953), II, 245–255; H. O. Evans, *Iron Pioneer: Henry W. Oliver, 1840–1908* (New York: E. P. Dutton & Company, 1942), p. 212.

[130] D. H. Weld, "Private Freight Cars and American Railways," *Columbia University Studies in History, Economics, and Public Law*, Vol. XXXI, No. 1 (New York: Columbia University Press, 1908), 23–25.

[131] Hidy and Hidy, *op. cit.*, pp. 10–11, 17, 20.

integrating an industry. Nonetheless legislatures and courts have insisted in regarding them as common carriers.[132]

In the census of 1880, an American geologist calculated that of the total capital, $364,909,324, invested in mineral enterprises, about 22 per cent was in plant, 6 per cent in working capital, and the remainder in real estate.[133] It is far from clear whether any of these figures took account of investments in research and transportation which were also essential to the utilization of natural resources. Since so much capital had to be staked for preliminary or accessory operations, it is doubtful if investors could have then paid a high price for the raw materials themselves. The government program of disposal has been censured as a "giveaway." While the corruption, carelessness, and shortsightedness which often characterized policy were deplorable, the reduction of fixed costs in the materials themselves, when other costs were often high, facilitated the rapid economic expansion of the nation. As someone observed, "Ore is a treacherous image when divorced from the dollar sign."

The high costs of finding, extraction, processing, transportation, and other factors led the natural resources industries in the direction of large-scale business operation. The rule or the law of the apex with its constant threat of litigation compelled copper producers in both Arizona and Montana to consolidate their holdings.[134] Large-scale operations, furthermore, gave corporations other advantages. It was the mining companies of substantial size which could afford to carry on their own geological work. Large holdings could be more economically exploited. In timber, for instance, protection against fire and trespass cost less proportionately for large than for small areas; logging and sawing operations were more efficiently conducted. "There is a very definite economic law, according to which timber lands gravitate into large holdings." Similar advantages accrued to large-scale operations in petroleum. Lease or purchase of extensive areas enabled drillers to put down their wells in the most efficient pattern and to manage the field so as to extract in the long run the greatest amount of crude oil. In refining there were economies in continuous distillation. At the turn of the century American firms were resorting to this method, first utilized abroad. In turn, refineries and pipe lines grew in scale to handle the more generous run-throughs required by the process. In the Mesabi iron ranges, only companies with large capital could buy or lease the large holdings essential for the installation of machines powerful enough to remove the overlay,

[132] Wolbert, *op. cit.*, pp. 112–113.

[133] Raphael Pumpelly, "Report on the Mining Industries of the United States," *Tenth Census of the United States, 1880,* XV, xxxiii.

[134] Cleland, *op. cit.*, pp. 101–102; Rickard, *op. cit.*, pp. 359–362.

construct the railroads to carry the ore out of the pits, and introduce such niceties as drying the ore to reduce the tonnage to be transported. Only in the bituminous business as a whole was there an exception to this trend to giantism.

The bigness which came to characterize most natural resource industries was not confined to them. It was characteristic of the trend in American business as a whole. This trend, already discussed in the case of railroads, was marked also in other areas of enterprise.

CHAPTER VIII

The Transformation of Industry

THE TRIUMPH OF THE INDUSTRIAL SPIRIT

WHILE it is natural to make generalizations drawn from twentieth-century World Wars about the stimulus war gives to industrialization, similar connections in the case of the Civil War are frequently exaggerated. Nonetheless the experience of the embittered years between 1861 and 1865 at some points was decisive. When the shoe factory shod armies and a ready-made clothing industry based on the sewing machine clothed them, when the mechanical reaper harvested the wheat to make them bread, it was hard to cling to old beliefs that industry was an inferior way of life. The thinking of the founding fathers on this score, for example Jefferson, seemed not only archaic but childish. Though the unacknowledged belief that agriculture was the most productive way to wealth lingered in some places among some people as a conviction or a mere ceremonial obeisance, those acquainted at first hand with the new way of life were writing, "The encouragement of the manufacturing industries is the most direct and most lucrative method of increasing the wealth of a community." [1] To attain this new status, men's minds must be both enterprising and bold. Apparently the war years stimulated the country's businessmen to rise to this challenge. At least in 1887, Edward Atkinson, cotton manufacturer and publicist, thought "The great railroad constructor, the manufacturer, and the merchant of to-day engage in affairs as an ordinary matter of business, which to their predecessors, or even to themselves in their early manhood, would have been deemed impossible of accomplishment in a whole lifetime." [2]

[1] S. C. Brown, T. N. Dale, R. H. Thurston, *Report of the New Jersey Commission Appointed to Devise a Plan for the Encouragement of Manufactures of Ornamental and Textile Fabrics* (Trenton: Naar, Day & Naar, 1878), p. 18.

[2] Edward Atkinson, "The Relative Strength and Weakness of Nations," *The Industrial Progress of the Nation* (New York: G. P. Putnam's Sons, 1890), p. 71.

Though opinion and sentiment is in the nature of the case immeasurable, it is feasible to measure the results within limits. In the case of American industrial achievement, it is, of course, difficult to find a common formula embracing mackerel and coarse cotton cloth, mercury and machine tools. The characteristic they had in common, money value, changed with changes in the value of money. Nonetheless hardy statisticians are ready to dare this and other logical difficulties. According to one such attempt, the index of manufacturing production stood at 7.5 in 1863 and 53.0 in 1897. Indeed in the earlier part of the post-Civil War era, production fulfilled the surmise of the Revenue Commission in 1866 that in this country production quadrupled every twenty-four years.[3] Within this over-all picture specific patterns changed. Within old industries new trends suddenly appeared, grew at an accelerated rate, reached a peak, and then slowed down. On the other hand retarded growth was also a common phenomenon. In extreme cases growth stopped entirely. Thus new metallurgical methods erased smelting with anthracite coal and the rolling of iron rails; lubricants from petroleum had very nearly the same effect upon the whaling industry.[4] Changes in these two categories paled in importance before the rapid appearance of new industries. These continually unsettled the economy and gave contemporaries the feeling they were standing always on the edge of a new age of wonders and miracles. The analogy to a Rip Van Winkle who had gone to sleep in 1860 and waked to bewilderment years later was a common one.[5] It was no longer possible by the end of the century to employ, as Carroll D. Wright had as late as 1880, the textile industry as the illustration par excellence of the nation's industrialization, nor to use the number of spindles for working cotton fibers as the favored index of manufacturing advance.[6]

But even traditional industries such as textiles shared in the progress of the age. In cottons, for instance, the number of spindles approximately quadrupled between 1860 and 1900.[7] Spindles ran faster and turned out more yarn, and inventors placed the operation of the loom upon so

[3] Warren M. Persons, *Forecasting Business Cycles* (New York: John Wiley & Sons, 1931), pp. 170–171; "Report of the United States Revenue Commission," *House Executive Document* No. 34 (s.n. 1255), 39th Cong., 1st Sess., p. 41.

[4] Arthur F. Burns, *Production Trends in the United States Since 1870* (New York: National Bureau of Economic Research, 1934), pp. xiv–xxi, 159, 161–162.

[5] O. H. Platt, "Invention and Advancement," *Proceedings and Addresses. Celebration of the Beginning of the Second Century of the American Patent System* (Washington: Gedney & Roberts, 1892), pp. 57 ff.

[6] Carroll D. Wright, "Report on the Factory System of the United States," *Tenth Census of the United States, 1880,* II, 533–548.

[7] Bureau of the Census, *Historical Statistics of the United States, 1789–1945*, p. 187.

automatic a basis that one operative could now tend as many as thirty.[8] American initiative and invention, aided by government policy, were also sufficient to mechanize in the decades following the Civil War a wholly new textile industry, that of throwing and weaving silk. Hitherto hand operations had been necessary to cope with the irregularity and fragility of the silk fiber.[9]

IRON AND STEEL

Of course the appearance and growth of new industries really constituted the major revolution in the economy. In manufacturing, steel played the primary role. In 1867 the country made only 1,643 tons of steel ingots, the tonnage thirty years later was 7,156,957.[10]

As it happened, the essential processes and machines for making steel—an iron so "decarbonized" as to be less brittle and more malleable—cheaply came in the fifties both in the United States and Great Britain. In this country William Kelly, a Kentucky ironmaster, noted almost accidentally that a stream of air directed upon hot pig iron did not cool it but made it glow more hotly. The consumption by the oxygen in the air of the carbon in the iron itself was the cause of this seeming paradox. In Great Britain Henry Bessemer, an all-round inventive genius who accumulated in the course of a lifetime 114 patents in many areas of manufacturing, observed the same phenomenon. In 1856 he read before the British Association of the Advancement of Science his epochal paper on "The Manufacture of Iron and Steel Without Fuel." With immense practical imagination he devised the essential equipment for accomplishing his purpose. The core of the apparatus was the Bessemer converter, a huge pear-shaped receptacle in which the molten iron was placed and through which a blast of air was driven. After the discharge of flame from the open end of the converter fell away, the converter was tilted and a flood of steel poured forth into a ladle or other carrier. Neither Kelly's nor Bessemer's process produced a uniform product unless spiegeleisen, a compound of iron, carbon and manganese, was added. Robert F. Mushet, son of a Scotch metallurgist, discovered the necessity

[8] Victor Clark, *History of Manufactures in the United States* (New York: McGraw-Hill Company, 1929), II, 386–389; J. W. Oliver, *History of American Technology* (New York: Ronald Press Company, 1956), pp. 393–394; M. T. Copeland, *The Cotton Manufacturing Industry of the United States* (Cambridge: Harvard University Press, 1912), pp. 80–93; T. R. Navin, *The Whitin Machine Works since 1831* (Cambridge: Harvard University Press, 1950), pp. 273–274.

[9] F. W. Taussig, *Some Aspects of the Tariff Question* (Cambridge: Harvard University Press, 1915), pp. 228–234.

[10] Bureau of the Census, *Historical Statistics of the United States, 1789–1945,* p. 187.

of this element. Of the Bessemer process, an American sponsor wrote, "No improvement in practical metallurgy since the time of Tubal-Cain has realized such magnificent results in increasing the quantity produced and diminishing the selling price of a metal." [11]

Contemporaneously with Bessemer, William Siemens, a trained Hanoverian engineer resident in Great Britain and like Bessemer an all-round inventor, and the Martin brothers of France put together several inventions and practices into the Siemens-Martin process of steel-making. Commonly known as the open-hearth process, the new furnace used exterior heat to heat and boil the charge of molten metal to which "scrap" (wrought iron and steel) was added. Less spectacular and less rapid than the Bessemer, the open-hearth process enabled steel makers to control the character of the material by sampling and analyses and to turn out steel to meet specifications more exacting than those of steel rails, for the making of which the Bessemer process seemed so well fitted.[12] Neither the original Bessemer nor open-hearth process could use phosphorous-bearing ores. In the seventies two English inventors after considerable experimentation hit upon the idea of using a lime or magnesian limestone lining in the convertor or hearth; either "basic lining" dephosphorized the melted iron and produced a valuable by-product as well.[13]

THE APPLICATIONS OF ELECTRICITY

With the exception of Kelly, non-Americans were generally responsible for the massive basic innovations creating a modern steel industry. In the case of the other great industrial newcomer of the period—electricity—Americans, generally speaking, took the leadership. One area to which the inventors applied this new mysterious force was commercial communication. S. F. B. Morse, an American artist and professor of painting and sculpture at the University of the City of New York, had in 1837 secured an American patent on the electro-magnetic telegraph.[14] Soon after the Civil War a young Scotsman, Alexander Graham Bell, had come to Canada and then to the United States. His family had for

[11] William F. Durfee, "The Development of American Industries since Columbus. The Manufacture of Steel," *Popular Science Monthly*, XXXIX (October, 1891), 743–749; XL (November, 1891), 15–18, 26.

[12] Allan Nevins, *Abram S. Hewitt, with Some Account of Peter Cooper* (New York: Harper & Brothers, 1935), pp. 236–245; "Sir William Siemens," *Dictionary of National Biography*, LII, 240–244; John Fritz, *Autobiography of John Fritz* (New York: John Wiley & Sons, 1912), pp. 166–168.

[13] "Sidney Gilchrist Thomas," *Dictionary of National Biography*, LVI, 190–192.

[14] Carleton Mabee, *The American Leonardo. A Life of Samuel F. B. Morse* (New York: Alfred A. Knopf, 1943), pp. 189–213.

generations been interested in ways of teaching the deaf to talk, and it was this endeavor which at first kept Bell employed in the United States. Invention bent, he eventually secured a research assistant, Thomas A. Watson, and sought to perfect a multiple telegraph to send several messages over the same wire. His experiments in this matter led him to believe he could successfully send the human voice by wire. In 1876 he dumfounded the Emperor of Brazil by his telephone at the Philadelphia Centennial Exposition—"My God, it talks!" That year Bell secured a patent for his device. Two years later the first exchange was opened in New Haven, and by 1895 the number of Bell-owned telephone installations was approximately 310,000.[15]

The telegraph and telephone, which electric batteries or cells could power, used comparatively a mere trickle of electricity. Such sources were too expensive for the commercial use of electricity in other applications. When G. F. Brush, a graduate in chemistry from the University of Michigan, was experimenting with arc lighting in the early seventies, he not only had to improve the mechanism of the light but build a dynamo as well.[16] Then in 1877 Thomas Alva Edison, already a successful and famous inventor in the area of the telegraph, turned to the problem, believed by some experts to be "insoluble," of subdividing electric current and leading it into incandescent lamps. His task was larger than discovering an element which would glow in a vacuum bulb without quickly burning out; he had to invent a whole new system of conductors, meters, and generators. The critical date in the invention was not, then, so much 1879, when a carbonized thread in a bulb stayed incandescent for forty hours at Menlo Park, but 1882, when the central station at Pearl Street in New York was put into commercial operation.[17]

In spite of Edison's highly imaginative and, in the main, highly successful solution of his problems, one defect remained—he utilized direct current. Because of the increased size and thus high cost of the conductors, it was not feasible to transmit such current more than one mile. Among those who realized this defect was George Westinghouse, an ingenious young man who had invented in the late sixties an airbrake for trains. Assembling a group of engineers and purchasing the rights of

[15] "Alexander Graham Bell," *Dictionary of American Biography*, II, 148–152; A. F. Harlow, *Old Wires and New Waves. The History of the Telegraph, Telephone, and Wireless* (New York: D. Appleton-Century Company, 1936), pp. 350–366, 376; N. R. Danielian, *A. T. & T. The Story of Industrial Conquest* (New York: Vanguard Press, 1939), p. 15.

[16] Harold C. Passer, *The Electrical Manufacturers, 1875–1900. A Study in Competition, Entrepreneurship, Technical Change, and Economic Growth* (Cambridge: Harvard University Press, 1953), pp. 14–16.

[17] *Ibid.*, pp. 78–97; Waldemar Kaempffert, *A Popular History of American Invention* (New York: Charles Scribner's Sons, 1924), I, 568.

various inventors, Westinghouse put together an alternating current system. This saved transmission costs by sending a high voltage current over a small wire; it secured safety of installation by installing transformers to step up the current at the sending end and step it down at the receiving end. Any doubts about the success of the system were pretty well dissipated in 1893 when Westinghouse secured the lighting contract for the Columbian Exposition in Chicago.[18] The general illumination of the White City and the machinery responsible for it made as tremendous an impression as did the derived classicism of the Fair's architecture.[19]

Westinghouse and Edison focussed at first upon electricity as a source of incandescent lighting. To employ it as a means of transmitting power was easy in theory, for the electric motor was essentially a dynamo running in reverse. During the early eighties Edison experimented with the electric motor as a source of traction, but he was too busy to give the project full time and energy and, curiously in contrast with his foresight on lighting, he failed to see that the greatest market for the electric motor was on street rather than for steam railways.[20] Contrariwise, F. V. Sprague, a graduate of the United States Naval Academy, was so distressed by the smoke of the locomotives used to haul cars through the tunnels on the Metropolitan District Railroad of London that he sought in electric traction a smokeless substitute. In alliance with Edison's organization, he worked on the problem, and in 1887 succeeded in electrifying a considerable part of the Richmond Street Railways. At the time he secured the contract, he wrote, "We had only a blueprint of a machine and some rough experimental apparatus. . . . Fortunately for the future of electric railways, the difficulties ahead could not be foreseen or the contract would not have been signed." Nevertheless Sprague's Richmond triumph set a pattern for urban transportation in the United States. Westinghouse succeeded somewhat later with an alternating current motor in the transportation field.[21]

POWER

From place to place during the eighties and earlier the direct current motor had been applied in a variety of industrial uses. While such a device, utilizing power brought over a wire from a prime mover, was far more efficient than the shafts, belts and pulleys required for

[18] Passer, *op. cit.*, pp. 129–143.

[19] Charles M. Lungren, "Electricity at the World's Fair," *Popular Science Monthly* XLIII (October, 1893), 721 ff.

[20] Passer, *op. cit.*, pp. 216–223.

[21] *Ibid.*, pp. 237–249, 256–258.

steam or water installations, it could not, since it was direct current, reach out for electricity generated at distant or otherwise unusable water-power sites, for example Niagara, or from steam generator plants possessing the advantages of scale. An alternating current motor was essential. In the early nineties, Westinghouse and his associates re-worked an induction polyphase motor, invented by Nikola Tesla, an Hungarian engineer who had immigrated to this country. At the Columbian Exposition Westinghouse demonstrated the usefulness of this innovation.[22] By 1902, when comparatively accurate figures were available, electrical energy provided 1,500,000,000 kilowatt hours for industrial use.[23]

In unanticipated ways the development of electric power provided a new discipline for prime movers, the means of producing power. Primitive industrial development, such as that of the United States in the pre-Civil War years, had relied largely upon water powers. This was one reason for the concentration of manufacturing in New England. Its numerous streams with their sequence of falls, its comparative regularity in rainfall, and its abundance of lakes and wooded areas for storage purposes enabled the census of 1880 to declare New England was entitled "to the first rank as a water-power district." [24] Even her water-power textile cities such as Lawrence and Lowell came to rely increasingly upon steam power; and the further expansion of water power depended upon the utilization of less advantageous sites and the construction of expensive works.[25] Nevertheless by 1880 water power was still "generally much cheaper than steam-power." [26]

But steam power had the immense advantage of mobility. Since it was not tied down by natural conditions, it could be set up near markets or cheap fuel supplies. Whereas in the earlier years of the century, despite the intentions of James Watt, the employment of steam to move trains or vessels had been the greatest stimulus to technical advance in boilers and engines, industrial needs now set the pace. Of the many wonders at the Centennial Exhibition of 1876, the most impressive was the monstrous Corliss engine in Machinery Hall. This reciprocating engine, with a fly wheel 30 feet in diameter and with the improvements in gears

[22] *Ibid.*, pp. 239–240, 276–282.

[23] Bureau of the Census, *Historical Statistics of the United States, 1789–1945*, p. 157.

[24] G. F. Swain, "The Water-Power of the Streams of Eastern New England," *Tenth Census of the United States, 1880*, XVI, 10.

[25] Copeland, *op. cit.*, pp. 29–30; Constance M. Green, *Holyoke, Massachusetts: A Case History of the Industrial Revolution* (New Haven: Yale University Press, 1939), pp. 19–29.

[26] G. F. Swain, "General Introduction," *Tenth Census of the United States, 1880*, XVI, xvii, xxxv.

and governors that George H. Corliss had devised, animated all the exhibits of machinery.[27] Corliss and other builders constantly sought to secure a rapid and steady flow of power and to effect economies in fuel consumption through condensers, extra cylinders, insulation and steam under high pressure.[28] Nonetheless, the reciprocating engine, with its constant change in direction of moving parts, was probably less efficient than a continuous rotary motion. In 1884 Charles A. Parsons, an English university man, undertook to solve the problems of a steam turbine. The structure of the water turbine gave him a pattern. Steam from jets pushed in a zig-zag path through stationary and rotating blades and sent the latter spinning. With the turbines it was possible to attain a high number of revolutions per minute.[29] By the end of the nineties both George Westinghouse and General Electric had hitched the turbine to the electric generator, a coupling which spurred the generation of electricity in central stations. The high speeds facilitated the use of smaller prime movers and generators and meant large savings in materials and in construction and installation costs.[30] Thus the electric power industry joined transportation as a stimulus to the development of steam power.

Naturally the total horsepower employed in manufactures greatly increased. Whereas in 1869 the installed horsepower devoted to manufacturing was 2,346,142, in 1899 it was 10,097,893. Of the latter total, water power provided about one-seventh; in 1870 it had been on a par with steam power.[31]

THE FACTORY

At the end of the eighties, two Southern friends of Edward Atkinson visited him in Boston: they were intent on learning the reason for the industrial supremacy of this busy Commonwealth. One day Atkinson took them to a textile factory town, where his friends felt they "had touched the secret of New England." The next day Atkinson led them "up a narrow court opposite the Old South Church, into a nest of buildings plastered all over with little signs, a busy hive of industry covering arts almost without number. In the first room we entered we found two

[27] Robert H. Thurston, *A History of the Growth of the Steam-Engine*, Centennial Edition (Ithaca: Cornell University Press, 1939), pp. 502–503.

[28] *Ibid.*, pp. 503–525, 544.

[29] *Ibid.*, pp. 527–529; A. P. Usher, *A History of Mechanical Inventions* (Cambridge: Harvard University Press, 1954), pp. 392–397.

[30] Passer, *op. cit.*, pp. 310–313.

[31] Willard L. Thorp, "The Integration of Industrial Operation," 14th Census (1920), *Census Monographs*, III, 33.

men beating out gold-leaf for the dentist; in the next we found a man and a boy seated by a little furnace and a little forge, shaping steel knife-blades, too busy to stop the little trip-hammer, or even to speak to us; in the next, half a dozen men working in wood, turning out athletic implements of various kinds; and so on." [32]

Writing for the census of 1880 several years earlier, Carroll D. Wright, as well informed as Atkinson, announced when he turned to the past, that "the history of the factory system becomes the history of the textile industries." But an examination of the contemporary scene led him to add, "In nearly all industries where the terms of the definition of a factory can apply, that is, where raw material can be converted into finished goods by consecutive, harmonious processes carried along by a central power, the factory system had been adopted. . . . Some of the remarkable instances of the application of this system are to be found in the manufacture of boots and shoes, of watches, musical instruments, clothing, agricultural implements, metallic goods generally, firearms, carriages and wagons, wooden goods, rubber goods, and even in the slaughtering of hogs. Most of these industries have been brought under the factory system during the past thirty years." [33] Finally in 1902 Congress officially recognized the factory system by providing that the collection of statistics of manufactures be "*confined to manufacturing establishments conducted under what is known as the factory system,* exclusive of the so-called neighborhood and mechanical industries." [34] In 1899 two-fifths of the 512,191 industrial establishments of the country were factories.[35] Not only were factories taking over production, but the scale of factories themselves was enlarging. In cotton textiles, for instance, the number of active spindles per establishment in 1879 was 14,091; in 1899, 18,058. In boots and shoes the physical product per establishment turned out in the former year was 64,053 and in the latter, 136,313.[36]

To define with any precision a factory is as difficult as to delineate the reasons for its rapid triumph in the last half of the nineteenth century. But if we are to rely upon Wright's contemporary emphasis "on consecutive, harmonious processes" the invention of critical machines or methods would seem to be decisive. The former need not be within the factory; for example, the commercial application of the refrigerated car

[32] Edward Atkinson, "Consumption Limited, Production Unlimited," *Industrial Progress of the Nation,* p. 22.

[33] Carroll D. Wright, "The Factory System of the Nation," *loc. cit.,* pp. 1, 16.

[34] Thorp, "The Integration of Industrial Operation," *loc. cit.,* p. 35.

[35] *Ibid.,* p. 38.

[36] *Ibid.,* pp. 55, 64.

to the carriage of meat products after the Civil War made possible the concentration of meat packing in factories.[37]

Usually these devices were within the producing unit itself. Thus the invention of several significant machines was a prerequisite for the shoe factory.[38] Sometimes to make a factory it was enough to arrange machines in a new order or on a different scale. Alexander Holley, scion of a Connecticut ironmaster's family and a graduate of Brown University, won his fame as a founder of the American steel industry by departing from European precedents. He used larger Bessemer converters, placed them so they could be easily serviced and repaired, and above all arranged his equipment better to secure a flow of the material. Improved furnaces heated the iron before it was charged into the converter and more mechanical ladles handled the steel. Later the hot pig iron was transferred directly from the blast furnace to the converter, and the ingots cast from the latter were removed from the molds while still hot, and after being heated to a uniform temperature they were taken directly to the rolling mill.[39]

THE ORGANIZATION OF FACTORY PRODUCTION

The "process" that predestined the factory was perhaps as much managerial as mechanical. The early manufacturers had been so impressed at the amount of capital investment required by their new machines as compared with simpler tools that some thought they would have to run their machines around the clock to get an adequate return on their enlarged overhead. In the post-Civil War period here under scrutiny mechanical engineers, factory superintendents, and others were preoccupied with the task of securing internal economy within the factory, with determining precisely the costs of producing particular orders, and with performing the industrial operation with the utmost efficiency.[40]

Of the many individuals thus involved, the one to emerge as the

[37] Oscar E. Anderson, *Refrigeration in America: A History of a New Technology and Its Impact* (Princeton: Princeton University Press, 1953), pp. 47–52.

[38] George A. Rich, "Development of American Industries since Columbus: Manufacture of Boots and Shoes," *Popular Science Monthly,* XLI (August, 1892), 500–511.

[39] Clark, *op. cit.*, pp. 265–266; American Institute of Mining Engineers, *Memorial of Alexander Lyman Holley, C.E., LL.D.* (New York: American Institute of Mining Engineers, 1884), pp. 66–71; W. F. Durfee, "The Development of American Industries since Columbus: The Manufacture of Steel," *loc. cit.*, LX, 30, 32.

[40] Henry R. Towne, "The Engineer as an Economist," *Transactions of the American Society of Mechanical Engineers,* VII (1885, 1886), 428–429; F. A. Halsey, "The Premium Plan of Paying for Labor," *Transactions of the American Society of Mechanical Engineers,* XII (1891), 755–777; F. W. Taylor, "A Piece-rate System," *Transactions of the American Society of Mechanical Engineers,* XVI (1895), 862–866.

most famous and on the whole the most influential was Frederick W. Taylor. As a young man of considerable education and private means, he had passed through a mechanic's apprenticeship and had in the Midvale Steel Company near Philadelphia graduated through various positions as foreman and boss to chief engineer.[41] In his estimation manufacturers had solved comparatively well the problems of financing and of sales; their great remaining risk was production failures. Whether output was small or large, the overhead costs—taxes, insurance, depreciation, interest, salaries, power—remained pretty much the same. The escape from this dilemma was a "*large volume of output*" and a low cost of production per unit of product.[42] Taylor proposed to secure these results through "a big day's work, both for men and machines." [43] After "scientific" studies, Taylor applied to the workers an incentive wage system.[44] After experimentation he discovered in a machine shop the speed at which machines must be run to do their best work.[45] The result of all this was a displacement in the proportion of factory personnel. There were fewer "producers" in the narrow, historical sense of the word; there were more "clerks in the factory." New roles and responsibilities were given to this planning department.[46]

Most of the pioneering work for the Taylor system took place in the eighties in the Midvale Steel Company.[47] But it was not until 1895 that Taylor unveiled his diagnosis and prescription in a paper, "A Piece-Rate System," read before the American Society of Mechanical Engineers.[48] This document was clear, complete and compelling. It so spilled over with insights and suggestions that his later papers, "The Art of Cutting Metals" (1907) and "Shop Management" (1903), were largely illustration, the refinement of details, or recommendations on how to introduce scientific management by outwitting the antagonism of workers and others.[49]

The contribution of Taylor and other engineers to the matter of factory organization was one more factor in hastening the trend toward large-scale production. As long as skill flowed from the ability and train-

[41] F. B. Copley, *Frederick W. Taylor, Father of Scientific Management* (New York: Harper and Brothers, 1923), I, 69–80, 147, 157.

[42] Taylor, "A Piece-rate System," *loc. cit.*, pp. 857, 867–868.

[43] *Ibid.*, p. 878.

[44] *Ibid.*, pp. 856–858, 887.

[45] *Ibid.*, pp. 867, 878.

[46] *Ibid.*, p. 862; F. W. Taylor, "On the Art of Cutting Metals," *Transactions of the American Society of Mechanical Engineers,* XXVIII (1906), 54.

[47] Copley, *op. cit.*, I, 150–152.

[48] Taylor, "A Piece-rate System," *loc. cit.*, pp. 856–882.

[49] Taylor, "On the Art of Cutting Metals," *loc. cit.*, pp. 38–58; F. W. Taylor, "Shop Management," *Transactions of the American Society of Mechanical Engineers,* XXIV (1903), 1340–1454.

ing of the individual worker the small plant could hire such workers on terms of equality with the large; when skill became associated with costly studies and planning departments—Taylor constantly emphasized this expense [50]—the advantage shifted to the plant which could spread these overhead expenses over its large production.

INDUSTRIAL RESEARCH

Perhaps such expenses could be postponed or avoided if American producers continued the traditional pattern of letting foreign nations do the "pure" research and inaugurate its practical application and then importing the results. When Henry Bessemer invented the steel-making process, rival American claimants vied for the American rights to use it. The prize fell into the hands of A. L. Holley, who was in England on journalistic and engineering duties. Holley acted for a Troy, New York, metallurgical company, Messrs. Winslow, Griswold and Holley. Z. S. Durfee, an American engineer who had gone to England on the same mission for a rival group, brought back as consolation prize an artisan experienced in steel making and a right to use the Mushet spiegeleisen process.[51] A little later Abram S. Hewitt, an eastern ironmaster who was making the grand tour of Europe as an American commissioner to the Paris Exhibition of 1867 and as a visitor to steel mills in England, France and Germany, wrote jubilantly to an associate: "You ought to come over . . . and examine all these new things." Among them was the open-hearth process, the wider usefulness and technical superiority of which Hewitt appreciated. He signed an agreement to take out in America a patent for the Siemens-Martin process and to share the royalties with the inventors.[52]

Such was the course of invention in the basic metallurgical process; a similar transformation eventually took place in the specialties. In the nineties American industry undertook the production of tin-plate, a product hitherto rolled from bars and coated with tin in Wales, whence the American organizers of tin-plating imported the techniques, the machinery, and even the workmen to use it.[53] In short the history of

[50] Taylor, "On the Art of Cutting Metals," *loc. cit.*, pp. 35–36; Taylor, "Shop Management," *loc. cit.*, pp. 1369–1370.

[51] R. W. Hunt, "A History of the Bessemer Manufacture in America," *Transactions of the American Institute of Mining Engineers,* V (1876–1877), 201–202; Durfee, "The Development of American Industries since Columbus: The Manufacture of Steel," *loc. cit.*, XL, 18–19.

[52] Nevins, *op. cit.*, pp. 240, 245–246.

[53] Rowland T. Berthoff, *British Immigrants in Industrial America, 1790–1950* (Cambridge: Harvard University Press, 1953), pp. 68–69; Taussig, *op. cit.*, pp. 175–189.

steel in the United States reflected the genial admission of Captain W. M. Jones, Carnegie's great production genius, who, speaking to the British Iron and Steel Institute in 1881 announced, "While your metallurgists as well as those of France and Germany, have been devoting their time and talents to the discovery of new processes, we have swallowed the information so generously tendered through the printed reports of the Institute, and have selfishly devoted ourselves to beating you in output." [54]

From time to time American manufacturers, confronted by some technological perplexity or commercial anxiety, sought scientific answers to concrete difficulties. Thus as the brewing industry was changed between 1873–1893, as it had not been changed for millenia, by the findings of such eminent scientists as Pasteur and Takamine, American brewers imported scientifically trained German brewmasters and summoned Takamine from his native Japan to apply his knowledge of a starch digesting enzyme to the fermentation of corn.[55] In the case of another scientifically derived product, flour, Cadwallader C. Washburn, a Minneapolis manufacturer, had long been interested in the possibility of milling a higher proportion of quality flours from the grain and in the successful handling of hard wheats grown in the American Northwest. These problems had been met in one way or another in central and eastern Europe, where rollers had taken the place of millstones in breaking the grain, and in France, where mechanical purifiers with air blowers had separated the particles of different kinds in the passing flow of wheat. In 1878–1879 C. C. Washburn accidentally built a mill somewhat larger than he intended. The additional area he set aside as an experimental unit and installed in it an automatic, all-roller graduated-reduction mill. Significantly enough, the resulting flour was called "patent flour." [56]

The case of just who should get the credit for introducing the laboratory and experiment into the steel industry is somewhat clouded. While Z. S. Durfee was in England buying or trying to buy patents, W. F. Durfee, a cousin, was constructing for the former's principals an experimental steel plant near the iron mills of Captain E. B. Ward at Wyandotte, Michigan. A chemical laboratory under the direction of a succession of scientists imported from abroad was attached to the works. Both laboratory and plant tested various pig irons to determine their suitability for the new conversion process, and in 1864 this organization turned out the

[54] B. J. Hendrick, *The Life of Andrew Carnegie* (Garden City: Doubleday, Doran & Company, 1932), II, 309–310.

[55] T. C. Cochran, *The Pabst Brewing Company: The History of an American Business* (New York: New York University Press, 1948), pp. 110–123; Bessie L. Pierce, *A History of Chicago* (New York: Alfred A. Knopf, 1957), III, 154.

[56] John Storck and Walter D. Teague, *Flour for Man's Bread* (Minneapolis: University of Minnesota Press, 1952), pp. 225–236, 245–254.

first pneumatic or Bessemer steel made in America. Meanwhile A. L. Holley had erected at Troy, New York, an experimental mill for Winslow, Griswold & Holley. It proceeded to test irons from various eastern sources. A participant in this trial-and-error later wrote, "In the light of our present chemical knowledge of the manufacture, it is amusing to think of firms sending a few tons of iron to Wyandotte, Troy, or even England, to be tried in actual practice, when a few hours of laboratory work would have settled the entire question."[57] The same magic wand touched the blast furnace operations, transforming ore into pig iron. When Carnegie put a German chemist to work at the beginning of the seventies upon the raw material, "Nine-tenths of all the uncertainties of pig-iron making were dispelled under the burning sun of chemical knowledge."[58]

About all these operations there was, at least until approximately 1880, something of a spasmodic and temporary character. Even in steel the laboratory at Wyandotte "was ultimately destroyed by the influence of incarnate, malicious ignorance."[59] Innovation in the traditionless electrical industries, however, was preceded by the recruitment of men of science or the resort to them and the establishment of a laboratory to attack a problem through common action. Since whole industries came into existence in this fashion, such research operations continued. With one assistant, Alexander Graham Bell carried on his experiments with the telephone in a workshop partially financed by two of his well-to-do clients. At a moment of discouragement he consulted the nestor of American science, Joseph Henry, director of the Smithsonian.[60] Thomas Alva Edison had accumulated enough money to set up his own laboratory at Menlo Park, New Jersey. To tackle the problem of the incandescent electric light he added to his research staff machinists, a glassblower, a chemist, and a mathematician.[61] George Westinghouse, who had accumulated means and a staff of engineers from his invention of the air brake, gradually fleshed out the staff, hitherto largely concerned with railroad signals and switches, with more electrical experts. One of the latter established a laboratory and proceeded to invent a workable alternating-current system.[62]

Attendant upon the trend from individual to group invention was, of

[57] Hunt, "A History of the Bessemer Manufacture in America," *loc. cit.*, pp. 202–205; Durfee, "The Development of American Industries since Columbus: The Manufacture of Steel," *loc. cit.*, XL, 19–25.

[58] Andrew Carnegie, *Autobiography of Andrew Carnegie* (Boston: Houghton Mifflin Company, 1920), p. 182; James M. Swank, "Statistics of the Iron and Steel Production of the United States," *Tenth Census of the United States. 1880,* II, 154.

[59] Durfee, "The Development of American Industries since Columbus: The Manufacture of Steel," *loc. cit.*, XL, 23n.

[60] Harlow, *op. cit.*, pp. 351–356.

[61] Passer, *op. cit.*, pp. 79, 88, 89; F. L. Dyer and T. C. Martin, *Edison, His Life and Inventions* (New York: Harper Brothers, 1910), I, 269–279, 327–332.

[62] Passer, *op. cit.*, pp. 128–137.

course, a greater reliance upon the trained man, the educated expert, and the technician. Prominent in the group was the "chemist," a word often loosely applied to any scientist. But chemists and chemistry had long played a leading part in the industrial transformation,[63] and their employment for iron and steel and electrical enterprises was not so much a break as a continuation.[64] In place of the artisan or all-round machinist, the engineer now stepped to the fore. Durfee and Holley, for instance, were both educated engineers; one attended the Lawrence Scientific School at Harvard, the other, Brown. The executive heads of Midvale Steel when Taylor worked there were both chemists trained at the Sheffield School. Once it had been sufficient for a gifted "empirical engineer" to draw patterns on the floor of the shop, to supplement the design with verbal instructions, and whenever the machine was finished say, "Now, boys, we have got her done, let's start her up, and see why she doesn't work." [65] Breakdowns were the steps to progress. Now, with the appearance of engineering as a science, the draughting room became the nerve center of production, and a flood of calculations and blueprints took the place of guess and try.

Even mathematics, the Queen of the Sciences, aloof and abstract, had a practical role in the new dispensation. Edison employed a mathematician to make the lengthy calculations for the application of Ohm's law to the operation of the incandescent lamp,[66] and in the nineties when General Electric was formed, the company proceeded to enlist in its "calculating department" an immigrant scientist, C. P. Steinmetz, who "abolished the mystery and obscurity surrounding alternating current apparatus and soon taught our engineers how to design such machines with as much ease and certainty as those employing the old familiar direct current." [67] Frederick W. Taylor, baffled by the twelve variables involved in the efficient operation of cutting tools, admitted that without the aid of his mathematical associate, Carl Barth, a graduate of the Technical School of Horten, Norway, "we should never have reached the present solution of the problem." [68] Barth, incidentally, also made improvements in the slide rule.

Since technologists have to be trained, the industrial needs of the age had repercussions upon education and the organization of the learned.

[63] Archibald Clow and Nan L. Clow, *The Chemical Revolution. A Contribution to Social Technology* (London: Batchworth Press, 1952), *passim.*

[64] Harold K. Work, "Metallurgy in the Nineteenth Century," *Journal of Chemical Education,* XXVIII (July, 1951), 364–367.

[65] Copley, *op. cit.*, I, 101, 111–112; "William Franklin Durfee," *Dictionary of American Biography,* V, 547; "Alexander Lyman Holley," *Dictionary of American Biography,* IX, 148.

[66] Passer, *op. cit.*, p. 89.

[67] J. W. Hammond, *Charles Proteus Steinmetz, A Biography* (New York: Century Company, 1924), pp. 204–210.

[68] Taylor, "On the Art of Cutting Metals," *loc. cit.*, pp. 34–35.

The supply of engineers provided by apprentice training and even West Point was no longer adequate. By the beginning of the Civil War, a variety of engineering schools had stepped into the breach. Though as usual the foresight, enterprise, and wealth of private persons were responsible for the foundation and conduct of these pioneer institutions,[69] the United States government in the Morrill Act of 1862 gave 30,000 acres of public land for every Congressman to establish in each state at least one college "where the leading object shall be, without excluding other scientific and classical studies, and including military tactics, to teach such branches of learning as are related to agriculture and the mechanic arts . . . in order to promote the liberal and practical education of the industrial classes in the several pursuits and professions in life." [70]

In even the most promising private and public institutions there was at first considerable hesitancy about what to teach and uncertainty as how to describe what was being done.[71] Still the number of graduates increased. In 1897 there were approximately 10,000 students in schools of technology at the level of higher education,[72] and observers of the educational scene were admitting that where the two had been linked as an objective of private and public instruction, "agriculture is overshadowed by mechanics." [73] More particularly the land grant colleges "now stand at the end of the Appian Way, to eager feet the noblest gateway to the Eternal City of industrial and commercial prosperity." [74] As the number of trained specialists increased, they naturally became aware of their common interests and of the need for educating each other and for enlarging and systematizing knowledge of their calling. Within the decade 1871–1881 the American Society of Civil Engineers, which had had an existence of sorts before the Civil War, was reorganized and both the American Institute of Mining Engineers and the American Society of Mechanical Engineers were founded.[75]

[69] Dirk J. Struik, *Yankee Science in the Making* (Boston: Little, Brown and Company, 1948), pp. 337–352; E. C. Kirkland, *Dream and Thought in the Business Community, 1860–1900* (Ithaca: Cornell University Press, 1956), pp. 83–95.

[70] 12 *United States Statutes,* 503–505.

[71] Wellford Addis, "Curricula of Professional Schools," *Report of the* [U. S.] *Commissioner of Education for the Year, 1889–1890,* II, 944–977; Kirkland, *op. cit.,* pp. 93–95.

[72] *Report of the* [U. S.] *Commissioner of Education for the Year, 1896–97,* II, 1652.

[73] C. S. Murkland, "Industrial Education," *Report of the* [U. S.] *Commissioner of Education for the Year, 1896–97,* I, 444–445.

[74] J. E. Stubbs, "Report of the Section on College Work to the Tenth Annual Convention of the Association of American Agricultural Colleges and Experiment Stations," *Report of the* [U. S.] *Commissioner of Education for the Year, 1896–97,* I, 430.

[75] R. H. Thurston, "Technical Education in the United States," *Transactions of the American Society of Mechanical Engineers,* XIV (1893), 918; *Scientific and*

While the publications of such groups made available the research findings and practical experience of their members—Frederick W. Taylor's papers appeared in the *Transactions of the Society of Mechanical Engineers* and elicited thereby much favorable comment [76]—institutional arrangements for research in technology and engineering lagged behind those provided for agriculture. The national government, for instance, passed no Hatch Act for manufacturing. Perhaps none was necessary. Celebrating the centenary of the Patent Office in 1891, one contributor detected four methods of investigation in America "in the interest of future invention. First, individual enterprise; second, schools and universities; third, learned societies and endowments; fourth, government aid." He continued, "To the modern investigator leisure and opportunities are necessary; in chemistry and physics, at least, apparatus and laboratories are indispensable; and few men working alone can command either the needful time or the bare material necessities. During this century nine tenths of the great discoveries have been made by men with institutions back of them." Of these institutions sheltering and encouraging industrial invention, the most significant had been schools and universities. Such generalizations reveal an overemphasis upon German patterns [77] and some obliviousness to what American industry itself was already undertaking in the way of research.

In general it would be wrong to create the impression that in the post-Civil War period an army of educated men bearing a banner with the slogan "We know, we can win" moved into the fortress of industry. The transformation of an art into a science or technology did not take place evenly, forthrightly, or unopposed. "Practical men" were suspicious, even hostile, to the new approach. Such men sneered at the scientists who improved the fermentation process as "beer doctors," and the steel laboratory at Wyandotte was derisively called "Durfee's 'pothecary-shop." [78] There was some justification for these attitudes. A master artisan such as John Fritz, largely ignorant of schoolrooms, could for instance devise the three high mill, an improved method of rolling steel,[79] and the improvements in the steam turbine had been "felt out" by makers who "had little

Technical Societies of the United States and Canada, 6th Edition (Washington: National Academy of Sciences–National Research Council, 1955), pp. 65, 95, 99; Fritz, *op. cit.,* pp. 294–295.

[76] Topical discussion by Gantt, *Transactions of the American Society of Mechanical Engineers,* XXVIII (1906), 283.

[77] F. W. Clarke, "The Relations of Abstract Research to Practical Invention," *Popular Science Monthly,* XXXIX (August, 1891), 541–543.

[78] Durfee, "The Development of American Industries since Columbus: The Manufacture of Steel," *loc. cit.,* XL, 23n; Pierce, *op. cit.,* p. 154; Copley, *op. cit.,* I, 101–102, 126–127.

[79] Fritz, *op. cit.,* pp. 108–115; R. W. Hunt, "President's Annual Address. The Evolution of American Rolling Mills," *Transactions of the American Society of Mechanical Engineers,* XIII (1891), 48–52.

understanding of the principles of their art." [80] The roster of American inventors includes many great men who had little advanced education. George Westinghouse went to Union College for three months; Edison "received almost no formal education of any kind." [81] Yet both in their electrical inventions saw ahead more clearly than men learned in the subject. When Lord Kelvin was telegraphing from England to the promoters of Niagara's power, "Trust you avoid gigantic mistake of alternating current," George Westinghouse had already installed several successful alternating current systems.[82] It was all very puzzling. As Edison's mathematician later wrote, "I cannot imagine why I could not see the elementary facts in 1878 and 1879 more clearly than I did. I came to Mr. Edison a trained man, a postgraduate at Princeton; with a year's experience in Helmholz's laboratory; with a working knowledge of calculus and a mathematical turn of mind." [83]

At a time when invention was being reduced to a system, it was still not unusual for science to learn from industrial advance rather than the other way around. In the steel industry "the practice of making and using steel far out-ran the underlying science." [84] As for the steam engine, the President of the American Society of Mechanical Engineers informed his fellow workers in 1886 that it "has grown by the survival of the fittest, and from the perfected steam engine has been worked out the theory of thermo-dynamics. The steam engine in its highest form preceded the theoretical knowledge which has been written up under the name of thermo-dynamics, just as the music of the great masters was written and played long before the science called acoustics had been worked out." [85] Perhaps the battle of education versus experience as chief prerequisite for invention was really a case of "no contest": there is no accounting for creativity. The mechanic or scientist who would merely refine the inheritance of the past could not serve the hurrying present. As one of Taylor's disciples put it, "The usual way of doing things is always the wrong way." [86]

[80] R. H. Thurston, "The Mechanical Engineer. His Work and His Policy," *Transactions of the American Society of Mechanical Engineers,* IV (1882–1883), 82.

[81] Passer, *op. cit.*, pp. 78, 129.

[82] *Ibid.*, p. 287.

[83] *Ibid.*, p. 89.

[84] Work, "Metallurgy in the Nineteenth Century," *loc. cit.*, p. 364; A. L. Holley, "Technical Education," *Memorial of Alexander Lyman Holley, loc. cit.*, pp. 205–207.

[85] Coleman Sellers, "President's Address, 1886," *Transactions of the American Society of Mechanical Engineers,* VIII (1886), 679–680.

[86] Copley, *op. cit.*, I, 112.

CHAPTER IX

Tariffs, Patents, and Other Intangibles

MINOR METHODS OF GOVERNMENT AID

IF science were to replace rule-of-thumb, obligations of a new magnitude were sure to confront government, for government must, as F. W. Clarke put it in 1891, be selfishly interested in science, since "no government could long exist were it deprived of all the resources for defense and inter-communication which science has invented." In brief, national safety and well-being dictated that government protect and aid industrial advance. Clarke found that in the realm of governmental promotion of science and invention "little need . . . be said." [1] As an overall description of the relations then existing between government and industry, this utterance had accuracy—relatively speaking. Certainly in variety and extent, government assistance to transportation, agriculture, and mining had been more customary and more generous.

What industry, like other economic activities, needed was venture capital. Here the national government saw few opportunities to contribute and did not embrace the few offered it. Though S. F. B. Morse and his associates in 1845 prevailed upon Congress to appropriate $30,000 for the demonstration telegraph line between Washington and Baltimore, they could not persuade Congress on the analogy of the post office to make the telegraph a government property or provide funds for extensions.[2] Perhaps the Pacific Telegraph Act in 1860 was an exception. This statute gave the constructors of the proposed line a right of way through the public land and a maximum subsidy of $40,000 a year for a period of ten

[1] F. W. Clarke, "The Relations of Abstract Research to Practical Invention," *Popular Science Monthly*, XXXIX (August, 1891), 544.

[2] Carleton Mabee, *The American Leonardo: The Life of Samuel F. B. Morse* (New York: Alfred A. Knopf, 1943), pp. 249–261, 282–286.

years for transmitting government messages. In essence this arrangement was a contract for carrying the mails and the subsidy was not given unless the line was open. Specific events, the shadow of disunion, for example, furnished a motive for the bill's passage.[3] It was thus hardly a concrete statement of a general policy of federal aid.

At the local level, however, government could and did come to the financial assistance of industry. Communities had once given land and water powers to the proprietors of essential industries, grist mills, for example. States also had long given to corporations theoretically serving a public interest, such as educational and religious institutions, orphanages, hospitals, and cemeteries, an exemption from taxation. In the first half of the nineteenth century states found it logical to extend a tax exemption, whole or partial, to the securities or franchises of banks and railroads, which obviously developed the economy.[4] In the eyes of many states and cities industry fell in the same category. Generally this favor relieved for a limited time a manufacturing enterprise from taxes on its real property in land and factories.[5] The case for this form of promotion had to be pretty convincing, for American democracy held deep-seated notions of equality in taxes. The result of an irrevocable exemption from taxation, said some dissenting justices of the Supreme Court, "would be to exempt the rich from taxation, and cast all the burden of the support of the government, and the payment of its debts, on those who are too poor or too honest to purchase such immunity."[6] Besides under this discrimination existing enterprises in effect paid a subsidy to new or competitive ones.

Another device for encouraging industry, a governmental contract for the purchase of articles and hence the provision of a sure market, was not so much a deliberate resort to promotional policy as incidental to governmental needs. Northern industries, just emerging from the depression of 1857, received large government contracts during the Civil War. While patriotism and individual pride often motivated the business response to these opportunities, government orders were also very profitable. As

[3] Robert L. Thompson, *Wiring a Continent: The History of the Telegraph Industry in the United States, 1832–1866* (Princeton: Princeton University Press, 1947), pp. 348–355, 515–517.

[4] James F. Colby, "Exemption from Taxation by Legislative Contract," *American Law Review*, XIII (October, 1878), 29–32; E. C. Kirkland, *Men, Cities and Transportation: A Study in New England History, 1820–1900* (Cambridge: Harvard University Press, 1948), II, 314–316; T. N. Cooley, *A Treatise on the Law of Taxation, Including the Law of Local Assessment* (Chicago: Callaghan and Company, 1883), pp. 9–11, 52–56.

[5] C. T. Main, "Valuation of Textile Manufacturing Property," *Transactions of the American Society of Mechanical Engineers*, XIX (November–December, 1897), 123; Testimony of C. H. McDermott, *Report of the Industrial Commission*, I, 103; Testimony of H. N. Eaton, *Report of the Industrial Commission*, VII, 366; Testimony of C. D. Wright, *Report of the Industrial Commission*, VII, 24.

[6] Colby, "Exemption from Taxation by Legislative Contract," *loc. cit.*, p. 38.

Abram S. Hewitt, the Eastern ironmaster, wrote, "I think the Ordnance Bureau will give us the business of making gun iron and the result will be to make the company a profitable concern." [7] Nor was such stimulus confined to wartimes. The Midvale Steel Company secured in 1875 an order for gun forgings for howitzers. "It was from this small beginning that Midvale's big government business grew." [8] There are grave doubts, however, whether such governmental business was really of decisive importance in peacetime. The armor plate which Carnegie furnished the new navy—its alleged imperfections once raised a fearful rumpus in the nineties—constituted only 3,000 tons of the concern's total annual production of 2,000,000 tons of steel.[9] Close as the Du Pont firm, manufacturers of explosives, had always been to the national government, its powder production was, with the exception of wartimes, primarily for civilian purposes—mining, construction, and the like.[10]

THE TARIFF AND BUSINESS

Governmental assistance through tax exemptions and through providing a market for industry pales during this period in comparison with assistance via the tariff. Even before the outbreak of the Civil War, Congress had begun a retreat from the liberal doctrines of an untaxed trade, as exemplified in the tariff of 1857, but the voracious financial needs of the Civil War and of handling the war debt after Appomattox quickened the change of policy.[11] At a time when a desperate government resorted to the printing of paper money, it was hardly likely that it would pause for a detailed scrutiny of customs duties or the academic discussion of general theory. What the Treasury needed was money in a hurry. Civil War tariff legislation with its high protective duties consequently paid little regard "to acknowledged politico-economic laws or precedents." [12]

[7] Allan Nevins, *Abram S. Hewitt, with Some Account of Peter Cooper* (New York: Harper and Brothers, 1935), pp. 194–195, 211–212; F. A. Shannon, *The Organization and Administration of the Union Army, 1861–1865* (Cleveland: Arthur H. Clark Company, 1928), I, 53–148; J. B. Hodgskin, "The Financial Condition of the United States," *North American Review*, CVIII (April, 1869), 525.

[8] F. B. Copley, *Frederick W. Taylor: Father of Scientific Management* (New York: Harper and Brothers, 1923), I, 114; David A. Wells, "The Meaning of Revenue Reform," *North American Review*, CXIII (July, 1871), 113.

[9] B. J. Hendrick, *The Life of Andrew Carnegie* (Garden City: Doubleday, Doran & Company, 1932), II, appendix p. 404.

[10] William Haynes, editor, *American Chemical Industry: The Chemical Companies* (New York: D. Van Nostrand Company, 1949), VI, 127–129; B. G. Du Pont, *E. I. Du Pont de Nemours and Company: A History, 1802–1902* (Boston: Houghton Mifflin Company, 1920), pp. 116–136.

[11] F. W. Taussig, *The Tariff History of the United States*, 7th ed. (New York: G. P. Putnam's Sons, 1923), pp. 135–139.

[12] "Report of the United States Revenue Commission," *House Executive Document* No. 33 (s.n. 1255), 39th Cong., 1st Sess., p. 2.

Once the war was over, though scattered reductions were made, a return to earlier policy proved impossible.[13] A general revision of the tariff in 1883 made few changes, and then in 1890 with the McKinley Act a new turn to protection took place. After a standstill in the Wilson-Gorman Act of 1894, protection reached its peak in the Dingley Tariff of 1897.[14]

Actually, words such as "extreme" or percentage figures for the level of duties on protected items—there was a free list—are misleading in the case of these particular enactments. Necessity remained throughout the years the mother of protection. There was a rough correlation between the passage of tariff acts and periods of prosperity and depression. In 1875 an across-the-board reduction of 10 per cent, made in 1872 before the panic of 1873, was quietly erased; [15] in the comparative prosperity of the early eighties even protectionists conceded the necessity of some reductions; [16] and in the nineties, though the connection between the tariff level and industrial prosperity had by this time become confused with morality and heresy, tariff acts came at critical times along the curve of business fluctuations.[17] Since these acts attempted to drive in span the mismatched horses of governmental revenue and industrial welfare, general arguments for policy and responses to conditions in the public or private sector of the economy were difficult to disentangle.

One school of thought maintained that tariffs should be for revenue only, that protective features were unwise and illegitimate. Theoretically these spokesmen based their case upon the classic arguments for the international devision of labor and enterprise; each region should devote its human and other resources to the productions in which it had a comparative advantage in costs and should exchange its products, thus cheaply made, for the products cheaply made elsewhere.[18] Nor was this argument merely speculative. Americans were quite aware that Great Britain was the greatest industrial nation of the world and were eager to equal or surpass her. The logical path to success was to imitate her policy, and Great Britain was the fortress of free trade. She imported cheap food and commodities for her working populations and cheap raw materials to be transformed into finished manufactured articles which she succeeded in selling abroad. She was a trading as well as a manufacturing nation.[19]

[13] Taussig, *op. cit.*, pp. 17–192.

[14] *Ibid.*, pp. 230–360.

[15] *Ibid.*, pp. 190–191.

[16] *Ibid.*, pp. 239–249.

[17] *Ibid.*, pp. 251–360.

[18] J. F. Tallant to Edward Atkinson, June 18, 1869, Atkinson Papers, Massachusetts Historical Society; A. T. Rice, "Maxims and Markets," *North American Review*, CXLVII (October, 1888), 461; David A. Wells, "How Shall the Nation Regain Prosperity?" *North American Review*, CXXV (September, 1877), 284–285.

[19] Rice, "Maxims and Markets," *loc. cit.*, p. 465; R. Q. Mills, "The Gladstone-Blaine Controversy," *North American Review*, CL (February, 1890), 151–160; "Re-

Consequently, American reformers of a moderate persuasion felt we should at least adopt free trade in raw materials.[20] The superabundance of federal revenues in the eighties seemed to justify a modest step in that direction. Thus, while Cleveland in his famous tariff message of December, 1887, could not forego completely a discussion of tariff theory, he drove home his argument otherwise: "Our progress toward a wise conclusion [the revision of taxation] will not be improved by dwelling upon the theories of protection and free trade. This savors too much of bandying epithets. It is a *condition* which confronts us, not a theory." [21] Of course the supporters of protection preferred to reduce the surplus and stimulate business by a more lavish and more embracing program of government expenditures.[22]

Such proposals were mere decorations for an occasion. The continuing argument for a protective tariff was that it was essential for industrial diversification and expansion. American investors would not undertake the establishment of untried or uncertain enterprises unless the tariff counterbalanced the cheaper costs of foreign competitors.[23] Nor did the case stop with benefits to capitalists. In the realm of costs the argument emphasized labor costs, the nominal rate of wages. Protection, therefore, was essential for workers as it enabled them to secure a higher level of wages; protection by creating new industries enlarged opportunities for employment. Arguments of this sort were peculiarly cogent at a time of depression psychosis. Even Cleveland had to recognize their appeal.[24] Others, somewhat more perceptive, such as F. W. Taylor, asserted the American rate of wages reflected the superior efficiency of the American worker, or could be made to do so if a scheme of scientific management were introduced.[25]

As science rode high, wide and handsome and rapid changes in economic affairs and in tariff acts unsettled calculations of businessmen, many felt that Congressional legislation, prone to the exchange of favors

---

port of the Special Commissioner of the Revenue," *House Executive Document* No. 27 (s.n. 1416), 41st Cong., 2d Sess., p. xxxviii.

[20] "Report of the Special Commissioner of the Revenue," *Senate Executive Document* No. 2 (s.n. 1276), 39th Cong., 2d Sess., pp. 34, 66.

[21] J. D. Richardson, *A Compilation of the Messages and Papers of the Presidents, 1789–1902* (New York: Bureau of National Literature and Art, 1903), VIII, 590.

[22] J. M. Laughlin, "The Evils of the Sub-Treasury System," *North American Review*, CXXXVII (November, 1883), 560; W. M. Grosvenor, "What Shall be Done with the Surplus?" *North American Review*, CXLIV (January, 1887), 81; Henry Rogers, "A Monetary Whim," *North American Review*, CXLV (October, 1887), 455; T. B. Reed, "Spending the Public Money," *North American Review*, CLIV (March, 1892), 319.

[23] W. E. Gladstone, James G. Blaine, "A Duel- Free Trade, Protection," *North American Review*, CLIV (March, 1892), 41–43, 47.

[24] Richardson, *op. cit.*, p. 341.

[25] F. W. Taylor, "A Piece-Rate System," *Transactions of the American Society of Mechanical Engineers*, XVI (June, 1895), 882.

and to partisan considerations, was no way to make a tariff; science should do the job. As soon as the Civil War ended, Congress established a United States Revenue Commission, whose chairman was David A. Wells, to study and make recommendations. Wells naturally thought the new device would avoid a slavery to current pressures or to private interests.[26] Though this particular reliance upon the expert did not last beyond 1870, Congress in 1882 established a Tariff Commission. Its chairman, John L. Hayes, was the Secretary of the Wool Manufacturers' Association, an effective lobby for protection! [27] As time went on and act succeeded act, the business world longed for an end to vacillation. Boards of Trade and Chambers of Commerce were diverted from "their own legitimate affairs" into "watching and protesting to Congress," wrote one dejected businessman.[28] And in the mid-nineties no less a business leader than Andrew Carnegie thought the tariff should be revised only once every ten years "except in an emergency," for business found it trying to adjust to frequent and violent changes.[29]

By this time, too, Congressional action in regulating business, for example the Interstate Commerce Act and the Sherman Anti-Trust Act, and in the realm of labor legislation had revealed unmistakably the inherent dangers in the ideological precedents furnished by protection. The advocates of free trade had long pointed out that, "The conditions of prosperity are in the main natural, the gift of God, entirely independent of laws. . . . If the whole truth were shown, it would be found that nearly every instance of growth that could be cited . . . has been made in spite of legislation and that legislation has usually been a hindrance." [30] Now they could ask, "Has not the long-continued existence of this system [protection] given a tendency to the hardly disguised socialistic movements of the present day?" [31]

[26] "Report of the United States Revenue Commission," *House Executive Document* No. 34 (s.n. 1255), 39th Cong., 1st Sess., p. 2; D. A. Wells to Edward Atkinson, April 6, 1865, Atkinson Papers, Massachusetts Historical Society; Same to Same, July 14, 1866, Same to Same, April 9, 1867, Same to Same, September 21, 1868; *Nation,* VIII (January 14, 1869), 24–25.

[27] Taussig, *Tariff History,* pp. 231–232; *Nation,* X (June 9, 1870), 359; (June 23, 1870), 398.

[28] Edward Kemble, "Business Revival," *North American Review,* CLIX (November, 1894), 612–614; *Nation,* X (April 14, 1870), 234.

[29] Andrew Carnegie, "What Would I Do with the Tariff if I Were Czar?" *Forum,* XIX (March, 1895), 25–27.

[30] D. A. Wells, "The Meaning of Revenue Reform," *loc. cit.,* p. 115; W. G. Sumner, "Evils of the Tariff System," *North American Review,* CXXXIX (September, 1884), 293.

[31] Edward Atkinson, "What Shall be Taxed? What Shall be Exempt?" *The Industrial Progress of the Nation* (New York: G. P. Putnam's Sons, 1890), pp. 262–263.

Whatever politicians or special interests believed or accomplished, there was contemporary though contradictory evidence that in the realm of theory and argument the case for free trade had prevailed. In 1880 Wells was writing to Edward Atkinson, "The thinking intelligent minds are all one way." [32] A few years later the editor of Lalor's *Cyclopaedia of Political Science* apologized for including in the work an article on protection. Something could indeed be said in favor of excluding it "since the cyclopaedia is a scientific work; and a consensus of political economists may be said to exist as to the truth, and therefore as to the expediency, of the principles of free trade." [33] So apologetic a tone for an article which derided protection as a system "clearly disastrous to the people" and "opposed to progress in wealth and civilization" and ascribed its existence to a hangover "of barbarism," was extraordinary.[34]

Clearly something other than inherent logic accounted for the continuance of the protective system. Though the South retained in general its traditional hostility to protection—"to be for free trade," commented Henry Adams, was like "having worn a rebel uniform or having been out with the Ku-Klux klan" [35]—most regions and the two political parties were split on the tariff question. The significant alignment was one of economic interests. Wedded to the protective tariff were a considerable number of farmers. Many received direct protection on the things they produced, wool, sugar, hemp, flax; some were impressed by the argument that the tariff gave them a home market.[36] However much figures demonstrated that the number of wage earners in protected industries was a minority of producers,[37] the dogma that a protective tariff increased wages and employment opportunities had a wide hold upon labor leaders and followers.[38]

[32] David A. Wells to Edward Atkinson, December 14, 1880, Atkinson Papers, Massachusetts Historical Society.

[33] John J. Lalor, ed., *Cyclopedia of Political Science* (New York: Charles E. Merrill & Co., 1888), III, 440.

[34] David H. Mason, "Protection in the United States," J. J. Lalor, ed., *Cyclopedia of Political Science,* III, 416.

[35] Henry B. Adams, "The Session," *North American Review,* CXI (July, 1870), 45.

[36] Taussig, *Tariff History,* pp. 248–249, 274–275, 291, 308–309; Testimony of Malachi F. Dodge, *Report of the Committee* [on Education and Labor] *of the Senate . . . 1885,* III, 127–135; Chester W. Wright, *Wool-Growing and the Tariff. A Study in the Economic History of the United States* (Boston: Houghton Mifflin Company, 1910), pp. 208 ff.

[37] Edward Atkinson, "Common Sense Applied to the Tariff Question," *Popular Science Monthly,* XXXVII (September, 1890), 593–596.

[38] Testimony of Edward King, John Garrett, and others, *Report of the Committee* [on Education and Labor] *of the Senate . . . 1885,* I, 696–698, 1122–1126, 1136; II, 9, 14–15, 16–18; III, 129–130, 593–599.

The real clash on the tariff was not between thinkers, and doers [39] or between the haves and have-nots, but within the ranks of businessmen themselves. Import duties on coal, iron ore, and pig iron, for instance, hampered iron and steel works in New England and elsewhere along the Atlantic coast.[40] A traditional industry such as cottons no longer needed protection on its commoner fabrics and favored a trade policy designed to expand international exchanges.[41] The powerful phalanx of railroad managers, promoters and investors on the whole preferred low or no duties on railroad iron and dispatched a lobbyist to Washington to forward their viewpoint.[42] The trading or mercantile community, including exporters, importers and, to a less extent, bankers, were not enthusiastic about protection.[43] Nor were capitalists of this persuasion without spokesmen. The *Nation*, in season and out, belabored the point that protection was against natural law and subverted the virtues, for example self-help, of private capitalists.

A split of this sort within the business community led to bitterness and extravagance. James M. Swank writing to Edward Atkinson, the most garrulous of free trade exponents, under the letter head of the American Iron and Steel Institute, a trade association revived in 1864 in large part to gain tariff favors,[44] anticipated apocalypse if the Association went over to Free Trade. "There will be little left of the great iron and steel industries of this country." [45] Since such thinking was "Pennsylvanian," it was not surprising that Atkinson wrote his wife during a journey in 1867 through that state that "her people are ignorant and her schools bad. . . . The business men are obstinate and pig headed." [46]

Few issues in American history have involved contemporaries in the expenditure of so much time and energy as has the tariff; few have called

[39] George P. Fisher, "The Writings of Mr. Roland G. Hazard," *North American Review*, CIX (October, 1869), 368–369.

[40] Nevins, *op. cit.*, pp. 262–263, 555; Taussig, *Tariff History*, pp. 270–271, 298–299; S. W. Mendum, "The Question Clubs and the Tariff," *North American Review*, CL (March, 1890), 303.

[41] Taussig, *Tariff History*, p. 243; "On the Collection of Revenue, by Edward Atkinson," *North American Review*, CV (July, 1867), 281.

[42] A. D. Chandler, Jr., *Henry Varnum Poor* (Cambridge: Harvard University Press, 1956), pp. 182–186, 238–244.

[43] *Commercial and Financial Chronicle*, XLVIII (March 16, 1889), 350–351; L (May 31, 1890), 757; *Twenty-first Annual Report of the Chamber of Commerce of New York, 1878–1879* (New York: Chamber of Commerce Press, 1879), p. 32; Testimony of John Wanamaker, *Report of the Industrial Commission*, VII, 468.

[44] Chandler, *op. cit.*, p. 243.

[45] James M. Swank to Edward Atkinson, January 2, 1889, Atkinson Papers, Massachusetts Historical Society.

[46] Edward Atkinson to Mary Atkinson, October 21, 1867, Atkinson Papers, Massachusetts Historical Society.

forth retrospectively more study and analysis. It should be possible consequently to know in a general way what the effectiveness of the tariff had been. Though the inflow of funds to the Federal Treasury can be stated, this test is a minor matter in a policy in essence promotional. Apparently protection in this period furthered within the boundaries of the United States the manufacture of certain woolens, for example worsteds; of certain metallurgical products, for example tin plate; and the growth of new industries such as silk.[47]

But the measurements of countervailing costs to consumers and to the economy, and the apportionment of responsibility for growth among several factors baffles ingenuity. F. W. Taussig, whose books sought to appraise tariffs in terms of performance, concluded, "To judge a very moderate measure like that of 1894 by its visible fruits is so difficult as to touch the bounds of the impossible. The effects on any particular industry —which are but a fragmentary bit of evidence as to the promotion of general prosperity,—are sufficiently difficult to trace. . . . Even after the lapse of time, there could hardly be such an unmistakable result one way or the other as to prevent doubt and dispute." [48] Andrew Carnegie, whose hankerings for a measure of protection were muted, counselled Edward Atkinson against spending too much time on the tariff. The steel king thought the tariff was "trifling." [49] On a public occasion he once announced that "Tariffs never bothered me very much." [50]

THE PATENT SYSTEM

A like judgment on the patent system, the other great aid of the national government to industry, would fly in the face of facts. The formative period of the patent system began with the Constitution which assigned without question to the Federal government the power to "promote the Progress of science and useful Arts, by securing for limited Times to Authors and Inventors the exclusive Right to their respective Writings and Discoveries." [51] By 1861 statute and practice had determined that the nation would not issue patents for the discovery of scientific principles—these belonged in the public domain—but only for novel and

[47] F. W. Taussig, *Some Aspects of the Tariff Question* (Cambridge: Harvard University Press, 1915), pp. 176–177, 217–218, 336.

[48] Taussig, *Tariff History,* pp. 318–319.

[49] Andrew Carnegie to Edward Atkinson, January 3, 1890, Atkinson Papers, Massachusetts Historical Society.

[50] Testimony of Carnegie, *Hearings before the* [Stanley] *Committee on Investigation of the United States Steel Company,* III, 2459.

[51] Henry S. Commager, editor, *Documents of American History* (New York: Appleton-Century-Crofts, 1949), p. 141; Max Farrand, editor, *The Records of the Federal Convention of 1787* (New Haven: Yale University Press, 1911), II, 505, 595.

useful machines and devices, that the duration of a patent grant should be seventeen years, and that a Patent Office was the proper administrator of these affairs.[52] In 1860 the Patent Office granted 4,363 patents for inventions; in 1897, 22,098.[53] If numbers be all, the patent system would thus seem to have succeeded in stimulating the course of invention. Certainly few would doubt the desirability, from a social point of view, of this objective; the method, the grant of an exclusive enjoyment for a period, was more questionable. But even Thomas Jefferson, on all fronts a foe of privilege, had thought the grant of a monopoly in the productions of the mind was an essential incentive.

More practically the inventors in the post-Civil War years generally secured the rewards for their discoveries. There were few parallels to the earlier experience of Eli Whitney and Charles Goodyear. Henry Bessemer, Alexander Graham Bell, Thomas A. Edison, George Westinghouse, for example, were rewarded for their innovations.[54] And this in spite of the fact, frequently observed in the history of invention, that a blueprint and a model were not necessarily a working machine and that the process a machine was designed to improve was not necessarily a commercially feasible one. To its success the contributions of speculators, investors, and organizers were also an essential prelude. The owners of the patents for the McKay stitcher for making shoes spent $200,000 before anything was realized on it,[55] and F. W. Taylor and his associates cut up more than 800,000 pounds of iron and steel and spent $150,000 to $200,000 of other people's money in the course of their experiments in cutting steel.[56]

Celebrating in 1891 the centenary of the patent system, President Harrison informed a convention of inventors and manufacturers that it was "a great step in the progress of civilization when the law took notice of property in the fruit of the mind." [57] In spite of the "applause" which greeted this evaluation, some contemporaries differed. A few denied

[52] A. Hunter Dupree, *Science in the Federal Government: A History of Policies and Activities to 1940* (Cambridge: Harvard University Press, 1957), pp. 9–14, 46–47.

[53] Bureau of the Census, *Historical Statistics of the United States, 1789–1945,* pp. 312–313.

[54] "Topical discussion by Allan Stirling on the Bessemer Process," *Transactions of the American Society of Mechanical Engineers,* XVIII (1896), 490.

[55] George A. Rich, "The Development of American Industries since Columbus: Manufacture of Boots and Shoes," *Popular Science Monthly,* XLI (August, 1892), 507.

[56] F. W. Taylor, "On the Art of Cutting Metals," *Transactions of the American Society of Mechanical Engineers,* XXVIII (1906), 35.

[57] *Proceedings and Addresses: Celebration of the Second Century of the American Patent System at Washington City, D.C. . . . 1891* (Washington: Gedney & Roberts Co., 1892), p. 23.

that the prizes of the patent system were necessary. It was claimed that the stimulus to invention was not gain but that inventors were the sharers in the mind of God and were driven to invention by a sort of Promethean compulsion to bring back from Heaven's Gate the application of science to art.[58] After all, it was the daughter of the Commissioner of Patents who chose the first message "What hath God wrought" for Morse's telegraph.[59]

Others, like F. A. Walker, President of Massachusetts Institute of Technology, felt the patent system was of minor importance. "While our patent laws have encouraged specific invention and have multiplied a hundred-fold the contrivances, great and small, useful and futile, which have been put upon the market . . . the *power to invent,* which inheres to so remarkable a degree in our people, was created altogether irrespective of, and long antecedently to, that system of legislation. It is with us an inheritance; and it is fairly a matter of question whether that inheritance has not been impaired rather than increased by our patent laws." Walker thought the immigration of "inferior" races and the absorption of wealth and effort by agriculture had slowed the exercise of this inheritance and the growth of manufactures.[60] The undemonstrable character of these assertions is certainly evidence that the causes of invention are largely conjectural.

Far more tangible were the business results of patent laws. Indubitably their operation heightened the uncertainty and wastefulness of industry. Often there was a prodigal expenditure of effort and money to invent something already invented but different enough not to infringe the patents of others and to be in turn patentable. Or there was the lavish and wasteful purchase of existing patents on the mere ground that they might be useful.[61] Such anxiety was understandable, for an invention for doing a thing in a better fashion could draw the value from preceding methods and render whole installations obsolete. As Holley observed in 1875, the steel industry "cannot be revolutionized all at once, however desirable the technical results might be; for that would bankrupt

[58] Chauncey Smith, "A Century of Patent Law," *Quarterly Journal of Economics,* V (October, 1890), 48–50, 58–61; O. H. Platt, "Invention and Achievement," *Proceedings and Addresses: Celebration of the Second Century of the American Patent System,* pp. 63–65; Holland Thompson, *The Age of Invention: Chronicles of America* (New Haven: Yale University Press, 1921), XXXVII, 165.

[59] Mabee, *op. cit.,* pp. 259–260, 275.

[60] F. A. Walker, "American Manufactures," *Discussions in Economics and Statistics* (New York: Henry Holt and Company, 1893), II, 179–189.

[61] Passer, *op. cit.,* pp. 144–145, 160–161, 277–279; W. T. Hutchinson, *Cyrus Hall McCormick: Harvest, 1856–1884* (New York: D. Appleton-Century Company, 1935), pp. 544–572.

the business at large." [62] In an era with enough uncertainties, the patent system with its threats of infringements, court suits, and damages presented producers with the additional prospect of losses of great magnitude. Everyone, for instance, seemed to have invented the telephone and clogged the Patent Office with applications or caveats on or about the time Alexander Graham Bell secured his patent. The Bell Telephone Company spent years fighting claimants in the courts. In 1887 the Supreme Court by a majority of 4 to 3 validated the Bell discovery.[63] The Company participated first and last in six hundred court cases, many of them against outright charlatans and fraudulent companies.[64] The possible jokers in the patent process were again revealed when George B. Selden, a patent attorney and scientific tinkerer, invented a road engine in 1879 and patented it in 1895. Though he never found the means to manufacture any automobiles, the federal courts for a long time declared he had anticipated many essential features of the motor car and Selden collected royalties from most manufacturers except Henry Ford.[65]

Uncertainties of this sort businessmen met, as they met others during this period, by cooperation. Steel manufacturers, for instance, were appalled by a possible controversy over the competing patents of William Kelly and Henry Bessemer. "Lawyers must be paid! Experts would not testify gratuitously! Costs of court would accumulate! Judges were doubtful! Jurors were uncertain, and then, if victorious, what would they gain? And if defeated, utter ruin would overwhelm them!" As a result they pooled, shared, and licensed patents through the trustees of a special corporation. A reduction in fees and royalties followed.[66] In the electrical industry Edison's firm long refrained from launching patent litigation against its rivals, including Westinghouse; but in the nineties both contestants initiated a multitude of suits. In 1896 General Electric and Westinghouse pooled their patents and agreed to pay royalties to the

[62] American Institute of Mining Engineers, *Memorial of Alexander Lyman Holley* (New York: American Institute of Mining Engineers, 1884), pp. 182–183; *Nation,* XXX (January 29, 1880), 72.

[63] Telephone Cases, 126 *United States,* 531, 573.

[64] A. F. Harlow, *Old Wires and New Waves* (New York: D. Appleton-Century Company, 1936), pp. 367 ff.; J. W. Stehman, *The Financial History of the American Telephone and Telegraph Company* (Boston: Houghton Mifflin Company, 1925), pp. 13–18.

[65] "George Baldwin Selden," *Dictionary of American Biography,* XVI, 567–568; Electric Vehicle Company *v.* C. A. Duerr & Company, 172 *Federal Reporter,* 923.

[66] W. F. Durfee, "The Development of American Industries since Columbus: The Manufacture of Steel," *Popular Science Monthly,* XL (November, 1891), 28–29; R. W. Hunt, "A History of Bessemer Manufacture in America," *Transactions of the American Institute of Mining Engineers,* V (1876), 201–202, 204; J. M. Swank, "Iron and Steel Production," *Tenth Census of the United States, 1880,* II, 861.

other if either exceeded sales quotas.[67] Earlier General Electric had been formed largely to consolidate companies possessing essential patents.

Clearly the patent system might lead to bigness, if not to monopoly.[68] Edison, opposing the General Electric consolidation, wrote, "If you make the coalition, my usefulness as an inventor is gone. My services wouldn't be worth a penny. I can invent only under powerful incentive. No competition means no invention." [69] Edison was exaggerating, in human fashion. The incentive of business advantage explained the institutionalization of invention through laboratories for research, experiment and technology. Larger concerns, if assured of gain, could afford the overhead investment in invention and distribute this fixed cost more advantageously over their larger output.

PRIDE AND PREJUDICE

More than any particular statute or judicial decision, the spirit of nationalism stimulated industrial development. The absence of centralized planning, direction and control did not mean the absence of a grand design. It simply meant that private persons formulated goals and devised the means to reach them. Inferiority to foreign producers was humiliating. From overseas Abram Hewitt wrote back to his brother: "They beat us to death in France." [70] One of Taylor's hearers years later thought that if the master's system were introduced, "No country in the world would compete with North America." [71] Of course America's chief competitor and examplar was Great Britain, the traditional sovereign of the industrial transformation: "England, our rival always, our friend in business never." [72] Against her were pitted American ingenuity and American enterprise. It was left to John D. Rockefeller, the tycoon of tycoons, to summarize with becoming serenity the spirit of the age: "I saw a marvelous future for our country, and I wanted to participate in the work of making our country great. I had an ambition to build." [73] This spirit was not confined to business leaders and publicists; it also infected engineers and workers.[74]

[67] Passer, *op. cit.*, pp. 329–334.

[68] *Ibid.*, pp. 324–327; A. A. Bright, *The Electric-Lamp Industry* (New York: Macmillan Company, 1949), pp. 143–148, 156–159.

[69] Passer, *op. cit.*, pp. 321–322, 352.

[70] Nevins, *op. cit.*, p. 240.

[71] Topical Discussion by H. Emerson, *Transactions of the American Society of Mechanical Engineers,* XXIV (1903), 1464.

[72] Rice, "Maxims and Markets," *loc. cit.*, p. 466.

[73] John Flynn, *God's Gold: The Story of Rockefeller and His Times* (New York: Harcourt, Brace and Company, 1932), p. 201.

[74] John Fritz, *The Autobiography of John Fritz* (New York: John Wiley & Sons, 1912), dedication and preface.

Surveying the "importation of the factory system to this country" for the census of 1880, Carroll D. Wright ascribed it to "patriotism and statute law . . . the result of both moral and economic forces." [75] Edward Atkinson provided specific explanations for American ability to compete with England and the Continent. "Our chief advantage" was in "an alleged versatility and power of adapting means to ends, and in great quickness of perception on the part of the working people in respect to the advantages to be gained by the adoption of new processes or inventions." The causes for this national characteristic were to be found in "First. Our system of common and purely secular schools attended by the children of rich and poor alike. Second. Manhood suffrage. Third. The easy acquisition of land. Fourth. The habit of saving small sums, induced by the establishment of savings-banks throughout the manufacturing states. Fifth. The absence of a standing army, and the application of revenue derived from taxes on the whole to useful purposes." [76] To these causes might be added the widespread conviction that production was the way to welfare. In sum, the character of American institutions, many of them outside the economy, explained the nation's industrial triumph.

[75] Wright, *loc. cit., Tenth Census of the United States. 1880.* II, 538.

[76] Edward Atkinson, "The Cotton Manufacture," *Tenth Census of the United States. 1880,* II, 949; O. H. Platt, *loc. cit.*, pp. 60–63.

CHAPTER X

The Organization of Production

THE DELIGHTS AND DANGERS OF SIMPLICITY

THE simplest form for the organization of production is the individual proprietorship in which an individual owns the property and manages manufacturing operations. But even in the early days of the industrial transformation the partnership, a scarcely more complicated form of organization, had brought together individuals in an industrial operation. This had been true, for instance, of the cotton mill in Rhode Island, commonly asserted to be the birthplace of the American cotton industry.[1] Both arrangements had many advantages. They made easy the entrance of individuals into industrial operations. Under the partnership, for instance, owners of diverse assets did not all need to furnish money. One might contribute a waterpower, another construction material for the mill, a third his skill as a workman, a fourth his ability as a marketer.[2] There was, furthermore, a widespread belief that in the more rudimentary forms of organization, the managers, since they had a genuine stake in an enterprise, would be more energetic, efficient and prudent in the conduct of its affairs. The sharpest of all stimuli, self-interest, would be directly at work. Mere agents would lack this motivation.[3]

The arguments for these arrangements were not confined to the economic sphere; they were just as likely to be political and social and wear an equalitarian air which appealed to strong strains in American

[1] C. F. Ware, *The Early New England Cotton Manufacture: A Study in Industrial Beginnings* (Boston: Houghton Mifflin Company, 1931), pp. 19–20.

[2] *Ibid.*, pp. 127–129; B. E. Hazard, *The Organization of the Boot and Shoe Industry in Massachusetts before 1875* (Cambridge: Harvard University Press, 1921), pp. 71–72.

[3] Ware, *op. cit.*, pp. 132–133; Louis Hartz, *Economic Policy and Democratic Thought: Pennsylvania, 1776–1860* (Cambridge: Harvard University Press, 1948), pp. 57–58; Testimony of Andrew Carnegie, *Hearings before the* [Stanley] *Committee on Investigation of United States Steel Corporation*, III, 2417–2418.

thought. This sort of thinking did not die away with the Civil War.[4] On the contrary it was probably one of the chief explanations for the measures taken thereafter to regulate big business enterprise.

Be that as it may, there were some disadvantages to the partnership form of organization. In 1899 John R. Dos Passos, a New York lawyer, "talking by the card of history," informed the Industrial Commission that partnerships, which went back to the time of the ancient Greeks, had demonstrated three defects: "Each partner was liable for the debts" of the partnership regardless of his exact contribution; "when one of the partners died the business was at an end"; and finally a creditor "could not bring suit against the partnership without suing each of the parties, which was very disadvantageous."[5] Contemporary practice also demonstrated the inflexibility of the partnership arrangement. When Carnegie and his associates were building at Pittsburgh and elsewhere their great industrial empire, they long operated under a partnership agreement. Since they feared that a partner or his heirs might transfer his share to hostile or incompetent parties and since they also wished to terminate the participation of anyone who became undesirable or failed to meet expectations or who could not get along with his partners, the members of the group signed an iron-clad agreement to the effect that, if two-thirds of the entire partnership voted for anyone's retirement from the firm, his partnership ceased and he must retire.[6] These and other provisions involved the Carnegie partnership in misunderstanding and litigation.[7]

THE CORPORATION

But contemporaries neither appraised nor utilized these more elementary forms of organization in a vacuum; they constantly compared them with alternatives, the chief of which was incorporation under charter from the state. Judged in terms of economic usefulness, the corporation had what the partnership lacked: the death or withdrawal of a shareholder did not terminate its existence; the individual investor might have his liability for a corporation's debt limited to the amount of his own investment; owners could easily give, sell, or otherwise transfer their shares. In short the corporation possessed a possible permanence which

[4] "Report of the Special Commissioner of the Revenue," *House Executive Document* No. 27 (s.n. 1416), 41st Cong., 2d Sess., pp. xxxiv–xxxvi.

[5] Testimony of John R. Dos Passos, *Report of the Industrial Commission*, I, 1146–1147.

[6] Testimony of Andrew Carnegie, *loc. cit.*, pp. 2348, 2397.

[7] B. J. Hendrick, *The Life of Andrew Carnegie* (Garden City: Doubleday, Doran & Company, 1932), I, 135, 300–301.

was one aspect of that stability upon which the age was so insistent. Finally, its stocks and bonds were a most effective means of marshaling the subscriptions of many investors into an aggregated capital for considerable enterprises.[8] This helped to explain, along with their public interest character, why the corporation first appeared in this country in banking and in transportation enterprises.[9] Corporate expansion was a necessary prelude to commercial, territorial and railroad expansion. "As handmaids, they marched together toward the goal of commercial, territorial, literary, moral and religious development which the Almighty has destined us to reach in this country." [10]

Such rhetoric could not entirely dispel doubts. On the economic and moral plane suspicion of the separation of managership and ownership persisted; only new methods of intra-corporate control and supervision and new incentives or "conscience" could bridge the gap.[11] In the larger field of ideals, a corporate charter had long been regarded as bestowing upon incorporators a privilege; such favoritism, it was said, was incompatible with a democratic society in which the same business opportunities should be open to all. The corporation, it was charged, was essentially a "monopoly" with all its inherent dangers and injustices; since it was only an artificial person it was "mercenary" and "soulless." [12] One way to handle these dangers was to cease issuing charters or to bestow them only upon small businesses.[13] Another solution was to reconcile anti-charter thought to the admitted economic need for corporations. One line of legislation, therefore, sought to protect the investor against the managers of "his" company through regulations about proxies, business decisions reserved for stockholders, details of annual meetings, and a requirement that directors, to qualify for their job, must own stock.[14]

[8] Testimony of F. L. Stetson, *Report of the Industrial Commission,* I, 981–982; Testimony of John R. Dos Passos, *loc. cit.,* pp. 1148–1149.

[9] William Miller, "A Note on the History of Business Corporations in Pennsylvania, 1800–1860," *Quarterly Journal of Economics,* LV (November, 1940), 154–158; W. C. Kessler, "Incorporation in New England: A Statistical Study, 1800–1875," *Journal of Economic History,* VIII (May, 1948), 47; G. H. Evans, Jr., *Business Incorporations in the United States, 1800–1943* (New York: National Bureau of Economic Research, 1948), p. 20.

[10] Testimony of John R. Dos Passos, *loc. cit.,* p. 1148.

[11] E. L. Godkin, "Idleness and Immorality," *Forum,* XIII (May, 1892), 335–338.

[12] Hartz, *op. cit.,* pp. 58–61, 69–79; William Jay, "The Corporation in Commerce," C. M. Depew, ed., *One Hundred Years of American Commerce* (New York: D. O. Haynes & Co., 1895), I, 47.

[13] *Nation,* XII (June 8, 1871), 398–400.

[14] John W. Cadman, Jr., *The Corporation in New Jersey: Business and Politics, 1791–1875* (Cambridge: Harvard University Press, 1949), pp. 301–326.

Corporate champions continually pointed out that corporations enrolled more investors than partnerships and that the trend was hence to a wider dispersion of ownership. Certainly the history of the Massachusetts textile corporations had demonstrated this before the Civil War, and in the nineties when the American Sugar Refining Company consolidated nine firms the average number of partners in each was three; afterwards the number of stockholders was "numbered by the thousands." [15] State legislation, also, sought to hasten the equalitarian trend by making the corporation the result not of a special but of a general enactment. Of the latter, anyone could take advantage. As we have seen, general incorporation had been applied to banking enterprises and to railroads. For a limited group of industries New York had passed such a measure as early as 1811.[16]

Beginning with the forties several states adopted constitutional provisions necessitating incorporation under general laws. Of these the first important industrial state was New York in 1846. By 1875, such arrangements had become so common that "special charters might be considered a thing of the past for most fields of enterprise in most states of the Union." [17] Somewhat paradoxically the procedure of general incorporation which appealed to corporate foes was also desired by advocates of incorporation. The new process by its simplicity and regularity eliminated the delays, expenses and legislative maneuvering involved in getting a special charter.

Among varieties of enterprises the advance of the corporation was uneven. By the last decade of the century in the three states of New Jersey, Ohio and Pennsylvania, incorporation for manufacturing purposes constituted the largest percentage of business incorporations.[18] Several years earlier in 1878, Carroll D. Wright, then Commissioner of Statistics for Labor in Massachusetts, stung by the charge that the Commonwealth was "corporation ridden," pointed out that in manufacturing there were 10,395 private establishments and only 520 corporations. In the former there were 15,733 partners; in the latter 26,058 stockholders. The private establishments employed 166,588 workers, paid $79,015,095 in wages, and manufactured goods valued at $351,325,814; the manufacturing corporations employed 101,337 persons, paid $38,860,174 in wages and produced goods valued at $180,810,519.[19]

[15] Ware, *op. cit.*, pp. 148–151; Testimony of F. B. Thurber, *Report of the Industrial Commission,* I, 7; Testimony of John R. Dos Passos, *loc. cit.*, p. 1148.

[16] W. C. Kessler, "A Statistical Study of the New York General Incorporation Act of 1811," *Journal of Political Economy,* XLVIII (December, 1940), 877–882.

[17] Evans, *op. cit.*, pp. 10–11.

[18] *Ibid.*, p. 66.

[19] *Ninth Annual Report of the* [Mass.] *Bureau of Statistics of Labor, 1878,* pp. 87–88.

THE COMBINATION MOVEMENT

No matter how enduring earlier forms of industrial organization were or how active constitutional conventions and state legislatures were on the premises, the spread of incorporation in the post-Civil War era was more the extension of an earlier movement than the beginning of a new one.

The real organizational problem of the decades after 1860 was a quite different one: the combination of corporations or the "trust [which] can, at will, abolish the law of supply and demand, [and] set aside the principle of competition which has governed the commercial world since the beginning of commerce." [20] In short the characteristic of the new period was the consolidation or combination movement. This was not a wholly novel phenomenon, for measures to attain a common industrial policy among several producers or to centralize and control an industry were well-nigh contemporaneous with the appearance of industrialism in the United States. As early as 1817 in the then comparatively unindustrialized West the salt producers of the Kanawha Valley had formed the Kanawha Salt Company, which was to set quotas of production for each enterprise, sell all the product, and determine the price.[21] When the revolutionized cotton industry came to America's shores, Almy and Brown through exhortation, if in no other way, assumed a leadership in setting prices for their own and others' yarn and sought to induce firms to act "in unison"; [22] and the "great corporations" which distinguished the industry north of Boston were generally owned and controlled by a core of common investors—Lowells, Cabots, Perkinses, Jacksons, Appletons, Dwights—whether the mills were in Maine, along the Merrimac, or in central Massachusetts. These enterprises exchanged patents and information about costs and tended to patronize the same banks and selling agents.[23] Nor was the combination movement confined to the United States. The same trend appeared in Great Britain and Germany and other countries of Western Europe.[24]

With the advent after the Civil War of high industrialism and a national railway network, the American movement toward combination

[20] V. H. Lockwood, "How to Reform Business Corporations," *North American Review*, CLXIV (March, 1897), 296.

[21] Louis C. Hunter, "Studies in the Economic History of the Ohio Valley," *Smith College Studies in History* (Northampton: Department of History, Smith College, 1934), XIX, Nos. 1–2, pp. 53–55.

[22] Ware, *op. cit.*, pp. 44–45.

[23] Vera Shlakman, "Economic History of a Factory Town: A Study of Chicopee, Massachusetts," *Smith College Studies in History* (Northampton: Department of History, Smith College, 1937), XX, Nos. 1–4, pp. 25–47.

[24] Testimony of F. B. Thurber, *loc. cit.*, pp. 8–9.

dwarfed most earlier examples. Initially the centralized organization of the new industries was informal. A group of producers with experience and with capital would proceed to bring various enterprises together through a community of interest, a joint participation in several partnerships and firms.

In the oil industry, for example, refining centers appeared in New York, Philadelphia, Baltimore, Pittsburgh, the Oil Regions, and Cleveland. In the last community John D. Rockefeller, "naturally an optimist" in his own words, who had acquired some means from a commission grocery business and who could borrow additional funds from his father or the banks, took the leadership. Gathering about him relatives and outsiders, "interesting and quick-minded men," [25] he formed in 1867 the partnership of Rockefeller, Andrews and Flagler. "The cause leading to the formation of this firm was the desire to unite our skill and capital in order to carry on a business of greater magnitude with economy and efficiency in place of the smaller business that each had heretofore conducted separately." [26] Three years later these associates and others chartered the Standard Oil Company of Ohio. The securities of this firm they gave to themselves in exchange for their own interests and used also to purchase the enterprises of oil men in Cleveland and in the other centers.[27] In this fashion they enlarged the number of able associates as well as extended the area of common policy. "This enterprise, conducted by men of application and ability working hard together, soon built up unusual facilities in manufacture, in transportation, in finance, and in extending markets." [28]

A somewhat similar development took place in iron and steel. In spite of the early Bessemer pioneering in New York State and Michigan, Pittsburgh became the steel city. Here the ore of the Great Lakes mines could meet most advantageously the fuels, coke and natural gas, of western Pennsylvania. Here also appeared Andrew Carnegie, an immigrant lad from Scotland, who even as a young man had acquired a considerable fortune from varied investments in railroads, petroleum, and metal works.[29] Like Rockefeller, Carnegie was a self-christened "sanguine man, optimistic to a degree." [30] When Carnegie wished to start an

[25] J. D. Rockefeller, *Random Reminiscences of Men and Events* (Garden City: Doubleday, Doran & Company, 1933), p. 20; R. W. Hidy and Muriel E. Hidy, *History of Standard Oil Company (New Jersey): Pioneering in Big Business, 1882–1911* (New York: Harper & Brothers, 1955), pp. 14–23.

[26] Rockefeller, *op. cit.*, p. 85.

[27] Allan Nevins, *Study in Power: John D. Rockefeller, Industrialist and Philanthropist* (New York: Charles Scribner's Sons, 1953), I, 82–87.

[28] Rockefeller, *op. cit.*, p. 83.

[29] Hendrick, *op. cit.*, I, 123–146.

[30] Testimony of Andrew Carnegie, *loc. cit.*, III, 2439.

enterprise or acquire an existing one, he usually would "get up a party" of his "dear friends" and "young geniuses." These recruits would contribute the necessary funds. On occasion, when their resources were inadequate, Carnegie would go outside the group to enlist other partners. Young men with managerial talents but without money were staked to the "party" and paid for this investment later through profits on their shares.[31] Carnegie, who expressed a preference for partnerships of one sort or another, did not achieve an overall incorporation of his enterprises until the nineties, when he was working to adjust quarrels among the partners and to sell out his holdings and retire. For this end the corporate form was prerequisite, for it put the properties in a salable form.[32]

INDUSTRIAL POOLS

Precorporate and private centralization of industrial policy and practice through a community of interest among investors and producers had the looseness and adaptability fitted to a period of rapid business changes. The arrangement also accorded with the individualism of the age. The persons concerned made their own decisions, usually without recourse to the state for authorization, and they could continue, though perhaps under somewhat different circumstances, to run their own businesses. As we have seen, the railroad pool had these qualities.

Indeed, the railroads introduced the pool into industry. Early in the seventies when Rockefeller and his allies were distressed at the chaotic condition of the oil business, the railroads were suffering from their usual competition with each other for the business of carrying oil. From the Pennsylvania and other interested railroads emerged the South Improvement Company scheme. Under its provisions the railroad carriers were to divide the oil business among themselves on a percentage basis; the oil refiners and shippers who were members of the scheme were to divide their business among the railroads according to the agreed pattern and were to receive for their endeavors as "eveners" a rebate on their own shipments. In order to administer the division effectively the "eveners" received information about the shipments of oil by their competitors and, as a sort of gratuity, a rebate on these too.[33] When this scheme collapsed, Rockefeller and refiners from centers other than Cleveland organized an "Association" whose central board of directors allotted

[31] *Ibid.*, III, 2353, 2356–2357, 2366–2367, 2405–2406; Testimony of Charles M. Schwab, *Report of the Industrial Commission*, XIII, 452, 459.

[32] Testimony of Andrew Carnegie, *loc. cit.*, III, 2372, 2377, 2386–2387; IV, 2538–2539; Testimony of Charles M. Schwab, *loc. cit.*, p. 449.

[33] Nevins, *op. cit.*, I, 102–110; Hidy and Hidy, *op. cit.*, p. 16; Ida M. Tarbell, *The History of the Standard Oil Company* (New York: McClure, Phillips & Co., 1904), I, 54–63.

crude oil to the refining centers on a percentage basis. Local boards made allotments to individual refiners. Members of the Association had to report all purchases and sales to the board of directors. Then and later the pool's management sought to buy all crude for refiners and negotiate all transportation agreements.[34]

The railroads were also allied with the makers of rails under the Bessemer patent. Because of the huge expense of establishing a rail mill, the number of rail producers was quite limited. At one moment the railroads were eager to favor producers along their own lines and granted them favorable railroad rates; at other times when railroads were rail purchasers rather than shippers, they would use their potential power as carriers to force down prices on the rails they bought.[35] Consequently the price of rails vacillated wildly. In 1887 in order to "steady prices," the producers established a pool[36] which allotted a quota to each manufacturer and provided financial penalties if the quota were exceeded; these fines were then distributed to producers who had not fulfilled their quotas. Though the pool denied it determined prices, the steel men, apparently after consultation with the officers of the chief railroads, were able to stabilize the price at $28.00 a ton.[37] Andrew Carnegie, who generally chafed at restraints because he could manufacture more cheaply,[38] thought this pool "perfect."[39] In the nineties manufacturers of other specialized steel products tried in vain to imitate the success of the rail producers.[40]

In attempts to secure harmony in the anthracite coal trade the railroads were even more to the fore. By the Civil War the coal railways had been built from the deposits to the markets and shipping points along the Atlantic coastline; of these centers New York was the most significant.[41] Theoretically the railways had it in their power to control coal production, for in their own right they often owned or leased coal lands and indirectly, through the supply of cars, they could control the production by independents. Between 1873 and 1896 the anthracite roads entered upon a succession of agreements or informal understandings.

[34] Nevins, *op. cit.*, I, 159–164, 212–214; Hidy and Hidy, *op. cit.*, pp. 17–19; Tarbell, *op. cit.*, I, 108–110.

[35] Testimony of Andrew Carnegie, *loc. cit.*, III, 2387–2388.

[36] Testimony of Percival Roberts, Jr., *Hearings before the* [Stanley] *Committee on Investigation of United States Steel Corporation*, I, 321–322.

[37] Testimony of James Gayley, *Hearings before the* [Stanley] *Committee,* I, 308–309; Testimony of Andrew Carnegie, *loc. cit.*, III, 2387–2388.

[38] Hendrick, *op. cit.*, I, 210–213; II, 50–52.

[39] Testimony of Andrew Carnegie, *loc. cit.*, III, 2387.

[40] Testimony of Percival Roberts, Jr., *loc. cit.*, pp. 347–348.

[41] Eliot Jones, *The Anthracite Coal Combination in the United States with Some Account of the Early Development of the Anthracite Industry* (Cambridge: Harvard University Press, 1914), pp. 4–20, 23–37.

Though there were differences in details of management, the general pattern set an overall total of shipments to tidewater and apportioned it among the railroads on a percentage basis; sometimes it provided a series of fines against overshipping, usually it effected price increases at tidewater markets.[42] Since most of these arrangements were short-lived and their abandonment brought chaos to the coal market, the Philadelphia and Reading Railroad in the nineties sought to accomplish a common policy through leasing rival coal roads and extending its own lines into the New England market. It overextended its financial resources, however, and collapsed in the panic of the nineties.[43]

Pools as a means of combination revealed certain defects. Their successful operation depended upon good times. When business was booming the members of the pools tended to stick to their agreements: "As a rule, troubles came during times of depression, when there was not sufficient business to go round and everyone was struggling to obtain enough to run full at the expense of his competitors."[44] Of course a return to *sauve qui peut* involved breaking the agreement. Outraged members could not resort to the courts, for pools were not legally enforceable. Since pools lacked sanctions,[45] they could not guarantee the regularity, uniformity and stability for which business was groping in a time of rapid and frightening change.

TRUSTS AND HOLDING COMPANIES

Rockefeller, in distress at the failure of his own pools, characterized them as "ropes of sand." In his case he had an existing community of interest to fall back upon. During the pool experiments the addition of new and able members had indeed enlarged the group.[46] Nonetheless this arrangement had its defects. It was poorly devised to protect the "common interest. . . . This condition of conflict will grow as the business grows—it will prevent harmonious pulling together."[47] The chief instrument of the group, the Standard Oil of Ohio, in the contemporary state of corporation law could generally neither own stock in other companies nor carry on business in other jurisdictions. When it did

[42] *Ibid.*, pp. 40–50, 55–58; M. W. Schlegel, *Ruler of the Reading: The Life of Franklin B. Gowen, 1836–1899* (Harrisburg, Pa.: The Archives Publishing Company of Pennsylvania, 1947), pp. 32–48.

[43] Jones, *op. cit.*, pp. 50–55; E. C. Kirkland, *Men, Cities and Transportation: A Study in New England History, 1820–1900* (Cambridge: Harvard University Press, 1945), II, 68–71.

[44] Testimony of Percival Roberts, Jr., *loc. cit.*, pp. 348–349.

[45] Testimony of C. C. Allen, *Report of the Industrial Commission,* I, 1181.

[46] Nevins, *op. cit.*, I, 175, 215–217.

[47] *Ibid.*, I, 387.

operate outside of Ohio, it confronted taxation additional to that in the home state. To expand foreign and domestic markets, the Standard group also required new agencies. In the competitive setting of the day, it was also desirable to keep their business operations concealed. A resort to the state for a charter would dissipate the benign secrecy of private operations.[48]

In this dilemma, the able counsel of the group, S. T. C. Dodd, proposed the adaptation of an old device, the trust. In 1882 the forty-one stockholders in the Standard Oil Company of Ohio signed a trust agreement establishing a board of nine trustees; to the trustees the signers transferred all the properties owned and controlled by themselves, receiving as receipts trust certificates. According to an article in the trust agreement, "It shall be the duty of said Trustees to exercise general supervision over the affairs of said Standard Oil Companies, and as far as practicable over the other Companies or Partnerships, any portion of whose stock is held in said trust. It shall be their duty as Stockholders of said Companies to elect as Directors and Officers thereof faithful and competent men."[49] As was to be expected in view of the prevailing distribution of shares, John D. Rockefeller and his allies were the trustees under the agreement.

Within a few months after the signing of this agreement the trustees incorporated the Standard Oil Company of New Jersey. With its stock and some cash they purchased from the Trust its refineries, shipping works, and other factories in New Jersey. At the time of this transaction, the company was simply implementing the precautionary purposes which it had been established to handle.[50] By the nineties a new role was thrust upon the New Jersey Company, largely as a result of the popular and judicial hostility aroused by the trust's power and the manner in which it was exercised. In 1892 a judicial decision in Ohio declared the purposes of the trust "to establish a virtual monopoly of the business of producing petroleum . . . and to control, . . . the price . . . [were] contrary to the policy of our state and void." The judge furthermore forbad the Standard of Ohio to permit its affairs to be directed by the trustees.[51]

It had happened that in 1889 the State of New Jersey had revised its corporation laws under the direction of J. B. Dill, an able corporation lawyer.[52] The new statute limited the taxes which could be levied upon a corporation to a small percentage upon its capitalization, and the eco-

[48] *Ibid.*, I, 388–393; Hidy and Hidy, *op. cit.*, pp. 40–45.

[49] Hidy and Hidy, *op. cit.*, pp. 46–49; Testimony of John R. Dos Passos, *loc. cit.*, p. 1142.

[50] Hidy and Hidy, *op. cit.*, pp. 47–51.

[51] Nevins, *op. cit.*, II, 229–232; Hidy and Hidy, *op. cit.*, pp. 217–219.

[52] "James Brooks Dill," *Dictionary of American Biography*, V, 309–310.

nomical way in which New Jersey managed its affairs assured that it "will not be driven to squeeze my corporations to make up a deficiency. The State of New York has a deficiency in its various departments, and its officials sit up nights to see how they can squeeze more money out of my corporations." [53] Furthermore New Jersey had aided incorporation by placing few limitations upon the purposes of a corporation, by permitting it to issue stock to the amount it saw fit, and by limiting the stockholders' liability. Corporations with a New Jersey charter could own real estate in other states and carry on business there and could own the stocks of other corporations.

This authorization to serve as a holding company enabled a New Jersey corporation to act as a centralizing agency in combination policy.[54] Furthermore this new device could be described in soothing words which, because they were new, did not arouse the hostility that its predecessors had. As Judge Gary informed an investigating committee, the Federal Steel Company, a New Jersey corporation, "is no more a trustee than you are a trustee of the stock you actually own in a corporation. . . . it is absolute owner and controls that stock just as much as you would if you as an individual owned it; no difference; no secret arrangement about it; no private understanding about it; no pool or any division in any way of business, business interests, or profits." [55] Finally New Jersey was just across the Hudson from New York City. It was thus easily accessible to the rising metropolitan center of American management and investment.[56]

In 1899 the Standard Oil group increased the capital stock of the Standard Oil (New Jersey) from $10,000,000 to $110,000,000. It exchanged this stock for that in forty constituent concerns. The New Jersey's Board of Directors was composed largely of those who had administered the affairs of the group since the 1870's.[57] A few years later John D. Rockefeller was asserting that while a corporation might be bad as well as good, "the corporation in form and character has come to stay—that is a thing that may be depended upon. Even small firms are becoming corporations, because it is a convenient form of partnership." Certainly the holding company signalized the final triumph of the corporation, for now corporations could be made to combine corporations.[58]

The history of the electric industries demonstrated the same advantages. In telephony, the inventors and their financial sponsors were

[53] Testimony of J. B. Dill, *Report of the Industrial Commission,* I, 1081; Testimony of F. L. Stetson, *loc. cit.,* p. 975.

[54] Testimony of J. B. Dill, *loc. cit.,* pp. 1081–1087.

[55] Testimony of Elbert H. Gary, *Report of the Industrial Commission,* I, 994.

[56] J. W. Cadman, Jr., *op. cit.,* pp. 174–177.

[57] Hidy and Hidy, *op. cit.,* pp. 219–226, 305–313.

[58] Rockefeller, *op. cit.,* p. 65.

the movers in the formation of a succession of firms in which they assigned themselves stock for previous scientific or financial contributions. These organizations centralized the industry. They leased their telephone instruments, protected by patents, to operating companies which raised money from local investors for the construction and operation of lines and exchanges. These operating companies paid a part of the rent in their own stock. By 1899 the core organization—since evolved into the American Telephone and Telegraph Company—had undertaken the construction and operation of long distance lines and, through a subsidiary, the manufacture of instruments.[59]

In the electric light industry, the Edison Electric Light Company secured a charter in New Jersey in 1878. In return for assigning to this concern his inventions and improvements, Edison received 2,500 out of its 3,000 shares and a cash payment earmarked for experiment. Powerful financial interests, such as the Morgan bankers and Henry Villard of the railroads, were also interested in the firm.[60] Once the electric light had demonstrated its feasibility, local investors were generally relied upon to finance the operating companies; the central organization provided advice and equipment, which was protected by patents, and received in return stock in the operating companies.[61] At the end of the eighties Henry Villard brought about the consolidation of various Edison companies into the Edison General Electric Company; almost at once it acquired the Sprague concern, the innovator in street railway equipment. In 1892 Villard and Morgan chartered the General Electric Company, which through exchanges of stock purchased the Edison General Electric Company and the Thomson-Houston firm. Thus General Electric brought together in a single concern manufacturers of alternating and direct-current equipment, of arc and incandescent lighting, and of electric equipment for transportation purposes. It also brought into the enterprise the superior managerial talents of the Thomson-Houston officials.[62]

THE EXTENT OF COMBINATION

By the nineties the combination movement had carried centralization of production, at least in some industries, to a high level. John D. Arch-

[59] J. W. Stehman, *The Financial History of the American Telephone and Telegraph Company* (Boston: Houghton Mifflin Company, 1925), pp. 4–12, 20–42.

[60] Harold C. Passer, *The Electrical Manufacturers, 1875–1900. A Study in Competition, Entrepreneurship, Technical Change and Economic Growth* (Cambridge: Harvard University Press, 1953), pp. 84–86.

[61] *Ibid.*, p. 118; Forrest MacDonald, *Let There Be Light. The Electric Utility Industry in Wisconsin, 1881–1955* (Madison: American History Research Center, 1957), pp. 33–90.

[62] Passer, *op. cit.*, pp. 102–104, 248–249, 321–329.

bold of the Standard testified that in 1898 the Standard group refined 83.7 per cent of the oil in the country; though this was a slightly larger per cent than five years earlier, it was probably smaller than in the 1870's.[63] Since the fate of the industry was closely intertwined with the methods and costs of transportation, it was not surprising that the Standard managers were alert to the significance of pipelines. In the seventies they established an affiliate to construct and operate these new means of moving oil and had won a resounding victory over the Pennsylvania Railroad which had undertaken the same business on a large scale.[64] As one of the Standard group wrote Rockefeller about local lines, "We must prevent all such enterprises from making headway and make it as discouraging as possible for any to start. No difference how small such an enterprise may start, we must prevent it from taking root as far as we can do so by legitimate & fair means." [65] Though outsiders first undertook the daring construction of trunk pipelines from the Oil Regions over the mountains to the eastern seaboard, the Standard was able to contain most of these rivals.[66] At the close of the nineties, its trunk-line mileage was 3,905 and its network of gathering lines was 10,749.[67]

Originally the Standard organization refined petroleum and distributed and marketed its products. It did not own oil-bearing lands or oil wells, nor was it an oil producer. As one of the Standard group wrote, "Our business is that of manufacturers and it is in my judgment, an unfortunate thing for any manufacturer or merchant to have the care and friction which attend speculative ventures." [68] Yet chance ultimately dictated a change in policy. The Standard managers acquired producing properties incident to other operations, became interested in drilling for and transporting natural gas, and ultimately confronted a declining oil production in the Pennsylvania fields and rising production in the Lima-Indiana field, whose crude their investigations had purified. Finally to protect themselves against threatened shortages and excessive vacillation in prices for crude—in brief to bring order into production—they began leasing properties and developing them. In 1898 their production accounted for 33.5 per cent of the country's output, incidentally their all-time peak. Retrospectively, Rockefeller thought the results of the decision in 1888 to enter production had been "most gratifying." [69]

Though no single group or firm had a predominant position in steel

[63] Testimony of John D. Archbold, *Report of the Industrial Commission,* I, 560; Tarbell, *op. cit.,* II, 221.

[64] Hidy and Hidy, *op. cit.,* p. 20; Nevins, *op. cit.,* I, 182–184, 231–249.

[65] Hidy and Hidy, *op. cit.,* p. 84.

[66] *Ibid.,* pp. 21–22, 76–87; Nevins, *op. cit.,* I, 345–381.

[67] Hidy and Hidy, *op. cit.,* p. 408.

[68] *Ibid.,* pp. 170, 177–178.

[69] *Ibid.,* pp. 176–188, 270, 278.

comparable to that of Standard, steel also exhibited a tendency to monolithic structures controlling the successive stages in manufacturing, to what observers called the integration of industry or vertical combination. Carnegie loved to shroud actuality with boasts and to terrify competitors, sometimes blandly, with figures of his comparative costs, real and possible.[70] Yet on one occasion Charles M. Schwab, the Carnegie Company's one-time president, said the concern manufactured "a larger general variety of steel articles than almost any other manufacturing concern." In general he calculated the firm turned out between 25 and 30 per cent of the nation's finished product of steel; specifying categories, Schwab thought of "structural materials of all descriptions, plates, things of that sort we made 50 per cent; in rails 30 per cent; in armor we made half." [71] In the nineties they secured ore deposits in the Great Lakes region. "The Carnegie Company were large miners of ore—mined all the ore they required themselves, to the extent of over 4,000,000 tons per year. They transported a large percentage of it in their own boats over the lakes; they carried a very large percentage of it over their own railroad to their Pittsburg [sic] works. . . ." [72]

Carnegie's nearest rival, the Federal Steel Company, was chartered in New Jersey in 1898 as a holding company. According to its president, Judge Elbert H. Gary, it was not a "trust," it was not seeking a "monopoly." Its characteristic feature was integration. "It takes the ore from the ground, transports it, manufactures it into pig iron, manufactures the pig iron into steel, and the steel into finished products, and delivers these products." It owned mines of ore and fuel, railroads and steel mills and produced 30 per cent of the steel rails in the country.[73]

Actually in the steel industry in the nineties, concentration of production was most marked in some finished products. After a rapid corporate evolution during the nineties, the American Steel and Wire Company assumed final form in New Jersey. According to the testimony of John W. ("Bet-you-a-million") Gates, its president, "We are owners of iron mines, miners of iron ore, owners of coal mines, miners of coal, burners of coke." More to the point at hand, the concern made 75 to 80 per cent of the iron rods in the country, 65 to 90 per cent of the wire nails, and "We have a monopoly of the barbed wire" industry.[74] This was not due so much to the energy, unscrupulousness, or talents of one of the most picturesque of the tycoons but to the fact that "we practically

[70] Hendrick, *op. cit.*, I, 210–213; II, 1.

[71] Testimony of Charles M. Schwab, *loc. cit.*, pp. 448–449.

[72] *Ibid.*, p. 448.

[73] Testimony of Elbert H. Gary, *Report of the Industrial Commission*, I, 982–985, 994–995; Testimony of Elbert H. Gary, *Hearings before the* [Stanley] *Committee on Investigation of United States Steel Corporation*, I, 67–68.

[74] Testimony of John W. Gates, *Report of the Industrial Commission*, I, 1005, 1009–1010.

own every patent on barbed fence wire and machinery in existence in the United States, and we claim that no one can manufacture barbed wire without infringing our rights." [75] About the same time, other organizers put together in New Jersey the American Tin Plate Company, which, according to critics, owned "practically every mill in the country, making tin plate for the general trade." [76]

In telephony the nineties witnessed some shrinking of the empire of the Bell companies. In 1893–1894 the expiration of the Bell patents apparently threw the door open to competitors. Most of them appeared in the Middle West and in New York State; some with imposing capitalizations prepared to move into Chicago and the seaboard cities. These efforts often assumed the panoply of a crusade. Their corporate names appropriated the appealing words, "Independent" or "Peoples' " company; their promises included a lowering of rates. In terms of numbers of stations, the threat of competition was impressive. Actually it was a false dawn, for early in the next century these enterprises usually revealed serious defects and the crusaders turned out to be speculators or promoters bent on a quick dollar. Also, the Bell companies had secured such a headstart toward a national network that these newcomers could not catch up.[77]

In the electric light and power industry operating companies tended to be like railroad corporations, "natural monopolies" controlling the business in a geographical area. The manufacturers of electrical equipment were in a different situation. Until the nineties the production of electric lamps was competitive; the chaotic depression years of that decade, however, led these enterprises to stabilize the industry through combinations or agreements. The significant patent pool between Westinghouse and General Electric in 1896 was the end product of this process. As well as bulbs, the pool also covered motors, dynamos, transportation equipment, and the like. After 1896 Westinghouse and General Electric were the only two full-line producers in the country. In spite of their understanding, competition continued between the two.[78]

Whatever may have been the personal drives to power and recognition or the individual ambitions that led to combination (Gates confessed, "We wanted to be the wire manufacturers of the world" [79]), the economic factor which explained them was the uncertainty and in-

[75] *Ibid.*, I, 1009.

[76] Testimony of W. T. Graham, *Report of the Industrial Commission,* I, 850, 856–857; Testimony of Byron W. Holt, *Report of the Industrial Commission,* XIII, 558–559.

[77] Stehman, *op. cit.*, pp. 51–59, 65–97; N. R. Danielian, *A. T. & T., The Story of Industrial Conquest* (New York: Vanguard Press, 1939), pp. 46–50.

[78] Passer, *op. cit.*, pp. 349–355.

[79] Testimony of John W. Gates, *loc. cit.*, p. 1033; J. W. Jenks, *The Trust Problem* (New York: McClure, Phillips & Co., 1905), pp. 73–74.

stability of business enterprise in this period. Rockefeller once observed of the early petroleum industry that it was an enterprise which did not require much capital and which provided great gains. "Naturally all sorts of people went into it; the butcher, the baker, and the candlestick-maker began to refine oil, and it was only a short time before more of the finished product was put on the market than could possibly be consumed." [80] Nor was the human desire for gain the only source of instability; geography and resources contributed uncertainty. Oil wells flowed and stopped; there were gluts and shortages. In 1862 monthly averages of the price of crude oil ranged per barrel from 10 cents to $2.25; between 1872 and 1874 the average wholesale price of kerosene in New York sank from a low of 21.75 cents per gallon to 10.75.[81] In general the words businessmen most frequently used to explain the situation they confronted were "chaos," "anarchy," "ruin," "failure," "instability."

To those engaged in the struggle for business survival these phenomena were the result of competition. One way to be fit to survive was to cut costs by effecting economies through a larger scale of operations in manufacture, transport, and marketing. As Rockefeller said of his concern, "We needed volume." He and his associates centralized administration of many refineries "with a view to securing greater economy and efficiency." [82] Another means of rescue was the combination or trust. Whatever the motive or method, according to the *Nation* "The one proposition an economist or politician can lay down with certainty is security is necessary to prosperity." [83]

Indeed the practitioners and apostles of combination were as sure on their side as the supporters of competition were on the other that consolidation was in accord with natural law. This was Carnegie's and Rockefeller's opinion,[84] just as it was of the latter's counsel, S. T. C. Dodd. "You might as well endeavor to stay the formation of the clouds, the falling of the rains, or the flowing of the streams, as to attempt by any means or in any manner to prevent organization of industry, association of persons, and the aggregation of capital to any extent that the ever-growing trade of the world may demand." [85]

On the other hand some who read the record were less certain about the predestination of the combination movement. The trouble was that

[80] Rockefeller, *op. cit.*, pp. 81–82.

[81] Hidy and Hidy, *op. cit.*, pp. 9, 17.

[82] Rockefeller, *op. cit.*, pp. 58, 82–83; Testimony of Charles R. Flint, *Report of the Industrial Commission,* XIII, 33–37.

[83] *Nation,* XXV (October 4, 1877), 207.

[84] Rockefeller, *op. cit.,* p. 132; Testimony of Andrew Carnegie, *loc. cit.,* III, 2346–2348, 2451.

[85] John Moody, *The Truth about the Trusts: A Description and Analysis of the American Trust Movement* (New York: Moody Publishing Company, 1904), foreword.

men did not leave the laws of competition alone. Contemplating the patterns of Rockefeller's price-cutting and railroad rebates, dissenters concluded that the oil king attained the growth of his concern not through the sweet persuasion of aloof negotiation, but through duress of circumstances of his own devising.[86] Sometimes business observers made distinctions between the kinds of competition that justified combination and that did not. A similar distinction had been attempted for the railroad world and a railroad director and industrialist, Percival Roberts, succinctly formulated the generalizations for industry. "Free competition within the rule of reason" was no excuse for combination; "cutthroat" or "destructive" competition was. The latter included selling below the cost of production.[87]

Perhaps the whole uproar over competition was an irrelevance. Mr. Dooley, the observant barkeeper of Peter Finley Dunne, once defined a trust as "somethin' for an honest, ploddin', uncombined manufacturer to sell out to." [88] In other words the motive for combination was not production control but financial gain. A shrewdly devised strategy of capitalization or recapitalization by itself brought profit. The primitive concept that capitalization of an enterprise should reflect the value of its physical property was discarded as old fashioned in the period of bigness and combination. For one thing property took on new forms. Patents, franchises, and relationships were property. In the eighties Jay Gould admitted that the $80,000,000 capital of the Western Union greatly exceeded the value of its "material property." On the other hand he would not part with his unexpired patents for several million dollars. The contracts with the railroads for the use of the telegraph were also highly valuable. "The father-in-law of Mr. Bell came to see me once," he said, "and told me that we could take the whole of the Bell patent and control it for $100,000. We declined to do it, and now it has a market value of nearly $20,000,000." [89] Firms which purchased natural resources found them more valuable than the price paid, either because the resources were more abundant than estimated or more limited.[90] Of course the real intangible was the earning power of the combination, presumably enhanced by the economies it brought about and the degree of market control it exerted. Though this was a matter of hope or calculation, it, too, could be capitalized.

Business leaders were almost universal in the belief that expectations

[86] Hidy and Hidy, *op. cit.*, pp. 33–34, Tarbell, *op. cit.*, I, 56–69, 156–168, 197–207.

[87] Testimony of Percival Roberts, Jr., *loc. cit.*, pp. 322–323, 349–350; Testimony of James Gayley, *loc. cit.*, p. 309.

[88] Moody, *op. cit.*, p. xiii.

[89] Testimony of Jay Gould, *Report of the Committee* [on Education and Labor] *of the Senate . . . 1885*, I, 878–885.

[90] Testimony of Andrew Carnegie, *loc. cit.*, III, 2401–2406.

should be handled in this fashion, whether the stock was sold to outside investors or turned over to the promoters and members of the consolidation. Paradoxically a procedure which locked into the economy a highly speculative element won the almost universal assent of business leaders bent upon stability. When Carnegie, for instance, incorporated the Edgar Thompson Company in 1874 he "naturally" capitalized it at its "actual" or "real" value, its "earning power," present and future. "We had a sure future that our iron, ore, everything, was growing more valuable." When asked if he expected that "in time, as the business progressed, it would grow in value, to equal the value of the stock issued?" Carnegie answered, "Yes, sir; and it always more than exceeded that, as you know." [91]

This colloquy is especially revealing, for it was the statement of an industrialist who in general was hostile to watered stock, deplored Wall Street, and focussed more upon manufacturing than financiering. When he at last incorporated the Carnegie Company of New Jersey, he made the value of individual shares $1,000 apiece "to keep them out of the stock exchange." [92] Rockefeller had somewhat the same outlook. The Standard rarely purchased properties at inflated values; the first step was a careful appraisal. Indeed this was a grievance of those whose property was acquired.[93] According to Rockefeller's later recollection, the "so-called 'octopus'" had no "'water' introduced into its capital (perhaps we felt that oil and water would not have mixed)." [94] This was a somewhat too genial view of the situation. In 1882 when the Trust was formed the total of trust certificates exceeded the book value of the properties by $15,000,000.[95] But Rockefeller was hardly a speculator.

Whereas the attitude of this earlier business generation had been in general conservative, by the nineties a new type had appeared on the American scene, the promoter of industrial combinations. Sometimes this individual was "chased" into performing these functions by manufacturers; [96] more often, outside the battle, he discerned the possibility of combinations. In any case, he usually secured a charter for the new centralized corporation and persuaded the producers to sell out to it. Of course, if he could use the securities of the new corporation for this purpose, so much the easier; otherwise he had to raise funds from the sale of stock or by loans from bankers. The promoter was apt to take the

[91] Testimony of Andrew Carnegie, *loc. cit.*, III, 2370; Testimony of James Gayley, *loc. cit.*, p. 309.

[92] Testimony of Andrew Carnegie, *loc. cit.*, IV, 2538–2539.

[93] Nevins, *op. cit.*, I, 133–146.

[94] Rockefeller, *op. cit.*, p. 62.

[95] Hidy and Hidy, *op. cit.*, p. 46.

[96] Testimony of D. G. Reid, *Report of the Industrial Commission,* I, 866; Testimony of William H. Moore, *Report of the Industrial Commission,* I, 959–961.

bulk of his pay in the stock of the consolidation. Since it was easier to persuade hard-headed producers to participate by paying them more than their property was worth and to capitalize hopes from combination, there was a tendency to water the capitalization. Preferred stock represented assets; the common stock was thrown in as a bonus to facilitate the formation of amalgamation.[97] Examples of the new type of organizer were: W. H. Moore, who put together the National Biscuit Company, the Diamond Match Company, and the American Tin Plate Company; C. R. Flint, the "Father of the Trusts," who after failing to consolidate the electric light and power industry, brought into being the National Starch Company and the United States Rubber Company and many other consolidations; and Elbert H. Gary, who helped John W. Gates consolidate the barbed wire industry and later create the Federal Steel Company of which he became the president.[98] Eventually the investment banker took over the promoter's role.

Probably because public opinion did not regard them as producers, promoters were put on the defensive in justifying their role. Both Flint and Moore emphasized it "was a very difficult thing" to organize these companies. Hard work, education, and the ability to be *"a disinterested intermediary,"* were required. Incidentally both Moore and Gary had the title "Judge." The consolidations made must not fail, for failure shadowed the reputation for judicious infallibility essential to promotion.[99]

Few businessmen were so well known to contemporaries or so faithfully remembered by history as those who flourished between the Civil War and the beginning of the twentieth century. It matters little if one calls them "captains of industry" or "robber barons"; they were men of ability. As Carnegie put it, "Take from me all the ore mines, railroads, manufacturing plants and leave me my organization, and in a few years I promise to duplicate the Carnegie Company." [100] W. H. Vanderbilt, outside the Standard group but well acquainted with it through business dealings, declared, "I never came into contact with any class of men as smart and able as they are in their business, and I think that a great deal of their advantage is to be attributed to that. They never could have got in the position they are in now without a good

[97] Testimony of W. T. Graham, *loc. cit.*, p. 862; C. R. Flint, *Memories of an Active Life: Men, and Ships and Sealing Wax* (New York: G. P. Putnam's Sons, 1923), pp. 305–306; *Report of the Industrial Commission,* XIII, Review of evidence, x–xi; Testimony of E. R. Chapman, *Report of the Industrial Commission,* XIII, 94.

[98] Testimony of William H. Moore, *loc. cit.*, pp. 939–940; Testimony of C. R. Flint, *Report of the Industrial Commission,* XII, 33–34; Flint, *Memories of an Active Life,* pp. 286–300.

[99] Flint, *Memories of an Active Life,* p. 294; Testimony of William H. Moore, *loc. cit.*, pp. 959–960.

[100] Hendrick, *op. cit.*, II, 5.

deal of ability, and one man would hardly have been able to do it. It is a combination of men. I don't believe that by any legislative enactment or anything else, through any of the States, or all of the States, you can keep such men down." [101]

Presumably such talents came from a family inheritance and from early training and experience. The general picture of the American industrial leader as one who began work at an early age and made his way to the top without means or educational advantages [102] is now pretty well discredited. Instead a study of the industrial élite during the 1870's in textiles, steel, and railroading has demonstrated that the industrial leader was then of American birth and that his father was in all likelihood born in America. The future business executive was born usually not on a farm but in a small community, or less frequently in a city. More certainly he came from a business family of standing in the community. In textiles 44 per cent of the business leaders had been to college; in steel 37 per cent. Nearly half the group did not take their first regular job until nineteen or over.[103]

COMPETITION OR MONOPOLY

In spite of the fears of reformers and the smug assertions of businessmen that they had got the situation stabilized in their favor, it is extremely difficult to decide whether the period of combination had left the economy more or less competitive, whether monopoly had conquered. If one's estimate of what happened relies upon language contemporary with the growth of bigness, "monopoly" did not mean control of the market or of prices; it was used as a synonym for any corporate organization or any giant enterprise. If one relies upon the more skilful tools of the modern economists, he discovers diverse definitions, some highly subjective, and may well conclude "no word is more difficult to define and no phenomenon more difficult to measure" [104] than monopoly. An historian is naturally sensitive to the charge of making "rather loose expeditions into history." [105] Still, if the risk be taken, scattered evidence inclines one to believe that the late nineteenth century was not char-

[101] Moody, *op. cit.*, p. 131.

[102] Testimony of John R. Dos Passos, *loc. cit.*, pp. 1165–1166.

[103] F. W. Gregory and I. D. Neu, "The American Industrial Elite in the 1870's," William Miller, ed., *Men in Business. Essays in the History of Entrepreneurship* (Cambridge: Harvard University Press, 1952), pp. 193–211.

[104] J. Potter, "Industrial America," H. C. Allen and C. P. Hill, eds., *British Essays in American History* (London: Edward Arnold, 1957), p. 291.

[105] George J. Stigler, *Five Lectures on Economic Problems* (New York: Macmillan Company, 1950), p. 51.

acterized by a very considerable decline of competition.[106] For one thing the spread of the railroad network continually breached the barriers of transportation costs behind which local monopolies had always nourished themselves. An enterprise does not need to be either national or large to be non-competitive. For another thing, it is difficult, though analytically not impossible, to reconcile the decline in prices, even in products such as kerosene which are automatically characterized as monopoly-controlled, with the decline of competition. Nor were all combinations of firms successful. A corporation lawyer observed, "Othello's great point was, I have had losses, too!"[107] The trust that succeeded in surviving was balanced by the trust that failed or escaped going under only by the most desperate expedients. Even as puissant a concern as General Electric narrowly escaped receivership and in 1899 wrote down its capital stock account by 40 per cent.[108] Though it is customary to deride the observations of big businessmen on competition and monopoly as hypocrisy, perhaps they knew what they were talking about when they asserted the "natural" state of business was competitive.[109] If at any moment competition did not prevail, it lurked on the horizon. Once a combination raised or administered prices, new capital and new managerial ability would flow into the field.[110] Even to an experienced member of the Standard's élite, this prospect seemed continuous, inevitable, and displeasing. He wrote to Rockefeller, "*Competitors we must have* . . . if we absorb them, be sure it will bring up another."[111]

In most cases the best testimony is that of a man convinced against his expectations. In the seventies, F. B. Thurber, a New York grocery merchant, was belaboring the railroads in New York State and elsewhere and organizing anti-railroad sentiment. Naturally he started out with a "strong prejudice" against trusts. "I believed they would tend to oppress the public with high prices and also that their political influence was to be feared." In 1899 before the Industrial Commission he chronicled their benefits, including the reduction of prices and "moderate margins of profit." "I had no conception . . . that there was any rational basis for their existence. But a careful study of their effect, ranging over a period of years, has materially modified my opinion."[112]

[106] *Ibid.*, pp. 51–54; G. W. Nutter, *Extent of Enterprise Monopoly in the United States, 1899–1939* (Chicago: University of Chicago Press, 1951), p. 44.

[107] Testimony of F. L. Stetson, *loc. cit.*, p. 973.

[108] Passer, *op. cit.*, pp. 326–329.

[109] Digest of evidence, *Report of the Industrial Commission*, 1, 220; Andrew Carnegie, "The Bugaboo of Trusts," *North American Review*, CXLVIII (February, 1889), 141–150; *Nation*, XLV (July 28, 1887), 68.

[110] Testimony of John R. Dos Passos, *loc. cit.*, p. 1151.

[111] Nevins, *op. cit.*, II, 76; Hidy and Hidy, *op. cit.*, p. 383.

[112] Testimony of F. B. Thurber, *loc. cit.*, pp. 3–18.

CHAPTER XI

Financing Expansion

SAVERS: INDIVIDUAL AND INSTITUTIONAL

IF the frequency with which an argument is repeated be the test of its validity, the usefulness of the corporation as a means of financing expansion was immense. About the amount of capital it and other devices were called upon to provide in the nineteenth century, there is still considerable uncertainty. Though after 1887 the statistical labors of the Interstate Commerce Commission give a sound basis for the capital requirements of the railroads, the census figures for the capitalization of industry adopt such varying definitions as to be of little value. As "suggestive" of the needs for capital an expanding economy presented, the *Commercial and Financial Chronicle* concluded that in 1887 alone there were on the New York Stock Exchange approximately $180,386,000 in new bond issues and $98,726,791 in new stock issues. The *Chronicle,* characterizing these sums as "large," pointed out they did not include listings on stock exchanges in other American cities, nor were "listings" the only way by which "floating capital . . . has taken fixed forms." [1]

Though part of this capital was invested in plant, equipment, and other overhead, American manufacturers had early discovered that, if they were to succeed in their enterprises, part of their original capital must be kept in fluid form for the purchase of supplies, the payment of wages, or for meeting the vicissitudes of production. Thus the great Massachusetts cotton-manufacturing corporations early in the nineteenth century planned to keep at least a third of their capital in mobile form and in practice invested only three-eighths in fixed property. And as Carnegie said later, "It is astounding the amount of working capital you must have in a great concern. It is far more than the cost of the works." [2]

[1] *Commercial and Financial Chronicle,* XLVI (March 10, 1888), 303–304.

[2] C. F. Ware, *The Early New England Cotton Manufacture: A Study in Industrial Beginnings* (Boston: Houghton Mifflin Company, 1931), pp. 19–22; Testi-

Generally speaking the rate of saving in the community responded to the challenges presented to it. The most thorough study of saving in the United States focusses unluckily though understandably on the twentieth century, but its authors conclude that in the nineteenth "real saving (adjusted for price level and population growth) has doubled every forty years." More specifically "there is . . . some evidence that the rate of growth of real saving per head was at a peak in the 1870's and 1880's."[3] As has already been hinted, the great corporations and combinations got their start from the accumulations of their founders and their friends. Rockefeller for some years before his oil venture had been a partner in a highly successful commission grocery business in Cleveland. From its large profits he secured the funds to start in the oil business. When he bought out his partner in the new enterprise, he borrowed an amount he hoped "would easily pay for the plant and good will."[4] On his part Andrew Carnegie, though less than thirty years of age, had at the close of the Civil War an income of nearly $50,000 a year from investments in oil, railroad supplies and equipment, and in railroads themselves, and was confessing to a friend, "Oh, I'm rich, I'm rich!"[5] At the beginning of new enterprises this transfer of funds from old ones was facilitated by the still small scale of production and the relative inexpensiveness of entry into business. The simple art of processing petroleum meant that in the sixties and seventies the cost of a small refinery was $10,000 and of a large one $50,000.[6] For the construction of Carnegie's first great steel works, the Edgar Thomson, the partners put in only $20,000 apiece "if I remember right," said Carnegie.[7] Apparently conditions of this sort were persistent and pervasive.[8]

By the nineties the larger scale of production and the course of combination altered circumstances. Then a corporation lawyer could recall the time when he was "proud" to organize corporations in New Jersey with a capitalization of $1,000,000; "to-day I sneak in at the back door because it is so small." When the Federal Steel Company was

mony of Andrew Carnegie, *Hearings before the* [Stanley] *Committee on Investigation of United States Steel Corporation*, III, 2421.

[3] Raymond W. Goldsmith, *A Study of Saving in the United States* (Princeton: Princeton University Press, 1955), I, 4–5.

[4] John D. Rockefeller, *Random Reminiscences of Men and Events* (Garden City: Doubleday, Doran & Company, 1933), pp. 40–41, 46–47, 80–81; Allan Nevins, *Study in Power: John D. Rockefeller, Industrialist and Philanthropist* (New York: Charles Scribner's Sons, 1953), I, 13, 35–36.

[5] B. J. Hendrick, *The Life of Andrew Carnegie* (Garden City: Doubleday, Doran & Company, 1932), I, 120–124.

[6] Nevins, *op. cit.*, I, 51–52.

[7] Testimony of Andrew Carnegie, *loc. cit.*, p. 2353.

[8] Donald Kemmerer, "Financing Illinois Industry, 1830–1890," *Bulletin of the Business Historical Society*, XXVI (June, 1953), 97–111.

capitalized at $200,000,000 it created a "furor" because this figure did not coincide with the "normal size" of a corporation.[9]

Individuals were not the only savers. Corporations, provided their relation of income and outgo were favorable, could also play the role. It was a fixed policy of the Standard group to plow back earnings into the business; for instance in the decade 1882–1891, dividends constituted only 58.1 per cent of net earnings.[10] In steel Carnegie was the evangelist of reinvesting profits, particularly in times of depression. In the nineties he asked his partners so frequently and insistently to deny themselves dividends and put earnings into plant that he wrung from one of his associates the lament: "It surely must be in manufacturing—say the Carnegie Steel Company—that man never is, but always to be blest." [11]

The corporation, financing its growth from growth itself, was not the only institutional investor. Another was the savings bank. Such institutions, philanthropic in tone, had been established in this country early in the nineteenth century to collect the small deposits of artisans, merchants, workers, and of the deserving poor, and to pay interest on them. At the beginning very little legal attention was directed to the investment policy of savings banks. Clearly the money had to be placed in sound securities—those, for instance, of the national, state or local governments.[12] Gradually the area of investment was enlarged to include investment in mortgages on land, in certain senior securities such as railroad bonds, and finally in the securities of other enterprises, particularly those located near at hand. State legislation decided what enterprises savings banks could aid.[13] Between 1875 and 1897 the total assets of savings banks increased from $896,197,000 to $2,198,824,000. In part this increase was due to an increase in the number of banks [14]—more importantly to the change in the character of their clients. Not the underprivileged but the comfortable middle class and businessmen put their savings in savings banks; deposits ceased to be skimmed from the pittances of the poor.[15]

[9] Testimony of J. B. Dill, *Report of the Industrial Commission*, I, 1086; *ibid.*, Review of the Evidence, XIII, xxxii–xxxiii.

[10] Rockefeller, *op. cit.*, pp. 89–90; Ralph W. Hidy and Muriel E. Hidy, *History of Standard Oil Company (New Jersey): Pioneering in Big Business, 1882–1911* (New York: Harper & Brothers, 1955), pp. 632–633.

[11] Hendrick, *op. cit.*, I, 197–199; II, 1–5.

[12] Fritz Redlich, *The Molding of American Banking: Men and Ideas* (New York: Hafner Publishing Company, 1947), Vol. II, Pt. 1, pp. 209–230.

[13] Testimony of George B. Chandler, *Report of the Committee* [on Education and Labor] *of the Senate . . . 1885*, III, 86.

[14] Bureau of the Census, *Historical Statistics of the United States, 1789–1945*, p. 266.

[15] "Report of the Special Commissioner of the Revenue," *House Executive Document* No. 27 (s.n. 1416), 41st Cong., 2d Sess., pp. xliii–xliv.

Actually savings banks were limited institutions in regional terms. They were concentrated in the Northeast and on the Pacific coast. In the post-Civil War period, other reservoirs of investment funds developed more rapidly and collected more ample assets—insurance companies. The popularity of insurance arose from the need of individuals to provide for their families in a changing, competitive society. In addition, aggressive administrators of insurance companies organized armies of salesmen.[16] The quaintly titled entry "admitted assets" of life insurance companies increased from $24,115,687 in 1860 to $1,344,903,198 in 1897; at the same time their "admitted surplus" mounted from $6,955,814 to $187,892,252.[17] The states which had statutes regulating insurance investment policy, originally limited as in the case of savings banks to governmental securities and to land mortgages, relaxed such restrictions. In 1875 New York, by repealing charter restrictions, in effect allowed insurance companies to invest in the stocks and bonds of private corporations. Massachusetts did away with all restriction in 1888. In the 1880's the Mutual Life Insurance Company of New York, one of the "big three"—for in insurance, as elsewhere, big business was developing —began edging into railroad securities and later into the securities of public utilities and banks. This sequence was not unique.[18]

THE DISTRIBUTION OF SECURITIES

New ways had to be found for the creators of stocks and bonds to distribute their wares. Before the war the states, with their programs of internal improvements, and the national government, particularly in time of war, floated the largest totals of securities. The first private corporations to match them were in the railroad field. Probably operating upon European precedents, incorporated banks, wealthy individuals, and private unincorporated firms or private bankers were the primary takers of securities. As purchasers, they might plan to own the securities themselves or to distribute them to other investors.[19] The financial needs of

[16] Douglass North, "Capital Accumulation in Life Insurance between the Civil War and the Investigation of 1905," William Miller, editor, *Men in Business. Essays in the History of Entrepreneurship* (Cambridge: Harvard University Press, 1952), pp. 239–246.

[17] Frederick L. Hoffman, "Fifty Years of American Life Insurance Progress," *American Statistical Association Publications,* XII (September, 1911), 729.

[18] S. B. Clough, *A Century of American Life Insurance: A History of the Mutual Life Insurance Company of New York, 1843–1943* (New York: Columbia University Press, 1946), pp. 175–191; R. C. Buley, *The American Life Convention, 1906–1952: A Study in the History of Life Insurance* (New York: Appleton-Century-Crofts, 1953), I, 112–114; J. O. Stalson, *Marketing Life Insurance. Its History in America* (Cambridge: Harvard University Press, 1942), 618–619; Hoffman, *op. cit.,* pp. 730, 732.

[19] Redlich, *op. cit.,* II, Pt. 2, pp. 305–355.

the Civil War gave a new impetus to the trend. As we have seen, the firm of Jay Cooke and Company took the whole of certain government loans and placed them with large and small investors by an advertising campaign and aggressive salesmanship. Since Appomattox did not put an end to the need of the national government for means to refund or otherwise manage its huge debt, Cooke's pioneering methods were refined and extended. By 1870–1871 he coalesced a group of eight firms into a syndicate which agreed to take whole issues of Pennsylvania Railroad securities and if the syndicate could not re-sell them they would purchase the securities in their own right. This was known as underwriting.[20]

Always conspicuous among underwriters were firms of private bankers. Their partnerships did not require a large preliminary investment, and the reputation for integrity and insight of the individuals composing them was their greatest asset.[21] Since partnerships in this area as in others were peculiarly vulnerable to the change of fortune of the individual members, there was a considerable business mortality of firm names. Thus few of the firm names prominent before the Civil War survived into the postwar period, and the collapse of the economy in 1873 wiped away others, including Jay Cooke's.

Successors sprang forward. Some were German Jewish houses, "the Dutchmen," such as the Seligmans and the Speyers. Perhaps the most conspicuous in this category was Kuhn, Loeb and Company, established in 1867. It stepped into power and prominence after 1875, when Jacob Schiff, an immigrant, entered the firm.[22] Of all the private banker firms the most famous was, of course, that of J. P. Morgan & Company. Morgan, born in America but educated in this country and abroad, was sent to New York in 1857 by his father, J. S. Morgan, an American private banker in London. For several years the son was associated with private bankers already functioning in this country; he also had the good luck to surround himself, at least in the later nineteenth century, with exceedingly able new partners.[23] Morgan became the "Jupiter" of American finance. Though private bankers played what seemed a disproportionate role in investment banking, two national banks in New York City, the First National Bank under G. F. Baker and, somewhat later, the National City Bank, extended their original function of buying national

[20] Henrietta Larson, *Jay Cooke, Private Banker* (Cambridge: Harvard University Press, 1936), pp. 105, 314–317.

[21] Redlich, *op. cit.*, II, Pt. 2, pp. 333–334, 381–382.

[22] *Ibid.*, II, Pt. 2, pp. 361–363; Cyrus Adler, *Jacob Schiff: His Life and Letters* (Garden City: Doubleday, Doran and Company, 1929), I, 8–9.

[23] Redlich, *op. cit.*, II, Pt. 2, pp. 382–384; F. L. Allen, *The Great Pierpont Morgan* (New York: Harper & Brothers, 1949), pp. 24–30, 32–39, 84.

bonds as a basis for their own banking business into the purchase of securities for customers. These two banks became members of syndicates and underwrote loans.[24]

Although financing the government was the seed bed for investment banks, a growing economy tempted venturesome bankers to wider fields. The first area outside of governments was railroads. At the end of the sixties, Morgan found himself the ally of officials trying to keep an up-state New York railroad out of the paws of Jay Gould and Jim Fisk; a few years later when W. H. Vanderbilt wished to sell some of his stock in the New York Central in order to quiet the charge of monopolist and diversify his holdings, Morgan arranged a syndicate to finance the purchase and then distributed the stock to European purchasers. From this time on Morgan was a railroad power.[25] The interest of the investment bankers in industrial securities quickened later. Perhaps one of the reasons for this tardiness was that governments and railroads had accustomed bankers and investors to bonds, and few industrial companies issued them. Nonetheless, as has been seen, some of Morgan's partners at the end of the seventies interested the financier in Edison's plans for electric light, and Morgan, along with Kuhn, Loeb and Company, had a leading role in the formation of the General Electric Company in 1892.[26] During the nineties the House of Morgan also became interested in the Federal Steel Company,[27] an interest which flowered in the later incorporation of the United States Steel Corporation. Other banking firms during the nineties became interested in the securities of American Telephone and Telegraph, Westinghouse, and other utilities and industries.[28]

At first the relation of the investment bankers to the enterprise whose securities they handled had been one of relative detachment. When they had sold the securities their function stopped. But investment bankers like promoters needed to have with investors a reputation for infallibility. The American investment banking houses often had their reputations sullied by the business policies of the concerns for which they had once been financial agents. The funds raised were misused; the reorganizations accomplished under banker's direction did not stick. Largely for defensive purposes, therefore, the investment bankers discovered the

[24] Redlich, *op. cit.*, II, Pt. 2, pp. 386, 388.

[25] Allen, *op. cit.*, pp. 30–35, 43–46.

[26] Harold C. Passer, *The Electrical Manufacturers, 1875–1900: A Study in Competition, Entrepreneurship, Technical Change, and Economic Growth* (Cambridge: Harvard University Press, 1953), pp. 101–103, 104.

[27] Testimony of E. H. Gary, *Hearings before the* [Stanley] *Committee on Investigation of United States Steel Corporation*, I, 203–204.

[28] Redlich, *op. cit.*, II, Pt. 2, pp. 386, 388.

wisdom of maintaining some sort of influence or control over their principals.[29] When Morgan sold abroad the Central's stock he became a member of its board of directors.[30] Regarding himself as a "merchant prince" or "gentleman," Morgan had a fastidious distaste for the rowdy tactics of many business contemporaries.[31] Like others, he deplored the competition and instability of the business world. Investment bankers generally became the advocates of order and harmony; in so far as their participation in railroads and industries permitted, they sought such ends through persuasion, agreement, and combination. Thus in 1885 Morgan prevented a war between the Central and the Pennsylvania, in which each proposed to blackmail the other with parallel lines; instead, after a long session on his yacht, he brought about harmony between the lines.[32] And the very next year representatives of the anthracite coal railroads, for some of which Morgan was banker, met at his invitation at his house. He opened proceedings with a little homily. They were there to "take counsel as to the possibility of preventing further injury to the interests they represented, by some concerted action looking to an arrest of the demoralization of business which resulted from the existing want of harmony." Curiously enough this fraternization resulted in a "Morgan pool" which assigned from a stated fixed tonnage a percentage of shipments to each road.[33]

COMBINATION AMONG INVESTMENT BANKERS

The investment bankers naturally sought to apply harmony to their own sphere. Immediately after the Civil War there was a good deal of scrambling, some of it pretty ill-natured, for the government refunding loans; later, oversights of this sort were corrected. As Schiff informed a Congressional Committee, it was not considered "good form to create unreasonable interference or competition. . . . After the negotiation has once begun a banking house should not endeavour to get it away from somebody else." [34] After the eighties, as a matter of custom clients were tied to certain banking houses and a breach of this practice led to retaliation. When the Philadelphia and Reading Railroad in its expansion sought to escape the Morgan suzerainty by a resort to other bankers, a

[29] *Ibid.*, II, Pt. 2, pp. 360–361, 377.

[30] *Ibid.*, II, Pt. 2, p. 383.

[31] Allen, *op. cit.*, pp. 67–73, 165, 183, 185–193; W. S. Rainsford, *The Story of a Varied Life: An Autobiography* (Garden City: Doubleday, Page & Company, 1922), p. 281.

[32] Allen, *op. cit.*, pp. 50–54.

[33] "Investigation of Labor Troubles in the Anthracite Regions of Pennsylvania, 1887–1888," *House Report* No. 4147 (s.n. 2676), 50th Cong., 2d Sess., p. lii.

[34] Redlich, *op. cit.*, II, Pt. 2, p. 379.

Morgan partner is said to have exploded, "That will be very bad for Speyers and the Reading"; [35] and Morgan proceeded to regain control of the railroad from a president who once declared, "I would rather run a peanut-stand than be dictated to by J. P. Morgan." [36] As supplement to the rather informal understanding that customers seeking credit should stick to one banker, there were occasionally tying contracts which bound them to do so.

Since middlemen bankers distributed securities, they would gain much in the direction of stability if purchasers could be counted on. By the nineties, consequently, investment bankers as owners of stocks and as directors had penetrated insurance companies. In the Mutual of New York, for instance, all the senior officers and all the members of the Finance Committee in charge of investments were directors of corporations or bankers, investment or otherwise. Among these was George F. Baker of the First National Bank of New York.[37] Kuhn, Loeb and Company also exerted an influence in the Mutual and in other insurance companies.[38] Indirectly or directly, investment bankers became interested, through stock ownership and through directorships, in banks like the Guaranty Trust Company of New York. Such banks could participate in underwriting securities and as commercial banks they could lend short-term funds, with securities as collateral, to finance speculation in such securities.[39] In brief, the Mutual Insurance Company owned a large block of stock in the Guaranty Trust Company "because we wanted a Trust Company which we could rely upon." [40] While the coalescing of investment bankers, insurance companies and banks into a monolithic structure went further in the twentieth century, the nineties started the process and gave a preview of what was to come.[41]

Of course banking integration could not control the key figure, the individual investor. Luckily circumstances during this period probably operated to increase his propensity and ability to invest in securities. In an agricultural community, the investor tends to regard land as the most desirable investment. Such habits might have hampered the transfer of

[35] Arthur Pound and S. T. Moore, eds., *More They Told Barron* (New York: Harper & Brothers, 1931), pp. 126–127.

[36] Lewis Corey, *The House of Morgan. A Social Biography of the Masters of Money* (New York: G. H. Watt, 1930), p. 202.

[37] Clough, *op. cit.*, pp. 188–191.

[38] Adler, *op. cit.*, I, 185–191.

[39] Clough, *op. cit.*, pp. 192–196.

[40] *Testimony taken before the* [Armstrong] *Joint Committee of the Senate and Assembly of the State of New York to Investigate and Examine into the Business and Affairs of Life Insurance Companies Doing Business in the State of New York* (1905), I, 200.

[41] H. U. Faulkner, *The Decline of Laissez Faire* (New York: Holt, Rinehart and Winston, Inc., 1951), pp. 37–44.

capital to industry had not the Civil War occurred and the embracing labors of Jay Cooke and his associates in behalf of their "popular loans" given thousands of persons their first experience of buying pieces of paper other than mortgages.[42] In so far as industrialization increased personal wealth it also furthered the habit of investment. The later statistical demonstration that non-farmers and the wealthier fraction of the community accounted for most of the community's savings [43] was well understood by contemporaries. As the president of the Chicago, Burlington and Quincy put it, the money that Huntington and Gould accumulate "does them personally very little good—a small part of their incomes may be invested in show or champagne, but more of it is invested in some form of industry." [44]

INDUSTRIAL DEVELOPMENT BY FOREIGNERS

The fact that "the Dutchmen" and J. P. Morgan had close alliances with foreign correspondents and agents in Frankfort and London hinted that American enterprise was counting upon foreign investors to provide it with funds. There were other institutional arrangements pointing in the same direction. As early as the 1830's the Rothschilds, the great European bankers, had an agent in New York in the person of August Belmont, and the house of Baring Brothers and Company of London, though less conspicuous in American financing after the Civil War than before, still retained an American representative.[45] Funds from abroad played a trivial role in American industry compared to those invested by foreigners in railroads or by Americans in manufacturing.[46] Indeed it might be stretching a point to speak of foreign industrial investment as such. In brewing, meat-packing, flour-milling, patent medicines, into which money from England flowed, the English practically purchased the properties, incorporated a second company in England to hold, as trustees, the American properties, and usually insisted that the American vendors, to whom a stock interest was assigned, continue the management on the spot.[47]

The foreign ownership of American securities far from met with

[42] Larson, *op. cit.*, p. 174.

[43] Goldsmith, *op. cit.*, I, 9.

[44] Charles Elliott Perkins to T. M. Marquett, Jan. 3, 1891, Perkins Private Letters and Memos, R. C. Overton.

[45] Redlich, *op. cit.*, II, Pt. 2, pp. 353, 356, 379, 388.

[46] N. T. Bacon, "American International Indebtedness," *Yale Review*, IX (November, 1900), 266.

[47] Erastus Wiman, "British Capital and American Industries," *North American Review*, CL (February, 1890), 225–228; Bessie L. Pierce, *A History of Chicago . . . 1871–1893* (New York: Alfred A. Knopf, 1957), III, 117, 150.

American approval. The chauvinistic argument assumed varied forms. Purists of the old school felt Americans should pay for the nation's imports with tangible exports and not by the shipment abroad of securities; the sale of any kind of American securities to aliens was a reflection upon the self-reliance and manliness of the American economy; the annual interest charges on such securities were a dangerous "drain" or "tribute." [48]

Yet the trickle of foreign money into American industries brought certain advantages. English investors, even more than American, were in favor of stability in business and reliability in management. Chastened by their experience with American railroads, they wanted to be sure that the properties they purchased amounted to something and were what they were pictured to be. Accordingly, as a prelude to negotiation they despatched to this country "an independent, impartial, and expert chartered accountant, from some well-known and long-established firm, whose position is sufficiently guaranteed by the fact that his firm are members of the Society of London Chartered Accountants, . . . famous the world over for their accuracy, probity and sound judgement in matters of book-keeping." [49] Members of these English accounting firms stayed on in this country to found branches of the parent group. Sobriety is not usually associated with alcohol, but the introduction of professional accounting into the United States was an attendant circumstance to the appraisal of breweries.

When Jay Cooke undertook the task of selling government bonds during the war, one of his first steps was to "peg the market." After all, if he took the securities at a guaranteed price, he had to be sure that the price on the public market was not so low as to undermine the undertaking. This market manipulation became necessary for all syndicates.[50]

THE EVIL UTILITY OF THE STOCK EXCHANGE

Like everything else in this period security markets were institutionalized and modernized. In 1869 three agencies for the handling of securities amalgamated into the New York Stock Exchange, an unincorporated organization with a limited number of "seats." There were still organizations outside its orbit: the Curb market for unlisted securities, and the consolidated exchange which handled predominantly mining securities. Still the Stock Exchange was the king-pin and most companies of importance sought to have their shares "listed" on it for trading pur-

[48] Wiman, *loc. cit.*, pp. 220–228; "Report of the Special Commissioner of the Revenue," *House Executive Document* No. 27 (s.n. 1416), 41st Cong., 2d Sess., pp. xxix–xxxi.

[49] Wiman, *loc. cit.*, p. 227.

[50] Larson, *op. cit.*, p. 175.

poses. In November, 1879 the Exchange attained a 700,000 share day; in December, 1886 the first million share day.[51] Railroad bonds and stocks were its chief pabulum until the late nineties. Between 1896 and 1900, however, the number of listed industrials rose from 20 to 46; the "big trusts" and combinations were listed almost immediately.[52] Overall annual transactions in bonds were several times greater than in stocks.[53] In theory the brokers on the Stock Exchange brought together the interests of buyers and sellers and thus provided a continuous market for securities and a valid quotation for them. One important broker, blandly mixing his metaphors, wrote, "Wall Street has been very aptly described as the 'business pulse of the nation' and that is what it is, in the truest sense of the term. As the mercury in the thermometer denotes the degrees of heat and cold, so do the fluctuations in the Wall Street markets show the rise and fall of the business activity of the country." Changes in security prices "are the results when natural conditions are allowed to prevail." [54]

Apparently the prerequisite for these "natural conditions" were purchases and sales for money by those who actually wished to own securities or divest themselves of such. Though it would be untrue to deny that such conditions prevailed on the Street, it was doubtful that they were either so universal or inevitable as to constitute "a natural law." Different procedures were facilitated by the fact that one could carry stocks on margin by putting up only a percentage of their value in cash and borrowing the remainder from the broker or through him from other brokers or banks. This was all the easier since the New York banks under the national bank law held the reserves of the nation's banking system and preferred to keep this money busy by loaning it in "call loans" with securities as collateral.[55]

As early as 1869 Charles F. Adams, Jr., could summarize the *argot*, the objectives and the methods of Wall Street: "A bull, in the slang of the stock exchange, is one who endeavors to increase the market price of stocks, as a bear endeavors to depress it. The bull is supposed to toss the thing up with his horns, and the bear to drag it down with his claws. The vast majority of stock operations are pure gambling transactions.

[51] Clough, *op. cit.*, p. 180; M. G. Myers, *The New York Money Market: Origins and Development* (New York: Columbia University Press, 1931), pp. 295–296.

[52] W. J. Schultz and M. R. Caine, *Financial Development of the United States* (New York: Prentice-Hall, 1937), pp. 434, 441; Myers, *op. cit.*, pp. 433–434.

[53] Clough, *op. cit.*, p. 382; Testimony of F. B. Thurber, *Report of the Industrial Commission*, I, 7; *Commercial and Financial Chronicle*, LV (August 20, 1892), 283; (December 31, 1892), 1097.

[54] Henry Clews, *The Wall Street Point of View* (New York: Silver, Burdett and Company, 1900), p. 2.

[55] Myers, *op. cit.*, pp. 134, 280–281.

One man agrees to deliver, at some future time, property which he has not got, to another man who does not care to own it. It is only one way of betting on the price at the time when the delivery shall be made; if the price rises in the meanwhile, the bear pays to the bull the difference between the price agreed upon and the price to which the property has risen; if it falls, he receives the difference from the bull. All operations, as they are termed, of the stock exchange are directed to this depression or elevation, of stocks, with a view to the settlement of differences. A 'pool' is a mere combination of men contributing money to be used to this end, and a 'corner' is a result arrived at when one combination of gamblers, secretly holding the whole or greater part of any stock or species of property, induces another combination to agree to deliver a large further quantity at some future time. When the time arrives, the second combination, if the corner succeeds, suddenly finds itself unable to buy the amount of the stock or property necessary to enable it to fulfill its contracts, and the first combination fixes at its own will the price at which differences must be settled." [56] In short not the law of supply and demand, not dispassionate and impersonal market forces, but the willfulness and power of individual operators, determined on many short-run occasions prices on the Stock Exchange.

Entirely aside from economic conditions apt to affect securities in general—and such knowledge was available to all—the situation in any particular company was best known to officials, promoters, or other insiders; their decisions and acts might also determine what the company did and what the securities sold for. It was therefore an era of "cliques," "gangs," and "rings." Few adopted the self-denying business creed of T. Jefferson Coolidge, a Boston capitalist, who resigned the presidency and a directorship in the Atchison, Topeka and Santa Fe for the work was "not only fatiguing but unprofitable, because as director and president I felt that my duty to my *cestuis que trust,* the shareholders, prevented me from taking advantage of any facts not known to all, and cut me off from speculations which might have been advantageous." [57] Illustrations of a contrary practice were commonplace. Certainly the classic derisory account of Wall Street operations is to be found in Charles Francis Adams, Jr., "A Chapter of Erie," an exposé of the subtlety and ruthlessness of Daniel Drew, the Treasurer and "Speculative Director" of the Erie Railroad. Whenever hard pressed for securities to discharge his future con-

[56] Charles F. Adams, Jr., and Henry Adams, *A Chapter of Erie and Other Essays* (New York: Henry Holt and Company, 1886), p. 7; See also *Commercial and Financial Chronicle,* XX (January 2, 1875), 5.

[57] T. Jefferson Coolidge, *The Autobiography of T. Jefferson Coolidge, 1831–1920* (Boston: Houghton Mifflin Company, 1923), p. 88; T. C. Cochran, *Railroad Leaders, 1845–1890: The Business Mind in Action* (Cambridge: Harvard University Press, 1953), pp. 123–124.

tracts, made when he was "short" of Erie stock, Drew would cause the railroad to issue shares by the barrow load, deluge the market with them, and break the price.[58] Henry Clews, a Wall Street broker and apologist, disclosed plenty of similar incidents.[59]

No arithmetical appraisal of the respective proportions of investing and gambling transactions on the Exchange is possible. Roger Babson's statement that "Probably four-fifths of the companies that are organized whether in the transportation, electric power, or industrial field, are organized primarily not to transport passengers or generate power or manufacture goods, but to get securities to sell" [60] is a guess spawned by the salesman's instinct. A further difficulty was drawing a demarcation line between gambling and speculation. After all it was to the advantage of the economy that those who had funds should place them in enterprises so well run they were likely to succeed and to withdraw them from enterprises likely to fail. This was speculation; it was also wagering.

Though gambling performances distorted or deflected the operation of the Exchange as a free market, it is doubtful if they offended American majority opinion. Americans had been speculators in land for generations. There is fascination as well as entertainment derived from wealth quickly gained by daring and by struggle. At the end of the sixties, E. L. Godkin of the *Nation* was observing, "So many great fortunes are now made, every year, by lucky strokes, or by a sudden rise in the value of property over the vast field opened, in our day, to enterprise and speculation . . . that the old mode . . . by slowly 'working one's way up,' by frugality, the practice of industry and by the display of punctuality and integrity merely, may be said to have fallen into disrepute." [61] Vanderbilt, Drew, Gould, J. H. Keene, and other colorful titans of speculation were in a way national heroes and entertainers. For instance, neither the sophisticated nor upright could avoid being beguiled by the antics of plunderers such as Jim Fisk.[62]

Of course in a democracy the avenues of wealth should be open to all. So there grew up along the fringes of Wall Street "bucket shops"

[58] Charles F. Adams, Jr., and Henry Adams, *op. cit.*, pp. 5–134.

[59] Henry Clews, *Fifty Years in Wall Street* (New York: Irving Publishing Company, 1908), *passim;* Margaret L. Coit, *Mr. Baruch* (Boston: Houghton Mifflin Company, 1957), pp. 62–88.

[60] Roger Babson, *Actions and Reactions: A Biography* (New York: Harper & Brothers, 1935), p. 85.

[61] E. L. Godkin, "Commercial Immorality and Political Corruption," *North American Review*, CVII (July, 1868), 249–252; Larson, *op. cit.*, pp. 78–79; S. F. Van Oss, *American Railroads as Investments* (New York: G. P. Putnam's Sons, 1893), p. 10.

[62] Allan Nevins and M. H. Thomas, eds., *The Diary of George Templeton Strong, Post-War Years, 1865–1875* (New York: Macmillan Company, 1952), IV, 408.

where the small-scale plunger could buy and sell a few shares on a margin of one per cent. Through this agency Wall Street clerks and small merchants formed their pools. As gamblers, the odds were stacked against them, entirely aside from the fact that they did not have the financial resources for a long battle nor the power nor inside information to make manipulation a sure thing. These small fry operated on hand-me-down "tips," "pointers," and "rumors." [63]

Clearly bankers, brokers, and other operators on Wall Street had to "manufacture public opinion" about the securities they were concerned with. This might involve no more than being kind to the gentlemen who wrote for the papers about the buying and selling of stocks. Thus the firm of Henry Clews fitted up a special "apartment" for the press and here the reporters for nineteen papers could write up their "money articles." [64] Or the speculator might have a journalistic organ of his own. Apparently by accident rather than by design Jay Gould acquired the New York *World*, once a religious newspaper. During his ownership the column "Wall Street Gossip" was certainly well named. "Items for investors" as a heading left more to surmise.[65] Best of all, of course, was to make slanted news which all papers would print. In this field Gould was certainly master of the revels. Early in 1882 when stock market operators accompanied an attack upon his "specialities" with the assertion that Gould was in need of money and was selling his securities rather than "protecting" them, Gould showed to a few friends his actual holdings in Western Union and various railroads. While the *Commercial and Financial Chronicle* was sufficiently impressed to comment, "The explanation for making this disclosure is so reasonable that it may be accepted as true," [66] "some of the wags" irreverently called it "the greatest show on earth." [67] In any case the assaults ceased, the shorts covered, and there was a spectacular recovery in prices. About two years later Gould, hammered by similar rumors about his circumstances, repeated the maneuver, revealing a "private vault" of "marvellous capacity" containing not less than $110 million in securities. Since "there was not the

[63] Clews, *Wall Street Point of View*, pp. 59–64; John Moody, *The Long Road Home, An Autobiography* (New York: Macmillan Company, 1934), pp. 66–67, 97–99, 122–130; *Commercial and Financial Chronicle*, XXXVII (April 18, 1883), 161.

[64] M. H. Smith, *Twenty Years among the Bulls and Bears of Wall Street* (Hartford: J. B. Burr and Company, 1870), pp. 519–520.

[65] J. W. Barrett, *Joseph Pulitzer and His World* (New York: Vanguard Press, 1941), pp. 57–61; F. L. Mott, *American Journalism . . . 1690 to 1940* (New York: Macmillan Company, 1941), pp. 433–434; Julius Grodinsky, *Jay Gould, His Business Career, 1867–1892* (Philadelphia: University of Pennsylvania Press, 1957), pp. 291–292, 294.

[66] *Commercial and Financial Chronicle*, XXXIV (March 18, 1882), 301.

[67] *Ibid.*, XXXIV (March 18, 1882), 308.

least proof that the suggestion of Mr. Gould's weakness had any basis other than in the imagination of those who circulated it," the market responded buoyantly.[68]

To the tolerant opinion of the Wall Street speculator there was a strong minority dissent. Moralists of an old school had no use for gambling, and a generation which turned itself inside out to crush the Louisiana lottery [69] was sure to produce critics who found Wall Street "a haunt of gamblers and a den of thieves." [70] Men in business and other callings who gave their lives to the productive process and saw in production, industrial or agricultural, the test of national welfare had little use for speculation on the Street. It diverted attention from "legitimate business." "Resolve to be business men, but speculators never," counseled Carnegie.[71] And Rockefeller was of much the same opinion.[72] Again, there has always been in America a suspicion of absentee management; the investment bankers were its apogee. As Morgan's pastor wrote: "Mr. Morgan and his business associates were dependent for their knowledge of the West on occasional junketing expeditions, hurriedly taken, in well-found Pullman cars, over thousands of miles of railroads that they controlled. Such expeditions were scarcely an adequate introduction to the millions whose well-being depended largely on these roads." [73] In addition to their isolation from social sympathy or social responsibility, the Wall Street gentry were given to self-satisfaction which easily toppled over into arrogance. As Clews boasted, "The New York Stock Exchange is organized after the same manner as a social club, such as the Union League, the Union or the Manhattan, and not under a special charter from the Legislature. Hence it is protected from the interference of that honorable body." [74]

SHEEP ARE MEANT TO BE SHORN

Paradoxically those advocating a reform of the system were hamstrung by the difficulty of defending the "victims" of Wall Street. Should one save fools from their folly? The old rule had been *caveat emptor*. Few in the nineteenth century advocated the disuse of this bracing therapy in the particular area of buying and selling securities. Naturally,

[68] *Ibid.*, XXXVIII (January 26, 1884), 97.

[69] Harry T. Peck, *Twenty Years of the Republic, 1885–1905* (New York: Dodd, Mead & Company, 1917), pp. 215–220.

[70] C. F. Adams, Jr., and Henry Adams, *op. cit.*, p. 95.

[71] Andrew Carnegie, "The Road to Business Success," *The Empire of Business* (New York: Doubleday, Page & Co., 1902), pp. 6–8, 16.

[72] Rockefeller, *op. cit.*, pp. 132–133.

[73] Rainsford, *op. cit.*, p. 290.

[74] Clews, *Fifty Years*, p. 95.

beneficiaries of the process rallied to its defense. C. R. Flint informed the Industrial Commission: "The evils which have developed in connection with the organization of industries are being corrected by natural law. The careless banker has lost his reputation; the careless investor has lost his money; and the result of it is, more care will be taken. The fact of it is that we have been, in a way, passing through a period of education." [75] F. L. Stetson, corporation lawyer and counsel to J. P. Morgan, took a sterner and wider view of the situation: "There is not anything yet that takes incompetents, lunatics, and paupers and makes them competent, responsible business men. You can not do it, and you have got to trust to the development that comes from the experience of having your property at risk. . . . As long as he thinks he is buoyed up by some life-preserver, he will not make a success, nor will the community and the world get on through the efforts of that kind of coddling." [76] The courts, in particular cases, accepted the same reasoning. If a buyer believed the statement of the seller about value, that was a matter of opinion and "the law supposes [the former] to have just as good opportunities for reaching a correct conclusion or forming a correct judgement." Only if the vendor willfully misstated a fact, and the purchaser had really suffered loss, could the latter sue with any prospect of success.[77]

The need of an expanding community for investment also accounted for the tolerance or indifference to the misdeeds of security sellers. General Dodge, a rough-hewn Western railroad builder of discernment and integrity, admired Jay Gould because he had developed the railroad network of the Southwest: "And when I compare where he put his brains and millions with those who have criticized so severely, who would not invest a cent, except it was secured and bought a safe interest, I feel it was to him that was due the credit instead of the criticisms." [78]

Meanwhile changing premises undercut these traditional apologies. As management drew farther apart from investment, it was silly to hold investors responsible for their miscalculations. Again stockownership was dispersing. Once it might have been plausible to assert that corners "chiefly affect the speculators themselves, and the community at large but little," [79] and "Whether stocks go up or stocks go down, as among

[75] Testimony of C. R. Flint, *Report of the Industrial Commission*, XIII, 93.

[76] Testimony of F. L. Stetson, *Report of the Industrial Commission*, I, 973; *Commercial and Financial Chronicle*, XX (March 13, 1875), 256; Testimony of J. J. Myers, *Report of the Industrial Commission*, I, 1137–1138.

[77] *Commercial and Financial Chronicle*, XVIII (May 9, 1874), 467–468; Testimony of John R. Dos Passos, *Report of the Industrial Commission*, I, 1163.

[78] R. C. Overton, *Gulf to Rockies: The Heritage of the Fort Worth and Denver and Southern Railways, 1861–1898* (Austin: University of Texas Press, 1953), p. 69.

[79] Clews, *Fifty Years*, p. 97.

the really active professional stocks, it does not matter a great deal. It is simply one of them skinning another." [80] But now there were thousands of stockholders and "nearly the whole country (including the typical widow and orphan) is interested in the stock market." [81] Furthermore the diversification of the economy and the multiplication of corporations created a situation too complex for the brokers and bankers themselves to understand or handle.

SECURITY TRADING AND REFORM

Measures of reform consistent with the ideology of businessmen and the public made proposals of self-reform or self-regulation attractive. To a limited extent that was what the Stock Exchange was already organized for. It drew up rules for the conduct of transactions. To be listed on the big board and thus eligible as collateral for loans and for trading, a security and the issuing company had to meet certain requirements, including a degree of publicity.[82] The Board could and did expel members for "obvious fraud," [83] and stop trading, as they did in the case of the Erie Railroad, in securities flagrantly manipulated.[84] That such punishment was more Pickwickian than painful was revealed by the maintenance of an "Unlisted Department" on the Exchange where in the nineties trading continued in the securities of the most notorious trusts.[85] Perhaps since the Exchange was a "club," it was best to fall back upon standards of behavior befitting a member. On this procedure the *Chronicle* made the derisive comment: "Corners have lately been out of fashion" possibly because "consolidation and watering answered the purpose much better. Cornering stocks is looked upon with much disapproval by a great majority of the respectable brokers, as it is considered very damaging to legitimate business." [86]

In the case of security trading, as in other aspects of the economy during this period, the provision of correct and adequate information was consistent with the American dogma of self-reliance. After all, the buyer might be expected to look after himself, if he only knew where to look. The result was a remarkable flowering of means for acquiring financial information. When he had founded the New York *Herald* in

[80] Testimony of F. B. Thurber, *loc. cit.*, p. 19.

[81] *Commercial and Financial Chronicle*, XXXIII (August 30, 1881), 118.

[82] *Report of the* [Pujo] *Committee on Banking and Currency of the House to Investigate the Concentration of Control of Money and Credit . . . 1913*, p. 36; *Commercial and Financial Chronicle*, XXI (October 30, 1875), 413.

[83] *Commercial and Financial Chronicle*, XXVI (January 19, 1878), 55.

[84] Van Oss, *op. cit.*, p. 126; Myers, *op. cit.*, p. 309.

[85] *Report of the* [Pujo] *Committee*, p. 37.

[86] *Commercial and Financial Chronicle*, XXXIII (September 10, 1881), 276.

the thirties, James Gordon Bennett wrote a "money article" dealing with activities of Wall Street. Bennett had a background of training in political economy and the personal courage and bounce fitting him for the task. Other New York papers soon followed suit with stocklistings and with analyses of stock market conditions.[87] There was a justified suspicion of the integrity of such information, for financial editors might use their columns to further their own or client's speculations.[88] Besides such columns shared the shallowness of journalistic reporting.

More thorough was the information in periodicals. In the forties Freeman Hunt, who had freelanced in various magazine fields, established the *Merchants' Magazine and Commercial Review.* In spite of a somewhat sycophantic approach to businessmen, this monthly magazine contained invaluable material on business enterprises.[89] In the middle of the next decade Henry Varnum Poor, editor of the *American Railroad Journal,* once devoted to aiding railroad promoters, orientated his publication to informing and protecting investors. The new direction quadrupled his subscription list.[90] After the Civil War these pioneering efforts at investigation, analysis, and communication were supplemented by a new and perhaps superior instrument. Hunt's *Merchants' Magazine* gave way to the weekly *Commercial and Financial Chronicle.* In 1875 the latter inaugurated a monthly Investors' Supplement. "We seek by bringing together every fact affecting the standing of any security, to render all the assistance possible to the investor. It is hardly necessary for us to remark how unsatisfactory is the ordinary publication from week to week of detached information. . . . We do not claim that these tables and accompanying facts are complete and perfect; nor will they ever be so in the fullest sense, but we expect to make them as nearly faultless as human agents can."[91] The lists in the *Chronicle* dealt, as was natural, largely with governmental and railroad securities.

In 1868 Henry Varnum Poor at the suggestion of his son began to collect information for his first *Manual of the Railroads of the United States.* Because of the superiority of his statistics and the independence of his analyses, the *Manual* enjoyed a monopoly for decades. By the early eighties it had 5,000 subscribers.[92] It undertook on a piecemeal basis to

[87] A. D. Chandler, Jr., *Henry Varnum Poor: Business Editor, Analyst, and Reformer* (Cambridge: Harvard University Press, 1956), pp. 221, 235; Mott, *op. cit.*, pp. 230–231; Smith, *op. cit.*, pp. 233–234.

[88] Smith, *op. cit.*, pp. 520, 526; Arthur Pound and S. T. Moore, eds., *They Told Barron: Conversations and Revelations of an American Pepys in Wall Street* (New York: Harper & Brothers, 1930), p. 312.

[89] "Freeman Hunt," *Dictionary of American Biography*, IX, 384.

[90] Chandler, *op. cit.*, pp. 206, 212–220, 222–224.

[91] *Commercial and Financial Chronicle*, XX (April 3, 1875), 323.

[92] Chandler, *op. cit.*, pp. 231–232, 250–256.

serve as a manual for industrial securities. In the nineties John Moody, who analyzed corporate securities for a Wall Street firm, conceived the idea of publishing such information in a volume. In 1900 he issued his first *Manual of Industrial Statistics;* It proved to be the "gold mine" he had anticipated.[93]

There were obvious shortcomings to the publicity ideology. First of all there were the difficulties of getting the information from private sources and of being sure that it was right. There was the deeper question of what people did with information after they got it. In theory the first two pitfalls could be avoided, if a law compelled companies to report their activities and financial condition to some public body. As we have seen, the multiplication and perfection of official reporting procedures were first applied to railroads and had been a prominent provision of the Interstate Commerce Act of 1887. Along the way the device had fallen far short of effectiveness. Poor had found the reports in only half the states were helpful in preparing his *Manual;* those of such key states as New Jersey, Michigan, and Wisconsin were so incomplete as to be of little value. National supervision was not necessarily much better. The *Commercial and Financial Chronicle* commented upon a report on the Union Pacific prepared by a government official: "The champions of government supervision and control of railroads may find somewhat of a damper thrown upon their enthusiasm when they reflect that it takes a government official nearly seven months after the close of any period to get up his report for that period. Why, even the railroads themselves do better than that."[94] Though there were members of the business community who felt that all businesses, including industries, should be compelled by national law, as in the case of banks, to issue reports after an examination by an expert accountant, such proposals faced the handicaps that most enterprises were not incorporated by the nation but by states, and did not wear so admittedly a public character as did utilities and railroads.[95]

In the want, therefore, of legally defensible grounds for interference, the case for publicity in industrial corporate affairs fell back upon the willingness of such firms to provide information. Fortunately, a considerable section of the business world wanted candor in such matters. For instance Judge Elbert H. Gary was an apostle for corporate disclosure. The Federal Steel Company had "no disposition . . . to conduct the business of the company to the prejudice or without the knowledge of the stockholders. We have sometimes been, I think, unreasonably an-

[93] Moody, *op. cit.*, pp. 88–93; Babson, *op. cit.*, pp. 139–141.

[94] *Commercial and Financial Chronicle,* XXXVIII (January 26, 1884), 98.

[95] Clews, *Wall Street Point of View,* p. 28; *Commercial and Financial Chronicle,* LIV (November 26, 1892), 88; Testimony of F. B. Thurber, *loc. cit.*, pp. 15, 16–17; Testimony of H. Campbell, *Report of the Industrial Commission,* XIII, 311.

noyed by inquiries from stockholders, our stock being largely distributed; still we have endeavored to take the pains to give such information as we had—all the information we had—to the stockholders, and be respectful. . . . I did not quite agree with some of the gentlemen that the affairs of a large corporation should be kept secret." [96] For Federal Steel and its successor United States Steel Gary insisted upon annual reports, the encouragement of stockholder participation in annual meetings, and the abolition of exclusive or prior information to directors for use in speculation.[97] The tendency of pioneers to adopt the policy that disclosure paid was hastened by the combination movement, for secrecy of operations had been primarily a necessity in the strategy of competition between small units.

Another way to protect investors and enforce public policy was to regulate directly matters of capitalization. From the fifties on, states, where the railroads were long matured, passed legislation specifying the proportion of bonds and stock they could issue, declaring that stock must be fully paid up in cash, prohibiting the declaration of stock dividends, and specifying that stock issued by going railroads must be sold at market value rather than face value, if the former were the higher. The purpose of these enactments was to bring about an identity between the road's capital structure and its "real" cost and to prevent the watering of stock upon which the roads could pretend they had to pay dividends.[98] As over half the states had no railroad legislation of this sort and the Interstate Commerce Act ignored matters of capitalization,[99] the issue was either not a burning one or else there was a well justified suspicion that in practice such regulations were a farce.[100] Perhaps this explains a lack of urgency in the later proposals to apply similar legislation to a wider area of business. The argument, too, that excessive capitalization might be advanced as a justification for higher prices had less application to industry, where decline of prices was more marked than increase. Besides it was felt "only time can prove" the value of trusts with "enormous capitalization." [101]

It was of course possible to elevate the argument from the frustrating

[96] Testimony of E. H. Gary, *Report of the Industrial Commission,* I, 996; Testimony of E. H. Gary, *Hearings before the* [Stanley] *Committee on Investigation of United States Steel Corporation,* I, 69–70; Van Oss, *op. cit.,* pp. 169–170.

[97] Ida M. Tarbell, *The Story of Steel: The Life of Elbert H. Gary* (New York: D. Appleton and Company, 1925), pp. 142–146.

[98] E. C. Kirkland, *Men, Cities and Transportation: A Study in New England History, 1820–1900* (Cambridge: Harvard University Press, 1948), II, 322–326; B. H. Meyer, *Railroad Legislation in the United States* (New York: Macmillan Company, 1903), pp. 162–163.

[99] Meyer, *op. cit.,* p. 163; Lewis H. Haney, *A Congressional History of Railways in the United States* (Madison: Democrat Printing Company, 1910), II, 309–310.

[100] Babson, *op. cit.,* pp. 87–88; Chandler, *op. cit.,* p. 261.

[101] Testimony of F. B. Thurber, *loc. cit.,* pp. 6–7, 17, 20–21.

realm of technical considerations to the stratosphere of morals. Perhaps for instance critics disliked overcapitalization not because totals of this sort caused high prices to consumers but because they made the rich richer through an excessive return upon their money. Why not then limit profits, particularly as the old concept of a "just rate" of interest still persisted? To this question Rockefeller gave the answer for his business generation: "In the early days there was often much discussion as to what should be paid for the use of money. Many people protested that the rate of 10 per cent was outrageous and none but a wicked man would extract such a charge. I was accustomed to argue that money was worth what it would bring—no one would pay 10 per cent, or 5 per cent, or 3 per cent unless the borrower believed that at this rate it was profitable to employ it. . . . All the arguments in the world did not change the rate, and it came down only when the supply of money grew more plentiful." [102]

Though there were plenty of voices doubting that the bankers and the apparatus they managed should produce such handsome rewards for the work done—after all it wasn't "production"—some saw that national growth depended upon saving and investment and that those who organized these operations, in spite of errors and unworthy intentions, performed, on the whole successfully, a vital function during this period. Common opinion has highlighted the criticisms made by the Pujo Committee, which investigated in the heart of the Progressive era the "concentration of control of money and credit." The Committee found in bankers' control a dangerous centralization of power and an abatement in competition. But the first paragraph in the conclusion of the report has been consistently ignored: "We are not unmindful of the important and valuable part that the gentlemen who dominate this inner group and their allies have played in the development of our prosperity. . . . Without the aid of their invaluable enterprise and initiative and their credit and financial power the money requirements of our vast ventures could not have been financed in the past, and much less so in the future." [103]

[102] Rockefeller, *op. cit.*, pp. 47–48.
[103] *Report of the* [Pujo] *Committee*, p. 159.

CHAPTER XII

Building American Cities

URBAN GROWTH AND THE WELFARE OF THE ECONOMY

TO those who believed that the welfare of the American economy depended upon the production of capital goods, the decade of the eighties brought forebodings. The most obvious support for this theory had been the construction of the railroad network. Its constantly extending mileage had given employment and business directly to thousands; it had also stimulated auxiliary activities such as the iron and steel industry and the engineering trades. Now railroad expansion was slowing down. What was to take its place? What power was now to pull the economy forward?

Though the answer was by no means obvious, the new generative factor was the growth of American cities. There had been cities, of course, in the colonial era, and in the first half of the nineteenth century population had gone cityward as well as westward. But after the Civil War the railroads and the industrialization of the economy compelled urbanization at rapid speed. In 1860 the number of places in the United States with a population of 8,000 or over was 141; in 1900, it was 545. At the same time there was a progressive increase in the absolute totals of urban dwellers. Whereas in 1860 just over 5,000,000 people lived in cities, in 1900 the urban population was just under 25,000,000. The eighties was the decade *par excellence* of urban growth; for those ten years the Federal Census reported "A very large increase in urban population." [1]

The startling accessions of population to cities came from two migrations: one from the country to the city and the other from abroad. On the whole the former, at least in quantitative terms, was probably the more important. Since the country-city migration was merely a population displacement within the national boundaries, it is hard to estimate its net effects. In 1891 the *Commercial and Financial Chronicle*, brooding

[1] *Twelfth Census of the United States. 1900*, I, *Population*, Pt. 1, p. lxxxiii.

over the decline of New Hampshire and Massachusetts small towns, expressed distress at this "decay" and "the melancholy story of the farming towns" but added that so long as Massachusetts "as a whole, is showing such vigor, there is no room for lamentations over the drift of population away from the barren hillsides." [2] On the other hand, immigrants from abroad represented an addition to the economy. These were producers and consumers the United States had not had before. And they came fast and numerously in the late nineteenth century. In 1882 their number, 788,992, set a record up to that time and one not to be surpassed until 1903.[3]

Though not all immigrants went to cities, and the enlarging population, wherever located, was a stimulus to the economy, there were differences between cities and rural regions which were of profound importance. The compacting and concentration of population stimulated economic activities, for example urban transportation and the provision of electricity from a central station, which a dispersed population in those days could neither have called into being nor supported. Where people were gathered in communities, standards of taste, convenience, and economic necessity compelled other improvements. For instance, officials of Augusta, Maine, complained in 1880: "The method of keeping . . . the main street in condition, is to haul on gravel in the summer and grade up in places where needed. In the fall and spring this makes a road-bed of 6 or 8 inches of mud. . . . Then in the spring our streets are scraped and the gravel that was hauled in is again carted out." [4] This was a road condition to which country dwellers had become, perforce, reconciled. It was humiliating to an aspiring city if "not a single paved street exists."

Furthermore, in the country the building of houses and barns was apt to be assimilated to the partially self-sufficing regime of the farm; in the urban communities it was set apart and organized into commercial construction, the building industry. In 1900, 63 per cent of the establishments in the building trade were located in the country's 209 cities and construction expenditures on farms constituted less than 10 per cent of the nation's total.[5] Finally, in the city considerations of the relation between sanitation and health, to mention no other factors, raised problems that had to be met by community rather than individual or familial

[2] *Commercial and Financial Chronicle,* LII (February 7, 1891), 221–222.

[3] Bureau of the Census, *Handbook of Historical Statistics, 1789–1945,* pp. 33–34.

[4] Census Office, *Tenth Census of the United States–1880,* XVIII, *Report on the Social Statistics of Cities,* Pt. 1, p. 7.

[5] *Twelfth Census of the United States. 1900,* VII, *Manufactures,* Pt. 1, p. cclvi; R. W. Goldsmith, *A Study of Saving in the United States* (Princeton: Princeton University Press, 1955), I, 619.

action. The provision of pure water and the disposal of waste meant that in the city reliance upon public policy in social and economic matters came earlier and went deeper than elsewhere in the United States.

The problems and challenges inherent in these figures and circumstances induced in some a state of ecstasy. As F. C. Howe of Cleveland was to write: "The possibility of a free, orderly, and beautiful city became to me an absorbing passion. . . . I had an architectonic vision of what a city might be. I saw it as a picture. It was not economy, efficiency, and business methods that interested me so much as a city planned, built, and conducted as a community enterprise. . . . The city was the enthusiasm of my life. And I saw cities as social agencies that would make life easier for people, full of pleasure, beauty, and opportunity." [6] Whatever Howe might dream, the city wore a very material aspect. It had to be built. To some extent the increase in municipal debt mirrored this necessity. Though such debts might occasionally represent operational costs they were primarily capital expenditures. In 1860 net municipal indebtedness in the country was estimated at $200,000,000; in 1880 it was $725,000,000, and in 1902 $1,433,000,000.[7] Whereas early in the period these sums were fed into the economy via city subscriptions to railroad securities or other forms of railroad subsidy, the revulsion against the railroad-aid policy in the hard times after 1873 meant that municipal expenditures for other purposes became more important.

Unhappily for purposes of historically measuring and tracing such expenditures, statistical data cannot be pushed very far back into the nineteenth century. But the investment in municipal water works in 1905 was estimated at "considerably more than a billion dollars"; [8] in gas works, plants and distributing systems, the sum in 1900 was $567,-000,506, about twenty times what it had been in 1860.[9] In 1860 neither central electric power stations nor electric railways existed. In 1902 the issued capitalization and funded debt of electric stations selling power in the commercial market was $627,515,875; [10] At the same date for street railways the capitalization and funded debt was $2,308,282,099.[11]

[6] F. C. Howe, *The Confessions of a Reformer* (New York: Charles Scribner's Sons, 1925), pp. 113–114.

[7] Paul Studensky, *Public Borrowing* (New York: National Municipal League, 1930), p. 13; *Commercial and Financial Chronicle*, XX (May 15, 1875), 463–464.

[8] D. F. Wilcox, *Municipal Franchises* (Rochester, N. Y.: The Gervaise Press, 1910), I, 399.

[9] *Twelfth Census of the United States. 1900*, X, *Manufactures*, Pt. 4, p. 705.

[10] Bureau of the Census, *Special Reports: Central Electric Light and Power Stations, 1902*, p. 16.

[11] Bureau of the Census, *Special Reports: Street and Electric Railways, 1902*, p. 11.

THE CHOICE OF PUBLIC OR PRIVATE ENTERPRISE

Cities could turn over the provision of municipal services to private enterprise or furnish them at first hand through municipal ownership and operation. Though state legislatures restricted the capacity of cities to go into debt and otherwise limited their functions, cities remained public corporations chartered for public purposes.[12] In favorable circumstances the legal hindrances to activity were not excessive. In 1897 the appellate division of the New York Supreme Court, validating New York City's issue of bonds for the construction and ownership of a subway, asserted that it was a principle of our nation's policy "to foster and protect private enterprise." Nonetheless the municipal ownership of a subway system was neither "socialism nor paternalism." There were other purposes cities could fulfill by their energy and expenditure. It was futile to formulate "a complete definition of 'a city purpose' . . . in view of the fact that reasons may arise which we are unable to foresee or now consider." [13] In the same decade the justices of the Massachusetts Supreme Court unanimously approved a wide area for the municipal provision of public services.[14]

If the city chose to fulfill its functions through the agency of a private corporation, the transfer of responsibility was usually effected by the grant of a franchise, either from the state or city government depending upon the date and jurisdiction. Such contractual documents permitted a private corporation to acquire property through eminent domain and to use the streets to lay pipes, install conduits, put down rails, or string wires. "The political science of the street is of fundamental importance in most municipal problems," commented one expert.[15] Since the streets were generally not wide enough to accomodate competitors, a franchise was usually equivalent to a monopoly grant.[16] The franchise grant might or might not contain time limitations, rate and service regulations, provisions for recapture, or provide for payments by the grantee. In other words, it roughly resembled the earliest railroad charters.

[12] Simon Sterne, "Administration of American Cities," J. J. Lalor, ed., *Cyclopedia of Political Science* (New York: Charles E. Merrill & Co., 1886), I, 460, 463–464.

[13] Sun Printing & Publishing Association *et al. v.* Mayor, etc. of City of New York *et al.*, 152 *New York*, 257; 46 *Northeastern Reporter*, 500.

[14] Opinion of the Justices to the House of Representatives, 150 *Massachusetts*, 592.

[15] D. F. Wilcox, *op. cit.*, II, 806.

[16] E. J. James, *The Relation of the Modern Municipality to the Gas Supply* (A Paper read before the Philadelphia Social Science Association. February 11th, 1886), p. 8; M. D. Hirsch, *William C. Whitney, Modern Warwick* (New York: Dodd, Mead & Company, 1948), p. 436.

THE IMPROVEMENT OF STREETS

Even the most confirmed advocate of private enterprise admitted that streets were a legitimate responsibility of government.[17] Expenditures for this purpose were, of course, not large so long as the making of streets did not depart widely from that of country roads. Cities graveled their streets or, as in Philadelphia, used an abundant supply of local materials for cobblestones. Though these methods had the advantage of cheapness, such streets were dirty, rough, noisy, uneven, damaging to traffic and uncomfortable for riders. The rationale for innovation was not long in coming. "Smooth and clean highways are a wise investment from every point of view, and that so long as the work is done in a thorough and scientific manner, the result is worth having, regardless of cost. No city should think itself rich enough to prosper without them, and no city is so poor that it can not afford them if it has any reason whatever for continued existence. Good roadways are cheap at any cost, and bad ones are so disastrously expensive that only a very rich country, like the United States, can afford them." [18]

Apparently about the time of the Civil War, eastern cities became aware of the possibilities and advantages of paving their streets with small granite blocks. Soon quarries in Massachusetts and Maine, along the coast or accessible to it, became interested in the paving-stone industry. A specialized craft of stone cutters recruited from Yankees and immigrants from the British Isles began hammering out the "New York block" eight to twelve inches long, seven to eight inches deep, and three-and-one-half to four-and-one-half inches wide. Coastal sailing vessels distributed the product to cities up and down the Atlantic and there were even some shipments to the interior.[19] On the whole cities without easy access to quarries relied upon other materials. After the mid-seventies pioneer communities in the Midwest were laying down brick pavements, a material far superior to wooden blocks, which in spite of their tendency to decay and heave, were also a contemporary fashion. Chicago was noted for its "floating pavements" of cedar block, "which are said to rise with the floods of water filling the roadways after heavy

[17] Charles E. Perkins, Memo, Jan. 26, 1885, Perkins Private Letters and Memos, R. C. Overton.

[18] Dr. Albert Shaw, quoted by N. P. Lewis, "Modern City Roadways," *Popular Science Monthly,* LVI (March, 1900), 525–526.

[19] *Sixth Annual Report of the Bureau of Industrial and Labor Statistics for the State of Maine, 1892,* pp. 204–206; *Sixteenth Annual Report of the Bureau of Industrial and Labor Statistics for the State of Maine, 1902,* p. 47; R. T. Berthoff, *British Immigrants in Industrial America* (Cambridge: Harvard University Press, 1953), pp. 78–81.

rainfalls."[20] Finally, taking a cue from the experiences of Paris and London, American cities about 1870 began the use of asphalt. At first the raw material came from the great Pitch Lake deposit in Trinidad; by the end of the century the refining of American crude oils was producing a domestic supply.[21]

Though cities owned the streets and could improve them through their own officials and employees, the task could also, without a franchise, be turned over to private contractors. Like all jobs, these contracts were much sought after and there frequently grew up a political alliance between the city government and favored contractors. The latter provided a labor force, frequently Irish or Italian, and the labor force provided voters at election time.[22]

WATER AND SEWERAGE

Cities had also to face the problem of providing abundant supplies of water for their own use, for fire fighting, for industrial purposes, and for their own populations. After research during the closing decades of the nineteenth century had validated the germ theory of disease, the water had to be pure. Building dams and aqueducts, installing pumping apparatus to raise the water to standpipes or high basins, laying out an elaborate distribution system of water mains was an expensive business. Generally speaking, whether the municipality should build and own the works or turn the job over to a private corporation depended upon the empirical consideration of what was the less painful way of raising the money. On the one hand municipal officials and citizens were loath to increase city debt; on the other, private capitalists, though they were sometimes granted subsidies and a monopoly of providing water service, hesitated to invest in enterprises in the determination of whose rates social and sanitary considerations were more important than the law of supply and demand.[23] Though ancient Rome had undertaken the task of water supply and classical precedents meant a great deal to Ameri-

[20] Lewis, *loc. cit.*, p. 530; V. S. Clark, *History of Manufactures in the United States, 1860–1893* (New York: McGraw-Hill Company, 1929), p. 494.

[21] Lewis, *loc. cit.*, pp. 534–539; R. W. Hidy and M. E. Hidy, *History of Standard Oil Company (New Jersey): Pioneering in Big Business, 1882–1911* (New York: Harper & Brothers, 1955), pp. 445, 773 n. 8.

[22] Hirsch, *op. cit.*, pp. 455–456; R. F. Foerster, *The Italian Emigration of Our Times* (Cambridge: Harvard University Press, 1919), pp. 353–355; Testimony of F. Ross, *Report of the Industrial Commission*, XV, 159.

[23] Blake McKelvey, *Rochester, The Flower City, 1855–1890* (Cambridge: Harvard University Press, 1949), pp. 32, 125, 135–136, 263–265; Bayrd Still, *Milwaukee, The History of a City* (Madison: State Historical Society, 1948), pp. 247–248; William D. Miller, *Memphis during the Progressive Era, 1900–1917* (Madison: American History Research Center, 1957), pp. 68–69.

cans, more influential in the United States was the example of its two leading cities. In Philadelphia the Fairmount works opened in 1799–1801, and in New York, where the original Croton system was opened in 1842, water works were municipal undertakings. Since New York had earlier experimented with private enterprise, its eventual choice of public ownership and operation was all the more influential.[24]

Interlocked with the water problem was the provision of improved sewage facilities. In some instances, as in Chicago and Milwaukee, the sewers emptied into the lakes from which the cities drew their water supplies; everywhere the wider employment of water closets raised problems of disposal. Slowly and quarrelsomely, most municipalities brought themselves to provide facilities through the sale of bonds and the levy of assessments upon abutting property owners. In Chicago the heroic measure of reversing the flow of the Chicago River, into which most waste was dumped, away from Lake Michigan and into the Mississippi was completed in 1871 at the cost of $3,000,000.[25]

LIGHTING

The provision of modern lighting facilities had, of course, to wait upon the course of invention. In 1816 Baltimore, the first American city to do so, introduced illuminating gas made from coal. In the seventies a dual transformation affected the gas industry. The Standard Oil group became definitely interested in piping and selling natural gas, used primarily for industrial and heating purposes, and also in the production of gas oil, a derivative from petroleum, which was used to produce water gas, a product with superior illuminating qualities.[26] These changes, of course, soon confronted the competition of electric lighting. Frank Brush's invention of an improved arc light devised a source of illumination peculiarly fitted for the outdoors. The Edison incandescent light early in the eighties was designed for interior use, and it was not until a later date that it competed with the arc light for street illumination. In any case, the advent of electrical lighting slowed the expansion of gas as an illuminant. In many ways the problems connected with lighting were like those of providing water. There was a dual market for the product—a private one, homes and businesses, and a public one, street

[24] *Tenth Census of the United States. 1880,* VIII, *Report on the Social Statistics of Cities,* Part 1, pp. 565, 812–813; Nelson M. Blake, *Water for the Cities* (Syracuse: Syracuse University Press, 1956), pp. 44–62, 100–171.

[25] Still, *op. cit.,* pp. 241–242, 363–365; Bessie L. Pierce, *A History of Chicago* (New York: Alfred A. Knopf, 1940), II, 330–334.

[26] *Twelfth Census of the United States. 1900,* X, *Manufactures,* Part 4, pp. 713–714; Hidy and Hidy, *op. cit.,* pp. 171–172, 451, 738 n. 5.

lighting. Both gas and electricity had to use the streets, the one for mains, the other for wires or conduits.

URBAN TRANSPORTATION

As cities grew in population and enlarged in area, a new problem emerged—urban transportation. Before the Civil War the omnibus and the horse-car furnished public conveyances. Horse-car lines were often adjuncts to speculation in suburban real estate. But these methods were hazardous, uncomfortable, and inefficient. They so heightened street congestion, already intense enough, that a person could proceed on foot more quickly to his destination.[27] More rapid means of locomotion had been introduced into the city incidental to the search by steam railroads for convenient urban terminals. Though railroads secured franchises permitting them to lay rails along the streets, such documents were usually foresighted enough to prohibit locomotives from traveling along city thoroughfares and to insist that there steam should give way to mule or horse-power.[28]

One obvious solution for the dilemma was to construct roadways at different levels and to permit locomotives and cars to travel the elevated one. Still there were real business uncertainties in such undertakings. In view of the proclivity of steam trains to jump the track or to run off bridges, elevated railroads threatened dangers.[29] There was also considerable doubt whether people would take the trouble to walk upstairs for improved transport.[30] Whatever the attitude of passengers, abutting property owners were quickly aware that an iron elevated structure along the street and the frequent passage of noisy trains was likely to diminish rather than enhance the value of their property. Nevertheless the need was so great that a Rapid Transit Commission appointed by the Mayor of New York recommended in the early seventies for two of the north and south avenues in the city an elevated system capable of carrying 15,000 passengers a day.[31] By the next decade elevated roads

[27] Harry J. Carman, "The Street Surface Railway Franchises of New York City," *Studies in History, Economics, and Public Law* (New York: Columbia University Press, 1919), pp. 29–30 note; Massachusetts: *Twenty-fourth Annual Report of the Board of Railroad Commissioners, 1893,* pp. 103–104.

[28] Carman, *op. cit.,* pp. 17–20, 33–35.

[29] "Report on the Meigs Elevated Railroad," Massachusetts: *Eighteenth Annual Report of the Board of Railroad Commissioners, 1887,* pp. 125–130.

[30] Henry C. Brown, *Valentine's Manual of Old New York, 1926* (New York: Valentine's Manual Inc., 1925), p. 21; *Commercial and Financial Chronicle,* XVIII (April 4, 1874), 339–340.

[31] Brown, *op. cit.,* pp. 19–22; James J. Swank, "Statistics of the Iron and Steel Production of the United States," *Tenth Census of the United States. 1880,* II, 150.

had demonstrated their success. Eastern cities imitated New York, and in the early nineties Chicago, destined to become the city of "El's," already had its lines.[32]

Eventually the elevateds were electrified. So were the surface lines. Cities, unless in special circumstances like San Francisco's, discarded the use of an endless cable beneath the pavement to tow cars and relied, particularly after Sprague's demonstration in Richmond, upon an overhead electric wire or an underground one with which a shoe from the car made contact.[33] By the nineties there "was an active 'boom' in electric railway building" and speculation. "It is stimulated by the apparent cheapness of electricity as compared with horse power, by the expectation of large profits, and in some cases probably by the hope of successful deals in the securities of the company." [34]

Private capitalists solicited and secured the franchises for these networks of urban transportation and operated the completed enterprises. Whereas local capital had once undertaken this task, capitalists without local ties moved into the enterprise.[35] A hope of steady dividends prosaically earned from operations was hardly their aim. Instead they applied to urban transportation the most dubious devices of speculation and personal enrichment developed in the railroad world: the construction company, the lease, consolidation, stock-watering and Wall Street speculation. In some cases those practicing these arts in the new area were railroad men; for instance, in the eighties Jay Gould applied his unquestioned talents to the New York elevated system. He transferred its complicated affairs to the arena of Wall Street, journalistic rumors, and the courts. Eventually the growing returns from the consolidations he put together placed the stock on a dividend basis and made it one of the "blue chips" in the Gould estate.[36]

In street railways a national "syndicate" appeared, originating in Philadelphia. Its leaders, Peter A. B. Widener and William L. Elkins, started their business careers, as had John D. Rockefeller, in the provision trades. Clearly this occupation as a training ground and reservoir of capital possessed a magic of its own. Dabbling in politics, Widener, Elkins, and others had by 1884 gathered within their Philadelphia Traction Company at least half the street car lines of the city. Elkins, who

[32] Pierce, *op. cit.*, III, 218–220.

[33] Hirsch, *op. cit.*, pp. 426–427; Stearns Morse, "Slots in the Streets," *New England Quarterly*, XXIV (March, 1951), 4–11.

[34] Massachusetts: *Twenty-fourth Annual Report of the Board of Railroad Commissioners, 1893*, p. 105.

[35] *Ibid.*, p. 106.

[36] Julius Grodinsky, *Jay Gould: His Business Career, 1867–1892* (Philadelphia: University of Pennsylvania Press, 1957), pp. 288–314.

had invested in oil and had sold out to the Standard, once remarked, "Give me the Broadway franchise and the coal-oil trade of Philadelphia and I will retire." [37] Actually this was a rather limited objective. In 1886 the Philadelphia group, with the alliance of broker Charles T. Yerkes, invaded Chicago. In the resulting process of consolidation and leasing, the capitalization of the various enterprises roughly doubled and cable cars superseded the horse-drawn ones.[38]

In New York City William Collins Whitney, a graduate of Yale and a reform anti-Tweed Democrat who had married a Standard Oil fortune, formed an alliance with T. F. Ryan, a Virginia farm boy now a broker. Whitney once remarked of his associate, "If Ryan lives long enough, he'll have all the money in the world." [39] Whitney and Ryan called to their assistance the Philadelphians Widener and Elkins and were also fortunate enough to retain as counsel Elihu Root to plot a path through the intricacies of New York law and politics, though in the latter area Whitney himself was adroit enough. These capitalists went ahead to consolidate all the surface lines of New York City. The first instrument was the Metropolitan Traction Company, a holding company incorporated in New Jersey. Like holding companies elsewhere, it exchanged its stock for the concerns it acquired; it also leased enterprises. In 1893 their corporate means of expansion became the Metropolitan Street Railway Company of New York. Whatever the legal form, the battle for consolidation was waged in the city and state governments and with frequent recourse to the courts. A trail of injunctions and receiverships marked this continual litigation. Nor were the vacillations of securities on Wall Street forgotten.[40]

Though Whitney's brother became the urban transportation magnate of Boston through his own efforts, the Widener-Elkins-Whitney-Ryan syndicate at the end of the century were reputed to have built up the street railway systems in New York, Chicago, Philadelphia, and Pittsburgh and in at least one hundred cities and towns from Maine to Pennsylvania. In addition they had become influential in gas and electric-lighting companies as far west as Omaha and as far south as St. Augustine. The united capitalization of their street railways was a billion dollars and of their lighting companies $300,000,000.[41]

[37] B. J. Hendrick, "Great American Fortunes and their Making: Street-Railway Financiers," *McClure's Magazine,* XXX (November, 1907), 32–37.

[38] *Ninth Biennial Report of the Bureau of Labor Statistics of Illinois, 1896,* pp. 56–58.

[39] Hirsch, *op. cit.,* p. 466.

[40] *Ibid.,* pp. 223–224, 226, 421–468; Philip C. Jessup, *Elihu Root* (New York: Dodd, Mead & Company, 1938), I, 146–153, 185–187.

[41] Hendrick, *loc. cit.,* p. 33.

THE MOVEMENT FOR MUNICIPAL OWNERSHIP

By the end of the nineteenth century there was a considerable movement for government ownership of certain industries. In its national phase this movement, which sometimes touched the railroads, focussed on the telephone and telegraph. But the objective eliciting the most expenditure of words and effort was the municipal ownership of public utilities. In one sense this is surprising, for earlier circumstances had certainly cast a dark shadow over the wisdom of enlarging both the sphere of municipal activity and the size of municipal debts. The experience of communities in financing railroad expansion had not turned out well; debt repudiations and scaling wrote an epitaph to the policy. What is more, events in New York City immediately after the Civil War unveiled a most discouraging example of municipal enterprise.

There the municipality had fallen into the merciless hands of a group of unsavory officials, whose leader was William Marcy Tweed, boss of Tammany Hall. With great persistence and courage, reform elements opposed to Tweed in 1871 finally rid the city of his tyranny and documented a noisome record of graft and corruption. The methods of the Tweed Ring in looting the city and enriching itself had diversity and also a certain simple charm. A favorite device was to suggest to contractors who worked for the city that they increase their bills and kick back the surplus to the conspirators. Thus a County Court House which really cost about $3,000,000 was made to stand on the books at $11,000,000. Toward the end of their rule, Tweed and his associates were taking as their own about 85 per cent of the city's expenditures. "If to the amount stolen outright is added the amount extravagantly and wastefully expended in sinecure offices, the performance of unnecessary work, fraudulent contracts, it is safe . . . to say that one-half the city debt of $130,000,000 represents absolute plunder," concluded Lalor's *Cyclopedia of Political Science.* An investigating committee estimated that if a private corporation had run the city, it could have done so for about one-tenth the stated costs.[42] Incidentally most of Tweed's expenditures were for unquestioned "public" purposes.

The Tweed experience bit deep. Methods of improvement, advocating city home rule and centralized and responsible city government, seemed inadequate to stem the "evils arising out of our attempts to rule the large populations of our cities, made up of foreign and floating

[42] Sterne, *loc. cit.*, pp. 464–465; J. F. Rhodes, *History of the United States from the Compromise of 1850* (New York: Macmillan Company, 1928), VII, 16–25; E. P. Oberholtzer, *A History of the United States since the Civil War* (New York: Macmillan Company, 1922), II, 581–595.

elements, through a government in form republican." The real cure, some felt, was the abandonment of democracy in the city and the restriction of the ballot to those owning property.[43] Americans were not allowed to forget the bearing of this episode upon municipal and state ownership. In 1891 Godkin, editor of the *Nation* and a fanatic for laissez faire, answered the question, What is the State? with an answer complete for New York City, "the little Tammany junta."[44]

If one were likely to forget this equation, events in Philadelphia reminded him of it. Acting on the assumption that gas lighting was a public function and should not be delegated to a private corporation, the city in 1841 took over the gas plant and entrusted its management to twelve trustees appointed by the Councils of the city government. Most paradoxically this arrangement was known as the "gas trust." It became a political machine. It employed 15 per cent more workers than necessary. Since it never established a depreciation fund, the original plant decayed and the mains leaked so badly that it was impossible to maintain pressure. Few extensions of service were made, and the coal used for the gas was purchased at extravagant prices. Finally, in 1880 a committee of investigation concluded: "One could not conceive a large business plant, run upon business principles, in such a condition without reflecting unfavorably upon its owners." After a decade of struggling with direct municipal operation, the Councils leased the city gas properties in 1897 to the United Gas Improvement Company for $10,000,000. This concern, a trust of quite a different character, owned plants in other cities. For a time the improvements in service and modernization which it introduced gained wide popular approval for it.[45] Be that as it may, the Philadelphia story of public ownership was characterized by one crusader for public ownership as "the most disastrous failure of its kind in the country. It was a huge inescapable argument against the advocates of public ownership. . . ."[46]

[43] Robert P. Porter, "The Municipal Debt of the United States," *Galaxy*, XXIV (September, 1877), 399, 404; *Commercial and Financial Chronicle*, XXII (May 27, 1876), Investors' Supplement, p. iii; XXIV (February 10, 1877), 123–125.

[44] E. L. Godkin, "The Economic Man," *North American Review*, CLIII (October, 1891), 500.

[45] Leo S. Rowe, "The Relation of Philadelphia to the Gas Supply," *Municipal and Private Operation of Public Utilities. Report to the National Civic Federation* (New York: National Civic Federation, 1907), Pt. II, v. 1, 588–664; Edward W. Bemis, "Municipal Operation *versus* Private Operation of Municipal Monopolies," *Report to the National Civic Federation*, Pt. I, v. 1, 149–155.

[46] John R. Commons, *Myself* (New York: Macmillan Company, 1934), pp. 111–112; Frederic W. Spiers, "The Philadelphia Gas Lease," *Municipal Affairs*, I (December, 1897), 718–729; W. S. Outerbridge, Jr., "History of the Philadelphia Gas Trust," in E. W. Bemis, *Municipal Ownership of Gas in the United States* (Baltimore: American Economic Association, 1891), pp. 155–169.

Despite such discouragements the advocates of municipal ownership had made considerable headway. The group was composed of college professors, mostly economists, who led a far from routine academic existence: John R. Commons and Richard T. Ely of the University of Wisconsin, E. J. James of the University of Pennsylvania, Edward W. Bemis, from the University of Chicago and eventually a consultant to cities desiring to install municipally owned gas works, and Frank Parsons, a lecturer in the law school of Boston University and a freelance teacher elsewhere.[47] Of the reformers, Parsons was the most important. His *The City for the People,* published in 1899, crammed together in encyclopedic style arguments in behalf of municipal ownership. Though its obliviousness to differing contexts or circumstances and its insistent note diminish its persuasiveness, the book reveals one intellectual prop of the group as a whole, reliance upon foreign precedents: Germany's railroads, Berlin's telephone, Glasgow's tramways and gas and electric works. A later volume by Parsons discovered the usefulness of New Zealand precedents.[48] Along with professors, American portraitists of Utopias played their part. In 1888 Edward Bellamy published *Looking Backward, 2000–1887.* An advocate of nationalized industries, Bellamy proposed as one preliminary step the public ownership of local public utilities.[49] Bellamy inspired an organized movement, whose Nationalist clubs and their agitation were one explanation for the passage in Massachusetts in 1891 of a statute permitting cities and towns to own their gas systems.[50]

A contemporary of Bellamy was Henry George. The classic statement of his position, *Progress and Poverty,* appearing in 1879, had focussed upon the evils arising from monopoly in land and proposed to abolish them by a single tax upon its unearned increment. Among the many converted by George's philosophy was Tom L. Johnson, a Cleveland millionaire with a fortune derived from, among other sources, street railways. Johnson saw monopoly in public utilities as one explanation for poverty. As a successful candidate for mayor of Cleveland, he devoted his immense knowledge and convictions to an attack upon urban monopoly or "Privilege." Since Cleveland was forbidden by law to own street railways, Johnson proposed as a solution the lease of the existing

[47] Commons, *op. cit., passim;* R. T. Ely, *Ground under Our Feet, An Autobiography* (New York: Macmillan Company, 1938), *passim;* Arthur Mann, *Yankee Reformers in the Urban Age* (Cambridge: Harvard University Press, 1934), pp. 126–144.

[48] Mann, *op. cit.,* pp. 139–141; L. S. Rowe, *Problems of City Government* (New York: D. Appleton and Company, 1908), pp. 330–349.

[49] Sidney Fine, *Laissez Faire and the General-Welfare State. A Study of Conflict in American Thought, 1865–1901* (Ann Arbor: University of Michigan Press, 1956), pp. 296–300.

[50] Bemis, *Municipal Ownership of Gas,* pp. 9–10; *Commercial and Financial Chronicle,* XLVIII (June 1, 1889), 713–714.

private lines to an operating company of five trustees appointed by the mayor of the city. The lines were to be limited to an agreed return upon their stock, and the rates they charged were placed upon a sliding scale, with a minimum of three cents, depending upon the level of earnings. To bludgeon the old companies into this agreement, Johnson threatened to build competitive lines on parallel streets and charge a three-cent fare.[51] There were mayoralty campaigns elsewhere—Chicago, for instance—which were won on the issue of municipal ownership.

In his ten-years war, Tom Johnson had the support of the Cleveland *Plain Dealer.* This was symptomatic, for the campaign for municipal ownership had considerable journalistic backing. For several years, before he established his Municipal Ownership League and ran for mayor of New York in 1905, William Randolph Hearst had been heating up the issue. In his early career in San Francisco he had been the advocate of municipal ownership of the city's water works; when he invaded New York with the New York *Journal* in the nineties he attacked the Gas Trust and proposed a muncipal gas works.[52] Certainly the conjunction of the professional reformers and the notorious editor of sensationalism was puzzling. Still it was not the first time in history that the dragon and St. George were on the same side.

Leaders to be effective had to have followers, and journalists had to have readers who could be persuaded. Generally the crusaders for municipal ownership pictured themselves as relying upon the "people" and it would be folly to deny that Hearst's sensational journalism had more positive influence in the crowded sections of New York than in the homes of tycoons.[53] But businessmen also had a stake in efficient municipal services and in low prices for them. They might use water, gas, and electricity in large quantities in business and industrial establishments. Also, since they paid wages, they were interested in lowering the cost of living for wage receivers. If street transportation were not available and cheap, they might have to erect company housing near places of work.[54] So even the apostles of laissez faire were willing to grant to

[51] F. C. Howe, *op. cit.*, pp. 85–137; Tom L. Johnson, *My Story* (New York: B. W. Heubsch, 1915), pp. 107–119, 156–166, 184–294; Herbert Croly, *Marcus Alonzo Hanna, His Life and Work* (New York: Macmillan Company, 1923), pp. 82–83.

[52] John K. Winkler, *William Randolph Hearst, A New Appraisal* (New York: Hastings House, 1955), pp. 136–142; Mrs. Fremont Older, *William Randolph Hearst, American* (New York: D. Appleton-Century Company, 1936), pp. 204–210, 561.

[53] Abram Hewitt to V. H. Rothschild, October 23, 1871, Allan Nevins, ed., *Selected Writings of Abram S. Hewitt* (New York: Columbia University Press, 1937), p. 387.

[54] Testimony of William Steinway, *Report of the Committee* [on Education and Labor] *of the Senate . . . 1885,* II, 1087.

municipalities a range of activities vouchsafed to few other forms of government.

Thus Charles E. Perkins, president of the Burlington Road, thought that "the inhabitants of a small, compact community, like a city, in the exercise of local self-government . . . may wisely and economically combine to procure gas, water, horse-cars, and perhaps other conveniences, granting special privileges in the streets, which are limited in number and extent, and limiting prices in consideration of such privileges. . . ." [55] An executive of the New York Edison Company, concerned as to where to draw the line between the permissible and the forbidden, concluded: "Good roads, it is conceded, must be provided by the commonwealth, as also sewerage; water supply is usually, though not always, considered a municipal function; lighting, communication and transportation are on debatable ground; there are few in this country who approve public bakeries or store-houses, although bread is a necessity of life. Somewhere within this range is the point where democracy becomes socialism. It is important to limit the function of the municipality at that point, and not be misled by the phrase that 'a city is a business corporation.' . . . The real limits of municipal activity must be found in an alert and wholesome public opinion which will prevent steps that lead by easy reaches into socialistic enterprises, pure and simple." [56]

Vague and fatuous though this distinction was, it had as much touch with reality as the prodigies of reconciling fact and theory undertaken by the advocates of municipal ownership. The strength of their attachment to municipal ownership and of their belief in democratic government confronted them with a dilemma when they looked realistically at the level of politics and political administration in the cities of America. So American advocates of municipal enterprise were compelled to dismiss the Philadelphia gas trust as "that parody on popular government" or elaborate a doctrine of purification in which theory refined fact. Thus it was private enterprise that corrupted city governments, and the responsibility of public enterprise would act as a cleansing agent.[57]

The main thread of their argument was not, however, circular or contradictory. Obviously a franchise was a privilege, a thing of value. Its recipients proceeded to capitalize it. Thus Whitney's consolidation in 1901 of New York street railways issued securities to a par value of $165,000,000; the net value of the physical property was $60,000,000.

[55] C. E. Perkins to the Cullom Committee on the Interstate Commerce Act, September 21, 1885, Perkins Papers and Memos, R. C. Overton.

[56] R. K. Bowker, "Public Control, Ownership or Operation of Municipal Franchises? With Special References to Electric Lighting," *Municipal Affairs,* I (December, 1897), 606.

[57] John R. Commons, "Municipal Electric Light," *Municipal Affairs,* I (December, 1897), 668–671; Bemis, *Municipal Ownership of Gas,* p. 17.

The differential was the capitalized value of the franchises which Whitney thought, being combined, were worth a good deal more than when they were separate.[58] It was performances such as these that gave substance to the frequent charge against the private managers of urban utilities that their stock was heavily watered. Without doubt there were many unfairnesses and short-cuts in this matter of capitalization. Also, as elsewhere in the economy, managers and investors were capitalizing on the basis of estimated earnings rather than actual investment.

Favoritism and extortion were not the whole explanation of this over-capitalization. While certain utilities such as water and gas works had been long enough in existence to be stabilized and the results of their operation anticipated, electricity as light and electricity as power for street railways were new arrivals. Technical advances and manufacturing changes were so rapid that costs, including that for equipment, fell rapidly; experience with these new industries was so lacking that there was a blindness to proper charges for depreciation. As in the case of new industries, there was a spectacular increase in patronage and use. In short, since over-optimism was common, business misjudgments about capitalization and profits understandably resulted.[59] The ideological case for capitalizing prospective earnings was posited, as in manufacturing, upon a certain check by competition. But of course in municipal utilities such competition was unfeasible. So advocates of municipal ownership correctly emphasized the inherent monopoly of public utilities as an explanation of their high and discriminatory charges.

ACHIEVEMENTS OF MUNICIPAL OWNERSHIP

In terms of adoption municipal ownership had considerable success. In provision of sewers it was universal; "Copies of sewer franchises are like rare books, hard to get." [60] In the case of waterworks, of the 3,326 installations in the United States in 1899 only 46.27 per cent were owned and operated by private owners, while 53.73 per cent were owned and operated by the communities in which they were located. At the same date, of the 965 gas works, 1.45 per cent were municipally owned; of the 3,032 electric light plants 15.17 per cent were municipal.[61] In street railways, private enterprise swept the boards. When the National Civic Federation investigated the merits of public and private

[58] Hirsch, *op. cit.*, pp. 459–460.

[59] E. S. Mason, *The Street Railway in Massachusetts: The Rise and Decline of an Industry* (Cambridge: Harvard University Press, 1932), pp. 12, 21.

[60] Wilcox, *op. cit.*, I, 451.

[61] *Fourteenth Annual Report of the* [U. S.] *Commissioner of Labor, 1899. Water, Gas, and Electric-Light Plants under Private and Municipal Ownership*, p. 13.

operation early in the twentieth century, it was compelled to turn to publicly owned tramways in England for a yardstick of performance.[62] As to the reasons for these variations the concentration of municipally owned gas and electric works in the smaller places gives a hint. Individuals as opposite as Tom Johnson and Charles E. Perkins believed the close oversight of operations justified municipal enterprise in such communities.[63] Waterworks which did not require a large labor force were less vulnerable to the spoils system and hence more acceptable to voters. Though private enterprise was historically entrenched in the gas business, electric light and power arrived later, at a time when the municipal ownership movement had acquired momentum.

In terms of comparative economic performance, it is hard to come by a dispassionate appraisal of the merits of public and private municipal enterprise during this period. The contemporary literature abounds with exceptions, assumptions, and short-run judgments. Though much ink had already been spilled on matters of rates, service and efficiency, the National Civic Federation, when it undertook an investigation in 1907, headed the introduction to its resulting volume with the assertion that until the Federation took up the matter "no definite effort had been made to determine impartially and scientifically the relative merits of private and public ownership and operation of public utilities." [64] However, in 1888 A. T. Hadley, an economist and president of Yale, had dared to appraise contemporary accomplishments. Sensitive to the larger context surrounding the movement for municipal ownership abroad and in America, he concluded: "What the advocates of state ownership really fail to show is the combination of liberal policy and wise administration in the same instance. . . . This is a damaging omission. As far as it exists, it renders the argument for state management of industry totally inconclusive. . . . Successful administration is found, but without the more liberal policy which is the main argument for government activity. Liberal policy is sometimes found, but is almost invariably accompanied by mistakes in administration." [65]

REGULATION OF MUNICIPAL ENTERPRISE

Between private and public ownership lay the compromise of public regulation of private enterprise. As we have seen, state and nation turned to this middle way in the case of railroads, but champions of municipal

[62] *Report to the National Civic Federation,* Pt. I, v. 1, p. 13n.

[63] Charles E. Perkins to the Cullom Committee, September 21, 1885, Perkins Papers, R. C. Overton; Howe, *op. cit.,* pp. 135–136.

[64] *Report to the National Civic Federation,* Pt. I, v. 1, p. 12.

[65] A. T. Hadley, "Some Difficulties of Public Business Management," *Political Science Quarterly,* III (December, 1888), 581–582.

ownership would have none of it. Tom Johnson, for instance, believed monopoly was more than a match for a prying or regulatory government. It would always win.[66] Moderates were more sympathetic to regulation, for state ownership "may be compared to a man who protects himself against a boy with a snowball by killing the boy. The social industrialism is no more necessary than the homicide is." [67] At different times in different jurisdictions legislation which had once let the government give franchises free or without stipulation, exacted, for this money-making privilege, a flat fee or a percentage of receipts, or stipulated the franchise must be sold at auction to the highest bidder.[68] Franchise grants were limited in duration and the city was authorized to recapture the property after a certain period. Rates and services were also regulated. All this resembled the old effort to regulate railroads through provisions in their charters.

As in the case of railroads, the regulatory movement gravitated into the hands of that new governmental discovery, the commission. In Massachusetts, for instance, street railways were placed under the control of the Massachusetts Railroad Commission when it was established in 1869.[69] Through the decades the degree of regulation over both means of transportation revealed the same evolution: rate-making changed from recommendations to mandates, and the Commission could prescribe measures for public safety and comfort, and finally in the nineties place severe limitations upon the methods of capitalization.[70] In 1885 the Commonwealth established a Board of Gas Commissioners and two years later changed its name to the Board of Gas and Electric Light Commissioners. Explicitly accepting the monopoly character of these new enterprises, the General Court authorized these Boards to investigate rates upon complaint and if they deemed proper, order a reduction in price and, in the case of gas, an improvement in quality.[71] The anti-stock watering statutes of the Commonwealth also caught within their dragnet the gas and electric utilities.[72]

As in the case of the railroad commission, these regulatory agencies

[66] Howe, *op. cit.*, pp. 132–134.

[67] G. K. Holmes, "State Control of Corporations and Industry in Massachusetts," *Political Science Quarterly*, V (September, 1890), 436.

[68] Hirsch, *op. cit.*, pp. 442–444, 447–450; Mason, *op. cit.*, pp. 134–137.

[69] Mason, *op. cit.*, p. 134.

[70] *Ibid.*, pp. 138–143.

[71] *Acts and Resolves . . . of Massachusetts . . . 1885*, pp. 769–772; *Acts and Resolves . . . of Massachusetts . . . 1887*, pp. 992–993.

[72] C. J. Bullock, "Control of the Capitalization of Public Service Companies in Massachusetts," *American Economic Association Quarterly*, X (April, 1909), 385–386, 398–404.

put great emphasis upon reports, publicity, and complaints of wrong from individuals. But a panegyrist of this device confessed it was of limited utility. It would work neither in a "corporation-ridden state" like Pennsylvania, nor "in South Carolina half of whose population ten years of age and over is illiterate." The prerequisites to success were "that a large body of the people of the state shall be intelligent and educated; that they shall be devoted to reading and discussion; that associated efforts shall be habitual and frequent; that population shall be considerably dense; and that resentment against wrong and whatever limits the common welfare shall be quick and energetic." [73] This proviso seemed to require, as in the case of most utopias, the regeneration of mankind or at the very least their elevation to the standard *homo sapiens* had attained in Massachusetts.

URBAN BUILDING

Private expenditures for residential and business purposes were the most important contribution American cities made to the economy.[74] An index of the dollar value of building permits in terms of 1913 dollars reveals how important this stimulus was. The index reached a peak in 1890 which was not approached again until 1925.[75] Such figures, as usual, obliterate distinctions. But so can the impressionistic, qualitative observations of travelers. In an oft-quoted sentence Lord Bryce, after excepting a few historic American cities, remarked, "American cities differ from one another only herein, that some of them are built more with brick than with wood, and others more with wood than brick." [76] Actually, building followed a straight-line evolution from wood to brick to stone. For stone was the prestige building material, granite enjoying the highest favor. Governmental buildings—customs houses, post-offices, courthouses, and jails—were built of it, as were buildings having a public aspect—banks, hotels, churches, markets, and railroad stations. Since granite was hard to work and therefore expensive, those with lesser means turned to softer stones, and brownstone fitted the prescription perfectly. Since its chief deposits lay along the lower Connecticut River, it could be shipped cheaply by water; the large blocks, straight from the quarry, were easily worked up and fitted near the spot of construction. Brownstone fronts

[73] Holmes, *loc. cit.*, p. 437.

[74] Goldsmith, *loc. cit.*, p. 619.

[75] John R. Riggleman, "Building Cycles in the United States 1875 to 1932," *Journal of the American Statistical Association*, XXVIII (June, 1933), 178.

[76] James Bryce, *The American Commonwealth* (New York: The Macmillan Company, 1915), II, 880.

dominated the domestic architecture of Boston's Back Bay and flowed like a chocolate tide along the avenues and cross streets of New York.[77] The birthplace of Theodore Roosevelt had a brownstone front; Commodore Vanderbilt gave the material a certain cachet when he built his palace on Fifth Avenue of it. To the Commodore, granite, like the law, was "too slow," and he wanted the building done before he died.[78] Of the stone buildings in New York, over three-quarters had brownstone fronts,[79] and its use penetrated even to Chicago.[80] The slate quarries, which furnished fire-proof roofing, and the lime quarries, whose product was processed in kilns to make interior finish plaster, were associated industries. All in all, the number of building stone quarries in the United States increased from 1,444 in 1850 to 5,764 in 1902.[81]

Houses with brownstone fronts usually had side and rear walls of brick. In some communities, for example Philadelphia, brick had been the traditional material for super-structures of the more pretentious early buildings. By century's end, even the slums of Philadelphia were brick single-family houses.[82] Since the costs of transportation increased rapidly with the distance such heavy materials were carried, nearly every city was rimmed with clay pits from which its buildings had been dug. Every state in the Union, except two in the Far West, reported brickyards. Nonetheless there was a tendency for the industry to gravitate to deposits of superior clay and to utilize at these locations brick-making machinery.[83]

In the United States even the interior structure of stone and brick edifices—flooring, beams, roofs—was generally of wood. Furthermore there were factors which made it the preferred material for the whole building. Forests were abundant. Moreover a revolutionary new technique for building houses and working wood kept prices down. In the

[77] "Report on the Building Stones of the United States and Statistics of the Quarry Industry, 1880," *Tenth Census of the United States. 1880,* X, 127, 282–286, 316–326; *Eighty Years of Progress of the United States* (New York: L. Stebbins, 1861), II, 355.

[78] Carleton Putnam, *Theodore Roosevelt* (New York: Charles Scribner's Sons, 1958), I, 20; Wayne Andrews, *The Vanderbilt Legend: The Story of the Vanderbilt Family, 1794–1940* (New York: Harcourt Brace and Company, 1941), p. 220.

[79] "Report on the Building Stones of the United States," *loc. cit.,* p. 314.

[80] *Ibid.,* p. 296; John Drury, *Old Chicago Houses* (Chicago: University of Chicago Press, 1941), pp. 67, 98.

[81] *Twelfth Census of the United States. 1900, Special Reports. Mines and Quarries, 1902,* pp. 785–788.

[82] "Report on the Building Stones of the United States," *loc. cit.,* p. 33; James Ford, *Slums and Housing, with Special Reference to New York City* (Cambridge: Harvard University Press, 1936), I, 267.

[83] V. S. Clark, *History of Manufactures in the United States, 1860–1893* (New York: McGraw-Hill Company, 1929), pp. 493–494; *Commercial and Financial Chronicle,* XXII (May 27, 1876), 508–510.

1830's an ingenious migrant from New England to Chicago invented the balloon frame. Previously a frame house had been composed of heavy timbers fitted together; the balloon frame used a multitude of lighter pieces and relied upon the exterior boarding to give the structure rigidity and strength. The house utilized the principle of the box.[84] Later, multiplication and refinement of woodworking machinery released workers from making blinds, sash, doors, and mouldings by hand in a shop during the winter and transferred this task to a shop using machinery all the year round,[85] thus doing the work more cheaply and in some instances performing prodigies hand workers could not attempt.[86]

The census of 1880 observed that, "Having a larger and more rapidly-increasing population than any other country that is noted for its consumption of iron, we are consequently the largest consumers of nails and spikes in the construction of dwellings and public buildings, stores, warehouses, offices and similar structures." [87] So pronounced were the advantages of wooden construction that great American cities clung to it even after the Chicago fire of 1871 demonstrated its danger.[88]

Whatever the building façade, the interior was mechanized. The American stove, "works of real art," "handsome, bright, cheerful, healthful, and clean," [89] and one of the early triumphs of American mass production, gave way to an industry of steamfitting and heating apparatus. The same domestic mechanization created the indoor bathroom and toilet, thus benefiting the porcelain industry.

American construction now began to utilize new materials of the industrial age. In New York City Peter Cooper, the ironmaster, decided to support the floors of his Cooper Union on horizontal rolled iron beams. By 1859 his plant was rolling beams 4 feet long and 9 inches deep.[90] Somewhat earlier Harpers rebuilt their burned down publishing plant with one seven stories high, using iron beams supported by iron columns; instead of brick or stone, it had a cast-iron front.[91] By the eighties architects were considering the feasibility of a building whose support was a

[84] Siegfried Giedion, *Space, Time and Architecture* (Cambridge: Harvard University Press, 1941), pp. 269–276.

[85] F. R. Hutton, "Report on Machine Tools and Wood-working Machinery," *Tenth Census of the United States. 1880,* XXII, 178–290; Testimony of Gabriel Edmonston, *Report of the Committee* [on Education and Labor] *of the Senate . . . 1885,* I, 548.

[86] John Maass, *The Gingerbread Age: A View of Victorian America* (New York: Rinehart, 1957), *passim.*

[87] Swank, *loc. cit.*, p. 151.

[88] Ford, *op. cit.*, I, 267; Edith Abbott, *The Tenements of Chicago, 1908–1935* (Chicago: University of Chicago Press, 1936), p. 10.

[89] Swank, *loc. cit.*, p. 150.

[90] Allan Nevins, *Abram S. Hewitt with Some Account of Peter Cooper* (New York: Harper & Brothers, 1935), pp. 114–119.

[91] Giedion, *op. cit.*, pp. 129–138; Brown, *op. cit.*, pp. 8–9.

metal frame or cage and whose walls were simply filler between the beams and columns. In 1885 the plans of a Chicago engineer, W. LeBaron Jenney, materialized in the ten stories of the Home Insurance Company building, the "first skyscraper."[92] Of course steel had now superseded iron. Whereas the census of 1880 had mentioned neither iron nor steel for buildings, the census of 1900 noted the production of 856,983 tons of structural shapes of iron and steel. Unhappily it did not specify what proportion went into buildings.[93]

The construction industry stimulated the economy directly. Materials had to be manufactured and put together or installed. Occupations ranging from sophisticated manufacturing such as wood working to the handicrafts of carpenter, mason, painter, plumber, and plasterer boomed. In 1900, expenditures on construction turned out an annual product valued at $1,946,000,000.[94] In the sixties an American calculator had surmised by extrapolation from data then available that there was "a vast annual demand for 130,000 new houses" and foresaw that the better construction and luxuries of a "modern house" with "modern improvements" constantly increased the expenditure per house. For the decade as a whole he put their total cost at $1,300,000,000. This was quite unlike the course of affairs in the "old and stationary countries of Europe," where "old cities" were already built and there was consequently "no active and continued demand for labor and capital to provide new dwellings to accommodate swelling numbers."[95]

The American ideal of owning one's home was deep-seated. Home ownership conferred prestige, showed others that the owner was getting ahead and reassured him that he was "Americanized."[96] In farming the dream was widely realized; in urban living, much less so. In New York City in 1900, rented homes constituted 87.9 per cent of the total; in Chicago 74.9.[97] Since urban population was notably on the wing, it relied on rented properties. Builders of all sorts relied in large part on borrowed money. The owner did not issue stock, he encumbered the property with a mortgage. Though most figures for construction in the late nineteenth century contain a good deal of surmise, it seems reasonably accurate to

[92] Giedion, *op. cit.*, pp. 138–142; Pierce, *op. cit.*, III, 499–500; C. M. Green, *American Cities in the Growth of the Nation* (London: John De Graff, 1937), pp. 119–120.

[93] *Twelfth Census of the United States. 1900,* VII, *Manufactures,* Pt. 1, p. cxlix; X, *Manufactures,* Pt. 4, p. 61.

[94] *Ibid.,* VII, *Manufactures,* Pt. 1, p. clxiii; Goldsmith, *loc. cit.,* p. 619.

[95] *Eighty Years of Progress of the United States,* p. 355.

[96] Abbott, *op. cit.,* p. 363.

[97] G. P. Watkins, "The Growth of Large Fortunes. A Study of Economic Causes Affecting the Acquisition and Distribution of Property," *Publications of the American Economic Association,* VIII (1907), 75; Abbott, *op. cit.,* p. 366.

say that the non-farm mortgage debt rose from $3,811,000,000 in 1890 to $4,661,000,000 in 1900.[98] While the major share of this mortgage debt was held by individuals, savings banks and insurance companies under legal restrictions were also large holders.[99]

Such arrangements facilitated home ownership without funds; they also aided speculative tenement building. Builders who went into this operation generally bought the land from an owner, borrowing money from him for the purchase; the latter frequently lent a portion of the funds for the purchase of material. When the building was done, the builder tried to sell it as soon as possible to an investor who would put in some money of his own and purchase the mortgages accumulated along the way. Land owner and builder hoped to make their gains by marking up the value of the property in the course of these transactions.[100]

By the mere fact of its existence, the city regulated the kind of edifices it had. Even with minimum planning, the city had to lay out the pattern of the streets. In Philadelphia the rectangular system or gridiron went back to its founder, William Penn. Between 1808 and 1811, three commissioners appointed by the New York state legislature laid out the gridiron plan of north and south avenues and cross streets for New York City and applied it from the old town of crooked streets on lower Manhattan to 155th Street. Chicago also had the gridiron. While this design had the advantage of fixing precise boundaries for property and thus facilitating its conveyance, it necessarily determined the size of the conventional lot: in New York, 25 feet frontage and 100 feet in depth, and in Chicago "the shoe-string lot," also with a 25 foot frontage but often 125 feet deep. Both sizes were ill-adapted for tenement construction, a tenement being a house occupied by three or more families.[101] When multi-family houses were built with higher standards they came to be called apartment houses and furnished abode for the well-to-do and middle classes.[102]

Although tenements appeared in New York as early as the 1830's, it was in the seventies, as congestion deepened, that the typical brick

[98] Leo Grebler, David Blank, Louis Winnick, *Capital Formation in Residential Real Estate* (Princeton: Princeton University Press, 1956), pp. 443–444.

[99] D. M. Fredericksen, "Mortgage Banking in America," *Journal of Political Economy*, II (March, 1894), 208–209.

[100] Robert W. DeForest and Laurence Veiller, editors, *The Tenement House Problem* (New York: Macmillan Company, 1903), I, 357–378; *Eighty Years of Progress of the United States*, p. 357.

[101] Ford, *op. cit.*, I, 83–84, 259–261; Abbott, *op. cit.*, p. 171.

[102] Brown, *op. cit.*, pp. 25–26; Pierce, *op. cit.*, III, 57–58, 500; Homer Hoyt, *One Hundred Years of Land Values in Chicago* (Chicago: University of Chicago Press, 1933), pp. 136–137.

tenement, five or six stories high, appeared, occupying most of the front part of the narrow lot. Since Chicago lots were a little deeper and the city could spread out over the prairie, tenements there became wooden houses two or three stories high. There was one on the front of the lot, one in the rear on an alley, and sometimes one between.[103]

Families were crowded into these dwellings until the density of population per square mile became record-making. In 1893 well over half the population of New York City lived in tenements; in thirty-two acres of the eleventh ward, there were 986.4 persons per acre, a density which only parts of Bombay approached.[104] The crowded urban regions by their filth and lack of ventilation bred more than their share of mortality and illness; to them also were ascribed prostitution, drunkenness, crime, poverty, and the break-down of family life. The more conservative feared they were seed beds of social discontent and revolution.

Charity societies, settlement houses staffed by professors, divines, and social service workers, and individual reformers such as Jacob Riis protested the growth of slums.[105] The particularities of their indictment and proposed remedies would seem to fall within the "public purpose," the responsibility for which in other matters majority opinion had often assigned to city governments. Some European precedents, to which American reformers were usually attune, pointed in the same direction. But though there were many who asserted that private philanthropy and the self-denial of rich men would remove the slum, rare was the proposal to do so through municipally owned housing.[106] For local authorities to spend public money "competing with private enterprise in housing the masses is bad principle and worse policy." Since housing was not a "natural monopoly," [107] public housing lacked that justification.

The answer was regulatory legislation. In New York after years of investigation and report, the legislature passed the first tenement house law in 1867. Successive years saw amendments or new acts until the passage of a general tenement house act in 1901, "the most significant regulatory act in America's history of housing." It was widely copied elsewhere. This act "would not have been possible except for the vogue of restrictive legislation that so largely dominated American

[103] Abbott, *op. cit.*, pp. 190–193.

[104] Ford, *op. cit.*, I, 187.

[105] *Ibid.*, I, 123–124, 172–175, 182, 199.

[106] *Ibid.*, I, 159–162, 175–178, 197–198; E. C. Kirkland, *Dream and Thought in the Business Community, 1860–1900* (Ithaca: Cornell University Press, 1956), pp. 44–45.

[107] E. R. L. Gould, "The Only Cure for Slums," *Forum*, XIX (June, 1895), 498; G. A. Weber, "Improved Tenement Homes for American Cities," *Municipal Affairs*, I (December, 1897), 752.

thought at the opening of the twentieth century."[108] Whereas in 1867 it had been thought sufficient to give each sleeping room ventilation by transom to another room or hall and to prescribe one toilet or privy for each twenty occupants, by 1901 the law restricted tenement houses to 70 per cent of the lot, required for every room a window opening upon street, yard, or court, compelled the installation of running water and a private toilet in each apartment, and prescribed a certain minimum of cubic feet of space for each occupant. The evolution of these requirements had been accompanied by a tightening of administration through the Board of Health or Building Department and had culminated in a Tenement House Department in 1901.[109] Some provisions of the act were to govern only future construction; others were to compel the alteration of "old-law tenements."

As in other aspects of the economy, the regulatory movement headed into a dilemma. If pushed far enough to accomplish the sanitary and social objectives sought for, it might so increase expenses of construction and hence rents as to defeat its purposes. For a while housing reformers were able to console themselves with the reflection that alterations in "old-law tenements" benefited the landlords by decreasing vacanies and increasing the rents which the occupants ought to be willing to pay.[110] But as congestion continued and new-law tenements were not constructed fast enough, and as apartments in old-law tenements continued in use into the twentieth century, regrets that regulation had not started earlier and chiding landlords for greed hardly seemed an adequate clarification of the situation.[111] What the reformers wanted was expansion under standards which the community could approve. But one employer had noted in the eighties, "Capitalists consider tenement houses a poor investment, paying poor returns."[112]

[108] Ford, *op. cit.*, I, 154, 205.
[109] *Ibid.*, I, 154–155, 217–223; Weber, *loc. cit.*, pp. 748–749.
[110] DeForest and Veiller, editors, *loc. cit.*, pp. xiv, xvi, xxvi.
[111] Ford, *op. cit.*, I, 202, 204.
[112] Testimony of William Steinway, *loc cit.*, p. 1087.

CHAPTER XIII

Serving and Controlling The Domestic Market

A DISTASTE FOR TRADE

THE worship of work is so deeply ingrained in the national character that it has been considered a distinctive American trait.[1] Hymn and verse, story and aphorism attest the ubiquity of this ideal. But Americans did not approve equally of all sorts of work. Laudable work involved manual effort, perspiration, getting dirty. President Francis Amasa Walker, contemplating the proposal to join his Massachusetts Institute of Technology with a liberal arts or classical university, thought the gain would be dearly bought if it brought his students "habitually in contact with young men, who regard labor as degrading, who look upon the rough clothes and stained fingers of the laboratory and the workshop as badges of inferiority in character or in social standing."[2] Probably this thoroughly American definition of work derived from an agricultural background and a reverence for Biblical injunction ("in the sweat of thy brow, thou shalt earn thy bread"). Persons outside of agricultural or industrial production did not meet either the historical or divine specifications.

Thus it was that David Wells bemoaned as a sign of degenerate days following the Civil War the "disproportionate growth" of cities and the accompanying movement of people from occupations deemed productive into those connected with commerce, trading or speculation. "The spirit

[1] A. M. Schlesinger, "What then is the American, This New Man?" *Paths to the Present* (New York: Macmillan Company, 1949), pp. 8–9.

[2] F. A. Walker, "Technological Instruction, Opening Address of the Chairman," *Proceedings of the International Congress of Education Held at Chicago . . . 1893* (New York: National Education Association, 1894), pp. 531–532.

of trading and speculation pervades the whole community." [3] At the end of the century, a New England journalist and salesman, lamenting that the region was more and more a wealth distributor and less and less a wealth creator, noted that a class valedictorian prophetically providing careers for his classmates did not put "one of that class into a sphere of life where they could produce a cent. They would be real-estate men, editors, doctors, lawyers—some profession, creating nothing." [4] Those standing behind a counter and selling silks, gloves, thread and laces, or keeping books, did not occupy a circle of detraction as low as "drones" and "dudes" who did no work at all, but clerks and bookkeepers were certainly nearly as bad as a "man milliner," a designation of extreme disapprobation.

Curiously enough, it remained for an American reformer to voice the traditional patrician distaste for trade. This attitude, as old as the classics, had descended through feudal and monarchical societies which Americans had theoretically put behind them. Nonetheless, in the eighties Edward Bellamy was writing of his ideal community, "according to our ideas, buying and selling is essentially anti-social in all its tendencies. It is an education in self-seeking at the expense of others, and no society whose citizens are trained in such a school can possibly rise above a very low grade of civilization." [5] More than other forms of business, the *Nation* agreed, retailing prevented a man from attaining the heights of culture: art and charity.[6]

No matter what public voices said on the matter, the number engaged in trade mounted. In 1870 there were 850,000 persons in trade, finance, and real estate; in 1900 the number was 2,870,000.[7] The proportion of the national income derived from trade rose from approximately 12 per cent in 1859 to 18 per cent in 1900.[8] Great merchants such as A. T. Stewart in New York, John Wanamaker in Philadelphia and New York, Potter Palmer, and Marshall Field in Chicago arose to challenge the business leaders in transport, manufacture and banking. Indeed "Down to 1868 the dry-goods kings were the greatest of American kings." [9] In 1888 John Wanamaker attained the distinction of being

[3] "Report of the Special Commissioner of the Revenue," *Senate Executive Document* No. 2 (s.n. 1276), 39th Cong., 2d Sess., p. 22; *ibid.*, No. 4 (s.n. 1416), 41st Cong., 2d Sess., p. xxxi.

[4] Testimony of Elisha Winter, *Report of the Industrial Commission*, "Education," XV, 68.

[5] Edward Bellamy, *Looking Backward, 2000–1887* (Boston: Ticknor and Company, 1888), p. 121.

[6] *Nation*, XXII (April 20, 1876), 259–260.

[7] Bureau of the Census, *Historical Statistics of the United States, 1789–1945*, p. 64.

[8] *Ibid.*, p. 14.

[9] *Nation*, XXXVII (August 30, 1893), 178–179.

chosen Postmaster-General in President Benjamin Harrison's cabinet.

Achievements of this sort were evidence of the strong economic forces pushing marketing of merchandise into a new prominence and into new forms. On the production side, these forces were epitomized by the larger quantity of commodities flowing from a dynamic industrialized economic order. The virtual completion of a national transportation system, furthermore, enabled manufacturers and traders to break down autonomous and limited marketing areas and to distribute products on a national scale. On the consumption side, growth of trade reflected the increase in national income and its diffusion on such equalitarian terms that mass rather than élite markets emerged. Furthermore, celebrated as American thrift was, the growth of trade implied that American income receivers had a propensity to spend as well as to save. Here again the democratic character of American life played a part. There were no historic social taboos limiting the purchasing aspirations of the masses. For the humble as well as the exalted, comfort and even luxury were possible—if one had the price.[10]

VARIED LAYERS OF MIDDLEMEN

To dispose of goods and to serve markets, a series of middlemen intervened between manufacturer and consumer. There are several explanations for their appearance—geographical apartness, financing of manufacturing and trading operations, difference between managerial talents required in production and in distribution. Whatever the reasons, goods passed through many hands on way to market. In discussing a sales tax in 1864, the Commissioner of Internal Revenue surmised that the portion of agricultural products going through commercial channels "may be sold once, twice, or thrice, while textile fabrics are sold five, six, or seven times before being consumed." [11]

To systematize or regularize the various stages in distribution is as hopeless as nailing down the weather. There were bewildering shifts of form and definition; there was a blurring of function, and the methods of marketing one product were not necessarily those for marketing another. Around mid-century the general structure might be said to be based on commission merchants, otherwise known as "selling agents" or "factors" or "first hands." Such firms generally took the product of a producer; according to John Wanamaker the former's "principal business was banking—to receive the goods and advance upon them.

[10] David A. Wells, *Recent Economic Changes* (New York: D. Appleton and Company, 1899), pp. 380, 386–389.

[11] "Annual Report of the Secretary of the Treasury on . . . the Finances . . . 1864," *House Executive Document* No. 3 (s.n. 1222), 38th Cong., 2d Sess., p. 61.

. . . The manufacturer drew bills on the commission man, who indorsed them. . . . and then the manufacturer had to find the facilities to use the paper when he got it; he had to find the banker to furnish the money, generally a local banker." The next stage was the jobber or "second hand."[12] He broke up the large assortments from the commission merchant into the smaller ones, "job lots," desired by retail merchants.

Since jobbers served retailers, they tended to move nearer their customers. Before the Civil War, jobbers' houses had been confined largely to the Atlantic coast; after the conflict and with the broadening of the market, jobbers moved into interior cities, Cincinnati, Chicago, and St. Louis. The jobber sold on credit to the retailer or other user.[13] As the products of manufacturers became more standardized and were branded, as commercial integrity became more common, goods could be bought from sample rather than from examination. The buyer no longer needed to go down to the city to make up his stock. Agents or drummers came to him.[14] Sometimes, however, when producers found they had more goods on their hands than the distributors would take, they would resort to an auction to get their product moving to retailers. In 1876 New England producers of textiles held in New York "the largest public sale of domestic goods ever known in this city." Not surprisingly "these large transactions rendered business quiet with commission houses and jobbers."[15]

However customary auctions may have been earlier in the century,[16] they became later a rather spasmodic way of jumping links in the distributive chain and avoiding the charges middlemen made for their services. Meanwhile other marketing changes were steadily and remorselessly eliminating or subordinating wholesalers. Perhaps the peak of wholesaling came around 1879, at least in the industrialized East.[17] The new industries, less bound by traditional arrangements and with products they had to promote or force into the market, were the leaders in displacing wholesalers. For instance, John D. Rockefeller was exceptionally elated by the achievement of the Standard in selling its products "direct to the consumer. . . . I have often wondered if the criticism which centered upon us did not come from the fact that we were among the

[12] Testimony of John Wanamaker, *Report of the Industrial Commission,* VII, 455.

[13] *Ibid.,* VII, 455; F. M. Jones, "Middlemen in the Domestic Trade of the United States, 1800–1860," *Illinois Studies in the Social Sciences,* XXI, No. 3 (Urbana: University of Illinois, 1937), 10, 14–16.

[14] Jones, *loc. cit.,* pp. 16–17.

[15] *Commercial and Financial Chronicle,* XXII (May 27, 1876), 514, 527; (June 17, 1876), 598.

[16] Jones, *loc. cit.,* pp. 33–43.

[17] Harold Barger, *Distribution's Place in the American Economy since 1869* (Princeton: Princeton University Press, 1905), p. 71.

first, if not the first, to work out the problems of direct selling to the user on a broad scale." [18]

This recollection was hardly a precise description of the Standard's operations; the oil company did not usually dispense with the retailer. It built its own marketing structure up to him. By the nineties the Standard group was constructing at chosen spots bulk facilities for storing its products; from these stations it distributed, by tank or other types of wagons, petroleum products to the retailer, be he grocer or hardware dealer or owner of a general store. The Standard thus made little use of independent merchants or jobbers. It retained within its own organization the profits and charges of distribution. Though some of its marketing organizations, for example the Waters-Pierce Oil Company in the Southwest, were powerful corporations, a Domestic Trade Committee at headquarters in New York formulated general policy. Marketing areas were given boundaries, production interrelated with distribution. Besides, in the competitive struggle control of a marketing organization gave the Standard an invaluable instrument for price-cutting, for pushing new products, and for searching for customers.[19]

During the same years, Gustavus F. Swift in fresh meat processing, James B. Duke in cigarettes, McCormick in harvesters, and the Singer Sewing Machine company built large marketing organizations. Sometimes, as in the case of Swift, it was the perishable nature of the product and the necessity of breaking down Eastern hostility to Western beef that led to the building of branch houses and refrigerated warehouses. In other instances as in the case of the International Harvester and Singer Sewing Machine, need for effective servicing of machines and for financing customers explained the change. Duke wanted an advertising more aggressive and a distribution more rapid than old-style commission merchants could give him.[20]

DEPARTMENT STORES

While the manufacturer in his search for vertical integration of his business was invading the sphere of the middleman, the retailer was eroding it from another quarter. The primordial American retail store had been the general store. When the local market was a crossroads in

[18] John D. Rockefeller, *Random Reminiscences of Men and Events* (Garden City: Doubleday, Doran & Company, 1933), pp. 57–58.

[19] Ralph W. and Muriel E. Hidy, *History of Standard Oil Company (New Jersey). Pioneering in Big Business, 1882–1911* (New York: Harper & Brothers, 1955), pp. 58–60, 290–301.

[20] A. D. Chandler, Jr., "Integration and Diversification as Business Strategies—An Historical Analysis," A Paper Given before the Business History Conference at the University of Illinois in February, 1959. (Mimeographed).

the country or in the village, it was not large enough to support specialized or "one-line" stores unless they were the shops of artisans. Depending upon where one stood in a general store, "It was possible to identify the distinctive smells of molasses, vinegar, damp cellar floors, fish, cheese, freshly ground coffee, rope, rubber boots, dress goods in bolts, leather goods, or kerosene." By twentieth-century standards, stores of the 1870's were "dirty unsanitary places, offering a limited range of quality in merchandise, and with no assurance that prices paid would guarantee colors, durability, or fit." [21] The general store operated on credit. The middlemen from whom it bought goods extended long terms to the store's proprietor, and he, in turn, furnished the same service—often at twelve months—to his customers, one reason being that customers bartered for store goods the products they had grown or made. "Settlement day" came once a year. Beyond this necessitous economic arrangement was the social one; credit was a sign of prestige. It bespoke the solvency of the grantee and the grantor. To have one's credit at the store cut off was the equivalent of a fall from grace.

One of the newcomers threatening the general store and the simple marketing arrangement of which it was the terminal unit was the department store. The paternity of this innovation is a matter of dispute. Since it is possible to list a number of big European stores antedating American ones, conceivably the former were precedents; [22] still, it is informative to note that in 1890 a visiting American was describing the Bon Marché of Paris, frequently cited as the first department store, as "near like Wanamakers in Philadelphia as any store I know of." [23] In short, it is likely that the department store in the United States grew out of American merchandising institutions. Sometimes wholesalers established department stores.[24] More often the parent stem of some retail dry goods establishment put out departmental branches. Macy's in New York, for instance, started retailing ribbons, feathers, lace, embroideries, and gloves. Then its founders added speciality imports from France and Germany, ready-to-wear goods, housekeeping articles like table linen and curtains, jewelry, decorative objects, china, silverware, kitchenware, birdcages, books. In a little over ten years after his New York opening in 1858, Macy was operating the outline of a department store,[25] which

[21] Lewis Atherton, *Main Street on the Middle Border* (Bloomington: Indiana University Press, 1954), pp. 43–49.

[22] Ralph M. Hower, *History of Macy's of New York, 1858–1919: Chapters in the Evolution of the Department Store* (Cambridge: Harvard University Press, 1943), pp. 70–73.

[23] John K. Winkler, *Five and Ten: The Fabulous Life of F. W. Woolworth* (New York: Robert McBride & Company, 1940), p. 98.

[24] Hower, *op. cit.*, pp. 143–145.

[25] *Ibid.*, pp. 46–47, 160–164.

probably accounts for Wanamaker's designation of the enterprise as the first department store in New York.[26]

The proneness of dry goods stores to become department stores is perhaps explained by the dominant role of women shoppers[27] (the sequence of additions at Macy's would accord with that hypothesis). This in itself was quite a revolution, for the old general store, like the saloon and the barbershop, had been a man's world.[28] In other instances a different course of development operated. As Wanamaker said, "Every great retail store is simply a small store highly developed. Its real foundation is the old-time crossroads country store. . . . It is a natural product evolved from conditions that exist as a result of fixed trade laws."[29]

An enumeration of origins is not always a sufficient statement of cause. In this country and abroad, the presence of a large, localized market furnished by the growth of cities explained the department store. Particularly important in this respect were improvements in urban transportation, enabling people in the suburbs to come into the city for their shopping.[30] Actually this centripetal pull also spurred the multiplication of specialized one-line retail stores.[31] Also, department stores forged ahead for other reasons. Potter Palmer was willing to accept the return of goods with which the customers were not satisfied—"Your money back if. . . ."[32] The high visibility and persistence of his advertising campaigns helps account for Macy's success[33] in spite of the fact that he sold only for cash while other department stores gave credit.[34] Since their large-scale operations and resulting dependence upon employees mitigated against setting of prices by haggling between clerk and customer, the department stores assumed leadership in applying the more efficient one-price or fixed-price system.[35]

[26] Testimony of Wanamaker, *loc. cit.*, p. 454.

[27] Lloyd Wendt and Herman Kogan, *Give the Lady What She Wants! The Story of Marshall Field & Company* (Chicago: Rand McNally & Company, 1952), pp. 27–34; "Changes in Conducting Retail Trade in Boston, since 1874," *Thirteenth Annual Report of the* [Mass.] *Bureau of Statistics of Labor, March, 1900*, pp. 4–5.

[28] Wendt and Kogan, *op. cit.*, p. 34; Atherton, *op. cit.*, p. 44; T. D. Clark, *Pills, Petticoats and Plows, The Southern Country Store* (Indianapolis: Bobbs-Merrill Company, 1944), p. 32.

[29] Testimony of Wanamaker, *loc. cit.*, pp. 451, 453; *Thirteenth Annual Report of the* [Mass.] *Bureau of Statistics of Labor*, pp. 58–64.

[30] Testimony of Wanamaker, *loc. cit.*, p. 455; Wendt and Kogan, *op. cit.*, p. 92.

[31] Testimony of Wanamaker, *loc. cit.*, p. 455; *Thirteenth Annual Report of the* [Mass.] *Bureau of Statistics of Labor*, pp. 6–35.

[32] Wendt and Kogan, *op. cit.*, pp. 34, 63, 75; Hower, *op. cit.*, pp. 94–95.

[33] Hower, *op. cit.*, pp. 51–62.

[34] *Ibid.*, pp. 18, 91, 118; Testimony of S. W. Woodward, *Report of the Industrial Commission*, VII, 734.

[35] Hower, *op. cit.*, pp. 88–90; Wendt and Kogan, *op. cit.*, p. 92; Testimony of Wanamaker and Woodward, *loc. cit.*, pp. 453, 733.

Department stores also had advantages in purchasing. Their ample resources lessened the need for long-term credit from intermediaries, and the scale of their orders made it possible for them to ignore jobbers and commission merchants and deal directly with manufacturers. "The manufacturer does not need to take the large risk he formerly took, because through the retailer in touch with the consumer he can find out exactly what his mills should make and often has the retailer's order before a thread is in the looms." Other risks and service charges were eliminated and the department store got the goods at a cheaper price, without which advantage their stores could not have operated at a profit. The fight to reduce costs and secure the economies of large-scale operations had also characterized the growth of industry and the expansion of railroads. In short, the competitive system and decline in prices led in merchandising as elsewhere to bigness; the department store was the equivalent of the trust or holding company in manufacturing.[36] As bigness took over the field, middlemen languished, and in city after city jobbers disappeared or declined in number.[37]

CATALOGUE HOUSES

From the seventies to the nineties some department stores undertook a mail-order business with many a doubt of its value and many a lament over its nuisance aspects.[38] This departure was not so much an innovation as a defensive measure against specialized mail-order houses. For these institutions, like the department store, were a challenge to the existing order of distribution. In a sense they *were* department stores. Though they were located in cities, they did not cater to an urban clientele but to an agricultural one. They were nonetheless an obvious response to the nationalization of the market accomplished by the railroads and facilitated by changes in communication and by the lowered postal rates and rural free delivery introduced by the post-office during the last three decades of the nineteenth century. Even before the Civil War there had been mail-order houses distributing a few standardized products; advertisements in newspapers and periodicals and in "mail-order magazines" had acquainted customers with their wares and ways.[39]

[36] Testimony of Wanamaker and Woodward, *loc. cit.*, pp. 455, 734; Testimony of Otto Young, *Report of the Industrial Commission,* VII, 696.

[37] Testimony of Woodward, *loc. cit.*, p. 736; *Thirteenth Annual Report of the* [Mass.] *Board of Statistics of Labor,* p. 56.

[38] Testimony of Wanamaker, *loc. cit.*, pp. 463–464; Testimony of S. W. Roth, *Report of the Industrial Commission,* VII, 706; Hower, *op. cit.*, pp. 119, 164, 269, 332–333.

[39] Boris Emmet and John E. Jeuck, *Catalogues and Counters: A History of Sears, Roebuck and Company* (Chicago: University of Chicago Press, 1950), p. 19.

Still it was not until 1872 that Aaron Montgomery Ward established the first great mail-order house in Chicago. Ward stated his philosophy and hopes thus: "Having had experience in all classes of merchandise, and traveling salesman, and a fair judge of human nature, [I] saw a great opening for a house to sell direct to the consumer, and save them the profit of the middleman." Since the Granger movement was currently out to supplant the nefarious middleman, Ward was able to describe his business as "The Original Grange Supply House." Though this association withered away, by the nineties Ward was listing 24,000 items in his catalogue and doing an annual business of over one million dollars.[40]

By this time he was facing a competitor in Sears, Roebuck and Company. R. W. Sears had the immense vitality and enthusiasm of a salesman and medicine man and was not above the sharp practice of the petty merchant. As an express station agent in the upper Middle West, his employers allowed him to do trading on the side. In the course of these activities he hit upon the possibility of selling American-made watches through his fellow express agents. A. C. Roebuck, his associate, was a watch repairer and assembler. Amidst vicissitudes and vacillations the firm grew. By 1893 the firm's catalogue offered, besides watches, jewelry, sewing machines, furniture, dishes, clothing, harness, saddles, firearms, wagons, bicycles, shoes, baby carriages, and musical instruments. Sears, Roebuck and Company had long since eliminated the express agent in favor of direct sales to consumers. In 1895 it moved to Chicago. Expansion pushed its gross sales from $296,368 in 1892 to $420,855 in 1894. Sears simply had to strike the rock of the rural mind with one of his magic advertisements or "special offers" and a flood of orders, which clerks could hardly handle, gushed forth.[41] His low prices stemmed from huge purchases direct from suppliers and manufacturers and from his selling solely for cash.

THE CHAINS

Along with the one-line store, the department store, and the mail-order business, chains were another response to changes in the market. In the sixties, George F. Gilman, a downeaster who had been a New York City dealer in hides, leather and teas, established the Great American Tea Company; for a while he seemed headed along the path of Ward and Sears, since he sold his teas and coffees by mail order to clubs of purchasers whom he enticed by low prices and prizes. By 1870 Gilman also had eleven store outlets. He was advertising as his great advantage

[40] *Ibid.*, pp. 2, 19–21.
[41] *Ibid.*, pp. 23–46, 59–67, 721 n. 9.

that by doing away with middlemen he saved "various profits and brokerages, cartages, storages, cooperages, and waste with the exception of a small commission paid for purchasing to our correspondents in China and Japan, one cartage, and a small profit to ourselves which, on our large sales, will amply repay us." While there was some truth in these boasts, Gilman's chief advantage seems to have been that he was competing with storekeepers who traditionally exacted a large mark-up on tea, a staple product which kept well.[42] All this was by-the-by, for in 1869 Gilman began employing a new business name, the Great Atlantic and Pacific Tea Company, and establishing retail outlets in the leading cities of the country. In 1878 he sold a half interest in the business to a fellow downeaster, George H. Hartford, whose family name was to become associated with the growth of the A & P. The partnership meanwhile added additional grocery products to tea and coffee. In 1902, after Gilman's death, the concern was incorporated in New Jersey. It had financed its expansion out of earnings.[43]

Almost contemporaneously F. W. Woolworth, a New York upstate farm boy and store clerk, conceived the idea of expanding a single counter devoted to five-cent items into a whole store carrying articles at five and ten cents. By 1879, when he opened his first permanent establishment at Lancaster, Pennsylvania, he had started and written off a fair number of experimental locations. During their pioneer period the five-and-tens were confined largely to middle-sized cities.[44] In 1886 Woolworth personally moved to New York, where he tried to break through the barricade of jobbers and purchase directly from the manufacturers. The latter tried to honor the old marketing arrangements, but Woolworth finally prevailed upon a candy manufacturer to sell him products he could retail for 5 cents the quarter pound. He followed this triumph by a trip to Europe, where he was able to buy inexpensive glassware, china, toys, and the like. By the mid-nineties, when Woolworth opened display stores in the big cities, manufacturers were more willing to deal with him. By this time Woolworth had twenty-eight stores; his yearly sales were $1,000,000. On the walls of a new Lancaster store opened to celebrate the coming of age of the system, Woolworth emblazoned in gilt: "Large purchases for cash direct from manufacturers explain the high values we offer." In a letter to his store managers in 1892 he wrote: "We must have cheap help or we cannot sell cheap goods." [45]

[42] Roy J. Bullock, "The Early History of the Great Atlantic & Pacific Tea Company," *Harvard Business Review*, XI (April, 1933), 289–298.

[43] Roy J. Bullock, "A History of the Great Atlantic & Pacific Tea Company since 1878," *Harvard Business Review*, XII (October, 1933), 59–69.

[44] Winkler, *op. cit.*, pp. 35–53.

[45] *Ibid.*, pp. 66–71, 79–101, 105, 109, 117, 130.

ADVERTISING

"Remember our advertisements are in our show windows and on our counters,"[46] Woolworth once reminded his managers. In this policy the king of the five-and-ten was certainly swimming against the tide of his times. For whatever the institutional marketing arrangements, advertising played a mounting role in marketing. No matter how large or accessible the market, it would not buy unless it were informed or stimulated to do so. Advertising "is the medium of communication between the world's greatest forces—demand and supply. It is a more powerful element in human progress than steam or electricity," wrote a New York agency in 1893.[47]

As the market grew too large to draw its information from town crier, handbills, or shop signs, merchandisers turned to newspapers,[48] whose front pages consisted of a series of small advertisements, set in agate in solid columns, usually without illustrations. Such advertisements announced the time tables of boats and railroads, the loss of property, and the arrival of goods—along with their prices—at some store or dealer. The advertiser generally wrote the copy himself. Middlemen appeared who purchased space in advance in a large number of papers, say one hundred, and then solicited advertisements to fill them; they made their profits by their commissions from newspapers and by buying space at wholesale and selling it at retail.[49] It was estimated that 11,000,000 advertisements appeared in 2000 American newspapers in 1847.[50]

After the Civil War, changes in methods of typesetting and the insistence of advertisers introduced display advertising into the newspapers. In New York City, Lord and Taylor and R. H. Macy pioneered in substituting a two column spread for one and attracting attention with illustrations and larger type faces.[51] The post-Civil War era also saw the spread of advertising to periodicals. Advertisers first resorted to the religious weeklies, a form not far removed from the newspaper. They were extremely popular and owing to their denominational sponsorship were supposed to tap a market of substantial readers.[52] Once under way,

[46] *Ibid.*, p. 138.

[47] Frank Presbrey, *The History and Development of Advertising* (Garden City: Doubleday, Doran & Company, 1929), p. 341.

[48] George Wakeman, "Advertising," *Galaxy*, III (January 15, 1867), 203; Presbrey, *op. cit.*, p. 181.

[49] Presbrey, *op. cit.*, pp. 179–181, 192–194, 206–208; Ralph M. Hower, *The History of an Advertising Agency, N. W. Ayer & Sons at Work, 1869–1929* (Cambridge: Harvard University Press, 1939), pp. 13–22.

[50] Presbrey, *op. cit.*, p. 210.

[51] *Ibid.*, pp. 245–248.

[52] *Ibid.*, pp. 281–282.

the rush to magazines proceeded apace. Advertising invaded the staid monthlies—*Scribner's, Harper's, Century,* and the *Atlantic*—and found in the nineties its perfect medium, in view of the feminization of American purchasing, in the women's magazines.[53] Advertisements in press and periodical increased 80 per cent in the eighties and about a third in the next decade.

Perhaps one-quarter of this increase went to periodicals.[54] The resort to magazines represented a great change in the source of advertising. Whereas local retailers once appealed to consumers within the limited range of a newspaper, now manufacturers and other producers were making customers in a national market aware of their products. By their demands these consumers could put pressure upon retailers to carry the product, and the whole chain of wholesalers would have to handle it. The makers of patent medicines—Castoria, Purina and Lydia Pinkham —had once done this through newspapers.[55] With the periodical, this hard core of national advertisers was joined by the soap makers ("Good morning, have you used Pears Soap?"), by food producers (Royal Baking Powder and Baker's cocoa), and by the manufacturers of new products (the sewing machine, the typewriter, the fountain pen, and, after the late eighties, the safety bicycle). About most of these products the public genuinely required information.[56] With efforts of this magnitude, the advertiser no longer relied upon his own inexperience. He turned to the expert. "The man," said a magazine article in 1869, "who has anything to sell now-a-days has attached to his establishment not only his salesman, but his poet." [57] A few years later the *Nation* commented, "The preparation and planning of advertisements of all sorts have assumed the proportions of a business by itself, to which the entire time and thought of a number of men are devoted." [58]

Advertising also burst out-of-doors. Every blank wall, barn or hoarding bore its message. So did curbstones and sidewalks. Pennants fluttered, sandwichmen paraded, vehicles covered with advertising lent color to the congestion of city streets, and billboards lined main-traveled thoroughfares and railroad lines.[59] By the nineties there was some shrinking from this exhibitionism. One advertising man observed: "The employment of natural scenery as a background for this work has fallen under

[53] *Ibid.*, pp. 337–343.

[54] Frank Luther Mott, *A History of American Magazines, 1885–1905* (Cambridge: Harvard University Press, 1957), pp. 20–21.

[55] Presbrey, *op. cit.*, pp. 290–297.

[56] Mott, *op. cit.*, pp. 22–28.

[57] Wakeman, *loc. cit.*, p. 204.

[58] *Nation,* XX (May 20, 1875), 342.

[59] Wakeman, *loc. cit.*, pp. 202–204.

public disapprobation and appears to be going into disuse." [60] If it were true that rock and mountain were safe from slogans, jingles, and names, it represented one of the few reversals good taste had imposed upon the ubiquitous vulgarity of the "golden age of advertising."

INDICTMENTS OF MERCHANDISING

Criticism was made of every feature, whether old or new, of marketing arrangements. Probably in no area of the economy was the charge of monopoly more frequently and more loosely applied. The old-time country store, it was said, was a monopoly, for it was the only local purveyor and thus able to charge extortionate prices.[61] Nor did newcomers escape censure. When the *American Grocer* was established in 1869 as a mouthpiece for the trade, it rode herd against the Great Atlantic and Pacific Tea Company with an article on "The Tea Trade and Certain Monopolies." [62] At century's end, when the Industrial Commission was probing the affairs of department stores, the trend of cross-examination revealed a fear that these big stores were monopolies. Criticism of this sort was all the sharper, for trade was actually a stronghold of small business. The limited amount of capital required to enter the occupation, the extension of credit by dealers, and the rudimentary form of business organization —there were few corporations, while partnerships and individual proprietorships were common—enabled the little men without many initial resources to have a go at success.[63]

Most charges of monopoly were fairly groundless. Even in the horse and buggy days, rural consumers had a choice of stores in several places and for major shopping operations made trips to the city.[64] The undoubtedly high mark-ups and prices were in large part phases of the long credits, expected and granted, and the spread of risks of bad debtors to the good customers.[65] While some of the practices complained of in the case of department stores were true, the presence of several such stores in the large cities and their unabating competition with each other guaranteed that the consumer was protected against the worst evils of monopoly.

[60] N. W. Ayer, "Advertising in America," Chauncey M. Depew, editor, *One Hundred Years of American Commerce* (New York: D. O. Haynes & Co., 1905), I, 83.

[61] Atherton, *op. cit.*, pp. 49–50.

[62] Bullock, "The Early History of the Great Atlantic & Pacific Tea Company," *loc. cit.*, pp. 293–294.

[63] Testimony of Wanamaker, Woodward, and Young, *loc. cit.*, pp. 452, 455, 459, 465, 697, 731–733.

[64] Atherton, *op. cit.*, pp. 50–54.

[65] Clark, *op. cit.*, pp. 316–319.

As advertising became "a monomania" [66] in the late sixties, criticism of it mounted. The necessity for it in an expanding and competitive industrial economy was obvious, however, even to the blue-blooded *Nation,* which, although not dependent on advertising, commended it as "a token of healthy energy, and the ingenuity used in it may even command admiration, though it can never be the index of any intellectual effort above the level of shrewdness." [67] The indictment against advertising was based first on the grounds of taste. To pay for constant iteration of one's name in the papers, especially in connection with pursuits purely acquisitive, offended the fastidious. Others felt lapses in literary and artistic judgment and even in estimates of utility might be but preludes to the "shrewdly dishonest" and the "indecent." [68] The main charge, however, was dishonesty. Exaggeration trembled on the brink of fraud. One abusing comment noted: "Surely there need be no sickness, suffering, or death, if men would only take the medicines brought to their notice through the journals." [69] Others identified fraudulent advertising with the department store pricing policy. Perhaps Macy introduced the system of marking articles 24¢, 49¢, 99¢, and $4.98 and thus avoiding multiples of five. These off-beat prices enabled the store to check on the honesty of clerks and to record fractional mark-ups, but critics thought them a means to tempt customers into a store and sell them a higher-priced article.[70] Advertising folk-lore relates the reply of an advertising writer to a merchant's query as to the possibility of something new in advertising copy. The answer was "Let's try honesty." [71] Some did. Among the pioneers in eliminating fakery were Wanamaker's and Macy's. The former's advertising counselor, John E. Powers, brought information back to advertising.[72]

A Lowell merchant said that while people for the sake of their prices patronized department stores, the latter were not "popular." Nonetheless distaste for these and other new institutions in the marketing area could lead to little in the way of prohibitory legislation. Sometimes legislatures forbad advertisers to use "mountainsides and boulders." [73]

[66] Wakeman, *loc. cit.*, p. 203.

[67] *Nation,* XX (May 20, 1875), 343.

[68] *Ibid.*, 342–343; Wakeman, *loc. cit.*, pp. 202–203; Bellamy, *op. cit.*, pp. 440–444.

[69] Wakeman, *loc. cit.*, p. 208.

[70] Testimony of Wanamaker, Roth, and Woodward, *loc. cit.*, pp. 460, 705–710; Testimony of D. R. Goudie, *Report of the Industrial Commission,* VII, 723–724.

[71] Presbrey, *op. cit.*, p. 303.

[72] *Ibid.*, pp. 303–318; Testimony of Joseph L. Chalifoux, *Report of the Industrial Commission,* VII, 342.

[73] *Nation,* XX (May 20, 1875), 343.

More customary was the adoption by city or state of a taxation system discriminating against the new forms of merchandising. After all, a charge for a license to carry on a trade, business or profession had a long tradition, and taxation, akin to licensing,[74] could be directed against alien firms and agents. It could be proportioned to the amount of business done or value of goods in stock. It could also be levied upon the individual departments in a department store as if they were separate enterprises, with the result "they would be obliged to disintegrate and divide up into a great many stores." [75] Once again the spirit of localism was called upon to buttress the static, the short-sighted, the unabashedly self-interested. Of course, it was argued that such measures were directed to preserving a cherished way of life. But the openly avowed aim of destroying marketing innovations, the misrepresentations of the practices of newcomers, and the autos-da-fé of mail-order catalogues promoted by local merchants [76] ill accord with protestations of lofty aims.

Nor in this period, whatever their later decisions, were judges disposed to look favorably upon such discriminatory tactics. "This kind of taxation is usually imposed at the instance and solicitation of domestic dealers, as a means of protecting them from foreign competition. And in many cases there may be some reason in their desire for such protection. But this shows in a still stronger light the unconstitutionality of the tax. It shows that it not only operates as a restriction upon interstate commerce, but that it is intended to have that effect as one of its principal objects. And if a state can, in this way, impose restrictions upon interstate commerce for the benefit and protection of its own citizens, we are brought back to the condition of things which existed before the adoption of the Constitution, and which was one of the principal causes that led to it." [77] It was no coincidence that the Supreme Court of the United States handed down this majority opinion in Robbins *v.* Shelby Taxing District in the same year, 1886, as the Wabash decision in the case of the railroads. The regulation of interstate commerce was a Federal matter.

Others also defended the new ways of doing things. Surveying changes in retailing with long perspective and ample detail in 1900, the

[74] W. C. Ford, "License Tax," J. J. Lalor, editor, *Cyclopedia of Political Science, Political Economy, and the Political History of the United States* (New York: Charles E. Merrill & Co., 1888), II, 768–770.

[75] Testimony of Goudie, *loc. cit.*, p. 725.

[76] Emmet and Jeuck, *op. cit.*, pp. 150–164; Bullock, "Early History of the Great Atlantic & Pacific Tea Company," *loc. cit.*, pp. 293–298; Bullock, "A History of the Great Atlantic & Pacific Tea Company since 1878," *loc. cit.*, pp. 65–67; Testimony of Goudie, *loc. cit.*, p. 725; Testimony of Chalifoux, *loc. cit.*, p. 342.

[77] Robbins *v.* Shelby Taxing District, 120 *United States,* 489, 498; See also Welton *v.* The State of Missouri, 91 *United States,* 275.

Massachusetts Bureau of Labor Statistics concluded: "The trend of modern business, quite apart from whatever unfair practices may exist among the unscrupulous, is toward concentration of capital and perfection of organization, the elimination of unnecessary expenses and a corresponding reduction of profit on the individual article accompanied by an enlargement of profit in the aggregate, which permits a lower price to the consumer. This is substantially the same movement that has taken place and is still going on in the industrial world. On the one hand the Department Store, on the other the factory, exhibit it in its highest form, but the same tendency is shown through every branch of trade, every avenue of industry. Its ultimate result, so far as the consumer is concerned, is a wider supply of commodities at lower prices. No such movement can take place of course, without arousing active opposition from those who suffer from it, or who are overcome by it, in the transition from the old to the new order." [78]

[78] *Thirtieth Annual Report of the* [Mass] *Bureau of Statistics of Labor,* p. 69.

CHAPTER XIV

The American Menace Abroad

THE SHAPE OF FOREIGN TRADE

THE free and largely unregulated flow of goods in domestic commerce prevents, at least for the period here under scrutiny, the accumulation of statistical data on its total amount or its constituent details. In foreign commerce things have been quite different. Probably the assumed superior merit of the foreign market and the flow of revenue from taxes on imports account for the greater attention given to international exchanges. In any case the fact that goods going abroad or coming thence have had to flow in certain well defined channels through customs houses and past government officials has facilitated the accumulation of a large mass of data and a considerable refinement of its details.

The value of merchandise imports and exports increased greatly from 1860 to 1897; from totals at the former date of $353,616,000 in the case of imports and $316,242,000 of exports to $764,730,000 and $1,032,-008,000 at the later date.[1] Foreign trade is peculiarly the barometer of the economic weather; it responds sensitively to depression and prosperity and more slowly to changes in production and consumption in both the sending and receiving nations. These increasing figures for the United States, therefore, somewhat mirror the expansion of economic activity here and elsewhere.

An expansion in the value totals of exports more rapid than in imports and a shift from an "unfavorable" balance of trade in 1860 to a spectacularly "favorable" one by 1897 raise somewhat more complicated issues. The figures of 1860 register a relationship between exports and imports which, with the exception of 1838–1849, had been characteristic of American foreign trade since the nation had been established.[2] After

[1] Bureau of the Census, *Historical Statistics of the United States, 1789–1945,* p. 244.

[2] Charles J. Bullock, John H. Williams, and Rufus S. Tucker, "The Balance of Trade of the United States," *Review of Economic Statistics,* I (July, 1919), 215–220.

1860 this historic pattern, with the exception of 1862 when exports exceeded imports by a mere million dollars, remained unbroken through 1873.[3] The business crisis of the latter year seemed to signalize a permanent revolution in foreign trade in merchandise. Beginning with 1874, American exports exceeded American imports in value until the end of the century. There were only three years, 1875, 1888, and 1893, when the country had an "unfavorable" balance of trade and that generally a small one. In the late seventies the excess of exports over imports attained spectacular levels. A discrepancy of almost equal magnitude was attained in the late nineties.[4]

The theory of international trade, buttressed by considerable empirical evidence, asserts, however, that it is impossible for any nation to have a favorable or unfavorable balance of trade. Over the long run the shipment of gold—for these were the days of the international gold standard—and invisible items of payment bring about an equilibrium in the balance of international payments. Thus the pre-Civil War excess of imports to which we have already alluded was met by payments from foreign shippers to the American merchant marine for the carriage of goods, by the investments of foreigners in the securities of American governments and enterprises, and, after the 1849 gold discoveries in the Far West, by the shipment abroad of specie. The continued excess of imports in the late sixties and early seventies was financed, after a preliminary hesitation in the Civil War, by the flow of European investment funds into American railroads and into United States bonds. Whereas in 1860 the Secretary of the Treasury estimated foreign investments in the United States at $400,000,000, by 1873 "it is certain" their total was "not less than $1,500,000." Funds were coming in faster than return payments for interest were going out.[5]

After 1873 when American exports generally exceeded imports, the invisible items which restored an equilibrium were payments to foreign shipowners and operators—for the American merchant marine declined as a carrier after the Civil War—and the payment of interest charges on European investments here. The latter exceeded the new investments made by Europeans. The extraordinary surplus of exports at the end of the nineties was also accompanied by a continuous inflow of gold.[6] Though there is something rather reassuring about a theory that demonstrates that in the end international indebtedness will be taken care of, enterprises had to operate on a short-run basis. If gold were coming into the country, banks, for instance, could relax their apprehension

[3] *Ibid.*, 221.
[4] *Ibid.*, 224, 228.
[5] *Ibid.*, 215–223.
[6] *Ibid.*, 224–229.

about reserves and lend more liberally. Consequently, in times of business crisis and at other critical moments (for instance, the resumption of specie payments in 1879) businessmen and government officials watched the balance of trade sharply and rejoiced when American exports were in lavish demand. In 1879, as we have seen, prodigious exports of wheat assured the success of resumption. But as the economy developed, the ability of crops to come to the rescue diminished.

THE SUPERIORITY OF EXPORTS

Though it is not the province of this volume to elaborate upon the role agricultural products played in exports, some statement of the elementary facts on this count is necessary for the understanding of the relative position of other merchandise items. In 1859, the last year before the war, the South provided $198,389,351 of the country's exported products; the value of all exports was only $80,000,000 more.[7] Though southern exports included tobacco, rice, and naval stores, cotton fiber was far and away the most important commodity. During the Civil War, as a part of its military-diplomatic strategy, the Confederate government resolved upon an embargo of cotton exports. The effectiveness of this embargo during all of 1861 and the earlier part of 1862 was "complete," "as near air-tight as human effort could make it." Though Europe escaped the fearful ultimate effects of a "cotton famine," cotton shipments in the last two years of the American Civil War came commonly from sources other than the United States.[8] In 1876 the reconstructed South was able to produce as much cotton as before the war, and in 1877 exports shot above three million bales for the first time since Appomattox.[9]

The late seventies also saw an increase in exports of northern agricultural products. The free-land policy, the colonizing activity and building of western railroads, the inrush of immigrants all operated to expand greatly the acreage devoted to wheat and corn. A series of innovations in handling, packing and shipping fresh beef stimulated the range cattle industry.[10] Then in 1879, a blight of bad weather fell upon English and European crops; this at a time the grain-growing regions in

[7] F. L. Owsley, *King Cotton Diplomacy, Foreign Trade Relations of the Confederate States of America* (Chicago: University of Chicago Press, 1931), p. 13.

[8] *Ibid.*, p. 43.

[9] Department of Commerce, *Statistical Abstract of the United States, 1913*, pp. 509, 668.

[10] *Commercial and Financial Chronicle,* XXXI (October 23, 1880), 416–417; F. A. Shannon, *The Farmer's Last Frontier, Agriculture, 1860–1897* (New York: Holt, Rinehart and Winston, Inc., 1945), pp. 190–195; Warren M. Persons, Pierson M. Tuttle, and Edwin Frickey, "Business and Financial Conditions following the Civil War in the United States," *Review of Economic Statistics,* II (July 26, 1920), 25–26.

the United States were so exceptionally favored that the average yield per acre and the total crop had never been equaled in American history. "It is the American supply alone," wrote the London *Economist*, "which has saved Europe from a great famine." The price per bushel and exports both rose rapidly.[11] 1879 was the pinnacle of an upward trend. Between 1875 and 1881 exports of wheat and wheat flour increased 162 per cent; exports of meat products doubled; exports of cotton increased 30 per cent.[12]

In the nineties the exports of agricultural products again made records. In 1892 when Europe had poor crops, the value of the wheat exports ($161,399,132) was the second greatest for any year in the nineteenth century; that of 1898 was not far behind. In 1896 for the first time in American history the exports of American cotton exceeded six million bales, and in the next two years seven million.[13] But whereas in 1880 the percentage of all domestic exports provided by agricultural commodities had been 84.3, a high water mark, in 1892 it was 79.1; in 1897 it was 66.8.[14]

Meanwhile in the ten years following 1890 the growth in the value of exports of manufactures had been greater than in the full century preceding that date. In 1900 they were 31.65 per cent of America's domestic exports.[15] Little wonder that Frank A. Vanderlip, once an official in the United States Treasury and in 1902 a New York banker, was writing jubilantly of the American "Commercial Invasion" of Europe. "American locomotives, running on American rails, now whistle past the Pyramids and across the long Siberian steppes. They carry the Hindoo pilgrims from all parts of their empire to the sacred waters of the Ganges. Three years ago there was but one American locomotive in the United Kingdom; today there is not a road of importance there on which trains are not being pulled by American engines. . . . We have been successfully meeting competition everywhere. America has sent coals to Newcastle, cotton to Manchester, cutlery to Sheffield, potatoes to Ireland, champagnes to France, watches to Switzerland, and 'Rhine wine' to Germany."[16] More prosaically, the first half dozen of our man-

[11] A. D. Noyes, *Forty Years of American Finance* (New York: G. P. Putnam's Sons, 1898), pp. 53–57.

[12] Bullock, Williams, and Tucker, *loc. cit.*, p. 225.

[13] Department of Commerce, *Statistical Abstract of the United States, 1913*, pp. 509, 637.

[14] *Ibid.*, p. 638.

[15] "Exports of Manufactures from the United States and their Distribution by Articles and Countries," Treasury Department, Bureau of Statistics, Monthly Summary of Commerce and Finance . . . April, 1903, *House Document* No. 15 (s.n. 4481), 57th Cong., 2d Sess., pp. 3241, 3243.

[16] Frank A. Vanderlip, *The American "Commercial Invasion" of Europe* (Republished from *Scribner's Magazine*, 1902), pp. 9–13.

ufactured exports were in order of value: iron and steel manufactures, refined mineral oils, copper, cotton manufactures, leather and manufactures thereof, and agricultural implements.[17] The first of these categories was a catchall for forty-four distinct articles or groups of articles of which various forms of machinery—including electrical machinery, sewing machines, typewriters, locomotives, cash registers, shoe machinery—constituted nearly one-half the total value.[18]

Displacements of this magnitude were bound to have repercussions upon other aspects of American foreign commerce. As for imports, "manufactures ready for consumption" slowly declined. Whereas in 1860 such products had constituted 48.68 per cent of American imports, in 1897 the figure was 26.48.[19] There was also a certain rearrangement of the channels of foreign commerce. As long as agricultural staples were America's chief exports and manufactured articles played a large role in her imports, trade was with western Europe, where industrial operatives depended upon American flour and pork and whence advanced manufacturers shipped their output to our comparatively undeveloped nation. Now that the United States in its production and commerce began to resemble western Europe, it might be expected that its manufactured commodities would go to the still newer parts of the world—Asia, Africa, Oceania, Canada, and Mexico. To a certain extent this was true. The growth in the exports of cotton cloth during the nineties "has been chiefly to Asia"; Asia along with Europe was "the chief market for American mineral oils"; but in agricultural implements, boots and shoes and copper, European nations remained easily the largest takers. As a market for American steel, Canada and Mexico became of great importance, but the United Kingdom and Germany in 1900 still took as large a value as North America outside the United States. Of the continents invaded by the trade in American manufactures, Asia, with the nearer countries of North America, proved the most promising. South America and Oceania were disappointing; Africa was a poor last. At century's end the United Kingdom and its dependencies were the largest consumers of manufactures of the United States.[20]

From his mountain watch-tower in the Berkshires, a Williams College economist at the turn of the century feared an intoxication over an extraordinary export trade might well lead the nation down the paths of wrong thought to the goal of mercantilist ideas, whose advocates had

[17] "Exports of Manufactures from the United States" . . . April, 1903, *loc. cit.*, pp. 3244–3245.

[18] *Ibid.*, pp. 3254–3255.

[19] Department of Commerce, *Statistical Abstract of the United States, 1913,* p. 645.

[20] "Exports of Manufactures from the United States" . . . April, 1903, *loc. cit.*, pp. 3255–3262, 3266–3267, 3270–3272.

rejoiced in a favorable balance of trade because it brought the precious metals into the realm and thus contributed to national wealth. Contrariwise, an excess of imports was deemed a first step to bankruptcy. Since Adam Smith had discredited this mercantilist concept in his *Wealth of Nations,* "few economists have thought it necessary to trouble themselves over imaginary evils resulting from the balance of trade." Yet an eminent business leader was now telling Americans it was the purpose of United States Steel through its export business "to bring to this country just as much money from foreign national countries or parts as we can possibly get. It seems to me that is for the interests of the country."[21]

Though it was fairly easy to demonstrate that the simpler concepts of advantages from an export surplus were misleading, it was clearly hard to eradicate variants and vestiges of the idea from the minds of even sophisticated people. For various reasons imports were felt to be bad. David A. Wells, whose ideas on foreign commerce avoided the more common mistakes, was distressed in the sixties that national consumption exceeded national production, and though he realized we could finance the then current excess of imports by the sale of American securities abroad, thought this was living by borrowing, a procedure to be deplored. It was not clear that Wells' ideas came so much from the mercantilist past as from the folklore of the American farm, the notion that a farm should be self-sufficient and its owner self-reliant. The Wells' dogma "Product for product is the absolute condition on which alone commerce is possible," smacks of the world of agricultural barter. Though Wells came pretty close to identifying imports with immorality, he did not take the final step.[22] That remained for Brooks Adams, one of the most complicated and doctrinaire minds of his era, who at the end of the century was asserting that the addiction of the English to sport and high living generally showed they were "as a nation, wasteful and profuse. . . . The effect of this lavish outlay for indulgences has been to cause the value of imports to gain on the value of exports, until the adverse balance approximates $800,000,000."[23]

Though opinion in high places cast a shadow of disapproval on imports, exports basked in the bright sunshine of favor, and the *Com-*

[21] Charles J. Bullock, "The Theory of the Balance of Trade," *North American Review,* CLXXIII (July, 1901), 111–114; Testimony of Elbert H. Gary, *Hearings before the* [Stanley] *Committee on Investigation of United States Steel Corporation,* I, 226.

[22] "Report of the Special Commissioner of the Revenue . . . Dec., 1869," *House Executive Document* No. 27 (s.n. 1416), 41st Cong., 2d Sess., pp. xxx–xxxi, lx.

[23] Brooks Adams, *America's Economic Supremacy* (New York: Harper & Brothers, 1947), pp. 139–141; Andrew Carnegie, "What Would I Do with the Tariff if I Were Czar?" *Forum,* XIX (March, 1895), 18–22; *Commercial and Financial Chronicle,* XLVIII (March 30, 1889), 412–413.

mercial and Financial Chronicle could picture agricultural exports as coming to the rescue of the American economy. But "the great preponderance of agricultural exports is an element of weakness as well as of strength." A poor crop meant an unfavorable balance.[24] Exports of manufactures were cherished for they eased the hardships of a maturing industrial order. When every depression, minor and major, was characterized by gluts, unemployment, overproduction, some observers were sure the United States had "too many factories" or carried on industrial operations too efficiently. In some industries the output of six months could supply the home market. From such dilemmas the foreign market was an escape.[25] Whether facts belied or reinforced analysis of this sort is a matter of opinion. In 1902 less than 9 per cent of the net value of manufactures was exported. But such an overall figure is inconclusive. In the cases of the chief manufactured exports of the United States, exports took 15 per cent of the value of iron and steel, 57 per cent of the value of refined illuminating oil, approximately 50 per cent of copper, 7 per cent of the value of cotton goods, 2 per cent of the value of boots and shoes and 16 per cent of the value of agricultural implements. In addition 5 per cent of the value of patent medicines and 25 per cent of sewing machines were exported.[26]

In the eyes of Brooks Adams, who could see a danger farther off than most men, any failure to dispose of America's surplus manufactures would spark a revolution, bring on international war, or lead to socialism. "Today the nation has to elect whether to continue to expand . . . or to resign itself to the approach of a relatively stationary period, when competition will force it to abandon the individual for the collective mode of life."[27]

Those less ridden with phobias or who saw that events had a way of opening exits from blind alleys found in the state of American commerce cause for optimism. England's example was in this era a pole, sometimes repelling, sometimes attracting. Though she may have had an unfavorable balance of trade, she was still the great trading nation of the world and her goods flooded the markets of every nation and con-

[24] *Commercial and Financial Chronicle,* XXXIV (April 1, 1882), 359.

[25] "Exports of Manufactures from the United States" . . . April, 1903, *loc. cit.*, p. 3241; "Report of the Secretary of the Treasury . . . on the Finances . . . 1884," *House Executive Document* No. 2 (s.n. 2291), 48th Cong., 2d Sess., pp. xi–xii; *Commercial and Financial Chronicle,* XXI (October 30, 1875), 424; (December 4, 1875), 523–524; David A. Wells, "The Meaning of Revenue Reform," *North American Review,* CXIII (July, 1871), 149–150; Testimony of J. L. Chalifoux, *Report of the Industrial Commission,* VII, 340.

[26] "Exports of Manufactures from the United States" . . . April, 1903, *loc. cit.*, pp. 3247–3252; R. B. Pettengill, "United States Foreign Trade in Copper," *American Economic Review,* XXV (September, 1935), 426–430.

[27] Adams, *op. cit.*, pp. 89, 93, 103.

tinent. It was all very well for the figures of American domestic production of coal, pig iron and steel to exceed, as they did by century's end, those of any other country in the world; but the achievement of selling goods in a home market protected by a high tariff was a limited one. The real test of industrial supremacy was selling goods in the international market in competition with goods produced in other nations.[28] Though Vanderlip was elated at carrying coals to Newcastle and selling cotton goods in Manchester and Brooks Adams chronicled England's loss of "energy," "initiative" and "diligence,"[29] the United Kingdom retained into the twentieth century its hold upon the largest percentage of the world's commerce, imports plus exports, and was in 1902–1906 still ahead of the United States in exports, though the gap had been greatly diminished in the preceding twenty years.[30]

The trend could unloose visions. If the United States produced no Milton to write, "Methinks I see in my mind a noble and puissant nation," it at least produced a grocer in Manchester, New Hampshire, who was "looking forward to-day to the time when this country shall emerge from its childhood into a vigorous young manhood, and with wise legislation shall look forward to the day in which we will become one of the leading commercial nations of the world. . . . In order to attain that position we must produce goods and products of as good quality and at as low a price as the western nations of Europe."[31] Sometimes Americans focussed so exclusively upon front-runner Great Britain they forgot there were other contestants. "The average American," commented the *Commercial and Financial Chronicle* in 1885, "will be surprised to find . . . that in the commerce with foreign nations, not only the British Isles but Germany and France also are much in advance of us."[32] And by the end of the century, Americans learned that "When Japan is fully equipped with the latest machinery it will . . . be the most potent industrial force in the markets of the world."[33] All of which, being translated, meant that producers in these various countries would be better able to sell in foreign markets than would producers in America.

[28] "Report of the Special Commissioner of the Revenue . . . 1869", *loc. cit.*, p. xxxviii.

[29] Adams, *op. cit.*, pp. 137–141.

[30] M. G. Mulhall, *The Dictionary of Statistics* (London: George Routledge and Sons, 1899), p. 129; A. D. Webb, *The New Dictionary of Statistics* (London: George Routledge and Sons, 1911), pp. 93–94.

[31] Testimony of H. K. Slayton, *Report of the Committee* [on Education and Labor] *of the Senate . . . 1885*, III, 99.

[32] *Commercial and Financial Chronicle,* XLI (August 1, 1885), 114–115.

[33] R. P. Porter, "Is Japanese Competition a Myth?" *North American Review,* CLXIII (August, 1896), 155.

THE EXPORT POLICY OF PRIVATE ENTERPRISE

Steps to the expansion of American exports were taken early by private enterprise. In the 1850's the manufacturers of American reapers, including Cyrus H. McCormick, had sent their machines abroad to be demonstrated at fairs, exhibitions and contests. After the panic of 1873 and during the ensuing depression, McCormick looked upon the foreign market as one to cultivate for its own profits and also a way to win for himself the recognition and honors which his thirst for fame required. His European ventures were made on his own account rather than on his firm's. Since the cost of transporting a reaper from Chicago to Liverpool was in 1862 $49.50, it seemed more profitable to license a foreign manufacturer to use the McCormick discoveries and patents. The road to developing a foreign market was a rocky one. Some countries, like Canada, whose western plains invited the reaper, had high tariffs upon imports; elsewhere the conservatism of farmers and the sharp practices of agents held down expansion. Still by the late seventies much had been accomplished. A new McCormick reaper works built in Chicago after the fire of 1871 could turn out a larger product than the domestic market could absorb; the movement of shipping agents to Chicago and their ability to forward shipments by through bills of lading reduced to $17.00 the cost of transporting a reaper from Chicago to Liverpool. The desire of foreign grain-growers to compete with American ones and the higher costs of agricultural labor in Europe brought about by migrations to the United States, stimulated the wider use of the reaper or other machinery, particularly in England and in Russia, where large fields were suited to mechanized agriculture.

McCormick's machines demonstrated their superiority. It was comparatively easy to find agents abroad or to appoint Americans who would work for a salary plus a commission on sales and who would buy consignments at wholesale and resell as they saw fit. By the time of McCormick's death in 1884, he had marketed abroad about 12,000 machines. The biggest market was Europe and England, though four thousand had gone to Australia and New Zealand. The business had been vexatious and not very profitable.[34] "Western Europe was the expensive business playground of the magnates of the industry in the United States. Their victories abroad were extremely flattering to their pride, and had an advertising value at home many times larger than the heavy cost involved," concludes McCormick's biographer.[35]

[34] William T. Hutchinson, *Cyrus Hall McCormick, Harvest, 1856–1884* (New York: D. Appleton-Century Company, 1935), pp. 405–447, 643–685.

[35] *Ibid.*, p. 686.

Certainly this generalization was not true of the Standard Oil group. Neither John D. Rockefeller nor his brother William, in charge of the export business, embarked upon that trade to win the Legion of Honor or be received by Napoleon, and neither demanded recognition as the "inventor" of petroleum. The impact of the Pennsylvania discoveries upon Europe had been immediate and immense. As a European scholar wrote later, "I have often heard the tale of how my grandfather, a merchant at Tromsoe, far north in Norway, who every year made a trip to Hamburg for his commodities, early in the 1860's brought home a petroleum lamp and at night placed it burning at the corner window on the main street. In a little while hundreds upon hundreds of townspeople crowded around the house and could hardly tear themselves away from the wonder they saw before their eyes." [36] At the beginning William Rockefeller and the Standard Oil Company of New York, primarily an export agency chartered in 1882, sold their products to American export merchants or to agents or branch houses of foreign importers. Of these products kerosene was the most important. The foreign market was willing to absorb a brand somewhat inferior to that marketed in the United States. Aside from producing this export brand and locating their refineries along the Atlantic seaboard, the participation of the Standard Oil men in the export process was not all embracing. They did, however, busy themselves over the quality of shipments, consider whether barrel or can was the best way of carriage, and occasionally send emissaries abroad to investigate conditions and promote the sale of their products.[37]

The competition in the European market of Russian oil produced in the Caucasus and financed by Rothschild and Nobel money shook the Standard into more effective marketing measures. Besides, by the eighties, Standard's methods of bulk distribution in the domestic market had taught it something, and in 1888 the American trust established the Anglo-American Oil Company, the first of Standard's foreign affiliates. The concern acquired a fleet of tankers, a method of shipment in which Nobel and Rothschild had pioneered, built bulk stations in England, owned tank cars and barges, and distributed through its tank wagons to retailers. On the Continent, Standard bought into oil marketing concerns which had tankers, depots, and business contacts. Sometimes the Standard owned a majority of the securities in these affiliates. As in America, the Standard sought to assure exclusive marketing areas to its agents or

[36] Halvdan Koht, *The American Spirit in Europe. A Survey of Transatlantic Influences* (Philadelphia: University of Pennsylvania Press, 1949), pp. 168–169.

[37] Ralph W. Hidy and Muriel E. Hidy, *History of Standard Oil Company (New Jersey). Pioneering in Big Business, 1882–1911* (New York: Harper & Brothers, 1955), pp. 122–144.

companies. These changes in promotion and marketing were essentially a holding operation, for exports from Russia continued to rise, and in 1891 the export value of American kerosene was less than it had been in 1888 or 1882.[38]

Meanwhile the Standard group had turned its attention to the Orient, where "teeming" millions were potential customers for kerosene and were not likely to shift to gas or electricity. Russian oil went thither through Suez and went more quickly than American from New York. Somewhat later the Royal Dutch Company was producing oil in Indonesia and expanding its Oriental markets. While the Standard had once been content to sell to merchants trading to the Far East, in the mid-nineties it established its own stations in Japan, China, and southeastern Asia, where agents sold to local distributors. The Standard packaged its kerosene in tin cans (the use of which as roofing and household utensils became a bench mark of American penetration into the Orient), sold lamps and wicks cheaply, and distributed pamphlets in native languages on the use of kerosene. When Standard, despite all these efforts, still fell short of meeting competition, it considered acquiring its successful rivals, but on this score it could not repeat its United States triumphs.[39]

What progress the Standard made was accompanied by a general din abroad to the effect that the concern was a menace, "the American trust." And American opinion occasionally reflected dissatisfaction with the practices attending American business expansion overseas. In view of differences in quality, grades, and foreign competitive situations, it was not surprising that American products seemed to sell abroad at lower prices than in the United States. A policy of dumping could not be blamed for this situation. The phenomenon was sporadic, even accidental. The combined copper producers of the Michigan peninsula provided an exception. A copper duty in 1869 operated to exclude foreign copper from the United States or raise the price; with this protection the American copper producers for over a decade regularly dumped abroad at a lower price the share not taken by domestic consumers.[40] Open dumping was sure to trigger a chauvinistic demand that American producers were bound to supply American consumers at as low prices as they did anyone. Again, Americans, quite accustomed to cooperative agreements among producers to divide markets, were quick to scent the possibility of Americans signing a treaty with foreign competitors for the same purpose.

[38] *Ibid.*, pp. 144–153.

[39] *Ibid.*, pp. 239–268.

[40] F. W. Taussig, *Some Aspects of the Tariff Question* (Cambridge: Harvard University Press, 1915), pp. 167–168; *Report of the Industrial Commission,* I, Review of Evidence, pp. 22–23; XIII, 725–772.

With some unimportant exceptions, international cartels did not, in this period, include American industry.[41]

GOVERNMENT POLICIES AND FOREIGN TRADE

Any popular or governmental hostility to business was a distinct liability, for foreign commerce had to rely upon favorable governmental policy. If, for instance, export trade was to be promoted, "it was fundamental that American producers sell at low prices. The foreigners will buy in the cheapest not the dearest market." Prices were the reflex of many conditions, including currency policies. Thus at the close of the Civil War Wells was bewailing the high level of American prices. In 1861 when gold and currency were at par, according to his statement, a foreigner could buy in this country with $1000 in gold 111⅑ dozen "ordinary, square-post cane-seat chairs," in July, 1864, 143 dozen, and in 1868, 102 dozen. "The foreign purchaser now goes to France or Germany."[42] With such an equivocal example at hand, it is not surprising that the theory as to why export prices worked out this way is complicated. With the greenbacks, as we have seen, there were two prices in the domestic market, one in terms of gold, one in terms of paper money. In the foreign market, with the international gold standard operating, prices and exchanges were in terms of gold. Foreigners did not use American paper money or possess it, or, according to the greenbacks' foes, have much faith in it. Other complications arose from the divergencies between the long and short term results of a paper currency, from the fact that some of the factors involved "could work either way." Still there was a popular opinion that in a country on paper, exports would be stimulated and imports would be hampered. As we have seen, the advocates of the greenbacks among industrial leaders regarded that currency as a disguised form of protection. On the other hand, Wells clearly thought that in the total situation as it was at that time, inconvertible paper hampered exports of manufactures and resumption and contraction would stimulate them by reducing prices.[43] However the greenbacks worked, they were a governmental influence brought to bear

[41] Hidy and Hidy, *op. cit.*, pp. 142–143, 250–252; Testimony of E. H. Gary, *Report of the* [Stanley] *Committee on Investigation of United States Steel Corporation,* I, 226–227; J. W. Jenks, *The Trust Problem* (New York: McClure, Phillips & Co., 1905), pp. 47–49.

[42] "Report of the Special Commissioner of the Revenue . . . January, 1869," *House Executive Document* No. 16 (s.n. 1302), 40th Cong., 3rd Sess., 11–12.

[43] *Ibid.*, pp. 11–12; F. W. Taussig, "International Trade under Depreciated Paper, A Contribution to Theory," *Quarterly Journal of Economics,* XXXI (May, 1917), 380–403; W. C. Mitchell, "Gold, Prices, and Wages under the Greenback Standard," *University of California Publications in Economics,* I (Berkeley: The University Press, 1908), 257–258.

upon foreign commerce which only government decision could exert.

There were other and clearer ways in which government policy increased costs and thus sent foreign purchasers elsewhere. A good share of American imports—dyestuffs, soda-ash, bleaching powders, tin, hides, raw silk, and wool—were raw materials later to be employed in the making of finished goods. The tariff on such raw materials should be lowered or abolished. "Give to the manufacturer his raw material cheap, and you enable him to manufacture cheap and sell cheap; and all the experience and all the laws of political economy, teach that with every reduction in the price of manufactured commodities in ordinary use, consumption and production increase in a far greater ratio." [44]

There was thus a very considerable movement just after the Civil War and sporadically thereafter to lower tariffs on such articles or to extend the free list to cover them. Whether this drive antagonized influential American groups or left them indifferent depended on circumstance. Raw silk, for instance, had always come in free. In spite of earnest efforts by the Department of Agriculture Americans have not yet succeeded in producing it profitably, even with the use of prison labor.[45] But the importation of wool alarmed American sheepmen from Vermont to California. In 1867 Congress adopted an ingenious "scientific" device to reconcile the interests of wool producers and manufacturers of woolens. A specific duty on woolen goods compensated the manufacturer for the increase in the cost of his raw material and an additional duty gave him protection on his finished product.[46] Nor did ingenuity stop there. "The McKinley Bill [of 1890] provided that ninety-nine per cent of the duty should be refunded upon foreign iron and steel used in manufacturing articles for export. . . . This gave American manufacturers all the benefits of free trade in their contests with foreign manufacturers through the world," commented Carnegie. He added "it should be a feature in all future tariffs." [47] By thus turning the doctrine of free raw materials inside out the protectionist forces deprived the tariff reform movement of some momentum.

A third cause for high prices, according to Wells, was taxation. Certainly immediately after the Civil War, with its high, well-nigh uni-

[44] "Report of the Special Commissioner of the Revenue . . . 1866," *Senate Executive Document* No. 2 (s.n. 1276), 39th Cong., 2d Sess., 34; "Report of the Special Commissioner of the Revenue . . . Dec. 1869," *loc. cit.*, pp. lxxiv–xcii.

[45] Taussig, *op. cit.*, pp. 222–224.

[46] Chester W. Wright, *Wool-Growing and the Tariff. A Study in the Economic History of the United States* (Boston: Houghton Mifflin Company, 1910), pp. 213–218.

[47] Andrew Carnegie, "My Experiences with, and Views upon, the Tariff," *Century Magazine,* LXXVII (December, 1908), 198; Andrew Carnegie, "The McKinley Bill," *Nineteenth Century,* XXIX (June, 1891), 1029–1030.

versal taxes, concern with their costs was understandable and legitimate.[48] Over the years, however, most American businessmen were not worried on this score. Instead, they realized that the favorable tax rate they enjoyed was one of the great assets of America vis-à-vis foreign competitors. The failure of the Confederacy to divide the nation and the fact that the United States had little to fear from its near neighbors made it unnecessary to maintain large armies or fleets. The government tax on beer was enough to float the American navy. If the United States had been in the position of France or Germany, it would have to maintain a standing army of 700,000. "More than one in twenty of all the adult males of working age within the limits of the country," testified Atkinson in the eighties, "would be withdrawn from their productive work, whereby the quantity of things to be divided between labor and capital, from each year's annual product would be so much diminished. Yet more: one more man in every nineteen of those remaining would be forced to labor in order to pay the taxes necessary to sustain the seven hundred thousand idle men gathered together in camp and barracks waiting for the work of destruction." [49] Carnegie believed likewise.[50] At the same time Vanderlip discovered abroad "that a most depressing influence on industries is exerted by the national tax-gatherer." America's system of federal taxation "helped," not "hampered," our industries.[51]

With a fascination akin to phobia, employers or their spokesmen in this country emphasized the importance of comparative labor costs in all production. At the end of the seventies, with the depression and the railroad strikes of 1877 still fresh in mind, the Secretary of State, W. M. Evarts, asked American consuls to investigate, among other things, the wage levels and cost of living among European workers. With the information at hand (and perhaps ignored) he summarized the situation and its remedy. "Within the last fifteen years we have demonstrated our ability, by the brilliant development of our own resources, to exclude, by honest competition, foreign manufactures, to a large extent, from our shores. The question which now peremptorily challenges all thinking

[48] "Report of the United States Revenue Commission . . . 1866," *House Executive Document* No. 34 (s.n. 1255), 39th Cong., 1st Sess., 13; "Report of the Special Commissioner of the Revenue . . . 1867," *loc. cit.*, pp. 26–27; "Report of the Special Commissioner of the Revenue . . . Jan. 1869," *loc. cit.*, pp. 21–22, 51–52.

[49] Testimony of Edward Atkinson, *Report of the Committee* [on Education and Labor] *of the Senate . . . 1885*, II, 223, 236; "Report of the Special Commissioner of the Revenue . . . 1868," *House Executive Document* No. 61 (s.n. 1332), 40th Cong., 2d Sess., pp. 12–15.

[50] Andrew Carnegie, "Americanism *versus* Imperialism," *North American Review*, CLXVIII (January, 1899), 5.

[51] Vanderlip, *op. cit.*, p. 24.

minds is how to create a foreign demand for those manufactures which are left after supplying our home demands. . . . This question appeals equally to the selfishness and patriotism of all our citizens, but to the laborer it appeals with tenfold force, for without work he cannot live, and unless we can extend the markets for our manufactures he cannot expect steady work, and unless our manufacturers can undersell foreign manufacturers, we cannot enlarge our foreign market. . . . If our workingmen, native and naturalized, will only read these reports in that national spirit with which I have endeavored to point out some of the principal features therein, and drive from their midst communism, strikes, and drink—evil spirits born of apprehension, and foreign to our country and our institutions . . . labor faithfully and intelligently like freemen; live within their means, like frugal and sensible men; and choke down all demagogical attempts to divide the American people into hostile ranks as capitalists and laborers, there can be no reasonable limit set to the development of our manufacture and commerce." [52]

One trouble with these proposals was their utter unfeasibility. While there were other men like Wells who saw in apparently high labor costs a handicap to American exports, they realized the undesirability of reducing wages in a democracy.[53] Perhaps it could be done by indirection if one first reduced the cost of living. But one could hardly ask American farmers, already rebellious enough, to accept the loss of protection on some of their products; nor could government dispense with duties on food imports, for example coffee and sugar, that were its chief revenue producers; nor was the response of workmen to Evarts' suggestion they be like Belgian workmen, who enabled Belgium to compete with England, Germany and France by being contented, frugal, "cheerfully complying with a reduction in hours [sic] and wages," [54] likely to encourage a belief Americans would do likewise.[55]

In the course of his mingled boasts and reproaches, Evarts noted that the American worker did from one-and-a-half to twice as much as the average European in a given time.[56] But the Secretary of State was either too blind, opinionated or cunning to draw the inference which could unloose the knot of the American dilemma. Years later, however, commenting on a paper of F. W. Taylor, a fellow engineer prophesied,

[52] Department of State, "State of Labor in Europe, 1878, Reports from the United States Consuls," *House Executive Document* No. 5 (s.n. 1875), 46th Cong., 1st Sess., pp. 37–38.

[53] "Report of the Special Commissioner of the Revenue . . . Jan. 1868," *loc. cit.*, pp. 28–29; "Report of the Special Commissioner of the Revenue . . . Jan. 1869," *loc. cit.*, pp. 67–69.

[54] "State of Labor in Europe, 1878," *loc. cit.*, p. 2.

[55] *Cigar Makers' Official Journal,* December 10, 1880.

[56] "State of Labor in Europe, 1878," *loc. cit.*, p. 36.

we must "capture the world's trade" and "substitute *production* and *operation* for construction." Otherwise "horrible depression." We must produce and distribute more cheaply. "Were Mr. Taylor's methods generally applied no country in the world would compete with North America." [57] Taylor's paper advocated: "High Wages and Low Labor Cost as the Foundation of the Best Management." [58] Taylor was not the first to point out that it was not comparative days' wages which counted but the labor cost per unit. This argument had been the stock-in-trade of the free traders; [59] it was significant that it had now penetrated to the ranks of employers and management.

PROTECTION AND FOREIGN TRADE

With most of these matters, admittedly the government could do little except by way of fringe legislation. But its power in the matter of the tariff was unassailable. Though before the Civil War it had occasionally been argued that the way to encourage exports was to reduce the duties on imports, in short to use the tariff itself as an instrument of promoting foreign trade, and though specific measures, like the reciprocity treaty with Canada in 1854, seemed to point in the same direction, a number of complications and extraneous considerations had precluded scientific evaluation of the policy. Still, in the eighties voices were again raised in behalf of modifying protection for this purpose. Wells, after a spell of writing about the balance of trade with what he no doubt regarded as persuasive indirection and statesmanlike moderation, flatfootedly announced: "All trade and commerce in the practical business of life, is the interchange of products and services and there can be no buying without selling, or selling without buying." One given reason for the new emphasis was the need for a foreign market during the industrial depression and business stagnation of the time; [60] perhaps another was the growing industrialization of the nation. In any case Congress paid little heed to these theories and its tariff of 1883 left the protective system pretty much as it had been.[61] The fact that a Tariff Commission

[57] Discussion by H. Emerson, *Transactions of the American Society of Mechanical Engineers*, XXIV (1903), 1462–1464.

[58] F. W. Taylor, "Shop Management," *Transactions of the American Society of Mechanical Engineers*, XXIV (1903), 1343–1344.

[59] J. B. Sargent, "Evils of the Tariff System," *North American Review*, CXXXIX (September, 1884), 291; W. C. Ford, "Commercial Superiority of the United States," *North American Review*, CLXVI (January, 1898), 79–81.

[60] David A. Wells, "Evils of the Tariff System," *North American Review*, CXXXIX (September, 1884), 277–278.

[61] F. W. Taussig, *Tariff History of the United States* (New York: G. P. Putnam's Sons, 1914), pp. 230–250.

theoretically framed the bill perhaps stimulated McCulloch to write that what the country needed was a "fair-minded" Commission to educate legislators, manufacturers and others to the fact that the tariff stood in the way of opening foreign markets to a "plethora" of manufactured goods and thereby prevented America from escaping a disastrous depression.[62]

The idea that the United States should have to make any modification of its tariff system in order to encourage exports was extremely distasteful to protectionists. Shipbuilder John Roach, declared of foreign purchasers, "They buy our cotton, our bread, our petroleum; they buy those things which they cannot produce themselves, and which man cannot exist without. Necessity compels them to buy such articles; but we hear the very flimsy argument, given in some of our New York papers occasionally, 'If we do not buy from them, they will not buy from us.' Will any man of common sense believe for one moment that the produce merchant of Liverpool who buys our bread, our meat, our butter, our cheese, and our petroleum will go to the iron-maker of Great Britain, and say to him, 'If they do not buy your iron in the United States, I will not buy their bread from them'? . . . Gentlemen, they have got to have our food; they cannot live without it, they cannot raise it themselves, and they cannot to-day produce their own cotton, and they must have ours. We do not want their woolen or cotton goods, or iron; we want their gold. . . ."[63] More piercing than this pirate yell was the proposal to do without foreign trade entirely, since the "Supreme Architect" had given this country vast and varied areas, every clime, and every resource. "We could build a Chinese wall around the country and be the happiest people on the face of the globe"—at least such was the opinion of a New York cigar manufacturer.[64] If losing vigilance we let foreigners into our protected market, "we should be reduced to a nation of cotton and corn growers and an overproductive agricultural nation"—a "calamity that would be worse than all the plagues or wars the world ever saw."[65]

Nonetheless the heresy that we might have to breach protection in order to market products abroad made headway. One path out of the doctrinal dilemma was reciprocity, for protectionists might support it without surrendering their principles. Moreover, in the case of our early

[62] "Annual Report of the Secretary of the Treasury on . . . the Finances . . . 1884," *House Executive Document* No. 2 (s.n. 2291), 48th Cong., 2d Sess., pp. xii–xiii.

[63] Testimony of John Roach, *Report of the Committee* [on Education and Labor] *of the Senate . . . 1885,* II, 89–90.

[64] Testimony of Walter E. Barnett, *Report of the Committee* [on Education and Labor] *of the Senate . . . 1885,* II, 841–842.

[65] Testimony of John Roach, *loc. cit.,* p. 90.

reciprocity treaties with Canada and the Hawaiian Islands, political and other non-economic conditions (the United States dreamed of annexing both) played a part.[66] Reciprocity was first made a general policy in connection with Latin America, whose raw materials, sugar, coffee, fruits, and the like, Americans imported in such quantities that we had with Latin American countries a perpetually unfavorable balance of trade. Since in this area European nations had a real commercial superiority, hemispheric sentiments of varied intensity and meaning came into play.[67] In the eighties James G. Blaine, Secretary of State, began a forceful advocacy of reciprocity with Latin America. According to his chief, Benjamin Harrison, "It will certainly be time enough for us to consider whether we must cheapen the cost of production by cheapening labor in order to gain access to the South American market" after we had tried other measures.[68]

Neither Blaine nor Harrison was able to prevail upon Congress to enact reciprocity in a liberal form. Instead, the McKinley Bill of 1890 admitted into the United States free of duty sugar, molasses, coffee, tea, and hides from countries which produced and exported them; but if these nations levied "reciprocally unequal and unreasonable" duties upon our exports the President was to re-impose duties upon sugar and other enumerated articles. While for political purposes it was canny to stress in this connection exports of American agricultural products to Latin America, Blaine had also in mind "agricultural implements and machinery, mining and mechanical machinery, structural steel and iron, steel rails, locomotives, railway cars and supplies, street cars [and] refined petroleum." [69] Little wonder that Carnegie, neither wheat grower nor pig keeper, was of the opinion that "our vigorous Secretary of State, Mr. Blaine, is the father of the reciprocity idea, which promises to strengthen his already commanding position among our statesmen." [70] Under the McKinley Bill a number of tariff agreements were made. "Tariff" Wilson dropped reciprocity from his measure of 1894; it was re-introduced in the Dingley tariff of 1897. Then action on and interest in this device petered out.[71]

[66] United States Tariff Commission, *Reciprocity and Commercial Treaties,* pp. 21–26; "Report of the Select Committee on Transportation-Routes to the Seaboard," *Senate Report* No. 307, Pt. 1 (s.n. 1588), 43rd Cong., 1st Sess., pp. 193–197.

[67] D. S. Muzzey, *James G. Blaine, A Political Idol of Other Days* (New York: Dodd, Mead & Company, 1934), pp. 426–438.

[68] J. D. Richardson, editor, *A Compilation of the Messages and Papers of the Presidents* (New York: Bureau of National Literature and Art, 1903), IX, 74.

[69] Muzzey, *op. cit.,* pp. 448–449.

[70] Andrew Carnegie, "The McKinley Bill," *loc. cit.,* p. 1030; Andrew Carnegie, "What Would I Do with the Tariff if I Were Czar?" *Forum,* XIX (March, 1895), 24–26.

[71] United States Tariff Commission, *op. cit.,* pp. 26–31.

THE AMERICAN MERCHANT MARINE

Among the other things President Harrison thought worth trying were "established and reliable steam communication" with South America and "convenient methods of money exchanges." [72] Here he put his finger on matters to which policy makers had given long and controversial attention. On the first count, "steam communication," the fundamental and inescapable fact was the decline of the American merchant marine in foreign commerce. As late as the early fifties, 70 per cent or over of the value of American imports and exports was carried in American vessels. Then a decline set in; during the Civil War the percentages fell into the twenties. By 1897 only 15 per cent of the value of imports and 8.1 per cent of the value of exports were carried in vessels of American registry.[73] Indeed the custom of shipping under foreign flags was so common that the payment to foreigners for freight services was a significant item in the American balance of payments. For the period 1874–1895, calculations of the net indebtedness of America in the matter of freight monies place the overall sum at $560,000,000 or $25,500,000 a year.[74] These figures help explain how the United States was able then to maintain pretty constantly a favorable balance of merchandise exports. They do not account for the decline of the American merchant marine in foreign commerce.

Unquestionably the Civil War was important. The depredations of Confederate sea raiders raised the war risks on American vessels to "an exorbitant figure; five, seven and one-half, and even ten per centum being demanded by insurance companies, over and above the ordinary risks. . . . The exaction of such exorbitant, although necessary, premiums must cancel the profits of almost any venture." So wrote an English pamphleteer.[75] Confronted by these facts, American shipowners began to sell their vessels to foreigners who could sail them under neutral flags. The raiders burned or sank about 110,000 tons of Northern shipping and caused the sale of 800,000 to foreign owners.[76] The polemics over the decline of the merchant marine emphasized the effect of the Civil War. But in the light of history, one suspects here an overemphasis, for nations

[72] Richardson, *op. cit.*, p. 74.

[73] J. F. Crowell, "Shipping Industry of the United States; Its Relation to Foreign Trade," Monthly Summary of Commerce and Finance, December, 1900, *House Document* No. 15 (s.n. 4129), 56th Cong., 2d Sess., p. 1408.

[74] Bullock, Williams, and Tucker, *loc. cit.*, pp. 226–227.

[75] George W. Dalzell, *The Flight from the Flag: The Continuing Effect of the Civil War upon the American Carrying Trade* (Chapel Hill: University of North Carolina Press, 1940), p. 239.

[76] *Ibid.*, p. 247.

whose shipping war has driven from the sea have rebounded to high place as shipbuilders and operators.

Meanwhile, there was under way a revolution in shipping. The success of the old merchant marine had been based upon the relative advantages this country possessed in building wooden sailing vessels, which were especially useful in carrying bulk commodities (cotton, wheat, coal and timber), for the delivery of which speed and punctuality were relatively unimportant. Such vessels were also useful for long distance trades along which coal was not available or too expensive. In the late nineteenth century sailing ships cheapened costs by increasing their size and thus carrying a larger cargo. Iron and steel hulls, though they fouled and thus slowed speeds expensively, did not require a hold full of struts, beams and braces to keep them rigid; and metal ships could be built larger. The application of power driven apparatus to handle sails, yards, anchors, and the like reduced crews and costs of operation. In special trades, such as carrying wheat from the Pacific coast to Europe, sailing vessels found employment until the eighties.

Meanwhile the evolution of the steamship—hull, power, and propulsion—was constantly making it a more effective instrument.[77] By 1860 Britain had already built an iron, screw-driven, steam fleet.[78] At later dates the compound engine with high steam pressures occupied less space in the hold and reduced the amount of coal required from ten to less than one pound per horsepower per hour.[79] Thus on long trades, vessels carried less fuel and spaced coaling stops farther apart. Contributory factors—for example, the Suez Canal, which after 1869 shortened the journey to the Orient,[80]—and the preference of the age for predictability and dispatch gave the nod to the steamship. Most of these vessels did not operate in lines; they were tramps, "cheaply built boats [that] are nothing but tanks with boilers and machinery in them." [81] This derogatory utterance by an American contains more than a hint of the craftsman's nostalgia for the old days.

On the whole, the builders and operators of the American merchant marine did not initiate these innovations nor were they able to participate

[77] G. S. Graham, "The Ascendancy of the Sailing Ship, 1850–85," *Economic History Review*, Second Series, IX (1956), 75–86; John G. B. Hutchins, *The American Maritime Industries and Public Policy, 1789–1914* (Cambridge: Harvard University Press, 1941), pp. 371–386.

[78] J. R. T. Hughes, "Discussion of Papers," *Journal of Economic History*, XVIII (December, 1958), 577.

[79] Graham, *loc. cit.*, pp. 86–88.

[80] Max E. Fletcher, "The Suez Canal and World Shipping, 1869–1914," *Journal of Economic History*, XVIII (December, 1958), 556–559.

[81] Testimony of W. H. T. Hughes, "Hearings before the [Farquhar] Committee of the House on Merchant Marine and Fisheries," *House Report* No. 1210 (s.n. 2810), 51st Cong., 1st Sess., pp. 2, 11–12.

as advantageously in the new pattern as they had in the earlier decades. Nor was it certain that they wanted to. As a government document observed at century's end, "In the economic development of a nation, it is frequently necessary to choose between dividing and concentrating the productive energies of its people. Labor and capital being limited quantities, it is necessary, it is natural and inevitable, that they should select the field of largest returns first and leave the less inviting avenues of enterprise until later. . . . This is why labor and capital devoted itself to economic pursuits on land and forsook the sea in the years during which the American people were occupied to their utmost in creating Commonwealths out of our public domain. From 1850 to 1890 our problems were internal. Most of them for most of the time were intensely exacting. . . . For the time being our hands as a nation were full—full of work as honorable as shipbuilding and ocean commerce, and far more urgent and fundamental. . . . It was inevitable that the decadence of our merchant marine should coincide with the development of our domestic resources. . . . There is no other cause needed to explain the result." [82]

When a trend is so "inevitable," a doubt as to the wisdom of reversing it rises. Foreign vessels, particularly English ones, carried American cargoes and carried them cheaply and well. An index number of American export freight rates fell from 117 in 1873 to 55 in 1897; it had been lower.[83] If purely commercial considerations rather than nationalistic discrimination and promotion had not governed carriers under foreign flags, the expansion of American trade that did take place would have been impossible. Nonetheless the argument that American ships must carry American goods persisted. At least in the controversy over the protective tariff, it is possible occasionally to touch factual bottom. But probe the merchant marine question as one will, one generally strikes bald assertion, folklore, emotion, the humiliation that America stood "in a discreditable attitude towards the people of other countries in this work. Year after year in places the American flag is not seen. I pray God I may yet be able to cross the Atlantic Ocean under my own flag, the stars and stripes. . . ." Finally, according to neo-mercantilist notions, the payment of freights to aliens took gold out of the country. Like an incantation, witnesses repeated "Trade follows the flag." Or, projecting their own chauvinistic impulses, they felt foreign vessels *must* discriminate against Americans.[84]

[82] Crowell, *loc. cit.*, pp. 1382–1383.

[83] Douglass North, "Ocean Freight Rates and Economic Development, 1750–1913," *Journal of Economic History,* XVIII (December, 1958), 549.

[84] *Ibid.*, p. 1406; Testimony of Ambrose Snow and S. W. Carey, "Hearings before the [Farquhar] Committee," *op. cit.*, pp. 27, 28.

Though most of the reasoning just quoted was highly subjective, it might be argued more realistically that the United States on the periphery of the world's network of steamship lines—Europe was their center—could benefit through the establishment of direct communications with certain markets. It might also be true foreign vessels were not eager to provide certain facilities, say refrigeration, needed for some American exports.[85] Even American railroads had been loath to provide refrigerated cars for the domestic dressed beef trade. In these instances, expense rather than malice explained the attitude. Admittedly these were peacetime considerations. The need of a merchant marine as an auxiliary to the nation's navy in wartime was a different but related problem. Also, if foreign carriers were imperiled by wars in which their nations were involved, the United States did not have vessels under a neutral flag with which to continue its foreign trade.

Though in this period every European maritime nation and Japan favored its merchant marine, the road to an effective American policy was tortuous and thorny. America's fundamental handicap was well stated by a government report: "Price is the key, the world over, to commercial primacy." [86] It cost more to build ships in America than elsewhere. By the nineties American yards were probably as well equipped mechanically as their foreign competitors, but they did not have enough work for individual yards to specialize in certain types or to standardize operations. The advantages of large-scale production could be attained only if one could "manufacture" ships rather than "build" them. But the shipbuilding industry did not reach this level. For one thing labor costs were higher in this country than in Europe. A workman along the Clyde would live on bread, cheese, and beer and meat twice a week. "Now when you get an American workman, he wants meat three times a day." [87]

The solution of letting American ship operators buy their vessels in the cheap foreign market, the solution of "free ships," was impossible, for American navigation laws of long standing denied American registry to foreign-built vessels. "There are three things, the importation of which is theoretically impossible, viz., counterfeit money, indecent publications, and ships," commented Wells.[88] Any proposed repeal of the restriction on ships raised a fearful clamor from American shipbuilders and, of course, flew in the face of the dominant protectionist philosophy. American ship operators confronted other higher costs, for it cost more in wages and food to run their vessels. "In Great Britain, the law says you

[85] Crowell, *loc. cit.*, pp. 1406–1407.

[86] *Ibid.*, p. 1380.

[87] Testimony of S. W. Carey, *loc. cit.*, p. 16; Crowell, *loc. cit.*, pp. 1387–1391.

[88] "Report of the Special Commissioner of the Revenue . . . Jan. 1869," *loc. cit.*, p. 37.

shall give a crew so much bread, meat, rice, raisins, dried apples, etc. When they [the seamen] go on a vessel under the American flag, they want a porterhouse steak, which costs as much as at the Fifth Avenue Hotel. . . . They want the best butter and the best of everything."[89] A modern, detailed estimate of the difference in labor costs in shipbuilding between Great Britain and the United States in 1900 set the percentage at 50 to 100 per cent less for the former, and of running expenses between American and foreign vessels at 25 to 50 per cent less for the latter.[90]

Though many of the causes for the inferiority of the American merchant marine were clearly beyond the reach of the statute book, Congress in 1864–1865 authorized a mail subsidy for a line giving a monthly service between the United States and Rio de Janeiro. While the subsidy lasted, the United States contributed $1,500,000 and Brazil $1,000,000. At the same time Congress authorized a subsidy of $500,000 a year for a monthly service from the Pacific coast to Japan and China via Hawaii. In the first decade of its subsidy, the Pacific Mail Company, which more or less provided this service, received $4,583,335.33. Seeking a more generalized policy, Congress under the guidance of Blaine passed in 1891 a Merchant Marine Act. Patterned after the French system of bounties, this measure rejected a general bounty for tramp vessels based upon the distance of their voyages, but did give bounties on a per mile basis for outward voyages on certain lines. The highest bounty, $4.00 per mile, was for 8000-ton metal screw vessels; the lowest, 66⅔ cents, for 1500-ton metal or wooden craft. In return for these various measures the United States received some lines which folded the day the money stopped, or limped along until they found a haven under a new subsidy bill. The stimulus to American exports was practically imperceptible in the statistical column.[91]

Support for this policy was not confined to Eastern capitalists who, lounging on piazzas of summer cottage or hotel, could gaze off over the romantic blue waves. At least one important labor leader was saddened because "we are almost entirely at the mercy of England and other countries in the matter of ocean carriage."[92] And the Secretary of the Chicago Board of Trade, miles from sea water, trumpeted: "Without delay the national government should restore our merchant marine and place her flag over American merchandise upon the high seas. . . . History teaches that national effeminacy accompanies the degeneracy of the merchant marine and that the decline of maritime power is followed

[89] Testimony of S. W. Carey, *loc. cit.*, p. 16.

[90] Hutchins, *op. cit.*, pp. 464, 520.

[91] *Ibid.*, pp. 527–537; Royal Meeker, "History of Shipping Subsidies," *Publications of the American Economic Association*, vol. VI, No. 3, pp. 157–169.

[92] Testimony of John Jarrett, *Report of the Committee* [on Education and Labor] *of the Senate . . . 1885*, I, 1137.

by the decadence of enterprise and commerce."[93] The lobbyists for shipping subsidies loudly proclaimed that their cause enlisted both Republicans and Democrats and "the only thing that limits it is the flag."[94] Nevertheless American maritime policy was a matter of too little and too late.

The truth is that part of the mercantile community, busy on foreign trade, was somewhat skeptical about American policy, past and proposed. The *Commercial and Financial Chronicle* sneered at the "senseless dogma of the American navigation laws."[95] And there were other interests. In the Farquhar Committee, Representative Fithian from Illinois asked: "I represent an agricultural constituency. My people produce oats, corn, wheat, pork, and beef. . . . How will this subsidy give to my people cheaper transportation of their products?" The answers to this query were gibberish.[96] As influential as regional opposition or the division of economic interests were inherent defects in the subsidy programs. A shrewd observer of the subsidy campaign concluded that Americans would tolerate protection as long as it was indirect, concealed and diffuse in its effects, as with the protective tariff, but they had little inclination to pay their taxes to the Treasury to be appropriated outright to individuals and corporations. The unpopularity of the latter heightened this reluctance.[97]

FINANCING FOREIGN TRADE

President Harrison had prescribed "convenient methods of money exchanges" as a stimulant for American commerce. At the time he spoke, the methods were traditional enough—they were British. Sterling as currency and exchange was respected around the world for its soundness and stability, and British banks, with branches in every port and a central banking system at home, facilitated its use. Throughout the nineteenth century British institutions had thus financed American commerce; British credit had supported it. According to the rubric, trade is always "following" something: in this case it followed not the flag but the

[93] Chicago Board of Trade, *Twenty-eighth Annual Report of the Trade and Commerce of Chicago for the Year Ending December 31, 1885* (Chicago: Knight and Leonard, 1886), pp. xix–xx.

[94] Testimony of J. M. Lachlan, "Hearings before the [Farquhar] Committee," *op. cit.*, p. 55.

[95] *Commercial and Financial Chronicle,* XXVIII (May 17, 1879), 488; XXIX (August 23, 1879), 184–185.

[96] "Hearings before the [Farquhar] Committee," *op. cit.*, pp. 55–59.

[97] P. M. Zeis, *American Shipping Policy* (Princeton: Princeton University Press, 1938), pp. 52–53; M. M. McKee, "The Ship Subsidy Question in United States Politics," *Smith College Studies in History,* VIII, No. 1 (October, 1922), p. 41.

loan. An American shipping goods to Latin America or Asia would draw a bill of exchange upon the purchaser and take it to an American banker. If the banker endorsed or accepted it, the bank had no further market for the bill or foreign acceptance, since there was no central bank to buy it and turn an instrument of trade into a liquid asset. Consequently Americans opened credit via American banks with English banks, who possessed the power of rediscounting their paper at the Bank of England. Likewise the foreign purchaser of American goods because of the ubiquity and skill of English banking institutions would rather buy merchandise for which he could pay in sterling. In the twentieth century a naturalized American banker, Paul Warburg, thought that under the American system we paid "an annual tribute of millions to Europe for the financing of our [foreign] trade, which is not only a wilful waste, but also a blemish on our financial standing." Americans paid several commissions rather than one and often European banks were unwilling to have American business constitute an undue proportion of their credit operations. This was prudence rather than chauvinism on the part of the foreign banker.[98] On the whole the United States did not throw off its inferior status until the passage of the Federal Reserve Act (1913) enabled national banks to open branches abroad and established a central bank which could discount the paper its members issued in foreign trade and until World War I sapped the strength of sterling and turned foreign purchasers, including Europeans, to a market where they had to use dollar exchange.[99]

INCIDENTAL IMPROVEMENTS

The age was committed to the thesis that if individuals had correct information they would make correct decisions. In the matter of foreign trade, they turned, as they had in other matters, to the government to provide it. The familiar evolution ensued. Data which the government had once collected for its own functions was now to be collected for the welfare of private persons. Government agencies had to expand their data collecting activity to new areas and furnish their findings more promptly and more frequently. Consequently, in 1866 Congress authorized the Treasury Department, which was concerned with the collection of duties, to establish a Bureau of Statistics to provide wider information on markets, trade, exchanges, and the like. The bureaucracy of the gov-

[98] Paul M. Warburg, *The Federal Reserve System, Its Origin and Growth* (New York: Macmillan Company, 1930), II, 227, 414.

[99] *Ibid.*, II, 413; H. P. Willis, *The Federal Reserve System, Legislation, Organization and Operation* (New York: Ronald Press, 1923), pp. 1226–1231, 1683, 1695; C. W. Phelps, *The Foreign Expansion of American Banks* (New York: Ronald Press, 1927), pp. 42–63, 68–70.

ernment was driven with so light a rein that the State Department, under whose jurisdiction were the consuls, also continued to furnish information about foreign commercial markets. In both departments reports were placed on quarterly, monthly, or daily basis. In 1903 this evolution reached an interim plateau with the establishment within the Department of Commerce and Labor of the Bureau of Manufactures, later the Bureau of Foreign and Domestic Commerce, whose "province and duty" was "to foster, promote and develop the various manufacturing industries of the United States and markets for the same at home and abroad. . . ." The Bureau concentrated on the export trade in manufactures.[100]

Meanwhile there was a good deal of complaint among shippers and producers over the calibre of American consuls. They were, it was said, ignorant of the language and culture of the countries to which they were assigned. This charge largely arose because the American Civil Service at that time consisted of political appointees, and changes in administration involved changes in personnel. There were other handicaps. As Governor Smyth of New Hampshire put it in the eighties: "I do not think that our Government . . . has made a proper effort for a market for our products abroad, . . . and with an energetic Government that will send active consuls abroad on good salaries instead of starving them, we can make markets all over the world, and establish factories all over the United States, and it would not hurt New England a bit."[101] The recommended solution was usually a career service of educated personnel. A strong motive for the establishment of business schools at the college or university level in the eighties and after was the training of more competent American representatives abroad.[102] In all this censure and recommendation there was a peculiarly graceless note. Private enterprise was asking the government to do what it had failed to accomplish. For it was common knowledge that American promoters and "drummers" abroad were hampered by their ignorance of foreign languages and business customs and antagonized foreigners by their com-

[100] L. F. Schmeckebier and G. A. Weber, *The Bureau of Foreign and Domestic Commerce. Its History, Activities, and Organization* (Baltimore: The Johns Hopkins Press, 1924), pp. 16–28; *Commercial and Financial Chronicle,* XIX (August 22, 1874), 178.

[101] Testimony of Frederick Smyth, *Report of the Committee* [on Education and Labor] *of the Senate . . . 1885,* III, 119–120; Charles D. Warner, "Our Foreign Trade and Our Consular Service," *North American Review,* CLXII (March, 1896), 274–286.

[102] W. R. Harper, *The President's Report: Administration: Decennial Publications of the University of Chicago* (Chicago: University of Chicago Press, 1903), I, xc–xci; W. B. Donham, "The Graduate School of Business Administration," S. E. Morison, ed., *The Development of Harvard University since the Inauguration of President Eliot, 1869–1929* (Cambridge: Harvard University Press, 1930), pp. 533–534.

placent Americanism. "One of the bad traits" we had inherited from England "is a feeling of superiority over the rest of the world." [103]

Though government policy could and did affect many items in the foreign interchanges of the United States, for example protective duties, it did not touch many others. Sometimes this was the result of a failure to act. Shipping legislation, for instance, left Americans still paying freight monies to alien shipowners. Sometimes in view of contemporary conceptions of what the government should or could do, policy makers never thought of taking action. There was, for instance, no legislation governing the flow of international investment. As we have seen, the billion and a half dollars Europeans had put into public and private American securities by 1873 helped finance the American surplus of merchandise imports.[104] Wells, a government official, might shake his head in disapproval at this capital movement as demonstrating that "the aggregate of national production does not maintain the same proportion as formerly to the aggregate of national consumption." With a strange inconsistency he was also sad because he was afraid it could not last.[105] Since nothing ever does, he was bound to be right. Following the collapse of 1873 foreigners began curtailing new investments in this country and selling their American securities. Though this phenomenon was repeated at other times of panic, the total of foreign investments in the United States generally increased until, in 1899, it was placed at $3,300,000,000.

Meanwhile such figures had lost a little of their direct importance. From 1874 to the end of the century American exports generally exceeded imports. Foreigners paid for them with gold and also through the interest payments Americans owed them on foreign investments. This latter sum for the period 1874–95 has been calculated at an average of $85,000,000 a year.[106] But this, too, couldn't last. Early in the twentieth century Vanderlip was writing, "One of the most unanswerable of financial conundrums is how the world has settled its debt to us in the past and is to settle it in the future." For a time Americans could repurchase American securities held abroad. Since this procedure had limitations, Vanderlip commented that in "the opinion of many European and not a few American financiers . . . ultimately the settlement of this trade balance must be effected by America investing in European interests and securities. A few years ago it would have sounded absurd

[103] J. W. Van Cleave, "What Americans Must Do to Make an Export Business," *The Annals of the American Academy of Political and Social Science,* XXIX (May, 1907), 471–472; Vanderlip, *op. cit.,* pp. 21–23.

[104] Bullock, Williams, and Tucker, *op. cit.,* pp. 223–224.

[105] "Report of the Special Commissioner of the Revenue . . . December, 1869," *loc. cit.,* pp. xxx–xxxi, lix.

[106] Bullock, Williams, and Tucker, *op. cit.,* pp. 225–229.

to have talked of the possibility of American capital seeking investment in Europe. The idea is hardly yet so familiar as to make it seem reasonable."[107] But Vanderlip saw signs of the new trend. The industrial character of American exports revealed triumph and opportunity. Now "It is New Europe, a land of undeveloped possibilities, abounding in opportunity for keen captains of industry. It is mature America, the exemplar of modern industrial methods, perfected mechanical ideas, and ripe economic policy."[108] Though this shrewd American banker may have rushed his prophecy a bit, he was not imaginative enough to foresee the national government making loans and gifts to foreign nations and thus incidentally financing American exports. But at the time he wrote, this procedure was inconceivable as a part of "ripe economic policy."

[107] Vanderlip, *op. cit.*, pp. 16–19, 38–39.
[108] *Ibid.*, p. 36.

CHAPTER XV

The Attack on Wealth

ALL ABOARD FOR ALTRURIA!

THERE was bound to be discontent. For one thing the period here under scrutiny witnessed two ravaging panics, those of the seventies and the nineties, and a third, that of the eighties, which might have had a blacker reputation in an era when comparisons were less favorable. The financial collapse of the stock market and the banking system and the enduring idleness of men and of capital in the ensuing depressions were convincing demonstrations that all was not well with the economy. In addition there was a host of bewildering changes in the organization and conduct of production and distribution. Competition was apparently giving way to combination and "monopoly." Workers were organizing, and labor disputes, unsurpassed in American history for their violence and for the numbers involved, raged through the country. At the same time, large fortunes were becoming larger. Where once $50,000 had been the measure of a "magnate," millions now became the standard.[1] Great wealth was not only accumulated but inherited, and Americans were contemplating a new phenomenon, the "idle rich" as Theodore Roosevelt called them.[2] Even those who profited handsomely were puzzled and dismayed by uncertainty and change.

The resulting flood of analysis and prescription attained its peak in three classics of reform literature. One was *Progress and Poverty*, which appeared in 1879. Henry George, its author, was a printer, economist, and prophet. A second was *Looking Backward*, by Edward Bellamy, who before the publication of this volume had been a somewhat obscure journalist and periodical writer. Finally in 1894 Henry Demarest Lloyd, once a writer for the Chicago *Tribune* but now a free-lancer with an

[1] Testimony of Richard J. Hinton, *Report of the Committee* [on Education and Labor] *of the Senate . . . 1885*, II, 438.

[2] E. L. Godkin, "Idleness and Immorality," *Forum*, XIII (May, 1892), 337–339.

independent income through marriage, published *Wealth Against Commonwealth.*[3]

It would be difficult to imagine three more unlike books. Henry George's volume was a text book on economic theory, written with eloquence and feeling. In the search for the cause of industrial depression and the increase at the same time of want and of wealth (a paraphrase of his book's subtitle), George concluded that the great evil was a monopoly of land and the increase of the rent which went to its owners as the community advanced in population and wealth. The unjustly large share returned to landowners meant a diminution in the share for labor in wages and for capital in interest. George proposed to deal with land monopoly by a single tax expropriating the entire return from the ownership of land as distinct from the improvements on it; as for other complete monopolies, like the railroads, telegraph and telephone and municipal utilities, the government should own and operate them. The return from the single tax would be appropriated for government activities in the field of culture and health. Thus George anticipated that government would become a "cooperative society" in which "the common property" would be administered "for the common benefit."[4]

Where George was all analysis, Bellamy and Lloyd wrote utopian fantasies. *Looking Backward* is designedly so. It is the chronicle of a proper Bostonian, "rich and also educated and possessing, therefore, all the elements of happiness enjoyed by the most fortunate," who, after being placed in a trance, awakes in 2000 A. D. in a transformed and, if it were possible, a more cultured Boston. It is a most ingratiating volume, written in good humor, without bitterness. It is an adventure tale with a romantic love interest, its heroine a nineteenth century figure, equipped with maiden blushes, tender hand-clasps, and "moistened eyes." The criticism of the economic and social order which the hero had left behind him, is almost incidental to a description of the arrangements and blessings of a new socialist age.[5]

Lloyd's book, in essence a prolonged attack upon the Standard Oil and its leader, was not meant to be a fantasy. But it has the form of one. It begins with a picture of the Pennsylvania oil fields in the early days, where everything was going splendidly until John D. Rockefeller, "President of the Light of the World," casts a blight on it. This ogre came from a "palace," where he dwelt with "a few men . . . in offices

[3] "Edward Bellamy," *Dictionary of American Biography,* II, 163–164; "Henry George," *ibid.,* VII, 211–215; "Henry Demarest Lloyd," *ibid.,* XI, 331–332.

[4] Henry George, *Progress and Poverty. An Inquiry into the Cause of Industrial Depressions, and of Increase of Want with Increase of Wealth. The Remedy* (New York: D. Appleton and Company, 1880), 237–266, 395–396, 408–410.

[5] Edward Bellamy, *Looking Backward, 2000–1887* (Boston: Ticknor and Company, 1881), *passim.*

rich with plate glass and velvet plush, singing a siren song which drew all their competitors to bankruptcy or insanity or other forms of 'co-operation'. . . ." As a result of their "necromancy," "less oil has flowed, less light shone, and there has been less happiness and virtue."[6] When he emerges from his extravagant rhetoric, Lloyd accounts for the growth of the Standard by a series of mean acts against widows and the handicapped, by traits of stinginess and hypocrisy, and the practice of corruption and privilege.

Though these charges had the paraphernalia of documentation and footnote reference, the handling of evidence is not persuasive.[7] Lloyd equated innuendo with fact—a fire in the refinery of a competitor is attributed by a newspaper "to a man running about the works in a mysterious way just before the flames broke out"[8]—constantly employed the device of guilt by association, and pushed inference so hard that he held the Standard responsible for iniquitous ship subsidy bills and transformed the Rothschilds, genuine and vigorous competitors of the Standard in the European oil market, into a secret marketing agency of Rockefeller, largely on the ground that the Rothschilds used Rockefeller's competitive methods and that "their policy has been never to engage in commercial enterprise on their own account."[9] The final sin of the Standard was "money-worship," the "old self-interest."[10] As antidote to the business monster materializing from the vapors of confusion, clamor, and abuse in Lloyd's pages, it is perhaps enough to quote J. W. Jenks of Cornell, a genuine expert on trusts, no stick-in-the-mud reactionary or kept economist: "I have known many of the trust leaders and advocates, and many of their chief opponents. In uprightness, sincerity, public spirit, patriotism, there is little difference among them. Likewise in earnest determination to look out for themselves and to protect what they consider their own, there is little difference."[11]

Be that as it may, in Lloyd's world of the future, "We are to apply the co-operative methods of the post-office and the public school to many other common toils, to all toils in which private sovereignty has become through monopoly a despotism over the public, and to all in

[6] Henry D. Lloyd, *Wealth Against Commonwealth* (New York: Harper & Brothers, 1894), pp. 42, 44, 45, 61, 465, 474–475.

[7] Allan Nevins, "Letter to the Editor of the *American Historical Review*," *American Historical Review*, L (April, 1945), 676–689; Chester McA. Destler, "Wealth Against Commonwealth, 1894 and 1944," *American Historical Review*, L (October, 1944), 49–72, and "Letter to the Editor of the *American Historical Review*, L (April, 1945), 689.

[8] Lloyd, *op. cit.*, p. 447.

[9] *Ibid.*, pp. 389–404, 443.

[10] *Ibid.*, pp. 494–515.

[11] J. W. Jenks, Address, *Chicago Conference on Trusts* (Chicago: Civic Federation of Chicago, 1900), p. 34.

which the association of the people and the organization of processes have become so far developed that the profit-hunting Captain of Industry may be replaced by the public serving Captain of Industry. But we are to have much more. We are to have a private life of a new beauty. . . . We are to be commoners, travellers to Altruria." [12] Thus Bellamy's and Lloyd's tales arrived at the same terminus—Government ownership and operation. But there were more specific details for Bellamy's utopia, and more sunniness in it.

Along with the conviction that the times were out of joint and should be set right, these three critics shared an immense popularity. By 1905, perhaps two million copies of *Progress and Poverty* had been printed. In the early nineties a million copies of *Looking Backward* were in circulation, and apostles of the author had founded a national movement, complete with journals and extensive organization.[13] *Wealth Against Commonwealth* enlisted the fervor of the "unknown host" of the like-minded, though not of the Standard associates in their "glass and velvet" lair.[14] That each of the books should have a wide appeal is not surprising in view of the fact that the three critics, no matter how radical their proposals, voiced popularly held and often contradictory attitudes. Thus, for Bellamy and Lloyd the competitive order was immoral since it gave the strong the right to destroy their rivals, neighbors and brothers.[15] Henry George, on the other hand, classified the proposal "that competition must be restrained" as one of the "ideas which bring great masses of men . . . under the leadership of charlatans and demagogues." As such it was "fraught with danger." [16] For a moment, until he recoiled from the greed and money-making involved, Lloyd admired "consolidation. . . . Men have become so intelligent, so responsive and responsible, so co-operative that they can be intrusted in great masses with the care of vast properties owned entirely by others and with the operation of complicated processes." [17] Bellamy was forthright: "Small capitalists . . . were totally incompetent to the demands of an age of steam and telegraphs. . . . Even [consolidation's] victims . . . were forced to admit the prodigious increase of efficiency which had been imparted to the national industries, the vast economies effected by concentration of management and unity

[12] Lloyd, *op. cit.*, pp. 534–535.

[13] Sidney Fine, *Laissez Faire and the General-Welfare State: A Study of Conflict in American Thought, 1865–1901* (Ann Arbor: The University of Michigan Press, 1956), pp. 290, 296–300.

[14] Caro Lloyd, *Henry Demarest Lloyd, 1827–1903: A Biography* (New York: G. P. Putnam's Sons, 1912), I, 191–201; Testimony of J. D. Archbold, *Report of the Industrial Commission,* I, 559.

[15] Fine, *op. cit.*, p. 298; H. D. Lloyd, *op. cit.*, pp. 495–499.

[16] George, *op. cit.*, p. 10.

[17] H. D. Lloyd, *op. cit.*, pp. 429–505.

of organization . . . as a means of merely producing wealth, capital had proved efficient in proportion to its consolidation. The restoration of the old system . . . might indeed bring back a greater equality of conditions with more individual dignity and freedom, but it would be at the price of general poverty and the arrest of material progress." [18]

In spite of their disagreements, George, Bellamy, and Lloyd reflected American insistence upon efficiency and upon production, pride in national greatness based on productivity, belief in natural law, preference for "economy" in government and mistrust of "restrictive" governmental legislation.[19] Nor was the transition to the new order to be difficult, although on this score Lloyd was obscure.[20] George's single tax, though it alarmed some, was so palatable to many businessmen that they became his admirers. Since his system was "but the triumph of common sense," Bellamy anticipated that the transition to it, in spite of some agitation and excitement would be an "evolution" effected by politics and enlightenment.[21] The persistence of the romantic type of femininity in Bellamy's utopia also promised that emancipated women would still be as consoling and as piquant as in the Victorian era.

This emphasis was of course necessary. If reformers are to do more than write books, they must persuade others to follow them. The majority of the discontented were not radical. Some were farmers, more concerned with the remedying of particular abuses than with the building of a brave new world; though there was labor discontent, except for a small minority, workers did not propose to alter fundamentals of society or economics. It was, in fact, the middle-class from which the armies of reform were in large part recruited. This group included people in the professions, made uneasy by the power and values of a rising business class, and also many businessmen themselves, to whom consolidation was a threat.[22] On this score as on others, business was not monolithic.

CONSOLIDATION, PRO AND CON

The successful businessmen of the era customarily defended consolidation because it lowered prices. As John D. Rockefeller put it, "We

[18] Bellamy, *op. cit.*, pp. 75–76.

[19] Bellamy, *op. cit.*, pp. 161, 290, 315–317, 354–355; H. D. Lloyd, *op. cit.*, p. 497; George, *op. cit.*, pp. 287–289, 409.

[20] H. D. Lloyd, *op. cit.*, pp. 517, 521.

[21] Bellamy, *op. cit.*, pp. 67–70, 77–81.

[22] Fine, *op. cit.*, pp. 295, 299–301, 346; Daniel Aaron, *Men of Good Will: A Story of American Progressives* (New York: Oxford University Press, 1951), pp. 55–171; Richard Hofstadter, *The Age of Reform from Bryan to F. D. R.* (New York: Alfred A. Knopf, 1955), pp. 213 ff.; Charles A. Barker, *Henry George* (New York: Oxford University Press, 1955), pp. 418, 511–517; Testimony of J. R. Dos Passos, *Report of the Industrial Commission*, I, 1156–1157.

think our American petroleum is a very cheap light. It is our pleasure to try to make it so."[23] And a similar defence was the most telling that the Standard's counsel, S. T. C. Dodd, could make.[24] In actuality the general price levels for manufactured as well as agricultural products declined from 1870 to the later nineties. At one point, a former foe of the railroads characterized the decade as "the consumer's millenium."[25] Granted all this, prices in highly controlled industries such as sugar, whisky, and certain iron or steel products sometimes rose after the successful formation of a combination—and like as not fell again later.[26] Experts in the matter of trusts were cautious on the interrelationship between trusts and prices. Jenks in 1899 was observing, "It remains still to be fully established what the effects are upon the prices of raw materials and finished products."[27] But critics of business price policy were in no mood to be patient. In their minds low prices were but an aspect of the fierce price wars, usually a prelude to consolidations. Once the consolidators had the consumer at their mercy, they raised prices to recompense their members for earlier losses. Critics also maintained that low prices sometimes merely reflected local price-cutting undertaken to ruin competitors. More useful in anti-trust polemics than instances of price-cutting was the assertion that the centralization of business gave a power that might be used in future to raise prices to extortionate levels. It was not actual prices but potential ones which were at issue.

A cognate defence of consolidation was that a large business could lower its costs through economies and efficiencies impossible to small enterprises. The former bought its materials in large quantities and more cheaply, dispensed with hordes of competing salesmen, utilized inventions and the most efficient plants, and employed the best managerial talent.[28] The telephone and telegraph, stenography and the typewriter "rendered possible and practical the concentration and consolidation under single management of a magnitude and multiplicity of business interests which a generation ago would have been physically impossible."[29] To this panegyric a perceptive critic entered a demurrer. Because of their nuisance value as competitors, consolidations included the weak

[23] Testimony of John D. Rockefeller, Report of the Committee on Manufactures, *House Report* No. 3112 (s.n. 2606), 50th Cong., 1st Sess., p. 389.

[24] S. T. C. Dodd, "Ten Years of the Standard Oil Trust," *Forum,* XIII (May, 1892), 308–310.

[25] Address of F. B. Thurber, *Chicago Conference on Trusts,* p. 135.

[26] Jeremiah W. Jenks, "Industrial Combinations and Prices," *Report of the Industrial Commission,* I, 39–57.

[27] Address of J. W. Jenks, *Chicago Conference on Trusts,* p. 31.

[28] William W. Cook, *The Corporation Problem* (New York: G. P. Putnam's Sons, 1891), pp. 215–216; Address of Azel F. Hatch, *Chicago Conference on Trusts,* pp. 66–67.

[29] Hatch, *loc. cit.,* pp. 65–66.

as well as the strong. Business combinations "are unnatural creations in that they load down the vigorous and prosperous concerns with the weight of the unprofitable and failing ones. The law of the survival of the fittest in manufacturing is one thing; the trust plan of turning strong establishments into a poorhouse for the preservation of weak concerns is quite a different thing." [30] Since even reformers like Lloyd and Bellamy granted the superior efficiency of combination, public opinion probably recognized that this was one of the "good" phases of big business.

But like the argument about prices, that about efficiency was largely an irrelevance. The significant thing about the anti-trust movement was that it paid only minor attention to economic analysis. A speaker before the Chicago Conference on Trusts, who received salvos of applause during his address and an ovation at its end, characterized the trust issue as "the great moral, social, and political battle that now confronts the whole Union. . . . We must place national righteousness above national wealth, ethics above economics, political principles above pecuniary profit, the Constitution above the commerce of the country." [31] When such highflying generalities were reduced to the specifications of an indictment, the objection to big business was that it did away with little business. If Lloyd's *omnium gatherum* can be said to have a consistent theme, it was that the Standard had driven out of business producers who wanted to stay in business. That bigness might benefit the consumer was not the question; more fundamental was the conviction that it was better for a man to be his own master than to be the employee of a large corporation. The former estate contributed to his dignity and independence and gave him an opportunity for self-development; the latter condition dwarfed his individuality, checked manhood, and made him a hireling.[32] The derivation of such attitudes from Jefferson and from an agrarian culture was obvious. That every man should have a business and the right to succeed in it (a sort of homestead thinking applied to industry) Jenks shrewdly remarked is "the question . . . perhaps the most vital one of the whole discussion. Only experience can give the final answer." [33]

The political argument against big business also considered the impact of bigness upon democratic government. How would it affect the Republic? It seemed axiomatic that by its magnitude and affluence big

[30] Cook, *op. cit.*, p. 228.

[31] Address of D. G. Wooten, *Chicago Conference on Trusts,* pp. 52–53.

[32] Address of J. W. Jenks, *Chicago Conference on Trusts,* p. 32; J. W. Jenks, *The Trust Problem* (New York: McClure, Phillips & Co., 1905), pp. 195–211; Address of John Graham Brooks, *Chicago Conference on Trusts,* pp. 57–58; Address of R. S. Taylor, *ibid.*, p. 73; Address of A. L. Weil, *ibid.*, p. 80; Address of Hazen S. Pingree, *ibid.*, pp. 263–267.

[33] Address of J. W. Jenks, *Chicago Conference on Trusts,* p. 33.

business was bound to get a better deal from government than would the inconspicuous citizen. "A Constitution adapted to three millions is certainly unsuitable to 125,000 magnates possessed of thirty-three thousand millions of Gold. The Constitution may prescribe one course, but you must perceive this Imperial golden treasury of these Republicans demands another." [34] How did the corporate system vis-à-vis the government work? "So long as the business of corporations is affected by government, just so long will corporations continue to bribe, brow-beat, and dominate public officials." [35] In short Lloyd and his sort describe the era, by innuendo if not by direct assertion, as one of crawling corruption of legislators, executives, and judges. Others felt that the very power of big business must overawe government. Political equality was impossible without economic equality. In the United States democracy had given way to plutocracy which "makes money and pleasure the objects of existence and the tests of success. Whatsoever is an aid to plutocracy is a danger to the republic." [36]

While this might have been the destination at which the nation had arrived, there is no clear evidence that it got there by the path asserted. As Jenks observed: "While it is probable that many individual cases . . . occur, and that corporations, both in self-defence and for the sake of furthering their own interests, do at times buy members of legislatures, it is likewise probable that the prevalence of this custom is not a little exaggerated by many people, and especially by certain sections of the press. It is certainly true that the character of individual legislators and their faithfulness to their trust are considerably better than is commonly assumed in popular discussion in the newspapers." [37] In sum, the picture of the era as graft-ridden stems in part from the human tendency in defeat to cry "foul play." Reformers who saw their measures rejected found it hard to conceive that the inexpediency or unacceptability of their proposals accounted for the outcome. Also, popular sentiment was likely to regard all attempts at lobbying or persuasion of legislators as essentially sinister.[38]

In the last analysis the criticism of the development and function-

[34] John H. Greene, *The Power-Holding Class versus the Public: Imaginary Dialogue of McKinley and Hanna. Prosperity, Trust and Imperialism* (Newport, R. I.: The Brotherhood of Liberty, 1900), p. 30.

[35] Cook, *op. cit.*, pp. 247–248.

[36] *Ibid.*, p. 249; John M. Bonham, *Industrial Liberty* (New York: G. P. Putnam's Sons, 1888), pp. 46, 57; W. J. Ghent, *Our Benevolent Feudalism* (New York: Macmillan Company, 1902), pp. 25–26; Address of A. L. Weil, *Chicago Conference on Trusts*, p. 93.

[37] Jenks, *The Trust Problem*, p. 192.

[38] Testimony of P. J. McGuire, *Report of the Committee* [on Education and Labor] *of the Senate . . . 1885*, I, 347–352.

ing of the economy was an attack upon the spirit and accomplishments of business and industrialism. It was an attack upon the way by which wealth was created and divided and upon the motivations of individuals engaged in the process. Wealth-making was greed and selfishness, the "old self-interest," and a culture in which acquisition was the aim was "material." As Bryan put it before the Chicago Conference on Trusts, "In the determination of questions we should find out what will make our people great and good and strong rather than what will make them rich." [39] No more millionaires, was the conclusion of Henry D. Lloyd.[40]

Abstractly considered, working for gain at furnace or furrow would seem as "selfish" and "material" as working in the "velvet and plate glass" counting house. Apparently popular impulse drew a line between them, perhaps because it conceived of the returns from business activity as a static single sum which was neither justly nor desirably divided. Also the investment and management of money did not fall within the definition of work. Bellamy's utopia significantly dispensed with "those gentry," the bankers and merchants.[41] More important as explanation for anti-business sentiment was the natural tendency to equate income with expenditures for consumption. An individual did not need millions to live. If he had large sums at his disposal, he or his descendants were apt to be lazy, and idleness was synonymous with mischief. The expenditures of the rich on "palaces" on Fifth Avenue or "cottages" at Newport, on yachts and gay parties seemed to prove the vanity, the frivolity, and voluptuousness charged against the upper economic classes.[42] When Carnegie advised society not to shoot its millionaires, he was not being entirely facetious. Carnegie argued that millionaires "labored on" to make things cheaper for others.[43] How convincing such arguments were is another matter.

PRELUDES TO THE SHERMAN ANTI-TRUST ACT

At a time when the Wholesale Grocers' Association of New York was resolving that "it is to the best interests of all true American citizens

[39] Address of W. J. Bryan, *Chicago Conference on Trusts,* p. 511; Bellamy, *op. cit.,* pp. 57–58, 67, 69–70, 179–184, 277–278; H. D. Lloyd, *op. cit.,* pp. 420–431, 492, 494–515, 519; Testimony of Reuben Carroll, *Report of the Committee* [on Education and Labor] *of the Senate . . . 1885,* II, 1099.

[40] H. D. Lloyd, *op. cit.,* p. 524.

[41] Bellamy, *op. cit.,* p. 117.

[42] Godkin, "Idleness and Immorality," *loc. cit.,* pp. 338–341; E. L. Godkin, "The Expenditures of Rich Men," *Scribner's Magazine,* XX (October, 1896), 495–500; E. C. Kirkland, *Dream and Thought in the Business Community, 1860–1900* (Ithaca: Cornell University Press, 1956), pp. 37–45.

[43] Andrew Carnegie, "Wealth and Its Uses," *The Empire of Business* (New York: Doubleday, Page & Co., 1902), pp. 138–140.

to use every endeavor to cause the most extreme legislation against the operation of trusts that can be had consistent with our state and national constitutions," clearly alarm was in the ascendence.[44] Of the many roads to safety, that of government ownership of enterprise, crucial to Bellamy's and Lloyd's proposals, was not taken, except in certain municipalities. Another way was to forbid outright monopoly or big business. Prior to the enactment of national legislation—the Sherman Anti-Trust Act in 1890—some states had taken action. By the end of the nineties fifteen states had constitutional provisions—Maryland's, for instance, read that monopolies "are odious, contrary to the spirit of a free government and the principles of commerce, and ought not to be suffered"—prohibiting trusts, and twenty-seven, had statutes. Most of these states were Southern and Western; few, if any, were important industrial and commercial states. The success of such measures depended upon care in defining terms and the specifications in their prohibitions. On the last count various legislatures had forbidden agreements to limit output, apportion territories, or to maintain, raise or lower prices. In general the enforcement of these acts was left to the attorney generals of the states.[45]

During the nineteenth century a few states made strenuous efforts to apply their anti-trust policy. In Texas, for instance, suit was brought against the Waters-Pierce Company, a Missouri corporation marketing Standard oil in the Southwest. The chief charge was that in contracting with purchasers to handle its oil exclusively the Waters-Pierce organization violated Texas law. It should, therefore, forfeit its license to do business in the state. The state courts and eventually the Supreme Court of the United States so found, and the license was revoked. To meet constitutional requirements, the lower court had to hedge its decision by declaring: "Nothing herein contained shall be construed to in any way affect or apply to or prohibit said defendant's right to engage in interstate commerce within this State." [46] Within three months of the decision of the United States Supreme Court, Texas gave a new Waters-Pierce Company a state license.[47] It may have been things of this sort that led Jenks to observe later that the prohibitions of state legislatures and courts "have had comparatively little, practically no effect, as regards the trend of our industrial development." [48]

[44] Address of F. B. Thurber, *loc. cit.*, p. 126.

[45] Henry R. Seager and Charles A. Gulick, Jr., *Trust and Corporation Problems* (New York: Harper & Brothers, 1929), pp. 341–348.

[46] *Ibid.*, pp. 349–352; Waters-Pierce Oil Company *v.* Texas, 177 *United States*, 28.

[47] Seager and Gulick, *op. cit.*, p. 352; Ralph W. Hidy and Muriel E. Hidy, *History of Standard Oil Company (New Jersey): Pioneering in Big Business, 1882–1911* (New York: Harper & Brothers, 1955), pp. 448–451.

[48] Jenks, *The Trust Problem*, p. 218.

Although usage customarily labels these state measures as "prohibitory" or "preventive," they were just as apt to be regulatory in so far as they undertook to discriminate between what was legal or illegal. A policy of regulating business was implicit in the American temper, for a democracy usually seeks to compromise or reconcile conflicting interests and viewpoints. Why not preserve the benefits of bigness and extirpate only its evils? A governor of West Virginia before the Chicago Conference on Trusts was ready to lay down stipulations: "If the advocates of and participants in the trusts could satisfy the masses upon the following propositions, they would then have but limited opposition in the years to come, viz: First, Will you and can you, in all cases, as you claim, agree to furnish a better and cheaper article to consumers of all the necessaries of life covered by your trusts and combines? Second, What do you propose to do with the tens of thousands of middle-men now employed, who of necessity must lose their present positions? And, third, What will become of the 'small dealers' scattered over our country from Maine to Florida, and from the surges of the Atlantic to the Sunset Sea, whose waves make music in the golden sands of California?" [49] The policy of making distinctions appealed also to those who asserted trusts were the result of "natural evolution," that they had "come to stay." To prohibit them was as impossible as to oppose machinery; it was retrogressive.[50] In short, "It will be folly to undertake reckless warfare for the annihilation of trusts, but the claws of the monster, if that it be, can be cut, and, under the restraining influence of good regulations this Behemoth, biggest born of commerce, may become a docile, harmless, and really amiable family pet." [51]

Besides, Americans had tried the way of regulation for the railroads. It was the way of experience. Ostensibly national legislation in the Sherman Anti-Trust Act rejected this precedent. Railroad monopolies were thought to be different from industrial combinations; the former were "natural," the latter were artificial. Furthermore it was dubious if legislatures had the wit to devise wise regulatory provisions and find able administrators to apply them, for business combinations were matters of great complexity, legal and economic. Also, it was doubtful if government agencies could escape the creeping corruption for which business was popularly thought responsible.[52]

[49] Address of G. W. Atkinson, *Chicago Conference on Trusts,* pp. 98–105.

[50] Address of A. F. Hatch, *loc. cit.,* pp. 67–68; Address of A. L. Weil, *loc. cit.,* pp. 94–95.

[51] Address of William Fortune, *Chicago Conference on Trusts,* pp. 55–56; Address of R. S. Taylor, *loc. cit.,* p. 77; Address of F. B. Thurber, *loc. cit.,* p. 124.

[52] Address of R. S. Taylor, *loc. cit.,* p. 74; United States *v.* Trans-Missouri Freight Association, 166 *United States,* 320, 321.

THE SHERMAN ANTI-TRUST ACT

The need for national legislation rather than state legislation in dealing with big business was obvious. "A national market has taken the place of the local market. . . . Uniformity of law and harmony of procedure is as essential as uniform railroad rates and absence of discrimination," observed the Statistician of the Interstate Commerce Commission.[53] No Supreme Court decision, as in the Wabash case, precipitated action. Instead, during the eighties the platforms of both major parties inveighed, albeit ambiguously, against the loss of the advantages of competition. Finally, by the end of the decade, Congress was ready for some sort of legislation. The legislative history of the bill reveals contradictions of purposes and uncertainties about methods. The bill, originally introduced by Senator Sherman of Ohio, ran the gamut of senatorial debate and amendment and referral to two different committees. In the House discussion was brief and inconclusive. Finally, with only one dissenting vote in both Houses, the Sherman Anti-Trust Act became law. Actually Sherman had little to do with the phraseology of the statute bearing his name. Senators, mostly Republican and mostly Eastern and mostly conservative—"great lawyers," to use W. H. Taft's phrase—put the bill in the form which prevailed.[54] The critical provisions were in the first two sections:

Section 1. "Every contract, combination in the form of trust or otherwise, or conspiracy, in restraint of trade or commerce among the several States or with foreign nations, is hereby declared to be illegal. Every person who shall make any such contract or engage in any such combination or conspiracy, shall be deemed guilty of a misdemeanor," and punished by fine or imprisonment or both.

Section 2. "Every person who shall monopolize or attempt to monopolize, or combine or conspire with any other person or persons to monopolize any part of the trade or commerce among the several States, or with foreign nations, shall be deemed guilty of a misdemeanor," and punished by fine or imprisonment or both. Section 8 made it clear that the words "person" or "persons" included corporations and associations. The act made it "the duty" of district attorneys of the United States and the Attorney General to institute proceedings in equity against violations of the act and also allowed "any person who shall be injured in his business or property by any other person or corporation by reason of

[53] Address of Henry C. Adams, *Chicago Conference on Trusts*, p. 39.

[54] Seager and Gulick, *op. cit.*, pp. 367–373; W. H. Taft, *The Anti-Trust Act and the Supreme Court* (New York: Harper & Brothers, 1914), p. 3.

anything forbidden or declared to be unlawful by this act" to sue in the federal courts and recover "three fold the damages by him sustained and the costs of suit." [55]

As to the intent and scope of the act, Senator Hoar from Massachusetts probably gave the most accurate and persuasive exegesis. The national government "is entering upon a new and untrodden field of legislation. It is undertaking to curb by national authority an evil which under the opinions which have prevailed of old under all our legislative precedents and policies, has been left to be dealt with either by the ordinary laws of trade or to be dealt with by the States. . . . We have affirmed the old doctrine of the common law in regard to all interstate and international commercial transactions, and have clothed the United States courts with authority to enforce that doctrine by injunction. We have put in also a grave penalty." [56] Though there was a common law in nearly every state, there was not any common law of the United States. This act elevated common law doctrines to the explicitness of a Federal Statute.[57] Since common law was at issue, it was natural to entrust the execution of the policy to courts rather than to commissions. Besides, if no Congressman knew what he wanted, the courts might find out. "Legislators madly dashed to the work, threw ink upon paper, and called it a statute and legislation, and they asked the courts to enforce it—enforce a statute based upon doubt and guess and speculation and against the natural laws of trade and business." [58] At least such was the opinion of a corporation lawyer.

Apparently Congress committed itself in the act to a belief in the beneficence of free and unlimited competition. In its deliberations it did not harken overmuch to the theory that combination was inevitable and that "deadly, brutal competition" was responsible for the appearance of combination.[59] Competition was the natural order; if it did not exist, it lurked on the horizon and only needed to be beckoned into action. If monopolies raised prices too high, the presence of higher profits would at once attract competitors. In a sense it made little difference who enforced the Sherman Anti-Trust Act, for the competitive order was self-enforcing. Anti-trust was not intended to supplant but to supplement the "ordinary laws of trade."

In the circumstances, it would seem legislation was a work of supererogation. Not at all. There was an urgent need to express a

[55] 26 *United States Statutes,* 209–210.

[56] Speech of Senator Hoar, *Congressional Record* [51st Cong., 1st Sess.], XXI, Pt. 4, p. 3146.

[57] *Congressional Record* [51st Cong., 1st Sess.], XXI, Pt. 4, p. 3152; Taft, *op. cit.,* p. 21.

[58] Testimony of John R. Dos Passos, *Report of the Industrial Commission,* I, 1143.

[59] Speech of Senator Platt, *Congressional Record* [51st Cong., 1st Sess.], XXI, Pt. 3, pp. 2729–2731.

"faith" in competition, boldly "to take some step, make a beginning to show we [the Senate] are opposed to trusts." [60] When this creed and subscription is coupled with the imposition of criminal penalties upon certain business acts, it is clear that the Sherman Anti-Trust Act accorded with the preference of the day for moral condemnation over economic analysis. The hard-headed or derisive who have referred to American anti-trust policy as a "myth," a "religion," a "babble of voices," a "moral pronouncement" would seem to be on the right path.[61]

It could be argued that words could exorcise trusts because words had brought them into being. "All monopoly is bottomed on legislation." [62] To illustrate this point, diagnosticians of bigness picked on the protective tariff—"The mother of all trusts is the customs tariff bill" [63]—the patent laws,[64] and, above all, the incorporation laws in the several states. Extremists proposed that legislatures stop issuing charters and that business return to the basis of a more individualistic and less "collective" form of association. Others were content with restrictions, such as limitations upon capitalization. Still others, in order to terminate the shameful competition between states to facilitate the act of incorporation and to dissipate the half-light of which jurisdictions could regulate, proposed Federal incorporation.[65] But proposals were not laws. Meanwhile it was up to the machinery of justice to "define" immorality by defining and punishing forbidden acts. In this complex task, the frequently mentioned common law was not helpful. There was not a single common law; there were common laws.[66] The courts had to decide which precedents and parts Congress had inserted into the Federal code.

THE JUSTICES TRY THEIR HAND

In 1895 in the first important anti-trust case before the Supreme Court, United States *v.* E. C. Knight Company, the Justices came up

[60] Milton Handler, "A Study of the Construction and Enforcement of the Federal Anti-Trust Laws," *Temporary National Economic Committee, Monograph* No. 38, p. 1; Speech of Senator George, *Congressional Record* [51st Cong., 1st Sess.], XXI, Pt. 4, p. 3148.

[61] Thurman Arnold, *The Folklore of Capitalism* (New Haven: Yale University Press, 1937), pp. 207–229; Handler, *loc. cit.*, p. 80; Walton Hamilton and Irene Till, "Antitrust in Action," *Temporary National Economic Committee, Monograph* No. 16, p. 11.

[62] Frederic C. Howe, *The Confessions of a Monopolist* (Chicago: The Public Publishing Company, 1906), p. v.

[63] Testimony of Henry O. Havemeyer, *Report of the Industrial Commission,* I, Testimony, 101–102; Address of D. G. Wooten, *loc. cit.*, pp. 49, 51; Address of J. G. Brooks, *loc. cit.*, p. 60.

[64] Jenks, *The Trust Problem,* pp. 56, 220–221.

[65] Address of D. G. Wooten, *loc. cit.*, p. 51; Address of E. C. Crow, *Chicago Conference on Trusts*, pp. 106–112.

[66] Handler, *loc. cit.*, pp. 2–8.

with a distinction, shattering to reformers and dismaying to many of the legal fraternity. In this case the doings under review were those of the American Sugar Refining Company, popularly known as the Sugar Trust. This Trust purchased through an exchange of stock certain refineries in Philadelphia; following this acquisition, it was alleged that it owned 98 per cent of the refining capacity of the country.[67] In their decision, all the Justices save one saw the act complained of as a commonplace business transaction. "The contracts and acts of the defendants related exclusively to the acquisition of the Philadelphia refineries and the business of sugar refining in Pennsylvania, and bore no direct relation to commerce between the States or with foreign nations. The object was manifestly private gain in the manufacture of the commodity but not through the control of interstate or foreign commerce." Clearly the Sherman Anti-Trust Act, which dealt with commerce, did not apply.[68]

This judicial obliviousness to motives and intentions was probably due to the fact that in an Anglo-American democracy, the law deals with facts and not dangerous or unwholesome thoughts. Furthermore, in this instance there was an absence of the classic forms of agreement and of a contract intending to control trade in the product.

Also it would seem the judges were helped to their distinctions by the way in which the Department of Justice prepared the case and presented it to the Courts.[69] The Department employed none of the available evidence on the sale of sugar in interstate commerce and of the control of sales and prices by the Trust. Attorney General Olney was more than reconciled to the decision. In a private letter he wrote: "You will observe that the government has been defeated in the Supreme Court on the trust question. I always supposed it would be, and have taken the responsibility of not prosecuting under a law I believed to be no good—much to the rage of the New York *World*."[70] Be that as it may, the decision of the Court had validated one of the most effective forms of business consolidation and control.

In following years, however, the Supreme Court did not continue down the path marked out in the E. C. Knight case. Two years later it was dealing with railroads which had formed the Trans-Missouri Freight Association, a pooling device to establish and maintain "reasonable rates" for freight carried by the eighteen participants in a zone lying between the Pacific and the first tier of states beyond the Mississippi or the Missouri Rivers. The railroads claimed the Sherman Act was not intended

[67] United States *v.* E. C. Knight Co., 156 *United States,* 2, 3.

[68] 156 *United States,* 17.

[69] Taft, *op. cit.,* pp. 56–57, 59.

[70] Quoted in Allan Nevins, *Grover Cleveland: A Study in Courage* (New York: Dodd, Mead & Company, 1932), p. 671.

to apply to transportation but to manufacturing activities. Mr. Justice Peckham, the spokesman for the bare majority of the court, dismissed the relevance of this argument with the wry observation, "To exclude agreements as to rates by competing railroads for the transportation of articles of commerce between the States would leave little for the act to take effect upon."[71] In this case, also, a written agreement dealing with commerce between the routes was unmistakably in evidence and at issue.

Accordingly, the consideration which bothered the Court was whether the Sherman Anti-Trust Act forbade unreasonable restraints on trade and commerce and permitted reasonable ones. It had been a feature of common law to permit agreements restraining commerce when they were ancillary to the main and legal purpose of the contract. For example, agreements by a freed apprentice not to compete with his master or by the seller of a business or occupation not to compete with the purchaser in the same locality were reasonable restraints and hence not void.[72] Justice Peckham admitted he was impressed by the argument that since competition between railroads might be ruinous to them and to the community, a pooling agreement might be reasonable. But he did not think Congress had, in passing the statute, revealed any intention to exempt reasonable restraints from legal prohibition, and it was not the Court's business to read distinctions of this sort into the statute.[73] In an opinion which was in general prolix and repetitious, the Justice was singularly succinct on one point: "Competition, free and unrestricted, is the general rule which governs all the ordinary business pursuits and transactions of life. Evils, as well as benefits, result therefrom. . . . No law can be enacted nor system be devised for the control of human affairs that . . . does not produce some evil results, no matter how beneficial its general purpose may be. . . . The Anti-Trust Act . . . renders illegal all agreements which are in restraint of trade or commerce. . . ."[74] Four Justices vigorously dissented from this decision.[75]

Although the majority gave a very small loophole for the current doctrine that legislation should preserve the good and prevent the evil results of big business, Mr. Justice Peckham held out a formless hope a year later in United States *v.* Joint Traffic Association. In this case the Court surveyed an agreement on rates, this time in trunkline territory. Once again he chanted the virtues of free competition, but on another matter added a somewhat waspish warning: "To suppose, as is assumed

[71] United States *v.* Trans-Missouri Freight Association, 166 *United States,* 303.
[72] Handler, *loc. cit.,* pp. 3–7.
[73] 166 *United States,* 321, 326, 330.
[74] 166 *United States,* 337, 341.
[75] 166 *United States,* 343.

by counsel, that the effect of the decision in the *Trans-Missouri case* is to render illegal most business contracts or combinations, however necessary and indispensable they may be, because, as they assert, they all restrain trade in some remote and indirect degree, is to make a most violent assumption, and one not called for or justified by the decision mentioned, or by any other decision of this Court." [76]

In 1899 Peckham wrote the decision for Addyston Pipe and Steel Company *v.* United States. Though the Justice had apparently become the majority's specialist on anti-trust, in this instance he relied heavily upon a preliminary decision handed down in a lower court by William Howard Taft. The Supreme Court affirmed that decision. At issue was an agreement between six manufacturers of cast-iron pipe. In thirty-six states, "pay territory," they agreed through various devices to collusive bidding on contracts for the delivery of iron pipe.[77] The defendants claimed their resulting prices were reasonable. Peckham imperiously thrust this observation aside: "We do not think the issue an important one, because . . . we do not think that at common law there is any question of reasonableness open to the courts with reference to such a contract. Its tendency was certainly to give defendants the power to charge unreasonable prices, had they chosen to do so." [78] Peckham, though he quoted considerably from Taft, did not see fit to repeat the latter's attempt to define precisely what reasonable restraints were, nor did he echo Taft's vigorous aversion to judges determining "how much restraint of competition is in the public interest, and how much is not. The manifest danger in the administration of justice according to so shifting, vague, and indeterminate a standard would seem to be a strong reason against adopting it." [79] Though the defendants were manufacturers, E. C. Knight did not save them. Unluckily for them, they had signed an agreement governing their sales. Though they controlled perhaps only 30 per cent of the national production, the Court found that the monopoly prohibited and punished by the Sherman Act did not have to be absolute. "It is the effect of the combination in limiting and restricting the right of each of the members to transact business in the ordinary way, as well as its effect upon the volume or extent of the dealing in the commodity, that is regarded." [80]

In sum, after a decade of interpretation and application, courts had found in the generalities of the Sherman Act a prohibition of price-

[76] United States *v.* Joint Traffic Association, 171 *United States,* 568.

[77] Addyston Pipe & Steel Company *v.* United States, 175 *United States,* 212–215.

[78] 175 *United States,* 238.

[79] Handler, *loc. cit.,* pp. 6–7.

[80] *Ibid.,* p. 30; 175 *United States,* 245.

fixing and of sharing the market. They had usually rejected distinctions between reasonable and unreasonable restraints and exalted competition as a sanctified economic order. In their decisions, the judges clearly felt more secure when confronted with an actual agreement, preferably a document. In the business world such an agreement was on the way to being antiquated. Businessmen and organizers had long since run past the milepost of pooling. The giants of the era were consolidations, mergers, combinations: they had come into being through an act of sale and purchase in which *per se* the court had found no illegality. The Justices were not solely responsible for this frustrating outcome; the caprice or negligence of enforcement officials and the shortcomings of litigation as a means of business control were also to blame.[81]

Except in the railroad field, where its impact on pooling was decisive, anti-trust policy neither dominated nor deflected the nation's economic course in the nineties. Looking back on that decade years later, Carnegie bewildered inquisitors by his nonchalance about the Sherman Act. "Do you really expect men engaged in an active struggle to make a living at manufacturing to be posted about laws and their decisions, and what is applied here, there, and everywhere?" [82] When badgered as to whether he might not have had advice of counsel, the steel king replied, "Nobody ever mentioned the Sherman Act to me, that I remember." [83]

On the question whether putting the Sherman Anti-Trust Act into comparative obscurity accorded with popular desire or not, the evidence is conflicting. In 1899 the trust issue still so "occupied the public mind" that the Civic Federation of Chicago assembled a conference on the subject. While its purpose was nonpartisan, the reporter of the occasion chronicled the loudest ovations and the most extravagant popular demonstrations for the politicians who unleased the rhetoric of an earlier day against the trusts. At the conclusion of Bryan's address, "The Man before the Dollar," the crowd rushed forward to grasp the hand of their spokesman and savior.[84] Meanwhile Congress had appointed an Industrial Commission, composed of Congressmen and representatives of various interests who, with the aid of experts, investigated trusts or industrial combinations. They filled volumes with testimony and research articles.

In 1900 the Commission presented its preliminary proposals. With the exception of certain suggestions for tightening up the regulation of

[81] Walton Hamilton, "The Problem of Anti-Trust Reform," 32 *Columbia Law Review* (February, 1932), 175.

[82] Testimony of Andrew Carnegie, *Hearings before the* [Stanley] *Committee on Investigation of United States Steel Corporation,* III, 2433, 2434, 2436; IV, 2479.

[83] *Ibid.,* III, 2455.

[84] *Chicago Conference on Trusts,* pp. 42, 53, 514.

the railroads, they focused exclusively upon protecting investors and members of corporations. The reformation they proposed was that of Wall Street and of corporation government. They did not advance any amendment or extension of the Sherman Anti-Trust Act. As for trusts, the Commission concluded: "Experience proves that industrial combinations have become fixtures in our business life. Their power for evil should be destroyed and their means for good preserved." The Commission was confident that the proposals it had made "will be of great service and will not endanger business prosperity." [85] The final report in 1902 went somewhat further. Stringent legislation should prevent "discriminating between customers, and cutting rates and prices in one locality . . . for the purpose of destroying local competition"; and a progressive franchise tax should be levied upon the gross earnings of corporations in interstate commerce, an instance of the attack on wealth. Existing antitrust acts should be vigorously enforced.[86] Apparently, like Christianity, the Sherman Anti-Trust Act had not failed—it had never been tried.

[85] Industrial Commission, *Preliminary Report on Trusts and Industrial Combinations,* I, 5–6.

[86] *Report of the Industrial Commission,* XIX, 643–652.

CHAPTER XVI

Recruiting and Training Workers

IN 1874 the *Commercial and Financial Chronicle* observed that American thought on population was historically different from European. The latter, influenced by Malthus, felt "the growth of population is an evil, and tends to increase poverty, starvation and license." "In this country the increase of population . . . is potentially a rich source of wealth."[1] A few months later the *Chronicle* was adding, "in England they have a million of idle paupers at one end and a million of idle aristocrats at the other." All are unproductive. Both Germany and France had a million in the army. In the United States "every man, woman, and child throughout the country is either doing something to help production or is preparing and looking forward to that work as one paramount object of life. This energetic spirit of self-help and self-reliance is stimulated both by our free institutions, by our boundless area of rich land" and by the absence of armies.[2]

Among the many intangibles about the labor force in the United States is a preliminary uncertainty over the numbers involved. Though Federal censuses have provided a mountain of data, the figures are somewhat unreliable because of the difficulty of defining a worker and of placing him in a defined occupation.[3] Estimates and corrections of census data indicate that in 1860 there were 1,930,000 workers in construction, manufacturing, and independent hand trades; 170,000 in mining; and 780,000 in transportation and other public utilities, trade, finance, and real estate. The total was lower than that for agriculture. In 1900 workers

[1] *Commercial and Financial Chronicle,* XIX (November 14, 1874), 490.

[2] *Ibid.,* XX (April 17, 1875), 368.

[3] P. K. Whelpton, "Occupational Groups in the United States, 1820–1920," *Journal of the American Statistical Association,* XXI (September, 1926), 335.

in the first category numbered 8,000,000, of whom nearly 80 per cent were in manufacturing; in mining, 760,000; and in the last category, 4,860,000, of whom those in transportation and public utilities were estimated at 2,100,000. The total was larger than that for agriculture.[4]

One important source of workers was immigration. Annual totals of arrivals, which had begun to fall off in the late fifties, continued to decline in the early sixties. In each of the years, 1861 and 1862, arrivals were below 100,000; to find similar figures the nation would have had to return to the early forties. After the Civil War immigration increased until it reached its nineteenth century peak in 1882 with 788,992. A decline then occurred; in 1898, the figures 229,299 hit the bottom of the trough.[5] With a consistency which is rare in such matters, there was a very high correlation between the total arrivals of immigrants and the indices of hard and good times in the United States. With prosperity, as between the Civil War and 1873 and in the early eighties, there was an increase of arrivals; in depression, as after 1873 and 1893, there was a decline. The correlation is even more impressive when the number of males, the chief source of workers, is alone considered, or when monthly variations are taken into account—immigrants tended to arrive in greater number in the spring, the forward edge of a seasonal increase in employment. If official figures of foreigners returning to their homelands were available for this period, as they were from 1907, they would probably reinforce the correlation.[6] In short, prosperity tempted Europeans to this country with job opportunities and furnished them in their homelands with the means to undertake the journey.

The sheer mass of arrivals was significant, for foreign "laborers" did the rough, heavy, disagreeable work. Partly this was the result of their pressing need for a job and their absence of industrial experience. When immigrants did have particular skills, their arrival in this country was crucial in a wide area of industrial undertakings. Thus when Boston dollars were developing the copper deposits in the upper peninsula of Michigan, miners from Cornwall, trained for generations in handling ores, thronged in to run the tunnels and shafts and extract the deposits. As Pennsylvania became the great anthracite and bituminous producer of the nation, miners from the pits of northern England, Scotland and Wales handled pick and powder beneath American soil. Even in industries as

[4] Solomon Fabricant, "The Changing Industrial Distribution of Gainful Workers," National Bureau of Economic Research, *Studies in Income and Wealth,* XI (1949), 42.

[5] Bureau of the Census, *Historical Statistics of the United States, 1789–1945,* pp. 33–34.

[6] Harry Jerome, *Migration and Business Cycles* (New York: National Bureau of Economic Research, 1926), pp. 33–40; *Commercial and Financial Chronicle,* XIX (November 14, 1874), 491; XX (May 15, 1875), 463.

well established as textiles, women weavers from Scotland and England came over for American mills; sometimes the employers met the delegations at the station with a brass band. To enter the silk mills Englishmen by the hundred came to Paterson, filling the depot with their belongings, "large, square boxes with ropes tied about them, the packages done up in coarse homespun canvas and the strings of tins and kitchen utensils," and bade fair to turn the New Jersey city into a second Macclesfield. Since new methods of making iron by puddling and rolling depended upon the skill and strength of English and Welsh workers, Welsh furnacemen were as much at home at "Pottsville, and Catasauqua, Hanging Rock, or Johnstown, as if those places were . . . Ebbw Vale, Yayscedwyn, Pontypool, and Rhymney." [7]

To depend upon the know-how or skill of a foreigner was so commonplace that in the eighties one American employer sneeringly asked another why he wanted technical schools in America. "I said, 'because if I want a draftsman or foreman, I want a well-equipped man, and I can't get him in the ordinary workman, unless he has had some opportunities of acquiring knowledge that he cannot get in a shop.' 'Well, is that the only reason? You could send abroad and get all that in men who have been trained in technical schools already established.' " [8] Whatever their specialized contribution, the number of immigrants in industry was significant in itself. Aliens in 1870 constituted 53.3 per cent of the labor force in mining; 37.6 per cent in certain textiles; and 43.4 per cent in branches of the iron and steel industry. By 1890 the percentages were respectively 49.1, 42.8, and 37.9.[9]

The other great resource for the labor force was native workers. Though it was the "business ambition of the young men and women which leads them . . . to gather at the manufacturing and mercantile centers," [10] migration of persons was not always necessary; industry or employment could move to them. Thus the campaign to build a cotton industry in the South in the eighties had to face genuine problems of providing capital and management but not that of providing labor. The readjustment of southern economy after the Civil War and the large number of whites, loosely described as "poor whites," who had never participated in its prosperity, made labor superabundant and

[7] R. T. Berthoff, *British Immigrants in Industrial America, 1790–1850* (Cambridge: Harvard University Press, 1953), pp. 32–34, 42, 50–54, 59–60, 63–64, 68–69, 84–85.

[8] Testimony of John W. Britton, *Report of the Committee* [on Education and Labor] *of the Senate . . . 1885*, II, 1129.

[9] Charlotte Erickson, *American Industry and the European Immigrant, 1860–1885* (Cambridge: Harvard University Press, 1957), Appendix II, pp. 190–191.

[10] *Eleventh Annual Report of the* [Mass.] *Bureau of Statistics of Labor. January, 1880*, p. 276.

cheap.[11] One contemporary calculated that in the South, "it would be easy to put 1,000,000 people to work manufacturing cotton, and never miss them from present employment." [12] The silk industry likewise moved to New Jersey and to Pennsylvania, where there was a labor surplus; in the latter state, the wives and children of coal miners constituted the labor supply.[13] Indeed the movement of industry toward pools of labor was usually a movement toward women and child laborers.

INDUCED MIGRATION

Infrequently, public policy directed its attention to recruiting labor and stimulating migration. In so far as American immigration legislation had historically placed few restrictions upon the migration and entrance of aliens, it could be said to have always exerted a negative influence in this direction. In this period the classic instance of a more positive policy was the contract labor law of 1864. With a timely glance at the labor shortage of the Civil War years, the act "to encourage immigration" exempted immigrants from the draft into the armed services. To overcome the immigrant's burden of paying an ocean passage, employers could enter into a contract with prospective immigrant workers to advance the money; this advance constituted a lien upon the recipient's wages for twelve months and upon any property he might acquire in this country.[14] This enactment in a sense did little but make enforceable at law previous informal arrangements and place the details of contracts under government supervision. More remotely its provisions were reminiscent of the arrangements of earlier centuries by which immigrants received the money for their trans-Atlantic passage by becoming on their arrival indentured servants.

Comparatively the contract labor law was of limited importance. Employers imported skilled workers under its provisions but found such arrivals were apt to drift away, contract or no, to rival establishments, other occupations, or to return to the home country.[15] More important than solicitation by employers was the activity of American consuls and of state commissioners of immigration, of agents for steamship and railroad companies, and of foreign-born labor agents or other contractors working from America. Also, earlier immigrant arrivals wrote about job opportunities to their relatives and friends and sent remittances

[11] Broadus Mitchell, "The Rise of Cotton Mills in the South," *Johns Hopkins University Studies in Historical and Political Science,* XXXIX, No. 2, pp. 161–189.

[12] *Ibid.,* p. 183 note.

[13] F. W. Taussig, *Some Aspects of the Tariff Question* (Cambridge: Harvard University Press, 1918), pp. 232–233.

[14] 13 *United States Statutes,* 385–387.

[15] Erickson, *op. cit.,* pp. 46–50.

to pay for their passage.[16] By and large America's reputation as the promised land of high wages and escape from terrifying conditions in the old world—famine or pogroms—were more influential in stimulating immigration than any policy, public or private.

American labor, however, had become convinced that the contract labor law was the means by which American employers lowered wages or imported strike breakers. Instead, employers usually operated through labor agencies to assemble foreigners who were already here. For instance, it was such an agency in California that in 1870 agreed to provide seventy-five Chinese coolie laborers to work in a struck shoe plant in North Adams, Massachusetts; the shoe manufacturer paid the company a fee of a dollar a man and also the transportation cost by emigrant train across the country. This singular and striking episode stirred wide curiosity, elicited approval from the business press, and naturally alarmed organized labor.[17] No matter how infrequently direct financing enabled aliens to reach jobs in America or how much the labor ideology of the brotherhood of all workers was denied by immigration exclusion, organized labor, particularly the skilled window glass workers, were agitating for the repeal of the contract labor law.[18] It was easy to blur the ideological flaw in their case by distinctions between "voluntary" and "imported" immigrants.[19] The arrival of the latter under the contract labor law was "unnatural." As a matter of fact, employers put up little opposition to repeal. They used the act sparingly and some of them were convinced that protective tariff legislation to be an harmonious and impregnable whole should keep "out of our country the competition of cheap foreign labor." [20] In 1885 Congress forbade the importation of contract labor.[21] In reality it only declared void pre-voyage contracts or understandings.

Chinese immigration to the West Coast of the United States was somewhat of an exception. Though most Chinese who came here were free or voluntary immigrants who had paid their fares in advance, they were emigrating at the same time under contracts to other countries in the West Indies and South America. When toward the close of the sixties the Central Pacific sent to China an agent who engaged several thousand Chinese laborers to work on the construction of the road and prepaid their passage, a similar situation seemed likely to arise in this country.

[16] *Ibid.*, pp. 44, 72–86.

[17] Frederick Rudolph, "Chinamen in Yankeedom; Anti-Unionism in Massachusetts in 1870," *American Historical Review*, LIII (October, 1947), 14–27.

[18] Erickson, *op. cit.*, pp. 50–54, 139–147.

[19] Testimony of William Weihe, *Report of the Committee* [on Education and Labor] *of the Senate . . . 1885*, II, 5, 7–8.

[20] Erickson, *op. cit.*, pp. 158–162.

[21] 23 *United States Statutes*, 332–333.

In their helplessness and strangeness, Chinese immigrants were also peculiarly dependent upon Chinese assistance in this country—notably the "Six Companies," a clan device—to secure jobs.[22] These facts lent themselves easily to distortion by those who resented the competition of the Chinese and envied them their success; the anti-Chinese case also merged easily into an anti-wealth or anti-corporate one. At first the legal harassment of these newcomers was confined to the state of California; in 1882 by the high-handed interpretation of a new treaty with the Chinese, the National Congress was able to suspend Chinese immigration for ten years. This temporizing policy was extended until 1902, when a statute imposed indefinite exclusion.[23]

DOMESTIC MIGRATION AND THE LABOR FORCE

Important as aliens were in forming America's industrial armies, employers relied for their recruits primarily upon domestic migrations. Unfortunately the numbers changing from non-industrial to industrial pursuits are largely conjectural. Beginning with the census of 1850, it is possible to learn the state of birth and of residence of the native population and consequently to describe states as having a population surplus or a population deficit; by designating certain states as industrial and others agricultural one can get a rough picture of industry-agriculture mobility. In the earlier part of the nineteenth century most of the Eastern states were losing population to the West in an agricultural and westward movement. By 1890, however, deficits in New Jersey, Massachusetts, and Rhode Island had become surpluses, and by 1900 the same was true for Connecticut. Perhaps we can infer that an expanding industrial economy in the Northeast had effected the shift in this balance.[24] Figures also are available for the relative or absolute decline of population in rural regions and its accompanying expansion in cities.[25] But not all rural dwellers were non-industrial, nor were all city dwellers employed in industry.[26]

Though we can be certain that native population moved into industrial employments, the stimulus to this mobility is obscure. Whether employers organized to recruit labor on a wide scale is unknown. Per-

[22] Mary R. Coolidge, *Chinese Immigration* (New York: Henry Holt and Company, 1909), pp. 41–54.

[23] M. R. Davis, *World Immigration with Special Reference to the United States* (New York: The Macmillan Company, 1936), pp. 309–314.

[24] C. Warren Thornthwaite, *Internal Migration in the United States* (Philadelphia: University of Pennsylvania Press, 1934), plates I and II, pp. 10–11.

[25] *Supra.*, pp. 237–238.

[26] Testimony of Joseph Medill, *Report of the Committee* [on Education and Labor] *of the Senate . . . 1885*, II, 964; Testimony of Charles Siedler, *ibid.*, II, 1158; Testimony of Edward Atkinson, *ibid.*, II, 344.

haps the want-advertisements of employers and labor agencies and letters and word-of-mouth from earlier migrants were, as in the case of immigration, the chief cause for migration.[27] In any case the government left the decision about migration and employment up to the individual. Whereas its land policy had directly effected agricultural migrations, it had no industrial migration policy, unless legislation aiding industry can be interpreted as migration policy. This is pulling a long bow.

WOMEN AND CHILDREN

Though the labor force was predominantly masculine, in 1870 the number of females over ten years of age engaged in manufacturing and mechanical industries was 353,997; in 1900 the number over sixteen was 1,199,452. The numbers in domestic and personal service were higher.[28] On their penetration into manufacturing and mechanical operations, the comments of the census of 1900 reflected upon the extent of women's emancipation: "Naturally no women were reported as United States soldiers, sailors, or marines; nor were any reported as firemen . . . as street car drivers . . . as telegraph or telephone linemen, as apprentices or helpers to roofers and slaters, or as helpers to steam boiler makers or to brass workers. But the reader may note with interest and perhaps some surprise, that 5 women were employed as pilots; that on steam railroads 10 were employed as baggagemen, 31 as brakemen, 7 as conductors, 45 as engineers and firemen, and 26 as switchmen, yardmen, and flagmen; . . . that as many as 185 were returned as blacksmiths, and 508 as machinists; that 8 were boiler makers . . . and 11 were well borers." [29] But the great industries that recruited women were the textiles and dress-making.[30] The reasons for the entrance of women into mill and factory and outdoor industrial labor were of course complex. Ideological notions of women's "place" played their part; but in the eyes of engineers the "woman question" was due to the invention of machinery which made industrial work lighter.[31]

If a child is defined as a person under sixteen years of age, agriculture throughout the whole period was the greatest field of their employment. Here they often worked for their parents—irregularly and without wages.

[27] Carter Goodrich and others, *Migration and Economic Opportunity* (Philadelphia: University of Pennsylvania Press, 1936), pp. 517–518.

[28] W. C. Hunt, "Workers at Gainful Occupations at the Federal Censuses of 1870, 1880, and 1890," *Bulletin of the Department of Labor* No. 11 (July, 1897), p. 397; Bureau of the Census, Special Reports, 12th Census, 1900, *Statistics of Women at Work,* p. 32.

[29] *Statistics of Women at Work, loc. cit.,* p. 31.

[30] *Statistics of Women at Work, loc. cit.,* p. 32.

[31] Discussion by J. L. Gobeille, *Transactions of the American Society of Mechanical Engineers,* XVI (1895), 896.

Such employment resembled doing farm chores. The number of children, mostly boys, thus engaged was somewhat more than doubled from 1870 to 1900; on the other hand, the number of children in non-agricultural pursuits increased in the same period a little less than three times.[32] The characteristic of child labor, aside from its cheapness, was its comparative absence of strength and of skill. Consequently in industrial pursuits, children were put to doing errands, to helping around machinery, or aiding skilled workers, as in coal mining and glass working, or to moving objects about the machines or mills. One employer rightly described child labor as "mainly running about the floor," [33] work nowadays performed by mechanical conveyors. During their middle teens children also went into industry as learners and apprentices. Children worked at street trades—shoe-shining, newspaper selling—and in stores as cash girls and stock boys.

The most important industrial employment for children was in textiles, where by 1900, 4.7 per cent of the gainfully employed children between ten and fifteen years of age were concentrated. Somewhat less than half of these were in cotton textiles. Children had worked extensively in the cotton mills since their establishment in the late eighteenth century; by 1900 they still constituted 13 per cent of the total number of wage-earners in that industry.[34] Whereas child labor of this sort had been signally characteristic of New England, it had declined there; at the same time it had grown in the South. In both regions children went into the mills with the rest of the family. "Though the *per capita* return is small, they [the family] obtain a considerable sum by having a large multiplier." [35] Children were also a form of old-age insurance. Though much derision has been poured upon the employers' statement that they employed children because of the importunities of their parents, the assertion was far from sheer hypocrisy. Parents lied about their children's ages and tampered with their work certificates in order to get them employed, and took them into the mill as their own employees in order to keep them off the record.[36] On the other hand employers frequently would not hire adult workers unless they had children.[37]

[32] Alba M. Edwards, "Comparative Occupation Statistics for the United States, 1870–1940," *Sixteenth Census of the United States. 1940. Population,* p. 97.

[33] Testimony of T. L. Livermore, *Report of the Committee* [on Education and Labor] *of the Senate . . . 1885,* III, 13–14, 16.

[34] "Report on Women and Child Wage Earners, 1910," vol. VI, *Senate Document* No. 645 (s.n. 5690), 61st Cong., 2d Sess., pp. 45–46.

[35] Testimony of F. K. Foster, *Report of the Committee* [on Education and Labor] *of the Senate . . . 1885,* I, 78.

[36] *Ibid.,* pp. 67–69; *Report of the* [Mass.] *Bureau of the Statistics of Labor . . . 1869 . . . 1870,* pp. 137–147.

[37] "Report on Women and Child Wage Earners . . . 1910," *loc. cit.,* p. 60; *Twelfth Annual Report of the* [Mass.] *Bureau of Statistics of Labor . . . 1881,* pp.

Before the Civil War, agitation, arguing primarily that industrial employment interfered with the education of young people, had resulted in legislation in the Northeast curtailing or prohibiting child labor in mills and factories. In the eighties and nineties enforcement through inspection and supervision tightened up both old and new legislation. In the South more lenient statutes permitted a continuation of old ways.[38] Technical changes in the direction of automatic operation also diminished the need for child labor. All in all, the number of children under sixteen years of age at labor in manufacturing industries, which had totaled 114,628 in 1870, reached its peak ten years later at 181,921, and then fell away at the century's end to 168,583.[39]

COMPANY HOUSING AND COMPANY STORES

In a southern textile town, "a covered wagon or mountain schooner drove up to the [mill] office. It was full of family and that was about all. . . . The man asked for work. Mr. Montgomery told the superintendent to find them a vacant house."[40] In hosts of industrial communities this was inevitable prelude to employment. In the case of natural resources, the housing of the workers had to lie near the deposits of ore. In the case of manufacturing dependent upon water power, the factory was often located in an unsettled country and factory owners in order to recruit employees had to provide housing. Nor was the obligation lacking in already settled regions. From Chicago, where George Pullman moved his car works to the suburbs and built the town of Pullman, to New York City, where William Steinway built a model community at Astoria near his pianoforte works, the story was the same.[41] Thus appeared the "company village" or the "company town." In appearance, comfort, and convenience they varied greatly. There was a wide difference between the unpainted wooden houses struggling up the barren hillside of a coal town[42] and Pullman, with its buildings of "advanced secular Gothic" along tree-shaded streets, and with the largest

469–470; Testimony of Thomas O'Donnell, *Report of the Committee* [on Education and Labor] *of the Senate . . . 1885*, III, 451.

[38] "Report on Women and Child Wage Earners . . . 1910," *loc. cit.*, pp. 47, 71–72, 75–128, 131–204, 207–209, 215–221.

[39] Bureau of the Census, *Abstract of the Twelfth Census of the United States. 1900*, pp. 300–301.

[40] Mitchell, *loc. cit.*, p. 167.

[41] R. T. Ely, "Pullman: A Social Study," *Harper's New Monthly Magazine*, LXX (February, 1885), 453; Testimony of William Steinway, *Report of the Committee* [on Education and Labor] *of the Senate . . . 1885*, II, 1085; *Sixteenth Annual Report of the* [Mass.] *Bureau of Statistics of Labor . . . 1885*, pp. 4–5.

[42] Testimony of Robert D. Layton, *Report of the Committee* [on Education and Labor] *of the Senate . . . 1885*, I, 17–19.

houses equipped with bathrooms,[43] or a New England textile village like Manchester, whose multiple dwellings and dormitories, built of brick and tidily arranged, resembled somewhat a college campus. Though all such rented or leased buildings might be called "tenements," they were usually different from the noisome buildings in New York City slums which the employers in the cigar-making industry purchased and then sublet to the cigar-makers. Such places housed the manufacturing operations and the living quarters of the workers, and the latter paid rent for both.[44]

In general rents in company edifices were lower than in other housing. In Pullman, for instance, they were about three-fifths what they were in Chicago,[45] and in New England textile cities of the Lowell type, quarters outside company housing cost two or three times the figure set by corporations.[46] Nor did the owners generally seek to make a profit from rents. What with the original investment and the high costs of maintenance, they were usually content to break even or to earn a nominal interest like 3 per cent.[47]

Though there were individual cases of hardship and injustice,[48] the charge that company housing exploited workers is largely baseless. After all, this was a recruiting device. Whether "paternalism" is good or bad is a matter of definition. If by it is meant a sense of obligation for the welfare of workers or even a spirit of *noblesse oblige,* paternalism would seem more commendable than harmful; if company town paternalism involved interference in the private lives of the inhabitants or gave the employer an immense advantage in his controversies with workers, the judgment might well be different. For example, in Pullman, in mining towns, and in cigar-workers' tenements, workers occupied their dwellings on leases that could be terminated on short notice. In many a struggle with organized labor, loss of job meant loss of home; employers dis-

[43] Ely, *loc. cit.*, pp. 455–457.

[44] Testimony of Samuel Gompers, *Report of the Committee* [on Education and Labor] *of the Senate . . . 1885*, I, 271–275; *Thirteenth Annual Report of the* [Mass.] *Bureau of Statistics of Labor. March, 1882*, pp. 271–299.

[45] Ely, *loc. cit.*, p. 457.

[46] John Coolidge, "Low-Cost Housing: The New England Tradition," *New England Quarterly*, XIV (March, 1941), 16.

[47] Ely, *loc. cit.*, p. 461; T. R. Navin, *The Whitin Machine Works since 1831: A Textile Machinery Company in an Industrial Village* (Cambridge: Harvard University Press, 1950), pp. 76, 440–442; S. E. Morison, *The Ropemakers of Plymouth: A History of the Plymouth Cordage Company, 1824–1945* (Boston: Houghton Mifflin Company, 1950), pp. 17–18, 94; Testimony of Thomas L. Livermore, *Report of the Committee* [on Education and Labor] *of the Senate . . . 1885*, III, 5; Testimony of H. T. Elmer, *ibid.*, III, 576.

[48] T. V. Powderly, *The Path I Trod* (New York: Columbia University Press, 1940), pp. 36–37.

covered they needed their housing for their new employees, the strike-breakers.[49]

The managerial headaches of company housing, as well as the criticisms of it, led many corporations to try to sell their property to employees or to encourage outside capital to provide these essential buildings. In Manchester the Amoskeag sold house lots at a largely nominal fee and specified the number of houses the lot should hold "so as to secure an open well-ventilated city." [50] In Fall River one mill loaned money to a group of leading citizens to provide a housing project.[51] In Homestead the Carnegie works lent money to employees for house construction at 6 per cent; it never foreclosed a mortgage upon the home of any of its laborers.[52]

Nor did the provision of community facilities stop with housing. Not infrequently the employer laid out parks and recreation areas, provided libraries, schools, theatres, and, at Pullman, a hotel, with the only "barroom allowed" in the village, and like as not aided the Knights of Pythias or the Odd Fellows to build halls for meetings and entertainments.[53]

Since these were not bread-and-butter matters, critics were quick to detect the imprisonment of labor in the "gilded cage" of materialism.[54] The most controversial of these conveniences was the provision of a store. The reasons for the "company store" were diverse. In earlier times when a merchant had organized domestic production around his central store, it had been natural to pay workers in the products they needed or had manufactured. Orders upon stores had adjourned the necessity of paying wages in cash and placed upon others than manufacturers the responsibility of accumulating working capital and advancing credit. John Roach, the shipbuilder, recalled the pay days of his younger years.

[49] "Treatise" by "a Pittsburgh Lawyer," *Report of the Committee* [on Education and Labor] *of the Senate . . . 1885*, II, 342–343; Testimony of Samuel Gompers, *ibid.*, I, 274; Ely, *loc. cit.*, p. 463; Gerald W. Johnson, *The Making of a Southern Industrialist: A Biographical Study of Simpson Bobo Tanner* (Chapel Hill: University of North Carolina Press, 1932), pp. 48–55.

[50] Testimony of Thomas L. Livermore, *loc. cit.*, pp. 192–193; Testimony of G. B. Whitman, *Report of the Committee* [on Education and Labor] *of the Senate . . . 1885*, III, 29.

[51] Navin, *op. cit.*, p. 73.

[52] Report of the House Committee on Pinkerton Detectives, *House Report* No. 2447 (s.n. 3142), 52nd Cong., 2d Sess., pp. x–xi.

[53] Testimony of L. D. Warren, *Report of the Committee* [on Education and Labor] *of the Senate . . . 1885*, III, 375–376; Testimony of William Steinway, *ibid.*, II, p. 1085; Testimony of A. Heber Newton, *ibid.*, II, 550–551; *Twelfth Annual Report of the* [Mass.] *Bureau of Statistics of Labor, January, 1881*, pp. 472–475; Ely, *loc. cit.*, pp. 458–459.

[54] Ely, *loc. cit.*, pp. 465–466.

The timekeeper would ask: "'John, how much money do you want this week?' 'Well, I would like to have one-half of my wages this week.' 'You can't have it. What do you want to do with it?' 'I want to get a suit of clothes.' And if the old books are not destroyed, whoever would go down now to Brooks Brothers' store . . . might find there an order on Brooks Brothers, given by the proprietor of the old Allaire works, for a coat for John Roach."[55]

Although the employer was unlikely to transform company housing from a means of recruiting labor into a means of making money, he was not always so restrained with the company store. He compelled workers to trade there either by contract or by paying in scrip exchangeable for commodities at the company store. He often marked up prices higher than in other stores or stocked shoddier goods. Like the rent for company houses, the amount of a worker's purchases was deducted from his wages. Withholding is usually a frustrating device, for one never handles the money one earns. The company stores and other forms of "pluck-me" payments became grievances which labor fought against.[56] In the mid-eighties an observer from outside the battle thought the abolition of "truck payments" would free the worker from "extortion" and "greed," but conceded their continuance might be necessary "where a railroad is building and there may be no shops along its line, or where mining is going on at any considerable distance from shops. . . ."[57] By the end of the century the growth of communities and the passage of legislation had pretty well done away with company stores and store orders.[58]

INDUSTRIAL DISCIPLINE

Once an employer had his workers at hand, he was confronted with the problem of organizing them and inducing or compelling them to conform to the requirements of industrial discipline, which was quite different from that they were accustomed to on farms in America or Europe or in artisan employments. Nearly every aspect of the industrial

[55] Testimony of John Roach, *Report of the Committee* [on Education and Labor] *of the Senate . . . 1885,* I, 996.

[56] Testimony of R. D. Layton, *Report of the Committee* [on Education and Labor] *of the Senate . . . 1885,* I, 32; Testimony of Samuel Gompers, *ibid.,* I, 367–368; Testimony of Adolph Strasser, *ibid.,* I, 451; Testimony of Samuel Gompers, *Report of the Industrial Commission,* VII, 614–615; Testimony of D. A. Hayes, *ibid.,* VII, 106, 109; Testimony of Carroll D. Wright, *ibid.,* VII, 13.

[57] Testimony of Francis Amasa Walker, *Report of the Committee* [on Education and Labor] *of the Senate . . . 1885,* III, 530–531.

[58] Testimony of Daniel O'Leary, *Report of the Industrial Commission,* VII, 27; Testimony of R. R. Wade, *ibid.,* VII, 72; Testimony of Carroll D. Wright, *ibid.,* VII, 13; *Report of the Industrial Commission,* V, 59–61.

A Cigar Shop. (John Mitchell, *Organized Labor,* p. 312)

Child Labor in a Model Textile Factory, Rhode Island. (Collection of Mrs. Byron Dexter)

A Model Garment-Making Factory. (John Mitchell, *Organized Labor,* p. 312)

Winslow Homer, New England Factory Life—"Bell-Time." (*Harper's Weekly,* July 25, 1868, p. 492)

The Corliss Engine at the Philadelphia Exposition, 1876. (Collection of Mrs. Byron Dexter)

The Allis Engine at the Columbian Exposition, 1893. (*Harper's Weekly*, 1894, p. 1034)

TESTING RAIL
ROLLING A RAIL
SAWING A RAIL
THE CONVERTERS
WATCHING THE CONVERTERS

◀ Bessemer Converter. (*Harper's Weekly,* March 25, 1897. Courtesy American Iron and Steel Institute)

The "Wedding of the Rails" of the Central Pacific and Union Pacific, 1869. (Collection of Mrs. Byron Dexter)

Governor Stanford's Train on Way to the "Wedding of the Rails" on the First Transcontinental, 1869. (Photo courtesy of Southern Pacific)

Oil Wells, Spindletop, Texas. (Reprinted from *The Lamp,* Standard Oil Company of New Jersey)

The Drake Well in 1861. (Drake Well Park Museum, Titusville, Pennsylvania)

Transporting Barrels on Oil Creek. (London *Illustrated News,* February 27, 1875)

"The Anarchist Riot in Chicago"—The Haymarket Bomb Outrage. (*Harper's Weekly*, May 15, 1886, pp. 312–313)

The First Meat Train Leaving the Chicago Stockyards under Escort of United States Cavalry—The Chicago Railroad Strike, 1894. (*Harper's Weekly*, July 28, 1894, p. 701)

Samuel Gompers in a Speaking Pose. (Samuel Gompers, *Seventy Years of Life and Labor,* 1925, I, p. 308)

Marcus Alonzo Hanna. (Herbert D. Croly, *Marcus Alonzo Hanna,* 1923, Frontispiece)

transformation of the country contributed to this problem and, so rapid was the pace of industrial advance, new complexities were constantly arising. New machines or the subdivision of operations without the introduction of machinery, as in meat packing, outmoded old skills.[59] In the end the enlargement of the scale of operations presented the greatest challenge to successful organization, for it put new strains upon direction and superintendence.

Where once a few workers had gathered in the shop under the immediate oversight of the boss-owner, labor forces were now numbered in the hundreds. Between 1879 and 1899 the average labor force in single steel works and rolling mills increased from 220 to 412, and individual railroad corporations by the late eighties had labor forces of 36,000.[60] It was no longer feasible for the boss-owner to reprove tardiness or absenteeism with a frown or a burst of profanity; the labor force had to be in attendance and had to be on time and punitive measures had to take another form. Even under hand methods of production, organizers had to be alert to waste and loss. Now employees of railroads were collecting fares without supervision and a system had to be devised to make sure they turned them over to the company. Materials, once kept under benches in sheds where the owner could keep an eye on them, now had to be in greater supply and issued scrupulously to workers. The worker had once provided his own simple tools, but now he ran costly lathes and planes and Bessemer converters which could be ruined by ignorance or carelessness. Orders, formerly "shoved along" through the shop by the boss, now had to be kept track of in more formalized fashion. Rough, hazy methods of calculating the cost of making an article or filling an order had once sufficed; now size and complexity, including the larger sums assigned to overhead costs, complicated the task of accounting within the works.

Whatever the system, success depended in the end upon the ability of the superintendent of the plant and of his subordinates. The foreman was the key. Admiral Dewey, according to an engineer, won at Manila Bay "because he had organized a trained human force that was irresistible, and they had absolute faith in him. He knew where to draw the line between comradeship with his men and respect for superiors, and he kept the line taut!" On the other hand the military analogy had limitations. A textile factory, turning out large quantities of standard fabrics might well have a hierarchical structure with superintendent, "overseers" of departments or rooms, first hands, second hands, and so on down the

[59] Walter E. Weyl and A. M. Sakolski, "Conditions of Entrance to the Principal Trades," *Bulletin of the Bureau of Labor*, No. 67 (November, 1906), pp. 681–685.

[60] E. C. Kirkland, "You Can't Win," *Journal of Economic History*, XIV (1954), 322.

ladder. But employers wanted help that was self-reliant and foremen who would discipline the shop "without reducing the manliness of the men." [61]

A NEW FORM OF EDUCATION

One result of the new pressures was a new form of education for industrial pursuits. Formerly a beginner had customarily learned his handicraft by indenturing himself for a period of years to a master. Nearly all the states had legislation regulating the conditions of apprenticeship; like the "blue laws" they were now anachronisms. One uncertainty was how much skill the new way of industry required. Some occupations, such as the building trade, depended, in spite of the woodworking factory, upon skilled workers to assemble and finish a building. In the coal mines, fathers continued to take their sons down to learn the trade at the seam's face. In industry in general, however, there was "automatic machinery . . . operated by a rough boy called in from the streets or farm." He learned his specialized task soon. But the automatic machines required machinists to design and construct them, to make adjustments, to detect "mysterious faults," and to repair or replace broken parts. There had not been enough skill in 1870 to keep automatic machines running if they had been available.[62]

Apprenticeship collapsed. There was no one in the factory to give the instruction. The foreman couldn't spare the time; the employer couldn't afford to pay wages to a skilled worker and lose his productivity while he instructed someone else, nor could he pay standard wages to a beginner.[63] The regular employees were alarmed at the presence of a worker paid on a sub-standard basis, and, since they believed in the law of supply and demand as a determinant of wages, were as unwilling to enlarge the labor force with apprentices as they were to have the employer import workers from abroad.[64] The evidence suggests that apprentices had a hard, dull time in the factory. Whether they suffered

[61] M. P. Higgins, "Education of Machinists, Foremen, and Mechanical Engineers," *Transactions of the American Society of Mechanical Engineers,* XXI (1899), 647, 655; Discussion by Haines, Williams, W. S. Rogers, *ibid.,* 717, 728, 736–739; Henry Metcalfe, "The Shop-Order System of Accounts," *ibid.,* VII (1886), 440–442.

[62] M. P. Higgins, "Education of Machinists, Foremen, and Mechanical Engineers," *Transactions of the American Society of Mechanical Engineers,* XXI (1899), 1118; Testimony of Francis Amasa Walker, *loc. cit.,* pp. 336–337.

[63] Testimony of P. J. McGuire, *loc. cit.,* p. 352; Discussion by L. S. Randolph and W. B. Parson, *Transactions of the American Society of Mechanical Engineers,* XXI (1900), 761–765.

[64] Testimony of W. H. Foster, *Report of the Committee* [on Education and Labor] *of the Senate . . . 1885,* I, 405–406; Testimony of M. D. Connelly, *ibid.,* I, 590–596.

more from the indifference of the employer or the callousness of fellow employees is difficult to ascertain. In any case, once a novice jumped the high hurdle of admission limitations that workers were always striving to erect, he was put on trivial tasks like "sweeping out" or did errands, and if he learned how to handle a simple machine he was kept at it, because he was thus more immediately useful than if he had been moved around the shop until he had learned many processes. Although the breakdown in apprenticeship was probably bearable in most instances and nostalgia over its passing was excessive, the old-fashioned ways did develop all-round talents and the habit of meeting production emergencies, qualities invaluable in foreman or superintendent.

The whole period was alive with experiment in new forms of industrial education. We have already noted the innovations—the Morrill Act and others—in the training of engineers. Since professional instruction of this sort was confined to higher education, the vital questions were the provision of preparatory work for such institutions, or of final training for those who were to remain privates in the industrial ranks rather than become "captains of industry." Little could be done with the instruction in the elementary public school, which had to concern itself with the inculcation of reading, writing, spelling and arithmetic. Those bent on reform, therefore, had to be content with tinkering with those subjects to make them "more practical" or with introducing supplementary subjects such as manual training and drawing to acquaint pupils with perception of form and space and to educate them through training the hand and the eye as well as the head.[65] Since such innovations could be denominated "general education," every student could be compelled to take them.

More vulnerable to change was the high school. In this era the public education movement was rapidly providing institutions for secondary schools and enacting compulsory attendance laws. Some thought these new schools should train students for entrance to the academic colleges, where they could be trained for the professions, for a life of scholarship, or the life of a gentleman. To many it seemed wiser in an industrial commercial culture, clearly on the march and clearly competing with rivals in Europe, especially Germany, for the high school to give instruction in the scientific principles applicable to industry. This meant more chemistry, physics, and mathematics perhaps through

[65] S. R. Thompson, "Relations of the Common School to Industrial Education," *The Addresses and Journal of Proceedings of the National Educational Association . . . 1877*, pp. 219–220; Testimony of Francis Amasa Walker, *loc. cit.*, pp. 336–338; R. H. Thurston, "Presidential Address. The Mechanical Engineer, His Work and His Policy," *Transactions of the American Society of Mechanical Engineers*, IV (1882), 100–101; Discussion by Webb, *Transactions of the Society of Mechanical Engineers*, VI (1885), 526–527.

calculus, and also instruction in the trades.[66] How specialized the latter instruction should be depended upon the size and wealth of the community, its distinctive industries, and the willingness of the laboring community to tolerate a method of educating workers which it did not control.[67]

Trade or industrial schools had to have a shop. Whether it should inculcate the skill of plumbers, carpenters or machinists in particular or just general mechanical aptitude was a matter of dispute. Many of the tangles inherent in establishing industrial schools at public expense were avoided if private philanthropy could be induced to finance them. So it happened that from Worcester, Massachusetts, where a group of enlightened industrialists founded and supported the Worcester County Free Institute of Industrial Science, to Terre Haute, Indiana, where Chauncey Rose, a man with a fortune derived from railroads and commerce, founded the Terre Haute School of Industrial Science, private persons with means were pioneers in the new education.[68]

Whether under private or public ownership, these schools were plagued with persistent dilemmas. In a fluid, individualistic society such as that of the United States it was impossible, for one thing, to single out those with mechanical aptitudes and compel or induce them to follow a course of training appropriate to their abilities.[69] For another thing, it was impossible to eradicate the notion of "general education." Even engineers were pointing out that man is more than a producer; he is a social and political being. Education must, therefore, set the character and habits for these functions.[70] Sometimes an even broader context was

[66] Thurston, "Presidential Address," *loc. cit.*, pp. 101–103; R. H. Thurston, "Technical Education in the United States: Its Social, Industrial, and Economic Relations to Our Progress," *Transactions of the American Society of Mechanical Engineers,* XIV (1893), 890–891.

[67] Discussion by G. W. Melville, *Transactions of the American Society of Mechanical Engineers,* XXI (1899), 686–688.

[68] E. C. Mack, *Peter Cooper, Citizen of New York* (New York: Duell, Sloan and Pearce, 1949), pp. 243–268; Worcester County Free Institute of Industrial Science, *Addresses of Inauguration and Dedication, Worcester, November 11 1868; Memorial Notice of John Boynton, Esq., Founder of the Institute; Memorial Notice of Ichabod Washburn, Founder of the Practical Mechanical Department,* pp. 9–11; J. E. Hoyt, "Manual Training in the Public Schools of the Smaller Cities," *National Educational Association . . . Proceedings and Addresses . . . 1896,* p. 771; "Chauncey Rose," *Dictionary of American Biography,* XVI, 156–157; G. L. Alden, "Technical Training at the Worcester Free Institute," *Transactions of the American Society of Mechanical Engineers,* VI (1885), 510–518.

[69] Discussion by Babcock, *Transactions of the American Society of Mechanical Engineers,* VI (1885), 545; Higgins, "Education of Machinists, Foremen and Mechanical Engineers," *loc. cit.*, pp. 667, 676.

[70] Discussion by R. H. Thurston, *Transactions of the American Society of Mechanical Engineers,* XXI (1899), 708.

employed. "The end and aim of life is not simply to equip professional men; it is not simply to equip people with the power to 'do business'; it is not *simply* to enable people to earn a living." [71] Admittedly it was hard to correlate general education with American industrial supremacy. But British observers ascribed the latter achievement to our great common school education.[72] Employers, also, were generally talking about the value for manufacturing of general intelligence and knowledge.[73] A narrowly vocational educational system would in a period of rapid technological change and in a people with "the Israelitish habits . . . in traveling about" produce only outmoded or useless skills.[74]

[71] Higgins, *loc. cit.*, p. 676; Discussion by George I. Rockwood, *Transactions of the American Society of Mechanical Engineers,* XXI (1900), 1140.

[72] Discussion by W. R. Jones, *Transactions of the American Society of Mechanical Engineers,* VI (1885), 539–540.

[73] *Report of the* [U. S.] *Commissioner of Education . . . 1870,* pp. 39–40, 451; *Circular of Information of the* [U. S.] *Bureau of Education for April, 1872,* pp. 35, 41.

[74] Testimony of Francis Amasa Walker, *loc. cit.*, p. 336.

CHAPTER XVII

The Employer and the Conditions of Labor

THE DAY'S WORK

ANOTHER problem requiring decision by managers was the hours of labor. The authority for a hard and long day's work was ancient and overwhelming. When God expelled mankind's first parents from the Garden of Eden, He announced to men: "In the sweat of thy face shalt thou eat bread till thou return unto the ground" (Genesis 3.19). The fourth of the commandments included the injunction: "Six days shalt thou labor and do all thy work" (Exodus 20.9). Also economic practice in pre-industrial occupations made a long day imperative. As one opponent of hour legislation observed: "I do not think any farmer would want to have his hours regulated by law." [1] The agricultural day was indeed from sun-up to sun-down. Nor was this the only example of the long day. When artisans made shoes by hand labor they worked eighteen hours a day. "There was no limit of time or of anything else. A man simply worked as long as he could." [2] When new methods of production by machine, factory and corporation came, a long day's work persisted. In 1860 the average except for favored skilled trades was eleven hours. Aside from habit and scriptural authority, the reason the new methods made so little change was that long and continuous operation of the new machinery seemed the best or only way to meet the larger investment in overhead costs. One of the most enlightened of employers who pioneered in reducing hours, one of the brothers Cheney of the silk mills of South Manchester, Connecticut, observed: "Where machinery comes in as a heavy element, a spindle is a spindle, and the more minutes it

[1] Testimony of Frederick Smyth, *Report of the Committee* [on Education and Labor] *of the Senate . . . 1885*, III, 126.

[2] Testimony of C. H. M'Dermott, *Report of the Industrial Commission*, XIV, 502.

runs in a day the more work it will turn off." [3] Since this was so, the pressures of the competitive order held every employer and manager to the same practices.

In the early eighties there was a considerable regional movement to secure the uniformity of a ten-hour day in the chief textile producing states. Many employers greeted the effort with a sigh of relief: "'It [ten hours] would be better for manufacturer and operative, if it could only be made universal,' and these words . . . may be fairly taken to express the united wisdom of the manufacturers of textile fabrics in New York and New England." [4] This modification of old attitudes could hardly be ascribed to scientific studies of personnel fatigue. Such studies did not exist at the time. The new attitude was based upon the observation that certain mills and certain districts which worked a shorter than customary day were still highly productive and met the competitive pace.[5] Incidentally, it was the small establishments trying to meet the low costs of the larger producers that kept in business by working their employees a long day.[6]

Also the notion was gaining that there was just so much work in a man and a shorter day was as likely to "get it out" as a longer one. Workers reported more punctually for labor and kept at it until closing time; there was less waste. "Skill in management and thoroughness in discipline are more important than the eleventh hour in the product of a mill; and thorough discipline is much more attainable under ten than under eleven hours. For men and women are flesh and blood, and they cannot be held up to such steady work during eleven hours as during ten; and overseers are flesh and blood, and cannot hold them up." [7] All this might be true enough, but employers found it hard to shake off the conviction that their employees were much better off in the factory than outside. In the former location they were at least at work; in the latter they were at leisure, and in the enjoyment of spare time the most unruly portion of the labor force, in employers' estimation, revealed a devotion to "Whiskey, Tobacco, Loafing." [8] Why reduce hours when it meant more time for this trinity of waste?

[3] Testimony of F. W. Cheney, *Report of the Industrial Commission,* XIV, 733.

[4] *Twelfth Annual Report of the* [Mass.] *Bureau of Statistics of Labor . . . 1881,* p. 458.

[5] *Ibid.,* pp. 457–460; Testimony of Bishop H. C. Potter, *Report of the Industrial Commission,* XIV, 10; Testimony of John Jarrett, *Report of the Committee* [on Education and Labor] *of the Senate . . . 1885,* I, 1148–1149.

[6] *Twelfth Annual Report of the* [Mass.] *Bureau of Statistics of Labor . . . 1881,* p. 467.

[7] *Ibid.,* pp. 460–462; Testimony of W. C. Redfield, *Report of the Industrial Commission,* XIV, 659, 663, 665.

[8] *Twelfth Annual Report of the* [Mass.] *Bureau of Statistics of Labor . . . 1881,* p. 467.

The varied aspects of the gospel of work also dictated management's attitude toward other interruptions to industrial discipline. Managers had to be constantly on guard against too many holidays and against vacations.[9] Undoubtedly the employers' attitude toward strikes was compounded of many elements, but it is not without significance that some employers attributed strikes to those who "prefer idleness to work," and felt strikers were "mostly of the nomadic or floating class." [10] Note, too, that government labor officials adopted as a measure of the cost of strikes "man-days idle" or "man-days lost." [11] The latter standard, as well as being a reflex of common attitudes, also commended itself by its mathematical ascertainability.

While these notions were frequently patronizing or self-righteous, employers applied the same strict standards to themselves. To one, "idleness was the most terrible punishment"; to another, his dearest wish was the ability to work right up to the finality "when man's work is done." [12] To well-to-do individuals who didn't work or didn't have to, the age applied the contemptuous designation of "dudes" or "drones." [13] Also in workaday relationships the aversion to idleness often had a beneficial aspect. It led managers in times of business hardship to keep their mills going. They liked to have it asserted "Our mills never stop." [14] There was a note of canniness here, as well as of pride. No employer wished to disperse his trained labor force; he had a dread of turnover. A stable labor force was also a prerequisite to loyalty and responsibility. So employers in hard times spread the work and often ran their mills as long as they were making enough to cover overhead. "We never want

[9] Testimony of F. J. Donaldson, *Report of the Committee* [on Education and Labor] *of the Senate . . . 1885,* II, 1033–1034; Joel Benton, "The Holiday Hallucination," *North American Review,* CXLVI (April, 1888), 472–473.

[10] "Treatise" by "a Pittsburgh Lawyer," *Report of the Committee* [on Education and Labor] *of the Senate . . . 1885,* II, 359–361; Testimony of Edward H. Ammidown, *ibid.,* II, 1135.

[11] Florence Peterson, "Strikes in the United States, 1880–1936," U. S. Bureau of Labor Statistics, *Bulletin* No. 651 (August, 1937), pp. 10–11; *Eleventh Annual Report of the* [Mass.] *Bureau of Statistics of Labor . . . 1880,* pp. 66–68; *Third Annual Report of the* [U. S.] *Commissioner of Labor, 1887,* pp. 18–28.

[12] Will and Maxine Schoyer, *Scaife Company and the Scaife Family, 1802–1952* (Pittsburgh: Davis & Warde, 1952), p. 101; Bliss Perry, *Life and Letters of Henry Lee Higginson* (Boston: Atlantic Monthly Press, 1921), p. 431; Testimony of T. M. Miller, *Report of the Committee* [on Education and Labor] *of the Senate . . . 1885,* II, 24–25.

[13] E. C. Kirkland, *Dream and Thought in the Business Community, 1860–1900* (Ithaca: Cornell University Press, 1956), pp. 159–161.

[14] Testimony of James Whitehead, *Report of the Industrial Commission,* XIV, 577; Testimony of George C. Richardson, *Report of the Committee* [on Education and Labor] *of the Senate . . . 1885,* III, 308.

to make a change in the general management of the help any more than we can avoid." [15]

WAGES

Interlocked with hours was the problem of wages. The latter, penetrating every aspect of the industrial structure, for instance costs of production, was complicated. Sometimes employers sounded as if the law of supply and demand operating in a free economy would dispel their perplexities without any decisive choice on their part. "The law of supply and demand regulates the labor market . . . the workingman must submit to that law, and . . . it is entirely useless for them to attempt to rebel against its inexorable and inevitable operation." [16] This did not mean that many employers subscribed openly to any iron law of wages, that wages should be only enough to enable the workers, or a working group such as a family, barely to survive.[17] Indeed there were numerous statements of a contrary doctrine. Many employers realized that high wages meant high consumption and that high consumption meant prosperity. "You cannot have low and depressed labor and a prosperous business or a prosperous country." [18]

In the totality of circumstances employers were prone to focus upon real wages, what money would buy in terms of goods. To an obsessive but perhaps understandable degree, they were therefore concerned with the details of the expenditures of the laboring classes. Figuratively they accompanied the worker and his wife to market and invaded the kitchen to see how meals were prepared.[19] In all these matters they were prone to espy extravagance and waste. But, of course, carelessness and unnecessary expenditures for living expenses paled before those for "lager

[15] Testimony of Charles L. Harding, *Report of the Committee* [on Education and and Labor] *of the Senate . . . 1885*, III, 292; Testimony of Charles D. McDuffie, *ibid.*, II, 61.

[16] Testimony of Frank K. Foster, *Report of the Committee* [on Education and Labor] *of the Senate . . . 1885*, I, 667–668; Testimony of Jay Gould, *ibid.*, I, 1090; Testimony of T. M. Miller, *loc. cit.*, p. 20; "Treatise" by "a Pittsburgh Lawyer," *loc. cit.*, p. 33; Testimony of Edward H. Ammidown, *loc. cit.*, p. 1135; *Commercial and Financial Chronicle*, XXV (August 18, 1877), 148.

[17] Testimony of John S. McClelland, *Report of the Committee* [on Education and Labor] *of the Senate . . . 1885*, I, 134.

[18] Testimony of George C. Richardson, *loc. cit.*, pp. 137–318; Testimony of Charles D. McDuffie, *loc. cit.*, pp. 67–68; Testimony of R. C. Search, *Report of the Industrial Commission*, VII, 132; W. E. Partridge, "Capital's Need for High-Priced Labor," *Transactions of the American Society of Mechanical Engineers*, VIII (1886), 272.

[19] Edward Atkinson, "The Missing Science," *The Industrial Progress of the Nation* (New York: G. P. Putnam's Sons, 1890), pp. 339–348.

and leisure." A curious bicker arose between owners and workers over who spent the more for liquor, champagne in one instance and beer in the other.[20] Disapproval of the worker's habits was not the only outcome of these preoccupations. From them flowed the employer's concern with training in domestic science, with the passage of restrictive liquor legislation, with a farm policy emphasizing the abundant production of fibers and food, with national legislation on currency and tariff.[21] Edward Atkinson's diverting apotheosis of Commodore Vanderbilt as a "communist" because he reduced freights on commodities from the Middle West, attained rhapsody in the rhetorical question: "Can the anarchist, the communist, the socialist, the protectionist, the free trader, the co-operator, the paper-money man, the knight of labor, the eight-hour man, or the sentimentalist invent or suggest any other method of changing the direction of the industry of the whole community, which would on the whole be so effective in improving the conditions of all, as one which would save five cents a day on food and fuel . . . ?" [22]

While the employer saw that wages must maintain employee purchasing power, he also felt they must not encroach upon corporate returns or profits for owner and manager. Workers agitating for increased wages constantly confronted the argument that a wage increase "was not in the business," that "we are selling too closely," or "competition is too great, we cannot afford it." [23] Workers were lucky if they were not asked to take a cut in wages in order that the business might go on. However, not all employers subscribed to the theory that this was the way out. One manager-engineer, more pioneering than the rest, described the policy of reducing wages as "easy," "obvious," "wrong." [24] Another recourse in meeting competition and depression was to introduce labor-saving machinery. But this cost money. Better still was a wage system which would make the industrial labor forces more careful, more self-reliant—"poor labor costs more to watch . . . than dear labor" [25]—and more productive. In addressing themselves to this challenge, the employers of the period showed great fertility of resource and attained a considerable degree of success.

[20] Testimony of John Jarrett, *Report of the Committee* [on Education and Labor] *of the Senate . . . 1885,* I, 1163–1164; Testimony of Joseph Medill, *ibid.,* II, 960–961; Edward Atkinson, "How Can Wages be Increased?" *Forum,* V (July, 1888), 498.

[21] *Commercial and Financial Chronicle,* XXII (January 1, 1876), 5.

[22] Edward Atkinson, "Remedies for Social Ills," *Forum,* VII (April, 1889), 157.

[23] Testimony of Robert D. Layton, *Report of the Committee* [on Education and Labor] *of the Senate . . . 1885,* I, 11–12.

[24] Discussion by W. E. Partridge, *Transactions of the American Society of Mechanical Engineers,* VII (1886), 469; W. E. Partridge, "Capital's Need for High-Priced Labor," *loc. cit.,* p. 269.

[25] Discussion by Henry Metcalfe, *Transactions of the American Society of Mechanical Engineers,* VII (1886), 487–488.

The most rudimentary of these devices was the inside-contracting system, most rudimentary because in many ways it utilized the arrangements and incentives of previous methods of production. Though the contract system had a multitude of meanings, it is used here to describe a system whereby one party provided the place of work and, in most instances, the machinery, purchased the raw materials, and sold the finished product. The "inside" contractor, who agreed to do the work, hired the workers in his group or gang, paid himself and them wages which, if he were to make a profit, had to be somewhat less than he received from the company under the contract price. He thus had an incentive to supervise the work sharply and expedite its accomplishment. The manufacturer was spared the headaches of hiring and firing workers, of training them, and of foremanship. This system of inside contracting was applied to a diverse group of industries which included on the one hand standardized articles suitable for interchangeable production, such as military equipment, machines, and stoves, and, on the other hand, non-standardized products such as ships.[26]

As an inheritance from old ways of doing things, contracting stepped into mining in work such as opening shafts and driving passageways and digging and dressing ore. The company furnished the powder, lights, and tools and charged them to the workers; the contractors employed the workers. Cornish miners introduced this system into the Michigan copper mines and the owners experimented with its application to some surface activities.[27] Similar arrangements prevailed in coal mining.[28] When a "job" came into some machine shops it was customary to have the men "bid on it."[29] Though inside contracting persisted in some occupations and establishments into the twentieth century, the system had many disadvantages. It posed the necessity of inspecting the work

[26] F. L. Deyrup, "Arms Makers of the Connecticut Valley, A Regional Study of the Economic Development of the Small Arms Industry, 1798–1870," *Smith College Studies in History,* XXXIII (1948), 101–102, 149–150, 161–162; Charles H. Fitch, "Report on the Manufactures of Interchangeable Mechanism," *Tenth Census of the United States. 1880,* II, 33–35; Henry Hall, "Report on the Ship-Building Industry of the United States," *Tenth Census of the United States. 1880.* VIII, 103; John Buttrick, "The Inside Contract System," *Journal of Economic History,* XII (1952), 205–221; Henry Metcalfe, "The Shop-Order System of Accounts," *Transactions of the American Society of Mechanical Engineers,* VII (1886), 466; Henry R. Towne, "Gain-Sharing," *ibid.,* X (1889), 608.

[27] William B. Gates, Jr., *Michigan Copper and Boston Dollars: An Economic History of the Michigan Copper Mining Industry* (Cambridge: Harvard University Press, 1951), pp. 98–99; N. P. Gilman, *Profit Sharing between Employer and Employee* (Boston: Houghton, Mifflin and Company, 1889), pp. 28–29.

[28] Ray Ginger, "Managerial Employees in Anthracite, 1902, A Study in Occupational Mobility," *Journal of Economic History,* XIV, 148.

[29] Discussion by Van A. Norris, *Transactions of the American Society of Mechanical Engineers,* XII (1891), 771; Discussion by William H. Weightman, *ibid.,* 773.

thoroughly and of taking care lest contracting workers use machinery carelessly. Managers had to re-calculate prices for contracting lest they paid the contractor too great a profit (10 per cent was thought about right). The system merged so much into other systems of employment and wages that the overlapping produced confusion about discipline, punctuality, and absenteeism.[30]

When managers came to the conclusion they might as well supervise one system as two, they recoiled from paying by day or week. Time wages gave no incentive for superior performance since, according to Emerson, "mankind is as lazy as it dares to be."[31] So they sought other devices. One was the sharing of profits or gain-sharing. Probably first tried abroad, profit-sharing in this country was actually more important as the symptom of a quest than as a way of paying wages. At the end of the eighties an advocate of the system listed only some thirty experiments with profit-sharing in the United States, in textiles, shoes, printing, soap, retailing, and some of these could be included only by broad definition.[32] One of the most persuasive proponents and practitioners of gain-sharing was Henry R. Towne, who placed the production of locks on an assembly basis of interchangeable parts at his Yale and Towne shop in Stamford, Connecticut. He employed three hundred workers.[33]

The ideological advantages of profit-sharing were easily stated. The antagonistic interests of management and labor dissolved into a harmony wherein each "as a partner" was concerned with the efficient operation of the whole course of production. Though Towne believed that profit-sharing was the "ultimate and final solution,"[34] as a practical incentive system it displayed shortcomings. The savings and efficiencies were so diffused through the whole industrial structure as to disappear as a stimulus to the individual worker. Nothing he could do, for instance, could effect economies in purchasing raw materials or the sale of the product or in interest rates. The lazy and the energetic alike benefited from profit-sharing; and the distribution of profits, necessarily at long intervals, had no immediate reflection in the take-home pay upon which

[30] T. R. Navin, *The Whitin Machine Works since 1831* (Cambridge: Harvard University Press, 1950), pp. 147–149; Henry Metcalfe, "The Shop-Order System of Accounts," *loc. cit.*, pp. 466–468.

[31] Edward Atkinson, "Consumption Limited, Production Unlimited," *The Industrial Progress of the Nation*, p. 11; F. A. Halsey, "The Premium Plan of Paying for Labor," *Transactions of the American Society of Mechanical Engineers*, XII (1891), 755.

[32] Gilman, *op. cit.*, pp. 296–330.

[33] "Henry Robinson Towne," *Dictionary of American Biography*, XVIII, 613–614.

[34] Discussion by Henry R. Towne, *Transactions of the American Society of Mechanical Engineers*, VIII (1886), 290; Henry R. Towne, "Gain-Sharing," *ibid.*, X (1889), 601–618.

the workers depended. Employers realized it was unfair to workers without financial reserves to share in losses and so had to guarantee a minimum wage. The whole thing, said one, "savors of patronage and paternalism." [35]

Both inside contracting and profit-sharing were compatible and indeed often indistinguishable from the piecework system which became in this period the favored method of paying incentive wages, of paying for service rather than for time.[36] In mining, the payment to miners for the amount of coal or ore they got out approximated piecework. In textiles, though the system was not feasible for spinners, weavers were paid by the yard or "cut." Piecework was commonplace in the metal industries and in machine shops large enough to have a considerable duplication of the product.[37]

Introduction of the piecework system involved difficulties. Employers were so sure that piecework rates, paid on the basis of previously estimated labor costs of production, would so increase the productiveness of their workers and thus their earnings (and their anticipations on this score were correct) that they initially reduced the price per piece under the new system and, as they gained experience, cut the piecework rate at intervals lest they pay "an extravagant price for the work." [38] There was, therefore, often labor hostility to the introduction of the system. Since any worker generally regarded himself as the equal of another, he was not to be put off by the reply that he should take his complaints of a difference in wage not to the foreman but to God: "He is the person for you to go to. He didn't make you quite as sharp as that fellow." [39] But since the system did actually increase the productiveness of the individual worker and eased the problem of supervision ("the works [seem] to run themselves" was a description of the result on the Pennsylvania Railroad) [40] its forward march continued. The constant experi-

[35] Discussion by J. L. Wells, *Transactions of the American Society of Mechanical Engineers,* VIII (1886), 287–288; William Kent, "A Problem in Profit-Sharing," *ibid.,* VIII (1887), 63 ff.; Discussion by Towne, *ibid.,* VIII (1887), 644–646; Towne, "Gain-Sharing," *loc. cit.,* p. 625; F. A. Halsey, "The Premium Plan of Paying for Labor," *Transactions of the American Society of Mechanical Engineers,* XII (1891), 757–758.

[36] Gilman, *op. cit.,* pp. 46–49.

[37] Discussion by Oberlin Smith, *Transactions of the American Society of Mechanical Engineers,* VIII (1886), 288; Discussion by T. J. Borden, *ibid.,* VIII (1886), 289; Memoir of Edward F. C. Davis, *ibid.,* XVI (1895), 1179.

[38] Discussion by G. L. Fowler, *Transactions of the American Society of Mechanical Engineers,* VIII (1886), 285–287; Discussion by Henry R. Towne, *ibid.,* VIII (1886), 290–292; Halsey, *loc. cit.,* p. 756.

[39] Discussion by Fowler, *loc. cit.,* p. 286; Discussion by W. H. Doane, *Transactions of the American Society of Mechanical Engineers,* VIII (1887), 658.

[40] Discussion by Fowler, *loc. cit.,* p. 658.

mentation with alternatives (bonus and premium plans) eased the advance.[41]

In 1895 F. W. Taylor descended into the rough-and-ready multitude of preceding plans with his paper on "A Piece-Work System." Since he summarized a decade of experimentation at the Midvale Steel Company, in its own right a pioneering organization, Taylor's pronouncement acted as a catalyst. This paper answered many puzzles, facilitated the application of the system to tasks hitherto thought to be beyond its reach, and dogmatized expertly. Though some of his original hearers expressed reservations, most were electrified by his insights and the novelty of his approach.[42]

The first step in the Taylor system was to acquire, through observation and analysis, an accurate knowledge of the time in which a job could be done. On this standard performance a base pay rate was fixed at a "figure which will allow the workman to earn scarcely an ordinary day's pay when he falls off from his maximum pace." A differential rate structure was then added which gave "a high price per piece in case the work was finished in the shortest possible time and in perfect condition." To this superior achievement the faster pace of the operative as well as his intelligence and skill contributed. The latter two qualities management also had to display. Management's innovations in eliminating waste motion, in expediting the flow of work, and in running machinery at its most efficient rate were integral to the Taylor system. This "scientific and practical" theory stressed that employers must not change the rates downward as the men earned more; such action disregarded the scientific accuracy of the original determination and deceived the men.[43] Nonetheless, Taylor did confront the facts of competition and depression and had to admit that at Midvale Steel the wage-rate was cut if conditions of wages throughout the country changed "as occurred very generally in the rate of wages paid in 1893." The differentials, however, persisted.[44] In spite of the payment of higher wages, the system paradoxically made for cheaper costs since a greater output lowered costs. Taxes, insurance, depreciation, rent, interest, salaries, office expenses, sales expenses, costs of power amounted to almost the same whether output was great or small.[45]

[41] Halsey, *loc. cit.*, pp. 755–760.

[42] Discussion by Halsey and others, *Transactions of the American Society of Mechanical Engineers*, XVI (1895), 884–899.

[43] F. W. Taylor, "A Piece-Rate System," *Transactions of the American Society of Mechanical Engineers*, XVI (1895), 856–884.

[44] Discussion by Taylor, *ibid.*, XVI (1895), 895.

[45] Taylor, "A Piece-Rate System," *loc. cit.*, pp. 867–868; Pamphlet by Edward Atkinson, *Report of the Committee* [on Education and Labor] *of the Senate . . . 1885*, II, 235.

As systems of wages and industrial discipline grew more numerous and as each was refined again and again, some managers naturally became weary of mastering details and doubted the worth of new ways. Those with long experience with piecework declared it no "cure-all" for labor troubles.[46] Impatient managers drew "laughter and applause" from their hearers when they advocated not these new systems but a return to the old method of discharging men who were "nursing" work and of rewarding those who were best.[47] But these critics were whistling against the wind.

From the contract to the piecework system, American industrial discipline stressed the distinctiveness and individualism of the worker. Day wages were "demoralizing and leveling." Piecework accorded with what "the strictest moralist could call justice." [48] High pay for good work; poor pay for poor. This individualistic emphasis naturally latched on to doctrines currently in vogue. "Distressing as it may be to the kind-hearted philanthropist or social reformer, the great law of the survival of the fittest will be fully exemplified." [49] In the eyes of those focusing on America's industrial rivalry with other nations, the form of the industrial discipline which had emerged accorded with Americanism. America was outdistancing Europe because "we have to some extent been forced to adopt the true theory of work and wages. Our present labor troubles largely come from the introduction of Old-World ideas and Old-World methods." The manufacturer must "seek for the highest-priced labor as giving him the best returns for his expenditure. His problem is to adopt a system which shall utilize skill and intelligence. These are imperative and universal laws, and apply to all branches of business." [50]

DIGNITY AND DEMOCRACY

In businesses which had attained a magnitude common in this period and which were organized in the corporative form by owners who were absentees, relations between employer and employee inevitably became impersonal and mechanical. Gompers complained: "The employees are not known as men at all but are known by numbers." [51] Those concerned with arriving at the correct formula for industrial dis-

[46] Discussion by Borden, *loc. cit.*, p. 289; Discussion by Hawkins, *Transactions of the Society of Mechanical Engineers,* XII (1891), 764–766.

[47] Discussion by Hawkins, *loc. cit.*, pp. 773–774.

[48] Taylor, "A Piece-Rate System," *loc. cit.*, p. 873.

[49] Discussion by G. L. Fowler, *Transactions of the American Society of Mechanical Engineers,* VIII (1886), 658.

[50] Partridge, "Capital's Need for High-Priced Labor," *loc. cit.*, pp. 269–270.

[51] Testimony of Samuel Gompers, *Report of the Committee* [on Education and Labor] *of the Senate . . . 1885,* I, 289–290.

cipline had to decide how far managers should come into contact with their workers. The problem exceeded the boundaries of mere economics; it was social and political, involving matters of recognition and status that were all the more explosive because they were emotional. Perhaps because textiles were organized on an hierarchical basis, it was felt desirable here to confine communication to channels. The agent of the Amory mills in Manchester announced as his policy: "I never do my talking to the hands; I do all my talking with the overseers."[52] Other motives, snobbery and pride rather than discipline, sometimes underlay management performance. Taylor could not condemn harshly enough "the employer who goes through his works with kid gloves on, and is never known to dirty his hands or clothes, and who either talks to his men in a condescending or patronizing way, or else not at all. . . ."[53] That such policies were not universal, Marcus Alonzo Hanna demonstrated. On his street railway in Cleveland he knew almost every employee by name.[54]

Outside of the workplace, the problem was somewhat different. Even the agent of the Amory mills said, "On the street I talk with my people and recognize them."[55] It was a commonplace for mill agents in the same city "to come out here with the boys, and parade the streets with the firemen and with the soldiers when asked, and they all go and sit down at their banquets."[56] On the other hand J. P. Morgan, attempting to observe the vague line separating gentlemen from those who were not, put laboring men outside the category and preferred not to invite them into his library, the locus of many of his business decisions.[57]

The real test was after all whether managers and workers lived together. On this score it is quite unfeasible to draw a conclusion from metropolises like New York. The key to policy, if found at all, is in designed industrial communities. Lowell, where the agent and his subordinate overseers were housed in superior dwellings that were still a part of a common housing plan, could be dismissed as the materialization

[52] Testimony of G. B. Whitman, *Report of the Committee* [on Education and Labor] *of the Senate . . . 1885*, III, 38.

[53] Taylor, "A Piece-Rate System," *loc. cit.*, p. 880.

[54] Herbert Croly, *Marcus Alonzo Hanna: His Life and Work* (New York: Macmillan Company, 1923), pp. 85–88.

[55] Whitman, *loc. cit.*, p. 38.

[56] Testimony of Frederick Smyth, *Report of the Committee* [on Education and Labor] *of the Senate . . . 1885*, III, 117.

[57] W. S. Rainsford, *The Story of a Varied Life: An Autobiography* (Garden City: Doubleday, Page & Company, 1922), pp. 280–282; F. L. Allen, *The Great Pierpont Morgan* (New York: Harper & Brothers, 1949), pp. 95–97.

of early nineteenth century paternalism.[58] It was less easy thus to treat South Manchester, Connecticut, where each of the Cheney brothers lived in dwellings "built where the wealth is produced . . . and all those who had a share in producing the wealth have as much good from the lawns and adornment . . . as those who dwell in the fine house. The grounds are laid where all who work in the mills can see the fruits of the labors." Yet Cheney denied he was in "the model-village line." "We are only conducting our business on business principles." [59] In his appraisal of Pullman, Richard T. Ely was gratified to observe "no favorable sites are set apart for drones living on past accumulations, and if a few short stretches are reserved for residences which can be rented only by those whose earnings are large, this is an exception; and it is not necessary to remain long in the place to notice that clergymen, officers of the company, and mechanics live in adjoining dwellings." [60]

Though such random samples perhaps do not constitute a policy, the fundamental attitude of managers toward social relations with workers was also revealed in a memoir of Eckley B. Coxe published in the *Transactions of the American Society of Mechanical Engineers.* One of the greatest of American coal producers, Coxe was a man of inherited wealth. Though he might have, therefore, led a life of "inglorious ease," he chose instead one of active business; also "he lived among his workmen." [61] It would seem that Hanna rather than Morgan was the *beau ideal* of management. In sum, the policy of the hearty handshake "pays because a man is more than a machine, and the policy which treats him as a machine ignores one of the greatest factors in production, viz. human nature," as well as the democratic climate of America.[62]

THE RIGHT TO DECIDE

Whether it be farmland or factory, ownership of property confers the right to enjoy and manage it. In the case of production this meant that the contributors of capital, the investors, rarely questioned their right

[58] John Coolidge, "Low-Cost Housing: The New England Tradition," *New England Quarterly,* XIV (March, 1941), 15, 21–23.

[59] *Twelfth Annual Report of the* [Mass.] *Bureau of Statistics of Labor. January, 1881,* pp. 473–475; Testimony of F. W. Cheney, *Report of the Industrial Commission,* XIV, 728–729.

[60] Richard T. Ely, "Pullman: A Social Study," *Harper's New Monthly Magazine,* LXX (February, 1885), 457.

[61] "Memoir of Eckley B. Coxe," *Transactions of the American Society of Mechanical Engineers,* XVI (1895), 1182–1185.

[62] Testimony of W. C. Redfield, *loc. cit.,* pp. 657–660; Gerald W. Johnson, *The Making of a Southern Industrialist: A Biographical Study of Simpson Bobo Tanner* (Chapel Hill: University of North Carolina Press, 1954), pp. 48–60.

to manage the enterprise at first hand or appoint the management. As John Roach informed the prospective employees in his shipyard, "While you are in my workshop you must conform to my rules. . . . You must not attempt to take the control of my workshop out of my hands." [63] The tendency to arrogance inherent in the private property system was heightened by the employer's attitude that as businessmen they were philanthropists in hastening development and providing employment. As John D. Rockefeller put it, "The best philanthropy . . . is, in my judgement, the investment of effort or time or money, carefully considered with relation to the power of employing people at a remunerative wage, to expand and develop the resources at hand, and to give opportunity for progress and healthful labour where it did not exist before. No mere money-giving is comparable to this in its lasting and beneficial results." [64]

Not only was it right and beneficent that owners should determine labor policy, it was ordained by natural law. "The democratic element in modern society is undoubtedly gaining in strength with every year, and there is no good reason for lamenting its advance. But it will never do away with the natural aristocracy which has made skill in the conduct of business the endowment or the acquisition of a few. The many must continue to follow, as they always have done, when they did not rush to disaster; and the select minority of Nature's choosing must continue to lead, if the many are to prosper." In short there must be an industrial élite. Those who brought money and labor together and avoided the failure which was the fate of most entrepreneurs must constitute it.[65]

Nonetheless the owner-organizer group saw its prerogative challenged by two not entirely unrelated forces. One was government legislation. This interference management questioned on grounds of right; even more on grounds of effectiveness. Natural law was the proper governor of industrial affairs; statute law, attempting to supersede or to improve upon it, was "arbitrary," "artificial," "violent," and futile.[66] Legislation on matters of wages and hours "is attempting to be wiser than the Creator," [67] the author of natural law. Though this was generally accepted doctrine, there were some who believed that a circumscribed

[63] Testimony of John Roach, *Report of the Committee* [on Education and Labor] *of the Senate . . . 1885*, I, 1004.

[64] John D. Rockefeller, *Random Reminiscences of Men and Events* (Garden City: Doubleday, Doran & Company, 1933), pp. 141–142, 144–145; E. J. Phelps, "Irresponsible Wealth," *North American Review*, CLIII (May, 1891), 528–529; Testimony of John Medill, *loc. cit.*, pp. 992–993.

[65] Gilman, *op. cit.*, pp. 7, 34–40.

[66] Charles Elliott Perkins, Memo, May 8, 1885, Perkins Private Letters and Memos. Richard C. Overton.

[67] "Views of Dexter A. Hawkins," *Report of the Committee* [on Education and Labor] *of the Senate . . . 1885*, II, 153.

interference on the part of government might be desirable when we knew more about sociology, the "science of society," [68] or necessary when natural conditions changed. Thomas Livermore, the Amoskeag agent, thought in the eighties that such a time might come "when all the cheap lands are taken up so that there is no employment, like that of farming, into which the overflow of labor can pour; but I suppose that time will be a long time removed." [69]

The second interference came from the labor unions. Their intrusion was a favorite theme of alarm and abuse when managers got together. R. W. Hunt informed his fellow mechanical engineers in a discussion on how to organize production, "there is another difficulty which has to be constantly encountered, and that is, some man who does not work for you will come in and be supported by your men in his right to assert his authority to discuss with you your relations with your employees." [70] By challenging the right of the manager to organize his labor force on such terms as he willed, the unions also introduced those uncertainties which businessmen in all areas during this period were attempting to eradicate. A few years later Hunt recurred to the theme in discussing the union's "walking delegate, who can, as a rule, neither read nor write a single sentence in the English language correctly. . . . (applause)." [71] This interference by labor management felt was not only unsettling and irresponsible, it was ignorant of business in general as well as of the affairs of the firm which employed it. Contrariwise, those in charge believed that "brains and capital must be classed together." In a humanitarian spirit the capitalist must do the business thinking for his men.[72]

[68] Testimony of Francis A. Walker, *Report of the Committee* [on Education and Labor] *of the Senate . . . 1885,* III, 325–326.

[69] Testimony of T. L. Livermore, *loc. cit.,* p. 22; Testimony of F. A. Walker, *loc. cit.,* pp. 327–328.

[70] Discussion by R. W. Hunt, *Transactions of the American Society of Mechanical Engineers,* XII (1890), 777.

[71] Discussion by R. W. Hunt, *Transactions of the American Society of Mechanical Engineers,* XXI (1899), 725–726; Testimony of C. L. Harding, *Report of the Committee* [on Education and Labor] *of the Senate . . . 1885,* III, 295; Testimony of George Storm, *ibid.,* II, 816.

[72] Discussion by W. E. Partridge, *Transactions of the American Society of Mechanical Engineers,* VIII (1886), 275–276.

CHAPTER XVIII

Workers' Organizations and Their Weapons

FUNDAMENTAL INFLUENCES: NATIONALIZATION, THE BUSINESS CYCLE

EMPLOYERS were not the only group perplexed by the necessity of adapting to an age of machines, national markets, and giant business corporations. Workers had to adjust to the same conditions. Some of these economic circumstances had peculiar importance for the wage earners. Whereas mere mileage had once protected workingmen, as it had producers, from the competition of their fellows, the completion of the railroad network and the cheapening of rates and fares meant the disappearance of protected local markets. Since products made in one place could now be sold at a distance, matters of wages, hours, and other labor conditions were no longer of purely local interest. If the mobility of commodities were not at issue, the mobility of workers was. Wage earners could now with relative ease move from place to place in search of jobs. As immigration was demonstrating, there was even an international mobility of workers. These considerations combined to stimulate the organization of workers on national lines. The labor union with the longest uninterrupted history in the country, the National Typographical Union, fittingly enough appeared in 1850–1852 on the forward edge of the railroad era. One of its purposes was, except under limitations, "to prevent the movement of printers from one locality to another." [1]

Though the nationalization of the economic structure pressed workers toward national unions, labor could not entirely dispense with the advantages of organizing on a more limited geographical basis. As in the earlier part of the nineteenth century, there were local unions in in-

[1] John R. Commons and others, *History of Labour in the United States* (New York: Macmillan Company, 1918), II, 58–59; G. R. Taylor, *The Transportation Revolution* (Holt, Rinehart and Winston, Inc., 1951), p. 285; George A. Tracy, *History of the Typographical Union* (Indianapolis: International Typographical Union, 1913), pp. 117, 137.

dustrial centers which often united into trades' unions or trades' assemblies. Such geographically limited groupings had the advantage of quickly rallying to the aid of other embattled organized workers within their own craft or shop. By coinciding in state and community with functional political units, local organizations were more effective in political activity if organized labor chose to undertake it. If American labor saw advantages in financing and operating cooperative stores to bring down the price of commodities, as in the Rochdale system in Great Britain, the locality was the appropriate unit for such activity.

A second factor at work upon the labor movement was the alternation of prosperity and depression. When the price level rose, workers felt the squeeze between their relatively fixed wages rates and the fluid cost of living, and they were naturally more prone to protest and to organize to redress matters. At the same time employers found it easier to pass along increased labor costs to purchasers. On the other hand, times of falling prices placed wage earners in a more passive position. The specter of unemployment alarmed them. Furthermore prices were falling, employers were not expanding their activity or able to pass along increased costs to others. Though there were many exceptions to the generalization, the breezes of prosperity fanned labor organization forward; the head winds of depression slowed its advance.

As the country's economy recovered from the panic of 1857 and ultimately entered the high prosperity of the Civil War and post-Civil War years, there was a surge forward in labor organization. In 1859 various local unions of moulders coalesced into the Iron Moulders' International Union. One of the products such workers made was cast-iron stoves, and manufacturers of this article in the various centers were competing bitterly with each other for the enlarged market of the time. Consequently William Sylvis, a leading spirit in the organization and one of the greatest labor leaders of the era, emphasized the need for "a national organization, embracing every moulder in the country, a Union founded upon a basis as broad as the land in which we live." [2] In the later years of the Civil War and until 1873 the number of national labor unions markedly increased. They appeared in construction, among skilled railroad workers (conductors, engineers, and firemen formed Brotherhoods), among cigar makers, telegraphers, and iron and steel workers (the Sons of Vulcan were organized in 1862). The shoemakers formed the largest union, the Knights of St. Crispin, with approximately 50,000 members in 1873.[3]

[2] Jonathan Grossman, *William Sylvis, Pioneer of American Labor* (New York: Columbia University Press, 1945), pp. 24–30.

[3] Commons and others, *op. cit.*, II, 45–47, 151; Lloyd Ulman, *The Rise of the National Trade Union* (Cambridge: Harvard University Press, 1955), pp. 3–7.

Bringing a central organization into existence through the device of federalism was a natural one in the United States, for that was the path the nation had followed toward unity. Federalism had flexibility and an obvious applicability where local units were already in existence. It was from local organizations, consequently, that the impulse came in the sixties to form more perfect unions. In 1866 delegates from locals, trades' assemblies, and nationals, and various individuals given the privilege of the floor if not the vote, assembled in Baltimore, passed resolutions, and established the National Labor Union, an organization notably deficient in funds and lacking precise definition of who was eligible for membership. In spite of these handicaps, the National Labor Union held annual congresses until 1872 when only seven persons attended the meeting.

Inside and outside the national trade unions, the labor union movement at this time, 1870–1872, had perhaps 300,000 members.[4] As for the National Labor Union, there seems little reason to question the appraisal of a later, shrewd observer, "It was a typical American politico-reform organization, led by labor leaders without organizations, politicians without parties, women without husbands, and cranks, visionaries, and agitators without jobs." [5] Perhaps its deliberations and pronouncements educated and inspired certain workers; more promisingly it gave its leaders and participants a pragmatic training in the task of organizing and administering a central labor union.

THE KNIGHTS OF LABOR

In December, 1869, a group of nine garment cutters assembled in the hall of the American Hose Company in Philadelphia. These "broad-minded, thinking" members of a defunct local union resolved to establish a successor society. Apparently the chief leadership for "something different from what we have ever had" came from Uriah S. Stephens, a would-be Baptist minister who was also a Mason, an Oddfellow and a Knight of Pythias. Approximately within a month, the group had founded a secret fraternal order with a ritual, christened it the Noble and Holy Order of the Knights of Labor, constituted themselves Local Assembly No. 1, electing Uriah S. Stephens the first Master Workman. It also demonstrated that it was not necessary for a labor organization to resort to a saloon for revival; the Knights of Labor moved forward on

[4] Commons and others, *op. cit.*, II, 47, 95–96, 101, 102, 155.

[5] Norman Ware, *The Labor Movement in the United States, 1860–1895* (New York: D. Appleton and Company, 1929), p. 11; G. N. Grob, "Reform Unionism: The National Labor Union," *Journal of Economic History*, XIV (1954), 135.

hot coffee and lemonade.[6] Within three years this primordial unit of garment cutters had taken in "sojourners" from other trades who were expected in turn to form assemblies of fellow craftsmen; and District Assembly No. 1 had been formed in Philadelphia. Resembling the old local trades' union or trades' assembly in its inclusiveness, District Assembly No. 1 became a sort of mother church for the Knights.

Nonetheless throughout the mid-seventies there were many efforts to provide a different sort of central organization for an order which was expanding in terms of territory and occupations as the depression years following 1873 destroyed many national unions and beat down their membership. The Knights of St. Crispin, for instance, were absorbed into the Knights of Labor. Finally the Knights of Labor reached a landmark of sorts when the Reading Convention of 1878 drew up a constitution establishing a General Assembly and elected Stephens Grand Master Workman. Though on paper the order was highly centralized, the local and district assemblies remained the center of activity and indeed pulled the central organization and its officers along after them. In 1879 the General Assembly took steps to lessen the secrecy and the religious character of the Order. The public associated secrecy with sinister activity because of the terrorism of the Molly Maguires in the coal regions; and the Catholic Church, the church of many of the members of the Knights, distrusted religious commitments incompatible with the Catholic faith. In 1879 the Knights elected Terence V. Powderly, a machinist and Catholic, as Grand Master Workman. He held this position until 1893.[7]

These organizational changes in the Knights were taking place as the late seventies lifted the load of the depression of 1873. New members or those in other organizations flocked to the Knights, and its connection with a campaign for the greatly desired eight-hour day spurred the movement forward. By mid-1886 the Order had 729,677 members. The number in 1879 had been 9,287.[8] Such a swarming left organizers and officials a little breathless and awed the public. The New York *Sun* observed, "The ability of the president and cabinet to turn out all the men in the civil service, and to shift from one post to another the duties of the men in the army and navy, is a petty authority compared with that of these five Knights [the General Executive Board]. . . . They

[6] T. V. Powderly, *Thirty Years of Labor, 1859 to 1889* (Philadelphia: T. V. Powderly, 1890), pp. 73–76; "Uriah Smith Stephens," *Dictionary of American Biography*, XVII, 581.

[7] Ware, *op. cit.*, pp. 1–3, 18–51, 55–64.

[8] *Ibid.*, pp. 66–72; Donald Kemmerer and E. D. Wickersham, "Reasons for the Growth of the Knights of Labor in 1885–1886," *Industrial and Labor Relations Review*, III (January, 1950), 213–220.

can stay the nimble touch of almost every telegraph operator, can shut up most of the mills and factories, and can disable the railroads."[9] Though Powderly and his associates neither possessed the authority thus ascribed to them, nor would have exercised it if they had, this editorial alarm revealed how impressive the success of the Knights had been. From 1886 the membership declined; by 1893 it was 74,635; the next year the Order's "importance as an industrial society ceased."[10] Failures in critical strikes and the public's unjustified association of the Order with violence partially accounted for the collapse.

THE AMERICAN FEDERATION OF LABOR

In 1886 when the Knights had their peak membership, there were 138,000 members in the American Federation of Labor.[11] Through the principle of federalism, the national unions formed the structure of this organization. Such of the national unions as had emerged from the depression years of the seventies had formed in 1881 the Federation of Organized Trades and Labor Unions. In 1886 these and other units established the American Federation of Labor. The generative force in this new organization came from a handful of national unions organized on craft lines, and from their leaders. The most influential of the latter were Peter J. McGuire of the Carpenters and Adolph Strasser and Samuel J. Gompers of the Cigar Makers. A quarrel with units of the Knights of Labor over organizing the cigar makers' trade explained the primacy of the Cigar Makers' International Union in the new organization. The latter recognized its paternity by electing Samuel Gompers its first president, a position he held, with the exception of one year, into the twentieth century.[12] In 1897 the membership of American trade unions, in and out of the A. F. of L., totaled 447,000; in 1900 868,500. The next year it was to cross a million for the first time. The steadiest growth had been generally in unions in building and printing.[13] The organizing success of the railroad brotherhoods was outside the A. F. of L.

THE ORIGINS OF UNIONIZATION

A sequential account of unionization may easily give the impression that there was a progress from failure to success, that the last phase had

[9] Quoted in Commons and others, *op. cit.*, II, 371.

[10] Ware, *op. cit.*, pp. x, 66.

[11] Leo Wolman, *The Growth of American Trade Unions, 1880–1923* (New York: National Bureau of Economic Research, 1924), p. 32.

[12] Testimony of Samuel Gompers, *Report of the Industrial Commission*, VII, 596–597.

[13] Wolman, *op. cit.*, pp. 33–35.

conquered earlier perplexities and difficulties, and that the latecomers had found the answers to hard questions. But to cap the National Labor Union with the Knights of Labor and the Knights with the Federation may well be misleading, especially when the actors in the drama themselves advance a similar version of development. Adolph Strasser, one of the pillars of the A. F. of L. "knew they [the Knights] could not live, had no historical existence, and could not survive. I knew that from the beginning." [14] Such complacency, however, does not answer the question as to why labor organizations grew in America where before the Civil War they had had comparatively little influence and had attracted still less general attention.

The better informed among employers, managers, and observers knew such arrangements existed overseas, but most were convinced they were a response to European conditions and that American circumstances made unions impossible. This analysis, coupled with the self-rectitude felt by employers about their own motives and achievements, led quickly to the belief that labor organizations were due either to the human perversity of idlers and agitators or to foreign influences. The first explanation was a reaction of sheer waspishness; the second had factual basis. In coal-mining, organization owed much to leaders like John Siney, a Lancashire Irishman, and John Mitchell, American born of Scotch-Irish parents; in iron and steel to John Jarrett, a Welshman. Immigrants from Lancashire provided what backbone the feeble unions in textiles possessed.[15] Germans, professing a wide spectrum of socialist belief, influenced the labor movement in some American cities.[16] But foreign birth did not usually provide leaders of national stature, at least in the first instance. The parents of William Sylvis were both American born; Terence V. Powderly was born in the United States of Irish parents; Samuel Gompers was born in London of Dutch-Jewish parents but came to this country at the age of thirteen.[17]

Labor leaders, with the zeal of an episcopate seeking to establish its superior sanctity, traced their descent unbroken from the trade guilds of the Middle Ages or, with equal emphasis, asserted that unions grew inexorably out of circumstances. There was always antagonism between the buyer and seller of labor, or at the very least difference of opinion about its worth. As Gompers summed it up: "If they [unions] are im-

[14] Testimony of Adolph Strasser, *Report of the Industrial Commission*, VII, 261.

[15] R. T. Berthoff, *British Immigrants in Industrial America* (Cambridge: Harvard University Press, 1953), pp. 91–98; Testimony of John Roach, *Report of the Committee* [on Education and Labor] *of the Senate . . . 1885*, I, 997.

[16] Howard H. Quint, *The Forging of American Socialism: Origins of the Modern Movement* (Columbia: University of South Carolina Press, 1953), pp. 6–13.

[17] Grossman, *op. cit.*, p. 17; "Terence Vincent Powderly," *Dictionary of American Biography*, XV, 142; "Samuel Gompers," *Dictionary of American Biography*, VII, 369.

ported then, as has been said, they were landed at Plymouth Rock from the Mayflower. Modern industry evolves these organizations out of the existing conditions." In sum, the labor leaders found their justification where the capitalists had theirs—in evolution and natural law.[18]

Commitment to a theory of history involves commitment to a course of action. American labor organizations were not revolutionary in aim or in method. They were conservative. Such foreign influences as they responded to operated in the same direction.[19] Again Gompers (could he have been reading Bellamy?) summed it up: "One would imagine by what is often considered as the solution of the [labor] problem that it is going to fall among us, that a world cataclysm is going to take place . . . that we will go to bed one night under the present system and tomorrow morning wake up with a revolution in full blast, and the next day organize a Heaven on earth. That is not the way that progress is made; that is not the way the social evolution is brought about. . . . We are solving the problem day after day. As we get an hour's more leisure every day it means millions of golden hours of opportunities, to the human family. As we get 25 cents a day wages increase, it means another solution, another problem solved, and brings us nearer the time when a greater degree of justice and fair dealing will obtain among men." [20]

ANTI-UNION POLICY

It was fortunate for the unions that they had behind them the momentum of history, evolution, and natural law, for employers and managers were, at least at the beginning, generally hostile to labor organizations. This hostility was based partly on a matter of right; it was also a matter of policy.[21] Owners and managers were struggling with might and main to rationalize business, to control its disorderliness and to make their decisions stick. It was bad enough to have such variables

[18] Testimony of Samuel Gompers, *Report of the Committee* [on Education and Labor] *of the Senate . . . 1885,* I, 373; Testimony of Samuel Gompers, *Report of the Industrial Commission,* VII, 618; John Mitchell, *Organized Labor. Its Problems, Purposes, and Ideals* (Philadelphia: American Book and Bible House, 1903), p. 239; *Official Journal of the Cigar Makers' International Union,* June, 1885.

[19] Clifton K. Yearley, Jr., "Britons in American Labor: A History of the Influence of the United Kingdom Immigrants on American Labor, 1820–1914," *Johns Hopkins University Studies in Historical and Political Science,* Series LXXV, No. 1 (1957), 313–317; Berthoff, *op. cit.,* pp. 100–101, 106.

[20] Testimony of Samuel Gompers, *Report of the Industrial Commission,* VII, 655; Testimony of Adolph Strasser, *loc. cit.,* p. 460.

[21] Minority Report of the Homestead Strike, *House Report* No. 2447 (s.n. 3142), 52nd Cong., 2d Sess., p. xix.

as government policy or directors' decisions complicating the situation. To let organized workers participate in managerial decisions when, at the very least, they did not and could not know the big picture of production and markets, prices and costs, was to court the whirlwind. Particularly was this felt to be true when the representative of the workers was the "Walking Delegate," an outsider not even in the pay of the employer.[22] Since union decisions might make the difference between bankruptcy and profit,[23] employers generally preferred to make their contracts with individual workers. John Roach, the shipbuilder, was expressing a common attitude when he said: "I say to the men, 'When you came to seek employment of me, you came in your own individual capacity, you presented yourself on your own individual merits, and it was upon that condition I hired you. Now, if you have any complaint to make, make it for yourself. I will hear it and try to treat you fairly. . . .' "[24]

This statement of policy was far too pretty and too simple: it did not really describe the methods by which employers sought to deal with their workers' unionization. Employers made it a condition of contracts with employees that the latter had not been and would not become members of any union, or presented workers with the choice of surrendering union membership or losing their jobs.[25] Such iron-clad contracts were an effective means for preventing the start of unionism or eradicating it if under way.

Also, anti-union management had a very useful weapon in their power of discharge. They used it with ingenious variety. Leaders in the union organization suddenly found themselves without work and without stated reasons. And since the blacklist often accompanied the discharge, the courageous or unruly among the workers found it impossible to obtain other jobs in the locality or region. How widespread blacklisting for union activity actually was is impossible to say, for it was often confused with agreements among employers not to hire or tempt away each

[22] Discussion by F. F. DuBrul, *Transactions of the American Society of Mechanical Engineers,* XXIV (1903), 1457–1460.

[23] R. P. Bolton, "The Construction of Contracts," *Transactions of the American Society of Mechanical Engineers,* XXII (1900–1901), 111–112.

[24] Testimony of John Roach, *Report of the Committee* [on Education and Labor] *of the Senate . . . 1885,* I, 1004.

[25] Berthoff, *op. cit.,* p. 94; Testimony of John Jarrett, *Report of the Committee* [on Education and Labor] *of the Senate . . . 1885,* I, 1120; Testimony of M. M. Garland, *Report of the Industrial Commission,* VII, 101; Marvin W. Schlegel, *Ruler of the Reading: The Life of Franklin B. Gowen, 1836–1889* (Harrisburg: Archives Publishing Company of Pennsylvania, 1947), p. 66; D. L. McMurry, *The Great Burlington Strike of 1888: A Case History in Labor Relations* (Cambridge: Harvard University Press, 1956), pp. 16–17.

others workers or to exchange honest estimates of the real skills of those they employed.[26]

Managers might utilize mass procedures when they found themselves heading into real trouble. In 1892 Henry Clay Frick was at odds over a reduction in wages with the Amalgamated Association of Iron and Steel Workers at the Homestead plant of the Carnegie group. An investigating committee of the Senate later reviewing the story commented in passing: "The parties being unable to come to an agreement that was mutually satisfactory, the company closed its works . . . and discharged its men. So far there was no violation of law by anyone." [27] The lockout, for this was one, was the strike in reverse. It was a way of firing the first shot, and many labor disputes sputtered over which came first, the strike or the lockout.

In the Homestead fracas, management intended to replace the strikers with a new labor force and to protect those of its current workers who were willing to continue at work. This structure of plan and procedure, perhaps instinctive and customary, never received a clearer justification than in the report, drawn up by Charles Francis Adams, Jr., on the strike of the locomotive engineers on the Boston and Maine Railroad in 1877. Adams was then chairman of the Massachusetts Railroad Commission; according to the gratified author he took great pride in the "salutory doctrines" stated in his report.[28] "Undoubtedly the employés of a corporation have a right to leave its service. They can do so singly or in a body. The community, however, has also rights in the matter. . . . On the other hand the corporation has an equal right to go into the labor market and employ substitutes in the place of those who have so left its service, and those substitutes are entitled to protection in working for it. They have a right to be guarded from intrusion while in the line of their duty, as well as from insults and violence." [29]

There is plenty of evidence of popular allegiance to this reasoning. The Committees of both House and Senate, investigating the Homestead Strike, agreed at this point on sound doctrine. The Senators declared: "employers have an undoubted right . . . to employ and dismiss men

[26] William F. Willoughby, "Employers' Associations for Dealing with Labor in the United States," *Quarterly Journal of Economics,* XX (November, 1905), 144–145; Topical Digest of Evidence, *Report of the Industrial Commission,* IV, 133–136; Commons and others, *op. cit.,* II, 415.

[27] Report of the Select Committee of the Senate on detectives and labor troubles, *Senate Report* No. 1280 (s.n. 3072), 52nd Cong., 2d Sess., p. xvi.

[28] Charles F. Adams, Jr., *Charles Francis Adams, 1836–1915: An Autobiography* (Boston: Houghton Mifflin Company, 1916), pp. 174–175.

[29] Report of the Massachusetts Board of Railroad Commissioners on the Boston & Maine Railroad Strike of February 12, 1877, Massachusetts *House Report* No. 102, pp. 15–16.

at pleasure" and "all good citizens will agree" that strikers should not "undertake forcibly to prevent others from working." [30] The Representatives concurred: "The right of a person or corporation . . . to employ any one to labor in a lawful business is secured by the laws of the land." [31] And eventually Charles W. Eliot, President of Harvard University, was defending before a largely labor audience the thesis that "a 'scab' might be a type of modern hero." To be sure the distinguished educator was making the argument on the basis of moral qualities rather than economic services.[32]

If employers were to combat their employees successfully they had to know what the latter were thinking and doing. Of course employers' hostility to labor organizations made it impossible to use the unions as a channel of information and communication. As time went by management apparently found it unsatisfactory to rely upon confidences given to or overheard by foremen or blabbed out in saloons by loose-lipped union members after meetings.[33] Instead it turned to detectives. Though there were many agencies that supplied such operatives, the most famous was that founded in 1850 by "the old gentleman" who had done police work for cities and the national government, Allan Pinkerton, and continued by his sons. Their first and most normal activity was "quiet work." They shadowed suspected embezzlers, employees getting into bad habits, and railroad conductors stealing money from their companies. To this they added "patrol work" in the guise of uniformed watchmen at race-tracks, building construction, or in places where police forces were inadequate or nerveless. Only a few great metropolises had professional police forces adequate to provide protection against marauders and depredators and frequent disclosures showed that even these forces were riven with politics. It is no accident that mining companies, usually located in wild country, and railroad companies, vulnerable to train robberies, were the chief patrons of Pinkertons. Just after the Civil War the Pinkertons undertook strike business and provided spies to penetrate unions and report on their membership and activities.[34]

Though faced with far from a clear cut capital-labor quarrel, F. B. Gowen, ruler of the Reading Railroad and allied mining enterprises,

[30] Report of the Select Committee of the Senate, *loc. cit.*, pp. iv, xiv.

[31] Report of House Judiciary Committee on the Employment of Pinkertons, *House Report* No. 2447 (s.n. 3142), 52nd Cong., 2d Sess., pp. xi–xiii.

[32] Henry James, *Charles W. Eliot, President of Harvard University, 1869–1909* (Boston: Houghton Mifflin Company, 1930), II, 155n.

[33] Powderly, *Thirty Years of Labor, 1859 to 1889*, p. 76.

[34] Testimony of Frank Murray, Testimony of Matt Pinkerton, Testimony of Ross K. Pinkerton, Testimony of Andrew C. Robertson, Testimony of Robert A. Pinkerton, Report of the Select Committee of the Senate, *loc. cit.*, pp. 5–9, 26–29, 224–225, 247–261.

naturally turned in the seventies to Pinkerton to furnish a detective to unearth the Molly Maguires, a secret subdivision of the Ancient Order of Hiberbians, which, largely for personal reasons, murdered those they disliked, including mine superintendents. Gowen publicly identified this terrorism with the vestiges of unionism in the Pennsylvania anthracite and coal regions. The discovery of the ringleaders of the Maguires and their execution is a classic in the history of detection.[35] If an employer wanted strikebreakers he advertised through Pinkerton, and if he wanted protection for strikebreakers and plant he turned to the same agency.[36]

Before Homestead, Pinkerton had worked in seventy strikes. In 1892 Frick engaged from the agency an army of three hundred men and planned to land them from barges at night on the river side of the Homestead plant. The river approaches, unlike the land ones, were unfenced and unpatrolled by strikers. Like many amphibious operations, this one went awry. The barges were delayed; strikers, organized like an army, got word of the maneuver, and soon firing broke out. The strikers had a cannon they could not depress enough to bombard the river, and their attempts to burn the barges by flaming oil were frustrated by an inauspicious wind. After casualties on both sides, the Pinkertons surrendered as "prisoners of war." As they were marched through the streets to a rink serving as a corral, women and children inflicted indignities of such nature upon them that a Congressional Committee felt it could not publicly describe them.[37] This dismal occurrence furnished provender for the platform of the Populist Party of 1892: "The urban workmen are denied the right to organize for self protection, imported pauperized labor beats down their wages, a hireling standing army, unrecognized by our laws, is established to shoot them down. . . ."[38]

UNION ACTIVITIES AND THE LAW

Unhappily for the unhindered advance of unionization, all the handicaps were not "unrecognized by our laws." A union wore the aura of "conspiracy," for it was considered a concert among many to cause the managers and owners of an enterprise such misery and loss as to compel them to grant the wage earners' demands. In England the law early in the nineteenth century considered unions criminal conspiracies and regarded as indictable most of the measures they took to secure their ends. In spite of the authority British precedents had in American

[35] Schlegel, *op. cit.*, pp. 76, 87–91.

[36] McMurry, *op. cit.*, pp. 96–113.

[37] Report of the House Committee of the Judiciary on the Homestead Strike, *loc. cit.*, p. ix.

[38] H. S. Commager, ed., *Documents of American History* (New York: Appleton-Century-Crofts, 1949), II, 143.

courts, an examination of the outcome of early nineteenth century courts cases indicates "it was never the law in the United States that labor unions are illegal per se." Though judges fulminated and courts issued indictments against criminal conspiracy, in the end attention was directed primarily to purposes and to the methods unions employed to secure them. Before the Civil War, courts had ruled that union activity to raise wages was legal,[39] and the famous Massachusetts decision, Commonwealth *v.* Hunt, in 1842, involving a strike to procure the discharge of a non-union worker, made explicit the doctrine that the legality of a combination depended upon purposes and means. In this instance the court validated both.[40] Though some states passed laws ostensibly exempting from prosecution an apparently wide variety of union purposes and methods, they had little success. On many occasions and in many jurisdictions, the courts paid little attention to such legislation—or to the doctrines of Commonwealth *v.* Hunt, for that matter.[41]

Events in the world of railroad enterprise led the way to new legal devices against unionism. While interruptions of production often inconvenienced the public, interruptions of railroad service were almost immediately disastrous to the community. In 1877 a series of strikes against reductions in pay and changes in working rules erupted on the nation's railroads. On railroads in receivership and hence under jurisdiction of the courts, judges issued orders or notices that any interruption to service would be punished as contempt of court. In the great railroad strikes of the mid-eighties, the courts began issuing injunctions for solvent roads. Somewhat later individual employers threatened by labor activity asked courts to intervene through injunctions to prevent irreparable injury to property. The courts also began to define property not only as physical objects but as relationships. A business, judges held, had the right of access to markets for its products and to hiring markets for workers.[42]

The passage of the Interstate Commerce Act and the Sherman Anti-Trust Act offered the possibility of basing such decisions not upon judicial construction of common law but upon the solid fact of policy embodied in statute. The Interstate Commerce Act was the less important. It did not mention labor directly but it made interstate commerce by rail the open responsibility of the national government. On the other hand the convenient vagueness of the Sherman Anti-Trust Act declared illegal

[39] Edwin E. Witte, "Early American Labor Cases," 35 *Yale Law Journal*, 825–827, 836.

[40] Commonwealth *vs.* John Hunt and others, 45 *Massachusetts* (4 *Metcalf*), 111; Leonard W. Levy, *The Law of the Commonwealth and Chief Justice Shaw* (Cambridge: Harvard University Press, 1957), pp. 183–206.

[41] Witte, *loc. cit.*, pp. 828–832.

[42] *Ibid.*, pp. 832–836.

"every contract, combination, in the form of trust or otherwise, or conspiracy, in restraint of trade and commerce among the several states." On the whole the question whether Congress intended the act to apply to unions remained unsettled.[43]

In the end the Pullman or Chicago Railway strike of 1894, one of the great labor outbreaks of this period, shed a revealing light on this legal development, as it did on so many other aspects of labor-management relations. The original impulse to this conflict was a disagreement between Pullman and his workers over a wage-cut. Some of the workers had been organized into the American Railway Union, whose president was Eugene V. Debs, a homespun American activist, and whose membership included railroad operatives. When the Pullman strikers appealed for help, the American Railway Union refused to move trains which included Pullman cars, and a rail blockade threatened to strangle Chicago's, if not the nation's, transportation system. The strike movement collapsed when Grover Cleveland's Attorney-General, Richard Olney, secured an injunction against the strike's leaders, an injunction prohibiting a wide range of strike activity, and when President Cleveland, over the protests of Governor John P. Altgeld of Illinois, sent Federal troops to the scene of disturbance.[44]

When the resulting injunction case, *In Re Debs,* came before the Courts, the lower Federal tribunal "mainly" based its issuance of an injunction upon the clause of the Sherman Anti-Trust Act which declared every conspiracy to restrain trade and commerce illegal. When the issues were brought in another guise to the Supreme Court, the judges neither affirmed nor condemned the use of the Sherman Anti-Trust Act; they passed it by, emphasizing "the general confusion into which the interstate commerce of the country was thrown; the forcible interference with that commerce; the attempted exercise by individuals of powers belonging only to government, and the threatened continuance of such invasions of public right,"[45] and the constitutional jurisdiction of the Federal government, Congress, courts, and President over interstate commerce. "The strong arm of the national government may be put forth to brush away all obstructions to the freedom of interstate commerce or the transportation of the mails. If the emergency arises, the army of the Nation, and all its militia, are at the service of the Nation to compel obedience to its laws."[46] Debs served a jail term for contempt of court.

[43] Edward Berman, *Labor and the Sherman Act* (New York: Harper & Brothers, 1930), pp. 13–54.

[44] Almont Lindsey, *The Pullman Strike: A Story of a Great Experiment and of a Great Labor Upheaval* (Chicago: University of Chicago Press, 1942), pp. 90–235.

[45] *In Re Debs,* 158 *United States,* 592, 600.

[46] *Ibid.,* 582.

Every morning of his imprisonment he put a fresh carnation in his buttonhole.[47]

Though the decision in the Debs case ran along a groove the courts had already marked out,[48] the many fascinating novelties of the Pullman strike startled contemporaries and have since occasioned much historical and legal writing on topics such as the use of Federal troops in a strike without a previous request by the state's governor, punishment without jury trial for violating an injunction rather than for committing an outright criminal act, the efficacy of industrial as contrasted with craft unionism, the danger of "judge-made law" in a democracy, and the sinuous path taken by the Attorney-General to his goal.[49]

Of central importance in the conflict was the role played by the General Managers' Association, formed in 1886 by twenty-four railroads "for the consideration of problems of management arising from the operation of railroads terminating or centering at Chicago." For many years the Association concerned itself largely with technical matters, but by the mid-nineties it was creeping into labor policy, and announced that it would assist each road on such matters as recruiting strikebreakers. In the Pullman strike it refused to deal with the American Railway Union and acted as a high command for the strategy of the railroads.[50] In sum, the many factors hampering union organization—refusal to recognize, use of Pinkertons, obtaining injunctions, furnishing strikebreakers—were being pulled together into a concerted anti-labor design by associations of employers.

EMPLOYERS' ASSOCIATIONS

Actually the activities of such associations cannot be fitted into a sinister, static and doctrinaire pattern. The earliest of such associations predate the period here under discussion; their multiplication came in the late eighties, and reached an impressive peak around the turn of the century.[51] A capsule history of one of the earliest of employer or-

[47] Ray Ginger, *The Bending Cross: A Biography of Eugene Victor Debs* (New Brunswick: Rutgers University Press, 1949), p. 168.

[48] Berman, *op. cit.*, pp. 57–64; A. T. Mason, *Organized Labor and the Law* (Durham: Duke University Press, 1925), pp. 119–142.

[49] Allan Nevins, *Grover Cleveland, A Study in Courage* (New York: Dodd, Mead & Company, 1932), pp. 611–628; Waldo R. Browne, *Altgeld of Illinois. A Record of His Life and Work* (New York: B. W. Huebsch, 1924), pp. 116–174; Harry Barnard, *"Eagle Forgotten." The Life of John Peter Altgeld* (Indianapolis: Bobbs-Merrill Company, 1938), pp. 280–317; Lindsey, *op. cit., passim.*

[50] Report of the U. S. Strike Commission on the Chicago Strike of June–July 1894, *Senate Executive Document* No. 7 (s.n. 3276), 53rd Cong., 3rd Sess., pp. xxviii–xxxi.

[51] Clarence E. Bonnett, *Employers' Associations in the United States: A Study of*

ganizations, the Stove Founders' National Defense Association, will reveal the complexities involved in forming judgments in this matter. Significantly this one appeared in an industry directly affected by the nationalization of the market. Nonetheless it arose as a result of a strike or lockout in Troy in 1886, brought on by a series of moulders' demands for an increase in wages aggregating 30 per cent. The Troy manufacturers "had contracts made that would take up most of the balance of the year; they had to finish up those contracts; they could not afford to quit." Later the Troy employers, who found themselves priced out of the stove market by their concessions to the workers, asked the latter to accept a reduction of wages on the ground that "We can not do a successful business until we are put on an equal basis with other sections of the country." When the Stove Founders' Defense Organization attained national stature, it tried to prevent piece-meal capitulation to the moulders by stiffening the morale of local employers, by providing strikebreakers in case of conflict, or by doing the work in the shops of unstruck members. As a strike fighter it met with great success.

Nevertheless by 1891 the Association was engaged in settling differences with the moulders through the annual negotiation of a national agreement governing wages, hours, and rules. The workers had learned they had to consider the interests of the manufacturers, the latter had learned that the workers had able representatives—"really business men—that is about the size of it. The way we look upon it is a proposition from either side is a business proposition, in which both are interested, and which ought to be settled fairly to the interest of both parties." [52] Actually employers' associations were often weak organizations, stingily buttressed with funds and weak in membership loyalty.[53] Nor were workers always hostile to such groups. Gompers informed an investigating group in 1900: "I believe in the organization of the employers; I believe in the organization of labor. I believe that the organized forces meeting with each other will be governed by reason, and that they will respect each other by reason of the power that they have. In the beginning they will fear each other, but in time that fear will wear off, and they will . . . try to avoid by every means within their power any open hostilities, the cessation of work, strikes, or lockouts." [54]

Typical Associations (New York: Macmillan Company, 1922), pp. 21–24; Willoughby, *loc. cit.*, p. 110.

[52] Testimony of Thomas J. Hogan, *Report of the Industrial Commission,* VII, 861–873.

[53] Testimony of W. H. Sayward, *ibid.,* VII, 856.

[54] Testimony of Samuel Gompers, *ibid.,* VII, 648.

AMERICAN IDEALS AND UNIONIZATION

It is debatable whether the hostility of employers was as important an obstacle to union organization as the indifference of the American worker. The Boston Herald wrote in 1877: "The young American mechanic of ideas [looks] out for Number One. He is not so anxious about the number of hours he shall work, or the pay he shall receive, or the privileges he shall enjoy." [55] Steeped in the national ethic of individualism and self-reliance ("every tub must stand upon its own bottom") the discontented American worker did not turn instinctively to associations as a means of redress but changed his job or bosses or transferred, if possible, to the ranks of the self-employed. At the end of the century one of the hardest tasks before the American Federation of Labor was organizing the unorganized majority.[56] In this task, in spite of influences to the contrary, there were underlying aspects of the American tradition upon which labor could count.

One of these was the Christian faith. That is not to say that organized Christianity favored the organization of unions and that all pastors and priests aided the movement. Rather, many conservative Protestant clergymen thundered in press and pulpit against the evils of the labor movement,[57] and Powderly's career, in spite of the fact that Cardinal Gibbons astutely prevented papal condemnation of the Knights of Labor,[58] was a long record of harassment and condemnation by Roman Catholic priest and prelate.[59]

But America was a Christian nation and the Bible narrative (Genesis 4.9) early raised the question, "Am I my brother's keeper?" and apparently answered it affirmatively. The union movement was able to utilize effectively the theme of brotherhood and fraternity. Particularly was this true of the Knights of Labor. Its motto was an "Injury to one is the concern of all." Its concept of brotherhood was wide enough to embrace as members Negroes, immigrants, women, and unskilled workers. Lawyers, bankers, gamblers, and liquor dealers were excluded from the movement.[60] Indeed the resemblance of the Knights to a church was

[55] Boston *Herald,* March 8, 1877, quoted in R. T. Berthoff, *British Immigrants in Industrial America, 1790–1950,* p. 88.

[56] Testimony of Samuel Gompers, *Report of the Industrial Commission,* VII, 605.

[57] Henry F. May, *Protestant Churches and Industrial America* (New York: Harper & Brothers, 1949), pp. 52–57.

[58] John Tracy Ellis, *The Life of James Cardinal Gibbons, Archbishop of Baltimore, 1834–1921* (Milwaukee: Bruce Publishing Company, 1952), I, 486–546.

[59] Terence V. Powderly, *The Path I Trod* (New York: Columbia University Press, 1940), pp. 317–382.

[60] *Ibid.,* pp. 61, 143.

striking. Its original name was the Noble and Holy Order of the Knights of Labor. Ofttimes the decision to join was akin to conversion. Powderly became dedicated to the cause of the workingman after an address by John Siney: "I could see Christ in his face and hear a new Sermon on the Mount." [61] Prospective members were theoretically examined in their labor faith much as deacons in a Protestant church might scrutinize the validity of the "experience" of a convert; and the initiate went through a ceremony in a "Sanctuary . . . furnished with an altar and a Bible." The concluding service had prayers and a hymn, recited by all:

> God of the granite and the rose,
> Soul of archangel and the bee,
> The mighty tide of being flows,
> Through all thy creatures, back to Thee.
> Thus round and round the circle runs
> Infinite sea without a shore
> 'Til men and angels, stars and suns
> Unite to praise Thee, evermore.[62]

To placate suspicious churchmen, particularly in the Catholic hierarchy, the Knights sloughed off much of this religious atmosphere. That did not mean that the labor movement up to that time could have got along without the idea of brotherhood. William Sylvis, leader of the National Labor Union, felt like Powderly that unionism was a divine cause,[63] and reluctantly came to believe that the solidarity he advocated must include Negroes; he had been favorable all along to woman's participation.[64]

On the whole the note of personal piety and sense of divine mission petered out in the leaders of the labor movement after the Knights. Gompers was too much of a secularist to claim Christ as a fellow worker or fellow agitator.[65] Brotherhood became less religious and also better implemented. Central to the Federation's success were the benefits which the union provided in sickness, death, and for periods of unemployment. These were partly expedient, for they kept members loyal through thick and thin; they were partly necessary, for neither government nor society had made arrangements for adequate economic and social secu-

[61] *Ibid.*, p. 35.

[62] *Ibid.*, pp. 43–53.

[63] Grossman, *op. cit.*, p. 273; Powderly, *The Path I Trod*, pp. 38–39.

[64] Grossman, *op. cit.*, pp. 226–232.

[65] Testimony of Samuel Gompers, *Report of the Committee* [on Education and Labor] *of the Senate . . . 1885*, I, 374; Testimony of John Jarrett, *ibid.*, I, 1160; Philip Taft, *The A. F. of L. in the Time of Gompers* (New York: Harper & Brothers, 1957), p. 334.

rity. They were also fraternal. "Benevolence and Humanity" was their first object. "It is an old maxim with us that no trades unionist can be buried in potter's field. We wish to have a trades unionist cared for even after death and given a decent burial." [66]

On many counts, the brotherhood of the Federation was less universal than that of its predecessors. In practice the central organization or its affiliates rejected a solidarity broad enough to include all foreigners, women, Negroes, and the unskilled. They recognized that these groups presented problems to organized labor, but in general the high command sought to deal with them in another way than through their regular organizations. Foreigners, for instance, should stay in their own country and Congress should restrict immigration. While women might plead to be organized, a more effective procedure was to make their labor so "expensive" that employers would not hire them to compete with men. Negroes in the South usually had separate unions.[67] Such divisive tendencies were due less to the abandonment of Christian principles than to expediency. Unions were clubs, and social affairs were a large part of their activities. Union members preferred to meet there people of their own background or color.[68]

Employers also preferred to deal with organizations composed of the idealized "American mechanic." Such organizations enabled managers to treat their operatives more selectively by rewarding differences in skill and ability differently. For obvious reasons union leaders did not emphasize this factor. They did, however, assert that organizations of skilled workers knew best the needs of their own members. For instance, how could assorted machinists, grocers, tea dealers, miners and the like know enough about the conditions of the cigar trade to make a contract with employers for the cigar makers? [69] By their possession of specialized talents skilled workers also had qualities which the employer was compelled to pay for; unskilled workers were not in such a position. Perhaps the accompanying decline in the concept of solidarity was bearable by the time of the A. F. of L.; predecessors of which, it was acknowledged, had prepared the way for the acceptance of unionism. Thus in 1886 a communication to the *Official Journal of the Cigar Makers' International Union* asserted: "The K. of L. has attained a thorough unification and identity of interests among the workers." It

[66] Testimony of Samuel Gompers, *Report of the Committee* [on Education and Labor] *of the Senate . . . 1885,* I, 371.

[67] Taft, *op. cit.,* pp. 302–317; *American Federationist,* I (1894), 66–67, 216; III (1897), 244.

[68] Testimony of Samuel Gompers, *Report of the Industrial Commission,* VII. 647.

[69] *Official Journal of the Cigar Makers' International Union,* April, 1886; June, 1886.

has done more toward this goal "than any other organization in existence." [70]

The notion of Christian brotherhood was not the only theme in American ideology which unionism could utilize. Another aspect of American tradition was the habit of majority action and decision. Labor unionists could assert on the one hand that the wishes and anarchical freedom of the individual worker should be subordinate to the good of the whole as seen by the majority of his fellows. On the other hand, they could argue against the employer for the sacred right of association. Labor organizations could justify their worth on the basis of the Declaration of Independence, the Federal Constitution, and the existence of political parties.[71]

Brotherhood and democracy were fused into an amalgam of the ideal worker, union variety. "If it be true that the principles of trade union are correct; that the best way for the individual to obtain and maintain his rights is by uniting with his fellow-men; that it is manly for the workmen of a trade to combine for the common welfare, then I say that the individual who belongs to that trade and does not join with his fellow-workmen is either unintelligent or unmanly. For if he has the intelligence and does not act accordingly, he must be actuated by selfish motives; and to maintain a full, generous manhood, one cannot be selfish and not interested in his fellow-men." [72] Unionism was manliness. To be non-union was to be a "sheep in the slaughtering pen." [73] Since manly qualities were derived from the American environment, it is not surprising they were also the ones admired by "the enemy." Managers and employers believed in self-help and self-reliance, and, as businessmen were currently demonstrating, they also relied upon association and combination as a means of solving their problems.

THE STRIKE

Though there was much in labor's abstract creed that might have appealed to employers, there was much that repelled. The first task of any union, therefore, was to win recognition as the bargaining agency for the workers involved. Usually this involved wrenching recognition from reluctant masters. It could not be done by the exercise of reason; it had to be done by pressure. The common weapon was the strike. A business generation intent on conducting its affairs rationally found this

[70] *Ibid.*, February, 1886.

[71] Mitchell, *op. cit.*, p. 239; *Official Journal of the Cigar Makers' International Union*, October 10, 1881; January 15, 1882; October 15, 1882.

[72] *Official Journal of the Cigar Makers' International Union*, February 15, 1883.

[73] *Ibid.*, October, 1885.

resort to conflict insupportable. Employers quickly hastened to point out to their workers that they couldn't win. Though they preferred generally to have others, often labor leaders or reformers, point out that capitalists had the largest resources and could repel an attack or last out a siege more easily than those who depended upon their daily wage for bread,[74] employers themselves stressed they were already on close margins of profit and that acceptance of the union's demands in the matter of wages, for instance, "was not in the business." [75] This argument was convincing enough to trigger labor's demand that the states or nation establish commissioners of labor statistics to provide accurate information on profits and other matters, to give the unions a look at the books [76] and to lead some unions to countenance wage-scales ("scales of prices") fluctuating with the market or selling price of services and commodities.[77]

In the flurry of controversy over strikes, state officials as well as labor leaders began counting strikes and trying to attach labels of success or failure to them. The resulting summations were inconclusive, for it was hard to define a strike and distinguish it from a lockout. Still, after making one of the earliest of such summaries for Massachusetts, Carroll D. Wright wrote that of the conclusions to be drawn from it "the first and most obvious is plainly this: *Strikes generally prove powerless to benefit the condition of the wage classes.*" He went on to add that strikes tended permanently to deprive strikers of work, for manufacturers moved their plants to more salubrious districts or introduced machinery displacing the skilled worker who had struck. "Lastly, *strikes lead to improvidence, and are demoralizing in their effect upon the workingman.*" [78]

Workers, even organized ones, were far from rejecting conclusions of this sort. The National Labor Union deprecated strikes except as a last resort,[79] and the Knights of Labor resolved in 1883 "that strikes are deplorable in their effect and contrary to the best interests of the

[74] Carroll D. Wright, "The Amalgamated Association of Iron and Steel Workers," *Quarterly Journal of Economics*, VII (July, 1893), 419; Testimony of George McNeill, *Report of the Industrial Commission*, VII, 114–115.

[75] *Official Journal of the Cigar Makers' International Union*, December 15, 1882; Testimony of Joseph Medill, *Report of the Committee* [on Education and Labor] *of the Senate . . . 1885*, II, 992–993; Testimony of R. D. Layton, *ibid.*, I, 10–11.

[76] Testimony of Adolph Strasser, *Report of the Committee* [on Education and Labor] *of the Senate . . . 1885*, I, 461–462; Testimony of P. J. McGuire, *ibid.*, I, 327–328; Testimony of F. K. Foster, *ibid.*, I, 86–88.

[77] Testimony of John Jarrett, *Report of the Committee* [on Education and Labor] *of the Senate . . . 1885*, I, 1119; "Treatise" by "a Pittsburgh Lawyer," *ibid.*, II, 341; Carroll D. Wright, "The National Amalgamated Association of Iron and Steel Workers, 1892–1901," *Quarterly Journal of Economics*, XVI (November, 1901), 42.

[78] *Eleventh Annual Report of the* [Mass.] *Bureau of Statistics of Labor . . . 1880*, pp. 65–71.

[79] G. N. Grob, "Reform Unionism: The National Labor Union," *loc. cit.*, p. 133.

order."[80] Actually the policy of the Knights was somewhat of a straddle. Its leaders believed in strikes only as a "last resort."[81] Needless to say, this approach hardly led to enthusiasm or vigor in their conduct.[82] The American Federation of Labor or its affiliates adopted in theory a somewhat harder policy. To Gompers, McGuire, and Strasser, the strike was not warfare but "reason"; strikes were never lost, for they were "educative." Like the pre-Civil War "turnouts," they educated the public in the grievances of labor, and, as McGuire said, "I don't know what the employers think. They are a rather stupid set. They never learn anything until it is very late and they have to be taught through a strike or two." Strikes also developed "grit" and "manhood" in the workers involved,[83] a variant of the old theme that the blood of the martyrs is the seed of the Church.

Actually all labor organizations were constantly searching for a substitute for the civil war that was the strike. Many outside the movement joined this quest. A magic word, "arbitration," was discovered. When the Knights of Labor used it, as they did frequently, they meant simply negotiation between the parties in interest. Arbitration was equivalent to recognition of the union and a subsequent agreement between employers and employees. To others, the word meant submission of the issue to outside parties for adjudication. This was the way courts and judges handled conflicts of interest. Naturally the essential maintenance of railroad traffic lent particular urgency to the search for a substitute for strikes. After considerable investigation, tentativeness, and bitter experience, Congress in 1889 provided for controversies which might "hinder, impede, obstruct, interrupt, or affect" the interstate transportation of persons and property. If disputants chose arbitration, each selected an arbitrator, and these selected a third. Otherwise, the President on his own volition could select three commissioners, one of whom should be the United States Commissioner of Labor. These agencies were to investigate the dispute and make recommendations, the enforcement of which depended apparently upon public opinion.[84] Since the first alternative was never used, and the second only once, in the Chicago Railroad

[80] Ware, *op. cit.*, p. 132.

[81] Powderly, *The Path I Trod*, pp. 104–105, 115.

[82] Ware, *op. cit.*, pp. 117–154.

[83] Testimony of Adolph Strasser, *Report of the Committee* [on Education and Labor] *of the Senate . . . 1885*, I, 463; Testimony of Samuel Gompers, *ibid.*, I, 366, 372; Testimony of P. J. McGuire, *ibid.*, I, 321–323, 354; Testimony of Samuel Gompers, *Report of the Industrial Commission*, VII, 600, 607, 608, 619–620; *Official Journal of the Cigar Makers' International Union*, January 15, 1883.

[84] C. P. Neill, "Mediation and Arbitration of Railway Labor Disputes in the United States," *Bulletin of the Bureau of Labor* No. 98 (January, 1912), pp. 26–27.

Strike of 1894,[85] Congress in 1898 passed the Erdmann Act, providing first for the voluntary submission of disputes to mediators and then, in case of their failure and in certain circumstances, to a board of arbitration. The findings of the latter were to be binding upon both parties for a year and enforceable in the courts.[86] In truth compulsory arbitration by outside parties was unacceptable to both parties in the dispute. Employers did not want those unacquainted with the business or unconcerned with its operation to determine what the earnings of the enterprise should be. Employees could not be made to work on terms not of their choosing—that was slavery.[87]

THE BOYCOTT

If this was as far as an overriding public interest could move, employees and employers in most industries preferred to stick to their own ways. In the case of unions, this meant a search for means of pressure other than strikes. One was the boycott, "a chameleon that is impossible of definition." [88] Actually the boycott in America generally took two forms. Workers, as producers, might refuse to work on material, for example wooden trim or stone, which they considered was produced under unfair conditions. As consumers, they could refuse to purchase goods made under conditions designated as unfair. If these boycotts were applied directly against the manufacturer whose policy furnished the grievance, they were primary; if they were employed to compel third parties (other producers, marketers, workers or consumers) to join the movement, they were secondary boycotts.[89] As might be expected, the Knights of Labor, in view of the primitive state of unionization and of their hostility to the strike weapon, were in the eighties great advocates of boycotts; indeed, the Knights had a "boycott Department." The international unions in the American Federation of Labor employed the boycott perhaps less systematically, though the *American Federationist* published a list of boycotted firms under the heading, "We Don't Patronize." [90]

The boycott ordinarily meant the workers did not assume the hazard of surrendering their jobs, and on the face of it seemed to involve less

[85] *Ibid.*, p. 28.

[86] 30 *United States Statutes,* 424.

[87] *American Federationist,* I (September, 1894), 147.

[88] Leo Wolman, "The Boycott in American Trade Unions," *Johns Hopkins University Studies in Historical and Political Science* (Baltimore: Johns Hopkins Press, 1916), Series XXXIV, No. 1, p. 10n.

[89] *Ibid.*, pp. 10–15.

[90] *Ibid.*, pp. 24–36; Taft, *op. cit.*, pp. 264–266.

open violence than labor conflicts. About their legality there was, nevertheless, considerable uncertainty. State courts tended to look upon secondary boycotts with disfavor but to regard primary ones as permissible.[91] The great punitive decisions against the legality of boycotts came after this period.[92] But, as it did so many issues, the Chicago Railroad Strike of 1894 raised that of the secondary boycott, for the members of the American Railway Union had refused to handle Pullman cars. On this particular point the court's decision avoided refinement of analysis by burying the boycott under the right of the national government to assure the running of trains in interstate commerce.

Boycotts were negative in character. The unions devised a more positive variant in the union label attached to goods produced under approved conditions. On the union label the high command of the A. F. of L. set great store.[93] It had all the advantages of the boycott and, besides, was legal.[94]

MORE AND BETTER STRIKES

Instead of inventing substitutes for the strike, union leaders spent considerable time and energy lessening the gamble involved in calling them. Since the strike was, after all, their most effective weapon, it was plausible not to abolish it but improve it. This was even true of the Knights of Labor, which deplored strikes; it was truer of the A. F. of L.

In both organizations the general pattern of control was to require at the local level a greater than a mere majority for an affirmative strike vote, and, even better, to transfer the decision to the high command of the union. It alone could authorize strikes and only "authorized" strikes were entitled to assistance from the strike fund or reserve which officers sought to accumulate, not at the local level but at the national one.[95] Local decisions were apt to be impetuous, taken in the heat of the moment when men were smarting under a particular grievance.[96] It took

[91] Harry W. Laidler, *Boycotts and the Labor Struggle: Economic and Legal Aspects* (New York: John Lane Company, 1913), pp. 177–199.

[92] Harold U. Faulkner, *The Decline of Laissez Faire, 1897–1917* (New York: Holt, Rinehart and Winston, Inc., 1951), pp. 298–299.

[93] Testimony of Samuel Gompers, *Report of the Industrial Commission,* VII, 628–630; *American Federationist,* II (July, 1895), 91; IV (August, 1897), 143–144.

[94] Laidler, *op. cit.,* pp. 169–170.

[95] Testimony of Adolph Strasser, *Report of the Committee* [on Education and Labor] *of the Senate . . . 1885,* I, 463; *Official Journal of the Cigar Makers' International Union,* January 15, 1883; September, 1883; October, 1885; *American Federationist,* I (September, 1894), 140–144; Testimony of Samuel Gompers, *Report of the Industrial Commission,* VII, 609; Ware, *op. cit.,* pp. 117–134; Ulman, *op. cit.,* pp. 155–173.

[96] Testimony of Samuel Gompers, *Report of the Industrial Commission,* VII, 607.

cool wisdom to decide when was the right time to strike. Only the central command could know the resources of the union and whether they were sufficient to last through a conflict; only they could know whether the general conditions of the market and industry held out some promise of success. For bitter experience had demonstrated that "justice" had little to do with a strike's success. "Justice is but an abstract theory." The facts showed that strikes in a falling market or in a period of falling prices were apt to be failures.[97] Ancillary to the centralization of decision-making was the union's insistence upon a closed shop and upon limiting the number of apprentices lest the employer build up within his enterprise a competing army of non-union mercenaries.[98]

Refine it as you would, the strike remained warfare. As long as the harsher aspects of its use were avoided, the case of unions was likely to make a greater appeal to "the common sense of justice" and to "public opinion." The latter "in a republic . . . is apt to sympathize with the laborers, as the more numerous party and presumably in greater distress." [99] Or as a much-buffeted Pinkerton operator once commented derisively, "The workingmen are always right." [100] But violence and rioting usually soon dissipated this inherent advantage.

The constant newspaper repetition of the surmise that labor disputes threatened to import the horrors of the "Paris Commune" of 1870 into the United States was not so convincing a demonstration of this popular attitude as the national reaction to the Haymarket Riot in Chicago on May 4, 1886. The setting of this incident was complex. Workers were organizing to attain through a version of a "general strike," if need be, an eight-hour day; a small group of radical thinkers, justly characterized as anarchists, who boiled with rhetorical violence over the unjust organization of society, had some followers in the Chicago working class movement. When police intervention in a long-continued strike in the McCormick works resulted in the death of a striker, the radicals called a meeting of protest in Haymarket Square. At first this proved to be a rather dull affair. As it was coming to a close a detail of police entered the square and called upon the meeting to disperse. A bomb fell near the head of the police column. One policeman was instantly killed and

[97] *Official Journal of the Cigar Makers' International Union,* October 10, 1881; October 15, 1882.

[98] Testimony of Samuel Gompers, *Report of the Industrial Commission,* VII, 620–621, 657; *Official Journal of the Cigar Makers' International Union,* October 15, 1882.

[99] N. P. Gilman, *Profit Sharing between Employer and Employee* (Boston: Houghton Mifflin and Company, 1889), pp. 4, 6; Herbert G. Gutman, "The Iron Workers' Strike in the Ohio Valley, 1873–1874," *Ohio Historical Quarterly,* LXVIII (October, 1959), 357–358.

[100] Testimony of Charles Remke, Report of the Select Committee of the Senate on the Use of Pinkertons, *loc. cit.,* p. 36.

six others were fatally wounded. In an atmosphere of national hysteria, some of the anarchists were arrested as accessories to murder and, though the bomb thrower was never identified nor any exact connection established between him and the anarchists, seven of the latter were condemned and sentenced to hang. Ultimately four paid this penalty. One committed suicide. Governor Altgeld in 1893 pardoned those whose sentences had been commuted.[101] Henry C. Adams, the economist and public servant, wrote to Henry D. Lloyd, "I cannot see but that it is a good law, upon which they are convicted; whether the evidence supported the theory or not, I cannot say." [102]

More to the point was the reaction of organized labor. Samuel Gompers, whose central organization had initiated the eight-hour drive, protested the conduct and result of the anarchists' trial and pled with the Governor to pardon the convicted men. Gompers tried "to keep a cool head," "to be manly and not cringing." [103] The journal of the Knights of Labor, which had opposed the eight-hour campaign, characterized the anarchists as "cowardly, murderers, cutthroats and robbers," deserving "no more consideration than wild beasts." Later, however, it doubted the wisdom of the executions.[104] In the interest of balance it should be pointed out that while Marshall Field and some capitalists were hot for execution, Potter Palmer, also a great merchant, appealed for leniency, and few worked more diligently to reverse an injustice and prevent its repetition than Lyman J. Gage, whose conservatism was attested to by his presidency of the American Bankers Association, his advocacy of the gold standard, and by his becoming Secretary of the Treasury in the McKinley administration.[105]

Some observers ascribe the cataclysmic decline of the Knights of Labor after 1886 to a very tenuous connection between that organization and one of the anarchists.[106] Anyway, as Gompers observed, the Haymarket "catastrophe" "halted our eight-hour program." [107] Verily violence was unhealthy. In spite of the danger of playing with fire, Gompers in the Homestead Strike (it involved a constituent member of the

[101] Bessie L. Pierce, *A History of Chicago* (New York: Alfred A. Knopf, 1957), III, 273–289; Henry David, *The History of the Haymarket Affair, A Study in the American Social Revolutionary and Labor Movements* (New York: Farrar & Rinehart, 1936), *passim.*

[102] Quoted in Pierce, *op. cit.*, III, 284.

[103] Quoted in Taft, *op. cit.*, pp. 66–67.

[104] Quoted in Pierce, *op. cit.*, III, 280; 385n.

[105] Pierce, *op. cit.*, III, 285–286, 288; "Lyman Judson Gage" *Dictionary of American Biography,* VII, 85–86.

[106] Ware, *op. cit.*, pp. 316–319.

[107] Samuel Gompers, *Seventy Years of Life and Labor, An Autobiography* (New York: G. P. Dutton and Company, 1925), I, 294.

A. F. of L.) enterprisingly took steps to discourage the arrival of strike-breakers and raised funds and contributed his abilities to the defense of the strikers indicted after the battle.[108] Two years later in the Chicago Railroad Strike the strikers apparently hoped for considerable assistance from the A. F. of L. Though no affiliate of the Federation was involved, Gompers was on friendly terms with Debs. But the Federation high command adopted a statement frowning upon a general strike. The Federation did not wish to be placed in a position of arraying the working classes "in open hostility to federal authority . . . nor will we occupy it without a protest." The Federation did organize a fund for the defense of Debs. The amount raised was about a fifth of that in the Homestead case.[109]

As a result of his varied experiences, Gompers a few years later was assuring the Industrial Commission that unions discouraged violence. "We are citizens of this country, as much interested in it, in its welfare and in its tranquility, as any man who makes up the great citizenship of the United States. We are opposed to riots and riotous conduct, be that during a strike or during industrial peace." This statement was a phase of labor's program of selling to employers and the public the idea that permanently organized workers constituted responsible unionism, that impromptu and *ad hoc* labor action was the real danger. A businessman could not have said it better than did Gompers: "We recognize that peaceful industry is necessary to successful civilized life." [110]

Some observers have asserted that the growth of unionism led to a growing "conservatism" in strike policy.[111] The figures do not support this conclusion. Taking 1881–1885 as a base for his calculations, Paul Douglas has demonstrated that in the remaining years of the nineteenth century the number of strikes and strikers considerably more than doubled. Both figures trailed along on a sort of high plateau from 1886 to 1900. While in the nineties the relative frequency of strikes in proportion to the number of industrial wage earners dipped somewhat, the percentage of all strikes ordered by labor unions increased from 53 in 1881–1885 to 67 in 1891–1895 and 62 in 1896–1900. "The conclusion seems inescapable that union organization is accompanied by a tremendous increase in the strike rate." [112]

[108] Taft, *op. cit.*, pp. 136–137.

[109] *Ibid.*, pp. 80–81, 83, 136; Ginger, *op. cit.*, pp. 148–150.

[110] Testimony of Samuel Gompers, *Report of the Industrial Commission,* VII, 604, 606–607, 610–611, 648.

[111] Testimony of Rufus R. Wade, *ibid.*, VII, 70.

[112] Paul H. Douglas, "An Analysis of Strike Statistics, 1881–1921," *Journal of the American Statistical Association,* New Series, XVIII (September, 1923), 869–872, 876–877.

CHAPTER XIX

Programs and Philosophy of Organized Labor

HAZARDS AND CHARMS OF POLITICAL ACTION

LABOR had always had an alternative to boycotts and strikes—politics. There was much to recommend it. Some issues—prison-made goods, immigration restriction, child labor—could only be handled by legislation, if at all. Economic pressure against employers could not repeal statutes hampering labor organizations or strike the blinders from the eyes of judges. Politics was a means of action as useful in a falling as in a rising market. It did not call for the men to leave their tools and machines; it simply asked them to go to the ballot box and vote their interests. This had the consecration of being the democratic and the American way. The auguries of success were favorable. As employers were all too well aware, there were more workers than there were managers,[1] and, besides, the former could call on reformers sympathetic to labor's cause. From Massachusetts, where an old pillar of anti-slavery, Wendell Phillips,[2] maintained the momentum of agitation in behalf of labor, to Illinois, where the members of Hull House, a Chicago settlement house, conducted investigations and drew up legislation, such outsiders lent aid.[3]

As in the case of economic pressure, resort to political action involved decisions by the union as to when to act and as to the methods employed. Through logic and pressing necessity, labor came quickly to see that it must aid in the defense of its oppressed members before the

[1] E. C. Kirkland, *Dream and Thought in the Business Community, 1860–1900* (Ithaca: Cornell University Press, 1956), pp. 127–132, 141–142.

[2] Testimony of George E. McNeill, *Report of the Industrial Commission,* VII, 113–114.

[3] Josephine Goldmark, *Impatient Crusader* (Urbana: University of Illinois Press, 1953), pp. 20–35.

courts, especially since judicial decisions concerned larger issues than the fate of individuals at the bar. Such occasional stabs at political action did not involve complex organization; appeals could be made for funds through existing labor journals and through correspondence. Legislation was a more subtle matter, for the simple constitutional right of petition required the maintenance of a lobby. Among other things, this was expensive. Though the National Labor Union demanded a lobby, it was not until the mid-eighties that Powderly was proposing that the Knights set up a lobby in every state capital and in Washington to push labor bills and keep tabs on legislators.[4]

But lobbies faced much the same difficulty as strike pickets; somehow they were more "educative" and "persuasive" when they represented strength and could promise rewards and threaten reprisals. One way to achieve this effectiveness was to vote for trade union members who ran for public office; a second was to vote for the friends and punish the enemies of labor, no matter on what ticket they were running, a procedure quaintly termed non-partisanship. The Knights adopted both these measures. In 1886 the General Assembly resolved: "We will hold responsible at the ballot box all members of Congress who neglect or refuse to vote in compliance" with the Knights' demands.[5] Thirdly labor could go it alone by establishing its own political party or combine with others to do so. The National Labor Union had done this in 1870–1872.[6] At the end of the seventies the Knights of Labor were half way in the Greenback-Labor Party and seemed likely to repeat the commitment in 1886, but the next year Powderly reverted to his fundamental non-partisan stand.[7]

The leaders of the American Federation of Labor and its constituent unions were generally non-political, though they were less vacillating than Powderly and more forceful verbally. In 1885 P. J. McGuire of the Carpenters was expressing his disillusionment with labor legislation. Such laws Democrats and Republicans made to fool the workers, not to be enforced. "We have come to the conclusion that wherever we can help ourselves we will do it, without asking the aid of the Government, and if we want to make a law we will make it in our own trades unions and try to enforce it through them by contracts with our employers." [8] Years later, Samuel Gompers summarized what history had taught him:

[4] Norman Ware, *The Labor Movement in the United States, 1860–1895* (New York: D. Appleton and Company, 1929), pp. 10, 358–359.

[5] *Ibid.*, p. 361.

[6] G. B. Grob, "Reform Unionism: The National Labor Union," *Journal of Economic History*, XIV (1954), 133–134.

[7] Ware, *op. cit.*, pp. 361–364.

[8] Testimony of P. J. McGuire, *Report of the Committee* [on Education and Labor] *of the Senate . . . 1885*, I, 340.

"An independent labor and progressive movement was inaugurated by the National Labor Union and David Davis of Illinois was nominated for the Presidency in 1872. The National Labor Union never held another convention. It had spent its force; it had nominated a candidate for president." [9]

It required conviction, courage and parliamentary skill for Gompers to keep the Federation on the non-political course, for the Socialist-Labor Party, boring from within the union ranks, sought direct representation at the Federation's meetings and, in the mid-nineties, presented an eleven-point political program introduced with a preamble proposing, as in Great Britain, "the principle of independent labor politics as an auxiliary to their economic action." The depression of 1893 and the hard knocks union organization had taken, as at Homestead, gave the Socialists their chance. In the main battle Gompers put down the insurgents, but at the Denver Convention of 1894 he lost the presidency of the Federation for the only time during his life as labor leader. In Socialist eyes the defeat of their program committed the Federation to an "opportunistic political line." [10] Such episodes also convinced believers in pure and simple trade unionism that association with reformers was not a one-way street.

While such evidence would seem to demonstrate that the conspicuous national organizations were moving from political to industrial weapons, other labor groupings provide evidence for a contrary conclusion. Since the structure of American political action was not corporate but geographical, political activity by organized labor naturally clustered about organizations on a geographical basis, state or urban aggregations. Since urban labor unions were apt to embrace more foreign or Socialist members, their influence helped to push central labor unions along the path of politics. Thus in New York City the call for the establishment of the Central Labor Union was issued in 1881 by a member of a Socialist local assembly of the Knights of Labor, and the Central's Declaration of Principles re-echoed Socialist slogans about the class struggle and the desirability of political action. Its constitution included the precautionary provisions that the union should have no permanent president lest he "sell out the union to any political party" and no public official or lawyer could be a delegate to the union. By 1886 the Central Labor Union was debating in an abstract fashion whether labor should take independent

[9] Samuel Gompers, *Seventy Years of Life and Labor, An Autobiography* (New York: E. P. Dutton and Company, 1925), II, 268.

[10] Howard H. Quint, *The Forging of American Socialism: Origins of the Modern Movement* (Columbia: University of South Carolina Press, 1953), pp. 60–71; Gompers, *op. cit.*, I, 356–360, 384–389, 391–397; II, 268–269.

political action or try to swing its followers from party to party in a balance-of-power policy.[11]

A famous boycott case in New York City in which the judge sentenced the boycotters to Sing Sing for "extortion" (they had collected $1000 from the employer through arbitration) gave urgency to a program of participation in politics and seemed to reenforce the necessity of independent political action.[12] Through a series of accommodations, the Central Labor Union nominated the single tax reformer, Henry George, for mayor. The Democrats under Tammany Hall nominated Abram S. Hewitt, the philanthropist employer, and the Republicans, young Theodore Roosevelt. The excitement of the campaign and the criticalness of the issue so infected the high command of labor that Terence Powderly and Samuel Gompers spoke and worked for Henry George. Hewitt won, George was second, Roosevelt third.[13] On their roles as participants, both Powderly and Gompers had sober second thoughts. The former wrote of 1887, "I am glad I didn't talk [for George] this year," [14] and the latter characterized the 1886 campaign as "this curious determination to disregard experience." [15]

The New York campaign of 1886 did not have to surmount all the customary handicaps to labor's political action. The George candidacy had a campaign chest, an *ad hoc* journal, a roster of speakers and a force of volunteer workers. But it collided with some powerful advantages of the established parties. This was a period of intense political loyalties, partly inherited from the Civil War days; the habit of independent voting was not widespread. Nor were all political issues aligned along the axis of the labor-capital controversy. Workers were citizens and party members before they were workers. Politics, like religion, was a divisive factor and astute labor leaders tried to keep it out of the labor organizations. That was why lawyers were not allowed in the Knights of Labor. This was a period when politics became a business, the period of the machine. Neither a successful lobby nor a third party could be improvised; politics required full-time, sophisticated attention, and labor leaders in politics were part-time amateurs who lacked know-how and staying power. Curiously enough their political ideology reflected that

[11] Peter A. Speek, "The Singletax and the Labor Movement," *Bulletin of the University of Wisconsin* No. 878, *Economics and Political Science Series*, VIII, 270–283; Testimony of P. J. McGuire, *loc. cit.*, pp. 808–813.

[12] Speek, *op. cit.*, pp. 304–307.

[13] *Ibid.*, pp. 69, 308–315; Charles A. Barker, *Henry George* (New York: Oxford University Press, 1955), pp. 453–481; Allan Nevins, *Abram S. Hewitt, with Some Account of Peter Cooper* (New York: Harper & Brothers, 1925), pp. 460–469.

[14] Quoted in Ware, *op. cit.*, p. 363.

[15] Gompers, *Seventy Years of Life and Labor*, I, 312.

of the employers. Politics was dishonest, a dirty business. The labor union cause, like private business enterprise, became a sort of holy grail, above or beyond politics.[16] Furthermore, like their business counterparts, some union leaders thought government action was really futile and wrong. P. J. McGuire affirmed, "I believe the Government had better keep its hands off private business as much as possible." [17]

LABOR LEGISLATION

Although labor legislation in extent and enforcement fell short of the expectations of the more hopeful, the record was not one of absolute failure. At the end of the century an agent of the Industrial Commission surveyed the status of protective legislation. Just over half the states had legislation prohibiting the labor of children in factories; the age limitation was ordinarily fourteen but some additional years were added if the children lacked education. The states which did not have child labor laws were generally in the trans-Mississippi West or in the South. Nearly every Eastern state had passed legislation regulating the hours of labor for women and minors of both sexes in factories and mercantile establishments. The general limitation was to ten hours a day and sixty hours a week, though Massachusetts had a fifty-eight hour week and Wisconsin a forty-eight. About half the states had factory acts, so called after the great English factory act of 1831, enforcing certain standards of safety and sanitation in factories and sometimes other establishments. There were almost no factory acts in the South or beyond the Mississippi. In the chief industrial states of the East and Midwest there were generally laws providing for the licensing, inspection and, in Pennsylvania, the prohibition of sweatshops. Such establishments usually produced clothing, artificial flowers, and cigars in tenements or houses. Practically all the states "in which mines of any character are located" had mining laws providing for mining inspectors to see that operators obeyed provisions for escape shafts, ventilation, safety lamps, and for care in carrying and hoisting products and personnel and in handling explosives. Laws on the statute books were not self-enforcing and much of this legislation perforce dealt with definitions and details of administration.[18]

That the trans-Mississippi West in general stood aloof from this movement was due to its agricultural preoccupations; that the South did so was due, in part, to its desire to establish industries and not handicap their advance. In truth, the cutthroat competition among states for industrial growth was one reason for the general slowness in passing this

[16] Speek, *op. cit.*, p. 281; Ware, *op. cit.*, pp. 355–356.
[17] Testimony of P. J. McGuire, *loc. cit.*, p. 328.
[18] *Report of the Industrial Commission*, V, 30–31, 39–42, 100–118, 232 ff.

legislation and laxness in enforcing it. The difficulty of securing uniform legislation, where the central government had limited powers within a federal system, exasperated both employers and employees,[19] and, among other things, explained the latter's disillusionment with political activity.

Some ascribed the movement for legislation to employers or to government officials, such as commissioners of statistics for labor, who had come to look upon themselves as the guardians of labor's interests.[20] Others, like McNeill of Massachusetts, felt that the "initiative" for such legislation came "in every instance" from labor men. More commonly the state of mind of the community was felt to be responsible. "I do not believe Massachusetts would have accomplished what she has done in the way of factory legislation unless there had been enough sense of justice in the leisure class and the educated class to uphold the work of the workingman, and not only uphold it but aid it actively." [21] As usual Gompers had the common sense of the matter: "What is everybody's business is nobody's business, and organized labor makes it its business and then has the sympathy of the general public to come in and aid." [22]

THE VALUE OF LABOR

Whether wrung at first instance from employers or realized at second hand in legislation, the program of organized labor took off from certain assumptions. Perhaps these are best summarized in the bald assertion of the Grand Secretary of the Knights of Labor: "We know we have produced the wealth." [23] The theory that labor was the source of all value was as commonplace with the Federation of Labor as it was with the Knights.[24] It followed that unions were concerned with attaining an acknowledgment of labor's nobility and dignity by community and employer. The reason the Central Labor Union of New York advocated in 1882 an annual Labor Day distinct from other national holidays was

[19] Testimony of S. B. Donnelly, *Report of the Industrial Commission,* VII, 280; Testimony of R. R. Wade, *ibid.,* VII, 75–76; Testimony of J. G. Schonfarber, *ibid.,* VII, 450.

[20] Testimony of G. W. Russell, *Report of the Industrial Commission,* VII, 338–339; Testimony of Mrs. Fanny B. Ames, *ibid.,* VII, 67–68; Testimony of T. C. Search, *ibid.,* VII, 135.

[21] Testimony of G. E. McNeill, *loc. cit.,* p. 113; Testimony of James Campbell, *Report of the Industrial Commission,* VII, 52; Testimony of Miss Clare de Graffenreid, *ibid.,* VII, 232.

[22] Testimony of Samuel Gompers, *Report of the Industrial Commission,* VII, 639.

[23] Testimony of R. D. Layton, *Report of the Committee* [on Education and Labor] *of the Senate . . . 1885,* I, 16.

[24] Testimony of P. H. McLogan, *Report of the Committee* [on Education and Labor] *of the Senate . . . 1885,* I, 578; *Official Journal of the Cigar Makers' International Union,* November, 1885.

that labor alone had no day which it could call its own.[25] Though at least one employer thought this holiday hardly attained its lofty objectives ("drunken rabble, harvest for saloon keepers"),[26] its implied tribute to work certainly ought to have won popular sympathy in a generation which worshipped work and suspected leisure. It did. In 1893 the committee of the Senate investigating Homestead casually remarked in an obiter dictum: "It should not be forgotten that labor is the source of all wealth." [27]

Even wider approval might have been forthcoming if labor's thoughts about its own value had been somewhat less exclusive and somewhat less oblivious of other factors in the productive process. Labor on the whole grudgingly allowed capital a place. After all, capital was "the fruit of labor" and interest "may probably be right." [28] Labor's blind spot was management.[29] "Do not let the man who has no money hire capital to build the factory and to buy the raw material, and pay interest on that money, and then hire money to pay his labor, and make a profit above all that, and hire a superintendent at a good salary to manage the business, and be himself one of the lords of the land—so-called." Paradoxically Gompers preferred the capitalist with an inherited status to the self-made man. It was the fortunes of this latter group—Jay Gould was usually the example—that seemed to be made by some dishonesty or magic; they could not be accounted for by "the natural increase of capital." Parasitic employers should "go into a workshop and earn an honest living instead of undertaking to make money from nothing, absolutely nothing." [30]

THE WAGES SYSTEM

No specific phase of labor union policy was more interpenetrated by the theory that labor created all wealth than was wages; for "the wage question is the labor question." [31] At first organized labor hoped to avoid the complexities, injustice, and industrial strife engendered by the wages

[25] Speek, *loc. cit.*, p. 279.

[26] Will and Maxine Schoyer, *Scaife Company and the Scaife Family, 1802–1952* (Pittsburgh: Davis & Warde, Inc., 1952), p. 139.

[27] Report of the Select Committee of the Senate on the Homestead Strike, *Senate Report* No. 1280 (s.n. 3072), 52d Cong., 2d Sess., p. xiii.

[28] Testimony of Samuel Gompers, *Report of the Committee* [on Education and Labor] *of the Senate . . . 1885,* I, 364.

[29] N. P. Gilman, *Profit Sharing between Employer and Employee* (Boston: Houghton Mifflin & Company, 1899), p. 7.

[30] Testimony of Samuel Gompers, *Report of the Committee* [on Education and Labor] *of the Senate . . . 1885,* I, 366; Testimony of P. H. McLogan, *loc. cit.*, p. 577.

[31] *Official Journal of the Cigar Makers' International Union,* October, 1885.

system. They would abolish it. In his own Moulders' Union and in the National Labor Union William Sylvis became the prophet of producers' cooperation. The moulders would build and operate their own factories and divide all the returns, be they profits or wages. Ultimately such cooperation would end poverty and elevate the workers spiritually and morally.[32] This did not mean that producers' cooperation had solely an idealistic motive; in periods of business depression or after strikes had failed, producers' cooperatives served the practical end of putting people to work.

From time to time the Knights of Labor were enthusiastic over cooperation. In 1885 its Grand Secretary, for instance, was rather impatient with his unions' concern with wages. This was a mere short-time matter "while we remain wage workers." Instead the Knights desired to solve the problem of just distribution "by going into business for ourselves, contributing our own money, and starting a business of our own."[33] Uriah Stephens, like Sylvis, was a zealot for cooperation, and Terence V. Powderly in his first annual address to the General Assembly in 1880 summoned the Knights to abolish the wage system and embark upon a crusade for cooperation "which will eventually make every man his own master—every man his own employer; a system which will give the laborer a fair proportion of the products of his toil. . . . There is no good reason why labor cannot, through coöperation, own and operate mines, factories and railroads."[34] There were always some among the Knights who dragged their feet on this issue; and by the end of the eighties the Order was retreating on this front as on most others.[35]

Though, as a central organization, the Knights of Labor undertook but one cooperative enterprise, a coal mine,[36] its constituent assemblies or trades embarked upon several experiments. Their number in the mid-eighties may have reached 135. They were most numerous in mining, coopering, and shoe-making, occupations in which individual skill continued to play a considerable part. Most cooperative ventures were small, the average amount of investment per establishment being $10,000.[37] Most cooperatives failed, and those that did not assumed an organizational form far from flawless. The original investors among the workingmen became a directoral élite interested in profits; they employed other

[32] Jonathan Grossman, *William Sylvis, Pioneer of American Labor* (New York: Columbia University Press, 1945), pp. 189–219.

[33] Testimony of R. D. Layton, *loc. cit.*, p. 5.

[34] Ware, *op. cit.*, pp. 320–329; Terence V. Powderly, *The Path I Trod* (New York: Columbia University Press, 1940), pp. 266–270.

[35] Ware, *op. cit.*, pp. 328–329.

[36] *Ibid.*, pp. 329–333.

[37] John R. Commons and others, *History of Labour in the United States* (New York: Macmillan Company, 1918), II, 430–438.

workers at wages, sometimes low ones, and they cut the price of their products to compete with unionized rivals. Surveying these failures and deviations, one observer came to the conclusion that they were due to the effort "to get rid of the *entrepreneur* or manager." In spite of labor's blind spot on this score, managerial talent was necessary and it was rare.[38]

Few experiments by organized labor have stirred so much interest as producers' cooperation and won so much approval, particularly among intellectuals. At one extreme E. L. Godkin of the *Nation* beat the drum for cooperation with the zeal of a Sylvis or a Stephens, and for much the same reasons.[39] At the other extreme a group of reformers like R. T. Ely and E. W. Bemis, for whom Godkin would have had only contempt, undertook a study of cooperative enterprises on a regional basis. According to R. T. Ely, who wrote an introduction for the essays published by the *Johns Hopkins Studies in Historical and Political Science,* the investigators found more significant examples of cooperation in the United States than in England and demonstrated that one of "the prime conditions of success of cooperation is moral integrity of the cooperators. The cause of failure is more frequently ethical than intellectual weakness. This is true of all popular movements and for the mass of men. . . . Christ uttered a scientific truth, confirmed by every careful and intelligent observation of economic phenomena when he said, 'Seek ye first the kingdom of God and His righteousness, and all these things [economic goods] shall be added unto you.'"[40]

The practical men heading the A. F. of L. who had to face the day-to-day problems of labor while expecting that "ultimately" after the passage of ages workers would become their own capitalists and their own employers,[41] in general accepted the wage system and sought to make the best of it rather than to escape to utopia on the installment plan. Since they still adhered to the labor theory of value, they naturally thought labor should have a "prior" claim to the results of the wealth-producing process and that wages should not be determined by profits or dividends. Employers who could not make a profit and pay workers their rightful share should be driven out of industry by the stern rule of the survival of the fittest.[42] As to the proper share for workers, labor

[38] F. A. Walker, quoted in Gilman, *op. cit.,* pp. 39–42; *Nation,* LXVI (June 7, 1888), 462–463.

[39] E. L. Godkin, "Co-operation," *North American Review,* CVI (January, 1868), 157, 175.

[40] E. W. Bemis and others, "History of Coöperation in the United States," *Johns Hopkins University Studies in Historical and Political Science,* VI, 7, 9.

[41] Testimony of P. J. McGuire, *loc. cit.,* pp. 354–355.

[42] Testimony of Samuel Gompers, *Report of the Committee* [on Education and Labor] *of the Senate . . . 1885,* I, 376–378.

leaders were apt to resort to generalities: it should be "just" and "reasonable" and "fair." Since these terms, however useful as slogans, were not self-defining, labor leaders advanced equivalents: a "living" wage, a "decent" wage, enough "to live comfortably." [43] To objectives, so stated, few could take exception; they were, however, a sort of time bomb planted beneath the wage policy of employers. Organized labor, for instance, was not greatly interested in real wages. Their conclusion that cheap goods meant cheap labor revealed a distaste for tying wages to the cost of living. "I believe in high wages and high prices for commodities. . . . When a man has good wages he can save something even if prices are high." Organized labor looked forward to a wage level which would give them a surplus above mere living.[44]

Another complaint of employers was that the unions hoped to set all workers' wages at a uniform standard and thus hampered the paying of wages based on differences in skill and industry. Although Gompers acknowledged that he preferred time to piecework for its "excellence and perfection," he nonetheless felt that superior workers should and would get higher wages. All the union insisted upon was the "life-line" of a minimum wage.[45] Actually the search for definitively just wages has the static quality of most formulas. The economy was dynamic; labor's wage theory was fluid and pragmatic. Said Gompers: "I know we are living under the wage system, and so long as that lasts, it is our purpose to secure a continually larger share for labor, for the wealth producers. Whether the time shall come, as this constantly increasing share to labor goes on, when profits shall be entirely eliminated, and the full product of labor, the net result of production, go to the laborer . . . I am perfectly willing that the future shall determine and work out." [46]

THE EIGHT HOUR DAY

While labor's wage policy was for more and more, its policy on hours was for less and less. On this question, to an exceptional degree in labor history, the unions operated on the basis of a thought-out creed, which, coming early in the period, resembled a theological doctrine. In the sixties, Ira Steward, a self-educated machinist of Boston, began

[43] Testimony of Samuel Gompers, *Report of the Industrial Commission,* VII, 614, 645; Testimony of J. S. McClelland, *Report of the Committee* [on Education and Labor] *of the Senate . . . 1885,* I, 144–145.

[44] Testimony of Robert Howard, *Report of the Committee* [on Education and Labor] *of the Senate . . . 1885,* I, 641–642; Testimony of W. G. Moody, *ibid.,* I, 739–740; Testimony of Edward King, *ibid.,* I, 689–690.

[45] Testimony of Samuel Gompers, *Report of the Industrial Commission,* VII, 605, 613.

[46] *Ibid.,* VII, 645.

propagandizing the advantages of the eight-hour day. This was daring, for two decades later at least one manufacturer thought "ten hours a day is about right for a day's labor." [47] Steward's visionary concept went further than a minor improvement in the status quo. He felt that the workers, having attained greater leisure, would look around and see how others spent it—even the exhibitionist expenditures of the rich had utility—and thus develop their own cultural and social interests. As a result of their uplifted status, they would demand higher wages. As Steward's wife, an able woman, put it in a jingle:

> Whether you work by the piece or work by the day
> Decreasing the hours increases your pay.[48]

When workers had wants and the means to satisfy them, there would be an end to the underconsumption responsible for unemployment and for business depression. The shortening of the work day need not reduce production, for improved methods and machinery would compensate.

While these happy outcomes might appeal to employers, Steward's further inference that eventually his system would so erode profits that the glory of the cooperative commonwealth would come in could hardly reassure them.[49] Quite clearly Steward's ideas, like those of Henry George and Edward Bellamy, involved a new order of society. Luckily they had the advantage of combining a short-range objective and a long-range cure-all. The latter, like most panaceas, was almost too easy and automatic. Since the shortened day fitted in with reformist optimism, with the efforts of practical men to cope with the unemployment of depression, and with the natural human desire to cut down hours of labor, the eight-hour program in one gloss or another colored the thinking of labor organizations for decades.[50] Originally workers expected to realize the program through agitation and legislation. The diversity of state jurisdictions and the consequent fear in each state lest producers in another get an advantage pointed to the desirability of Congressional legislation. Nearly everyone agreed, however, that the Constitution had given the central government no power directly to regulate hours in private industry.

[47] Testimony of T. M. Miller, *Report of the Committee* [on Education and Labor] *of the Senate . . . 1885,* II, 24.

[48] Commons and others, *op. cit.,* II, 90n.

[49] Dorothy W. Douglas, "Ira Steward on Consumption and Unemployment," *Journal of Political Economy,* XL (August, 1932), 532–543; John R. Commons and J. B. Andrews, *A Documentary History of American Industrial Society* (Cleveland: Arthur H. Clark Company, 1910), IX (1860–1880), 277–329.

[50] G. E. McNeill, editor, *The Labor Movement: The Problem of Today* (Boston: A. M. Bridgman & Co., 1886), pp. 470–482; Testimony of Samuel Gompers, *Report of the Industrial Commission,* VII, 622–627; Testimony of Adolph Strasser, *Report of the Committee* [on Education and Labor] *of the Senate . . . 1885,* I, 459–460.

Within the limited area of its own workers, Federal legislation was possible. In 1868 a Federal statute declared, "That eight hours shall constitute a day's work for all laborers, workmen, and mechanics now employed . . . by or on behalf of the government of the United States." [51] For this measure it is hard to unearth any immediate political explanation. The National Labor Union under William Sylvis had made the eight-hour day an important part of its program, and on its behalf Sylvis and others lobbied with the President and with Congress.[52] A Senator also acknowledged that the "experiment" had "been discussed before the country." [53] Perhaps a stronger wave than usual in the ebb tide of Civil War reform carried the measure to safety on the beach. However murky the background, the act naturally aroused expectations, for the phrasing was explicit and it covered wage earners in private establishments working under government contracts. These factors, along with the example of the nation as a "model employer," could have had great weight. Actually administrative officials and the courts made the act a nullity. They held it was directive and not mandatory, that wages would have to be reduced with a reduction of hours. Workers had little choice but to continue under previous stipulations.[54]

This experience, along with their general hesitancy about politics, turned organized labor to the alternative weapon of economic pressure. It had always been their chief means against private employers. General campaigns for the eight-hour day, as contrasted with sporadic demands in particular establishments or occupations, were waged on an urban basis, for instance in New York City in 1872,[55] but the national movement for the same purpose waited until the mid-eighties. Even then there was an atmosphere of the accidental about the drive. That stumbling forerunner of the A. F. of L., the Federation of Organized Trades and Labor Unions, in order to recoup its waning strength resolved in 1884, "that eight hours shall constitute a legal day's labor from and after May 1, 1886, and that we recommend to labor organizations throughout this jurisdiction that they so direct their laws as to conform to this resolution by the time named." Persuasion or the threat of action or a general strike might bring employers to compliance.

[51] 15 *United States Statutes,* 77.

[52] Grossman, *op. cit.,* pp. 238–244; Testimony of Adolph Strasser, *loc. cit.,* p. 458.

[53] Speech of Senator Wilson, *Congressional Globe,* 40th Cong., 1st Sess., 1867, p. 413.

[54] Matthew A. Kelly, "Early Federal Regulation of Hours of Labor in the United States," *Industrial and Labor Relations Review,* III (April, 1950), 372–374; United States *v.* Martin, 94 *United States,* 400.

[55] Henry David, *The History of the Haymarket Affair: A Study in the American Social-Revolutionary and Labor Movements* (New York: Farrar & Rinehart, 1936), pp. 157–158.

The resolution did not necessarily enlist the support of the larger and rival Knights of Labor. Although the course of Powderly and other leaders was certainly equivocal, the membership of the Knights, according to the evidence, was enthusiastic for the eight-hour drive. Thus, as it turned out, there was a widespread rank-and-file support for action. Politicians and even a portion of the press gave approval. The momentum thus generated carried furthest in metropolitan areas. Even before the date set workers were striking for and securing a shorter day's work. Chicago, with 80,000 participants and strikers, mounted the biggest drive.[56] Then the Haymarket episode, as we have seen, shattered the movement. In the nineties the American Federation of Labor attempted to put together again the pieces of the eight-hour philosophy but in a different frame. Such constituent unions as were eager for a reduction of hours and well-heeled enough to undertake a strike were to be backed by the Federation and financially supported by it. A series of galloping strikes would thus attain eight hours for organized workers. This tactic met with both success and failure, but by the end of the century the Federation discarded even this effort.[57] Though the movement had shortened hours, it had not attained, except in special instances, the eight-hour optimum. To Gompers the issue in 1901 was still a "burning" one, and for reasons which Ira Steward would have commended.[58]

A HARMONY OF BELIEFS

We have noted that the philosophy of labor frequently resembled that of managers and employers. A belief in natural law and in practical measures are cases in point. Also labor tended to accept the values of the society about it and wished simply to share in them more generously. Nor was there much divergence in group attitudes over the fundamentals of the economic order or the features currently attending its hasty and disturbing development. For labor as for capital, production was a goal; the former relished the fact that "we are producing wealth to-day at a greater ratio than ever in the history of mankind." [59]

One means to this end was machinery, and labor, instead of smashing machines, admired the inventive genius which created them and

[56] *Ibid.*, pp. 162–177; Philip Taft, *The A. F. of L. in the Time of Gompers* (New York: Harper & Brothers, 1957), pp. 14, 16–17, 63–64; M. C. Cahill, *Shorter Hours: A Study of the Movement since the Civil War* (New York: Columbia University Press, 1932), pp. 152–159.

[57] Taft, *op. cit.*, pp. 142–146; Cahill, *op. cit.*, pp. 161–164.

[58] Testimony of Samuel Gompers, *Report of the Industrial Commission*, VII, 622–625, 652; Gompers, *Seventy Years of Life and Labor*, I, 309–310.

[59] Testimony of Samuel Gompers, *Report of the Industrial Commission*, VII, 606.

advocated their introduction.[60] The eight-hour day program was postulated upon the introduction of machinery which would, in spite of fewer hours, maintain production. Labor's complaint was that it did not get its share of the advantages of machinery. The solution, most often commended for its ideology and ingenuity, was the one the International Typographical Union followed when the Merganthaler linotype machine threatened in 1887 and after to destroy the old-fashioned type-setting by hand. The president of the International Union shrewdly observed, "Those familiar with the productiveness of machines are agreed that hand work cannot begin to compete with them, and it is therefore futile to attempt to stay the tide of their introduction." The union accepted the machine. However, by its insistence that they be operated by already skilled operatives it prevented extensive technological unemployment and it used the productiveness of the machines to facilitate a shorter working day. The union also insisted on a minimum wage.[61] For the industrial picture as a whole Gompers was explicit: "In the great race for the production of wealth we do not want to go back to the primitive methods; no sane man wants that." [62]

The collective action of the labor union was, according to its leaders, an evolution in response to circumstance. Were they able to apply a similarly benevolent judgment to parallel developments—the business combination, big business, the trust? Hostility to the trust on the part of the Knights smacked more of agrarian than industrial criticism.[63] Gompers was unwilling to embark upon a "general proposition." "We view the trust from the standpoint that they are our employers, and the employer who is fair to us, whether an individual, or a collection of individuals, an aggregation of individuals in the form of a corporation or a trust, matters little to us so long as we obtain the fair conditions." [64] The general opinion of labor leaders added up to a tentative willingness to tolerate combinations, for the latter seemed to hold out the promise of more stable wages, a better guarantee of continuous work, and also an easier way to establish common conditions of labor than by dealing with hosts of small competitors.[65] On the asserted lowering of prices by big

[60] H. A. Meier, "Technology and Democracy, 1800–1860," *Mississippi Valley Historical Review*, XLIII (March, 1957), 631.

[61] George E. Barnett, *Chapters on Machinery and Labor* (Cambridge: Harvard University Press, 1926), pp. 8–23; Testimony of Samuel Gompers, *Report of the Industrial Commission*, VII, 615–616.

[62] Testimony of Samuel Gompers, *Report of the Industrial Commission*, VII, 621.

[63] Address of I. D. Chamberlain, *Chicago Conference on Trusts* (Chicago: The Civic Federation of Chicago, 1900), pp. 366–370.

[64] Testimony of Samuel Gompers, *Report of the Industrial Commission*, VII, 621.

[65] Summary by Mr. Farquhar, *ibid.*, VII, 643; Address of Henry White, *Chicago Conference on Trusts*, pp. 325–328.

business, Gompers pointed out labor was not greatly interested in this accomplishment—"I am not a cheap man, anyway"—and that prices tended to decline largely because of mechanization. He did fear that trusts had a tendency and ability "to prevent the will of the people by buying up legislators." As for trust policy, the government had better leave combinations alone, for the "State is not capable of preventing development or natural concentration of industry." Instead of regulating business, the Interstate Commerce Act and the Sherman Anti-Trust Act had been turned against labor to deprive it "of the benefit of organized effort." [66]

When anti-business statutes were dismissed as "panaceas" by labor's spokesmen, it was unlikely that its high command would be enthusiastic over proposals seriously challenging an owner's right to manage his property. The cooperative enthusiasms of the Knights contained no threat of confiscation nor idea of government direction. Within the A. F. of L. an energetic socialist minority differed from the officers on the fundamental issue of private enterprise. In the nineties this faction sponsored a program calling for the municipal ownership of public utilities, the nationalization of telegraphs, telephones, railroads and mines, and the "collective ownership by the people of all means of production and distribution." Against this last proposal, article 10, Gompers and his allies fought with skill, determination and success. After the failure of the A. F. of L. to endorse public ownership, socialist influence fell off.[67] Perhaps no point illustrated better the tolerance of the unions for private enterprise than the consistent refusal of their leaders to count among its failures the panics and depressions of these years. "I think that panics come, not through those men's [employers'] idiocy or incompetency, but are attributable to causes not generally understood." [68]

Since the expressed thought of the leaders of organized labor was at bottom conservative and empirical and becoming more so and treasured the same scheme of values as did ownership-management, it would seem that the latter group might well vouchsafe the dearly-sought recognition the former strove for. Increasingly it did. Every great labor crisis, which in theory should have closed the ranks of employers, produced at least one capitalist of purest ray serene with courage and insight enough to look beyond doctrinaire partisanship. After the great railroad strikes of the seventies, culminating in the destructive Pittsburgh rioting

[66] Testimony of Samuel Gompers, *Report of the Industrial Commission,* VII, 643, 654, 655.

[67] Quint, *op. cit.,* pp. 66–71; Taft, *op. cit.,* pp. 71–74; Gompers, *Seventy Years of Life and Labor,* I, 391–394.

[68] Testimony of Samuel Gompers, *Report of the Committee* [on Education and Labor] *of the Senate . . . 1885,* I, 378; Testimony of Adolph Strasser, *ibid.,* I, 459–460.

of 1877, Congress investigated the alarming situation. The chairman of the committee was Abram S. Hewitt, a Representative and a noted iron-master. In 1878 Hewitt was observing in an address, "A new power has entered into the industrial world, which must be recognized. . . . It must be heard. Its just demands must be heeded. . . . The great result achieved is that capital is ready to discuss. It is not to be disguised that till labor presented itself in such an attitude as to compel a hearing capital was unwilling to listen; but now it does listen. The results already attained are full of encouragement." [69]

Again after Haymarket, when the air quivered with hysteria, Andrew Carnegie cut down the danger of revolution to pygmy size, and concluded: "The right of the working-men to combine and to form trades-unions is no less sacred than the right of the manufacturer to enter into associations and conferences with his fellows, and it must be sooner or later conceded. . . . My experience has been that trades-unions upon the whole are beneficial both to labor and to capital." [70] Carnegie went so far as to doubt the wisdom of the conventional belief that an employer should hire strikebreakers.[71] And in the labor disturbances of the 1890's, Marcus Alonzo Hanna derided the philanthropic façade of the town of Pullman and exploded: "A man who won't meet his men half-way is a God-damn fool!" [72] The suspicion that Hanna only inferentially advocated union recognition soon vanished when he became the chief participant in the efforts of the National Civic Federation, whose members included labor leaders and capitalists, to abate industrial conflict by persuasion and mediation.[73] And it was practical men in "the upper" and "lower classes," not economists, who led the way to the acceptance of unionism. At least that would seem to be the gravamen of an address delivered in 1888 to his fellow economists by their president, Francis A. Walker.[74]

In truth, it is as misleading to write the history of labor between 1860 and 1900 in terms of labor upheavals or uprisings as it is to detect in every local breakdown of orderly development the pattern of a general strike or any other form of proto-revolutionary action. This was a

[69] Allan Nevins, *Abram S. Hewitt, with Some Account of Peter Cooper* (New York: Harper & Brothers, 1935), pp. 413–414.

[70] Andrew Carnegie, "An Employer's View of the Labor Question," *Forum,* I (April, 1886), 119.

[71] Andrew Carnegie, "Results of the Labor Struggle," *Forum,* I (August, 1886), 549–550.

[72] Thomas Beer, *Hanna* (New York: Alfred A. Knopf, 1929), pp. 132–133.

[73] Herbert Croly, *Marcus Alonzo Hanna* (New York: Macmillan Company, 1903), pp. 386–388; Taft, *op. cit.,* pp. 225–229; Marguerite Green, *The National Civic Federation and the American Labor Movement, 1900–1925* (Washington: Catholic University Press, 1956), pp. 1–36.

[74] F. A. Walker, "Efforts of the Manual Laboring Class to Better Their Condition," *Publications of the American Economic Association,* III, No. 3 (1888), pp. 7–13.

period when the immense productive powers of the country were in transition from one system to another. The great problem was adjustment. Some turbulence was bound to attend the search for answers to the questions of what was fair and just and to the even more searching query of what was feasible and possible. That labor did not crystallize into a permanent party of discontent, nor come to regard itself as a group apart from the community with no responsibility for the common welfare,[75] was a tribute to the discernment, foresight and flexibility of both labor and capital.

[75] Testimony of Samuel Gompers, *Report of the Committee* [on Education and Labor] *of the Senate . . . 1885,* I, 382; Testimony of Edward King, *ibid.,* I, 561; Testimony of Samuel Gompers, *Report of the Industrial Commission,* VII, 610.

CHAPTER XX

Multiplication, Division, Materialism

THE TOTALS OF WEALTH

IN 1869 David A. Wells, whose perspicacity has often been mentioned in these pages, felt that the inflation of the time had hit the workers harder than the capitalist and that the rich were becoming richer and the poor poorer.[1] The idea, constantly repeated, endured. In 1895 the Massachusetts Bureau of Labor Statistics gave the concept a full rehearsal. "That the rich are becoming richer and the poor poorer, is frequently asserted to be one of the results of the prevailing industrial system. The belief that the facts support this assertion finds constant expression in speeches, magazines, books, newspapers, and conversation, and while the impatience of a few inspired by this belief leads at times to violent outbreaks against the social order, there are many of a milder nature who are dissatisfied because the ideal [a more equal division] of wealth is not more closely attained." [2]

Certainly the industrial years, covered by this volume, greatly increased the national wealth, a concept defined as the sum of the values of property within the nation. Figures of this sort, going back to the seventeenth century, originally overemphasized the nation's treasure in the precious metals; by the nineteenth century the concept stretched to cover land, natural resources, plants and railroads: national wealth was a "national inventory or stocktaking." [3] It consisted of things that could be seen, counted, and appraised. Perhaps a more informative substitute

[1] Report of the Special Commissioner of the Revenue, *House Executive Document* No. 16 (s.n. 1372), 40th Cong., 3d Sess., pp. 15–18.

[2] *Twenty-fifth Annual Report of the* [Mass.] *Bureau of Statistics of Labor. March, 1895*, p. 51.

[3] Census Office, *Special Reports. Wealth, Debt, and Taxation, 1907*, pp. 3–22.

for the last word was "assessed." For one of the reasons for using this concept of national wealth was the existence of data which tax officials, usually local ones, all over the nation had assembled. By a resort to arithmetic, it was possible to elevate "the appraised value" to "the true value," "the fair selling price of property." No matter how crude such data were, the period here under scrutiny exhibited a "gratifying" increase in national wealth. Its "estimated true value" in 1860 was $16,-159,616,068; in 1900, $88,517,306,775.[4]

By dividing these dollar totals by the number of inhabitants, enumerators concluded that the "true wealth" per capita had risen between 1860 and 1900 from $514 to $1,165.[5] These figures do not reveal how wealth is really distributed. Per capita wealth is the wealth no capita has. From the few figures available it is clear that there was a very high concentration of wealth. Between 1879 to 1881, approximately 15 per cent of the estates of males probated in Massachusetts were under $500; 65 per cent—this figure includes the former—were under $5,000; roughly a half of one per cent were $50,000 or over. In sum the richest 2 per cent of the population owned two-thirds of the state's wealth.[6] Little wonder that popular opinion tended to focus on the fact of large fortunes.[7] One writer, a corporation lawyer and convert to Henry George, asked, as others have since, "Who owns the United States?" and announced that 40,000 persons owned over one-half the national wealth. By extrapolating from individual fortunes and their rate of increase, he concluded at the end of the eighties "the American billionaire might reasonably be looked for within . . . [forty years] . . . and several billionaires might be expected within sixty years."[8] Incidentally, John D. Rockefeller, the closest competitor, never made it.[9]

There were many unsatisfactory aspects about the concept of national wealth. Somehow or other, it connoted a static condition, clearly

[4] *Ibid.*, pp. 4–7; Carroll D. Wright, *Outline of Practical Sociology* (New York: Longmans, Green, and Co., 1909), pp. 309–311.

[5] Census Office, *Special Reports. Wealth, Debt, and Taxation, 1907*, p. 44; Edward Atkinson, "How Can Wages be Increased?" *The Industrial Progress of the Nation* (New York: G. P. Putnam's Sons, 1890), p. 149.

[6] Willford I. King, *The Wealth and Income of the People of the United States* (New York: Macmillan Company, 1915), p. 79; *Twenty-fifth Annual Report of the* [Mass.] *Bureau of Statistics of Labor. March, 1895*, pp. 266–267.

[7] N. P. Gilman, *Profit Sharing between Employer and Employee* (Boston: Houghton Mifflin and Company, 1889), p. 2.

[8] T. G. Shearman, "The Owners of the United States," *Forum*, VIII (November, 1889), 262–273; T. G. Shearman, "The Coming Billionaire," *Forum*, X (January, 1891), 548.

[9] Allan Nevins, *Study in Power: John D. Rockefeller, Industrialist and Philanthropist* (New York: Charles Scribner's Sons, 1953), II, 404–405.

at variance with the country's coursing economic development. It was a carcass rather than a living body. Furthermore, when individuals or groups proposed in the interest of allaying discontent or enlarging the public welfare a different distribution of wealth, the concept of it as a lump of property values stood in the way. The American system of government protected property rights; "Every government has been a rich man's government" [10] and anyway, what would a division amount to? Arithmeticians and social philosophers were quick to make the necessary calculations and to discover that the redistribution of the wealth of rich men would mean the transfer of a mere pittance to the less fortunate and "it would not help the poor to have everybody poor." [11] A scholar in 1896 concluded: "The future laws which shall make better or worse the distribution of property are likely to accomplish their end, not by the bodily transfer of property from one class to another, but by making more equal or unequal the distribution of the future incomes of the people." [12]

In the nineteenth century the lack of statistical sophistication and the absence of data prevented anything but a start being made on determining the amount and distribution of the national income, defined as "the net product of or net return on the activity of individuals, business firms, and the social and political institutions that make up a nation." [13] In the twentieth century statisticians have far surpassed the tentative efforts of the Federal censuses and of individuals such as Edward Atkinson, to arrive at conclusions. According to the estimates of one of these experts, the functioning of the economy in the era covered by this volume greatly increased the national income. With adjustments made for changes in the price level, the average per year increased from $9,300,000,000 in the period 1869–1878 to $24,200,000,000 in 1889–1898. Per capita this meant an increase from $215 to $357.[14] Such increases, greater than in other industrialized countries and than in America before 1860, led one informed statistician to conclude in 1915: "Beginning with

[10] E. L. Godkin, "The Real Problems of Democracy," *Atlantic*, LXXVIII (July, 1896), 9–10.

[11] E. L. Godkin, "The Democratic View of Democracy," *North American Review*, CI (July, 1865), 115; Testimony of Edward Atkinson, *Report of the Committee* [on Education and Labor] *of the Senate . . . 1885*, III, 342; *Nation*, VIII (April 15, 1869), 290; Frederick B. Hawley, "The Proportion of Wages to Other Forms of Income," *Quarterly Journal of Economics*, II (April, 1888), 363–364.

[12] C. B. Spahr, *An Essay on the Present Distribution of Wealth in the United States* (New York: Thomas Y. Crowell, 1896), p. 73.

[13] Simon Kuznets, *National Income: A Summary of Findings* (N. Y.: National Bureau of Economic Research, 1946), p. 1.

[14] *Ibid.*, pp. 32–33.

1870, there has been an increase in the national dividend so enormous that it cannot logically be ascribed to anything but the tremendous advance in productive power due to the revolution by improvements in industry which have characterized the last half century. It seems improbable that any other great nation has ever experienced such sweeping gains in the average income of the inhabitants." [15]

Not only did national income increase, its division among various economic activities altered. Thus between 1869–1879 and 1889–1899, the percentage distributed to agriculture declined from 20.5 to 17.1. Meanwhile that for manufacturing rose from 13.9 to 18.2, for mining from 1.8 to 2.5. The share of construction, transportation, and service declined slightly.[16] While these figures might partially account for the presence of agricultural discontent, they have little bearing on the division of income between capital and labor, between rentier, manager, and wage earner. Between 1860 and 1900 the percentage of national income going into wages and salaries rose from 37.2 to 47.3; in rent it fell from 8.8 to 7.8; and in interest rose only from 14.7 to 15; the share to profits fell from 39.3 to 30.3.[17] Whereas in 1860 the sum of all the returns paid for wages was approximately the same as for profits, in 1900 the sum for wages was much the larger.[18]

Before 1890 most data on wages are highly speculative. In so far as wages can be stated, they are wage rates without allowance for the degree of unemployment; they are not useful, therefore, for ascertaining a worker's annual income. When all reservations have been made, there is little question that money wages, "nominal wages," rose during the late nineteenth century. The index of money hourly wages for men in all industries practically doubled between 1860 and 1890; it shrank a bit in the mid-nineties. Since the index of commodity prices fell rapidly after 1865, the purchasing power of wages, "real wages," often attained a spectacular improvement. At no time during the depressions of the seventies and nineties did an index of wages in purchasing power sink as low as in 1860 and the preceding fifties; in intervals of prosperity the power of wages over goods was much more favorable than in the good old days.[19] Little wonder, when Mr. Gompers was asked in 1900, "You would not agree to the statement sometimes made that the conditions of the working men are growing worse and worse?" he answered, "Oh, that is perfectly absurd." [20]

[15] King, *op. cit.*, p. 34.
[16] Kuznets, *op. cit.*, p. 40.
[17] *Ibid.*, pp. 49–51; King, *op. cit.*, pp. 156–164.
[18] King, *op. cit.*, pp. 162–169.
[19] *Ibid.*, pp. 189–193.
[20] Testimony of Samuel Gompers, *Report of the Industrial Commission*, VII, 645.

THE AMERICAN STANDARD OF LIVING

For rich as for poor, measurements of the resulting standard of living depend upon other factors than prices and the ability to pay them. A standard of living, for instance, also depends upon the overall technical level an economy has attained. The backwardness of the plumbers' art may thus account alike for the noisome toilets of a tenement and the fact that a bath tub costing $7000 in a tycoon's palace built by McKim, Mead, and White had its outlet sloping toward the tub. A standard of living also depends upon what people think they ought to have and do have in terms of services and commodities. Thus a cotton operative comparing 1848 with 1883 confessed: "We get many things now that we did not have then. . . . We have gas to pay for now, and ice, and such things." [21] To those leading the procession, the well-being of those farther down the line seemed fabulous. In 1880 the President of the American Society of Mechanical Engineers informed his hearers that the American cotton industry made and sold cotton goods so cheaply "that the very beggars in our metropolitan cities, and the 'tramps' sleeping in our fields or under the roof that shelters our cattle, wear a finer fabric than kings could boast a century ago." Though this seems a somewhat ambiguous endorsement of the functioning of the economy, he thought the "golden age" and the "millenial period" were at hand.[22]

To most people a millennium implies spiritual overtones. So does the standard of living. Though most intangible items elude the quantifier's grasp, an exception is the length of the working day. Whereas at the beginning of the Civil War, the ten-hour day prevailed in the building trades and in certain skilled occupations, the average day the country over was eleven hours. Gradually the standard day shrank. By century's end the work week was 57.3 hours, and Gompers, president of the A. F. of L., was estimating that the average hours of labor of the American worker were 9 to 9½ a day.[23]

[21] Testimony of A. M. Keniston, *Report of the Committee* [on Education and Labor] *of the Senate . . . 1885*, III, 267–268; Edward Atkinson, "Low Prices, High Wages, Small Profits," *Industrial Progress of the Nation* (New York: G. P. Putnam's Sons, 1890), p. 127.

[22] R. H. Thurston, "President's Inaugural Address," *Transactions of the American Society of Mechanical Engineers*, I (November, 1880), 4; R. H. Thurston, "Trend of National Progress," *North American Review*, CLXI (September, 1895), 297–312; Testimony of Andrew Carnegie, *Hearings before the* [Stanley] *Committee on United States Steel Corporation*, III, 2443–2444; Charles S. Ashley, "The Distribution of Wealth," *Popular Science Monthly*, XXIX (October, 1886), 729–730; *Tenth Annual Report of the* [Mass.] *Bureau of Statistics of Labor . . . 1879*, pp. 90–95.

[23] P. H. Douglas, *Real Wages in the United States, 1890–1926* (Boston: Houghton Mifflin Company, 1930), p. 208; D. D. Lescohier, *History of Labour in the United*

Less measurable satisfactions and benefits were flowing from public education, an advantage of American life increasingly available to children whose earnings parents could forego or whom parents could support. Indeed compulsory education acts made it imperative that parents make this sacrifice or break the truant laws. Though education was a community enterprise and thus not at first hand dependent upon the economy, in the last analysis American productivity and wealth furnished the taxes for the improved curriculum of the grades and the establishment and spread of the public high school.[24]

For a generation which made a gospel of work and which worked hard, it was somewhat paradoxical to estimate the achievements of the economy in terms of fewer hours at labor and more at leisure. The nature of work itself was a more acceptable measure. Certainly the economic development of the nation and the organization of business enterprise had greatly altered the nature of work. Though it placed millions under an industrial discipline to which they had to conform, it freed others from forms of labor which Americans had long felt were characterized by a stultifying dependence and inferiority. No change, for instance, in the labor force was more startling than the failure of the numbers in personal and domestic service to increase as rapidly as those in other industrial divisions.[25] More Americans proportionately than ever before could boast they wore no man's livery, and housewives and others began the long lamentation over the difficulty of getting maids, cooks, and the like.

Meanwhile, within the employment categories reflecting at first hand the industrial transformation, the number in unskilled laboring positions vis-à-vis those in directing or superintending capacities declined. Taylor's efficiency system, for instance, depended upon the multiplication of clerks and specialized foremen. Most categories about skilled and unskilled workers, as well as most judgments based upon them, are transitory things; but perhaps it was plausible to distinguish, as the census did, a class of labor "comprising those employments which are, as a rule, the more laborious, and in which the bulk of the work done does not call for a high degree of mechanical skill or ability, such as agricultural labor-

---

States, 1896–1932 (New York: Macmillan Company, 1935), III, 97–109; Testimony of Samuel Gompers, *Report of the Industrial Commission,* VII, 622; Edgar W. Martin, *The Standard of Living in 1860* (Chicago: University of Chicago Press, 1942), pp. 343–346.

[24] E. C. Kirkland, *Dream and Thought in the Business Community, 1860–1900* (Ithaca: Cornell University Press, 1956), pp. 53–60.

[25] William C. Hunt, "Workers at Gainful Occupations at the Federal Censuses of 1870, 1880, and 1890," *Bulletin of the Department of Labor,* No. 11 (July, 1897), pp. 397–398.

ers, boatmen, fishermen . . . sailors, draymen, hostlers . . . messengers, packers, porters, miners, quarrymen, servants, and the like." The percentage of the population gainfully employed in this category declined between 1870 and 1890. "The increased proportion of workers is found generally in the higher walks of business life and in those occupations which call for skilled labor principally rather than in the lowest or more laborious forms of employment." [26] Invention sought to replace mere muscular strength with power and to place on a mechanized basis tasks which the day regarded as "brutalizing" or "degrading." This was as true of farm as of factory.[27] As one engineer summarized it in 1899: "We know that in these latter days, it is *intelligent* labor rather than *hard* labor that counts." [28]

In spite of the economic advance of all classes in this period, the statement that the rich were getting richer and the poor poorer persisted in one form or another. Perhaps the fact that journalists just before the Civil War put the number of millionaires in metropolitan Eastern cities at less than a hundred but by the nineties were reporting 4,407 millionaires in the country as a whole [29] provided evidence for this notion. On the other hand Carroll D. Wright, the most social-minded of American statisticians, could hardly contain his impatience with the inaccuracy of the observation: "a wandering phrase, without paternity or date; it is not authority but familiarity that has given it weight. . . . To the investigator the real statement should be, The rich are growing richer; many more people than formerly are growing rich; and the poor are better off. If the sum total of wealth were stationary, any increase in the wealth of the rich would be an exploitation of the poor. . . . But the sum total of wealth is not stationary; it increases with great rapidity, and while under this increase the capitalistic side secures a greater relative advantage than the wage-earner of the profits of production, the wage-earner secures an advantage which means the improvement of his condition." [30] In 1900 Mr. Gompers' judgment of the rich-richer and poor-poorer concept was "a catch phrase." [31]

[26] *Ibid.*, pp. 415–416, 420, 423.

[27] David A. Wells, *Recent Economic Changes and their Effect on the Production and Distribution of Wealth and the Well-Being of Society* (New York: D. Appleton and Company, 1899), p. 373.

[28] Discussion by S. W. Baldwin, *Transactions of the American Society of Mechanical Engineers*, XXI (1899), 725.

[29] Herman E. Krooss, *American Economic Development* (New York: Prentice-Hall, 1955), p. 24; Sidney Ratner, editor, *New Light on the History of Great American Fortunes: American Millionaires of 1892 and 1902* (New York: Augustus M. Kelly, 1953), pp. 90–91.

[30] Wright, *op. cit.*, pp. 343–345; Gilman, *op. cit.*, pp. 2–3.

[31] Testimony of Samuel Gompers, *Report of the Industrial Commission*, VII, 654.

WAS IT ALL WRONG?

To many sensitive observers of the era both the qualitative changes in the way the country's work was performed and the growth in production, wealth, and wages were beside the point. Tests such as these, critics asserted, merely proved the nation's achievement was not ideal or spiritual but material. E. L. Godkin, editor of the *Nation,* scolded the rich for "the worship of wealth, in its coarsest and most undraped form . . . that is, wealth as a purveyor of meat, drink, clothing, and ornamentation, which . . . 'makes hay' of all noble standards of individual and social conduct." [32] And few can read the literature of business apologetics without realizing it was unpleasantly easy for the well-to-do to identify progress with material things.[33] Such identification was not a class matter. The American standard of living sought by organized labor was no more exalted. Godkin, who liked to censure impartially, concluded, "The poor are less discontented when they consume more of the necessaries and luxuries, because . . . as a rule, physical comfort among the great bulk of mankind tends to produce happiness" and that the masses in a democracy inherently elevate "material luxury into the great end of social progress." [34]

Though the charge of materialism has been often stated, repetition does not establish its truth. Since Americans have always been uneasy at being considered unspiritual, participants in the economic development of this era were far from disposed to accept the indictment of materialism or the sneer hidden in it. Some advanced a theory of knowledge stressing that the mental emerged from the practical. That the hand educated the mind was a favorite argument of the advocates of vocational education; "motion" is "the dawn of the soul." [35] Furthermore mechanism facilitated the cultural advance of the day. Mechanics had built the paper mill, the printing press, and the telegraph, "the life-blood of today." "Suppose the hammer . . . was blotted out of existence." The act "would bring us back to living in mud huts with nothing to eat but roots and herbs and nuts." [36] Finally mechanisms were the result of in-

[32] E. L. Godkin, "Idleness and Immorality," *Forum,* XIII (May, 1892), 340.

[33] Will and Maxine Schoyer, *Scaife Company and the Scaife Family, 1802–1952* (Pittsburgh: Davis & Warde, 1952) p. 103; Andrew Carnegie to W. E. Gladstone, February 7, 1890, Carnegie Papers, Library of Congress.

[34] E. L. Godkin, "Aristocratic Opinions of Democracy," *North American Review,* C (January, 1865), 198–199; E. L. Godkin, "The Economic Man," *North American Review,* CLIII (October, 1891), 499.

[35] Flora J. White, "Physical Effects of Sloyd," *Journal of Proceedings and Addresses of the National Education Association . . . 1896,* pp. 760–761.

[36] John E. Sweet, "President's Address, 1884," *Transactions of the American Society of Mechanical Engineers,* VI (1884), 31–35.

vention. Bessemer, Bell, and Edison were the heroic exemplars of a procedure which discovered nature's laws and harnessed natural forces for the service of men. Their accomplishment was akin to the "divine." The power loom embodied and represented thought as much as did the book. "What is there in the world of science, and the wonders of art, or the wisdom of letters that can more than stand side by side with any one of a dozen of our leading inventions?" [37]

Finally those operating on a level more mundane than the stratosphere pointed out that the attainment of welfare made possible by the economic order was an essential prelude to shattering the age-old handicaps to a cultural awakening. No doubt a Chicago University professor's conclusion that Rockefeller had done more for the world than Shakespeare was calculated to make the judicious as well as the genteel grieve; [38] it accorded nonetheless with an assertion by Charles Elliott Perkins, president of the Chicago, Burlington, and Quincy Railroad: "Have not great merchants, great manufacturers, great inventors, done more for the world than preachers and philanthropists? . . . Can there be any doubt that cheapening the cost of necessaries and conveniences of life is the most powerful agent of civilization and progress? Does not the fact that well-fed and well-warmed men make better citizens, other things being equal, than those who are cold and hungry, answer the question? Poverty is the cause of most of the crime and misery in the world—cheapening the cost of the necessaries and conveniences of life is lessening poverty, and there is no other way to lessen it, absolutely none. History and experience demonstrate that as wealth has accumulated and things have cheapened, men have improved . . . in their habits of thought, their sympathy for others, their ideas of justice as well as of mercy. . . . Material progress must come first and . . . upon it is founded all other progress." [39]

In terms of economic factors we can ascribe the achievement of the era to a sequence of important inventions which from science and technology flowed swiftly into production. As new goods, made in new ways, came upon the market, they were originally expensive. Experience in production and the quick application of mass methods of manufacture

[37] Sweet, *loc. cit.*, pp. 35–36; Discussion by W. R. Jones, *Transactions of the American Society of Mechanical Engineers*, VI (1884), 539–540; Oberlin Smith, "The Engineer as a Scholar and a Gentleman," *Transactions of the American Society of Mechanical Engineers*, XII (1890), 42; M. P. Higgins, "Education of Machinists, Foremen, and Mechanical Engineers," *Transactions of the American Society of Mechanical Engineers*, XXI (1899), 1115–1118.

[38] Kirkland, *op. cit.*, pp. 165–166.

[39] Charles E. Perkins, Memo, 1888, Perkins Private Letters and Memos R. C. Overton; Discussion by R. H. Thurston, *Transactions of the American Society of Mechanical Engineers*, XXI (1899), 704.

and distribution soon made them cheaper. The structure of the economy was still so competitive that the advantages of the new system flowed into the hands of consumers. The effective organization of labor prevented the sequestration of gains in the hands of lenders and managers.

But the generation which accomplished all this had a distaste for explanations so matter-of-fact. They preferred to ascribe the industrial triumph to "character." Education should teach character, and charity or relief should take care, according to the most prominent social worker of the time, lest it undermine "the character of a poor man—for it is his all." [40] In the cluster of specific qualities upon which the business and industrial discipline placed a premium, a changing economic scene brought about some shift. Whereas in the earlier days of commerce frugality, industry, punctuality, and integrity had been the road to fortune, wealth now came "rapidly" through "lucky strokes" and "bold and ingenious combinations." [41] In spite of the authority and astuteness of this observation (it came from E. L. Godkin of the *Nation*), the generation did not cease to admire or practice the traditional virtues; it simply added to them an appreciation of the ones the new day required—alertness, activity, and audacity. In a period of transition and depression, alive with dangers and uncertainties, the useful qualities were "hustle," ambition, dedication to the job, and above all, the willingness to take risks and strike out along new paths. They called it "gumption," they called it "pluck." [42]

This individualistic industrial ethic of self-reliance was certainly both bleak in terms of social relationships and deficient in the reflective or contemplative qualities.[43] But its positive aspects, carried to the pitch of genius by business leaders and enjoying the approbation of the majority of ordinary Americans, were neither mercenary nor ignoble. Exercised in relative freedom and with a conscious view to national greatness as well as private gain, the talent for business enterprise was the

[40] Josephine Shaw Lowell, *Public Relief and Private Charity* (New York: G. P. Putnam's Sons, 1884), p. 92.

[41] E. L. Godkin, "Commercial Immorality and Political Corruption," *North American Review*, CVII (July, 1868), 249–252.

[42] E. L. Godkin, "Commercial Immorality and Political Corruption," *loc. cit.*, pp. 250–254; E. L. Godkin, "The Democratic View of Democracy," *North American Review*, CI (July, 1865), 116; E. L. Godkin, "The Danger of an Office-Holding Aristocracy," *Century Magazine*, XXIV (July, 1882), 290–291; Kirkland, *op. cit.*, pp. 157–158; *Nation*, XXVII (August 8, 1878), 78; R. H. Thurston, "Technical Education in the United States: Its Social, Industrial, and Economic Relations to Our Progress," *Transactions of the American Society of Mechanical Engineers*, XIV (1893), 862; Andrew Carnegie, "The Road to Business Success," and "How to Win Fortune," and "Business," *The Empire of Business* (New York: Doubleday, Page & Co., 1902), pp. 3–18, 105–114, 119–122, 205–216.

[43] *Nation*, XI (November 3, 1870), 292.

source of that abundance which, in later days, democracy would administer differently. And today many nations seeking industrialization would be fortunate if they had, not so much America's resources, but the national qualities which gave birth to our industrial strength and the institutions under which these qualities flowered to achievement.

Bibliographical Notes

CHAPTER I BUSINESS VICISSITUDES

GENERALLY speaking, historians have not yet given business-cycle theory a wide acceptability. Perhaps one reason is the technical complexity of its erudition; another the self-imposed limitations upon its coverage, for instance its relative preoccupation with measurement and relative neglect of causation; and a third, the controversies, often highly doctrinaire, among business-cycle theorists. Consequently historians have clutched gladly at any explanation, stated in non-technical language, which seems related to historical data and in which chronology plays a part. For these reasons, entirely aside from any other merit, W. L. Thorp, *Business Annals* (New York: National Bureau of Economic Research, 1926) has had an enduring value. The historical sections in Joseph A. Schumpeter, *Business Cycles: A Theoretical, Historical, and Statistical Analysis of the Capitalist Process,* 2 volumes (New York: McGraw-Hill Book Company, 1939) can be generally understood without resorting to the theoretical apparatus accompanying them. Rendig Fels, *American Business Cycles, 1865–1897* (Chapel Hill: University of North Carolina Press, 1959) is a shorter account from an essentially Schumpeterian point-of-view. Charles Hoffmann, "The Depression of the Nineties," *Journal of Economic History* XVI (June, 1956), 137–164, though somewhat more eclectic, seems to precede from Schumpeterian premises. For the business climate as it appeared to contemporaries, there is no substitute for the annual reports of the Secretary of the Treasury, of the Comptroller of the Currency, or for the *Commercial and Financial Chronicle.* Joseph Dorfman, *The Economic Mind in American Civilization, 1865–1918* (New York: The Viking Press, 1949) and Paul Barnett, *Business Cycle Theory in the United States, 1860–1900* (Chicago: University of Chicago Press, 1941)—the last somewhat impatient with the untidiness of the conceptions with which it deals—organize contemporary thinking more systematically.

CHAPTER II GOVERNMENT FINANCE, CURRENCY, AND BANKING

On matters of government policy, D. R. Dewey, *Financial History of the United States* (New York: Longmans, Green & Company, 1956) has not been superseded. Paul Studenski and Herman E. Krooss, *Financial History of the United States* (New York: McGraw-Hill Book Company, 1952) brings the insights of the newer economics to bear. Alexander D. Noyes, *Forty Years of American Finance, 1865–1907* (New York: G. P. Putnam's Sons, 1909) has the advantage of contemporary experience and of mingling economics and politics, but is too severe with those who disagree with sound policy, as the author sees it.

The most valuable books on details in this chapter are the following: For treasury policy, Esther R. Taus, *Central Banking Functions of the United States Treasury, 1789–1941* (New York: Columbia University Press, 1943), although, perhaps, its brevity prevents seeing all the implications. On banking, Fritz Redlich, *The Molding of American Banking: Men and Ideas. Part II, 1840–1910* (New York: Hafner Publishing Company, 1951) has a pioneer approach and an inclusiveness of interest. It is one of the genuinely original works in a rather over-treated field. F. Cyril James, *The Growth of Chicago Banks* (New York: Harper & Brothers, 1938) Vol. I, is really a history of banking for the United States as a whole. Margaret G. Myers, *The New York Money Market: Origins and Development* (New York: Columbia University Press, 1931) shows how things worked out in America's financial capital. Consult also Andrew M. Davis, *The Origin of the National Banking System* (Washington: Government Printing Office, 1910); O. M. W. Sprague, *History of Crises under the National Banking System* (Washington: Government Printing Office, 1910); and David Kinley, *The Independent Treasury of the United States and Its Relations to the Banks of the Country.* (Washington: Government Printing Office, 1910).

Wesley C. Mitchell, *A History of the Greenbacks with Special Reference to the Economic Consequences of Their Issue, 1862–65* (Chicago: The University of Chicago Press, 1903), the standard treatment, is nevertheless under the spell of the preoccupations of the time it was written. D. C. Barrett, *The Greenbacks and Resumption of Specie Payments, 1862–1879* (Cambridge: Harvard University Press, 1931) echoes Mitchell on the early period and adds little for the later. Three of the essays in C. M. Destler, *American Radicalism, 1865–1901* (New London: Connecticut College, 1946) provide the best summary of intellectual greenbackism. A. B. Hepburn, *A History of Currency in the United States* (New York: Macmillan Company, 1915) covers currency and banking. On the silver crisis of the nineties, James A. Barnes, *John G. Carlisle, Financial Statesman* (New York: Dodd, Mead & Company, 1931), utilizing the sources exhaustively, is the authoritative treatment.

Of biographies of other participants in the financial drama, Henrietta Larson, *Jay Cooke, Private Banker* (Cambridge: Harvard University Press, 1936) and E. P. Oberholtzer, *Jay Cooke, Financier of the Civil War,* 2 vols. (Philadelphia: George W. Jacobs and Company, 1907) are outstanding.

CHAPTER III–VI TRANSPORTATION

In spite of the flood of writing about railroads, there are few systematic studies of the railroad business in the United States and of the practices and policies of its management. Two contemporary analyses of primary importance are Charles F. Adams, Jr., *Railroads: Their Origin and Problems* (New York: G. P. Putnam's Sons, 1878) and Arthur T. Hadley, *Railroad Transportation: Its History and Its Laws* (New York: G. P. Putnam's Sons, 1886). The preliminary chapters in S. F. Van Oss, *American Railroads as Investments: A Handbook for Investors in American Railroad Securities* (New York: G. P. Putnam's Sons, 1895) are also well worth perusal in spite of their pronounced conservative bias. The annual progress of the railroad network is best followed in the introductions to Poor's *Manual of the Railroads of the United States,* the first of which, aside from a preliminary history, appeared in 1868–1869. For the years 1880, 1881, 1882, 1883, and 1885, these introductions go beyond mere statistical accumulations and discuss policy and practice. Beginning with 1888 Poor's should be supplemented by the *Annual Report of the Statistics of Railways in the United States to the U. S. Interstate Commerce Commission.*

Of the secondary works on the railroads, T. C. Cochran, *Railroad Leaders. 1845–1890, The Business Mind in Action* (Cambridge: Harvard University Press, 1953) assembles valuable data which often strain at the schematic hitching post to which the author has tied them. E. C. Kirkland, *Men, Cities and Transportation: A Study in New England History, 1820–1900,* 2 vols. (Cambridge: Harvard University Press, 1948) is a regional study of railroads after they were built as well as a-building. Robert E. Riegel, *The Story of the Western Railroads* (New York: Macmillan Company, 1926), has the same advantage. Unhappily not all important railroads have competent histories for the period and many minor roads have been glorified *in extenso.* Exceptions to this generalization are Nelson Trottman, *History of the Union Pacific: A Financial and Economic Survey* (New York: The Ronald Press Company, 1923), somewhat too censorious on the early period; Richard C. Overton, *Burlington West: A Colonization History of the Burlington Railroad* (Cambridge: Harvard University Press, 1941); and George H. Burgess and Miles C. Kennedy, *Centennial History of the Pennsylvania Railroad Company* (Philadelphia: The Pennsylvania Railroad Company, 1949); Jules I. Bogen, *The Anthracite Railroads* (New York: The Ronald Press Company, 1927) and J. B. Hedges, *Henry Villard and the Railways of the Northwest* (New Haven: Yale University Press, 1930). In Charles F. Adams, Jr. and Henry Adams, *Chapters of Erie and Other Essays* (New York: Henry Holt and Company, 1886) the former has written two classic essays on episodes in the Erie's history.

For an understanding of the first transcontinental, the testimony in The Report of the Select Committee to Investigate the Alleged Crédit Mobilier Bribery, *House Report* No. 77 (s.n. 1577) 42d Cong., 3rd Sess., and in Report of the Commission and of the Minority Commissioner of the United States Pacific Railway Commission, *Senate Executive Document* No. 51 (s.n. 2505), 50th Cong., 1st Sess. is essential. Of the biographies of railroad men, most are "authorized" in some way and reveal little. Wheaton J. Lane, *Commodore Vanderbilt: An Epic of the Steam Age* (New York: Alfred A. Knopf, 1942); M. W. Schlegel, *Ruler of the Reading: The Life of Franklin B. Gowen, 1836–1889* (Harrisburg: Archives Publishing Company of Pennsylvania, 1947); and Oscar Lewis, *The Big Four: The Story of Huntington, Stanford, Hopkins, and Crocker, and of the Building of the Central Pacific* (New York: Alfred A. Knopf, 1938) are exceptional studies. For railroad financiers Henrietta Larson, *Jay Cooke, Private Banker* (Cambridge: Harvard University Press, 1936), has not superseded Ellis P. Oberholtzer, *Jay Cooke, Financier of the Civil War,* 2 vols. (Philadelphia: George W. Jacobs and Co., 1907) on Cooke's railroad activities. Lewis Corey, *The House of Morgan. A Social Biography of the Masters of Money* (New York: G. Howard Watt, 1930) is journalistic on Morgan, and Julius Grodinsky, *Jay Gould, His Business Career, 1867–1892* (Philadelphia: University of Pennsylvania Press, 1957) is expert.

The national government has collected railroad information, sometimes continuously, sometimes spasmodically. In the latter category are the *Annual Reports on the Internal Commerce of the United States,* Bureau of Statistics, Department of the Treasury. The first appeared in 1876; the last in 1891. These ten volumes, mostly by Joseph Nimmo and William Switzler, are a mine of information. The *Tenth Census of the United States. 1880,* vol. IV inaugurated new fullness of reporting. At the end of the period the Industrial Commission, in volumes IV and IX of its *Report,* collected testimony and prepared monographs, admirably indexed and digested, on transportation. Prolonged investigation preceded most proposals for national legislation. Outstanding are Report of the Select Committee on Transportation-Routes to the Seaboard (Windom Report), *Senate Report* No. 307, Pt. 1 (s.n. 1588), Pt. 2 (s.n. 1589), 43rd Cong., 1st Sess.; and Report of the Senate Select Committee on Interstate Commerce (Cullom Report), *Senate Report* No. 46, Pt. 1 (s.n. 2356), Pt. 2 (s.n. 2357), 49th Cong., 1st Sess. On state activity in the same field, the most influential document is State of New York, 1879, *Proceedings of the Special Committee on Railroads appointed under a Resolution of the Assembly to Investigate Alleged Abuses in the Management of Railroads* (Hepburn Investigation), 5 vols.

On the financing of the railroad network there are two useful introductory volumes: W. Z. Ripley, *Railroads, Finance and Organization* (New York: Longmans, Green & Co., 1915) and F. A. Cleveland and F. W. Powell, *Railroad Promotion and Capitalization in the United States* (New York: Longmans, Green & Co., 1909). Both reflect the preconceptions of the progressive era in which they were printed. On the morbidity of railroad enterprises consult the admirable Stuart Daggett, *Railroad Reorganization* (Cambridge: Harvard University Press, 1908) and E. G. Campbell, *The Reorganization of the American Railroad System, 1893–1900* (New York: Columbia University Press, 1938).

Carter Goodrich has completed his study of government assistance and planning of transportation enterprises. Of his articles on this theme the most useful for this period are Carter Goodrich, "Local Government Planning of Internal Improvements," *Political Science Quarterly,* LXVI (September, 1951), 411–445; Carter Goodrich and Harvey H. Segal, "Baltimore's Aid to Railroads. A Study in the Municipal Planning of Internal Improvements," *Journal of Economic History,* XIII (Winter, 1953), 2–35; Carter Goodrich, "The Revulsion Against Internal Improvements," *Journal of Economic History* (November, 1950), 145–169; and Carter Goodrich, "Public Aid to Railroads in the Reconstruction South," *Political Science Quarterly,* LXXI (September, 1956), 407–442. Since my chapters were written, Goodrich has collected these articles and other material in his *Government Promotion of American Canals and Railroads, 1800–1890* (New York: Columbia University Press, 1959).

To the local theme attention is paid in B. U. Ratchford, *American State Debts* (Durham: Duke University Press, 1941) and R. C. McGrane, *Foreign Bondholders and American State Debts* (Durham: Duke University Press, 1935). For governmental assistance in the states of the West consult J. N. Primm, *Economic Policy in the Development of a Western State, Missouri, 1820–1860* (Cambridge: Harvard University Press, 1954); F. W. Merk, *Economic History of Wisconsin during the Civil War Decade* (Madison: Madison Historical Society, 1916); and E. S. Beard, "Local Aid to Railroads in Iowa," *Iowa Journal of History,* L (January, 1952) 1–34. The best study for any governmental unit is for an eastern state; Harry H. Pierce, *Railroads of New York, A Study of Government Aid, 1826–1875* (Cambridge: Harvard University Press, 1953). On national policy, the first half of L. H. Haney, *A Congressional History of Railways in the United States* (Madison: Democrat Printing Company, 1910) deals with land grants and other assistance. J. B. Sanborn, *Congressional Grants of Land in Aid of Railways* (Madison: Bulletin of the University of Wisconsin, 1899) is the old standby and Thomas Donaldson, *The Public Domain, Its History with Statistics* (Washington: Government Printing Office, 1884) is the mine from which most material has been dug.

For the land grant controversy see also Robert S. Henry, "The Railroad Land Grant Legend in American History Texts," *Mississippi Valley Historical Review,* XXXII (September, 1945), 171–194 and also "Comments on Henry's Article" in the same volume (March, 1946), 557–576. There will always be "new light" on this issue. The latest new light is in Paul W. Gates, "The Railroad Land Grant Legend," *Journal of Economic History,* XIV (Spring, 1954), 143–146. On the administration of these grants by the railroads or the government consult D. M. Ellis, "The Forfeiture of Railroad Land Grants, 1867–1894," *Mississippi Valley Historical Review,* XXXIII (June, 1946), 27–60; J. B. Rae, "Commissioner Sparks and the Railroad Land Grants," *Mississippi Valley Historical Review,* XXV (September, 1938), 211–230; J. B. Hedges, "The Colonization Work of the Northern Pacific Railroad," *Mississippi Valley Historical Review,* XIII (December, 1926), 311–342; P. W. Gates, *The Illinois Central Railroad and Its Colonization Work* (Cambridge: Harvard University Press, 1934); and Overton, cited above. Of the many governmental investigations of public aid to railroads made during the nineteen forties, the best summary is Board of Investigation and Research, Public Aids to Domestic Transportation, *House Document* No. 159 (s.n. 10963), 79th Cong., 1st Sess.

Facts on railroad rates are provided in detail in Report by Mr. Aldrich from the Committee on Finance, Wholesale Prices, Wages, and Transportation, *Senate Report* No. 1394, Pt. 2 (s.n. 3074), 52d Cong., 2d Sess., and Interstate Commerce Commission, *Railways in the United States in 1902,* Pt. II, *A Forty Year Review of Changes in Freight Tariffs.* The best treatment of the attempt to stabilize rates on oil is in Allan Nevins, *Study in Power: John D. Rockefeller, Industrialist and Philanthropist,* 2 vols. (New York: Charles

Scribner's Sons, 1953), and on meat in Report of Special Senate Committee on the Transport and Sale of Meat Products, *Senate Report* No. 829 (s.n. 2705) 51st Cong., 1st Sess.

The consolidation movement is dealt with in the Report of the Industrial Commission, elsewhere cited, and in Interstate Commerce Commission, *Intercorporate Relationships of Railways in the United States as of June 30, 1906,* Special Report No. 1. On pools and related organizations, Charles S. Langstroth and Wilson Stilz, *Railway Coöperation: An Investigation of Railway Traffic Associations* (Philadelphia: University of Pennsylvania, 1899) is the most general approach. On a single example, Julius Grodinsky, *The Iowa Pool, A Study in Railroad Competition. 1870–84* (Chicago: The University of Chicago Press, 1950) is the best study. For pools in the South and trunk-line territory, the best approach is through the testimony of Albert Fink scattered through government investigations cited above, and often separately printed. His report on the "Adjustments of Railroad Transportation Rates to Seaboard Cities" is in John B. Daish, *The Atlantic Port Differentials* (Washington: W. H. Lowdermilk & Co., 1918).

Most histories of railroad regulation are characterized by woeful omissions in terms of time and locality. Because it escapes these deficiencies, B. H. Meyer, *Railway Legislation in the United States* (New York: Macmillan Company, 1903) still remains useful. W. Z. Ripley, *Railroads, Rates and Regulation* (New York: Longmans, Green, & Co., 1912) is good on the theoretical side. A useful summary of statutory provisions arranged in tables is provided by Interstate Commerce Commission, *Railways in the United States in 1902,* Pt. IV, *State Regulation of Railways.* Frederick Merk, "Eastern Antecedents of the Grangers," *Agricultural History,* XXIII (January, 1949), 1–8, provides background for the movement in the regions where it was of earliest importance. See also Kirkland, *Men, Cities and Transportation* for the New England experience. For the movement in the West, Solon J. Buck, *The Granger Movement* (Cambridge: Harvard University Press, 1913) is the best summary of provisions and accomplishments. That the Granger legislation had often a paradoxical relationship to Grangers is revealed in E. S. Beard, "The Background of State Regulation in Iowa," *Iowa Journal of History,* LI (January, 1953), 1–36; Mildred Throne, "The Repeal of the Iowa Granger Law, 1878," *Iowa Journal of History,* LI (April, 1953), 97–130; George H. Miller, "Origins of the Iowa Granger Law," *Mississippi Valley Historical Review,* XL (March, 1954), 657–680; and R. T. Daland, "Enactment of the Potter Law," *Wisconsin Magazine of History,* XXXIII (September, 1949), 45–54. Robert S. Hunt, *Law and Locomotion. The Impact of the Railroad on Wisconsin Law in the Nineteenth Century* (Madison: State Historical Society of Wisconsin, 1958) deserves imitation for other states.

Proposals to stimulate water competition are in the Windom Report, cited above, and in Report of the United States Deep Waterway Commission . . . 1896, *House Document* No. 192 (s.n. 3327), 54th Cong., 2d Sess. In New York the canalers' side influences N. E. Whitford, *History of the Canal System of the State of New York* (Albany: Bradlow Printing Company, 1906), while the railroad side is in the introduction to Poor's *Manual for the Railroads of the United States for 1881.* On the Mississippi River Basin, Louis C. Hunter, *Steamboats on the Western Rivers* (Cambridge: Harvard University Press, 1949) is standard.

On the wider subject of national regulation, S. W. Briggs, *History of Bills and Resolutions introduced in Congress respecting Federal Regulation of Interstate Commerce by Railways, etc., from the Thirty-seventh Congress to the Sixty-second Congress, Inclusive 1862–1913* is a summary and a guide. The Windom and Cullom Reports of course are essential reading. L. H. Haney, *A Congressional History of Railways in the United States* (Madison: Democrat Printing Co., 1910) gives excerpts from Congressional debates. The agitational literature is extensive. I have found Simon Sterne, *Railways in the United States. Their History, Their Relation to the State and an Analysis of the Legislation in regard to their Control* (New York: G. P. Putnam's Sons, 1912), along with Adams and Hadley, the most perceptive. James F. Hudson, *The Railways and the Republic* (New York: Harper & Brothers, 1886) has lots of facts but is quite one-sided. See also A. B. Stickney, *The Railway Problem* (St. Paul: D. D. Merrill Company, 1891) by a "liberal" railroad president. On the functioning of the Interstate Commerce Commission, I. L. Sharfman, *The Interstate Commerce Commission: A Study in Administrative Law and Procedure*, 4 vols. (New York: The Commonwealth Fund, 1931) is for this period rather brief and conventional. Reliance must be placed on the annual reports of the Interstate Commerce Commission, on its cases, and on the court decisions. J. W. Bunting, *The Distance Principle in Railroad Rate Making* (Geneva, N. Y.: 1947) and M. B. Hammond, *Railway Rate Theories of the Interstate Commerce Commission* (Cambridge: Harvard University Press, 1911) pay random attention to this early period in the Commission's history.

Lee Benson, *Merchants, Farmers, and Railroads: Railroad Regulation and New York Politics, 1850–1887* (Cambridge: Harvard University Press, 1955); Alfred D. Chandler, *Henry Varnum Poor, Business Editor, Analyst, and Reformer* (Cambridge: Harvard University Press, 1956); and George R. Taylor and Irene D. Neu, *The American Railroad Network, 1861–1890* (Cambridge: Harvard University Press, 1956) are all outstanding works; their authors generously permitted me to read portions or all of their original manuscripts.

CHAPTER VII NATURAL RESOURCES

For the development of natural resource industries, aside from lumber, the best general introductions are in T. A. Rickard, *A History of American Mining* (New York: McGraw-Hill Company, 1932) and A. B. Parsons, editor, *Seventy-five Years of Progress in the Mineral Industry* (New York: American Institute of Mining and Metallurgical Engineers, 1947).

The material available on separate industries is extensive. For the lumber industry, Frederick Merk, *Economic History of Wisconsin during the Civil War Decade* (Madison: Historical Society of Wisconsin, 1916) is an excellent introduction; and P. W. Gates, *The Wisconsin Pine Lands of Cornell University: A Study in Land Policy and Absentee Ownership* (Ithaca: Cornell University Press, 1943) an admirable continuation. R. F. Fries, *Empire in*

Pine: The Story of Lumbering in Wisconsin, 1830–1900 (Madison: State Historical Society of Wisconsin, 1951) and A. M. Larson, *History of the White Pine Industry in Minnesota* (Minneapolis: University of Minnesota Press, 1949) are both admirable state surveys. It is regrettable that the industry in the Far West and in the South lacks comparable treatment. There is random information in Part III of Charles S. Sargent, "Report on the Forests of North America," *Tenth Census of the United States. 1880*. The maps are especially valuable. The student can also learn much from the biographies of lumber kings: Isaac Stephenson, *Recollections of a Long Life: 1829–1915* (Chicago: Privately Printed, 1915) and R. N. Current, *Pine Logs and Politics, A Life of Philetus Sawyer, 1816–1900* (Madison: State Historical Society of Wisconsin, 1950).

Within the larger area of minerals, the pioneering role of the precious metals can be traced in Oscar Lewis, *Silver Kings: The Lives and Times of MacKay, Fair, Flood, and O'Brien, Lords of the Nevada Comstock Lode* (New York: Alfred A. Knopf, 1947), which concentrates strongly on the personal side, and in R. W. Paul, *California Gold, The Beginning of Mining in the Far West* (Cambridge: Harvard University Press, 1947). The latter is outstanding on the institutional side and has an excellent succinct account of mining law. On the minor metals consult W. B. Gates, Jr., *Michigan Copper and Boston Dollars: An Economic History of the Michigan Copper Mining Industry* (Cambridge: Harvard University Press, 1951) and R. G. Cleland, *A History of Phelps Dodge, 1834–1950* (New York: Alfred A. Knopf, 1952).

On the coal industry, the best description of methods and technology is H. M. Chance, "Report on the Mining Methods and Appliances Used in the Anthracite Coal Fields," *Second Geological Survey of Pennsylvania: 1883* (Harrisburg: Second Geological Survey, 1883), which pays some attention to bituminous. See also E. W. Parker, "Coal-Cutting Machinery," *Transactions of American Institute of Mining Engineers*, XXIX (1899), 405–459. J. T. Lambie, *From Mine to Market: The History of Coal Transportation on the Norfolk and Western Railway* (New York: New York University Press, 1954) is practically a history of bituminous in the region served by that railroad. See also H. N. Eavenson, *The First Century and a Quarter of the American Coal Industry* (Baltimore: Waverly Press, 1942). On iron mining, H. R. Mussey, *Combination in the Mining Industry. A Study of Concentration in Lake Superior Iron Ore Production* (New York: Columbia University Press, 1905) and F. P. Wirth, *The Discovery and Exploitation of the Minnesota Iron Lands* (Cedar Rapids, Iowa: The Torch Press, 1937) cover the whole story in that region. The two biographies, H. O. Evans, *Iron Pioneer: Henry W. Oliver, 1840–1904* (New York: E. P. Dutton & Company, 1942) and Hal Bridges, *Iron Millionaire. Life of Charlemagne Tower* (Philadelphia: University of Pennsylvania Press, 1952) are documented and highly informative. Paul De Kruif, *Seven Iron Men* (New York: Harcourt, Brace & Company, 1929) on the Merritts is impressionistic. Allan Nevins, *Study in Power, John D. Rockefeller, Industrialist and Philanthropist* (New York: Charles Scribner's Sons, 1953) also discusses the Merritts.

For the material on the petroleum industry in this chapter, consult primarily Paul H. Giddens, *The Birth of the Oil Industry* (New York: Macmillan

Company, 1938). R. W. Hidy and M. E. Hidy, *History of Standard Oil Company (New Jersey): Pioneering in Big Business, 1882–1911* (New York: Harper & Brothers, 1955) is fuller on a later period. S. W. Tait, Jr., *The Wild Catters: An Informal History of Oil Hunting in America* (Princeton: Princeton University Press, 1946) combines the virtues of being useful and spirited.

On government land policy and natural resources, the standard treatments are B. H. Hibbard, *A History of the Public Land Policies* (New York: Macmillan Company, 1924) and R. M. Robbins, *Our Landed Heritage: The Public Domain, 1776–1936* (Princeton: Princeton University Press, 1942). On the matters in this chapter it is still necessary to turn to Clarence King, "The United States Mining Laws and Regulations Thereunder," *Tenth Census of the United States. 1880,* XIV and to the encyclopedic Thomas Donaldson, *The Public Domain. Its History with Statistics.* John Ise, *The United States Forest Policy* (New Haven: Yale University Press, 1920) and his *The United States Oil Policy* (New Haven: Yale University Press, 1926) see evils on every side but conclude they were apparently necessary. A resort to government documents, for example *Annual Reports of the Geological Survey,* and *Mineral Resources of the United States,* an annual census beginning with 1884, is essential. G. P. Merrill, *Contributions to a History of American State Geological and Natural History Surveys,* Smithsonian Institution, United States National Museum, Bulletin 109 gives the prelude to national policy, whereas Testimony before the Joint Commission on the Organization of Certain Bureaus, *Senate Miscellaneous Document* No. 82 (s.n. 2345), 49th Cong., 1st Sess. is invaluable on purposes, procedures, and difficulties. Brookings Institution for Government Research, *The U. S. Geological Survey: Its History, Activities and Organization* (New York: Appleton & Company, 1918) is brief on history.

The conservation movement stimulated a cluster of biographies and autobiographies: A. A. Schenk, *The Biltmore Story: Recollections of the Beginning of Forestry in the United States* (St. Paul: Minnesota Historical Society, 1955) and Gifford Pinchot, *Breaking New Ground* (New York: Harcourt, Brace & Company, 1947) are in the latter category; A. D. Rodgers, III, *Bernhard Eduard Fernow: A Story of North American Forestry* (Princeton: Princeton University Press, 1951) is in the former. We have no biography of F. B. Hough. See his "On the Duty of Government in the Preservation of Forests," *Proceedings of the American Association for the Advancement of Science,* XXII, 1873, B1–B10. Julius B. Cameron, *The Development of Governmental Forest Control in the United States* (Baltimore: Johns Hopkins Press, 1928) is more interesting than a book on such a topic has a right to be.

Many of the works already cited include a discussion of transportation in relation to natural resources. See in addition, Commissioner of Corporations, *Report on Transportation by Water in the United States,* Parts 1, 2. On more specialized trades consult W. G. Rector, *Log Transportation in the Lake States Lumber Industry, 1840–1918* (Glendale, California: Arthur H. Clark Company, 1953); E. C. Kirkland, *Men, Cities and Transportation: A Study in New England History, 1820–1900,* 2 vols. (Cambridge: Harvard University Press, 1948); Louis C. Hunter, *Steamboats on the Western Rivers. An Economic and Technological History* (Cambridge: Harvard University Press, 1949); Harlan

Hatcher, *The Great Lakes* (New York: Oxford University Press, 1944); Harlan Hatcher, *Lake Erie* (Indianapolis: The Bobbs-Merrill Company, 1945); G. S. Wolbert, Jr., *American Pipe Lines, Their Industrial Structure, Economic Status, and Legal Implications* (Norman: University of Oklahoma Press, 1952); and L. D. H. Weld, *Private Freight Cars and American Railways* (New York: Columbia University Press, 1908).

CHAPTERS VIII AND IX INDUSTRY

The most inclusive treatment of manufactures in this period is Victor Clark, *History of Manufactures in the United States, 1860–1893* (New York: McGraw-Hill Book Company, 1929). Unfortunately the author made no effort to write an interesting narrative. The history of invention in the United States still awaits adequate treatment. Waldemar Kaempffert, editor, *A Popular History of American Invention*, 2 vols. (New York: Charles Scribner's Sons, 1924) lives up to its title. John W. Oliver, *History of American Technology* (New York: The Ronald Press Company, 1956) is not wholly reliable. A. P. Usher, *A History of Mechanical Inventions* (Cambridge: Harvard University Press, 1954) has four stimulating introductory chapters on the general setting of invention.

Of course there are treatments of special industries. In this connection the student who wants to get back as near as may be to the contemporary scene should read the series of articles on "The Development of American Industries since Columbus" in *Popular Science Monthly* in the early nineties. Equally valuable is the attention paid to industry and the factory by the Census of 1880. In addition to the statistics, Volume II contains useful special reports. On the textile industries consult Arthur H. Cole, *The American Wool Manufacture*, 2 vols. (Cambridge: Harvard University Press, 1926); M. T. Copeland, *The Cotton Manufacturing Industry in the United States* (Cambridge: Harvard University Press, 1912); and, more particularly, T. R. Navin, *The Whitin Machine Works since 1831: a Textile Machinery Company in an Industrial Village* (Cambridge: Harvard University Press, 1950). On brewing, T. C. Cochran, *The Pabst Brewing Company* (New York: New York University Press, 1948) is excellent; and on the direct and indirect effects of refrigeration, O. G. Anderson, Jr., *Refrigeration in America: History of a New Technology and Its Impact* (Princeton: Princeton University Press, 1953) is the authority. On the steam engine, Robert H. Thurston, *A History of the Growth of the Steam-Engine*, Centennial Edition (Ithaca: Cornell University Press, 1939) is standard. For the shoe factory, Blanche E. Hazard, *The Organization of the Boot and Shoe Industry in Massachusetts before 1875* (Cambridge: Harvard University Press, 1921) is excellent on the early period. George A. Rich, "Manufacture of Boots and Shoes," *Popular Science Monthly*, XLI (August, 1892), 496–515 continues the story.

Victor Clark, cited above, treats iron and steel well. His book should be supplemented by the articles of W. F. Durfee on "The Manufacture of Steel," *Popular Science Monthly*, XXXIX (October, 1891) 729–749, XL (November, 1891), 15–40 and of R. W. Hunt, "A History of the Bessemer Manufacture in America," *Transactions of the American Institute of Mining Engineers*, V

(1876–77), 200–216. Of the biographies of steel men, John Fritz, *The Autobiography of John Fritz* (New York: John Wiley & Sons, 1912) gives a worm's eye view; Burton J. Hendrick, *Life of Andrew Carnegie*, 2 vols. (New York: Doubleday, Doran & Company, 1922) and, better yet, Allan Nevins, *Abram S. Hewitt with Some Account of Peter Cooper* (New York: Harper & Brothers, 1955) view things from the top level.

For the electrical industries, A. F. Harlow, *Old Wires and New Waves* (New York: D. Appleton-Century, 1936) is indispensable though somehow disappointing. Luckily for the telegraph, there is an admirable account in Carlton Mabee, *The American Leonardo: A Life of Samuel F. B. Morse* (New York: Alfred A. Knopf, 1943). A. A. Bright, Jr., *The Electrical Lamp Industry: Technological Change and Economic Development from 1800 to 1891* (New York: Macmillan Company, 1949) is straightforward. Harold C. Passer, *The Electrical Manufacturers, 1875–1900: A Study in Competition, Entrepreneurship, Technical Change and Economic Growth* (Cambridge: Harvard University Press, 1953) is a much more sophisticated and subtle book. Something additional can still be learned from F. L. Dyer and T. C. Martin, *Edison, His Life and Inventions*, 2 vols. (New York: Harper & Brothers, 1910).

There is, so far, no adequate history describing the interrelationships of research and industry in the late nineteenth century. A. H. Dupree, *Science in the Federal Government: A History of Policies and Activities to 1940* (Cambridge: Harvard University Press, 1957) pays some passing attention to this matter. Kendall Burr, *Pioneering in Industrial Research: The Story of the General Electric Research Laboratory* (Washington: Public Affairs Press, 1957) has a useful first chapter on antecedents. The treatments on separate industries, cited above, are useful. On education, Dirk J. Struik, *Yankee Science in the Making* (Boston: Little, Brown & Company, 1948) has some stimulating things to say about the earlier period.

On other government assistance to manufacturing, the taxation system still awaits treatment. This assertion does not apply to the tariff. Here for thirty years the works of F. W. Taussig, *The Tariff History of the United States* (New York: G. P. Putnam's Sons, 1914), and *Some Aspects of the Tariff Question* (Cambridge: Harvard University Press, 1915) have blanketed the field. It is time for a second look at the system. Joseph Dorfman, *The Economic Mind in American Civilization, 1865–1918*, 3 vols. (New York: The Viking Press, 1949) treats the more respectable theorists, but the investigation should press down into the periodical and political literature and private papers. F. P. Summers, *William L. Wilson and Tariff Reform* (New Brunswick: Rutgers University Press, 1953) shows what can be accomplished. On this matter as on others in this chapter, scholars will benefit from a perusal of the Edward Atkinson Papers in the Massachusetts Historical Society.

In the patent system there was much interest in the thirties. Most attention to the earlier period has been colored by the preoccupations of the new deal era. An example is F. L. Vaughan, *The United States Patent System: Legal and Economic Conflicts in American Patent History* (Norman: University of Oklahoma Press, 1956). In addition to the material on the electrical and telephone industries, some of the papers and addresses in the *Proceedings and Addresses at the Celebration of the Beginning of the Second Century of the American Patent System at Washington City, D. C., April 8, 9, 10, 1891* (Washington: Gedney & Roberts Company, 1892) have value.

CHAPTER X THE ORGANIZATION OF BIGNESS

Many of the works cited in the bibliography of the previous chapter include material for this as well. The best cross section of the consolidation movement is provided by the *Report of the Industrial Commission* at the turn of the century. This investigating group mustered a considerable degree of expertise. Its general tone is, however, pronouncedly against big business. The evidence has been digested or summarized, but the student should turn to the original testimony, to which these summaries are but a useful guide. The Industrial Commission reported on many things: the material on business organization is primarily in volumes I and XIII; volumes VII and VIII contain additional matter, however the spine title may read. In briefer compass, Henry R. Seager and Charles A. Gulick, Jr., *Trust and Corporation Problems* (New York: Harper & Brothers, 1929) has a series of historical vignettes. More contemporary is John Moody, *The Truth about the Trusts* (New York: Moody Publishing Company, 1914).

Works on individual industries are essential. For the petroleum industry, Allan Nevins, *Study in Power: John D. Rockefeller, Industrialist and Philanthropist,* 2 vols. (New York: Charles Scribner's Sons, 1953) is organized on conventional lines but has masses of material. Ralph W. Hidy and Muriel E. Hidy, *History of Standard Oil Company (New Jersey): Pioneering in Big Business, 1882–1911* (New York: Harper & Brothers, 1955) pays particular attention to the structure of business organization and policy but it does not supersede Nevins. The more one reads in this interesting field, the more remarkable appears John D. Rockefeller, *Random Reminiscences of Men and Events* (New York: Doubleday, Doran & Company, 1933). I. M. Tarbell, *The History of the Standard Oil Company,* 2 vols. (New York: McClure, Phillips & Co., 1904), once the standard treatment, has now become a museum piece of historical polemics.

For iron and steel, Burton J. Hendrick, *The Life of Andrew Carnegie,* 2 vols. (New York: Doubleday, Doran & Company, 1932) is useful in spite of the author's tendency to stand back and admire, frequently with exclamation marks. The combined testimony of Andrew Carnegie, Elbert Gary, Charles M. Schwab, and John W. Gates in the *Hearings before the* [Stanley] *Committee on Investigation of United States Steel Corporation,* 8 vols., is enlightening. On other industries from the organizational point of view consult for coal: Eliot Jones, *The Anthracite Coal Combination in the United States* (Cambridge: Harvard University Press, 1914), and M. W. Schlegel, *Ruler of the Reading: The Life of Franklin B. Gowen, 1836–1889* (Harrisburg: Archives Publishing Company, 1947); for cotton, Caroline F. Ware, *The Early New England Cotton Manufacture: A Study in Industrial Beginnings* (Boston: Houghton Mifflin Company, 1931) and Vera Shlakman, "Economic History of a Factory Town," *Smith College Studies in History,* XX, Nos. 1–4 (Northampton, Mass.: 1935);

on salt, Louis C. Hunter, "Studies in the Economic History of the Ohio Valley: The Beginnings of Industrial Combination," *Smith College Studies in History,* XIX, Nos. 1–2 (Northampton, Mass.: 1934).

On electricity, Harold C. Passer, *The Electrical Manufacturers, 1875–1890: A Study in Competition, Entrepreneurship, Technical Change, and Economic Growth* (Cambridge: Harvard University Press, 1953) is admirable on the national scene and Forrest McDonald, *Let There Be Light: The Electric Utility Industry in Wisconsin, 1881–1955* (Madison: The American History Research Center, 1957), a much needed book, helps to dispel darkness about what was going on at the local level. On telephony, J. W. Stehman, *The Financial History of the American Telephone and Telegraph Company* (Boston: Houghton Mifflin Company, 1925) is much to be preferred to the highly doctrinaire N. R. Danielian, *A. T. & T.: The Story of Industrial Conquest* (New York: The Vanguard Press, 1939). The only summary of the careers of the business generation is F. W. Gregory and Irene D. Neu, "The American Industrial Elite in the 1870's," William Miller, editor, *Men in Business: Essays in the History of Entrepreneurship* (Cambridge: Harvard University Press, 1952).

G. Heberton Evans, Jr., *Business Incorporations in the United States, 1800–1943* (New York: National Bureau of Economic Research, 1948) is a statistical survey, as is William Kessler, "Incorporation in New England: A Statistical Study, 1800–1875," *Journal of Economic History,* VIII (May, 1948), 43–62, and William Miller, "A Note on the History of Business Corporations in Pennsylvania, 1800–1860," *Quarterly Journal of Economics,* LV (November, 1940), 150–160. John W. Cadman, Jr., *The Corporation in New Jersey, Business and Politics, 1791–1875* (Cambridge: Harvard University Press, 1949) is more verbal about a significant state. E. M. Dodd, *American Business Corporations until 1860 with Special Reference to Massachusetts* (Cambridge: Harvard University Press, 1954) has a much broader frame of reference. The controversy over what a corporation signifies and what its advantages and disadvantages are may be followed in Louis Hartz, *Economic Policy and Democratic Thought: Pennsylvania, 1776–1860* (Cambridge: Harvard University Press, 1948) and Oscar Handlin and Mary F. Handlin, *Commonwealth: A Study of the Role of Government in the American Economy, Massachusetts, 1774–1861* (New York: New York University Press, 1947).

CHAPTER XI FINANCING EXPANSION

The conceptual framework for a study of financing American business and the statistical details to fill it out are in the course of being provided. The National Bureau of Economic Research has published several studies, but the summary has not yet appeared. Heavy reliance in this realm must be placed upon Raymond W. Goldsmith, *A Study of Saving in the United States,* 3 vols. (Princeton: Princeton University Press, 1955). Though much of the material is of interest only to technicians, and the data do not at all points push back into the nineteenth century, the summaries and general organization of the book help make it of value.

Though the history of investment banking was incomprehensibly neglected for years, Fritz Redlich in Chapter XXI of his *The Molding of American Banking: Men and Ideas, Part II, 1840–1910* (New York: Hafner Publishing Company, 1951) has provided the best summary. He appends an excellent bibliography. Two excellent biographies give an insight into the business: Henrietta Larson, *Jay Cooke, Private Banker* (Cambridge: Harvard University Press, 1936) deals with one of the earliest investment bankers, and Alfred D. Chandler, Jr., *Henry Varnum Poor, Business Editor, Analyst, and Reformer* (Cambridge: Harvard University Press, 1956) is actually more than a biography, describing the evolution of promotion and financing with particular emphasis on railroads. Certainly a biography of Morgan should be urbane, if anything, and F. L. Allen, *The Great Pierpont Morgan* (New York: Harper & Brothers, 1949) has this quality and others. Lewis Corey, *The House of Morgan, A Social Biography of the Masters of Money* (New York: G. H. Watt, 1930) is doctrinaire and unreliable, but catches, through its numerous quotations, the color of the times. Cyrus Adler, *Jacob H. Schiff, His Life and Letters,* 2 vols. (New York: Doubleday, Doran & Company, 1929) furnishes some additional details.

So far we lack a history of Wall Street as an institution. Margaret G. Myers, *The New York Money Market: Origins and Development* (New York: Columbia University Press, 1931) pays some attention to the stock exchange. Henry Clews, *Fifty Years in Wall Street* (New York: Irving Publishing Company, 1908) and his *The Wall Street Point of View* (New York: Silver, Burdett & Company, 1900) show that a banker can be artless. M. H. Smith, *Twenty Years among the Bulls and Bears of Wall Street* (Hartford: J. B. Burr & Company, 1875) is an example of the tricks-and-traps-for-the-unwary school. For those who believed information would suffice to cure Wall Street, the biography of Poor, cited above, is best. John Moody, *The Long Road Home* (New York: Macmillan Company, 1934) is more important than Roger W. Babson, *Actions and Reactions: An Autobiography* (New York: Harper & Brothers, 1935).

On auxiliary institutions see Redlich, cited above, for savings banks, and Shepard B. Clough, *A Century of American Life Insurance: A History of the Mutual Life Insurance Company of New York, 1843–1943* (New York: Columbia University Press, 1946) for a narrative of one of the "big three" of insurance companies in the investment banking nexus. The investment problems of a somewhat less spectacular concern are covered in Harold F. Williamson and Orange A. Smalley, *Northwestern Mutual Life: A Century of Trusteeship* (Evanston: Northwestern University Press, 1957). See also Douglass North, "Capital Accumulation in Life Insurance between the Civil War and the Investigation of 1905," in William Miller, editor, *Men in Business: Essays in the History of Entrepreneurship* (Cambridge: Harvard University Press, 1952). On foreign investment in industry Erastus Wiman, "British Capital and American Industries," *North American Review,* CL (February, 1890), 220–234 and N. T. Bacon, "American International Indebtedness," *Yale Review,* IX (November, 1900), 265–285 are useful contemporary accounts. Charles F. Adams, Jr., "A Chapter of Erie" in his and Henry Adams' *Chapters of Erie and Other Essays* (New York: Henry Holt & Co., 1886) is a classic narrative of one Wall Street performance; and Julius Grodinsky, *Jay Gould, His Business Career, 1867–1892* (Philadelphia: University of Pennsylvania Press, 1957) is a narrative of the policies and practices of a great Wall Street speculator and manipulator.

The material on individual industries often treats matters of finance. For the railroads, consult T. C. Cochran, *Railroad Leaders, 1845–1890* (Cambridge: Harvard University Press, 1953) and E. C. Kirkland, *Men, Cities and Transportation: A Study in New England History, 1820–1860,* 2 vols. (Cambridge: Harvard University Press, 1948). For the oil industry, Ralph W. Hidy and Muriel E. Hidy, *History of Standard Oil Company (New Jersey): Pioneering in Big Business, 1882–1911* (New York: Harper & Brothers, 1955) and Allan Nevins, *Study in Power: John D. Rockefeller, Industrialist and Philanthropist,* 2 vols. (New York: Charles Scribner's Sons, 1953) are very illuminating. The more one reads the later works, the more revelatory John D. Rockefeller, *Random Reminiscences of Men and Events* (New York: Doubleday, Doran & Company, 1933) seems. On iron and steel, in addition to B. J. Hendrick, *The Life of Andrew Carnegie,* 2 vols. (New York: Doubleday, Doran & Company, 1932), consult Ida M. Tarbell, *The Life of Elbert H. Gary: The Story of Steel* (New York: D. Appleton & Company, 1925) and the testimony in the *Hearings before the* [Stanley] *Committee on Investigation of United States Steel Corporation,* 8 vols.

In the last analysis, any history of financing expansion must rely upon the files of the *Commercial and Financial Chronicle* and also upon *The Report of the Industrial Commission,* particularly on testimony and analysis in volumes I, VII, VIII and XIII. Books such as J. W. Jenks, *The Trust Problem* (New York: McClure, Phillips & Company, 1905) and John Moody, *The Truth about the Trusts. A Description and Analysis of the American Trust Movement* (New York: Moody Publishing Company, 1904) are largely derivative from this *Report.* The *Report of the Committee* [Pujo] *to Investigate the Concentration of Control of Money and Credit* (1913) is in general too late for this period and is vitiated by some built-in preconceptions.

CHAPTER XII BUILDING AMERICAN CITIES

Over twenty-five years ago in his *The Rise of the City, 1878–1898* (New York: Macmillan Company, 1933) Arthur M. Schlesinger posed a challenging hypothesis to historians of America. Aside from a more frequent and glib resort to the words "urban influences" and scholarly work in some areas, the response to this challenge has been disappointing. Particularly is this so in the area of the economic effect of the city. There have been some excellent histories of separate cities that have paid attention to these matters: Bayrd Still, *Milwaukee: The History of a City* (Madison: State Historical Society of Wisconsin, 1948); Blake McKelvey, *Rochester, the Flower City, 1855–1890* (Cambridge: Harvard University Press, 1949); and the magnificent Bessie L. Pierce, *A History of Chicago,* 3 vols. (New York: Alfred A. Knopf, 1937–1957), which in the last volume comes down to 1893. As is perhaps natural, the tendency even in books of merit, as in C. M. Green, *American Cities in the Growth of the Nation* (London: The Athlone Press, 1957) is to emphasize national economic history that took place in these cities and to individualize urban communities rather than to generalize from them as institutions or aggregates. As a consequence, if he wishes a cross-sectional picture, the student of economic history is driven back to censuses, very uneven in their concerns, and to much earlier works, usually written by those outside the historical discipline.

The best summaries of municipal borrowing are found in A. M. Hillhouse, *Municipal Bonds, a Century of Experience* (New York: Prentice Hall, 1936); Paul Studenski, *Public Borrowing* (New York: National Municipal League, 1930); and "Public Indebtedness," *Tenth Census of the United States. 1880,* VII, 521–891. On the provision of municipal services, I have found the most useful to be D. F. Wilcox, *Municipal Franchises,* 2 vols. (Rochester, N. Y.: The Gervaise Press, 1910). In spite of its tremendous length and pro-municipal ownership slant, this is a sophisticated work, in places a witty one. *Fourteenth Annual Report of the* [U. S.] *Commissioner of Labor, 1899, Water, Gas and Electric-Light Plants under Private and Municipal Ownership* is a factual summary, somewhat exasperating to use. The same might be said of National Civic Federation, *Municipal and Private Operation of Public Utilities,* 2 vols. 3 pts. (New York: National Civic Federation, 1907). This work also includes plenty of opinion and ideology; the municipal ownership advocates seem to have achieved a genuine coup d'état in capturing this report.

On the matter of street improvements, there are only scattered facts here and there. On waterworks, Nelson M. Blake, *Water for the Cities* (Syracuse: Syracuse University Press, 1956) is extremely interesting but unfortunately is largely confined to the pre-Civil War period and to four cities: Boston, New York, Philadelphia, and Baltimore. On the gas industry, consult Arthur L. Hunt, "Gas, Manufactured," *Twelfth Census of the United States. 1900,* X, 705–722. Edward W. Bemis, *Municipal Ownership of Gas in the United States* (Baltimore: American Economic Association, 1891), though strongly biased, is indispensable. On electric light and power, Harold C. Passer, *The Electrical Manufacturers, 1875–1900: A Study in Competition, Entrepreneurship, Technical Change and Economic Growth* (Cambridge: Harvard University Press, 1953) is very sound on business matters; Forrest McDonald, *Let There Be Light: The Electric Utility Industry in Wisconsin, 1881–1955* (Madison: American History Research Center, 1957) adds indispensable elaboration for the local level. There is a great deal of information in the Bureau of the Census, *Electrical Industries* [1902] in the volumes on central stations and electric railways. On the tycoons of city transportation, Burton J. Hendrick, "Great American Fortunes and Their Making: Street-Railway Financiers," *McClure's Magazine,* XXX (November, 1907), 32–48 is better than his narrative in *The Age of Big Business* (New Haven: Yale University Press, 1921), and both fall short of completeness and understanding. For Chicago, consult Pierce, cited above, and *Ninth Biennial Report of the Bureau of Labor Statistics of Illinois: Franchises and Taxation, 1896.* On New York City, Harry J. Carman, *The Street Surface Railway Franchises of New York City* (New York: Columbia University Press, 1919) furnishes a reliable historic framework. Julius Grodinsky, *Jay Gould, 1867–1892* (Philadelphia: University of Pennsylvania Press, 1957) has a chapter on the elevateds. Mark D. Hirsch, *William C. Whitney, Modern Warwick* (New York: Dodd, Mead & Company, 1948) and Philip Jessup, *Elihu Root,* 2 vols. (New York:

Dodd, Mead & Company, 1938) have been criticized for not glowing with indignation over their subjects' activities; this is really their strong point. Edward S. Mason, *The Street Railway in Massachusetts: The Rise and Decline of an Industry* (Cambridge: Harvard University Press, 1932) is the most balanced appraisal I have encountered.

The municipal ownership movement has left traces in John R. Commons, *Myself* (New York: Macmillan Company, 1934) and R. T. Ely, *Ground under Our Feet: An Autobiography* (New York: Macmillan Company, 1938), and is attended to more fully in the very appealing F. C. Howe, *The Confessions of a Reformer* (New York: Charles Scribner's Sons, 1925) and Tom L. Johnson, *My Story* (New York: B. W. Huebsch, 1915). Arthur Mann has a most persuasive chapter on Frank Parsons in the former's *Yankee Reformers in the Urban Age* (Cambridge: Harvard University Press, 1954).

There is still an unhappy ambivalence in treatments of housing and construction. Books tend to ideological or aesthetic dogmatism on the one hand or a plodding assembly of facts on the other. On construction materials beyond Victor Clark, *History of Manufactures in the United States, 1860–1893* (New York: McGraw-Hill Book Company, 1929) one can go only to the census. On stone, see "Report on the Building Stones of the United States and Statistics of the Quarry Industry," *Tenth Census of the United States. 1880,* X, and G. P. Merrill, "Stone," *Twelfth Census of the United States. 1900. Special Reports, Mines and Quarries, 1902,* pp. 785–834. The latter also contains articles on cement, clay, and gypsum. The most useful bridge between economics and aesthetics is Sigfried Giedion, *Space, Time and Architecture, the Growth of a New Tradition* (Cambridge: Harvard University Press, 1941). His *Mechanization Takes Command. A Contribution to Anonymous History* (New York: Oxford University Press, 1948) is suggestive but more specialized. The housing of the masses has attracted considerable historical attention, some of it of a very high order. The best general survey is James Ford *et al., Slums and Housing with Special Reference to New York City: History, Conditions, Policy,* 2 vols. (Cambridge: Harvard University Press, 1936). Gordon Atkins, *Health, Housing, and Poverty in New York City, 1865–1898* (Ann Arbor: Edwards Brothers, 1947) is admirable in conception and execution. The articles in R. W. DeForest and Lawrence Veiller, editors, *The Tenement Problem,* 2 vols. (New York: Macmillan Company, 1903) lean to tendenz. For Chicago, there are two excellent works, Hosmer Hoyt, *One Hundred Years of Land Values in Chicago* (Chicago: University of Chicago Press, 1933) and Edith Abbott, *The Tenements of Chicago, 1908–1935* (Chicago: University of Chicago Press, 1936), which, in spite of its dates, pays ample attention to the nineteenth century. Leo Grebler, David M. Blank, and Louis Wimmick, *Capital Formation in Residential Real Estate* (Princeton: Princeton University Press, 1956) goes back into the nineteenth century largely by working from data of the twentieth.

CHAPTER XIII THE DOMESTIC MARKET

The only considerable treatment of trade in the United States for this period is Harold Barger, *Distribution's Place in the American Economy since*

1869 (Princeton: Princeton University Press, 1955). It was undertaken under the auspices of the National Bureau of Economic Research. As in the Bureau's customary projects, the main emphasis is statistical, but within this framework, as with Barger's other work, there is considerable qualitative treatment and interpretation. The only treatment on the middlemen's structure is for an earlier period: F. M. Jones, "Middlemen in the Domestic Trade of the United States, 1800–1860," *Illinois Studies in the Social Sciences,* XXI, No. 3 (Urbana: University of Illinois, 1937). In view of its title there is a surprising amount of historical material in Paul H. Nystrom, *Economics of Retailing,* vol. I (New York: The Ronald Press Company, 1930). Along with Barger, this remains the best general introduction. The history of separate industries sometimes includes material on marketing. Notable examples are A. H. Cole, *The American Wool Manufacture,* 2 vols. (Cambridge: Harvard University Press, 1926); Ralph W. and Muriel E. Hidy, *History of Standard Oil Company (New Jersey): Pioneering in Big Business, 1882–1911* (New York: Harper & Brothers, 1955); and T. C. Cochran, *The Pabst Brewing Company: History of an American Business* (New York: New York University Press, 1948).

On particular retailing institutions, T. D. Clark, *Pills, Petticoats and Plows: The Southern Country Store* (Indianapolis: Bobbs-Merrill Company, 1944) deals with the exceptional functions of the southern general store. Lewis E. Atherton, "The Pioneer Merchants in Mid-America," *University of Missouri Studies,* vol. XIV, No. 2 (Columbia: University of Missouri Press, 1939) deals with the whole mercantile structure in the West. Students should read the unusually winning chapter on the general store in Lewis E. Atherton, *Main Street on the Middle Border* (Bloomington: Indiana University Press, 1954). On the department store, Ralph M. Hower, *History of Macy's of New York, 1858–1919: Chapters in the Evolution of the Department Store* (Cambridge: Harvard University Press, 1943) has the advantage of dealing with an important firm and of placing its development in a general context. Lloyd Wendt, and Herman Kogan, *Give the Lady What She Wants!* (Chicago: Rand McNally & Company, 1932) is a popularized history of Marshall Field's enterprises. Herbert Adams Gibbons, *John Wanamaker* (New York: Harper & Brothers, 1926), though a little sticky, is not undiscriminating. The testimony of Wanamaker and others in volume VII of *Report of the Industrial Commission* is largely about department stores. Luckily for the mail order houses we have Boris Emmet and John E. Jeuck, *Catalogues and Counters: A History of Sears Roebuck and Company* (Chicago: University of Chicago Press, 1950). Though occasionally awkward in organization and expression, this is a thoroughly scholarly work, a rare thing in the merchandising area. On the chain stores, there are for the A & P two articles by Roy J. Bullock in the *Harvard Business Review,* XI, XII (1933). John K. Winkler, *Five and Ten, The Fabulous Life of F. W. Woolworth* (New York: Robert M. McBride & Company, 1940) is far more than a popularization. Though Frank Presbrey, *The History and Development of Advertising* (New York: Doubleday, Doran & Company, 1929) comes from the profession, it is candid, complete, and sophisticated. James P. Wood, *The Story of Advertising* (New York: Ronald Press Company, 1958) goes a little deeper, particularly on the organization of the advertising business. Ralph M. Hower, *The History of An Advertising Agency. N. W. Ayer & Son at Work, 1869–1939* (Cambridge: Harvard University Press, 1939) is a technical study of a sample organization. G. P. Rowell, *Forty Years an Advertising Agent, 1865–1905* (New York: Franklin Publishing Co., 1906) carries anecdotage to its limits. There is considerable attention to advertising in Frank L. Mott, *A History of American Magazines, 1885–1905* (Cambridge: Harvard University Press, 1957).

CHAPTER XIV THE AMERICAN MENACE ABROAD

In contrast to domestic trade, the material on foreign commerce is abundant. The government has poured forth a flood of statistics, the more generalized of which are in the Bureau of Census, *Historical Statistics of the United States, 1789–1945*, and *Statistical Abstracts* for various years. The best succinct approach to the statistical and historical picture is Charles Bullock, John H. Williams, and Rufus S. Tucker, "The Balance of Trade of the United States," *Review of Economic Statistics,* Preliminary volume I (1919), 215–234. "Exports of Manufactures from the United States and Their Distribution by Articles and Countries . . . 1790–1902," *Monthly Summary of Commerce and Finance, April, 1903* (s.n. 4481) also provides the background material for this chapter.

The efforts of private industries to promote foreign commerce are excellently described in William T. Hutchinson, *Cyrus Hall McCormick, Harvest, 1856–1884* (New York: D. Appleton-Century Company, 1935) and Ralph W. Hidy and Muriel E. Hidy, *History of Standard Oil Company (New Jersey): Pioneering in Big Business, 1882–1911* (New York: Harper & Brothers, 1955). As for government policy and foreign trade, the more generalized effects of the currency situation are treated incidentally in many government reports—notably of the Treasury and of the Special Commissioner of the Revenue—during the late sixties. See also W. C. Mitchell, "Gold, Prices, and Wages under the Greenback Standard," *University of California Publications in Economics,* I (March 27, 1908) (Berkeley: The University Press, March, 1908). On the tariff, F. W. Taussig, *The Tariff History of the United States* (New York: G. P. Putnam's Sons, 1914) and *Some Aspects of the Tariff Question* (Cambridge: Harvard University Press, 1915) are the standard treatments. Essentially Taussig wrote to a formula: the arguments for the protective tariff are wrong, for in operation their effect was contrary to that asserted, damaging rather than beneficial. This is important information to have but it is not the whole story. Unfortunately Edward Stanwood, *American Tariff Controversies in the Nineteenth Century* (Boston: Houghton Mifflin Company, 1903) is too partisan and too prolix to fill in the gaps. Festus P. Summers, *William L. Wilson and Tariff Reform* (New Brunswick: Rutgers University Press, 1953) shows how a tariff is really made. Of studies of the tariff and particular commodities, in addition to Taussig's *Some Aspects of the Tariff Question,* cited above, see especially Arthur H. Cole, *The American Wool Manufacture,* 2 vols. (Cambridge: Harvard University Press, 1926) and Chester W. Wright, *Wool-Growing and the Tariff, A Study in the Economic History of the United States* (Boston: Houghton Mifflin Company, 1910). On the reciprocity movement the best summary is United States Tariff Commission, *Reciprocity and Commercial Treaties.*

On shipping and shipping policy, John G. B. Hutchins, *The American Maritime Industries and Public Policy, 1789–1914: An Economic History* (Cambridge: Harvard University Press, 1941) is a particularly broad-scale amalgam of descriptive history and economic analysis. It is the kind of book one does not need to go beyond. Nonetheless, as its subtitle suggests, the emphasis is economic. Marguerite M. McKee, "The Ship Subsidy Question in United States Policy," *Smith College Studies in History,* vol. VIII, No. 1 (October, 1922) (Northampton: Department of History, 1922), and P. M. Zeis, *American Shipping Policy* (Princeton: Princeton University Press, 1938) are, therefore, useful supplements. Even George W. Dalzell, *The Flight from the Flag: The Continuing Effect of the Civil War upon the American Carrying Trade* (Chapel Hill: University of North Carolina Press, 1940) on the Civil War and American shipping gets into policy.

On general governmental assistance to foreign trade, short of high policy, L. F. Schmeckebier and G. A. Weber, *The Bureau of Foreign and Domestic Commerce. Its History, Activities, and Organization* (Washington: The Brookings Institution, 1924) is a useful guide. Though it is heresy to say so, F. A. Vanderlip, *The American "Commercial Invasion" of Europe* (New York: Scribner's Magazine, 1904) is more accurate than Brooks Adams, *America's Commercial Supremacy* (New York: Harper & Brothers, 1947) and almost as interesting. To get the flavor of argument, consult J. F. Crowell, "Shipping Industry of the United States. Its Relation to the Foreign Trade," *Monthly Summary of Commerce and Finance. December, 1900* (s.n. 4129), probably sober enough to reach the status of history; or the testimony, far short of soberness, at any of the hearings, for example the Farquhar, listed in Hutchins' bibliography. Royal Meeker, *History of Shipping Subsidies* (New York: American Economic Association, 1905), displays some erudition and a passionate contempt for subsidies.

Clyde W. Phelps, *The Foreign Expansion of American Banks. American Branch Banking Abroad* (New York: Ronald Press Company, 1927) is mainly on twentieth century history and policy.

CHAPTER XV THE ATTACK ON WEALTH

Because the anti-trust movement impinges upon so many areas of American history, including that of general reform, its bibliography is very extensive. The following notations, therefore, are not meant to exclude other publications. The treatment of the movement in the nineteenth century once relied rather extensively upon the early chapters in John Chamberlain, *Farewell to Reform: Being a History of the Rise, Life, and Decay of the Progressive Mind in America* (New York: Liveright, 1932). This reliance is unfortunate, for Chamberlain's case is highly tendentious. A more recent and reliable survey of reform thought is Sidney Fine, *Laissez Faire and the General-Welfare State: A Study of Conflict in American Thought, 1865–1901* (Ann Arbor: University of Michigan Press, 1956). Though like most works on this subject, it contains predilections, it is objective enough to include a rare treatment of laissez faire theory. Edward C. Kirkland, *Dream and Thought in the Business Community, 1860–1900* (Ithaca: Cornell University Press, 1956) focuses primarily on business thought on social issues though there are random divergences to the economic field. On individual reformers, Daniel Aaron, *Men of Good Hope: A Story of American Progressives* (New York: Oxford University Press, 1951) manages to get behind the haloes. Reformers are lucky in their biographers: Arthur E. Morgan, *Edward Bellamy* (New York: Columbia University Press, 1944) and Charles A. Barker, *Henry George* (New York: Oxford University Press, 1955) are sympathetic and scholarly. Caro Lloyd, *Henry Demarest Lloyd, 1847–1903: A Biography,* 2 vols. (New York: G. P. Putnam's Sons, 1912) is less critical. The flavor of reforms comes best through the works of reformers themselves: Henry George, *Progress and Poverty: An Inquiry into the Cause of Industrial Depressions and of Increase of Want with Increase of Wealth: The Remedy* (New York: D. Appleton and Company, 1880); Edward Bellamy, *Looking Backward, 2000–1887* (Boston: Ticknor & Company, 1888); and Henry D. Lloyd, *Wealth Against Commonwealth* (New York: Harper & Brothers, 1894).

Of the many works on trusts and legislation, J. W. Jenks, *The Trust Problem* (New York: McClure, Phillips & Co., 1905) is a contemporary classic; Henry R. Seager and Charles A. Gulick, Jr., *Trust and Corporation Problems* (New York: Harper & Brothers, 1929) is an excellent guide to a longer period of development. Of the compilations of opinion, Chicago Conference on Trusts, *Speeches, Debates, Resolutions, List of Delegates, Committees, etc., Held September 13th, 14th, 15th and 16th, 1899* (Chicago: The Civic Federation of Chicago, 1899) is in a class by itself. Volumes I and XX in the *Report of the Industrial Commission* include important testimony and recommendations. James W. Bridge, editor, *The Trust, Its Book: Being a Presentation of the Several Aspects of the Latest Forms of Industrial Evolution* (New York: Doubleday, Page & Company, 1902) is a useful anthology of articles.

On anti-trust legislation, the derisive and satirical—for example, Thurman Arnold, *The Folk-Lore of Capitalism* (New Haven: Yale University Press, 1937)—have been so persuasive as to create a stereotype. Walton Hamilton and Irene Till, "Antitrust in Action" *Temporary National Economic Committee, Monograph* No. 16 (Washington: 1940) is in the same tradition, but its approach is somewhat historical. Milton Handler, "A Study of the Construction and Enforcement of the Federal Antitrust Laws," *Temporary National Economic Committee, Monograph* No. 38 (Washington: 1941) proceeds on the assumption that the policy is something more than necromancy. In treating a long array of cases under topics, its analysis is essential. Hans B. Thorelli, *The Federal Antitrust Policy: Origination of an American Tradition* (Baltimore: Johns Hopkins Press, 1955) bids fair to be the "definitive" scholarly work on the background and early interpretation of the Sherman Act. There is an informative contemporary flavor to William H. Taft, *The Anti-Trust Act and the Supreme Court* (New York: Harper & Brothers, 1914) and to William W. Cook, *The Corporation Problem* (New York: G. P. Putnam's Sons, 1891).

CHAPTERS XVI–XIX LABOR AND CAPITAL

It is a curiosity that writing on the problems of the labor force has been almost exclusively from the point of view of workers and their unions. While this is a legitimate interest, it is only a partial one. The one exception of any scope to this generalization is David Lescohier, in *History of Labour in the United States, 1896–1932,* volume III (New York: Macmillan Company, 1935). This work continues the earlier two volumes of the same title by John R. Commons. Lescohier's treatment, beginning nominally with 1890, really focuses on the twentieth century nor does it include employer policy on all labor matters. Consequently students of the subject must rely upon widely scattered source material—notably the testimony in the *Report of the Committee* [on Education and Labor] *of the Senate . . . 1885.* The first three volumes, like the rest inadequately indexed, contain the most important testimony. Another batch of testimony is in VII and XIV of *Report of the Industrial Commission:* this report has admirable summaries and indexes. Finally there is the file of the *Transactions of the American Society of Mechanical Engineers.* These began in 1880. The mechanical engineer, while he once may have been merely a technician, soon found himself in positions of management responsibility. Thus the *Transactions,* in presidential addresses if nowhere else, reflect a concern with the details of industrial discipline. The file is particularly useful on industrial education and systems of wage payments. Most of the papers, sometimes the presidential addresses, are followed by the printed record of the discussions at the meeting. Incidentally one will learn more about the Taylor system in the *Transactions* than elsewhere. I find it hard to reconcile most of what has been written in a secondary way about Taylorism with this contemporary setting.

This bibliography does not pretend to list all useful works on immigration even in an industrial sense. Harry Jerome, *Migration and Business Cycles* (New York: National Bureau of Economic Research, 1926) interrelates the immigration statistics and mobility with economic conditions in the United States. Early in the twentieth century a U. S. Immigration Commission issued a nineteen volume Report on "Immigrants in Industries," *Senate Document* No. 633 (s.n. 5669–5684), 61st Cong., 2d Sess. Vols. XIX and XX summarize the findings. Some of the material is applicable to the late nineteenth century; the Commission's preoccupation with a distinction between "old" and "new" immigration is of dubious worth. The long drought, largely inexplicable, of scholarly works in this area has at last been broken by Rowland T. Berthoff, *British Immigrants in Industrial America* (Cambridge: Harvard University Press, 1953) and Charlotte Erickson, *American Industry and the European Immigrant, 1860–1885* (Cambridge: Harvard University Press, 1957). The latter concentrates on contract labor and legislation concerning it. To fill the gap for the immigration of "celestials" there is an early "classic," Mary R. Coolidge, *Chinese Immigration* (New York: Henry Holt and Co., 1909). Even practitioners in the field of internal industrial migration admit the imperfections of their accomplishment. Carter Goodrich *et al.*, *Migration and Economic Opportunity, A Report of the Study of Population Redistribution* (Philadelphia: University of Pennsylvania Press, 1936) focuses largely on the twentieth century and has the shortcomings of most studies which are a prelude to the formation of national "policy." One of the supporting monographs, C. Warren Thornthwaite, *Internal Migration in the United States* (Philadelphia: University of Pennsylvania Press, 1934) is succinct and has useful maps. What is really needed is a study for the late nineteenth century, equivalent to those made for the Negro migrations of the twentieth century.

On the housing of employees there is a good deal of scattered material in sources already discussed as well as in the reports of state Commissioners of Labor. T. R. Navin, *The Whitin Machine Works since 1831: A Textile Machinery Company in an Industrial Village* (Cambridge: Harvard University Press, 1950) brings together material for more than one enterprise. S. E. Morison, *The Ropemakers of Plymouth: A History of the Plymouth Cordage Company, 1824–1949* (Boston: Houghton Mifflin Company, 1950) describes another housing project. The history of the company store has yet to be written.

So greatly have both popular and informed attitudes about women in industry and business altered that a great deal of earlier writing in this area is in danger of seeming merely "quaint," it is certainly slanted, though not blatantly. Within the framework of the crusade for protective legislation for women, the flavor of a "cause" has even governed the simple determination of what statistical material to compile. These generalizations are less true of research and writing on child labor. Still, both areas are a fine field for the "devil theory of history" and for tear-jerking. For these reasons the scholar will find somewhat unsatisfactory the nineteen volume study "Report on Condition of Women and Child Wage-Earners in the United States," *Senate Document* No. 645 (s.n. 5625–5703), 61st Cong., 2d Sess., prepared under the direction of the Commissioner of Labor. In spite of its length, the coverage is not complete. U. S. Bureau of the Census, *Statistics of Women at Work. Twelfth Census of the United States. 1900* and J. A. Hill, *Women in Gainful Occupations, 1870–1890,* [1920] *Census Monographs,* X are both more objective.

The material on industrial education is vast but, so far, largely unorganized. It is to be found in the proceedings of engineering societies and of the National Education Association, and in the reports of the United States Bureau of Education. Edward C. Kirkland, *Dream and Thought in the Business Community, 1860–1900* (Ithaca: Cornell University Press, 1956) has a chapter on what some businessmen thought on the matter. Samuel Rezneck is currently exploring engineering education, particularly in relation to the Rensselaer Polytechnic Institute. See his "The Engineering Profession Considers Its Educational Problems," *Association of American Colleges Bulletin,* XLIII (October, 1957), 410–418 and "The Man Who Made Rensselaer into a Polytechnic Institute," *Rensselaer Alumni News,* XXIII (January, 1957), 6–10. Paul Douglas, "American Apprenticeship and Industrial Education," *Columbia University Studies in History, Economics, and Public Law* (New York: Columbia University Press, 1921) is partly history and partly educational prospectus. Walter E. Weyl and A. M. Sakolski, "Conditions of Entrance to the Principal

Trades," *Bulletin of the Bureau of Labor,* No. 67 (November, 1906) is a sophisticated treatment.

On management's attitude toward hours, wages, and the like, it is necessary to resort to *Transactions of the American Society of Mechanical Engineers* and to testimony before government bodies. The reports of the Massachusetts *Bureau of Statistics of Labor* for 1870–74 and 1881 contain much testimony from management on hours. On wages, N. P. Gilman, *Profit Sharing Between Employer and Employee: A Study in the Evolution of the Wages System* (Boston: Houghton Mifflin and Company, 1889) provides both fact and contemporary opinion. But there is no substitute for the papers and discussions in *Transactions of the American Society of Mechanical Engineers,* particularly the ones contributed by F. W. Taylor, W. E. Partridge, Henry R. Towne, Henry Metcalfe, and F. A. Halsey. Of the biographies of capitalists, Herbert Croly, *Marcus Alonzo Hanna: His Life and Work* (New York: Macmillan Company, 1923) has an exceptionally perceptive analysis of Hanna's labor policy.

The classic treatment of labor primarily from the workers' viewpoint is John R. Commons, *et al., History of Labour in the United States,* 4 vols. (New York: The Macmillan Company, 1918–1935). For the post-Civil War period, the last three volumes are necessary; they cover most phases: working conditions, legislation, labor organization, and ideologies. In a way this pioneer work out of Wisconsin has been almost too successful; not that it has imposed upon other work its value judgments, but its emphasis and approach have been so unquestioned that only recently have scholars broken away to ask new questions and even make new factual contributions. One of the earliest deviants from the pattern was Norman Ware, *The Labor Movement in the United States, 1860–1895: A Study in Democracy* (New York: D. Appleton & Company, 1929). This is still a persuasive and refreshing book. More recently Lloyd Ulman in *The Rise of the National Trade Union: The Development and Significance of Its Structure, Governing Institutions, and Economic Policies* (Cambridge: Harvard University Press, 1955) has written a stimulating analysis of topics in labor union practice and policy and called in question the general theories of causation and development stated by Commons and Perlman. A contemporary account, strangely neglected, that is informed in its questions and shrewd in its insights is E. Levasseur, *The American Workman.* Translated by T. S. Adams, this work constitutes Extra Volume XXII in the *Johns Hopkins Studies in Historical and Political Science* (Baltimore: Johns Hopkins Press, 1900).

Though Ware is peculiarly good on the Knights of Labor, there is no substitute for T. V. Powderly, *The Path I Trod* (New York: Columbia University Press, 1940). His *Thirty Years of Labor, 1859 to 1889* (Philadelphia: T. V. Powderly, 1890) is less interesting.

The American Federation of Labor has received extensive treatment. Samuel Gompers, *Seventy Years of Life and Labor: An Autobiography,* 2 vols. (New York: E. P. Dutton & Company, 1923) is not as enlightening for its subject as either of Powderly's volumes is for his. R. H. Harvey, *Samuel Gompers, Champion of the Toiling Masses* (Stanford: Stanford University

Press, 1935) refuses to be overawed by its subject; but Louis S. Reed, *The Labor Philosophy of Samuel Gompers* (New York: Columbia University Press, 1930) misses an opportunity. Philip Taft, *The A. F. of L. in the Time of Gompers* (New York: Harper & Brothers, 1957), based upon wide sources, is better for the period before 1900 than Lewis L. Lorwin, *The American Federation of Labor: History, Policies, and Prospects* (Washington: The Brookings Institution, 1933) which reduces the early years to a prelude to later development.

Other labor leaders' experiences and thoughts may be found in Jonathan Grossman, *William Sylvis, Pioneer of American Labor: A Study of the Labor Movement during the Era of the Civil War* (New York: Columbia University Press, 1945); Joseph R. Buchanan, *The Story of a Labor Agitator* (New York: Outlook Company, 1903); John Mitchell, *Organized Labor: Its Problems, Purposes and Ideals* (Philadephia: American Book and Bible House, 1903); and George A. McNeill, editor, *The Labor Movement: The Problem of Today* (Boston: A. M. Bridgman & Company, 1887). However there is really no substitute for the compendium of opinions printed in *The Report of the Committee* [on Education and Labor] *of the Senate . . . 1885,* 4 vols.; and the *Report of the Industrial Commission,* especially volumes V, VII, and XIV. That this testimony often gives a stream-of-consciousness effect is all the better.

Whatever may be the defects of treating labor history in terms of labor crises, the existing treatments of such crises contribute a broad setting and are thus helpful. On the Molly Maguires, Marvin W. Schlegel, *Ruler of the Reading: The Life of Franklin B. Gowen, 1836–1889* (Harrisburg: Archives Publishing Company of Pennsylvania, 1947), and J. Walter Coleman, *The Molly Maguire Riots: Industrial Conflict in the Pennsylvania Coal Region* (Richmond, Va.: Garrett and Massie, 1936) destroy the conventional narrative. Henry David, *The History of the Haymarket Affair: A Study in the American Social-Revolutionary and Labor Movements* (New York: Farrar & Rinehart, 1936) is authoritative, as is the account in volume 3 of Bessie L. Pierce, *A History of Chicago,* 3 vols. (New York: Alfred A. Knopf, 1957). Since there is no comparable secondary account of Homestead, it is necessary to read both the reports and the testimony in Report of House Committee on the Judiciary, *House Report* No. 2447 (s.n. 3142, pt. 1), 52d Cong., 2d Sess., and Report of the Senate Select Committee, *Senate Report* No. 1280 (s.n. 3172), 52d Cong., 2d Sess. Though Almont Lindsey, *The Pullman Strike: The Story of a Unique Experiment and of a Great Labor Upheaval* (Chicago: University of Chicago Press, 1942) is sound, the contemporary investigation, United States Strike Commission, Report on the Chicago Strike of June–July, 1894, *Senate Executive Document* No. 7 (s.n. 3276) 53rd Cong., 3rd Sess. should not be neglected. Donald L. McMurry, *The Great Burlington Strike of 1888: A Case History in Labor Relations* (Cambridge: Harvard University Press, 1956) shows what can be done when a modern point-of-view gets to work on adequate documentation.

Standard treatments on various phases of labor organization are Leo Wolman, *The Growth of American Trade Unions, 1880–1923* (New York: National Bureau of Economic Research, 1924) and his "The Boycott in American Trade Unions," *Johns Hopkins University Studies in Historical and Political Science,* Series XXXIV, No. 1 (Baltimore: The Johns Hopkins Press, 1916); and Marion C. Cahill, *Shorter Hours: A Study of the Movement since the Civil War* (New York: Columbia University Press, 1932). C. K. Yearley, Jr., "Britons in American Labor. A History of the Influence of the United Kingdom Immigrants on American Labor, 1820–1914," *Johns Hopkins University Studies in Historical and Political Science,* Series LXXV, No. 1 (Baltimore: The Johns Hopkins Press, 1957) needs to be supplemented by the material in Berthoff, cited above. In general, the history of regional labor groupings has been neglected. P. A. Speek, "The Singletax and the Labor Movement," *Bulletin of the University of Wisconsin,* No. 878, *Economic and Political Science Series,* VIII, No. 3 (Madison, 1917) provides material for New York.

In governmental publications there is a vast accumulation of material. First the United States Commissioner of Labor and later the Department of Commerce and Labor, are notable for their annual reports and also their *Bulletins.* It is surprising that more attention has not been given to the reports of state Bureaus of Statistics of Labor. For instance, those of Massachusetts, begun in 1869 and under the direction of Carroll D. Wright, achieved a high level of distinction.

CHAPTER XX MULTIPLICATION, DIVISION, AND MATERIALISM

Though the measurement of national wealth and income has long been a concern of writers on our economic development and in the period covered by this volume became a great controversial issue—"the social question," the question of the proper division of wealth and income—the factual material is scattered and difficult to come by. At least this is true compared to the material and analysis available for the twentieth century. Wellford Isbell King, *The Wealth and Income of the People of the United States* (New York: Macmillan Company, 1915) was a pioneer volume in the area. In spite of this and in spite of its curious preoccupations—for it is a book very much of its time and place—the volume remains highly valuable. Charles B. Spahr, *An Essay on the Present Distribution of Wealth in the United States* (New York: Thomas Y. Crowell & Company, 1896) is a doctrinaire document compiled upon the premise that "the common observation of common people is more trustworthy than the statistical investigations of the most unprejudiced experts." This general observation seems childish in view of Robert F. Martin's *National Income in the United States, 1799–1938* (New York: National Industrial Conference Board, 1939) and the work of the National Bureau of Economic Research. The latter's prolonged statistical findings have been verbalized in Simon Kuznets, *National Income: A Summary of Findings* (New York: National Bureau of Economic Research, 1946). While both these volumes are more full on the twentieth century, they do penetrate back into the later nineteenth century. F. H. Streightoff, "The Distribution of Incomes in the United States," *Columbia University Studies in History, Economics, and Public Law,* LII, No. 2 (New York: Columbia University Press, 1912) is a study of the early twentieth century with some historical background.

As for standards of living, so far no study comparable to Edgar W. Martin, *The Standard of Living in 1860: American Consumption Levels on the Eve of the Civil War* (Chicago: University of Chicago Press, 1942) is available for the end of the century. The overall and courageous attempt to nail down a standard of living in Chester W. Wright, *Economic History of the United States* (New York: McGraw-Hill Company, 1941) does not make 1900 a stopping point in the longer period, 1840–1930. If we avoid the tyranny of mere date lines, there is much material in Bureau of Labor Statistics, U. S. Department of Labor, *How American Buying Habits Change* (1959). It deals primarily with the twentieth century.

On wages, the best volume is Paul H. Douglas, *Real Wages in the United States, 1890–1926* (Boston: Houghton Mifflin Company, 1930), but for want of data it does not deal with the period before 1890. Presumably these deficiencies will be remedied by two studies of the National Bureau of Economic Research now in preparation: C. O. Long, *Wages and Earnings in the United States, 1860–1890* and Albert Reis, *Real Wages in Manufacturing: 1890–1914.* Data on hours of labor are also elusive. Marion C. Cahill, *Shorter Hours: A Study of the Movement since the Civil War* (New York: Columbia University Press, 1932) deals largely with ideological and agitational matters. There is a considerable body of material on these elusive questions in the reports of the state labor commissioners—notably those of Massachusetts in the late seventies and early eighties.

The over-all estimate of the economic order set forth in this chapter is not derived from other American histories as much as from contemporary material in periodicals, from the testimony collected in the *Report of the Industrial Commission,* and from the statements of the business community either in biographies of businessmen or in such series as the *Transactions of the American Society of Mechanical Engineers.*

Index